Meaning and order in Moroccan society

For Margaret,
from all three of
us, with love and
memories
Burt, Hilly, Lany

Meaning and order in Moroccan society
Three essays in cultural analysis

Clifford Geertz
Professor of Social Science
The Institute for Advanced Study
Princeton

Hildred Geertz
Professor of Anthropology
Princeton University

Lawrence Rosen
Professor of Anthropology
Princeton University

With a photographic essay by **Paul Hyman**

Cambridge University Press
Cambridge
London   New York   Melbourne

Published by the Syndics of the Cambridge University Press
The Pitt Building, Trumpington Street, Cambridge CB2 1RP
Bentley House, 200 Euston Road, London NW1 2DB
32 East 57th Street, New York, NY 10022, USA
296 Beaconsfield Parade, Middle Park, Melbourne 3206, Australia

First published 1979

Printed in the United States of America
Typeset by Huron Valley Graphics, Ann Arbor, Michigan
Printed and bound by Halliday Lithograph Corp., West Hanover, Massachusetts

Library of Congress Cataloging in Publication Data

Geertz, Clifford.
Meaning and order in Moroccan society.

1. Morocco – Social life and customs.
2. Sefrou, Morocco – Social life and customs.
I. Geertz, Hildred, joint author.
II. Rosen, Lawrence, 1941– joint author. III. Title.
DT312.G37   301.29′64   78–54327
ISBN 0521221757

To the memory of Lloyd A. Fallers

Contents

Acknowledgments

We have, as all anthropologists, incurred an enormous series of debts to a large and varied group of people who have at one point or another vitally assisted our work. It is impossible to name them all here. Instead, we should like to thank first the officials of the Moroccan government from the ministries in Rabat to the local Sefrou administration and, in particular, the pasha, qadi, and qaid of Sefrou. Second, and most important, we should like to thank those who worked with us in Sefrou answering our questions, inviting us into their homes, taking us to "events," and generally attempting to assist us in understanding their form of life. Third, several people have read in manuscript form the essays included in this book and made specific and useful criticisms; we should like to thank them by name. For Lawrence Rosen these persons include Mustapha Benyaklef, Kenneth Brown, Edmund Burke III, Thomas A. Dichter, Ross Dunn, Dale Eickelman, Ernest Gellner, David Hart, Amal Rassam, and John Waterbury. For Clifford Geertz: Robert McC. Adams, Karen Blu, Kenneth Brown, Robert Cooter, George Dalton, Dale Eickelman, Shelomo Goitein, Albert Hirschman, Michael Meeker, William Sewell, Jr., Norman Stillman, Avrom Udovitch, Nur Yalman, and Aram Yengoyan. For Hildred Geertz: Daisy Dwyer, Dale Eickelman, Paul Rabinow, Amal Rassam, and Renato Rosaldo.

Financial support for Rosen's work has been provided by the National Institutes of Health, the Center for International Comparative Studies of the University of Illinois in Urbana, and the Institute for Advanced Study, Princeton, on the basis of grants from the Carnegie and Russell Sage foundations. Clifford Geertz's work was supported by the National Institute of Mental Health, the Committee for the Comparative Study of New Nations of the University of Chicago, and the Institute for Advanced Study. He would like to thank Amy Jackson for her extensive secretarial assistance. Hildred Geertz's work was

ix

Acknowledgments assisted by the Division of Social Sciences and the Committee for the Comparative Study of New Nations of the University of Chicago, the latter under a grant from the Carnegie Corporation.

We are grateful for all this assistance.

x

Transcription note

The problem of transcribing spoken Arabic remains a vexed one. The orthographies that exist are designed for classical Arabic, which, for the most part, exists only in literary form. One is caught between what one hears said and what one sees written, and thus, – a worse fate yet –between the passions of linguists and those of philologists. Here, we have sought to render what we have heard, with the exception that minor regional dialectical variations – rather pronounced in Sefrou – have been ignored for a Moroccan standard that, though it does not yet entirely exist, is rapidly coming to do so.

The transcription is that used in the most generally accessible Arabic-English dictionary, H. Wehr's fine *Dictionary of Modern Written Arabic* (edited by J. M. Cowan, Ithaca, 1976), with some adjustments to the special demands of Moroccan colloquial. The most important of these are the introduction of a *g* where necessary; the use of *e* for the short vowel represented in Wehr as *a* in cases where, as is common in Moroccan, that vowel is even further shortened so as to become a neutral midvowel, rather like the *e* in "glasses," the *u* in "butter," or the *e* in "bet"; and the omission of *t*, *d*, and *z*, which do not appear in Moroccan speech. Definite articles are transcribed as *l-*, *š-*, *b-l-*, *d-*, *j-*, *r-*, and *t-*.

In order not to clutter the text with italics and diacritics, Arabic words are strictly transcribed in each essay only the first time they appear, except when their appearances are widely separated. Otherwise they are rendered unitalicized in the most common English orthography for Arabic, in which neither vowel length nor consonant strength (e.g., *s* against *ṣ*, *h* against *ḥ*) is indicated, and *k* is *kh*, *s* is *sh*, *ḡ* is *gh*. As the strict transcriptions are indicated in the index, this system should make it possible for the Arabist to determine what the word in fact "really" is, while leaving the non-Arabist free from distracting technicalities.

xi

Transcription note   Neither place names nor personal names are strictly transcribed; the former are rendered as one is likely to find them represented on maps. Berber words are indicated by a preceding *Br.;* classical Arabic forms by a *cl.;* Hebrew words, by an *Heb.*

We are indebted to a number of our Arabist colleagues for generous help in these matters, but leave them unnamed for fear of implicating them in the errors that remain.

Introduction

The study

The movement of anthropologists toward a concern with complex agrarian societies has accelerated over the past quarter century until now it probably accounts for the bulk of the work in the field. Yet many problems of method, theory, and data presentation remain, and the sense that the classical monograph forms of anthropology – the "people" study (Nuer, Tikopia, Trobriand, Navajo) and the "community" study (Chan Kom, Amazon Town, Ramah, Lesu) – are awkward and ungainly in this context grows steadily deeper. Studies of "the Chinese," "the Brazilians," or "the Arabs," though suggestive, seem to claim too much for local findings; studies of this or that village, town, or settlement as such, though informative, seem caught in a kind of data parochialism. Committed by training and heritage, and in most cases by conviction, to microsociological investigation, anthropologists working in places like India, Mexico, or (the case at hand) North Africa find themselves faced with what looks like a Hobson's choice between dissipating the circumstantiality their narrowed focus provides in order to escape a sense of inconsequence and resigning themselves to adding a few footnotes to broader streams of scholarship in which they play no central role.

Matters are not, perhaps, all that desperate. Not only do important contributions continue to be made within the older formats that are neither provincial nor globalistic – as witness, so far as Morocco is concerned, David Hart's recent "people" study of the Aith Waryaghar and Kenneth Brown's "community" study of Salé – but a growing number of problem-oriented works – Dale Eickelman's on maraboutism, Vincent Crapanzano's on popular psychiatry, for example – manage to connect local findings with general considerations with great effectiveness.[1] Yet, the search for more adequate ways to render the special contribution of nook-and-cranny anthropological work to the   1

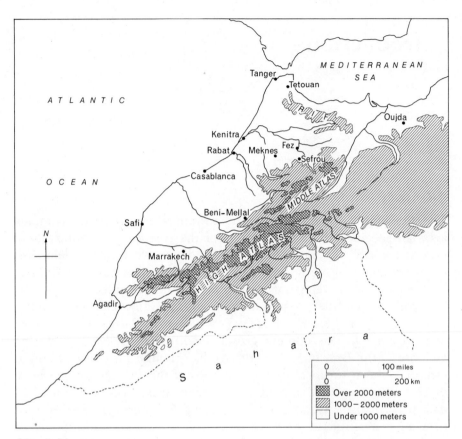

Map 1. Morocco

wider, multidisciplinary effort to comprehend . . . Morocco . . . the
Maghreb . . . the Middle East . . . the Third World . . . the Modern
World Order . . . continues, because new approaches to new issues in
new settings demand them. As in any other field, genres evolve as intentions do.

In such terms, the present work, in its organization and in the
assemblage of ideas that in an overall way animates it, is but another
attempt, hardly final and in no way ideal, to find a form in which
particular facts can be made to speak to general concerns. The research on which it was based was mostly conducted between 1965 and
1971 in a single small-city-and-dependent-environs of north central
Morocco: Sefrou (see Maps 1–4). It was carried out by several hands,
all of them American and all but one of them associated with the
University of Chicago, working in tandem in such a way that their

2

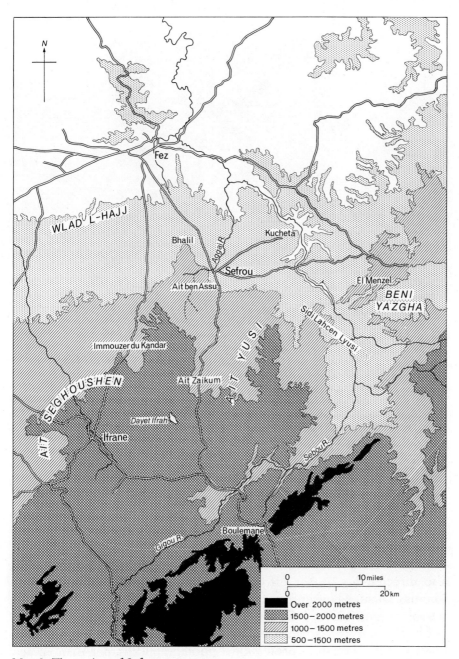

Map 2. The region of Sefrou

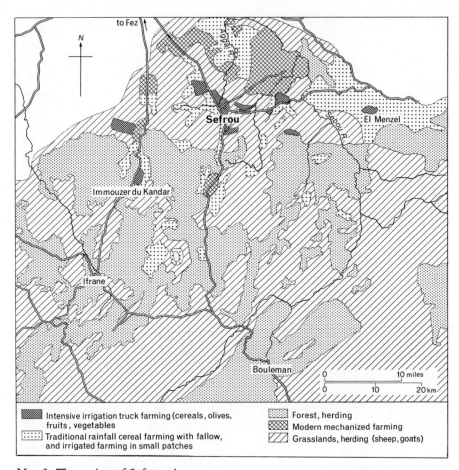

Map 3. The region of Sefrou: the economy

stays in the field were arranged in chain-link fashion so as to provide
almost continuous coverage during the whole six-year period, without
more than one or two, occasionally three, being there at once.[2]

All the researchers sought to gain a general picture of the ecology,
economy, history, social structure, and culture of the region, but each
also directed his or her efforts toward two or three special topics:
Thomas Dichter concentrated on adolescence, youth culture, and the
school system; Clifford Geertz on religion, the market, and ecology;
Hildred Geertz on kinship and family, the role of women, and oral
poetry; Paul Hyman, a professional photographer rather than an anthropologist, on catching the look of the place, its people, and its life;
Paul Rabinow on religious, political, and economic life in a particular
village; and Lawrence Rosen on urban social structure, law, and

4

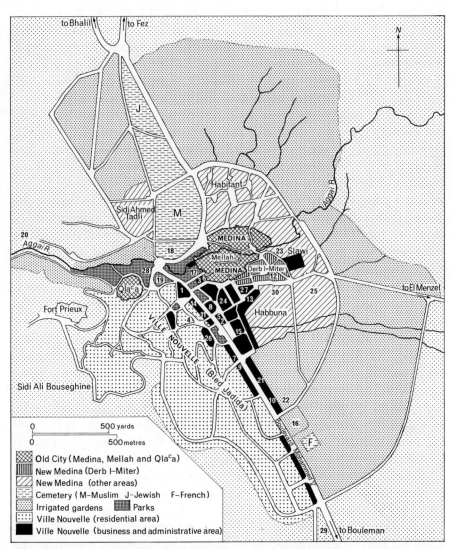

Map 4. The town of Sefrou: major areas. *Key*: 1. Super-Qaid's office; 2. Qaid's office; 3. Pasha's office; 4. Police station; 5. Civil court; 6. Qadi's court; 7. Gendarmerie; 8. Rural tax office; 9. Forestry and irrigation office; 10. Fire house; 11. Post office; 12. Nadir's office; 13. Hospital; 14. Bank; 15. Movie house; 16. Soccer field; 17. Swimming pool; 18. Bus and taxi station; 19. Tennis club; 20. Power station; 21. Livestock market; 22. Vegetable market; 23. Dry-goods and rug market; 24. College; 25. Lycée; 26. Former Jewish school; 27. Jewish school; 28. Public prayer ground (mṣellā); 29. Military barracks; 30. Prison.

5

Berber village organization.[3] But, though a multiple effort, the work was not closely integrated – a team study in the proper sense. Each investigator worked in his own way on his own problems, and normally alone, and there was, from the very start, no intention – indeed, there was a conscious disintention – to produce a unified, joint report governed by a consensual interpretation of pooled data. This is still the case, and the present book does not represent such a report.

Instead, it represents three separate sorties (four, if as they should be, Hyman's photographs are seen as perceptions, not illustrations) designed to depict the way in which the people of Sefrou relate to one another within a complex structure of historically created cultural symbols. The focus of each essay is different: The first is concerned with the general shape of Sefrou social organization; the second with a single major institution; the third with a particular dimension of everyday life. Different, too, are their scale and purpose: The first is comprehensive and summary; the second, bounded and analytic; the third, thematic and intensive. And so too, their structure: the first, discursive; the second, monographic; the third, systematic. Insofar as they converge, it is in their view of how collective meaning and social order come together in Moroccan life.

What we all hold is not any particular interpretation of any particular aspect of Moroccan society (there are, indeed, some sharp differences among us on a fair number of matters), any overarching "theory of society," or even any shared attitude toward the moral and political implications of what we imagine we have found out (save, of course, that there are some). What we all hold is the view that the systems of meaning, whether highly explicit like Islam or rather less so like hospitality, in terms of which individuals live out their lives constitute what order those lives attain. We see social relationships as embodying and embodied in symbolic forms that give them structure, and we are concerned to identify such forms and trace their impact.

It is in this *"famille d'esprit"* sense only that the following work represents a collective enterprise. As such, it is a product, not merely of the authors of the several essays, or of all of them together, but of all those who worked in Sefrou. Paul Rabinow, who was to have contributed a study of his own but was prevented from doing so by other obligations, was directly involved in the planning of the book from the beginning and has allowed us to incorporate some of his materials in the discussions of ecology and social organization of Sidi Lahcen Lyusi. Thomas Dichter has not been directly involved in this book, but both through his thesis and through extended discussions with those who have been
6 involved, he has contributed importantly to it.

The place

Sefrou is the name for both the city and the countryside that surrounds it. Although finer discriminations, geographical and social, are constantly employed in this extremely variegated region, residents usually apply the generic term *bled* to embrace the whole of it. Ideally, the term means "region" or "locality," and insofar as a locality can refer to a wide range of entities bled can, depending on the context, mean "city" and "country," "town" and "village." But the term bled projects a deeper sense of place than the merely locational: It also conveys a sense of relation between men and the landscape they inhabit. It is the region from which a particular individual or group draws its nurture, its sustenance, its most distinctive traits and ties. To identify someone as being from bled Sefrou – to say he is a "Sefroui" – is to imply those characteristics of manner, knowledge, relationships, and modes of interaction that have come to be associated with it, to connect a "who" with a "where."

This sense of place as an index or source of social identity is more directly implied in the idiom *mūl l-bled* (pl. *mwālīn l-bled*). Mul means "owner," and to speak of someone as mul l-bled, when referring to a given parcel of land, is simply to mean that he has possession or control of that property. But the phrase is also used to refer to the natives of a particular region, the people who characterize – and are characterized by – that place. Virtually every plot of land in the Sefrou region – each garden, field, and irrigation ditch – has a name, and every part of the region has one or more specific designations. To speak of particular individuals or families as mwalin l-bled, however, is to imply that they are the true embodiments of that which is distinctive to the locale, the people who carry its distinguishing qualities with them even when they leave the place or become a minority among the hosts of newcomers. To know a man's origins, the place in which his people are mwalin l-bled, is to know something of the ways he may think, act, and form relationships with others.

Physically, bled Sefrou refers both to the city proper and to the territory for which it constitutes the urban hub. The city of Sefrou is situated near the northern edge of the region just at the point where the foothills of the Middle Atlas Mountains meet the western plain of Morocco. Although the 30,000 inhabitants of the city have important ties to the large metropolis of Fez, which can be reached by a half hour's bus ride to the north, it is toward the south that most of the city's activities have long been directed. Here, in a 30-kilometer-wide strip that cuts through the foothills and plateaus of the Middle Atlas   7

Mountains, lies the territory of the Ait Yusi Berbers. Nearer to the city are found several larger settlements, among them the saintly complex of Sidi Lahcen Lyusi and the Arab-speaking village of Bhalil.[4]

But to see bled Sefrou as a place on the cartographer's map – a roughly bounded area containing various populations and settlement types – is to miss its true character. Bled Sefrou is really a social space – a network of relationships mediated by markets, public institutions, local identities, and densely interwoven bonds of kinship and alliance. No less importantly, it is a conceptual domain – a perceived set of populations, territories, pathways, and meeting places that are intimately, if not always harmoniously, linked to the nurturance and identity of those who live there. As an indigenous conceptual category, bled Sefrou underlines the interdependency, as well as the interaction, of its component parts. It stresses the conceptualization of the region as an arena within which social life is played out through institutions that crosscut internal divisions of geography and society, even as the substance and course of social life are deeply influenced by the contexts in which its various manifestations are found. So conceived, bled Sefrou also presents itself as an appropriate unit for analysis. It establishes, as the subject of study, a cultural field comprising a number of domains and frameworks within which Sefrouis' own concepts of selfhood and social relationship can be explored for their bearing on the organization of collective life.

The landscape

The interplay of environment and culture is one of the basic themes to which anthropologists have devoted themselves. If their studies have established anything, it is that the environment is no mere given, no neutral constant, no passively endured condition. Rather, it is an integral part of man's life-world, as deeply shaped by social conditions as social conditions are mediated by it. The natural setting is more than a context to adapt to, a store of resources to draw on, or a stage on which the drama of social life is played out; the ways in which a civilization works out its relation to its setting over a long period of time makes the environment a vital aspect of that civilization itself. To explore the irrigation or land use patterns of people in the bled Sefrou is to explore how its inhabitants use the available resources, how they make the resources a part of their own social drama, and how their ecological adaptations relate to other aspects of their culture.

The Sefrou region, like most of Morocco, is characterized by a
highly irregular and uncertain set of climatic conditions and a wide

variety of microenvironments capable of responding quite differently to the alterations of the weather. The French, in grand colonial fashion, simply divided the country into "useful" and "useless" Morocco, a distinction that embraced in the former the wheat lands of the nation's western plain and foothill oases and included in the latter the mountains and deserts surrounding them. But Sefrouis themselves draw a finer distinction among three main ecological zones: the plains (*weṭya*), the mountains (*jabel*), and the piedmont (*dir*).

Extending back from the Atlantic coast almost to the edge of the Middle Atlas Mountains, the Moroccan plains embrace most of the western part of the nation. As the main wheat-growing section of the country it was the area in which colonial farming was most actively pursued, and the foothills lying at its edge were used as winter pasturage by highland tribes until the French began limiting access to these sites. Although subject to wide climatic variations, the plains afford comparatively good conditions for the intensive cultivation of wheat and barley.

The Middle Atlas Mountains begin immediately south of the city of Sefrou. Although they rise in places to peaks of 3,000 meters, the Middle Atlas are mainly composed of a series of forested hills broken in spots by highland plateaus and small protected valleys. Herds of sheep and goats are grazed throughout the zone, and small-scale farming on the more accessible hills and plateaus is interspersed with irrigated cultivation in many of the valleys. The area is less densely populated than the plains, but pockets of more concentrated settlement exist around available sources of water. Of the 55,000 hectares of mountainous terrain in the Sefrou region, only about 10,000 hectares is cultivable land, and much of this must be left fallow in any given year. Overgrazing and extensive wood cutting have sharply reduced the forests near Sefrou, and erosion has become a serious problem.

Lying between the mountains and the plains is the dir, or piedmont zone. The dir–an Arabic term related to *darra* ("to flow copiously, be abundant") and *dirra* ("breast")–is a zone some 10 to 15 kilometers wide that runs along the foot of the mountains just before they join the plains. Here, springs bubble up from beneath the surface to supply a relatively stable source of water for irrigation and larger concentrations of population. It is within this oasislike zone that all the larger settlements of the area–most notably, the city of Sefrou–are found.

The interaction of these three ecological zones is intimately related to the overall climatic features of the region. The climate of the area is characterized mainly by its variability and unpredictability. For any given feature–temperature, rainfall, hours of sunlight, wind–the range of variation over a series of years is quite extreme. More importantly, perhaps, the variation within each year can be enormous. The response to this situation – by farmers, herdsmen, and merchants alike – takes the cultural form of a complicated set of strategies affecting all domains of life. Diverse crops are planted within a single garden or field to hedge against uncertain weather and markets; rights to fields or pastures are distributed in various microecological niches to spread the risk of changing circumstances; social ties are formed beyond the bounds of kinship or locality to cope with the whole range of environmental and social uncertainties, religious rituals are employed to coerce supernatural aid against the fluctuation of the elements. All these strategies intertwine and have mutual effects extending far beyond the confines of any simply adaptive solution.

The environmental uncertainties themselves are very real. Take, for example, the variation in temperature for a given month over several years. In June of 1958 the mean temperature varied from 87 to 48 degrees Fahrenheit, a range of 39 degrees in a single month. The following year the range was only 7 degrees (66 to 59); the third year, 19 degrees (85 to 66). Equally large fluctuations could be cited for any other month of the year. Indeed, no significantly predictable pattern emerges over longer spans of time. This is not to say that there is no regularity whatsoever, but only that changes of a magnitude that can seriously affect agricultural productivity occur as a matter of course, and the Moroccan farmer must arrange his affairs to compensate for this unpredictability.

The variation in temperature, which has an impact on growing cycles and evaporation rates, is matched by the more serious variation in rainfall. Because most of the plains and mountain regions are unirrigated, crops are dependent not only on the sheer quantity of rain that falls but, more importantly, on when it comes. Both these factors are extraordinarily erratic. For example, over one five-year period the total rainfall in the Sefrou region varied from 379 to 728 millimeters. In October 1956 there was 7 millimeters of rain; the following October there was 105; and in October of the third year, 55 millimeters. The variation is equally great within and among other seasons of the year. It is no comfort to the Moroccan farmer to say that the average rainfall in October of 1956–8 was 55.6 millimeters because the actual distribution of rainfall could never be even roughly guessed in advance.

The consequences of this environmental variation are diverse. Harvests, naturally, fluctuate considerably as the weather shifts. Between 1952 and 1962 the national output of cereals, measured in millions of

quintals, was as follows: 22, 32, 36, 28, 30, 18, 25, 26, 21, 10, 22. For
a country in which a year's harvest of the staple crop can vary over a
range of 26 million quintals (roughly 3 million tons), and where the
change from one year to the next may be of the order of 100 percent,
this is indeed a precarious situation. True, severe droughts and floods
occur infrequently, and the availability of foreign aid has eased some
of the insecurity. Most important for our present purposes, however,
is the fact that the success or failure of crops is itself unevenly and
uncertainly distributed over a given region. Adjoining hillsides in the
bled Sefrou may have very different yields in a single year, and people
have, therefore, arranged their ties and their concepts of the social
world in which they live to account for these events.

To say that the environment suffuses social and cultural life is not to
reduce the one to a function of the other or to conceive of the natural
setting as a thing apart from social life. Tracing the relationships that
surround the approach taken by the Sefrou people to their environment, one can see the importance of a town like Sefrou, which is set
in the intermediate dir zone and whose steady supply of water and
interstitial position makes it a natural entrepöt for the region. Similarly, one can see how the uncertainties of the environment have
influenced the interdependence of all three zones, rendering the bled
Sefrou an interacting entity in which simple dichotomies of urban and
rural possess little explanatory force. Moreover, one can see that although there is no necessary reason why people of the area have
adapted as they have, the environment and their view of it are as
much a characteristic part of the social being of the Sefrou people as
their kinship, their politics, or their religion. Indeed, the relationship
of each of these domains and the commonality of many of their defining features are particularly striking.

Situated in the piedmont, between mountain and plain, and surrounded by a wide expanse of irrigated gardens, the city of Sefrou has
often been referred to by travelers as an oasis. In many respects its
physical design and setting convey an almost storybook vision of a
Middle Eastern city. The old city, or *medina,* is surrounded by a high,
crenelated wall pierced in a number of places by gates that were
formerly used to seal the city off nightly from the gardens and countryside beyond. Within, the city is further subdivided by a number of
quarters and byways. Rows of small shops, specialized trade areas,
narrow streets lined by the characterless facades of dwelling places,
and all those features – mosques, baths, fountains, ovens – that give to
this Islamic city its distinctive urban character are found within the
walls. With the exception of a small urban sector, the Qlaᶜa, located 11

just to the east of the medina, Sefrou was, until the beginning of the colonial period, wholly contained within its ramparts.

With the advent of the Protectorate, the design of the city began to change. It was the policy of the Protectorate's first resident general, Lyautey, that the structure of indigenous cities be supplemented, rather than fundamentally altered, by the French presence. Accordingly, a new area, the Ville Nouvelle, was constructed along the eastern edge of the oasis' gardens. This sector now comprises a long street with cinemas, shops, cafés, and government buildings, as well as a number of residential streets lined by Western-style villas. After World War II, several new residential areas were constructed just outside the walls of the old city. These "new medina" areas contain houses of more traditional design, but the streets, laid out in rectangular pattern, are wide enough to carry the automobiles and trucks that are unable to traverse the narrow streets of the medina proper. Many of the residents of these new medina areas are better off financially than those who continue to live in the old city proper, although some of the oldest and most important families of the city still occupy sections of the medina.

The postwar years also saw a substantial influx of rural people to the city. The poorest of these immigrants tend to reside in the mellah, the former Jewish quarter. Those who can afford to often move later into other sections of the city, including a barrackslike set of structures, called Slawi, originally built to house victims of a flood that occurred in 1950.

Physically, then, the city of Sefrou has long been characterized by the presence of those institutions–economic, cultural, and administrative–that could serve as an urban focus for the surrounding region. The waters of the Aggai River and its network of irrigation canals gave to the city a reliable agricultural baseline that contrasts with the more uncertain supply of rainfall available in the countryside. Far from being a totally self-contained unit closed off from the surrounding hinterland, the city of Sefrou is, and probably always has been, thoroughy intertwined with the ecology and the history of the whole region.

The past

Just as their working of the environment becomes an integral part of the culture and organization of a people's distinctive existence, so too their history–seen not solely as a succession of people, places, and events, but as a gradual alteration of patterns, associations, and concepts–is a vital aspect of their characteristic nature. The history of

Sefrou and its region—at least as it bears on an analysis of contemporary social life—situates and indeed serves to explain how the concepts and institutions distinctive to this place in this setting inform the actions of its residents.

The city of Sefrou was probably established in the ninth century, when the founder of Fez, Idris II, is said to have settled there briefly. Not, however, until the latter part of the seventeenth century, with tribal movements and the restructuring of governmental legitimacy, did the Sefrou region begin to crystallize in a still recognizable form. The great Berber dynasties of the eleventh to fifteenth centuries—the Almoravids, the Almohads, and the Merinids—arose from the mountain and desert fringes of the country and, fueled by religious zeal, successively established themselves as the primary forces. Moreover, they helped to establish the pattern of a central government, or *makzen,* that was focused on a few major families and that sought—through alliance and military foray, intrigue and negotiation—to maintain solidity at the center and control over the tribes on the periphery. Regions of governmental control and local independence—*bled l-makzen* and *bled s-sība*—were not, however, geographically defined because constellations of power were numerous, shifting, and not organized along simply territorial lines. Even when makhzen dominance was amenable to actual enforcement—especially in the major cities—it was constantly subject to internal and external pressures. Rather than hierarchical, the pattern of political organization, from this formative period, became horizontal, and the bases of recruitment, alliance, and power were fractionated and multiple.

The period from the mid-fifteenth to the mid-seventeenth centuries was one of great disequilibrium throughout Morocco. European intrusion and the decline of the last Berber dynasty led to the dissolution of the country into a host of competitive, independent centers of power. Partly in reaction to the Christian intrusion on the coast, partly as a result of the threat to Moroccan civilization posed by the Christian recovery of Spain, and partly owing to intellectual influences from the Middle East, there developed throughout Morocco a number of mystical sects, headed by men (called *murābtīn*) conceived to be divinely inspired and divinely propelled. Although the most important of these maraboutic centers were defeated in the latter part of the seventeenth century, the emergent dynastic regimes sought to reestablish the makhzen on a more solid foundation by fusing the moral intensity of the Berber dynasties and the maraboutic centers with claims of legitimacy based on descent from the Prophet Mohammed. Founded in 1668, the still-ruling Alawite dynasty thus incorporated 13 features of genealogical and charismatic legitimacy while nevertheless constituting a regime that, like its predecessors, was confronted with multiple sources and centers of power and itself only as good as its powers of intrigue and enforcement.

In the early period of the Alawite dynasty, local marabouts continued to threaten the existence of the regime even as they sought to associate themselves with the sources of legitimacy now mobilized around it. In the Sefrou area, for example, a scholar and saint, Sidi Lahcen Lyusi, whose descendants still constitute the main saintly focus of the tribal region surrounding the city, sought to have his own legitimacy as a descendant of the Prophet underwritten by the Alawite sultan.

The seventeenth century was also a period of great movement of the Berber tribes in central Morocco. Propelled, in part, by drought in the Sahara, segments of a loosely organized Berber confederation pushed into the Middle Atlas Mountains and down onto the plains beyond. Separate groupings, hiving off all along the way, settled in the area and engaged the Alawite sultans in battle and alliance as each group sought to establish itself in the area. In the Sefrou region the Ait Yusi tribe predominated, and, like other loosely organized groupings throughout the Middle Atlas, lived in agonistic symbiosis with one another and the settled, mainly Arabic-speaking townsmen of Sefrou and other urban centers.

Contemporary residents of the bled Sefrou are not unmindful of this history, and because many of its institutional features – the sherifian dynasty of the Alawites, the spiritual force of saints, the aggressive individualism of each nodal point in the body politic – are very much a part of their present-day lives, this history is, whether or not they are conscious of its details, very much a part of what they now are. But it is in more recent and more localized events, persons, and periods that the consciousness of the people described in this book was formed, and their delineation of that history points up the contexts in which their own historically based perceptions have been forged.

The decade from 1894 to 1904 is notable to the Sefrou people as the period dominated by Qaid Umar al-Yusi. A Berber from high up in the mountain reaches of the Ait Yusi territory, Umar was one of those rural figures who created a network of alliances of such significance that the makhzen, by officially appointing him as *qaid* ("administrator") of the region, hoped to contain or coopt his power. Umar's appointment followed an all-out fight with a rival Berber contender, after which – in a highly unusual move – he was appointed not only qaid of the region but its urban analogue, *pasha* of the town, as well. His days were those in which caravans still moved through Sefrou to

14

the Sahara, when almost all the Arab townsmen were engaged in some
form of agricultural activity, and when a powerful local figure ratified
by a weak central government could control the entire region so long
as he was able to keep one step ahead of his ever-present rivals.

The assassination of Umar in 1904 came at a time when the Moroccan government, headed by the ineffectual sultan Mulay Abdel Aziz,
was under constant pressure from European intrusion. Beginning with
the direct incursion of the French in the Casablanca area in 1907 and
continuing until the actual formation of the French Protectorate in
1912, the disarray of the makhzen was reinforced, was part of, the
widespread political disorder on the local level. The little makhzen of
Qaid Umar and the interlocking relations between tradesmen, agriculturalists, and tribesmen that characterized the economy and social
organization of his time, were replaced, in this disorderly period, by a
weak form of collegial rule by notable families in the city and the
oscillation of rural figures competing for the role Umar had formerly
played.

But the arrival of the French had unalterably changed such roles.
Establishing a kind of colonial police rule through the pasha Lamouri,
the French consolidated their contol of Sefrou and the Ait Yusi territory and, after World War I, gradually began to obtain the best areas
on the plains for colonial farms. A separate European quarter was also
constructed alongside the old walled city of Sefrou. The early colonial
period saw a greater distinction drawn by the French between the city
and the countryside and among various sectors of the population than
had characterized the area in earlier times. Later, during the high
colonial period of the interwar decades, when the technological and
economic impact of the French was more significant, the institutional
differentiation of city and countryside, Arab and Berber, became even
more important. New marketplaces were constructed in the countryside, new administrative boundaries were drawn throughout the region, the population of the city grew as rural people came in search of
jobs and education, and an elaborate infrastructure of roads and communications accelerated the contacts of people within and beyond the
city and its surroundings.

Already in the 1930s the first elements of modern Moroccan nationalism were clearly in evidence. The attempt to split Berbers and Arabs
by means of the Berber Dahir of 1930, which sought to place the
Berbers under French rather than Islamic legal jurisdiction, actually
reinforced the ties between city and countryside, and the deposition
and exile by the French of the sultan Mohammed V in 1953 coalesced
sentiment around the nationalist movement. Some rural people worked   15

with the irregular Army of Liberation, and many of the urban people contributed to the activities of the nationalist political party, Istiqlal. The importance of the Sefrou region to the newly independent government was demonstrated by the fact that, following the return of Mohammed V and the acquisition of national independence in 1956, the pasha of the city, Si M'barek Bekkai, was appointed the nation's first prime minister, and the qaid of the Ait Yusi, Qaid Lahcen Lyusi, was designated the country's first minister of interior.

In the years since Independence the city has grown at an accelerated pace, as rural migrants have sought what schooling and employment are available in the city. Most of the Jews of Sefrou, once a major presence there, have departed since Independence, seeking in the cities of the Atlantic coast and abroad the opportunities Berber immigrants now seek in Sefrou.

Through these periods of rapid but clearly distinguishable change the present inhabitants of the Sefrou region have come to receive and work with the categories and conventions, political forms and cultural concepts that inform their view of their social world. It is not just that the aged remember a time when rival Berber tribesmen shot at one another from the city's rooftops or that today's youths focus their ambitions on obtaining jobs in the national bureaucracy. It is, rather, that the concerns with which the institutions of kinship, marriage, trade, and the like are approached vary with the historical career of the groupings involved, and hence the means by which culture is shared and interpreted within these groupings are linked to the changing circumstances of experience and perception. But for all that, the institutions of social life and the categories of persons and relationships employed remain common among the various generations and segments of the Sefrou population, and it is in the flexible application of these concepts and institutions that the shared distinctiveness of the region is to be found.

The authors of this book caught a particular society in a particular place at a particular time. From that encounter, as unique to us as to those we confronted, we have tried to construct a picture – or, more accurately, a related set of pictures – of what that society is like, how it got to be that way, and, so far as we can figure it out, why. To this last question – unanswerable, unavoidable, and the one by which such enterprises as this are justified – our response has been to conceive of social order as meaningful form and to conceive of meaningful form as embedded in the life, from one angle deeply singular, from another deeply familiar, the Sefrouis live.

1. Hart, D., *The Aith Waryaghar of the Moroccan Rif*, Tucson, 1976; Brown, K., *People of Salé: Tradition and Change in a Moroccan City 1830–1930*, Cambridge (Mass.), 1976; Eickelman, D., *Moroccan Islam*, Austin, 1976; Crapanzano, V., *The Hamadsha: A Study in Moroccan Ethnopsychiatry*, Berkeley, 1973.

2. The researchers and the periods they spent in the field are as follows: Clifford and Hildred Geertz: summer 1963, general survey by C. Geertz; July to November 1964, Rabat; July 1965 to August 1966 and July 1968 to March 1969, Sefrou; Lawrence Rosen: January 1966 to August 1967 and summer 1969, Sefrou; Paul Rabinow: 1968 to 1969, Sidi Lahcen Lyusi; Thomas Dichter: October 1969 to February 1971, Sefrou. The entire project was conceived and organized by Clifford Geertz. With the exception of Paul Hyman, the photographer, the researchers worked mainly in colloquial Moroccan Arabic and, occasionally, in French.

3. The following studies, directly related to research in the Sefrou region, have previously been published by members of the project:

Clifford Geertz: *Islam Observed*, New Haven, 1968; "The Wet and the Dry: Traditional Irrigation in Bali and Morocco," *Human Ecology*, 1:23–39 (1972); " 'From the Native's Point of View,' On the Nature of Anthropological Understanding," in Basso, K., and H. Selby (eds.), *Meaning in Anthropology*, Albuquerque, 1976, pp. 221–37; "Art as a Cultural System," *MLN*, 91:1473–99 (1976); "The Bazaar Economy: Information and Search in Peasant Marketing," *American Economic Review*, 68:28–32 (1978).

Lawrence Rosen: "The Structure of Social Groups in a Moroccan City" (unpublished Ph.D. dissertation, University of Chicago, 1968); "A Moroccan Jewish Community During the Middle Eastern Crisis," *The American Scholar*, 37:435–51 (1968); " 'I Divorce Thee,' " *Trans-action*, 7:34–7 (1970); "Muslim-Jewish Relations in a Moroccan City," *International Journal of Middle East Studies*, 3:435–49 (1972); "Rural Political Process and National Political Structure in Morocco," in Antoun, R., and I. Harik (eds.), *Rural Politics and Social Change in the Middle East*, Bloomington, 1972, pp. 214–36; "The Social and Conceptual Framework of Arab-Berber Relations in Central Morocco," in Gellner, E., and C. Micaud (eds.), *Arabs and Berbers: From Tribe to Nation in North Africa*, London, 1973, pp. 155–73; "The Negotiation of Reality: Male-Female Relations in Sefrou, Morocco," in Beck, L., and Keddie, N. (eds.), *Women in the Muslim World*, Cambridge (Mass.), 1979, pp. 561–84.

Paul Rabinow: *Symbolic Domination: Cultural Form and Historical Change in Morocco*, Chicago, 1975; *Reflections on Fieldwork in Morocco*, Berkeley, 1978.

Thomas Dichter: "The Problem of How to Act on an Undefined Stage: An Exploration of Culture, Change, and Individual Consciousness in the Moroccan Town of Sefrou, with a Focus on Three Modern Schools," (unpublished Ph.D. dissertation, University of Chicago, 1976).

4. The area for which Sefrou constitutes an important urban focus also includes a number of other localized groupings, among them the Ait Seghoushen, Beni Warrain, Beni Yazgha, Beni Mguild, Beni M'tir (Ait N'dhir), and those groupings living on the Sais Plain. These groups were the subject of brief, often narrowly limited, inquiries by members of the project.

Social identity and points of attachment: approaches to social organization
Lawrence Rosen

An approach to social organization

Although one can readily specify, and even directly observe, some of the social units that characterize life in the Sefrou region, it is far more difficult to establish categories of analysis that are true to the essential qualities of these social units. One can point to an urban quarter or circumambulate a rural settlement, step across the line separating irrigated oasis from rolling plain, or gather in collective celebration the members of a family or tribe. But studying the organization and dynamics of each such entity reveals that the structural forms alone do not wholly or unambiguously define the actual relationships they embrace. Watching kinsmen bargain over the nature of their mutual obligations or witnessing the resident of a given locale establish a personal network of affiliations, one appreciates that the question of what is a family, a quarter, or a tribe demands an analytic, rather than a typological, response.

In order to explore the actual formation and operation of social ties in the Sefrou region, it may, therefore, prove more fruitful to begin, not with resultant groupings, but with some of the concepts through which individuals establish their own and each others' social attachments, and to analyze how these attachments are drawn upon to form a series of highly contextualized social bonds. To comprehend the organization of social life in the Sefrou region, one must understand the conceptual structures – the collective images – through which the people sometimes experience, interpret, judge, and create their ties to one another.

Specifically, we shall be concerned here with analyzing two major sets of concepts that suffuse the organization of social life in the 19 region. The first set of concepts bears on the question of social identity. Each individual in the area draws a large part of his or her identity from those others with whom common ties of origin, locality, and kinship are shared. Moreover, the various concepts that contribute to this identity imply certain expectations and possibilities that may be tapped in the process of giving specific content to any relationship defined on the basis of common ancestry, shared locality, or similarity of origins. How these features of personal identity are actualized for the formation of interpersonal ties depends, second, on a series of concepts used in the negotiation of reciprocal relations. It is in the employment of the concepts of obligation and propensity, constraint and negotiation that the possibilities inherent in various modes of affiliation are themselves defined and realized.

One of the most striking features of social life in the Sefrou region that such an analysis reveals is the great emphasis placed on the individual. All societies, of course, are composed of individuals, but in Sefrou the cultural stress and repercussions of individual action – the free play of personality – determine, to an extraordinarily high degree, the shape and operation of everyday social life. Among the people of Sefrou, as the following discussion will argue in detail, ties of kinship do not determine forms of behavior, obligations of support, or networks of exchange; nor does residence or linguistic affiliation establish political alliance or economic association. The rules of behavior symbolically associated with these social frames are viewed by the Moroccans as relational possibilities, available social resources, rather than entailed obligations or incontrovertible rights. Tribe, family, and quarter, in this vision, become social fields in which independent lines of force, centered around nodes of interpersonal contact, are organized into distinct networks, personally serviced and situationally varied.

Moreover, the ways in which people in the Sefrou region conceptually divide the universe of social experience and establish their personal relationships crosscut each of the separate domains of economic, political, and social life. Contractual elements suffuse kinship relations, political alliances vary with shifting genealogical referents, and legal decisions are shaped by a multiplicity of interpersonal perceptions and ties. City and countryside, tribe and quarter thus become heterogeneous social fields, conceptual entities, in which certain institutions are found and others are not. An understanding of social life in Sefrou must account not only for the distinctive qualities of the institutional frameworks and their attendant cultural concepts, but also for the cultural stress on the processes through which individuals marshal their social resources to create personal webs of affiliation. This approach to social organization will be applied in the present discussion to an understanding of the ecological, political, legal, and social life of the Sefrou region.

Social and political organization: the rural pattern

Ecology and social structure: themes and variations

Just as biologists have found in the concept of ecology a useful framework for studying the relations between an environment and the forms of life found within it, so, too, anthropologists have come to analyze a society's placement on the land as a complex set of relations involving numerous aspects of physical, social, and cultural factors. From an ecological perspective, the artifacts of human existence are an integral part of the natural setting, and neither the environment nor the ways a civilization has worked out its relation to that environment can be understood apart from one another. An analysis of land use patterns or systems of irrigation is, therefore, more than a description of geographical givens and the social forms found in conjunction with them: It is also an exploration of the ways in which the people of a region have made their setting a part of their own social drama and how their cultural and social forms constitute a portion of the whole ecological pattern.

The Sefrou region is characterized by three major ecological zones, each of which contains a series of discrete microenvironments. The first zone, the plains, extends from the Atlantic littoral almost to the edge of the Middle Atlas Mountains. Here, in what the French used to call *le Maroc utile,* the climate, though subject to wide variation, affords relatively good conditions for intensive cultivation of grain. By contrast, the mountainous zone of the Middle Atlas is far less intensively cultivated. Herds of sheep and goats pasture throughout the zone, and small-scale farming is practiced on the more accessible hills and plateaus. In some places, irrigated gardening is possible, and the general pattern of scattered settlements is broken where populations have gathered around more stable or significant sources of water.

Between the mountains and the plains lies the piedmont zone, or *dir.* Running intermittently along the juncture of mountain and plain, the piedmont is characterized by a number of springs that well up from beneath the surface to supply a more consistent source of water for irrigation and population support. It is in this interstitial, oasislike   21 zone that the larger settlements of the region – in particular, the city of Sefrou – are found.[1]

For each of these three zones – plain, mountain, and piedmont – the range of climatic variation, within a year as well as among different years, is significant. Where temperature in a single summer month one year may vary only a few degrees Fahrenheit, temperature in the same month another year may vary as much as 40 degrees. More seriously, rainfall is unequally varied. Whereas winter is normally the season of greatest rainfall, in some years more rain falls in a single summer month than during an entire winter.[2]

Moreover, this extreme variability of climatic conditions has a spatial, as well as a temporal, vector. Within the mountains, for example, it is not uncommon for one hillside or valley to receive adequate and timely rainfall, while an adjacent area receives insufficient or inappropriately timed amounts. In both the mountains and the plains, therefore, one can differentiate a wide range of microenvironments, each of which has its own distinctive qualities. Recognizing these local conditions and the general climatic uncertainty, the people of the Sefrou region have organized their technology, their social ties, and their concepts of the world accordingly. Arrangements are often worked out for the movement of herds to greener or warmer pastures; parcels of both dry and irrigated land are sought to balance the unpredictable; crops are planted that require different amounts or schedules of watering.

Even in the oasis of Sefrou and other portions of the piedmont, where supplies of water are more regular and substantial, farmers hedge against uncertainties of climate, market, and political circumstance. More significantly, perhaps, each of the three zones forms part of an interdependent unit in which access to markets and the availability of different resources link the people into a complex whole. Despite the differences of zone or niche, the problem of unpredictability is broadly shared, and the social arrangements by which all the people of the region confront this situation, though notable for their local variations, display thematic similarity. For this reason one may speak of the entire area – bled Sefrou – as an interacting whole and at the same time draw analytic distinctions among its constituent populations.

The city of Sefrou lies at the base of the Middle Atlas Mountains at the point where the mountains join the Sais Plain. Although there are very significant relations with those who live on the plains side of the piedmont, it is largely in the piedmont itself and in the mountains to the south that the city's hinterland is to be found. The rural area surrounding the city is inhabited primarily by Berber speakers who identify themselves as belonging to various segments of the Ait Yusi "tribe" (Ar. *qbīla*; Br. *taqbilt*). The territory of the Ait Yusi ranges in width from 10 to 40 kilometers as it cuts through the heart of the Middle Atlas Mountains from Sefrou and the Sais Plain in the north to the valley of the Mulwiya River some 75 kilometers to the south. Three distinct regions, running from north to south, can be distinguished within this area: (1) the foothills and intermittent strips of irrigated land that extend from the Sais Plain through the plateau of Amekla, (2) the forests and mountain pastures that traverse the region of the Guigou River, and (3) the high plateau and mountains of Enjil. The official Moroccan census of 1960 lists some 130 separate Ait Yusi settlements (of quite unequal size and definition) with a total population of almost 60,000 persons. Although the vast majority of the people are native Berber speakers, several Arab-speaking settlements are situated within the Ait Yusi territory – particularly near Sefrou – and are, depending on the perspective and purpose invoked, regarded as integral parts of this otherwise Berber-speaking tribe.

The Ait Yusi territory thus cuts through each of the major ecological zones and a number of constituent microenvironments. In order to see how different Ait Yusi groups have worked out their social and political ties, as part of their overall ecological situation, we shall consider three particularly revealing examples. Two of the groupings described live in the piedmont zone and one in the mountains, but each has important ties to portions of the other ecological zones. Moreover, each example allows us to concentrate on particular features of many rural groups in the region without slighting the features that are broadly characteristic of the entire bled Sefrou. We shall look at the landholding pattern at Azghar, where the idiom of segmentary tribal structure is coupled with a separate set of principles for the distribution of shares in the land; the Sidi Lahcen Lyusi complex, where saintly and nonsaintly lineages have organized themselves to work a system of irrigation; and the Ait ben Assu cluster, whose internal organization is built on a characteristic amalgam of kin and contractual ties.

Azghar: collective landholding and segmentary idiom

Some 19 kilometers south of Sefrou, in the broad and reasonably fertile plateau of Amekla, lies a large plot of land called Azghar. The land itself comprises several thousand hectares and is held collectively by a number of different segments of the Ait Yusi tribe. How this land is conceptually divided and how its actual distribution relates to

23

Social identity and points of attachment

this conceptual scheme illustrate the relation between cultural categories and forms of social organization that will be seen to recur in numerous domains of life in the Sefrou region.

The people who hold land at Azghar are all identified with various segments of the Ait Yusi tribe. In order to understand how their affiliation as members of these segments relates to their social and political organization, it is important to understand how the Ait Yusi and its constituent units are conceptualized.

If you ask Berbers in the Sefrou region what exactly are the composition and internal structure of the Ait Yusi tribe, the answer is usually couched in terms of the utilization and defense of territorial resources or a genealogical hierarchy or both. In the first instance, it is said that the Ait Yusi are those persons who share the pastures, forests, and waters of Ait Yusi territory that are not otherwise restricted by individual or collective rights. Moreover, these persons help defend these resources, as well as the more restricted ones, against outside incursion. However, because the territorial boundaries are vaguely delimited, subject to political decisions made by the national government, and capable of being altered by particular Ait Yusi through sale or purchase, this definition is by no means one that correlates exactly with a set of physical boundaries or precisely sanctioned rights and duties.

Similarly, the genealogical structure, though conceptualized in terms of named segments, is not a simple representation of solidary social units. More knowledgeable, usually elderly, informants generally refer to the following subdivisions, more or less elaborated, in describing the tribe:[3] The Ait Yusi as a whole, they say, is divisible into two main units, the Ait u M'nassaf and the Ait Amur u Yahia. These, in turn, are divided into, in the first case three and in the second case five, superordinate segments of quite unequal size. Each of these units is further divided into from two to eight semiendogamous, roughly localized, maximal patrilineages, which are themselves divided into several localized medial lineages whose members claim but cannot always demonstrate the genealogical ties that link them together some five generations past. Finally, these medial lineages subdivide into a set of minimal lineages of three to five demonstrable generations' depth. The number of households, and beneath that, of families that make up a minimal lineage vary somewhat. So, too, does the range of relatedness of persons living in a given settlement, a unit to be considered in more detail below.

In theory this arrangement has much the appearance of a hierarchy
24 of units that, if classical segmentary theory were applicable, would be

characterized by the opposition of units of the same level of segmentation and the coalescence of such units at ever higher points on the genealogical charter.[4] But as we implied at the outset, in the case of the Ait Yusi, if not of many other Moroccan tribes, this chart of relationship is neither a precise diagram of sociologically real groups nested in corporate solidarity in an all-embracing hierarchy nor an archaic survival that, like the fossil record of a given species, refers only to some dead or reconstructed list of predecessors. Rather, such genealogical ties – at every level of segmentation from tribe to individual family – constitute a set of cultural categories, conceptual discriminations that often serve less to organize specific relations between groups of individuals than to provide a framework, a set of initial relationships, a lexicon of possible affiliations upon which individuals can draw in forming their personal networks. The organization of social life at Azghar exemplifies these principles.

The people who partake of the land at Azghar conceive of their collective interest as being divided into twelve units or shares, six of which are apportioned between each of two superordinate segments of the Ait u M'nassaf portion of the Ait Yusi tribe: the Ait Mekhluf and the Ait Feringu. The six shares of the Ait Mekhluf are further divided among each of six localized groupings; those of the Ait Feringu are divided through an intermediate genealogical level among two groups of five localized kin groups each. The actual subdivisions of the Ait u M'nassaf portion of the Ait Yusi are indicated in the following outline:

Ait Mekhluf (6 shares)
1. Ait Khalifa (1 share)
2. Ait Musa (1 share)
3. Ait Said u Lahcen (1 share)
4. Ait Haynajen (1 share)
5. Ait Buzian (1 share)
6. Ait Zaikum (1 share)

Ait Feringu (6 shares)
A. Ait Mohammed (3 shares)
7. Ait Ishu
8. Ait Hend
9. Ait Lahcen
10. Ait Reqia
11. Ait Azu
B. Ait Rezuk (3 shares)
12. Ait Ibu^{c}a
13. I^{c}arasen

25

14. Ait Lahcen Buqaya
15. Ait Ali Buqaya
16. Ait Miskin

Despite this conceptual division of interests along the lines of an elaborated genealogy, it would be seriously misleading to characterize the organization of the groups involved as one that simply conforms to the principles of segmentary structure. The twelve shares that constitute the total interest in the land are entirely abstract units: They do not represent parcels of land occupied by genealogically determined groupings. The segmentary image is appropriate to higher-order relationships, but not to the internal operations of the enumerated localized kin groups. The formal distribution of land is entirely in the hands of each of the sixteen localized groupings listed, and the principles of distribution invoked by each do not necessarily replicate one another. One group may allot a parcel to each head of a household; a second may grant plots on the basis of household size; and a third may assign rights to individual men who are away in the armed forces. In pre-Protectorate times the collective land of various Moroccan tribes is said to have been subject to periodic reallocation, and this appears to have been true in Azghar as well.[5] The last general redistribution was in 1913, shortly after the beginning of the Protectorate. Some of the individual segments have subsequently been reapportioned.

Reallocation and the ban on alienation of collective holdings to outsiders offer the potential for maintaining a shared interest in the land at Azghar. However, despite the conceptual stress on genealogically linked groupings as the units of which the collective enterprise is constituted, it is significant that the land is not distributed in terms of the segments' genealogical proximity to one another. Although the idiom of segmentarity is employed, it plays no role as a principle for ordering land distributions among newly proliferated segments. Indeed, it cannot play this role because the distribution of shares in Azghar is fixed at the higher genealogical levels and subject to the flexible application of quite a different set of principles at the lower levels. The actual distribution of land, far from being determined by a proliferating genealogy, is, in the first instance, a function of the rules of allocation used by each of the localized shareholding groups. These rules, however, are neither rigid nor all-embracing. Indeed, in keeping with the general absence of corporate activity, the distribution of allotments within any segment depends mainly on the ways in which individual members are able to marshal support based on ideals of kinship affiliation and bonds of personal obligation to enforce their claims against those of weaker persons.

26

That the conceptual and relational aspects of Sefrou life do not constitute simple mirror images of one another poses a difficult theoretical problem for the ethnographer. One approach would argue that the conceptual order is almost wholly divorced from the social order, that the abstract image of relatedness embodied, for example, in the idiom of segmentation is connected, not to the organization of interests in physical and political resources, but to other concepts (honor, descent, sexual differentiation) that give individuals a sense of meaningful attachment to an ongoing moral and social community.[6] From this theoretical perspective, the concept of segmentation can be understood only in relation to other conceptual domains that collectively project a distinctive commonsense view of reality. To partake of such a ramified conceptual order would, from this point of view, tell individuals who they are rather than what they should do.

An alternative approach would see the differentiation of conceptual and relational domains primarily in adaptive terms. The concept of segmentation provides a framework for coalescence when mutual interests must be served; organization in terms of personal affiliation allows individual assessments and strategies as the primary adaptive mechanism in a political and environmental situation that is as varied as it is unpredictable.[7]

Whatever the merits of these alternative emphases to other parts of the Middle East, the approach that appears to conform most closely with the Sefrou material combines elements of both these interpretations. Clearly, identification with other segments at Azghar and throughout the Ait Yusi territory serves as an important indicator of personal identity and attachment to a recognizable order in an uncertain world. But this conceptual, even psychological, emphasis is not without practical attachment to the perceived world of social relations. Although it is not the dominant organizing principle of resource allocation – and probably never was – the image of segmentation reinforces the common basis of personal identity, the potential of rallying nonobligatory support, and the justification of common claims at the same time that it permits the actual organization of resources according to principles that reside beneath and beyond the image of strict segmentation. The perpetuation of this dual order thus unites, at the one extreme, location of the self and other within a meaningful conceptual order, and, at the other, the continuance of a repertoire of relational possibilities that can be tuned to accord with those aspects of life that are not wholly accounted for by the segmentary image.

Even within the Azghar region the multiplicity of resource bases and the range of alternative social ties are characteristically varied.

Social identity and points of attachment

27

Several other properties, besides the collective land, are used by the constituent segments represented at Azghar. Near each of their localized settlements individuals also have interests in additional fields and gardens. For example, one of the localized groupings with interests at Azghar, the Ait Zaikum, also possesses two irrigated plots of land. Each year one of the two parcels receives all the water from two nearby springs, and the other is left fallow. Each individual member of Ait Zaikum owns a set of strips in both parcels, so that each year he will have both irrigated land and grazing land. Each of the two plots is divided into thirteen sections, which represent a day and a night of water, so that any one section gets irrigated once every thirteen days. Within each of these sections are eight to twelve individually owned plots that receive timed allotments of water during the period their section is irrigated. These hours are rotated between day and night, so that no one person always has work during the nighttime.

In a fashion similar to that at Azghar, each of the thirteen sections of irrigated land possesses a name that is said to belong to an ancestral figure but that no longer corresponds, if it ever did, to actual groups of descendants. All plots are individually owned and can be accumulated, sold within the Ait Zaikum, or inherited. Thus, as at Azghar, the division into named sections is fixed at the higher level, where it is symbolized in terms of a genealogical charter, whereas at the lower level there is great flexibility. Resources are thus distributed in accordance with principles quite different from those that might follow from genealogical relatedness alone.

Because the land tenure systems are flexible and diverse, they can be easily adjusted to the realities of specific political fluctuations and local ecological variation. Relations that are broadly conceptualized in the language of segmentary organization are, on the ground, arranged with no direct recourse to a hierarchy of corporate groupings. The conceptual regularity and organizational malleability, coupled with the distribution of different types of holdings in different fields and locations, help assure a degree of security for just about everyone in all but the worst of years.

Sidi Lahcen Lyusi: the cultural ecology of a saintly village

The linkage of conceptual forms based on a genealogical idiom and organizational forms grounded in personal contract is found in many parts of the Sefrou region and in many other domains besides resource allocation. A further example of the relation between concep-

28

tual categories and social forms is supplied by a study of the cultural ecology of the major saintly complex of the Ait Yusi territory.

Running along the floor and sides of a long valley in the foothills of the Middle Atlas Mountains some 32 kilometers to the east of Sefrou is a cluster of settlements called Sidi Lahcen Lyusi. The name derives from a seventeenth-century saint who is purportedly buried in one of the settlements and from whom many of the villagers claim descent.[8] This settlement is also known as Tamzazit, the name it bore when the local Berbers invited the saint to settle there. He accepted because of the abundance of land, water, and game found there, all signs of *baraka* ("divine grace"). A third name for the settlement is Roda, literally "cemetery," indicating that the saint's tomb is located there.

The village of Sidi Lahcen Lyusi is composed of five smaller settlements, of unequal size and importance, spread out along the sides of the valley. The smallest consists of one large compound perched on the side of a hill; the largest, Roda, accounts for about half of the 900 inhabitants of the village. Although each settlement is named, the villagers divide the whole cluster into "upper" and "lower" sections of the village. This distinction is basically topographical, but also has sociological and ecological ramifications. The upper settlements lie next to each other on a small plateau. Houses, stores, and a small mosque are located on this plateau as well as a government-constructed and maintained market and schoolhouse. The only source of water for drinking and irrigation is transported through a crude canal from a large spring named *cain s-sultān* ("the sultan's spring") located 5 kilometers further up the valley. Sitting on this plateau, the upper settlements are directly exposed to the elements and, therefore, tend to be cooler in winter and hotter in summer than the more protected lower settlement. Several hundred meters down the valley lies Roda, the main cluster of Sidi Lahcen. The settlement's houses, stores, large whitewashed mosque, and prominent green-tiled tomb are nestled against the flanks of the valley's slopes. The flat central area in front of the tomb and mosque serves as the center of the village and the location of the saint's festival (*musīm*) held twice each year.

Sidi Lahcen himself was said to have had four married sons, and each of the four named groupings of the village's *wlād siyyid* ("descendants of the saint") traces its pedigree back to one of these sons. There is a loose correlation between settlement and saintly lineage, but the strength of this correlation is greater on the conceptual than on the sociological level because members from all the named groups of descendants live in each of the main settlements. The essential difference sociologically between the upper settlements and the lower 29 ones is that approximately one-half of the inhabitants of Roda are not saintly descendants, whereas almost all the inhabitants of the upper settlements claim such descent. Altogether, the reputed descendants of the saint make up roughly three-quarters of the total population. Those lineages that make no claim to saintly descent stem from one of two sources: They are either members of the *wlād ʿabad* (literally "sons of the slaves"), who supposedly lived in the village before the arrival of the saint, or they derive from individual families who moved into the village during the period of intense unrest that preceded the entry of the French in 1912. These nonsaintly families do not form a cohesive social whole; they are, however, set off in terms of cultural identity from the saint's descendants.

During the past three centuries the physical shape of the Sidi Lahcen complex has altered as political and environmental circumstances have varied. The structure of the village as a whole is based on two essential elements: the presence of a long, flat runway (*waṭiya*), where large numbers of people can gather for the saint's festival, and the existence of an adequate water supply. There are only three places in the valley where these requirements can be met, and each has been used at different times in the history of the village.

In the seventeenth century – at least according to legend – the village was centered in the middle of the valley. This flat central area was supposedly the site of Sidi Lahcen's first house. There is a spring nearby, and the houses of the village are said to have been clustered around it. When Sidi Lahcen died, he was buried next to his house, and it was there that the tribesmen first came to celebrate his musim.

By the middle of the nineteenth century, the shape of the village had altered. The shift may have been occasioned by the weakening of the main spring, which today would be insufficient to meet the villagers' needs. The locus of the village shifted to the eastern side of the valley where more water was available and an open flat area could accommodate the musim participants. It was in this place, according to legend, that the saint's horse knelt as he entered the valley.

At the turn of this century the locus of the village moved again, largely in response to the political unrest of the period and the role the saintly village played at that time. A large tomb was constructed for Sidi Lahcen at the edge of the southern end of the valley. As the insecurities of dissidence increased, the villagers, together with a number of people fleeing the hostilities of the surrounding countryside, clustered around the tomb seeking its supernatural protection. The tribesmen noted the alteration sarcastically: "Berbers," they said, "live alone protected by the gun, Arabs huddle together protected by their saint." But for local

30

Arab and Berber immigrants the site had its advantages: Next to the tomb is the largest spring in the village and just below the tomb is a large flat area where musims are held to this day.

Politics, environment, and the role of saints as protectors have all shaped the village of Sidi Lahcen over time. Similarly, the pattern of social relations reflects an intricate adaptation to the ecology of the region. The people of Sidi Lahcen harvest a variety of crops on their dry land, and additional irrigated plots allow the cultivation of varied garden produce. Cash income, however, is derived not from these crops but from the 20,000 olive trees planted around the edges of the fields in the valley. Practically all the trees and land at Sidi Lahcen are private property (*milk*), there being no collective land and only a few small parcels of property held for the benefit of religious institutions (*ḥabus*). Although the olive crop is essential for the purchase of goods from outside the village, the trees are poorly cared for and rarely, if ever, trimmed. The olives are harvested by beating the trees with large poles – a process that shortens the life and productivity of the trees.

Most of the villagers attempt to keep three or four separate plots in different parts of the area. This distributes the risk of crop failure over several microecological niches. Indeed, fragmentation of landholdings through inheritance – which could result in one brother having a field high on the slope, another having a strip on the other side of the valley on flat terrain – may have had its adaptive value. However, as population has risen and the limits of agricultural expansion have been reached, fragmentation and repeated cultivation of the land pose serious problems. Because few animals are grazed in the valley and the use of chemical fertilizers is inhibited by inadequate loan programs, land fragmentation, and village factionalism, few farmers have been able to follow the example of one rich man who increased his crop yields 300 percent with modern technology. Although the farmer in question owns some 30 hectares of land, of which 10 hectares are irrigated, other villagers are entirely landless. Most of the people, however, hold only about 2 hectares of dry land and 1 hectare that is irrigated. This uneven distribution of resources is compounded by the uneven quality of the plots involved.

As population and political climate have altered, the lands of Sidi Lahcen have been enlarged. From the core area near the settlements, villagers were unable to extend their cultivation eastward over the rolling hills formerly used as grazing lands by transhumants from the Middle Atlas Mountains. In order to regulate tribal movements, the French limited access by transhumants to the area and offered land

31

titles to villagers settling in the region. Although the land involved is of poor quality and the springs that irrigate one-fifth of the new land are unreliable, the fact that the overall land base of the village has been nearly doubled has contributed to relative well-being in the area.

The existence of new lands has affected the arrangement of social and ecological patterns in the village. In both the core and frontier areas, however, it is the long-established relation between genealogical relatedness and the organization of the irrigation system that has helped shape life in the village.

In order to understand the relation between the conceptualization of the irrigation system and the actualities of its operation, it is important to note that two main types of irrigation systems are found throughout the Sefrou region.[9] The first system is usually referred to as *l-ma b-saᶜa* ("timed water"). In this system water flowing into any irrigation ditch is carefully timed. Moreover, in systems of this sort water is usually owned separately from the parcel of land. The owner is, therefore, free to use his allotted period to irrigate property anywhere in the system or, indeed, to buy and sell water without regard to any particular plot. The second system is called the *mubiḥ* ("sequential") system. Each garden within the system is irrigated in sequence, each receiving a full portion of water before the next is granted its turn. Moreover, water and land are linked to one another, and an owner can neither sell water independently of the land nor move it around to another part of the system. The owner of a garden possesses the right to use water for his specific plot of land but possesses no right to alienate the water. This concept is reflected in the term mubih itself, which is derived from a root (*bāḥa*) meaning "to regard as public property, as ownerless."

In Sidi Lahcen the timed system of irrigation predominates. The totality of irrigation time is divided into ten named "days" of sixteen hours each and twelve named "nights" of eight hours. Water during either the day or night may be owned in units of as little as fifteen minutes, although blocks of an hour are closer to the norm. The owner of a given allotment of time may use his water on any field regardless of its location in the system. However, because water must be present at the next owner's site of selection at the time his period begins, water is seldom moved far from its subsequent point of usage lest valuable irrigation time be lost in transport alone.

As in the collective land at Azghar, the arrangement of the irrigation system is conceptualized in terms of genealogical groupings. The ten named "days" are divided into four for the wlad siyyid in Roda, four for the nonsaintly wlad ᶜabad, and two for the wlad siyyid of the

32

upper settlements. Each day of sixteen hours is further divided along such conceptually corporate lines. Thus day 2, called the "Day of Ait Sidi Mohammed," after one of the sons of the saint, is divided into four named subgroupings such that one has an allotment of eight hours, two others have three hours and forty minutes each, and the fourth has a period of only forty minutes. However, whole groupings do not own the water, nor is actual ownership of water in each period limited to persons identified genealogically with the named divisions. For example, the eight hours of the first quarter is owned by six men who come from three separate lineages, the second by five men from two lineages, the third by three men from two lineages, and the fourth by three brothers. In other "days" and "nights" individual owners are also drawn from a mixed range of close and distant, saintly and non-saintly lines. Thus the conceptual framework is not correlated with actual ownership. Indeed, to the best of our knowledge, it never was. Rather, the conceptual system projects an overarching level of relatedness, legitimized by common acknowledgment of putative descent, that serves to order the basic structure of the irrigation system at the same time it allows maximal adjustment to ecological, political, and personal necessity at the most basic operative level.

The malleability of actual irrigation practices within a received organizational context is made visible during the course of disputes. One such incident will serve as illustration. The 6-kilometer-long irrigation canal that carries water down from Ain Sultan is divided into sections corresponding to the irrigation "days" and "nights." Each man who owns a period of water is responsible for cleaning a length of the canal in proportion to the amount of time he possesses for irrigation. The work is supervised by an elected official (*jāri*), who is often one of the poorest men in the village. In this particular settlement, the jari is given little authority and less respect.

In the early days of June it is decided by an informal, word-of-mouth consensus that the time to begin the summer's irrigation activity is at hand. In 1969 this process commenced with a meeting called after prayers at the local mosque. As there is no overarching political organization or established hierarchy in the village, men spoke in turn as the issues concerned them. A jari was reelected without dispute. The order of the "days" was established by having the village's Quran teacher (*fqīh*), an outsider, pick a name out of a bowl. It is felt by the villagers in Sidi Lahcen that if the cycle of days and nights began each year with day 1 this would be unfair to those with time in later days. Consequently, the cycle remains fixed, but it is put into operation at a randomly chosen day.

33

This part of the proceedings went quite smoothly. But the one remaining task the community had to perform, cleaning the canal, occasioned some revealing debate. It was proposed that instead of having each person clean his designated section of the canal – a procedure that usually occasioned much fighting about exact boundaries and degree of care devoted to the task – this year the work should be organized on the basis of *twīza*. A twiza is a customary form of mutual aid among the inhabitants of a rural area. It usually involves free help given by the members of a community to someone who needs special help in plowing, building a house, or the like. The person who is being helped feeds the workers while they are helping him, just as he will be fed on the days he helps them. Mutual aid may be based on any of a number of ties: kinship (lineal, collateral, or affinal), territorial proximity, friendship, or some combination of the above.

In general, calls for twiza aid are difficult to refuse because they are generally the reactivation of debts incurred at other twizas, and it is believed that the avoidance of such obligations may result in supernatural punishment. In this case, the proposal was presented separately by two men at the meeting, but was greeted with a great deal less than universal enthusiasm. The two men, one a descendant of the saint and the other not, were, as was quickly noted, among the men with the most water time. Their proposal, therefore, seemed self-serving. Perhaps as important for the community decision was the accusation that even if there was a twiza these men would not do their fair share of the work. They would, it was contended, send their young sons (as they had in the past), who were notorious loafers. The proposers, however, reemphasized the moral overtones of twiza and invoked, with great rhetorical verve, the ties, favors, and services they claimed to have rendered to the community at large and to particular individuals in the past. This moral blackmail seemed to be gaining the upper hand, although clearly most of the villagers were quite displeased about it. They recognized that refusing a twiza proposal was not an action to be taken lightly. The tide was finally turned, however, when a man from one of the saintly lineages, the *nāib* ("foreman") of a rich nonsaintly villager, argued that although he had as much or more to gain from the twiza as others he would vote against it. The twiza proposal, he argued, was insincere, would increase village strife, was not traditionally applied to canal cleaning, and would mean that the work on the canal would be sloppy and hasty. His speech – an eloquent Moroccan blend of concrete material considerations, political finesse, and rhetorical flourish – received generalized support, and the meeting dispersed without a vote.

34

Irrigation at Sidi Lahcen is, then, organized on the principle of individual ownership of water at the same time that the overall system is conceptualized as a genealogically ordered entity. The interplay of these two forces contributes to an image of fundamental regularity, while permitting great flexibility of operation. This flexibility is further enhanced by the fact that several other minor springs within the irrigation perimeter operate on the mubih, or sequential, system, and a wide variety of different crops is planted throughout the valley. Moreover, as the dispute over canal cleaning indicates, the system is integrated through the competition of individuals operating within the broad rules of the game. No organized political structure administers the irrigation system: Rather, the free play of individuals maneuvering in accordance with the accepted conventions of interpersonal relatedness, in the irrigation system as in other domains of life in the region, gives shape and distinctiveness to the social system.

Ait ben Assu: social organization in a Berber settlement

It is not solely in the domain of ecological adaptation that the repertoire of social ties is tapped by individuals in the formation of their personal networks of affiliation. Politics, family life, and the marketplace constitute similar frameworks within which individuals adjust social relations to the exigencies of their own perceived situations. One of the crucial ties drawn on in this process is that of kinship, and its structural confines and operational possibilities can be seen at work in a Berber village of the region.

Just south of the city of Sefrou, in a broad, partially irrigated valley, lies a small Berber settlement. The people who live there usually refer to themselves as the Ait ben Assu, a segment of the larger group of nonlocalized kinsmen called Iawen. Like most of those in the countryside around Sefrou, the Ait ben Assu settlement, or *duwwar,* is composed of several homesteads, many of which share adjoining walls and animal enclosures. Most of the duwwars in the immediate Sefrou region are more dispersed and unbounded than this one, but even here separate houses dot the nearby fields. About 0.5 kilometer up the valley lie two Arabic-speaking settlements, Upper and Lower Senhadja; on a high promontory overlooking them all stands the settlement of Sidi Youssef, whose Arabic-speaking inhabitants claim descent from a local saint and, through him, to the Prophet Mohammed.

Until the turn of the century most of the Iawen people lived in tents about 8 kilometers south at a place called Mezdou. Unlike the transhumant groups living higher up in the mountains, who migrated

35

with their herds over considerable distances, the Berbers of Iawen, like most of the herders in the Ait Yusi territory near Sefrou, were agriculturalists as well as herdsmen. Each group of localized kinsmen had its own territory within which certain portions were cultivated and others left fallow. Any uninhabited lands within the tribal territory could be used for grazing, but special arrangements were necessary if animals were driven onto another group's cultivable terrain.

During this period all the Iawen in the area shared a common storage bin (*mers*), which was divided into a number of private compartments. Each family had its own section in the mers and stored food and personal goods there. All the goods in the mers were private property, but were lodged together for purposes of protection. While the main body of the group moved about as a unit, one or more small tents inhabited by guards were left at the site of the mers and the nearby crops. In the winter, most of the group moved to winter pasturage, returning in the spring to their native district where the crops would be harvested. Today, most people have permanent dwelling units and private storage bins under their own floorboards, and only a small portion of the group stays in the tents near the now diminished flocks.

The Iawen have continued to follow a mixed agricultural and herding pattern. They keep their flocks near their own duwwar in the summer and even during particularly warm and snowless winters. Ample common pasturage is available on a first-come, first-served basis. If the winter is cold, the flocks are moved down to the Beni Mansour area, east of Sefrou, where a few men or boys living in tents watch over the herds. No specific pastures are set aside in this area, and any uncultivated plot may be used for grazing. Although herdsmen continue to assert their right as Ait Yusi to run their herds onto any available land, individual Iawen groups have established understandings with the local people for the use of particular sites. There is usually enough available space so that fights are avoided, although the introduction to some areas of governmental regulations and grazing charges has led to considerable trouble in recent years for groups who must drive their herds long distances from the mountains.

The present settlement of Ait ben Assu was formed just before the Protectorate, in the period of disorder that followed the death of the powerful Qaid Umar al-Yusi. At that time most of the Iawen lived in tents about 8 kilometers south at Mezdou. At the outset of the disorder the Arabic-speaking people of Senhadja – particularly one rich man – sought the protection of one of the Iawen Berbers who, together with several kinsmen, then moved down to form the Ait ben

Assu settlement. Of the remaining Iawen, two main settlements were formed near Mezdou, the Ait Bouteyeb and the Ait Chou duwwars. The other Iawen groups, both quite far south in the Enjil and Guigou regions, are also recognized as distantly related groupings.[10]

The Ait ben Assu settlement contains a little under 200 people, who make their living from the grain crops grown on the surrounding dry land, the garden produce of their irrigated plots, and–because the settlement is somewhat unusual for its number of young entrepreneurs–from the buying and selling of sheep throughout central Morocco. Formally, the inhabitants are related to one another and to individuals and groups outside the confines of their duwwar in an ever more embracing system of real and presumed ties of kinship and proximity. There are, however, no rigidly bounded groupings of kinsmen, and therefore the terms used to refer to collections of kinsmen may be shifted to suit individual circumstances and goals. The Berber term *iḡes* (pl. *iḳsan*), which like the Arabic *ᶜadem* literally means "bone," basically implies a patrilineal group whose members can specify their descent from a common ancestor usually no more than three to five generations past. The ighes is usually a localized grouping. A few settlements in the Sefrou region may be composed of a single ighes, but usually several related ones inhabit the same duwwar. This localized group of several ikhsan (usually called a *feḳeḍa*, from the word *feḳḍ*, meaning "thigh"), whose members usually claim, but cannot actually enumerate, their specific relatedness, generally bears the name of their settlement–in this case Ait ben Assu. Outsiders who have come to live in the settlement are not considered genealogical members of the Ait ben Assu fekheda, but they are identified by the settlement name, and, with the passage of time, intermarriage, and the general lack of concern with specific genealogical ties, come to be regarded as belonging to that unit.

Above the level of the ighes and fekheda is the *ferqa* ("division" or "section"). In the Ait ben Assu case, Iawen as a whole–particularly their own duwwar and the two at Mezdou–may be referred to as a ferqa. Finally, there is the "tribe" as a whole, the qbila, a term usually applied to the Ait Yusi.

It would, however, be misleading to think of these levels of association as representing bounded groups of kinsmen, sociologically distinct groups, for whom terms like lineage or clan would be appropriate. Instead of a set of discrete, hierarchical units combining at even higher points on a genealogical charter, the present-day ighes, fekheda, ferqa, and qbila may be regarded as conceptual categories that can be applied to a shifting range of kinsmen.[11] Each implies a level of 37

closeness and degree of idealized aid, but individuals apply the terms
differentially as situations and purposes change. Thus, some speak of
Ait ben Assu as an ighes when trying to convey – or conduce – a sense
of obligatory support, and others – or the same individual at another
time – call it a qbila in order to emphasize its separateness from larger
associations. For this reason these groupings are sometimes referred
to as patronymic associations rather than as set groups whose structure
is to be understood in terms of a genealogically based ordering.

It is, therefore, impossible to understand the organization of social
relations in this area by simply referring to genealogically related
groups whose momentary reference is posited in terms of a hierarchy
of relatedness. To see how groupings crystallize and how the repertoire of conceptual categories is adduced to articulate these relationships, we must look at the ways cultural concepts and relational
conventions contribute to the establishment of greater or lesser networks of affiliation.

Each Friday evening, after prayers at the duwwar's squat and rather
shabby mosque, the adult men of Ait ben Assu gather at the home of
one of their number. The host's dependent women prepare several
dishes, while the men, seated in the long, narrow room that doubles as
living room and bedroom, are served by their host. The gathering is
highly informal, with scattered conversations going on all over the
room as the twenty-odd men lounge barefoot on the mats and cush-
ions, eating, smoking, and drinking glass after glass of sweet mint tea.
Politics, agriculture, scandals, gossip, weather, the market in Sefrou –
all are touched on by one or another of the men present. Someone
mentions that he needs a bit more water for his garden, and others
note who might have a portion that could be borrowed for the appropriate time slot. A small group in the middle of the room mentions a
rumor that the government is going to give out some of the former
colonial lands in the area, and even those at the far end of the room
who have had only one ear for this discussion look attentively as an
older man with an elegant white beard quietly explains the unlikeli-
ness of such an occurrence. Later, someone mentions that the teacher
in their mosque school is due to be paid, and with considerable joking
and sometimes a little moralizing, several of the men who have been
doing well in the sheep trade are cajoled into paying a larger portion
of his fee than they paid last year. Before midnight, the men begin to
wander out of the room, slip into the shoes they had left by the door,
and, with no particular acknowledgments to their host, work their way
down the steep staircase and back toward their own houses.

38   If you ask someone present what this gathering was all about, he

may refer to it as the *jamāᶜa* ("gathering") of the Ait ben Assu. And when you have seen a few more such gatherings, you become used to the informality, the lack of clear authority, the ongoing negotiations by which affairs that affect the men of the duwwar as a group or as individuals are conducted. True, there are certain matters that concern them as a body – support for their mosque teacher, setting a time for the celebration centered around a saintly figure said to be buried in their graveyard, sending some men off to the festivities marking the anniversary of the king's ascension to the throne. And equally true, it is not hard to discern who the influential figures are to whom others listen and how the pressures of opinion and the talents for bargaining lead to acceptable decisions that can be loosely characterized as consensual. But equally striking is the fact that there is no formal political structure to the duwwar, no offices or prerogatives, and that what affairs of the community are involved in such sessions are considered and resolved in the free play of personalities rather than in the implementation of official duties.

There are, of course, some wider political institutions in which the Ait ben Assu are involved, but here, too, formal positions do not tell the full story. The Ait ben Assu and the three Arabic-speaking settlements of the valley are grouped under a single government-appointed sheikh and administrative district, but, as we shall see, these institutions involve a minimal number of important administrative affairs affecting the lives of the Ait ben Assu. In the pre-Protectorate period, when feuds and weak political control were more often the rule than the exception, a jamaᶜa might elect a battle chief, assess money, conscript fighters, and decide whether to enter into any particular dispute. But with the "pacification" of the area by the French and under the administration of the independent Moroccan government, the need for localized defense has declined and with it the need for the somewhat more formal (but still quite ad hoc and personalistic) arrangements of the past.

Just as the term duwwar implies a residential aggregation within which certain mechanisms and initial relationships exist that particular persons can play on for the formation of their own social networks, so too with the categories and concepts relating to kinship. The ethnographer of Morocco, is, in some ways, the victim of the history of his own profession in that he must constantly employ terms – such as lineage, kindred, tribe, or settlement – that imply a far greater range of structural regularities and operational consequences than is appropriate for the description of this particular society. The effort to strip away the meanings normally associated

Social identity and points of attachment

39

with these terms and to find terms more consistent with the range of leeway built into the Moroccan conceptual scheme becomes central to accurate ethnographic description.

The consideration of kinship in Ait ben Assu raises this point most strikingly. Each of the different forms of kinship affiliation – within the nuclear family almost as much as beyond – implies not so much a set of behavioral norms concerning support, deference, or obligation as a minimally bounded set of possibilities that can be adduced or ignored, utilized or avoided as individual situations and purposes vary. Considerable leeway is afforded the individual in choosing whether he will act toward a particular kind of relative in a way ideally implied by their particular tie. For example, a great deal of flexibility is involved in the determination by two cousins or two brothers of how useful or desirable it is to support or interact with one another in a strictly normative fashion. The ties afforded by birth become bases on which particular and rather self-consciously contractual arrangements are worked out between different pairs of individuals.

Similarly, at the level of broader associations kin ties alone constitute a basis of affiliation rather than a charter of prescribed rules. The laws of inheritance may clearly specify which relatives are to inherit set proportions of an estate and, if there is any communal property (there is none within any segment of the Iawen), what limits are placed on its alienation. But beyond these minimally corporate characteristics, the standards of actual behavior depend not on an elaborated set of kin roles but on a series of personally centered, dyadic contractual relations. In order to illustrate more directly the ways in which a single person plays on the social and cultural resources available to him to develop an intricate and extensive network of personal ties, it may prove useful to consider in some detail the career of one particular man. Although, as we shall see, his is a more than usually successful career of interpersonal manipulations, there is much that is typical in his career, and hence much to be learned from it about Moroccan social ties generally.

The structure of personal networks: a case study

Mohand u Hussein is an Iawen man in his mid-thirties who, over the past few years, has begun to build up a significant network of allies and dependents. Beginning with a small parcel of dry land and some sheep given him by his father, Mohand set about accumulating a modest number of personal holdings. When his first group of sheep became marketable, Mohand asked his father to arrange with a friend for

Mohand to take his own sheep down to Fez the next time his father's friend drove his truck there. With the proceeds Mohand increased his flock, purchasing sheep from as far away as the other side of the Middle Atlas and marketing them with the friend's help at times when prices were high in Sefrou and the large cities of central Morocco. Some of the sheep were kept with Mohand's distant relatives at Iawen of Enjil, with whom he formed the same sort of partnership as with nonrelated shepherds near his own duwwar and with whom he frequently ingratiated himself by means of small gifts and favors.

Following one particularly good year, Mohand began to increase and diversify his holdings. From a woman in his duwwar whose husband had recently died Mohand purchased a garden plot that received only a small amount of water from the irrigation system and had, therefore, been used mainly for grain crops up to that time. With his father's help he bought an additional period of irrigation time from another farmer, planted several garden crops, and, having marketed them in Sefrou, repaid his father and held his new plot free. In order that he might devote his own time to other projects, Mohand sought a person willing to work the garden for him. In doing so he had to decide among several individuals who applied for the task and several alternative sharecropping arrangements.

The generic name for a sharecropper is *kammās* (literally "one who possesses a one-fifth share").[12] The name derives from the fact that a grain crop is divided into five parts, of which one goes to the man who works the plot, one to the owner, one to the person who rents the land, one to the supplier of the seed, and one to the supplier of the animals (or tractor) that plow the land. The proportion of the harvest any man gets depends on how many of the above factors he is responsible for. If a man simply works another's land, he receives only one-fifth of the crop. However, if he also supplies the seed and plow team, he receives three-fifths of the harvest, and so on for other combinations. It is also possible to subdivide various categories (i.e., to share seed expenses, or for one to supply seed and another fertilizer, and then split that one-fifth of the harvest). Agreements between landowners and/or renters and sharecroppers are usually of one season's duration, and although they are not written down their terms are usually made known to others who can bear witness to the arrangement.

Both the term khammas and the five-part division of the crop are specific to the cultivation of grain crops on dry land. A different set of arrangements and a different set of terms are applicable to the cultivation of irrigated land. Here the general term used for a sharecropper is *rba*^c ("one who possesses a one-fourth share"). Unlike the khammas

41

system, the term rba^c does not seem to derive from a fourfold division of the input, but simply from the usual proportion of the crop earned by the sharecropper for supplying all the labor on the garden. Just as a khammas may actually earn more than one-fifth of the crop, so too one referred to by the generic term rba^c may earn more than one-quarter of the garden crop depending on his other inputs. More specifically, there are three kinds of rba^{c}s: (1) the *rba^c* system proper, in which the sharecropper receives one-fourth of the harvest and the owner provides all necessary supplies for cultivation; (2) the *tulut* ("one-third") system, in which the owner and sharecropper split the expenses of cultivation equally and the sharecropper gets one-third of the harvest; and (3) the *ness* system, in which the sharecropper buys everything necessary for cultivation and receives one-half of the crop.

Thus, the khammas or rba^c gets varying proportions of the crops he works depending on the amount of labor and/or capital he invests in the enterprise. Having sufficient capital for the enterprise and eager to increase the number of those who would look on him as their patron, Mohand chose the most needy of several cousins in his settlement, agreed to give him one-quarter of the future crops in return for his labor, and turned his own attention to other concerns.

In order to extend his own ties beyond the bounds of their localized kinsmen, Mohand's father had arranged to marry Mohand to a girl from a neighboring Berber settlement. The couple lived in Mohand's father's house, but after a few years of marriage, the stillbirth of two children, and the livebirth only of a daughter, Mohand's relations with his wife deteriorated to the point where he divorced her. He made an agreement with his former wife and her kinsmen that he would pay a fixed sum for the support of the daughter, who would remain in her mother's custody. Several years later, however, the former wife, at her father's insistence, filed suit for an increase in child support. Mohand won the court case, but the father of his former wife, in an attempt to force Mohand to accede to the requested increase, made a sacrifice at the door of a close friend, a man who was also Mohand's maternal kinsman.[13] This kind of sacrifice, called an *^{c}ar,* (literally "a curse"), places the recipient in the position of having to accede to the request of the supplicant or risk supernatural punishment.[14] In this case, Mohand's maternal kinsman did indeed intercede to request that Mohand pay the desired stipend despite his victory in court. Wanting to maintain good relations with this maternal kinsman–who, after all, was a knowledgeable trader and useful ally in his own right–Mohand agreed to pay a slightly higher amount and to prepay a full year's child support.

42   The following year Mohand, in partnership with his father and

brother, bought several pieces of dry and irrigated land in the Beni Mansour area of the Lower Aggai River. This region, about 25 kilometers east of Sefrou, was the area in which people from all the Iawen fractions had rented grazing land in particularly severe winters on previous occasions. Here, Mohand utilized a second type of agricultural labor arrangement, that of the contract worker, or *resemi*. A resemi is a hired agricultural worker who receives a salary, year-round living quarters, some meals, and any other fringe benefits his employer grants him. The resemi does not, however, receive any of the crops he helps to raise. Mohand knew several men in the area quite well and made the following agreement with them: Each would receive free accommodation in a house constructed on the land, a stipend of $1.20 for each of the five or six days per week he worked during the six- or seven-month-long agricultural season, 60 cents for each night of overtime labor spent doing irrigation, and one free meal per day. During the off-season the resemi was free to continue living in the house supplied him while tending his own sheep or picking up some odd jobs.

The advantage of this particular sort of arrangement for the worker is security: His income is not directly dependent on the success or failure of the crop; he does not have to invest any capital of his own in a place to live or risk debts to purchase seed, animals, or fertilizer; and his relationship with his employer usually results in an arrangement in which various kinds of help can be expected from the landowner. But the resemi arrangement is more than a straightforward economic agreement in which the hired hand's labor is purchased with a guaranteed salary and benefits rather than as a joint risk venture. In actual practice it is also a patron-client relationship in the broadest sense of the term, an arrangement that partakes of many of the social standards, implications, and consequences characteristic of rural, mainly Berber, social life. A resemi's employer (often referred to with the French *patron* and less often with the Arabic *sīdu*, or "master") also gives his employee additional allotments of food, gifts on the holidays, personal loans, and various other sorts of aid not required by their formal arrangement. Thus a complex set of social ties often develops around this ostensibly economic arrangement, one that grants a measure of security to the worker at the same time it affords an employer like Mohand the opportunity to call on the resemi's generalized support in any situaiton that may arise.

Within the settlement of Ait ben Assu proper, Mohand always participated in the mutual aid (*twīza*) rendered kinsmen and neighbors at the time of planting and harvesting. Once he had established himself as a landholder at Beni Mansour, he volunteered to help others there at those busy moments, knowing he could then call on these same people to help him plant and reap his own crops. He never engaged in this kind of mutual aid with his kinsmen at the other two Iawen settlements, but had it suited his purposes he no doubt would have done so. Indeed, as a general rule, Mohand avoided obligations to, or deep involvement with, any relatives outside his immediate family because, as he said, "they would then always come to me and say: 'We're from the same family [ᶜā'ila] so do this for me.' And I would have to say: 'We're just from the same fraction [ferqa, in this case Iawen as a whole], and I have to take care of my close family here at Ait ben Assu'". Mohand, like others in the area, knew full well that choosing to accede to requests made on the basis of kinship proximity was almost entirely up to the individual, and that each of the terms involved – ᶜa'ila, ferqa, and so on – has quite a wide range of applicability. Thus, when Mohand wanted his distant kinsmen at Enjil to keep some of his sheep – mainly so relatives in his own settlement would be less sure of his real worth and less likely to pressure him for aid – he would talk to these people using such phrases as "We're from a single family [ᶜa'ila]," the term most commonly associated with the immediate family. And when he wanted to put off a close relative, he would refer to their attachment with terms like ferqa and even qbila, trying to define the situation as involving the far vaguer ties of distant kinship.

Mohand's ties with his own kinsmen, then, had to be negotiated personally rather than simply invoked in normative fashion. For example, when a kinsman from Iawen of Mezdou wanted Mohand to act as his intermediary in settling a land dispute with one of Mohand's business acquaintances, he was unable to get Mohand to intervene on the basis of their bond of relatedness. Only after he made an ᶜar sacrifice did Mohand agree to become involved. That the ᶜar is used between kinsmen – mainly those who do not live in the same duwwar – shows clearly that blood ties alone are not always sufficient to constrain particular forms of behavior.

Mohand's ties within his own immediate family were themselves subject to considerable stress soon after his divorce. He arranged to marry his father's brother's daughter, but soon after the arrangements were completed he announced that he was moving out of his father's house and setting himself up in a new place next door. In some respects this was a necessary move. If Mohand was to entertain others in his own guest room and ingratiate himself with potential allies by offers of hospitality and displays of generalized reliability, he had to

44

be able to receive others in his own house and in his own name. His father, however, wanted Mohand to remain under his wing, so he sent several close relatives and friends to Mohand to say that it was shameful to leave his father's house and that his father was getting old and needed Mohand's help. Mohand argued that his move was not a break with his father but an assertion of his own independence, and he remained firm in his decision. The resultant move next door proceeded without incident or significant alteration in Mohand's relationship with his father.

Mohand's network of ties continued to be expanded over the following years. His tactics were those of any "big man" in the making. When he wanted a favor from a petty bureaucrat from the Ait Khalifa fraction, he refered to the pact of mutual protection and nonaggression (*uṭada*) that had been formed between their two fractions in pre-Protectorate times.[15] Although such pacts certainly require no forthcoming considerations at present–indeed, some people do not know who their utada-mates used to be–Mohand was able to frame his request in this idiom effectively even though it was clearly not the only factor involved in his relation with the government official. Mohand also supported the Mouvement Populaire, the Berber-oriented political party, in several elections and was rewarded by being made the supplier of sheep to a number of large party gatherings.

Two final indications of the lines of sentiment and affiliation developed by Mohand are also worth noting. Each year a devout Muslim is supposed to give one-tenth of his income to charity. Mohand, who says he owes his good fortune to Allah, is, unlike many other people in this region, careful to give the stipulated amount to the needy. But because there are so many in need, Mohand finds himself in a position of having to decide who should benefit from his beneficence–and indeed how he may himself benefit thereby. Mostly he gives gifts of grain and butter to close relatives in his own duwwar, particularly elderly ones with few resources of their own. Some goes to his mother's brother, for whom Mohand feels a particular affection. But the remainder goes not to his other poor relatives at the Iawen fractions of Mezdou but to some of the poor people at Beni Mansour, where his landholdings have, by now, become rather substantial.

A similar interest informs Mohand's thinking on the subject of his daughter's future marriage. By his second wife, Mohand has had a daughter who, when she was fourteen years old, was considered eligible for marriage. At that time Mohand was approached by an intermediary representing a man from Sidi Youssef–an Arab, a descendant of that settlement's saint and a descendant of the Prophet Mohammed.

45

Mohand, however, was unimpressed. He regards the people from Sidi Youssef as haughty, and he claimed that because the Arabs seclude their women far more than do the Berbers he would make both his wife and his daughter unhappy by agreeing to such a union. Accordingly, he told the intermediary that his daughter was too young to marry, and when he learned that the Sidi Youssef man was nevertheless preparing to make an ᶜar sacrifice at his door, Mohand let it be known that he would then ask an outrageously high brideprice in order to block the marriage. Privately, he said he would rather marry his daughter later to someone from Beni Mansour or from an outside fraction than to someone from among his own close kinsmen.

The pattern of Mohand's associations and the tactics he follows in arranging them are clear. Like others of the region, Mohand calls on a wide variety of institutionalized relationships in the quest of his own particular goals. He knows that the initial relationships of blood and proximity are resources rather than determinate obligations and that there are few who have either the expressed desire or, more importantly, the clear power to require adherence to some overarching scheme of rigid role behaviors. He knows, too, that since one possesses virtually no rights in this society except those that can be forcefully and personally secured, the development of a network of reciprocally obligated persons holds the central position in this system of social organization. He clearly seeks to be a man of whom others say, *"ᶜand-u klām"* ("he has words, power, the final say"). The establishment of a varied set of interlocking ties serves this end at the same time it embeds him ever more deeply in conventions that render his actions more predictable and acceptable, more complete and unblemished, more closely coordinate with that which is evaluated as true and real.[16]

But there is more to the process than a mechanical invocation of approbation through right action, more than an automatic creation of reputation (*sumᶜa*) by undertaking prescribed endeavors. The connection between concept and relationship is reciprocal and mutually causative. Not only are interpersonal ties subject to the dynamics of individual strategies, but the concepts that shape and situate these relations possess a high degree of malleability and open-endedness. Mohand not only negotiates his contacts with others, he negotiates the meaning and application of the terms that will shape these relations and their significance. He may employ the sliding references of kinship—applying such terms of ᶜa'ila, ferqa, and qbila to draw closer or pull back from the generalized obligations implied by these associational terms—or he may try to impose his definition of obligation (*ḥaqq*) on a situation not otherwise conceived of in these terms.[17] In the marketplace of possible relations and meanings, no less than in the relationships of the marketplace, Mohand, in a fashion characteristic of the Sefrou region, bargains for and with a view of social reality in which the resources of estate, connection, rhetoric, and the sheer force of personality all play major roles.

The structure of local government in the countryside

Just as the contexts of ecology and tribal organization provide frameworks within which various aspects of the available conceptual and relational possibilities are forged into distinctive patterns, so too is this interplay discernible in other domains. Like the marketplace or the duwwar, the institutions and processes of political life provide distinctive institutions and concepts that interdigitate with those of other social and cultural realms. And like these other contexts, formal offices and legal prerogatives, party affiliations and conventional alliances may be seen as resources whose implications and arrangement depend on the ways they are conceived of and implemented in actual situations.

Local government, in both the city and region of Sefrou, is, in its formal aspects, an entity created, controlled, and staffed by the national governmental authorities in Rabat. Two parallel structures exist: one for municipalities, another for rural districts. But the lines of authority and decision making that appear so simple and straightforward on an organizational chart belie a far more complicated set of relationships. The present discussion, as well as a later one centered on urban administration and politics, show how the lines of formal authority and those of actual political organization interact and in what sense the processes involved contribute to the relations among conceptual categories, contractual processes, and the malleability of social ties.

Rural administration

The formal organization of local governmental administration is rather simple. The urban and rural administrations converge, at their highest point, in the king and the Ministry of the Interior, and at their most immediate juncture, in the governor of one of the country's sixteen provinces. Each province, in turn, is, for purposes of rural administration, divided into a series of *cercles* headed by a "superqaid" (*qaid l-mumtaz*). In the Province of Fez, for example, there are (1967) five cercles, one of which, the Cercle de Sefrou, is headquartered in the city   47 of Sefrou but covers the rural area nearby. This cercle, in turn, is subdivided into *circonscriptions,* each headed by a qaid. A circonscription basically includes a number of rural settlements scattered over the countryside and organized into small administrative clusters for each of which a sheikh is appointed. These sheikhs, the lowest-level appointed officials, are charged with conveying governmental policy to the rural people and expressing the latter's interests to higher officials.[18]

However, a simple enumeration of the table of organization of the administrative hierarchy only scratches the surface of the political realities. Even on the purely formal level several factors must be noted. In pre-Protectorate times the qaid of a given region was usually a local man charged with the governance of a particular tribe or major division thereof. With the powers of the central government often quite weak – particularly in more outlying areas of difficult terrain, such as the areas back of Sefrou – the qaid of a given region was at the least semiautonomous and at most openly rebellious. Once the French had "pacified" a region of rural Morocco – and the last such area, in southern Morocco, held out until 1934 – a French official was placed over the appointed qaid, and in many cases, former qaidal areas were redrawn to make French control easier.[19] It would, however, be misleading to assume from this that tribes formed coherent political and administrative entities in the pre-1912 era and were simply broken up during the French period to further colonial goals. Sometimes this was the case, but more often political and social boundary lines were simply not coincident, and the internal political affiliations that characterize any given tribe or tribal section were easily rearranged to fit the administrative subdivisions made by the French officials. This ameboid quality of tribal political organization in the Sefrou area underlines the facts that tribes as such were not by definition cohesive political units and that the processes of political alignment were and, as we shall see, are still not totally attached to any particular social form or institution.[20]

When independence was achieved, the Moroccan government retained most of the territorial divisions used by the French. However, within a few years after Independence the government sought to professionalize the corps of qaids and superqaids. Accordingly, three main policies were established: (1) to institute a school for the training of future qaids, (2) to concentrate the attention of qaids on advancement through the bureaucratic ranks and on channeling all their expectations on the favors that flowed through that hierarchy, and (3) to move qaids out of the areas where they were born to areas where they

had no significant local ties. As a result, most of the qaids in

Morocco – and all of them in the Sefrou region – come from somewhere else and have their attention focused far more on advancing within the palace-controlled bureaucratic hierarchy than on developing local ties. This restrains the formation of local followings and requires that most local power figures operate without any official position in their own region.

Qaids and superqaids tend to remain in the Sefrou region for only a few years before being transferred elsewhere. Coupled with other aspects of administrative policy, this means that the rural areas are really rather lightly governed. The qaid keeps an eye on the overall economic and political climate, he consults with people about local problems, and with the aid of the gendarmerie, he maintains law and order. But there are a great many matters – economic, social, and cultural – with which he is relatively unconcerned and for whose solution governmental programs are few, weak, or nonexistent. Moreover, because he does not expect to remain long, the qaid or superqaid tends not to learn much about the people in his region. Instead, he relies on local assistants who remain in the area for long periods, if not for a whole career. These latter are, moreover, local people who really know the area well. In the Sefrou area there is a man whose official position is only that of clerk in the office of one of the local qaids, but who in fact runs most of the functions of that office. Indeed, he does this so well that there have been periods of several months between the tenure of the last qaid and the arrival of a new one during which he has effectively performed all the functions of his superior. The same is true in the Cercle of Sefrou for the khalifa (assistant) of the superqaid. But whereas the latter eventually was given a formal post of his own, the clerk of the qaid does not really expect – or, in his personal case, wish – to move from his present position.

The second aspect of this system of rural administration to which we referred earlier is the lack of fit between the formal administrative positions and the locally important political personalities. More precisely, there is a lack of coincidence between the lines of power and influence embodied in the administrative hierarchy and those that can be tapped by local people in an attempt to resolve their particular problems or further their own interests. Not only are there several other political institutions operative within the rural area that can be called upon to further individual and collective goals, there are also certain aspects of local political culture that permit alternative routes of access to those who occupy important decision-making positions. Political parties and the bonds that link a particular individual to a person with political connections of his own are among the most

Social identity and points of attachment

49

important of these nongovernmental political ties, and inasmuch as they are characteristic of political life in city and country alike they can be treated as a separate topic in their own right.

National political organization

Political parties in the Sefrou region are, for the most part, rather poorly organized. In the period leading up to Independence the only significant national political party, the Istiqlal party, was fairly well represented in the Sefrou region. Almost everyone now claims to have supported its programs, and in fact a number of local people were actively engaged in, or contributed funds to, its undertakings. In the countryside, the Army of Liberation – a more militant, even terrorist, organization – had the active support of many of the Berbers. Following Independence, political parties throughout Morocco took on a new importance. With the demise of the old system of tribal qaids and the inauguration of an independent Moroccan bureaucracy, political party affiliation became one of the most significant channels for acquiring a wide range of patronage benefits.[21] The Istiqlal party underwent a major schism, and several separate parties, from the Berber-oriented Mouvement Populaire to the leftist Union National des Forces Populaires (UNFP), began to compete for positions of power and influence.

The dominant power on the national scene, however, was obtained by the sultan, Mohammed V, and following his death in 1961, by his son, King Hassan II. By deftly playing the leaders of one party against those of the other and focusing the dependence of political appointees on the administrative hierarchy rather than on political parties, the monarchy became the central, and at times almost the only, effective national political institution.

The Sefrou area was not without representation among the new government's highest officials. Si M'barek Bekkai, the appointed pasha of Sefrou in the final days of the Protectorate, became the first prime minister of Morocco. His local ties were not, however, as extensive or important as those of Qaid Lahcen Lyusi, who as the qaid of the Ait Yusi was able to keep much of the Central Atlas region from supporting the puppet sultan placed on the throne by the French when Mohammed V was sent into exile. Upon his triumphal return as monarch of an independent nation, Mohammed V called on Qaid Lahcen to be his first minister of the interior. From this position Qaid Lahcen was, until his later fall from grace, able to do many favors for 50   people in and around the city of Sefrou.[22]

Typically, political influence throughout Morocco tends to operate on a personal rather than an institutional basis. This is as true for the operation of political parties as for bureaucratic favors and is shown most clearly, perhaps, in the various elections that have been held in the Sefrou region since Independence.

The most important election in the Sefrou region was the 1963 parliamentary election.[23] At that time each of the major parties in the country was represented: the Front pour la Defense des Institutions Constitutionelles (FDIC), an ad hoc coalition supporting the king; Istiqlal, still faithful to the monarchy but eager for a greater voice in government through an effective parliament; and the UNFP, led nationally by Mehdi ben Barka, later kidnapped and killed in Europe under circumstances that led to indictments by the French court against high Moroccan officials. The candidate for the Sefrou region seat from the king's coalition was the minister of commerce and industry, who also happened to be the brother of the pasha of Sefrou. He was opposed by two local men, one put up by Istiqlal and the other representing the UNFP. The exact details of this election – and its repercussions for later elections – need not concern us here.[24] What is important to note is simply that although most people in the city seem to have been sympathetic to the FDIC coalition, and most of the rural Berbers continued to identify with one of the coalition parties – namely, the Mouvement Populaire – in the event the FDIC minister was rejected and the Istiqlal candidate elected to office. The reason most people gave for this action was simply that the Istiqlal candidate was a local man who would share the benefits of his office with local people, whereas the government minister was not from their own region and not likely to further the fortunes of anyone but himself.

In short, as this and several other elections show, political parties in the Sefrou region are not strongly organized entities toward which firm institutional or ideological ties are felt to exist. Rather, they are frameworks for the development of attachments to politically useful others, coteries of individuals with diverse personal interests who have never been effectively organized by the party leaders into cohesive and enduring groups.

In many respects, this approach to political parties is but a reflection of certain aspects of political life in the Sefrou region generally. As we have seen, social groupings in the Sefrou area do not operate as solidary units that can demand a high degree of loyalty from, or exercise significant control over, the actions of those who have been born or recruited to positions of membership. Rather, the emphasis throughout the city and region of Sefrou is on personal connections con-

51

structed in face-to-face relations with particular individuals through a set of mutually accepted, customary forms of affiliation and reciprocation. One can call on ties of kinship, idealized bonds of tribal affinity, and acceptable norms of residential interdependence as bases from which to start building networks of personal affiliation. But the actual ability of each individual to elicit particular forms of behavior from others on the basis of these initial ties and each person's capacity to arrange his ties with the greatest tactical skill are paramount in the development of a set of dependable personal relationships.

What regularizes this otherwise disconnected and confused quest for personal aggrandizement is, of course, the fact that the number of ways in which such interpersonal ties can be established with any degree of certainty that their terms will be honored is relatively limited. If hospitality is offered a guest, some reciprocation must be given if one is not to be thought totally devoid of all good sense by one's neighbors. If an agreement for economic cooperation is not honored, others will be reluctant to enter into similar contracts with the violator. If a supernaturally sanctioned sacrifice is made as part of a request for aid, failure to accede to the request may be taken as a sign of nonconformity and unpredictability on the part of the one who fails to respond properly. And if ties of kinship are consistently ignored, their utility in later circumstances will be undermined. In short, the ways in which personal ties are contracted in Sefrou society are not without limit either in their number or in their repercussions, and this set of regularized forms of association gives the political domain, like others, its distinctive design.

Moreover, the link between local political ties and the pattern of national politics is less a bridge between alternative systems than a congruity of similarly structured systems of varying size. The pattern of local "big men" effectively coalescing a series of different personal ties into an elaborate set of useful relationships is, in many instances, quite analogous to the tactics employed by nationally important personalities. The same patterns of ingratiation and favor granting, individually negotiated ties and personally serviced obligations, inform both local and national followings. Moreover, in the virtual absence of any corporate groupings capable of sustaining support for particular positions rather than particular personalities, followings remain as brittle and tentative for the one as for the other. The constant quest is for dependents whose personal indebtedness makes their actions comparatively predictable, their future aid comparatively reliable.

One of the consequences, however, of personally centered networks of obligation is that the lines of actual power and influence are by no means necessarily those of the formal political hierarchy. In fact, given the highly personal nature of political ties in Morocco generally, it is very likely indeed that if any individual has a problem in his own locale he will seek a person who can help him from any place in the country, any position in the official hierarchy, and on the basis of any personal connection that best serves his particular purpose at that moment. Being highly mobile people, Moroccans think nothing of traveling several hundred kilometers to see a cousin who might be influential to one's present cause or spending hours to see a contact in a government ministry in the capital. A view from the heights of the national bureaucracy in Rabat can often yield a particularly truncated view of the lines and types of attachments through which local disputes or political interests are intertwined with persons and policies on the national level. To illustrate exactly what is implied here, let us look at a particular case study from the Sefrou region.

Social identity and points of attachment

The Dayat Ifrah dispute

Some 40 kilometers south of Sefrou, along the western edge of the Amekla Plain, lies a small lake called Dayat Ifrah. It rests just along the traditional border between two Berber tribes, the Ait Yusi to the east and the Ait Seghoushen to the west. In the period just before the beginning of the French Protectorate, Qaid Hadou u Said (the father of Qaid Lahcen Lyusi, the first Moroccan minister of the interior, and himself a former qaid of the Ait Yusi tribe) offered the land immediately surrounding the lake to a Saharan group called the Ait Daud u Musa. The latter settled on the flat, arable land around the lake, and the rock-strewn hills bordering their land on three sides were occupied by herders from various fractions on the Ait Yusi. It was clearly understood at the time that everyone had equal access to the waters of the lake as well as to pasturage on any uncultivated plots within both groupings' territories. However, in recent years, the Ait Daud u Musa people began to plant lentils and grain crops on almost all their own land. This not only led to the restriction of available pasturage for the herds of all concerned, but resulted in additional herds being grazed on the territory occupied solely by the Ait Yusi. Tensions increased until a brief incident involving members of each group touched off a direct confrontation.

According to various informants, one day an Ait Yusi woman went down to the lake to get some water. An Ait Daud u Musa man grabbed her water jug, smashed it to pieces, and told her that the Ait Yusi had no right to the waters of the lake. The woman returned 53

home and told her menfolk what had happened. As word of the
incident spread, men from the Ait Yusi fractions that had always used
the lake began to drive their herds down onto the Ait Daud u Musa
land and to set up their own tents, thus demonstrating their right not
only to water from the lake but to pasturage on the Ait Daud u Musa
land as well.

Reconstructing the exact chronology at this point is not easy, but if
the sequence is unclear the overall trend of succeeding events is far
more certain. Realizing that they were outnumbered, the Ait Daud u
Musa sought allies. They went to a number of influential men in the
Ait Seghoushen tribe, including the head of the local commune rurale,
and made ᶜar sacrifices. Apparently, the important men of the Ait
Seghoushen needed little convincing. They agreed with the Ait Daud
u Musa that the latter had always been members of the Ait Seghoushen tribe and that although it would be unseemly to become em-
broiled in any physical confrontation they would indeed try to intercede with the appropriate authorities on behalf of their "brothers."
Accordingly, the matter was taken up with the local qaid, who for-
warded the dossier to the provincial governor. Meanwhile, the qaid of
the Ait Yusi began to look into the matter. Together with several
uniformed assistants, he went up to Dayat Ifrah to investigate the
claims made by the Ait Yusi. However, a group of Ait Daud u Musa
women attacked the investigating officials, who then called on the
governor to send in the mobile guard to keep the peace. The fact that
several of the offending women were actually sent to jail did nothing
to dampen tempers.

During the following months each side collected allies and prepared
arguments that, it was hoped, would convince the minister of the
interior to rule in its favor. Each of the Ait Yusi fractions in the area
concerned chose a representative for an ad hoc assembly to direct the
group's actions. First, the representatives agreed that each person
from the fractions involved would pay one sheep for each of his
shepherds, the sheep then being used for costs sustained in bringing
their argument before the ministry of any court of law. No chief was
elected (as in a pre-Protectorate war council): Instead, they operated
on the same general basis of consensus that is said to characterize the
assembly of an individual settlement. The representatives also decided
to consult Qaid Lahcen Lyusi, who was spending part of his retirement
in a house in Sefrou. At first the Qaid expressed his support of the Ait
Daud u Musa, as it was his father who had given them their land. But
eventually the qaid decided to support the claims of the Ait Yusi, over
whom he served as qaid for many years before going to Rabat. He

54

even produced a document that said the land given to the Ait Daud u Musa had always been Ait Yusi territory and was never the property of people from Ait Seghoushen. This document was presented as proof of the claim that the Ait Daud u Musa were settled on traditionally Ait Yusi land and that any claims the former might make either to the lake or to the surrounding hills were totally invalid.

The Ait Yusi also tried another tactic. They sent one of their number, a very well connected local figure who also held a minor elective post, to see a man who was a member of a local family from which a number of qaids had originated and who was now serving as superqaid of a cercle near Casablanca. It was hoped that this man might be able to help the cause of the people from his home area by having a word or two with the minister in Rabat.

Meanwhile, the Ait Daud u Musa were preparing their own case. They had persuaded the big men of the Ait Seghoushen to acknowledge not only that they were really members of that tribe rather than of the Ait Yusi, but that they had been under the administration of the same officials who dealt with the Ait Seghoushen for some time. They noted, for instance, that when the Protectorate began the French divided the Ait Daud u Musa into two sections, of which one paid its share of the *tertib*[25] tax to the Ait Yusi qaid, and the other paid its share to the Ait Seghoushen administrator. They also noted that even before the Protectorate began the Ait Daud u Musa land had been divided into privately owned and fully alienable plots. Moreover, they pointed to the fact that once the system of tertib taxes was dropped the Ait Daud u Musa fell under the complete administration of the qaid of the Ait Seghoushen. Finally, the Ait Daud u Musa claimed that not only was the land immediately surrounding the lake theirs but that they were also the true owners of the hills the Ait Yusi claimed belonged to them. The Ait Daud u Musa based this claim on the fact that they used the rocky hills for grazing on a regular basis, whereas the Ait Yusi used the hills only during the summer, and that the latter's use of the land was based on understandings that obtained between the two groups for many years.

After considerable delay the minister issued his ruling. He said, first, that the Ait Yusi definitely have the right to water their animals at the lake – which was itself declared government property – and he ordered the Ait Daud u Musa not to interfere with the Ait Yusi's right of access to the lake over a path to be set aside for that purpose. The land immediately around the lake, the minister said, is indeed Ait Daud u Musa land because they have occupied it unchallenged for so many years, but it actually belongs to the tribal fraction as a whole

55

rather than to any particular individuals. Accordingly, the land must now be split up equally among the six lineages of the Ait Daud u Musa and no one may alienate his parcel outside this group. Because the right of mutual access for purposes of grazing was recognized by all parties as part of a specific agreement to that effect rather than as a nonnegotiable right, the parties were left to formulate a new agreement on this matter. Finally, the minister reaffirmed the Ait Yusi claim to the hills surrounding the Ait Daud u Musa territory and published this affirmation separately in the *Bulletin officiel*.

Careful consideration of the Dayat Ifrah dispute reveals a number of distinctive characteristics about the local political process and its relationship to the formal political hierarchy. Consider the question of the identity of the Ait Daud u Musa. Tribes and fractions in the Sefrou area are, as we have seen, not corporate entities whose various subdivisions relate to one another according to any rigid charter of genealogical or residential affiliation. Those who reside in the territory claimed and protected by a given tribe or fraction are generally recognized as part of that larger grouping: The view is an assimilationist one more than an absorptive alignment of totally discrete units. The Ait Yusi had regarded the Ait Daud u Musa as part of their own grouping by virtue of their occupying traditionally Ait Yusi land, and the former would seem to have acknowledged this status by having fought with the Ait Yusi–even against the Ait Seghoushen–in pre-Protectorate battles. But when the dispute broke out, the Ait Daud u Musa not only turned away from the Ait Yusi but actively declared that they had been, in fact, Ait Seghoushen all along. The big men of the latter area accepted this claim on the basis that the Ait Daud u Musa had been under the administration of Ait Seghoushen qaids for some years. Thus, the identification in terms of which group had the greatest amount of control over Ait Daud u Musa affairs could as well be made for the Ait Seghoushen as for the Ait Yusi. As a vehicle for gaining allies, there was no compunction on anyone's part about claiming alternative and mutually contradictory tribal identities.

The quest for allies did not, of course, end with historical reconstructions or manipulated identities. It also extended to seeking out persons who, by their connections to others in power, might affect the eventual judgment. In this respect, the action of the Ait Yusi in seeking out a local man holding a position in the government hierarchy somewhere else was quite typical. This "shadow qaid" system is one in which a locally important person who has been moved by the government to a post elsewhere may play a very significant role in the decisions made in his original territory–indeed, a greater role than that of the local qaid, who in turn, may be more involved in matters *Social identity and* that concern his own natal region.[26] A displaced authority, quite dif- *points of* ferent from and even contradictory to the formal system, may be *attachment* operative in a wide range of disputes and political issues.

The Dayat Ifrah dispute also indicates the resources of local political culture that may be utilized by the various parties. The ᶜar sacrifice places the burden of aid on the individual or individuals to whom the sacrifice is made, and although the Ait Seghoushen avoided physical involvement, they were obviously unwilling to give up their recognition of the validity of this device generally for the short-term gain of avoiding this particular dispute. On the other hand, Ait Yusi fractions not directly involved in the dispute were unwilling to join in on the basis of some idealized notion of tribal solidarity lest they be drawn into innumerable affairs involving other members of their vaguely defined "tribe."

And finally, it was clear to everyone that the dispute would probably erupt again at some later date, either among the Ait Daud u Musa themselves (who were opposed to relinquishing their private ownership rights and organizing their holdings into a collective) or between the original disputants. The never-ending, almost Byzantine qualities of such local disputes were only the final, and by no means the least typical, aspect of this entire affair.

The urban pattern

What has been said of the overall process of rural social organization is, to a remarkably high degree, appropriate for the urban area as well. Indeed, the more closely one looks at a wide range of institutions and practices throughout the Sefrou region, the more one sees that city and countryside are not polar opposites or even fixed nodes on a broad continuum. Rather, each partakes of the other, shares in its processes as well as its history, *is* part of the other. To study the ecology, social forms, and political relations of the city proper is, therefore, to focus momentarily on one facet of what must constantly be seen as a variegated whole.

Ecology of the oasis of Sefrou

Travel accounts and government planning reports often speak of the "oasis of Sefrou." The term oasis is, at least in a topographic sense, appropriate, for the city itself is set in the midst of gardens whose irrigated greenery forms a sharp contrast, particularly in the summer 57 months, to the surrounding countryside. The old walled city, or *medīna,* accounts for only 8 hectares of terrain; the water of the Aggai River, which passes through the heart of the medina, is presently used to irrigate several hundred hectares of garden land.[27] Prior to the arrival of the French, there were even several large gardens within the tightly packed confines of the medina itself. The garden area has, however, been sharply reduced over the last forty years. In the late 1920s the French began building a separate settlement, the Ville Nouvelle, in the gardens that lay along the western edge of the oasis. More important perhaps has been the growth, following World War II, of a series of residential areas just outside the walls of the medina. These "new medina" settlements have sharply cut into the extent of the city's gardens.

Ecologically and economically the city has long possessed a mixed urban-rural quality, depending on the products of the farmers and herders of the surrounding countryside as much as the latter have depended on the institutions and goods of the city. Today, 18 percent of the town's population is directly involved in agricultural activity. This figure must, however, be taken with care because it is a characteristic of the economy of Sefrou that men are engaged in many activities simultaneously. Even those who devote substantial amounts of time to agriculture are more than likely engaged in other activities as well. Urban Arab merchants, and formerly many of the Jewish merchants, have shares in land or animals cared for by rural residents, and many of the city's recent rural immigrants continue to maintain interests in, and devote some of their time to, their rural properties. In general, though, there has been a decline, over the past fifty years, in the proportion of the population primarily engaged in agriculture owing to the general decrease in garden space and the opening up of new commercial and administrative opportunities.

Some of the gardens are worked by their owners, but in many cases a sharecropper tills the land under the khammas or rba[c] arrangements described earlier for the countryside. Moreover, most of these sharecroppers come not from the fractions of the Ait Yusi or from the city of Sefrou itself, but from the nearby Arabic-speaking village of Bhalil.

Most of the gardens in the oasis are relatively small. Of 1,260 plots listed in a 1955 government survey, only 9.4 percent were larger than 1 hectare and the mean was about 0.25 hectare. Moreover, it is rare for a single family to own more than 4 hectares in a single canal system or 6 hectares overall.[28]

Although no cadastral survey of garden sites exists, it is possible to make certain general observations about landownership in the oasis. A comparison of air photos from the years 1936 and 1960 indicates that the size of the entire oasis has not changed in that time or for any other period on which documentation is available. Moreover, the air photos show no physical evidence (fences, tree lines, etc.) of significant subdivision of plots within the period covered by these documents. This is not to say that land fragmentation had ceased by 1936. Land records, court records, and numerous informants attest to the continued subdivision of land through inheritance. However, in recent years, as the city has expanded into the surrounding gardens and land prices have risen, there has been a greater tendency for heirs to divide the profits reaped from the sale or rental of individual plots. The result has been a decrease in the amount of land devoted to irrigated gardening, a shift toward crops that can be sold for high prices in the major urban markets, and a decline in the amount of garden crops produced and sold in the oasis itself. The viability of the remaining gardens depends largely on the continued functioning of the city's irrigation system.

The water used to irrigate the gardens surrounding Sefrou is derived entirely from the Aggai River, a narrow and rather shallow watercourse that begins in the hills to the west of the city and runs down to the Sebou River. The river itself is formed by two branches that originate in the hills west of the oasis. From the juncture of the two streams the river flows eastward, cascading down a waterfall some 20 meters high, continuing down a long narrow valley (along which is located an electrical generating plant), cutting through the heart of the medina of Sefrou, and continuing on through the rolling hills of Koushetsa to the Sebou River.

No exact figures are available on the amount of water carried by the river, but the supply is reasonably plentiful and regular even during the hot summer months.[29] Irregular rainfall patterns have, however, resulted in occasional flooding in the medina. A flash flood ripped through the lower part of the city in May 1916.[30] A much more serious flood occurred in 1950 when branches carried downstream by heavy rains formed an artificial dam that broke loose in the middle of the night, allowing the flood waters to damage numerous buildings and kill several residents. The government responded by deepening the bed of the river and reinforcing its channel within the medina.

The irrigation of the Sefrou oasis is accomplished by means of five canal systems, each of which leads off the Aggai at a point above the medina. The area watered by each, the quantities of water involved, and the complexity of distribution among subsidiary channels vary considerably. However, the system as a whole has remained basically the same for a very long time indeed.

59

The irrigation system of Sefrou operates on the mubih system, in which garden and water are inseparable and plots are watered in succession. The garden owner can neither sell his water independently of his land nor move it around to some other plot in the system. Because water is relatively plentiful and secure, garden owners can be reasonably assured of a steady supply of water. Ultimately, however, the water and canals belong to the state, which can take allotments of water without compensation for such public works projects as running the local generating plant. Moreover, the state possesses ultimate control over the administration of the irrigation system, although this control has mainly been exercised to take water allotments for the generating plant. The actual organization of the irrigation system remains close to its traditional form. Specifically, there exists for each of the five canal systems in the oasis a jari who oversees the maintenance and distribution of water in his portion of the system. Each jari is formally appointed by the pasha (in consultation with the owners of gardens in that portion of the system), but he is actually paid by the farmers themselves. Between the months of March and October he keeps a constant check on the system, seeing to it that the various sections of the canal are opened at the proper time, that the individual gardeners do not allow their gardens to be irrigated out of turn, and that the channels are kept free of blockage. He also checks to make sure that once a year each of the garden owners undertakes to give a thorough cleaning to the portion of the canal that runs through his property.

In case of disputes the garden owners first appeal to the jari for arbitration. There is also a system of collective meetings of the men with fields in the same section. They debate communally various decisions and minor alterations of the system in their own subsection, such as extra water for a particular garden. This group, which puts the system into concrete operation, has a leader (*amin*), who is frequently a rich old man appointed for life by the landholders in that particular section. Like the jari he may be called on to help settle disputes. If all else fails, the dispute is moved to the courts. Although he does not formally have power over such matters, the pasha of Sefrou often acts as mediator in the dispute, using the jari as an expert witness.

Thus, in the oasis of Sefrou, as in Sidi Lahcen and Ait ben Assu, the irrigation system is technologically and organizationally simple. Its operation requires little specialized knowledge or attention. It shares none of the overall genealogical conceptualization found in parts of the countryside, although it too is a system in which every garden has a name that is said to refer to an original owner. Although water is

60

more plentiful than in most parts of the countryside, disputes are common and somtimes quite heated. As in family life or the marketplace, relations in the irrigation system carry the common theme of social organization in the region: An overall moral and legal code serves as the context in which individuals contract and contend with one another, adjusting their personal needs more through direct confrontation – a kind of agonistic individualism – than through elaborately constructed group relations.

Social geography of the city of Sefrou

For the stranger who first sees Sefrou from one of the encircling hills, perhaps the most striking feature of the city is its great beauty.[31] From the top of Jbel Sidi Ali Buseghine, beside the tomb of the saint for whom the hill is named, or better yet from the adjoining Jbel Sidi Ali Benziyan, on which the French-built Fort Prieux still stands, one can look out over the gleaming white city, past the encircling gardens, to the dun-colored countryside beyond. From this vantage the city itself appears rather homogeneous. Only a few really distinctive features stand out: the minarets of the three main mosques of the medina, a modern apartment building on the far northern side, the separate enclave of the Qlaᶜa, the newer sections that have been built outside the walls of the old medina, and the villas and business district of the French-built Ville Nouvelle. Only when one descends to the streets of the old city proper is the appearance of simple uniformity and homogeneity dispelled.

The medina itself is entirely surrounded by a high crenelated wall into which five major gates (as well as several smaller and more recent gates) have been cut.[32] The huge wooden doors that now stand permanently open recall the period, lasting into the early part of this century, when the entire city was closed off each night against the outside world. Within the walls, the narrow streets form an incredible tangle of byways and deadends, meandering market streets and dank, covered corridors. The buildings, their characterless plaster walls presenting a solid front against the street, give virtually no hint of the size or quality of the dwelling that lies on the other side of a solid wooden door or a small grillwork window. It is only from within that one can obtain a clear impression of the quality of a given residence and the amount of space it actually encompasses. The houses of more wealthy people generally contain a central, enclosed courtyard with a series of guest rooms and sleeping rooms arranged around the periphery of both floors. The kitchen is usually at the rear of the first floor, al- 61 though the women of the household spend much of their time on the flat, concrete rooftop. Since World War II, many of the wealthier families have built houses of a similar style in one of the new quarters outside the city's walls, and their former residences have frequently been subdivided into several apartments. But from the outside there is no way of telling for certain whether a door will lead into the house of a rich man, a subdivided apartment complex, or a dark and musty cellar dwelling.

To gain a very rough grasp of the old city one can start at its geographical center, beside the deeply entrenched channel through which the Aggai River bisects the town. Here, as along several of the main streets winding toward various gates, are located a number of small shops. Cloth merchants sit in the cubicles that line a covered street at whose far end stands the unprepossessing doorway of a mosque. Clusters of fresh mint and cones of solid sugar stand out in the grocery stalls; farther along, on one side of a narrow bridge, the sellers of day-old bread display their wares. In the small streets to the side one finds cooked-food stalls, tiny cafés, and the shops of the few remaining metalworkers and jewelers. One long, gently winding street is lined with the shops of pack-saddlemakers and blacksmiths and contains the entrance to the courtyard of an old inn, now converted into a complex of small apartments. The tangle of unpaved streets that spreads out on all sides is clogged with people, refuse, piles of goods, stone-throwing children, and the excrement of innumerable donkeys.

If the Western visitor finds himself confused and disoriented in the welter of narrow streets and cul-de-sacs, or incapable of directing himself by reference to notable landmarks, his may only be a more extreme and disconcerting reaction than that experienced by some of the rural visitors to the weekly market or, indeed, by some of the Sefrouis themselves. There are, however, at least two significant categories people employ in referring to and orienting themselves within the old city: small streets of neighbors (sg. *derb*) and the various urban quarters (sg. *ḥuma*).[33] Throughout the medina's labyrinth of streets there exist several derbs, or alleyways, often leading to a deadend, which usually bear the name of a particular family. Indeed, until well into the Protectorate most of the houses in a particular derb were occupied by a group of relatives. Although this physical proximity should not be taken as evidence of any greater solidarity than pertained among families that were more dispersed, to be able to identify the derb in which a man's family lived afforded a significant index of that person's place on the social map. In recent years, many of the

62 former residents of the medina have moved to houses outside the

walls, and individual derbs are now occupied by persons of more diverse social and familial backgrounds. However, the concept of a derb as a social and geographical subdivision of the medina still remains significant.

A second way to look at the city is in terms of a quarter, or huma. The exact boundaries, and indeed the exact number of quarters, are not as clearly determined as the contemporary administrative divisions bearing some of the same names suggest. Most people nowadays list five quarters in addition to the *mellāḥ,* or Jewish quarter, but the list may run as high as ten or twelve because particular derbs may also be referred to as quarters. In pre-Protectorate times there were some seventeen gates that closed off particular sections of the medina at night or during disorders, but these did not correlate exactly with the boundaries of the quarters. Moreover, the minimally corporate activities of urban quarters in pre-Protectorate times and their present administrative aspects should not be taken as indications that they presently have any true corporate character.

Derb and huma are, then, two different ways in which people conceptualize the city of Sefrou, two parallel sets of symbols by which an order is imposed on an urban agglomeration lacking in an overall urban design as easily grasped as a grid or radial plan. In sociological terms, people do not identify themselves as "members" of a particular derb in a given quarter, for these are alternative rather than hierarchical symbolic orders. Nor is the street or quarter in which one lives a sure index of social standing or occupational pursuit. In the past, one's family, job, economic standing, religious brotherhood affiliation, and so on, tended to clump so that reference to any one of these features afforded an insight into each of one's other affiliations. But this was only a probabilistic insight and one that, given the economic heterogeneity of families and quarters in the past as much as in the present, added to but did not fully reflect the individual ties and traits on which the social organization of the city rests to the present day. Derb and quarter afford cognitive handles by which the medina is made comprehensible–"imageable," to use Kevin Lynch's phrase–to those who live, work, and move around in it.[34]

One quarter of the medina deserves special attention–the mellah, the old Jewish quarter. Until recent years the Jewish community accounted for a substantial part of the city's population. As Table 1 shows, the Jews composed fully half of the population of the city until around the advent of the Protectorate in 1912. Thereafter, the size of the Jewish community grew to more than 5,700 in the postwar period, but began to decline sharply after independence was obtained in

63

Table 1. *The population of Sefrou 1883–1960*

Year	Muslims	Jews	Europeans	Total Moroccans	Total
1883	2,000	1,000	–	3,000	3,000
1903	3,000	3,000	–	6,000	6,000
1913	–	–	–	6,400	6,400
1917	4,150	2,950	–	7,100	7,100
1926	4,894	3,444	140	8,338	8,478
1931	5,635	4,046	218	9,681	9,899
1936	7,288	4,346	246	11,634	11,880
1941	9,095	5,474	339	14,569	14,908
1947	11,342	5,757	495	17,099	17,594
1951–2	11,520	4,360	710	15,880	16,590
1960	17,583	3,041	337	20,624	20,961

Source: Figures cited for each year are derived from the following sources. *1883:* Foucauld, D., *Reconnaisance au Maroc 1883–1884,* Paris, 1888, p. 38; *1903:* Aubin, E., *Le Maroc d'aujourd'hui,* Paris, 1908, p. 396; *1913:* Caix, R., "La Population du Maroc," *L'Afrique franqise,* 23:180 (1913); *1917:* Périgny, M., *Au Maroc: Fès, la capitale du nord,* Paris, 1917, pp. 288–9; *1941:* Institute des Hautes Etudes Marocaines, *Initiation au Maroc,* Paris, 1945, p. 256; *1947:* Chouraqui, A., *La Condition juridique de l'Israélite marocain,* Paris, 1950, p. 33. The figures for 1926, 1931, 1936, 1951–2, and 1960 come from the official census for each of those years.

1956. At the time of fieldwork in 1967, the Jews in Sefrou numbered about 600, and by 1972 little more than 200 persons.[35]

Throughout most of their history, the Jews of Sefrou lived in the mellah. In most Moroccan cities, the mellah is located at the edge of the medina, but Sefrou is unusual in that the mellah is situated in the geographical center of the city, entirely surrounded by Muslim residential quarters. In the past, access to the mellah was through a single gate at the end of a bridge over the Aggai River, but in recent years an additional opening has been cut in the opposite wall of the quarter. To accommodate the dense population, apartments in the mellah rose three to four stories high, their common backs forming a wall within the city's wall. Perhaps out of reluctance to tie up available capital or perhaps as a means of securing the safety of their homes and shops, relatively few of the buildings in the mellah ever seem to have actually been owned by the Jews. Many of the structures were and are the property of the religious foundation (habus), leased by the Jews from the Muslim authorities. Others were owned by individual Muslim landlords. Those properties that were owned by Jews appear more often to have been held by the community as a whole than by individual proprietors.

After World War II, and particularly after Moroccan Independence 64 in 1956, the Jews of Sefrou began to move into other areas of the city.

They settled in Derb l-Miter, an adjacent new medina area, and especially in the Ville Nouvelle. This move was dictated as much by demographic necessity as by changing sociopolitical circumstances. By the 1950s the population density of the mellah had reached an extremely high figure. Moreover, as the Protectorate waned and Independence began, many Jews who lived in small towns in the Middle Atlas and Saharan regions moved into Sefrou. These rural Jewish immigrants probably numbered only several hundred, but even if some of the Sefrou Jews had not regarded them as uneducated and rather uncouth it was certainly an addition the mellah could ill afford to absorb. As the Jews moved out, the mellah became the habitat for poor Muslim immigrants from the countryside. With the founding of the State of Israel, the advent of Moroccan Independence, the death of Sultan Mohammed V in 1961, and the wars in the Middle East, most of the Jews have left Sefrou for Israel, France, and the cities of the Moroccan coast. The diminution – and probable demise – of the Jewish community of Sefrou is not the result of any breakdown in Muslim-Jewish relations, but stems from the Jews' general uncertainty about the stability of the Moroccan economy and the opportunities that would be available to their children in contemporary Morocco.[36] During the period of fieldwork, the Jewish schools still operated and Jews were still seen in the marketplace, but the familial hierarchy, the elaborate internal institutions, and the economic importance of the Jewish community, like the mellah community itself, were almost entirely gone.

In some respects the comments made about the medina apply as well to parts of the city lying beyond the medina's walls. Certainly the Qlaᶜa, a separate enclave whose high buildings form a common wall for the whole settlement, is much like any quarter of the old city proper. Its inhabitants, nevertheless, express a distinct identity that is, at times, opposed to that of "Sefroui" (a person from Sefrou), and its history has been one of closer ties to the rural areas lying just to the west, overt opposition to the inhabitants or administrators of Sefrou at various times during the late nineteenth century, and a tendency to farm the gardens of the western slope bounding the city until, through a series of intermediate steps, the land was used for the development by the French of the Ville Nouvelle.

Under the administration of the first resident general of the Protectorate, Marshal Lyautey, Europeans were discouraged from involving themselves directly in the daily life of the native Moroccans.[37] Throughout Morocco, "new cities" were built next to the existing medinas, and villas, business districts, and most administrative offices were located in these new areas. In Sefrou, it was in the western hills

65

rimming the oasis that the French built their new quarter, complete
with a post office, cafés, a hotel, gas stations, and public gardens.
Villas now occupy most of the gardens that formerly covered the area,
and the physical contrast with the medina could not be more striking.

Less striking, however, is the contrast between either of the old or
new cities and the areas that have been developed on the other three
sides of the medina. Beginning in the 1920s, but particularly after
World War II and the achievement of national independence, the
gardens immediately surrounding the medina began to be sold off for
residential buildings.[38] Streets were laid out on a simple grid pattern,
the metric rigidity giving its name to the first of these quarters to be
developed, Derb l-Miter. The houses erected along these new, wide
streets are, for the most part, rather traditional in design: bland, whitewashed walls punctured by grillwork windows surrounding a central
courtyard, guest and living rooms. Those new quarters closest to the
medina merge with the old city quite fully, and were it not that the
streets are broad enough to carry motor traffic – of which there is
none in the medina – it would be hard, without looking up at the
Moorish ramparts, to say exactly where the one ends and the other
begins. The quarter that has been built up on the west side of the Fez
road, like that on the far southern end of the oasis, is more dispersed,
with separate houses, including some villas, set among the garden
tracts that remain undeveloped.

Two other settlements, one lying within the city limits, the other
just outside, bear mentioning. After the 1950 flood washed away a
number of homes and shops along the river's edge, the government
moved quickly to erect a series of barrackslike structures just west of
the medina on an open tract of land. Owned and operated by the
government, this development, named Slawi, became at first the residence of many of those left homeless by the flood. Later, however, as
more and more people from the countryside moved to the city, Slawi
became a second-stage area. That is to say, the cheapest and least
desirable residences became those of the mellah and other decaying
portions of the medina proper, and Slawi became one of the places to
which people later moved when they were able. Until the recent
construction of concrete walls, the front of each of the apartments at
Slawi had an enclosure made of branches, cardboard, tin sheets, and
tar paper. The shantytown appearance was quite misleading, for in fact
it was and is to the medina that the poorest of rural immigrants
invariably gravitate.

A second settlement, called Cher ben Sefar (*cher* being the Berber
equivalent of duwwar, or settlement), is located just outside the mu-

nicipal boundaries to the east. It is the closest thing to a shantytown in Sefrou, a small group of twelve to fifteen dwellings, many now made of stone, that were erected by squatters from the countryside unable or unwilling to move into Sefrou proper. It is built on a rocky hillside that lacks running water, and the residents must, therefore, make frequent trips to fountains in the city. The municipal government and the rural administrator have continually tried to avoid the question of Cher ben Sefar's status – the city refuses it utilities, the qaid threatens to tear it down – but it now seems firmly emplaced, and as mortar and stone replace cardboard and branches, it takes on the appearance of a very small duwwar right on the city's doorstep rather than of a shanty-town, or bidonville, of the sort found in many larger Moroccan cities.[39]

Thus Sefrou divides roughly into three main entities: the medina, the Ville Nouvelle, and the new medina areas just outside the old city's walls. However, with the exception of the Ville Nouvelle and to a limited extent the old mellah, none of the quarters of the old city or any of the four main residential areas beyond its ramparts is in any sense sociologically homogeneous. The ethnic and social backgrounds of the city's inhabitants are quite mixed for any given area. Except for the Jews, by 1960 localized in a street of the Ville Nouvelle and a small area of one of the new quarters, and the remaining Europeans, who live in the villas of the Ville Nouvelle, the various social groups into which the Muslim population can be divided are quite evenly scattered throughout the city.

In some respects, though, the contrast among these three main divisions of the city is quite sharp. A few statistics will help convey the extent of these differences.[40] For example, in 1960 43 percent of the population of Sefrou lived in the medina, an area that, for all the complexity of its internal geography, encompasses only about 8 hectares of land. Accordingly, the population density is incredibly high – 1,117 persons per hectare, or about three times the density of Manhattan. The new medina areas and the Ville Nouvelle, with their gardens and open public spaces, are far less densely settled, the former areas averaging 150 persons per hectare, the latter just 12. A somewhat better index of actual living space is afforded by the figures concerning the average number of persons living in the dwellings of each area: In the quarters of the medina the average figure is 11; in the new medina areas, from 5.4 to 8.5. In terms of household facilities, almost all the houses of the new medina quarters are supplied with electricity, compared with 85 percent of the houses in the medina, but as many as 20 percent of the buildings in these newer areas

67

lack toilet facilities. In short, the quality of the buildings, the availability of various facilities, and the spaciousness of living arrangements are progressively better as one moves from the medina to the newer quarters outside its walls and up into the Ville Nouvelle. The economic status of the occupants of these three areas varies accordingly.

By and large, the medina has, particularly in recent years, become home for poorer people of rural origins, who have come to live, for longer or shorter periods of time, in the city, as well as for the poorer elements of the indigenous population itself. In particular, the mellah, which was still mostly inhabited by Jews at the time of the 1960 census, has been given over almost entirely to the poorest of rural immigrants. The new medina areas have, for the most part, become the home of older Sefrou families who have moved out of the medina, rural immigrants who are somewhat better off financially, and intermediate-level civil servants (e.g., schoolteachers, clerks) many of whom have come to Sefrou from other parts of Morocco. Finally, the Ville Nouvelle is populated largely by higher-ranking civil servants (a significant number coming from Fez), the Europeanized *commerçants,* the few remaining Frenchmen, and most of the remnants of the Jewish community. Thus, a rough social distribution is discernible, with the older urban types and more sophisticated "middle-class" elements of the population relinquishing the geographical and historical center of the city to those poorer rural people who have come to live in the city within recent years.

This is, however, only a very rough overview of the contemporary urban population, and except for certain general implications for economic standing, it conveys little of the complexity of urban social organization or the many facets of social stratification. In order to describe the structure of urban social patterns and the macrosociology of urban groupings, it will be necessary to consider the categories and institutions of Sefrou society in somewhat greater detail.

Government and politics in the city and region of Sefrou

The present governmental structure of municipalities such as Sefrou is, like that of the countryside, largely an amalgamation of features dating from the pre-Protectorate government of the sultan and those introduced by the French during the colonial period. Before the arrival of the French, cities like Sefrou were usually governed by a *pasha* chosen by the sultan from among the important families of the city, and directly responsible to the sultan's regional representative (*kalīfa*), himself often a close relative of the monarch. Civil order was handled

by the pasha, the Islamic law judge (*qāḍī*), the market official
(*muḥtaseb*), and, in the case of the imperial cities of Rabat, Marrakech,
Fez, and sometimes Meknes, the sultan himself. Because the Protectorate was organized to give the appearance of full respect for indigenous governmental institutions, the French did not destroy this system. Instead, they established one that was separate, though clearly
superior, to that of the pre-Protectorate period. A French *controleur
civile* sat beside each rural administrator, and each of the larger municipalities had French officials directly overseeing appointments and
most daily operations.

Sefrou, as a smaller city that had been on the edge of governmental
control throughout much of the pre-Protectorate period, was only a
partial exception to this general pattern. For most of the late nineteenth and early twentieth centuries, Sefrou was controlled by the
immensely powerful qaid of the Ait Yusi tribe, Umar al-Yusi, who
held officially warranted power in the city of Sefrou as well as in the
surrounding region. With his demise, Sefrou came under the administration of the pasha of Fez Jdid.[41] After the French arrived, a succession of pashas, including Si M'barek Bekkai, later the first prime
minister of independent Morocco, governed the city under the overall
aegis of the colonial government.

The independent Moroccan government has, since 1956, adhered
to a rather simple organizational form for most of the cities in the
nation. The pasha, appointed like all officials by Rabat, reports directly to the governor of his province – in the case of Sefrou, to the
governor of the Province of Fez. The governor, in turn, is directly
responsible to the Ministry of Interior, which is in charge of all matters of internal administration and civil order in the nation. The lines
of formal control reaching out from Rabat are, therefore, short and
tightly controlled. Moreover, it is the general policy of the central
government to appoint to positions of local authority individuals who
are from regions other than that over which they have formal administrative duties. Although this policy appears to be followed more carefully in rural areas than in the cities, and although there are clear
exceptions to the general rule, Sefrou itself has not had a local man as
pasha since before the Protectorate; the present pasha came to Sefrou
from Fez. Perhaps more important than his place of origin, however,
is the fact that the present pasha is a distant relative of the king. The
pasha's brother has also held several important ministerial posts in the
central government and has stood for election to parliament from the
Sefrou constituency.

Within the municipality proper, several positions and bureaus are 69 directly ranked beneath the office of pasha. In addition to the khalifa, who is formally charged with little more than keeping the shop when the pasha is away, there is a municipal accountant, a clerk, a chief of the licensing bureau, an office of public works, and an office of civil registration and statistics. The city government (*baladīya*) also includes a tax office and a network of low-level officials appointed to each of the administrative quarters of the city. This latter official, the *muqaddem*, is the agent of the baladiya most closely in touch with the minor affairs of everyday life in the city, and a closer look at his activities is, therefore, revealing.

In pre-Protectorate days, each of the urban quarters had its own muqaddem, who was chosen by the men of that quarter to represent their interests to the governing officials. At present, the four muqaddems perform a wide variety of functions. They certify that an individual is poor enough to receive handouts of grain from the municipal poorhouse or is eligible for the public works projects reserved for the poor. Because many rural people have flooded into the city in recent years – particularly during slack agricultural periods – and because a wide variety of fee waivers is available to the officially poor, this power of certification is of considerable significance to a number of people in the city. More important, perhaps, is the fact that the muqaddem, togther with a representative from the tax office and a respected resident of the quarter, go from house to house once a year assessing taxes to be paid to the central government. In general, the muqaddem is expected to know everyone in the quarter he covers, to keep a close eye on their general affairs, and to have his finger constantly on the economic, social, and political pulse of the area of the city he supervises. Appointed by the pasha, the muqaddems should be acceptable to the people of their districts. However, the fact that the same muqaddems have held office in Sefrou since Independence, when those appointed by the French were (with one exception) removed from office, should be interpreted as meaning only that they are regarded as not wholly unacceptable to the residents of their respective quarters.

Each morning the four muqaddems report to the chief of muqaddems in the pasha's office on events of the preceding day and night. Usually, this is a routine report, but it does indicate that the chief of muqaddems is indeed in close touch with the city, and if it were not also clear that this individual is personally rather important in Sefrou politics, this fact alone might hint as much.

All this is not to say that Sefrou is a closely watched town in a political, much less openly repressive, sense. Formally, the local police

70

are responsible to the governor of the province rather than to the pasha, but a certain amount of deference is shown the pasha by the police commissioner, and the pasha, in turn, may try to keep certain matters from becoming police affairs (e.g., in the case of rape a quick marriage is usually arranged, through the offices of the pasha and the qadi). `

One other urban governmental institution deserves to be mentioned: the City Council (*majlis l-baladīya*). This is an elective body formally charged with approving the municipal budget and, therefore, overseeing a wide range of city affairs. In fact, the council is quite without power, and its actions are simply those of a rubber stamp. In the early 1960s some members of the council took their duties so seriously as to challenge the budget submitted to them by the pasha. However, after the governor of the province was called up to Sefrou to clarify for the recalcitrant council members precisely what was expected of them, the members ratified proposals submitted to them by the pasha without hesitation.

Although the council as a formal body is without significant powers, elections to positions on the council have generated quite a bit of interest. Two elections for a new council were held in the period leading up to our own research: in 1960 for all twenty-one seats and in 1963 for an expanded twenty-three-seat council.[42] Electoral districts were roughly equal in terms of population except that the four seats alloted the Jewish community in 1960 were retained in 1963 despite the diminution of that segment of the population. Candidates were affiliated with the various political parties, those of the Istiqlal party winning most of the seats in 1960 and those of the coalition put together by the king for the 1963 parliamentary elections winning the majority in that year's elections. Yet despite these party attachments and the rather hectic politicking that characterized the elections, it was neither because of partisan differences nor because of the importance of the council as a governmental body that the elections elicited so much attention. Rather, interest ran at a fairly high level because of the patronage benefits it was hoped might accrue to any of the council members or their supporters. This pattern of personal politics aimed at acquiring specific connections that can be used in the pursuit of variously defined goals is, as we have already seen in the rural context, characteristic of the local political process of the entire Sefrou region.

Politics is a term that always covers a wide range of activities, from formal administrative procedures to the vaguest of instrumental relations. In the city and region of Sefrou, however, it is rather difficult to factor out a distinct set of domains of political life and to analyze them

71

in terms of their individual characteristics. One can set forth, as we have tried to do in the preceding pages, the formal attributes of rural and urban, national and local political institutions, and to indicate the particular ways in which these institutions ideally operate in a variety of specific situations. In fact, however, these formal institutions of political life do not, in and of themselves, tell all, or even much, about the intricacies of local-level politics. To understand more fully what is really going on in any political situation, a careful analysis of the individual ties of the personalities must also be considered, for political activities, like social activities generally, are very personalistic in orientation.

Consider once again the position of a local qaid. Strictly speaking, he is charged with maintaining order and administering government programs in the region under his control. In fact, the extent to which he really becomes involved in, or even knowledgeable about, the affairs of his region varies tremendously. In the Sefrou region, for example, there is a local man, himself a former qaid, who is regarded by most people as the real leader of the Ait Yusi even though he holds no official post and performs no formal functions. He is called upon to mediate various disputes, and when the help of outside personalities is desired, often intercedes on behalf of his fellow Ait Yusi with a political party official or government agent. His is always the biggest tent at the main celebration of the tribe's major saint, and it is he who offers the most lavish hospitality during the yearly Cherry Festival in the city of Sefrou. Yet if a particular dispute leaves him in the position of having to decide against a part of his "constituency" – as was the case in the Dayat Ifrah incident – he may simply avoid all involvement and leave it up to the nonlocal qaid, or his superior, to render the final decision. Similarly, as we have seen, the qaid or some other person located in one area may be called on by people of his region of origin to mediate a dispute or influence a decision that is not formally within his jurisdiction. When one begins to consider the channels through which decisions affecting local interests are made, the network of interpersonal ties involved often tends to become extremely complicated.

Indeed, the kind of power a local official can effectively employ in any situation depends as much on these personal ties as on his officially sanctioned authority. The pasha of Sefrou has come to be the major figure in the city's administration not just because of the resources on which he can draw as the government-appointed head of the city, but because of his personal ability to distribute patronage benefits effectively, to sustain the interests of those persons in the city who have connections that reach farther up in the government, to play on his brother's position in the national cabinet, and to play on various governmental offices and personnel in such a way as to allow them to take the blame for any unpopular moves.

Of course, the pattern of local politics is deeply affected by the institutions and machinations of national political figures and national political parties. In general, people in the Sefrou area feel no lasting attachments to any of the organized political parties. In an election, it is the combination of a candidate's personal attachments – only one of which is his party affiliation – that really counts. There has been considerable disillusionment with each of the national parties, and voting patterns are as likely to be evidence of frustration with the promises of each party as of support for particular individuals. Except for the UNFP, which has ceased to operate publicly in most of the country since the death of its leader Mehdi ben Barka, the various parties maintain small offices and hold infrequent gatherings in the city. But their supporters are few, their financial support minimal, and their organization practically nonexistent on the local level. Even in the relatively heated contest for parliament in 1963 or in local elections to the municipal council or Chamber of Agricultural Representatives, it was clear that people preferred to keep sharp lines from forming between various segments of the population because of political party ties lest such firm attachments interfere with each person's ability to form personally useful associations across any social boundary in the future. The educated and more "modernized" urbanites are the only ones who seem to take political issues and ideological disputes seriously, and even they have shown that their support for the Istiqlal party, for the idea of a parliament, or for particular aspects of Moroccan foreign policy is by no means fully formed, rigidly honored, or consistently applied.

In sum, political activity in the Sefrou area is generally directed toward the acquisition of some individual goal – obtaining a work permit to go abroad, getting certification of poor status entitling one to government welfare allotments, winning a municipal building contract or permit – and often the quest for useful allies is simply a hedge against future uncertainties. The hierarchy of government officials has been kept in tight check by the powers in Rabat, and the officials' local ties are, particularly in the rural areas, often rather shallow and tentative. Political alignments form and re-form with great rapidity and ease, and processes that are discernible on the local level not only bear great similarity to those on a national level but constitute a vital aspect of the overall political structure of the nation.

The legal system

Each of the domains of social life in the city and region of Sefrou possesses distinctive characteristics: modes of political alliance, conventions of economic affiliation, forms of kinship relatedness. However, in each of these domains common features are discernible: symbols of personal identity, crosscutting ties of personal relationship, applications of the accepted modes of establishing obligation. No less than other institutions, the legal system of the Sefrou area evinces at once the distinctive features of a system of adjudication and the characteristic modes of interpersonal attachment found in other domains of Sefrou social life. To look at the legal system of Sefrou is to look at a portion of the social organization of the region that has an internal history and a set of institutions that are as revealing in their distinguishing features as they are typical in the ways they partake of the broader culture of the area.

The Sacred Law of Islam is often regarded as the heart and soul of any Islamic community. Because it defines and regulates not only the principles and rituals of formal religious practice but much of the organization of political and legal activity proper, it can be seen as suffusing and characterizing almost the whole of Islamic life. In the present section, however, we shall be concerned only with the strictly legal aspects of Islamic law practiced in the city and region of Sefrou, as well as with the recent "secular" additions to the legal system. In particular, we shall concentrate on the development of judicial organization and the operations of the local court of religious law–the qadi's court. Finally, we shall try to indicate some of the ways in which the law can be seen as a focus through which a greater understanding of certain aspects of contemporary Moroccan social life can be perceived, and the ways in which the legal system itself articulates with other institutions of public and political life.

Judicial organization

In the period leading up to the inauguration of the French Protectorate, the judicial system of Morocco was neither very elaborate nor very centralized.[43] In each locality, several tribunals exercised authority within their respective jurisdictions. The court of the *qāḍī* (the religious law judge) was concerned with the direct application to specific cases of the principles of religious law (*šraᶜ*) as formulated by the great scholars of the Malikite school of Islamic law. Appointed by the sultan, the qadi was, particularly in the case of urban areas, either a local person noted for his learning or someone who had received appropriate training – usually at the Qarawiyin, the great mosque-university in Fez – and did not meet with the active disapproval of the community's leading citizens. The nature and extent of a qadi's powers were not determined solely by the formal mandate accorded him by the sultan. The reach and, in many instances, the content of his decisions depended in no small part on the acceptable foundations of judicial reasoning, the other personnel involved in the judicial process, the interests of certain segments of local society, and the network of personal affiliations established by the qadi himself.

Traditional Islamic law has often been characterized as a jurist's or scholar's law rather than a judge's law. In the Moroccan case, however, the legal system was somewhat more mixed. In formulating their opinions, qadis did not limit themselves to solutions based only on the classical sources of Islamic law – the Quran, the traditions of the Prophet (*sunna*), the process of analogic reasoning (*qiyās*), and the consensus (*ijmāᶜ*) of the early Islamic communities. At times they also formulated a preferred opinion (*istiḥsān*), one that could not be derived by strict analogy from the major sources of the law but that could nevertheless be rationalized as serving the public interest (*istiṣlāḥ*). These preferred opinions were largely derived from the advisory statements (sg. *fatwā*) that had been obtained by litigants from religious law scholars (*ᶜulamā*, sg. *ᶜālim*). Depending on the wisdom or reputation of the alim, these approaches might then be regularly adopted by qadis in many parts of the country. Moreover, there developed in Morocco a distinctive form of case law. It was recognized that through the concept of *ᶜamal* (judicial practice) the opinions of local courts, often based on local customs (*ᶜurf*) or the discretion of local qadis, could achieve widespread recognition, even though the approach differed from that which scholarly consensus had established as the preferred solution to an issue. These judicial practices were collected and published by Moroccan scholars, often in the form of mnemonic manuals for use by students and judges. Thus, a qadi could employ any one of a number of devices – doctrinal solutions, scholarly orientations, local customs, judicial practices – in reaching his decision on a given case. It also meant that the qadi could, and in many instances had to, be responsive to the will of local people and local interests.

In Sefrou, despite its small size, there were, in the years leading up to the Protectorate, several people who were recognized as ulama, and whose advisory opinions were sought in legal actions. In the late nineteenth century, and possibly for some time before, all the ulama

75

were formally employed as notaries in the court, though not all notaries were regarded as ulama. On occasion they would meet as a group,
in solemn session, to issue a collective opinion. This was referred to as
the bringing of an ᶜar – the shaming by the ulama (ᶜ*arra dyal
l-ᶜulamā*) – or as mediating a legal case (*kaysafaru nāzila*). Both these
usages reflect the spiritual force of the ulama's decisions (most of the
ulama are also descendants of the Prophet) and the role of these men
as society's mediators and arbitrators. However, when the opinions of
the ulama or qadi clashed with the interests of local powers, the result,
as in the Sefrou case, could prove disastrous.

It was during the time of Qaid Umar al-Yusi, older informants say,
that Sefrou suffered the loss of its ulama. Umar had insisted that the
qadi of Sefrou register a number of land transfers that had been
obtained by the qaid through coercion. The qadi refused the registration and condemned Umar's actions as sinful. Hearing that Umar
intended to have him murdered, several Sefrou elders warned the
qadi and aided his escape from the city. Umar had a more cooperative
man appointed in his place, but the ulama warned the new qadi that if
the deeds were registered he would be committing a grave sin. Umar's
reaction was swift and ruthless. He had four of the ulama scourged
through the streets – their hands tied, their feet bare, their mouths
stuffed with hot peppers, and their necks joined by a single rope. The
ulama were then cast into prison, where they died.

In all probability Umar was not the first – though the ferocity of his
response assured he would be the last – to misuse the ulama of Sefrou.
More to the point, however, is the fact that the presence of a multiplicity of legal personnel and bases for achieving a legitimate judicial
approach yielded a system that lacked in centralization and tight-knit
development what it possessed in flexibility and local distinctiveness.
No opinions of the qadis of pre-Protectorate Sefrou have been found,
but if the evidence of aged informants and records from other locales
may be trusted, it appears likely that the people of Sefrou – particularly some members of more notable families – were able to have a
substantial impact on the kinds of judgments, both familial and commercial, reached by the qadi. Indeed, this repertoire of legal concepts
and officials granted to the domain of law the same kind of malleability and personalism found in other fields of activity.

The qadi's court was not the only judicial forum operating in pre-
Protectorate Sefrou. All criminal matters, and some civil ones, were
handled by the pasha or the qaid sitting as sole judge. Their precise
jurisdiction and their choice of punishments were a function of personal power, and their judgments, though occasionally based on local

custom, were largely unbounded by any systematized body of law. In the marketplace, the *umāna* ("reliable commercial witnesses") and the *muḥtaseb* ("commercial norm applier") served to contain potential disruption. In Berber territories, Berber customary law (Br. *izerf*) was applied, and the descendants of saints – particularly those from Sidi Lahcen Lyusi – or specialists in Berber law from nearby tribes were often called upon to mediate or arbitrate disputes. In short, a wide range of legal institutions existed in the Sefrou region, and the precise powers of the legal personnel fluctuated with personal reputation, the balance of local interests, and historical circumstance. The establishment of the Protectorate changed much of this pattern. In addition to other reforms, the French instituted appeals courts, registration procedures for real properties, separate courts for Europeans, and strict supervision of existing courts by French civil or military officials.[44] At first the French granted formal judicial status to each assembly (*jamāᶜa*) of the rural Berber tribes, but in the famous Berber Dahir of 1930 the French went so far as to create Berber customary law tribunals and to grant to French courts control over virtually all criminal matters occurring in Berber territories.[45] This was rightly seen by all Moroccans as a divide-and-conquer tactic, and the furor raised by the Berber Dahir contributed significantly to the rise of nationalist sentiment.

Following Independence in 1956, the Moroccan government undertook its own series of judicial reforms. At present (1972), the organization of the legal system is roughly the following.[46] At the local level there is a single court, the *sadad,* which is divided into two branches. The first is the qadi's court, which, as in pre-Independence times, rules on matters of personal status, inheritance, and property disputes that involve only proofs of right originally issued by a qadi's court. The second branch of the sadad – for which the term *sadad* alone is usually applied – is concerned with criminal, civil, and commercial law. All disputes involving more than 900 dirhams, however, receive first consideration in the regional tribunal; cases involving less than 300 dirhams cannot be appealed beyond the level of the sadad.

The regional tribunal (*maḥkama l-iqlīmīa*), which for the Sefrou district is located in Fez, is both the court of first instance for disputes involving substantial sums of money and the appellate court for all other matters coming from the sadad or qadi's courts. The regional tribunal, in turn, is succeeded in the judicial hierarchy by the appeals court (*maḥkama l-isti'nāf*), of which there are three for the entire nation. Finally, there is the supreme court in Rabat (*majlis l-ᶜala*), which is itself divided into several chambers to hear final appeals.

Appointments to the position of qadi or *ḥakem* (the latter being the

77

term applied to a judge in the sadad branch of the local court) are made by officials of the Ministry of Justice. Until recently, the qualifications for appointment to the post of qadi related only to training in classical religious law, and qadis were, therefore, assigned only to that branch of the local court. However, the rules were subsequently changed, and a qadi must now be competent to deal with cases that come before all branches of the local court. Nevertheless, in most areas, Sefrou among them, there is one official called the qadi who usually handles nothing but cases within the jurisdiction of the qadi's court, except for emergencies, when he may substitute for a judge in the other branch.

There have also been significant changes in the sources of the law since Moroccan Independence. Instead of the prior reliance on uncodified religious law or French-influenced civil and criminal laws, new codes have been promulgated in several areas with which the local court is concerned. Within the jurisdiction of the qadi's court, for example, the ruling body of law is now the *Mudawwana* ("Code of Personal Status"), which was formulated in 1958.[47] This code – which deals with such matters as marriage, divorce, filiation, child custody, support, and inheritance – is very close to the principles of religious law practiced in the pre-Independence period. Unlike the modern codes of most other Middle Eastern countries, it makes few breaks with the past. Although it seeks to regularize such matters as the age of marriage and the need for a bride to consent to her union, both the stipulation that local custom may arbitrate against particular rules and the way in which the law is actually applied tend, as we shall see, to reinforce rather than undercut most preexisting tenets of Moroccan family law. In order to see just how this system of law actually works out in practice, let us consider in some detail the operation of the qadi's court in Sefrou as it existed at the time of our research.

The qadi's court in Sefrou

The qadi's court in Sefrou covers a jurisdiction that includes the city of Sefrou proper, the nearby village of Bhalil, and the portion of the Ait Yusi territory that lies immediately around the city. The court itself is staffed by several officials, each with a clearly prescribed range of formal duties and powers. In addition to the qadi himself, there are six ᶜ*adūl* (sg. ᶜ*adel*), or notaries. For any document made out in the qadi's office to be legally valid – documents such as marital contracts and land transfers – the signatures of two adul are an indispensable requirement. The adul usually work as teams, and because they are

78

paid a set fee for each document they sign they tend to develop a clientele of their own – persons who prefer the relative privacy and ease of working out personal arrangements that come from having adul who regularly handle their legal affairs. All but two of the adul in Sefrou at present are from the local area, and those who were born elsewhere have worked in Sefrou for some time. In pre-Protectorate times, each quarter of the city chose two adul from among its own members, but now adul are all appointed to handle whatever business comes to them. Adul with a particularly large or well-to-do clientele can make 2,000 to 3,000 dirhams (about $400 to $600) per month – a substantial sum in a place like Sefrou.

Various matters come before the court that require the testimony of ostensibly impartial experts. It is often necessary to determine the exact boundaries of an untilled piece of property, for example, or to compute the support that should be paid for the maintenance of a child. Accordingly, the court has a number of experts (*kubbarā*) who undertake such tasks at the request of one of the disputants or of the court itself. Given the nature of their jurisdiction and the varying standards of evidence, some of these experts are attached to the sadad branch (those who are experts on construction and commercial trans-actions), and the qadi's court has two pairs of experts who determine the costs of both clothing and household furnishings. The adul them-selves determine food values.

The qadi's court also has attached to it several matrons (sg. *ᶜarīfa*); one works in the women's section of the jail, and another serves as a policewoman, entering the woman's bath in case of fights or searching female suspects. A third matron serves as court expert on matters concerning female litigants (e.g., determining pregnancy and bodily injury), tasks that may also be assigned to a local doctor. Most impor-tantly, however, this matron also runs a house to which a woman can be sent by a husband who has just divorced her and wants to be sure his recently repudiated wife does not become pregnant before the expiration of the waiting period, during which her pregnancy is auto-matically attributed to the divorcing husband.

Two lesser court officials should also be mentioned, men of less important formal rank, but not necessarily of informal influence: the clerks (*kātib*) and uniformed aides (sg. *mkazni*). The clerks are simply in charge of keeping various records: They take notes of all court proceedings, send out summonses, handle correspondence to the min-istry, and register the petitions of all new litigants. Of at least equal importance, however, is the fact that, because of their knowledge of Islamic law and the workings of the local court, clerks are often asked 79 for advice on a wide range of legal matters and often advise persons how or whether to bring a matter to court. Depending wholly on their individual personalities and points óf view, the clerks can play a very important role indeed in the everyday operation of the legal system. The uniformed aides, on the other hand, are just messenger boys and sergeants-at-arms. In the qadi's court in Sefrou, however, one aide also acts as translator in the court's proceedings and, owing to his bombastic personality and the willingness of the qadi, he interprets far beyond the dictates of literal translation and has a clear impact on the order, and hence the development, of many proceedings.

Finally, it should be noted that a public prosecutor (*wakīl d-daula*) is attached to the court system. His main concern is with criminal matters, and he generally acts as liaison with the local police, pasha, qaid, and other bureaucratic offices. Although appointed through the Ministry of Justice, he may, depending on local politics and personalities, be more responsive to the qaid or pasha than to his superiors in the court hierarchy. His is also the power of enforcement of all judicial decrees, and in this respect he is the keystone of much of the system of local justice. Not surprisingly, the activities of his office were less amenable to direct investigation than were those of the court proper. However, a detailed study was made of the qadi's court in Sefrou, and it is to the analysis of this material that we shall now direct our attention.

In order to institute a proceeding before the court of the qadi, a petitioner must file a complaint (*mqal*) in which he or she sets forth the nature of the case to be brought, the person or persons charged as defendants, and exactly what the plaintiff wishes the court to do about the situation. This document is usually made out by the clerks, but it may be made out by a public scribe, a friend, or the complainant himself. The clerks then notify the parties involved and add the case to the docket.

A person who appears before the qadi's court may or may not choose to have someone else represent him. He may hire a formally trained lawyer (*muḥāmi*) if the case is sufficiently important or if he is sufficiently well-to-do. There used to be several lawyers in Sefrou, but at the time of fieldwork there were none; this necessitated the expense of bringing a lawyer up from Fez. Much more frequently, a person appoints a relative or friend to act as his *wakīl* ("legal representative"). A wakil can receive one of three different kinds of appointments: He (or she) can be granted full power of attorney without restriction of time or scope; he may be given full powers only for one particular case; or he may be appointed simply as one's spokesman. In

80

the first two cases, the wakil's powers include the right to sign documents and institute proceedings on behalf of the person he represents, as well as to commit the latter to swearing a holy oath in support of his claims. Most of the people who come before the court with a wakil to represent them grant the latter a limited power of attorney – for which the appropriate certificate must be obtained – and most, but certainly not all, of these are instances in which a woman assigns a father or brother or some other male relative to represent her. However, it must be stressed that many women speak for themselves – often with great force and resolution. Any stereotyped view of the Moroccan woman as shy about speaking up on her own behalf, whether in the court or in the street, would be thoroughly demolished by sitting in on an actual court session.

The court meets in public session once or twice a week, the remainder of the time being taken up with the supervision of other court business and the preparation of decisions. The qadi of Sefrou, a small man with a hoarse voice, green-tinted spectacles, a bright red fez, and a laconic style, sits behind a table on the dais at one end of the narrow courtroom while petitioners wait in the outdoor courtyard for their cases to be called. To the casual Western observer the actual proceeding appears quite disorderly. From the moment the first question is posed by the qadi until the last petitioner is hustled out of the room by a uniformed aide, there is virtually no end to the shouting, the argument, the interruption, and the indecorous remark. Everyone, from the bearded elder to the young girl, speaks up readily, whether or not he or she has been addressed by the court. Through this seeming confusion, however, there runs a conscious method. For the qadi is often as interested in turning people loose to confront one another as the latter are intent on convincing viewers of the proceedings, passersby in the street, stray anthropologists, clerks, aides, and even the qadi himself of the justice, or at least the reasonableness, of their claims.

The qadi begins by ascertaining who the parties are in the dispute and what, if any, documents they have to validate their claims. These documents are the most central form of evidence allowed before the court, and indeed if such documents have been rendered valid by the necessary signatures of two notaries they are very hard to break.[48] For example, if a dispute involves a marriage contract in which it has been stipulated that a portion of the unpaid brideprice must be given to the wife on her demand, this document carries great weight in the decision. If direct documentary proof is lacking, somewhat more indirect documentary proof may be sought. To sustain a claim, an individual

81

may get three, and preferably twelve, eligible witnesses to swear before two notaries to the facts asserted by one of the disputants. If a particularly strong document is desired, each of these witnesses will also be asked to appear one at a time before two pairs of notaries who determine whether the testimony of each of the witnesses is absolutely consistent with that of the others. Such documents may be obtained, for example, as proof of marriage by two people who never obtained an adul-witnessed contract, or to sustain one's claims to ownership of a piece of property by right of lengthy and undisputed occupation.

The unsworn testimony of petitioners, and even the documents they produce, may be totally contradictory. In this case, the court can require that one or both of the parties support his or her testimony with a holy oath.[49] The standard procedure is for the plaintiff (or the court) to demand that the defendant take an oath. If the latter does so, his or her innocence is assumed and the matter is settled – unless the plaintiff also takes an oath. It is, however, extremely rare for both parties to swear contradictory oaths: Only one such case was reported in the records studied. If, on the other hand, the defendant refuses to take an oath and the plaintiff does, the case is awarded the latter. If both parties or neither party swears an oath once requested, the case is dismissed. The oath itself is in no set form and may be taken anywhere, the most usual places being at a mosque, a saintly shrine, or in the lodge of a religious brotherhood (*zāwia*). The oath is often, but not necessarily, witnessed by notaries.

The force that oath taking possesses in resolving court disputes that have reached an impasse should not be underestimated. The overwhelming majority of people have a real fear that a false oath will result in harsh supernatural punishment, and on more than a few occasions individuals have maintained their testimony right up to the moment of oath taking, at which point they have refused the oath and surrendered the case. It must also be stressed that no punishment accompanies the discovery that one or another of the parties has been lying. The punishment, if it can be called that, is simply for the liar to lose his or her case.

What exactly is the nature of the cases that come before the qadi and how are they handled? As we noted earlier, the qadi's court mainly handles cases involving the laws of personal status and land disputes that involve no documents or documents made out by the court notaries, rather than a matriculated title issued by the government. Matters of personal status involve a wide range of disputes. A detailed breakdown of the 409 cases that came before the court dur-

82

ing 1965 shows that fully 31 percent (127 cases) were suits filed by women charging failure of support by their husbands (*nafaqa*). This support could refer to what was owed the woman either in the normal course of marriage or during the three-month period before a registered divorce becomes final. Only slighltly fewer cases (121, or 30 percent) were requests by a husband to have a runaway wife returned to his bed and board (*nušuz*). Thereafter, the number of cases involving the same sort of dispute falls sharply: 22 cases charged the husband with some sort of misconduct (*ḥussen l-muᶜašara*), 20 cases involved land disputes, 13 concerned child custody (*ḥaḍāna*), 8 dealt with inheritance, and 3 were requests by women for divorces issued by the qadi (*taṭlīq*). Of the remaining cases, the dossiers of 36 were unavailable because they were still involved in appeals or were in use by court officials, and 59 dealt with a host of different matters including visitation rights, partnerships in a given property, complaints about smoke issuing from a habus-owned bakery, disputes over a notarized sale, and fights over who has the right to presents brought to the shrine of a local saint. A similar statistical range and catalogue of cases could be cited for other years of the court's operation as well.

The overall caseload of the court is rather significant. For each year from 1961 to 1965 the number of cases brought before the court were: 379, 430, 420, 381, and 409. These statistics include cases that received a full hearing as well as those that were settled out of court before a final judgment was rendered. In 1965, about 60 cases were appealed to the regional tribunal: None was appealed higher. In general, during these five years, approximately 10 to 15 percent of the decisions of the qadi's court were appealed. Although precise statistics have not been compiled, it is clear that the higher court shows no reluctance in reversing qadis' decisions, and indeed at least one qadi in the recent history of Sefrou has run into trouble with his superiors because of the frequency with which his rulings were struck down by the higher court.

Most of the cases the court hears involve only the most routine applications of the law. Whether the facts in the case are curious or dull, the legal issues proper are seldom very interesting. A few ordinary cases, briefly related, give the flavor of the majority of disputes heard:

Case 1965/227. A woman claims that her husband deserted her three months ago and has given her no support since that time. She also says he took some of her things with him. She asks for the return of her things, support of 120 dirhams per month, for her husband to be made to return and act properly, and for him to find them a new place to live away from his family. The

Social identity and points of attachment

83

husband appears in court and, after voluntarily returning his wife's things, is ordered by the qadi to pay support of 100 dirhams per month and find a new residence apart from his father's household.

Case 1965/406. The plaintiff claims to have bought some land from the defendant – a sale witnessed by four other people – but the defendant would not come before notaries to make out the papers. The court says the plaintiff needs such a document of ownership: Even if he had more witnesses a sale not conducted before notaries would not be a legal one. The court also says that anyone who pays for property without getting such a document is a bit odd. The case is thrown out of court.

Case 1965/369. The petitioner sues his former wife stating that she has had custody of their daughter since the time of their divorce three months ago. Now that his former wife has remarried, however, he wants the child turned over to him. The court so rules.

Each of these cases involves little more than a brief investigation of the facts and a rather straightforward implementation of the law. In the first case, the plaintiff exercises her right to reside in a dwelling place not shared with members of the husband's family – a right of which women are well aware and often exercise to escape a bad relationship with the husband's mother. The second case shows how important notarized documents are for land transactions, so important that they usually constitute the only evidence the court will recognize of such a sale. Finally, in the third case cited, article 105 of the Mudawwana clearly states that if a divorced wife marries a person who is neither a close relative nor, in the case of a daughter, the marital guardian of the child, the mother must return the child to its father unless the mother is herself the child's marital guardian (which she would not be if her husband or any of his close agnates is still alive) or if the child will nurse from no one else.

Cases of this sort often involve the application of clear legal precepts to situations that can be unambiguously defined by the court. But court cases are, on occasion, considerably more complex than those noted above. This complexity often arises not from the issues of law themselves but from those aspects of the case that do not form part of the official record. Consider, for example, the following materials from the record of a 1959 case (No. 1959/444) involving a runaway wife:

October 26, 1959: petition. The plaintiff states that he paid a brideprice (ṣdāq) of 37,500 francs for his wife, the defendant, and that she herself received the money. He then wanted her to come before the notaries to have the marriage contract made out, but the defendant constantly postponed doing so. However, they lived together as man and wife until nine days ago when she

84

ran away. He is suing for her to be made to return to him and to come before notaries to have a proper marriage contract made out.

November 10, 1959. The defendant has hired a lawyer, who denies the plaintiff's charges and claims that the defendant does not even know this man. The plaintiff, in turn, says he will bring proof of his claims.

February 22, 1960. After having been granted three delays, the plaintiff brings documents in which twelve persons testify that the plaintiff (aged sixty, unemployed) is indeed married to the defendant (aged forty-five) and that they have lived as man and wife for seven months. The witnesses have no knowledge that the husband ever divorced the defendant. These facts they know because they are neighbors of the principals. A second document states that a second pair of notaries has also heard testimony from each witness in turn and all give the same evidence. The documents are signed by the notaries and their signatures are certified by the qadi.

The court then rules that whereas the defense counsel has no further comment to make after these documents were read the plaintiff is adjudged the legal spouse of the defendant. The latter is, therefore, ordered to return to the plaintiff's home and live with him in peace. As for making out a marriage contract, the court says that the notarized documents mentioned above serve in place of, and indeed have greater force than, a marriage contract, and any further papers would be superfluous.

April 12, 1961. The case has been carried to the appellate court, which takes note of the witnessed documents stating that the couple lived together for seven months as man and wife. They also note that neither the woman nor her lawyer showed up for the first three appellate court dates. In view of all these facts, the lower court decision is sustained and the wife charged costs of 10 dirhams.

The dossier also contains a letter from the qadi to the public prosecutor noting that he wanted to inform the defendant of the appellate ruling, but she could not be found at the address given. The prosecutor is asked to find her and see to it that the judgment is carried out.

Again, on the surface this case appears rather uncomplicated. In fact, the part of this dispute that came out in court was but the tip of the iceberg. Talking with some of the people from the disputants' home settlements produced a slightly different picture. According to the informants, the plaintiff is an elderly man who used to be well-off but who has squandered a lot of his money in recent years. He has married a number of times, keeping each wife for a short while and then divorcing her. The defendant soon realized this and decided she really did not want to be married to him after all. She wanted the plaintiff to divorce her, but he refused, apparently hoping that the woman would agree to a *ṭalāq kulᶜ*, a form of divorce in which the woman "redeems" herself by paying the man a given sum of money. The defendant then turned to her distant relative, the public prosecu-

85

tor, to persuade the plaintiff to divorce her, but the husband would not heed the prosecutor's appeals. After the court ruled that the woman had to return to her husband, the defendant refused and was actually sent to jail for her refusal. People in the settlement told the husband that the entire affair was shameful, that this was not a proper marriage, and that any woman who goes to jail will probably run around with other men as well. A talaq khul^c was finally arranged in which the woman kept her original brideprice payment, but the husband did not have to support her during the three months before their divorce became final. Within a few months the plaintiff had married and divorced still another young woman.

The purposes and repercussions of this case were not part of the evidence presented the court or part of the official record. Clearly, the wife avoided registering the marriage for fear she would have to buy her way out of it, and she actually preferred, as a surprising number of women do, to go to jail as the only technique for getting her husband to grant her a reasonable divorce. Her lawyer, who had a very bad reputation in Sefrou, could have tried to get twelve witnesses to testify that the husband had a habit of marrying women, making their lives miserable, and then making them pay him to divorce them, but the lawyer failed to do so. Considering the relative powerlessness before the law of a woman in the defendant's position, her's was really the only tactic available – and one that does not carry any great stigma.

Out-of-court factors are usually much more significant than in-court considerations in the Sefrou region.[50] Again, statistics give some indication of this. In as many as half of the suits filed in any one year, the case is dropped by the plaintiff partway through the proceedings. Many cases are initiated either as a way of making the defendant give serious consideration to an extrajudicial resolution of the dispute or as simple harassment. The court itself is well aware of this situation, and the qadi may throw out a case if he feels the plaintiff is just playing around with the law. On other occasions, he encourages the use of go-betweens in settling a case out of court. This is particularly true when the disputants are members of some of Sefrou's more notable families. Indeed, in cases involving such people, the qadi may be consulted informally and asked to help settle the matter without any suit being filed at all. Particularly in pre-Protectorate times, but to no small extent at present, disputants would ask a descendant of the Prophet, a member of a saintly lineage, or a highly respected person to mediate their arguments. Often it is the families of the parties involved, rather than the principals, who seek such a remedy. In Qu-
86 ranic law as well as in the present code there is an injunction to the

effect that in case of marital dispute intermediaries should be appointed to help solve the matter. In fact, however, this is never done officially in the Sefrou court, and when it is done unofficially the solution has no binding legal effect, its utilization being wholly a matter of judicial discretion.

The role of the judge is very significant in almost all matters that come before the court.[51] One of the most interesting ways this personal factor enters into legal actions is the manner in which the qadi chooses to read and apply various local customary practices. Even in the Code of Personal Status there are a number of situations in which the qadi is granted the right to allow local customs to inform particular decisions. Consider, for example, the *mutaʿa* payment, which is given by a husband as consolation to the wife he is divorcing. This payment is in addition to the cost of the woman's support, which must be paid by the husband during the three-month period (*ʿidda*) used to determine whether the wife has become pregnant by the divorcing husband. However, the law says only that this payment should be "proportional to his [the husband's] ability and the situation of his wife" (Mudawwana, article 60). It is, therefore, up to the qadi to determine how much, if anything, should be paid. In Sefrou, the court claims to use as a rule of thumb a charge against the husband of one-third of the original brideprice, unless the latter was particularly high, low, or long ago. In fact, the qadi has a pretty good idea of what constitutes a reasonable level of support for people of various backgrounds, and he applies these standards–these personal interpretations of what is customarily acceptable–to each situation individually.

Qadis throughout Morocco frequently follow local custom in such other matters as determining whether the bride's dowry should be recorded along with the brideprice in the marriage contract. In Sefrou, this dowry is not recorded, thereby affording the wife the advantage of claiming virtually all household goods–those bought during the marriage as well as those she brought to it–as part of her personal dowry.[52] The court may also bend the rules on the minimum age of marriage for girls (legally set at fifteen) if, in a particular area, girls generally marry earlier. If the court itself marries a girl off, either because she has no relative to act as her marital guardian or in some cases of rape, the court is enjoined to marry her to someone "of equal status."[53] The judge may take this to mean someone of the same ethnic background, the same economic standing as the girl's parents or guardian, or some other social standard recognized by the qadi and/or the local community. Finally, the judge has some leeway in the way in which a second divorce of the same couple may be 87 registered and how much, if any sum, must be paid the wife if they are again reconciled.

The qadi may also consult Malikite legal texts for guidance on problems not directly covered in the codes. The qadi of Sefrou claims that the three questions of this type most frequently presented to him deal with the extent to which a husband owes his wife support when she runs away from him, what actions invalidate one's right to custody over a child, and what kinds of absence from one's land result in the loss of certain rights over it. Indeed, insofar as the law itself is concerned, it is particularly in property matters that the qadi has to search most carefully in the written sources to formulate a particular decision. In the absence of specific, codified rules, which take precedence over all other sources, it is to the books of legal interpretation, to his own sense of what is right and practicable, and to his view of acceptable local practices that he will, in that order of priorities, turn for guidance in making his judgments.

Finally, before considering some general points of law and social life in the Sefrou region, some note ought to be made about the question of corruption in the court. This is a difficult matter to handle with discretion and due regard for the laws and customs concerning defamatory statements. Several facts are, however, indisputable. Since Independence, two qadis of Sefrou have been removed from office for unprofessional conduct. Moreover, it is a simple fact of life that one's land is less likely to be assessed at a very high value at the time of any land transfer if the court officials do not, at the same time, find themselves in the awkward position of living beyond their own means. In short, corrupt practices, which could be documented in embarrassing detail if necessary, are present and even somewhat regularized in land transactions, but such practices are by no means so pervasive in most matters of personal status as to undercut the judicious implementation of the law by the officials of the qadi's court. Indeed, by the standards of most Western countries or other developing nations, it can probably be said that for the kinds of cases that come before the qadi the level of dishonesty and corruption is well within the bounds of ordinary and acceptable judicial practice.

Law and society in the Sefrou region

The legal system of contemporary Morocco can be seen as a focal point of a broad range of social, political, and economic activities. At the level of the higher appellate courts – and particularly in those
chambers that deal with administrative procedures, electoral disputes,

and military justice – considerations of national political policy are particularly evident. At the local level, appointment to the position of chief judge of a cercle or even to the post of qadi is probably not within its political overtones, but the jurisdiction of local courts is sufficiently circumscribed and the involvement of other local administrators so much more central that strictly political matters form a relatively small part of the courts' overall operations. The impact of the local courts, particularly the qadi's court, is far greater in the domain of everyday social life.

The institution of the Code of Personal Status in 1958 significantly affected the way in which social problems, particularly problems involving marriage, divorce, and child custody, are treated in a region like Sefrou. although the law itself retains many features of traditional Malikite law and the Quranic basis of that law, the very fact that it has been given the status of a "secular" codified law is of considerable importance. In the first place, as Coulson has noted, laws now receive codified status in many Islamic countries if, instead of positively conforming to religious doctrine, they simply do not contradict that doctrine too sharply.[54] For example, the Quran grants a man the absolute right to divorce his wife when and if it pleases him, and there is solid doctrinal foundation to support his divorcing his wife irrevocably (i.e., with three pronouncements of divorce, all at the same time). The authors of the new code, however, have fragmented that form of triple divorce into three separate actions and have even allowed a certain amount of discretion to the court about how and with what effect each of these divorces may be registered. This is seen, however, not as a clear implementation of Quranic doctrine, which in some ways it obviously is not, but simply as an acceptable procedure that does not contradict that doctrine.

A second effect of the codification of the law is to regularize, and in some respects limit, the actions of the qadi. Although it could readily be shown that qadis never dispensed justice casually and that they gave careful consideration to Islamic law sources and local practices alike, the present law clearly limits the range of decisions that can be reached by giving the 1958 Code preemptive status over all other sources of law. Other traditional practices, such as the use of oaths, continue to limit the judge's discretion in matters of fact finding, while retaining a religious sanction of considerable social force.

It is also clear that, under the present qadi of Sefrou at least, justice is dispensed not so much unevenly among disputants of different social backgrounds, as with greater care and interest for some than for others. When a poor villager from Bhalil or a somewhat

89

downtrodden Berber from the countryside comes before the clerks, the notaries, or the qadi, the tone of voice, the admonitions, the depth of investigation, the rapidity with which judgments are reached, and the comments that follow clearly indicate that the court officials, who either represent or pretend to represent the status of learned defenders of Islamic civilization, consider some of the litigants as uncouth charges whose lives must be kept in strict rein by punitive laws and unyielding administrators. When a dispute involves persons from the urban Arab elite, however, not only is more consideration granted, but, more importantly, a much wider range of evidence is considered in order that underlying bases and consequent ramifications of the dispute may be fully understood. Where a case involving the runaway wife of a poor man elicits little investigation beyond the fact that the woman had no reason valid to the court for leaving her husband, a similar case involving an old Sefrou family yields a deeper consideration of all the relationships involved and a far greater effort to reach an out-of-court resolution that takes account of all the problems.

This is not to say that access to the apparatus of the legal system is in any clear way restricted to particular kinds of persons. The cost of a law case is very low, and poor people can get all fees waived without great difficulty. There are few delays in having one's case heard, although cases tend to be postponed by one or another of the parties as a battle of wills, fought outside the court at least as much as within, is joined. Cases tend to drag on for years as suits and countersuits, appeals and delays, are used to establish the most effective position in an out-of-court settlement. People make considerable use of the courts, and the level of awareness of what the law says, as well as the way it is implemented, is surprisingly high.

This is particularly true for the women. The legal system clearly disfavors women in a host of ways – in the witnesses needed, the equal rights denied, and the attitude of the all-male judiciary. Women do, however, have more legal safeguards than are generally realized, ranging from controls over their movement and residence to their rights to a judicial divorce. They also have economic and social pressures that can be brought to bear on a husband. In general, the practice of these rights requires the help of some male benefactor, but there is no question that women are seldom shy about using whatever resources are available to them to further their own claims.

The formal institutions of law in Sefrou clearly partake of the broader culture in which they are situated. The great Islamic law scholar Joseph Schacht once wrote:

As regards the formal character of positive law, the sociology of law contrasts two extreme cases. One is that of an objective law which guarantees the subjective rights of individuals; such a law is, in the last resort, the sum total of the personal privileges of all individuals. The opposite case is that of a law which reduces itself to administration, which is the sum total of particular commands. Islamic law belongs to the first type ... A typical feature which results from all this is the private and individualistic character of Islamic law. However prominent a place a programme of social reform and of improving the position of the socially weak occupied in the Koran, Islamic law, in its technical structure, is thoroughly individualistic.[55] *Social identity and points of attachment*

This individualistic character is at the very heart of any understanding of contemporary Moroccan law, and indeed of Moroccan social life in general. Certainly in the pre-Protectorate period, when a wide range of legal institutions and rationales allowed local qadis to accommodate themselves to local circumstances and individual cases, this individualistic element was very much in evidence. Post-Independence reforms have limited the powers of the qadi, but contractual stipulations and the totality of a person's social ties still play major roles in the resolution of legal disputes. The qadi's court is neither a microcosm of Sefrou life nor the primary forum for interpersonal relations. Just as one finds processes, forms of reasoning, and standards of conduct that are distinctive to the domains of family life, religion, and the marketplace, so, too, the legal system has its own set of distinctive features. At the same time, it is very much a part of the broader conceptual and relational structure of Sefrou life. In the modes by which court officials assess litigants and draw bounds of relevance around disputes, in the use of law as a resource for personal network formation, and in the influence of local custom and interests on national institutions, the legal system encompasses many of the features that are typical of social and cultural life throughout all domains of social action in the Sefrou region.

Social identity, cultural concepts, and the organization of personal networks

In societies characterized by sharply delineated corporate groups, the attributes and actions of particular individuals may, to a great extent, be understood in terms of the conditions and consequences of group membership. But where groups participate in few, if any, corporate endeavors and are arranged as nonexclusive categories, associations based on shared background or circumstance may form points of attachment that contribute to a person's overall identity and network of personal relations. Each of these points of attachment constitutes at 91 once a cultural domain (a focal point of meaningful concepts encased in recognizable symbols) and a relational framework (a set of social resources whose various possibilities may be drawn upon as context and purpose suggest). It is appropriate, therefore, in trying to understand Sefrou as a field of social action, to look at the categories of affiliation the people of this region mark as significant, to note the contribution of each to individual identity, and to explore the mechanisms by which the components of social identity are used to shape networks of personal relations.

Points of attachment: origins, locality, and relatedness

The social identity of an individual is constructed out of a wide range of attachments, each of which is itself defined by a series of cultural concepts. These sources of personal identity can be grouped into conceptual clusters whose general features are frequently referred to by the people of Sefrou and whose particular components form a repertoire of relational possibilities. Here, we shall consider three of these conceptual clusters: those that concern origins, locality, and relatedness.

A crucial aspect of an individual's social identity is embraced in the Arabic term *aṣl* (pl. *uṣūl*). Asl means "origin," "root," and "source." It also carries the meaning of "rules," "principles," and "fundamentals." Ramifications of the same root also mean "authentic," "traditional," "strength of character," and "nobility of descent." To ask, as the Sefrou people constantly do, where a man's asl is from (*menayn aṣl-u*) is to inquire into his social background, his origins, the place and people to which his roots extend. Moroccans tend to believe that social geography contributes heavily, perhaps even determines, much of a person's character. To speak of one's origins is to imply the social and physical context of one's nurturance, or those of one's ancestral line, and its influence on one's contemporary existence.

To what locale or group an individual's origins are traced varies, even for a single person, with the context and purpose of the issue. Because, as we shall see, the concept of "origins" overlaps those of "locality" and "relatedness," one's asl may be couched in terms of the place or kinsmen with whom one is linked. Asl, however, usually carried an implication of past time; it is that context from which the individual stems, the situation that contributed to his distinctive antecedents. Those antecedents may be regional or ethnic and often constitute the basis for one of the many names utilized by or attributed to the individual.[56] Thus a person may be referred to in various contexts

92

in terms of the place from which his people "originate"—*Sahrawi* ("from the Sahara"), *Jebli* ("from the Jebala, the foothills of the Rif mountains"); the tribe or fraction he stems from—*Seġušni* ("from the Ait Seghoushen tribe"), *Iᶜaweni* ("from the Iawen fraction of the Ait Yusi"); or by reference to places or groups that are clearly identified as Arab or Berber.

Like locality and relatedness, attachments based on origins are important because they imply a distinctive set of personal characteristics and modes of affiliation. Each setting, each sociogeographical entity, is characterized by traits and qualities perceived as unusual to that context. The key term here is *qāᶜida* ("custom," "mode"), from a root meaning "to sit," "remain," or "abide." Moroccans are extremely sensitive to differences of local custom and constantly seek information about how people from different backgrounds speak, conduct themselves, appraise, and form relationships with others. Knowledge of origins is not, therefore, a matter of antiquarian interest or mere palaver about real or invented descent: It is conceived of as information useful to the current establishment of interpersonal ties.

Often an inquiry, particularly to a third party, about the origins of a man or woman is answered in terms of the person's being Arab or Berber. These categories have often been treated in the literature as actual groupings possessing highly distinctive social and cultural characteristics.[57] It is true that one finds customs and practices among some Berbers not found among some Arabs, and that the range of variation within each category—even in an area as small as the Sefrou region—is often very great. Indeed, for any feature one might consider—religion, social structure, cultural concepts—the overlap is so great as to defeat any assertion of total distinctiveness. Rather, the distinguishing feature is language: Arabic speakers as opposed to Berber speakers. The former of these categories refers to those who speak colloquial Moroccan Arabic but no Berber; the latter refers to those who speak a dialect of Berber (in the Sefrou area, the Tamazight dialect) whether or not they also speak Arabic. Almost all men, and most women, in the Sefrou area who speak Berber also speak Arabic, usually with a high degree of competence. In the city proper, of those Muslims who responded in the 1960 census, 77 percent were Arabic speakers and 12 percent were Berber speakers.[58] However, as the result of subsequent rural immigration, the proportion of Berber speakers has probably risen to 30 or 40 percent.

Notwithstanding the absence of any uniform distinction between Arabs and Berbers as sociocultural entities, knowledge of a person's Arab or Berber origins is regarded as useful information about that 93

Table 2. *Social group distribution of adult Sefrou Muslims*

Social origin	Number	Percent
Sefrou Arabs	3,936	41.6
Rural Arabs	2,635	27.9
Rural Berbers	1,362	14.4
Other urban Arabs	499	5.3
Bhalil Arabs	451	4.8
Fez Arabs	310	3.3
Other urban Berbers	144	1.5
Sefrou-born Berbers	117	1.2
Total	9,454	100.0

person's social identity. Like other indicators, it suggests probable modes of association, existing sets of affiliations, and dominant perceptual orientations that may influence mutual evaluations and relationships. Just as a white-collar professional in America may assume that a blue-collar worker he encounters is likely to have a certain income level, educational background, and set of political views, so Arabs and Berbers make certain assumptions about each other's occupation, income, and perspective. Moreover, with the aid of the 1960 census data it is possible to break down the population of the city of Sefrou not only into Arabs and Berbers but into a set of categories relating to "locality" and "origins," and to note some of the key factors concerning socioeconomic positions of each category. Table 2 shows the division of the adult Muslim urban population according to social origins as of 1960. The largest segment of the Sefrou population was composed of people actually born in the city. In recent years, however, the significant influx of rural Berbers has probably made that grouping at least as numerous as Arabic speakers who have come to the city from their native rural homes.

Information about locality and origins can also inform fairly reliable guesses about a man's most probable occupation. The census shows, for example, that although native Sefrouis are distributed throughout the various occupations in approximately the same proportion as they are represented in the population at large, each of the other social groupings shows a tendency to concentrate in particular endeavors. Among these other groups of urban origin it is clear that, the Fez-born Arabs generally hold better occupations proportional to their size than any other segment of Sefrou society. Better educated and more skilled, these Fassis (people from Fez) are employed primarily as teachers, clerks, and skilled artisans. At the other extreme come the

Arabs from the nearby town of Bhalil. Employed as artisans, farm and garden laborers, and in low-level civil service posts, the people of Bhalil constitute the least skilled and educated portion of the population. Berbers from cities other than Sefrou work primarily as small-shop keepers or have been placed in Sefrou by their governmental employers, whereas Arabs from cities other than Sefrou are somewhat better represented in the white-collar and artisan sectors though less well represented in the civil service. The two percent of the working force made up of Sefrou-born Berbers seems to be polarized between white-collar civil servants and manual laborers.

What is particularly striking about each of these urban-born groupings, is that they are rather weakly represented in the various craft groups and, with the exception of the Bhalil people, hold above-average jobs with good representation in the civil service. Insofar as the government generally chooses to place civil servants, particularly police and court officials, in cities other than those from which they originate, for fear of favoritism to local friends and family, this representation may in part be accounted for not by social and economic but by simply political circumstances. This policy also accounts for the small number of civil servants among those Arabs originating from Sefrou itself: most of these are employed as artisans pursuing traditional skills, merchants operating on a small scale, gardeners, and unskilled workmen.

Because the Arabs and Berbers of nearby rural origins constitute the most significant groups of newcomers to the city and its occupational structure, it is worthwhile to look at these two groupings in somewhat greater detail. Clearly, the rural-born workers occupy a position that is in many ways very close to, if not slightly higher than, that of the Sefrou Arabs and significantly below all other groups except the Bhalil people. Moreover, though there is considerable similarity in occupational distribution of the rural Arabs and Berbers, rural Arabs are well represented in the crafts, while Berbers are not. Their distribution in civil posts and the manual labor force is fairly close.

Of somewhat greater interest, however, is the relation between the length of time rural Arabs and Berbers have lived in Sefrou and the quality of the jobs they hold. An inverse relation of only slightly irregular consistency exists between the length of time a person has lived in Sefrou and the quality of the job he holds. In other words, people who have recently come to town tend to have better jobs than people who have resided in Sefrou for as long as twenty years. The trend reverses itself among those who have been in the city for longer than twenty years, but it is still clear that these latter people do not 95 hold jobs of as high a quality as those held by people who came within the past decade. A quarter of those rural people living in Sefrou who came to the city after Independence are between thirty and forty years of age, and fully one-half are between thirty and fifty years old; they are also better educated and better off than their fellow countrymen who have lived in the city for longer periods.

It is, therefore, possible to draw statistical correlations between social background and contemporary circumstances, and to observe the context and extent of reference to another's place or group of origin. But the concept of asl, and the groupings it serves to delineate, do not correspond to entities that move across the field of social life as fixed and solidary units. Rather, the groupings implied constitute conceptual categories, useful indexes of the customs and attributes of those who derive a portion of their identity from this background. Social origins have a deep, though variable, impact on the contacts that may be used to obtain a job or a mate, and they may be extremely helpful in predicting the ways others may be induced to act.[59] But origins do not define the whole person: They must be understood in combination with several overlapping domains of interpersonal perception.

One of the most important contributors to social identity is embraced in the concept of "locality." Here, the key word is *bled,* which means "region" or "locality."[60] Various kinds of localities may be referred to by this term, so that, depending on the context, bled may mean "city" or "country," "town" or "village." Throughout this discussion, we have taken as our unit of study *bled Sefrou,* the locality that embraces the city and its surrounding countryside. But bled Sefrou also implies a social, as much as a geographical, space. It is an arena within which social life is played out through a complex series of intersecting relations, institutions, and circumstances. Moreover, bled Sefrou is a conceptual entity, a vaguely bounded context in which characteristic customs and actions are rendered meaningful through a recognized, if contestable, store of symbolic forms.

Just as one's asl constitutes a prior source of characteristic qualities and affiliations, identification with a particular locality, or bled, contributes to one's present nurture and hence to one's current traits and ties. It is not that one loses one's origins as a Berber by moving to an Arabic-speaking city, or that one ceases to have Arab origins when one's fraction becomes engulfed in the Berber-speaking Ait Yusi tribe. Instead, these conceptual categories overlap and interpenetrate, the emphasis given each cultural order being drawn upon by individual actors as predicament and purposes vary. To speak of a man's bled, therefore, is to attribute, evoke, induce, or compel an element of

another's identify that suggests how he most probably views and re- *Social identity and*
lates to others. *points of*

Asl and bled, as sources of social identity, may be seen to intersect *attachment*
most directly in the allied concept *mūl l-bled* (pl. *mwālīn l-bled*). Mul
means "owner" or "controller." When one speaks of a plot of land,
mul l-bled means "the owner of that parcel." A wife is referred to
idiomatically as *mwālīn ḍ-ḍar,* "the 'owner' of the house." Mul also
implies a kind of dialectic between the possessor and the thing possessed: A thing or a place is partly characterized by its mul, just as the
mul is characterized in part by the object of his or her control. To
invoke the plural, mwalin l-bled, is to refer to those individuals or
families who lend to and derive their characteristic qualities from the
locality with which they are associated. They are the embodiments of
its distinguishing features, qualities they may carry with them even
though they move to another locale or find themselves outnumbered
by recent immigrants. They combine asl and bled in the sense that
their origins are tied to a given locale whose salient features they
ideally personify.

Indeed, one of the striking aspects of Moroccan society generally is
the degree to which various localities are differentiated. The people of
adjacent cities, such as Rabat and Salé, or of neighboring villages and
regions consciously mark themselves off from one another.[61] The
inhabitants of each locale, particularly those who would regard themselves as the mwalin l-bled of that place, frequently cite as distinctive
the speech, mannerisms, customs, and history of the area. Identification with a particular bled must, however, be seen as a cultural
marker, rather than as a label for a distinct class, group, or faction that
is clearly bounded and exclusive. Attachment to a bled is one of the
diacritics of personal identity that may be exploited or ignored as
individuals set about discerning who others are and what sort of impact they may have on one's own network of alliances.

Just as the categories of Arab and Berber can be subsumed within
the open-ended concept of origins, so the general concept of bled
encompasses many finer discriminations. In particular, people are
quick to note whether one's bled is a city or a rural area. The distinction between *mdini* ("city dweller") or *weld l-mdīna* ("son of the city")
and *ᶜarūbi* ("countryman") is more subtle and ambiguous than simple
inspection suggests. For just as urban and rural areas are characterized
by frameworks and institutions of political, economic, social, and religious life that crosscut physical perimeters, people do not perceive of
and relate to one another along an invariant city-country axis. The fact
that a person comes from a rural locale or an urban district may, like 97

Arab or Berber origins, supply an index to his likely associations and modes of perception. Indeed, the fact that rural people are constantly moving in and out of the city of Sefrou – and like all Moroccans think nothing of traveling substantial distances in search of markets, jobs, or allies – lends to their site of residence a feature of social identity that others may use to discern probable customs and contacts.

In recent years, this movement of rural people has been accompanied by a tendency for many countrymen to settle more or less permanently in the city. The reasons for migration to the city most often cited by inhabitants of the countryside surrounding Sefrou are the greater availability of jobs and increased educational opportunities for children. Some people see in the city greater opportunity for advancement and the chance to be less dependent on particular relatives; others simply prefer the more varied social life of the urban environment. It is worth noting, however, that one-quarter of the people who migrated to the city between 1955 and 1960 were between thirty and thirty-nine years of age, and one-half were between thirty and fifty years old. During the period surrounding national independence, therefore, most of those who came to live in Sefrou had already tried to make a go of it in the countryside before seeking the alternatives of urban life.

Characteristically, rural immigrants still possess significant ties to the rural areas from which they come. Although no precise figures are available, it is clear that many individuals retain some interest in a parcel of land in the countryside, usually one that has proved incapable of supplying an adequate income. A relative or friend, seen on market days in Sefrou, may care for the land, and a visit at harvest or for special occasions may be the only time the rural immigrant returns to his native settlement. Others merely use Sefrou as a secondary place of residence. A wealthy man may have one wife in the city, another in the country, and spend part of every week in each of his homes. It is, however, true that, with few exceptions, rural people who have significant properties in the countryside do not move permanently to the city. As we have seen, a person really only has as many rights as he can actually enforce. He must, therefore, constantly establish his presence among those upon whom he depends and for whom he is a reliable ally if he is properly to service the network of ties necessary to sustain his own rights and interests.

Origins and locality provide elements of identity that are differentially perceived and utilized. The same is true of a third overlapping conceptual domain, which may be roughly glossed under the English rubric "relatedness." The Sefrou people themselves use no single term

98

to convey this concept. Instead, they use a series of terms based on the root *w-l-d,* as well as specific terms designating particular types of relatedness.[62] The root verb *walad* means "to beget," "generate," "give birth." A *weld* (pl. *wlād*) is a "son" or "descendant"; the term *wālīd* designates a "parent." These forms convey a generalized notion of relatedness based on common descent, without invoking its exact limits or determinative principles. Various modes of relatedness constitute points of attachment that are vital to the perceptions and relationships that contribute to individual social identity.

Ties to kinsmen are of indisputable importance to people in the Sefrou region. Although kin groups seldom act as corporate units, and personal relations must be constructed with kinsmen every bit as much as with outsiders, the bond of a common bloodline forms an important sociological indicator and resource. We have seen how people, like the Berber entrepreneur Mohand, use the sliding scale of kinship referents to establish any of a number of actual relationships with kinsmen. And we have seen, too, that whereas tribal fractions may invoke an image of relatedness based on an idiom of ramified descent, the fact that such relatedness does not prescribe attendant relations does not prevent it from offering a foundation for asserting useful attachments.

The same is true of two other examples of relatedness that have been touched on peripherally and that can be used as examples of relatedness and social identity. Throughout the Arab world one finds individuals and families who claim to be lineal descendants of the Prophet Mohammed. In Morocco, these descendants of the Prophet, or *šurfa* (masc. sg. *šarīf,* fem. sg. *šarīfa*), are divided into two main lines: the Alawites, who have held the throne since the seventeenth century, and the Drissin, who claim descent through Mulay Idris, who brought Islam to Morocco. Unlike other Moroccans, the shurfa are, by and large, careful to preserve documentary evidence of their descent in the form of genealogies attested to by each succeeding monarch. In Sefrou, there are several Alawite shurfa families – all rather distantly related to the king – and a larger number of families who can document their Drissi shurfa descent. A great many others claim Drissi descent, and although no one asks them to verify it, there is widespread skepticism of such persons' claims.

One of the reasons no one expects firm validation of claimed sherifian descent is that there are virtually no rights or perquisites that accrue to an individual by virtue of such status alone. True, one can be called by the title Mulay or Sīdi, and one can receive a modicum of deference, but no elaborate set of advantages is automatically asso-

99

ciated with this identification. Rather, it offers the individual a basis, or competitive advantage, for claiming to possess the spiritual power (*baraka*) ideally associated with descent from the Prophet. A sherif may, then, be called upon to mediate disputes or represent others as a go-between, and in the absence of further knowledge about him as a person, he will often be regarded as worthy of considerable respect. But informants are quick to assert, and equally quick to show by their actions, that sherifian status alone means little unless a person actually displays the features ideally associated with one of his background. Shurfa may be rich or poor, educated or ignorant, dark-skinned or light, but unless they can cumulate significant ties with others and indicate that they are indeed personally worthy of the respect due those who live up to their spiritual descent, the deferential title accorded them rings hollow indeed.

The same analysis applies to the descendants of saints (*wlād siyyid,* literally "sons of the saint"). Saints in Moroccan Islam are persons who, whether or not they were also descendants of the Prophet, are believed to have possessed supernatural grace. In their tombs, they are said to be still alive, and, as protectors and intercessors for those who seek their help, capable of dispensing favors in the everyday world. In the city of Sefrou, the main saintly shrine is Sidi Ali Buseghine, a green-roofed, whitewashed mausoleum perched on a hill overlooking the city. It is visited by people from all over the Sefrou region and beyond, who leave gifts that are then apportioned among the contemporary descendants of the saint.[63] Because of the money involved, wlad siyyid possess a degree of corporateness lacking in almost all other Sefrou region groupings and are more careful to guard their identity. Because each individual – male or female, child or adult – possesses a turn in rotation for receiving the goods and money brought to the shrine on that day, there is also a tendency for marriages among wlad siyyid to be more endogamous than among most other families.[64] Similar patterns are discernible among other saintly lineages in the region, including the descendants of the patron saint of the Ait Yusi, Sidi Lahcen Lyusi. Like the shurfa, the wlad siyyid are in closer proximity to a source of supernatural benevolence than others. But unless people believe that, on the basis of their actions, they do indeed possess the qualities ideally associated with their group, the wlad siyyid are regarded as no better, and perhaps quite a bit worse, than anyone else. Identity as a saint's descendant thus offers a basis for claiming certain characteristics and for establishing useful ties with others, but assures no permanent advantage.

100   Three conceptual domains – origins, locality, and relatedness – are

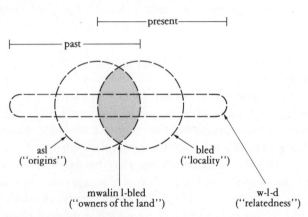

Figure 1. Social identity: points of attachment.

discernible as symbolic orders through which individuals are attached
to particular kinds of others and from which they derive important
aspects of their identity. These points of attachment are not the only
sources of personal identity that could be enumerated. The domains
discussed here may, however, be regarded as fundamental bases to
which individuals can look for possible relationships as they set about
constructing a network of personal ties. And from sources of identity
such as these one gains a sense of how another's probative character
and relationships may be joined to one's own web of associations.

The conceptual domains enumerated are neither exclusive nor
firmly bounded. Origins may be defined in terms of locality, and both
may intersect ties of relatedness. The relationship of each of these
orders, may be roughly diagramed as shown in Figure 1. As the dotted
lines on the diagram indicate, the concepts involved are open-ended;
depending on the context and purpose, they can be extended or contracted to cover a variety of circumstances and groupings. Asl and
bled may be roughly demarcated on an axis of past and present; relatedness crosscuts, and is not limited by the other domains. Mwalin
l-bled, whether or not they are also related to one another, combine
features of past and present, locality and origins.

Actualizing relationships: reciprocity and negotiation

If the concepts of origin, locality, and relatedness constitute touch-
stones of identity and connectedness, it is in the actual establishment
of social ties that these cultural resources are articulated. Without
ignoring the roles of chance, personality, and irrational behavior, it is
possible to delineate some of the mechanisms by which attachments   101

Meaning and order
in Moroccan society

are regularly crystallized into relationships and conceptual domains are precipitated into contextualized meanings.

Central to this understanding is the fact that the concepts of relationship, like symbolic systems generally, are fraught with ambiguity, complex associations, and multivocality.[65] Concepts such as asl and bled, like those denoting kin ties or personal qualities, are capable of being applied to a wide range of referents and capable of taking on different connotations as the context of their usage varies. For example, a person's asl may be posited in terms of his being a Berber. But where this characterization may be used in one instance to imply the range of allies he might draw on in a given dispute or the tendency to allow women to move about more freely, in another context it may be used to imply affinity to that which is most authentically Moroccan. Indeed, many of the concepts that deal with relational qualities lack specific meaning until one of its users succeeds in getting it applied as he wishes. For example, the concept *ḥaqq* ("obligation," "right," "truth," "reality") may be regarded as a hollow form until someone can make it apply to a given relationship and suffuse it with particular implications. Indeed, many of the linguistic symbols of Moroccan usage are themselves essentially negotiable concepts, the vehicles by and through which individuals bargain out the relations they are going to have with one another.[66]

This element of negotiation leads to a second mechanism of social relationship: the dynamics of uneven exchange. If one looks at the multiplicity of relationships that surrounds the life of any individual in the Sefrou region, it is readily apparent that these relationships carry with them some form of debt or obligation, some kind of privilege or possibility, some type of expectation or interdependence. Whatever the specific mechanism through which they are established and whatever their overall patterning for a particular person, the relationships that constitute a personal network are based on some real or potential inequality, some complex distribution of personally based dominance and dependence. There is, in virtually every social relation, a clear element of competition, of seeking to place oneself in a position in which others are dependent on oneself or in which one can have some assurance of another's specific aid, as a way of insuring oneself against the uncertainties of daily life. Because inherent forms of relationship – ties of kinship or fractional affiliation – carry with them few if any firmly sanctioned guarantees of another person's actions, it becomes necessary to establish for oneself a variety of personal relations based on some clearly understood sense of mutual obligation. Whether as cause or effect, this personal network of indebtedness

102

carries with it two other major premises of social organization: the reciprocal quality of all social actions and the regularized means through which such ties are formed.

In Sefrou society virtually all acts toward another person imply some sort of reciprocal action on the other's part. If a Moroccan wishes to indicate that he is doing something without any expectation of a possible return, he uses the borrowed French or Spanish term *fabur* ("favor"). Otherwise, the key term involved is the notion of *ḥaqq* ("obligation"), which implies that some sort of debt is always created in another by virtue of one's own actions. Earlier, for example, in tracing part of the career of the young Berber entrepreneur Mohand, we saw how he constantly ingratiated himself with others by gifts, offers of hospitality, and aid as an ally or intermediary. And we saw how others tried to create in him some obligation through their financial aid or by making an ᶜar sacrifice. Moreover, because the kind of reciprocity involved is as generalized as it is recurrent, a debt contracted in one form may be called up at a later date in quite another form. A man who has given another financial aid in time of need may request in return the hand of a daughter or his debtor's vote in a political election. However, because, in many cases, the exact nature of what and how much is expected by way of return has not been specified, the actual definition, extent, and transference of any debt may be the subject of considerable negotiation. One individual may, therefore, claim that a particular action (e.g., offering hospitality while the other is visiting the market at one's settlement) obliges the other to reciprocate in a way that seems inappropriately excessive (e.g., by intervening on one's behalf with a friend in the government) such that the entire matter becomes the subject of considerable bargaining, rhetoric, emotion, and often conflict.

The interchangeability of the forms of reciprocation coupled with the assumption that all acts imply or create some form of real or potential obligation make each person's network of social relations an intricate web of indebtedness. Knowing what another's place is in such a web of mutual obligations and contractual ties is a very important piece of information, for it tells one the kinds of ties another possesses, the constraints on his actions toward oneself, the probability of his acting toward particular others who are his social debtors or creditors in particular ways, and his general reliability as a person to be involved in one's own network of affiliations. Indeed, it is when people seek to cancel these debts, rather than rework them into some other form, that a great deal of uncertainty and a greater likelihood of conflict result.

103

As a general feature of the social life of the city and region of Sefrou, the interlocking systems of personal debt relations give a certain solidarity and predictability to the actions of the people who share one's environment. But the fact that such ties are formed in regularized ways, and canceled or renegotiated in regularized ways, places certain boundaries on the range of possible ties that are in fact formed by the people of this society. Many of these regularized and, in the sense of being normatively defined and at least minimally sanctioned, institutionalized forms of association have already been indicated. There are the mutual aid pacts and ᶜar sacrifices of the countryside and the formal bonds of marriage, sharecropping, and legal inheritance of the whole region. There are also the more ambiguous, but nevertheless critical, expectations associated with hospitality and physical proximity. And there are the ad hoc and often quite brittle friendships, sometimes accompanied by particular terms of address and a degree of homoerotic behavior. In short, there is a wide variety of kinds of contracts individuals can estabish with one another, contracts whose terms, in effect, are open to considerable negotiation and even violation, but whose general forms are sufficiently limited and publicly acknowledged to contribute a significant degree of regularity to what might otherwise appear as totally irregular self-aggrandizement.

The development of such networks of personal affiliation ties in closely with the sources of one's personal identity, for it is one's identity as a kind of kinsman, as a descendant of the Prophet, as a person of a particular ethnic and regional background that gives one a base for establishing particular kinds of ties with others. When Mohand is approached by a cousin for the loan of some grain, or when a sherif from an old Sefrou family is sent as an intermediary to settle a dispute, there is no question that the identity, as a kinsman or a sherif, establishes an important basis from which particular forms of action can be undertaken. But rather than being effective by virtue of the invocation of some particular status, such characteristics offer, at best, a selective competitive advantage over others who do not possess such characteristics and, at worst, are evaluated as totally irrelevant and meaningless in the context of the situation. What counts is the cumulation of particular features within the single individual and that person's ability effectively to induce another to act toward him in the ways ideally associated with his personal set of characteristics.

Because it is not some simple set of inherent statuses, some set of hierarchically arranged solidary groupings of social categories that is central to the overall pattern of social interaction in the Sefrou region,

104

it is reasonable to interpret the system of social stratification as one of
individuals rather than of groups or categories. For example, if one
draws a series of status pyramids based on economic resources or
educational background, these would describe the analytic positions
into which people fall in monetary or educational terms only rather
than the all-pervasive systems of social stratification by which the
people themselves place and act toward one another. A better image
of social stratification is constellations in which big men standing at
the center develop a range of personal associations of greater or lesser
extent and variety. The overall picture shows larger and smaller galaxies, sets of galaxies, and constellations, each of which is ordered out of
the same catalogue of possible forms of relationships but each of
which has a quality and patterning distinctive to itself. It is possible to
see through this image how each individual falls into some place in
one or more clusters of individuals and to specify his actual network
of social ties in relation to those of others rather than as the simple
implementation of a place in the overall social stratigraphy.

Focusing on the range of personal identifiers and the conventions of
reciprocity and negotiation also permits us to view the structure of
group relations in more dynamic and processual terms. Consider, for
example, the concept of a tribe. If one approaches the Ait Yusi tribe
as a series of discrete entities, each of which possesses similar characteristics and each of which is nested in a hierarchy of genealogically
defined units, one is quickly struck by the absence of any exclusive
principle that orders the arrangement of units into a regimented series
of economic, political, or religious relationships. Not only do interpersonal ties crosscut group affiliations, but even within any given unit
relationships are constantly being negotiated. Group affiliation, rather
than a structure entailing and prescribing set actions, constitutes one,
among many, of the structural skeletons around which individuals may
attempt to construct a corpus of interpersonal ties. To maintain a
concept of genealogical relatedness is to hold out, for the day when it
may prove useful, an inherently malleable basis for conceptualizing
and rationalizing a network that will have been built up through a
number of dyadic bonds. Instead of being exclusive, the concepts of
segmental attachment and personal networks are concurrent, indeed
interdependent, conceptual domains that contribute to the social identity, shaped by the conventions of reciprocity and negotiation, on
which constellations of personal bonds may be constantly built and
rebuilt.

Drawing on the conceptual sources of social identity and conventions of interpersonal relationship, individuals build up networks of 105

alliances whose weblike structures vary in strength and scope with the capacities of the person who stands at the center. Each framework of social activity has its distinctive characteristics, but the conceptual and relational resources upon which individuals draw crosscut these separate domains. Relations with kinsmen are negotiated like any other exchange; political alliances are worked up through the molding of identities and attachments; the bounds of a legal dispute vary with the perception of a litigant's background and circumstances. Social groupings are the product of the mutual contingency of concepts and relationships, and their nature varies as the frameworks they provide are filled in by individual effort.[67]

Notes

1. On the ecology of Morocco generally, see Despois, J., *L'Afrique du Nord*, Paris, 1964; Martin, J., H. Jover, J. Le Coz, G. Maurer, and D. Noin, *Géographie du Maroc*, Paris, 1964. On the physical geography and flora of the Sefrou region, see Martin, J., "Recherches morphologiques sur la bordure septentrionale du causse de Sefrou (Moyen Atlas marocain)," *Revue de géographie du Maroc*, 10:31–46 (1966); and Lecompte, M., "La Végétation du Moyen Atlas Central," *Revue de géographie du Maroc*, 16:3–34 (1969).

2. See Coté, A., and J. Legras, "La Variabilité pluviométrique interannuelle au Maroc," *Revue de géographie du Maroc*, 10:19–30 (1966). On the relation between ecology and agricultural production in various regions of Morocco, see Beguin, H., *L'Organisation de l'espace au Maroc*, Paris, 1974; Cerych, L., *Européens et Marocains 1930–1956*, Bruges, 1964; El Ghorfi, N., *Contributions à l'édification d'une politique agricole*, Rabat, 1964; Villeneuve, M., *La Situation de l'agriculture et son avenir dans l'économie marocaine*, Paris, 1971.

3. For listings of the constituent fractions of the Ait Yusi collected by French officials in the early period of the Protectorate, see Capitaine Reisser and Capitaine Bachelot, "Notice sur le Cercle de Sefrou," *Bulletin de la société de géographie du Maroc*, 4:29–51 (1918); and Anon., "Les Tribus du Maroc oriental, notice dressée par les officiers de renseignements du Cercle de Fez," *Reneignements coloniaux* (supplement à *l'Afrique Français*, July 1912), 7:293 (1912). A tribal map for the same period will be found at Anon., "Les Tribus de l'est de Fez, notice dressée par les officiers de renseignements du Cercle du Fez," *Renseignements coloniaux* (supplement à *l'Afrique française*, June 1912), 6:211 (1912).

4. The classic statement of segmentary theory is that of Evans-Pritchard, E.E., *The Nuer*, Oxford, 1940. Among the most important sources dealing with the applicability of segmentary theory to the organization of North African tribes are the following: Gellner, E., *Saints of the Atlas*, London, 1969; Hart, D., *The Aith Waryaghar of the Moroccan Rif: An Ethnography and History*, Tuscon, 1976; Vinogradov, A., *The Ait Ndhir of Morocco: A Study of the Social Transformation of a Berber Tribe*, Ann Arbor, 1974; Favret, J., "La Segmentarité au Maghreb," *L'Homme*, 6:05–11 (1966); Hart, D., "Segmentary Systems and the Role of 'Five Fifths' in Tribal Morocco," *Revue de l'occident musulman et de la Méditerranée*, 3:65–95 (1967); Peters, E., "The Proliferation of Segments in the Lineage of the Bedouin of Cyrenaica," *Journal of the Royal Anthropological Institute*, 90:29–53 (1960). See also the recent discussion of Bedouin tribal organization in Marx, E., "The Tribe as a Unit of Subsistence: Nomadic Pastoralism in the Middle East," *American Anthropologist*, 79:343–63 (1977). For an application of segmentary theory to the structure of Moroccan national politics, see Waterbury, J., *The Commander of the Faithful: The Moroccan Political Elite – A Study in Segmented Politics*, New York, 1970.

The literature on Moroccan tribal organization is quite large. Among the most important additional sources for this study are: Berque, J., *Structures sociales du Haut Atlas*, Paris, 1955; Montagne, R., *Les Berbères et le makhzen dans le sud de Maroc*, Paris, 1930; and Berque, J., "Qu'est-ce qu'une 'tribu' Nord-Africaine?" in his *Maghreb: histoire et socitées*, Gembloux, 1974, pp. 22–34. A useful bibliography is contained in Hoffman, B., *The Structure of Traditional Moroccan Rural Society*, The Hague, 1967.

5. On collective landholding among Moroccan tribes, see Amar, E., *L'Organisation de la propriété foncière au Maroc: étude théorique et practique*, Paris, 1913; Couleau, J., *La Paysannerie marocaine*, Paris, 1968; Guillaume, A., *La Propriété collective au Maroc*, Rabat, 1960; Le Coz, J., *Le Rharb, fellahs et colons: études de géographie régionale*, Rabat, 1964; Milliot, L., *Les Terres collectives: études de législation marocaine*, Paris, 1922; Lieutenant Tassoni, "Contribution à l'étude du régime coutumier des terres collectives: les terres de Djemaa au Maroc," *Revue algérienne, tunisienne, et marocaine de législation et de jurisprudence*, pp. 100–24, 133–57 (1928); Verdier, J., P. Desanti, and J. Karila, *Structures foncières et développement rural au Maghreb*, Paris, 1969; and Vinogradov, *op. cit.*, pp. 87–95.

6. For a discussion and application of this theoretical approach, in a significantly different context from the present discussion, see Meeker, M., "Meaning and Society in the Near East: Examples from the Black Sea Turks and the Levantine Arabs," *International Journal of Middle East Studies*, 7:243–70, 383–422 (1976). This approach is developed in Schneider, D., *American Kinship: A Cultural Account*, Engelwood Cliffs (N.J.), 1968; and "Some Muddles in the Models: or, How the System Really Works," in Banton, M. (ed.), *The Relevance of Models for Social Anthropology*, London, 1965, pp. 24–85.

7. See Sahlins, M., *Tribesmen*, Engelwood Cliffs (N.J.), 1968.

8. The saint and his descendants have been the subject of a historical study by Berque, J., *Al-Youssi: problèmes de la culture marocaine au XVIIIème siècle*, Paris, 1958; a comparative analysis by Geertz, C., *Islam Observed*, New Haven, 1968; and a field study by Rabinow, P., *Symbolic Domination: Cultural Form and Historical Change in Morocco*, Chicago, 1975. The present discussion of Sidi Lahcen Lyusi was contributed by Paul Rabinow.

9. See Geertz, C., "The Wet and the Dry: Traditional Irrigation in Bali and Morocco," *Human Ecology*, 1:23–39 (1972). For a similar distinction in medieval Spain, see Glick, T., *Irrigation and Society in Medieval Valencia*, Cambridge (Mass.), 1970. On the general question of water law in Morocco, see Bruno, H., *Le Régime des eaux en droit musulman*, Paris, 1913; Sonnier, A., *Le Régime juridique des eaux au Maroc*, Paris, 1933; Loubignac, V., "Le Régime des eaux, le nantissement et la préscription chez les Ait Youssi du Guigou," *Hespéris*, 25:251–64 (1938); Roche, P., "L'Irrigation et le status juridiques des eaux au Maroc (géographie humaine, droit et coutumes)," *Revue juridique et politique d'outre-mer* 19:55–120, 537–61 (1965). For a detailed description of irrigation and social organization in the Rif Mountains, see Hart, *The Aith Waryaghar*, pp. 107–16. Irrigation in the oasis of Sefrou is discussed in Annex A.

10. Writing in 1918, Reisser and Bachelot (*op. cit.*, p. 44) described the Iawen people in the following terms: "Les Iaouine (100 tentes) sont dispersés depuis N'Jil des Ikhataren jusqu'à Senadja (près de Sefrou). Ils n'ont jamais joué un rôle important chez les Ait Youssi. Avant notre venue, on les connaissait surtout commes des coupeurs de route. Sauf ceux qui habitent près de Sefrou, qui sont dans une situation aisée, les Iaouine sont pauvres. Ils comprennent: Les *Iberittene* (45 tentes) Mesdou; les *Ait Ichou* (20 tentes) Anoceur et Guigou; les Ait Chtab (25 tentes) Guigou; les *Ait Tratir* ou *Iberdour* (10 tentes) N'Jil."

11. There is every indication that the pattern described here is not a recent development. Older informants consistently describe relationships in pre-Protectorate times in terms consistent with an interpretation based on shifting kin referents and malleable group formation. The existence in the past of feuding, collective oaths, and formal bonds of alliance only added to the repertoire of relational possibilities; it did not rigidify social relationships into concrete, corporate groupings whose precipitation and career were determined irrespective of individual manipulation. Although a fuller demonstration of this argument will be the subject of a later work, evidence in support of the present interpretation will be found through a careful reading of the reports made by French ethnographers in the nineteenth and early twentieth centuries.

12. On sharecropping arrangements in Morocco, see Lesne, M., *Evolution d'un groupement Berbère: les Zemmour*, Rabat, 1959, pp. 246–54; and Stewart, C., *The Economy of Morocco 1912–1962*, Cambridge (Mass.), 1964, pp. 17–20.

13. Such a mediator is known as a *wasīta* (literally a "middleman" or "go-between"). The use of an intercessor is crucial to a wide range of social and economic relations.

14. Discussions of the *ᶜar* as applied in various social and political situations will be found in Westermarck, E., *Ritual and Belief in Morocco*, Vol. I, London, 1926, p. 518; and, *Memories of My Life*, New York, 1929, pp. 244–5; Crapanzano, V., *The Hamadsha*, Berkeley, 1973; Eickelman, D., *Moroccan Islam*, Austin, 1976, pp. 149–53; Hart, *The Aith Waryaghar*, pp. 305–7; Rosen, L., "Rural Political Process and National Political Structure in Morocco," in Antoun, R., and I. Harik

(eds.), *Rural Politics and Social Change in the Middle East,* Bloomington, 1972, pp. 214–36.

15. The commencement of a utada (also *tada* or *tata*) pact was generally symbolized by males of each group suckling at the breasts of the women of the allied group. See generally, Lesne, *op.cit.,* pp. 58–62; Bruno, H., and G.H. Bousquet, "Contributions à l'étude des pactes de protections et d'alliance chez les Berbères au Maroc central," *Hespéris,* 33:353–7 (1946); Magnin, J., "Note sur les alliances traditionalles dans le Moyen-Atlas septentrional," *Anthropos,* 47:784–94 (1952); Marcy, G., "L'Alliance par collactation (tada) chez les Berbères du Maroc central," *Revue africaine,* 2:957–73 (1936).

16. On the concept of klam, see also Eickelman, *op.cit.,* pp. 143–4.

17. On the concept of haqq, see Geertz, C., " 'From the Native's Point of View,' On the Nature of Anthropological Understanding," in Basso, K., and H. Selby (eds.), *Meaning in Anthropology,* Albuquerque, 1976, pp. 221–37; and Rosen, "Rural Political Process." The process of negotiating meaning is explored in greater detail in Rosen, L., "The Negotiation of Reality: Male-Female Relations in Sefrou, Morocco," which is published in Beck, L., and Keddie, N. (eds.), *Women in the Muslim World,* Cambridge (Mass.), 1979, pp. 561–84.

18. Various aspects of the structure of local administration are discussed in Ashford, D., *Political Change in Morocco,* Princeton, 1961; Leveau, R., *Le Fellah marocain défenseur du trône,* Paris, 1976; Waterbury, *op.cit.,* pp. 280–7; Chambergeat, P., "L'Administration et le douar," *Revue de géographie du Maroc,* 8:83–6 (1965); Marais, O., "Élites intermédiaires, pouvoir et légitimité dans le Maroc indépendent," *Annuaire de l'Afrique du Nord, X, 1971,* Paris, 1972, pp. 179–201; Michel, H., "Administration et développement au Maghreb," in Ruf, W., et al., *Introduction à l'Afrique du Nord contemporaine,* Paris, 1975, pp. 283–99; Nicholas-Mourer, H., "Les Collectivités locales dans l'administration territoriale du royaume du Maroc," *Annuaire de l'Afrique du Nord, II, 1963,* Paris, 1964, pp. 107–60; Pascon, P., "Désuétude de la Jemaa dans le Haouz de Marrakech," *Les Cahiers de sociologie,* 1:67–77 (1965); Rousset, M., "Le Rôle du ministère de l'intérieur et sa place au sein de l'administration marocaine," *Annuaire de l'Afrique du Nord, VII, 1968,* Paris, 1969, pp. 91–106.

19. See generally Bidwell, R., *Morocco under Colonial Rule: French Administration of Tribal Areas, 1912–1956,* London, 1973.

20. Sensitive accounts of the organization of various Moroccan tribes in their resistance to the French will be found in Dunn, R., *Resistance in the Desert: Moroccan Response to French Imperialism, 1881–1912,* Madison, 1976; Hart, *The Aith Waryaghar;* and Burke, E., *Prelude to Protectorate in Morocco,* Chicago, 1976. For the dubious argument that the only useful definition of tribe is that of a grouping created in response to contact with a superordinate political entity, see Fried, M., *The Notion of Tribe,* Menlo Park (Calif.), 1975.

21. On the nationalist period in Morocco, cf. Abun-Nasr, J., *A History of the Maghrib,* 2nd ed., Cambridge (Eng.), 1975; Ashford, *op.cit.;* Berque, J., *French North Africa: The Maghrib Between Two World Wars,* London, 1962; Berrady, L., et al., *La Formation des élites politiques maghrebines,* Paris, 1973; Halstead, J., *Rebirth of a Nation: The Origins and Rise of Moroccan Nationalism, 1912–1944,* Cambridge (Mass.), 1967; Hermassi, E., *Leadership and National Development in North Africa,* Berkeley, 1972; Lacouture, J. and S., *Le Maroc à l'épreuve,* Paris, 1958; Laroui, A., *Les Origines sociales et culturelles du nationalisme marocaine (1830–1912),* Paris, 1977; Le Tourneau, R., *Evolution politique de l'Afrique du Nord, 1920–1961,* Paris, 1962; Leveau, *op.cit.;* Moore, C., *Politics in North Africa,* Boston, 1970; Palazzoli, C., *Le Maroc politique,* Paris, 1974; Waterbury, *op.cit.,* pp. 33–58.

22. On the importance of Si Bekkai and Qaid Lahcen Lyusi as representatives of the Gallicized and traditional sectors from which government administrators were drawn, see Leveau, *op.cit.,* Part 1. For Qaid Lahcen's role in a more recent local dispute, see later in this essay, under 'The Dayet Ifrah Dispute."

23. See Chambergeat, P., "L'Election de la Chambre des Représentants du Maroc," *Annuaire de l'Afrique du Nord, II, 1963,* Paris, 1964, pp. 85–106.

24. Rosen, "Rural Political Process."

25. The *tertib* was an agricultural tax instituted in the last quarter of the nineteenth century. See Salmon, G., "Le Tertib," *Archives marocaines,* 2:154–8 (1905); and Stewart, *op. cit.,* pp. 26–7.

26. I am indebted to Clifford Geertz for suggesting the idea of a "shadow qaid" system. Compare the present argument with the analysis of rural elites in Leveau, *op. cit.*

27. The overall size of the oasis varies with the definition of its boundaries. A former pasha of the city cited a figure of 7,000 hectares: Lahbib, Si Bekkai ben Embarek, "Sefrou," *Bulletin économique et sociale du maroc,* 15:237 (1952). The proportion used as irrigated agricultural land is considerably less. On July 27, 1955, a government order fixed the proportion of water allocated to each irrigated parcel in the oasis of Sefrou. See *Bulletin*

officiel, no. 2255, Jan. 13, 1956, pp. 23–35. The survey enumerated water rights in 624 hectares of land irrigated by the five canal systems of the oasis. Many of the parcels listed were, however, being used as house sites, public gardens, and for other nonagricultural purposes. It is, therefore, impossible to tell exactly how much of the land involved was used for agricultural production. The author of a government report issued in 1949 placed the irrigated agricultural portion of the oasis at no more than 215 hectares: Nazelie, X., "Mémoire de stage: essai sur l'aménagement des ressources hydrauliques locales de la région de Sefrou" (Paris?), Ecole Nationale d'Administration, Promotion "Europe," Section "Affaires Extérieures," November 1949 (mimeographed), p. 10. Additional construction of houses on former garden lands has further reduced the portion of the oasis devoted to agriculture, both irrigated and dry.

28. *Bulletin officiel,* No. 2255. Again, it must be remembered that the plots involved are not necessarily devoted to agricultural uses. Further details on irrigation and land holding in the oasis will be found in Annex A.

29. The 1949 hydrological report stated that the Aggai River discharges 600 liters of water per second. Nazelie, *op. cit.,* p. 10.

30. Archives of the Alliance Israélite Universelle, Series Maroc LXXVI E, Letters 1802 (May 26, 1916), 2041 (July 8, 1916), and 2200 (July 28, 1916). These letters were written by M. Nigrine, director of the Alliance school in Sefrou. Letter 2041 also refers to a flood in Sefrou in 1889.

31. Sefrou has been mentioned by numerous travelers in their accounts of Morocco. Many of these accounts are cited in Colin, G., "Sufruy," *Encyclopedia of Islam, IV,* Leiden, 1934, pp. 499–500.

32. The wall is said to have been constructed around 1820 by Sultan Mulay Sliman. Lahbib, *op. cit.,* p. 234.

33. On alleys and quarters in Morocco, see Brown, K., *People of Salé: Tradition and Change in a Moroccan City, 1830–1930,* Manchester, 1976; Le Tourneau, R., *Fès avant le Protectorat,* Casablanca, 1949, pp. 217–31; Adam, A., *Casablanca, essai sur la transformation de la société marocaine au contact de l'occident,* Paris, 1968; Adam, A., "Urbanisation et changement culturel au Maghreb," *Annuaire de l'Afrique du Nord, XI, 1972,* Paris, 1973, pp. 215–32; and Eickelman, D., "Is There an Islamic City? The Making of a Quarter in a Moroccan Town," *International Journal of Middle East Studies,* 5:274–94 (1974). See also the discussion of urban organization in Lapidus, I., *Muslim Cities in the Later Middle Ages,* Cambridge (Mass.),

1967, pp. 85–95. For analyses of the structure of North African cities, cf. Stambuli, F., and A. Zghal, "Urban Life in Pre-Colonial North Africa," *British Journal of Sociology,* 27:1–20 (1976); Beguin, *op. cit.*; Blake, G., "Morocco: Urbanization and Concentration of Population," in Clarke, I., and W. Fisher (eds.), *Population of the Middle East and North Africa,* New York, 1972, pp. 404–23; Boughali, M., *La Représentation de l'espace chez le marocain illetré: mythes et traditions orales,* Paris, 1974; and Petonnet, C., "Espace, distance et dimension dans une société musulmane: à propos Bidonville marocain de Douar Doum à Rabat," *L'Homme,* 12:47–84 (1972).

34. Lynch, K., *The Image of the City,* Cambridge (Mass.), 1960.

35. A figure of 199 is given for 1972 in Stillman, N., "Sefrou Remnant," *Jewish Social Studies,* 35:255–63 (1973).

36. On the Jewish community during the period of fieldwork, see Rosen, L., "A Moroccan Jewish Community During the Middle East Crisis," *The American Scholar,* 37:435–51 (1968), and "Muslim-Jewish Relations in a Moroccan City," *International Journal of Middle East Studies,* 3:435–49 (1972). By 1976 only five or six Jewish families remained in the city, and almost all the community institutions had ceased to operate.

37. Scham, A., *Lyautey in Morocco: Protectorate Administration 1912–1925,* Berkeley, 1970.

38. On the growth of Moroccan cities generally in the postwar decades, see Escallier, R., "La Croissance urbaine au Maroc," *Annuaire de l'Afrique du Nord, XI, 1972,* Paris, 1973, pp. 145–73.

39. The most striking example is Casablanca. See Adam, *Casablanca;* and Adam, A., "Le 'Bidonville' de Ben Msik à Casablanca," *Annales de l'Institut d'Etudes Orientales,* 8:61–199 (1949–50). See also Petonnet, *op. cit.*

40. The statistics cited are taken from the 1960 census.

41. Le Tourneau, *Fès avant le Protectorat,* pp. 264–5.

42. On the local elections in 1963, see Chambergeat, P., "Les Elections communales au Maroc," *Annuaire de l'Afrique du Nord, II, 1963,* Paris, 1964, pp. 119–28.

43. On judicial organization in the pre-Protectorate period, see Tyan, E., *Histoire de l'organisation judiciaire en pays d'Islam,* 2nd ed., Leiden, 1960; Bruno, H., "La Justice indigène au Maroc," *L'Afrique française,* 43:74–6, 161–4 (1933); Péretié, A., "Organisation judiciaire au Maroc," *Revue de monde musulmane,* 13:509–31 (1911).

44. On the legal system during the Protec-

torate period, see Caillé, J., *Organisation judiciaire et procédures marocaines*, Paris, 1948; Girault, A., *Principes de colonisation et de législation coloniale: la tunisie et le Maroc*, 6th ed., Paris, 1936, pp. 359–406; Marty, P., *La Justice civile musulmane au Maroc*, Paris, 1933; Milliot, L. (ed.), *Recueil de jurisprudence chérifienne*, 4 vols., Paris, 1920–52; Scham, *op. cit.*, pp. 162–90.

45. Plantey, A., *La Réforme de la justice marocaine: la justice makhzen et la justice berbère*, Paris, 1952. On the effect of the Berber Dahir in a city of the Moroccan coast, see Brown, K., "The Impact of the *Dahir Berbère* in Salè," in Gellner, E., and C. Micaud (eds.), *Arabs and Berbers*, London, 1972, pp. 201–16.

46. See Haddou, C., *L'Organisation judiciaire du Maroc*, Casablanca, 1969; Salacuse, J., *An Introduction to Law in French-Speaking Africa, Vol. 2, North Africa*, Charlottesville (Va.), 1975. A somewhat outdated but nevertheless useful source is Morère, M., *Manuel d'organisation judiciaire au Maroc*, Casablanca, 1961. On the supreme court, see Ardent, P., and L. Fougere, "A propos de la Cour suprême marocaine," *Revue internationale de droit comparé*, 3:738–45 (1965).

47. The official translation of the Mudawwana has been reprinted from the *Bulletin officiel* in the *Revue marocaine de droit*, 10:254ff., 399ff. (1958); 11:49ff., 126 ff. (1959). An annotated translation (which is not accurate on all points) will be found in Colomer, A., *Droit musulman*, t.1, *les personnes–la famille*, Rabat, 1963, and *Droit musulman*, t.2, *la succession–le testament*, Rabat, 1968. Among the works analyzing the new code are Anderson, J.N.D., "Reforms in Family Law in Morocco," *Journal of African Law*, 2:146–59 (1958); Lapanne-Joinville, J., "Le Code marocain du statut personnel," *Revue marocaine de droit*, 11:97–125 (1959); and Gallagher, C., "New Laws for Old: The Moroccan Code of Personal Status," *American Universities Field Staff Reports, North Africa Series*, 5:1–11 (1959).

48. On the role of documents in Moroccan property law, see, for example, Pansier, J., "Les Moulkias et leur force probante," *Revue marocaine de droit*, 1:5–13 (1965).

49. On the taking of oaths in Moroccan proceedings, see Decroux, P., "Le Serment en droit marocaine," *Revue marocaine de droit*, 285–90 (1950); and Peyronnie, G., "Le Serment judiciaire dans de droit malekite et dans la jurisprudence marocaine," *Revue algérienne, tunisienne et marocaine de législation et de jurisprudence*, 1:34–43 (1934).

50. For an excellent analysis of the relation between the formal institutions of law and the social context of disputes, see Dwyer, D.,

"Cultural Conceptions of Conflict and Variability in Conflict Boundaries: A Moroccan Example," *Journal of Conflict Resolution*, 20:663–86 (1976).

51. See Rosen, L., "Equity and Discretion in an Islamic Legal System," ms. available from author.

52. Rosen, L., " 'I Divorce Thee,' " *Transaction*, 7:34–7 (1970).

53. On the concept of marital equality, see Ziadeh, F., "Equality (Kafa'ah) in the Muslim Law of Marriage," *American Journal of Comparative Law*, 6:503–17 (1957). On the roles and status of women in an area adjacent to the Sefrou region, see Maher, V., *Women and Property in Morocco*, Cambridge (Eng.), 1974.

54. Coulson, N., *Tensions and Conflicts in Islamic Jurisprudence*, Chicago, 1969, p. 107.

55. Schacht, J., *An Introduction to Islamic Law*, Oxford, 1964, pp. 208–9.

56. On personal names and social identity, see Geertz, " 'From the Native's Point of View.' "

57. Early French ethnographers, however, did not consider the Arab-Berber distinction particularly significant. The development of French perceptions of Moroccan social categories was closely related to the course of French involvement in the country. See Burke, E., "The Image of the Moroccan State in French Ethnological Literature: A New Look at the Origin of Lyautey's Policy," in Gellner and Micaud (eds.), *op. cit.*, pp. 175–200.

58. An additional 9% consisted of children under one year of age, and 2% failed to respond.

59. This argument is developed in more detail in Rosen, L., "The Social and Conceptual Framework of Arab-Berber Relations in Central Morocco," in Gellner and Micaud (eds.), *op. cit.*, pp. 155–74.

60. Cf. Rabinow, *op. cit.*, pp. 27–8.

61. On the distinction in identity between the people of Rabat and Salé, see Brown, *People of Salé*, pp. 52–8.

62. On the concepts associated with affinity and relatedness, see Eickelman, *Moroccan Islam*, Chaps. 4, 5.

63. Actually, they acknowledge their descent from the saint's servant, a fact that shows how tenuous genealogical links may be in assessing descent from a saint. There are frequent court cases in Morocco concerning who is really a descendant, and thereby entitled to a share in the gifts, and the Wlad Sidi Ali Buseghine have themselves been involved in at least one internecine lawsuit over whether the gifts should be distributed according to families or individuals. The court opted for the latter solution.

64. See Rosen, L., "The Structure of Social Groups in a Moroccan City," Unpublished Ph.D. dissertation (University of Chicago, 1968), p. 155.

65. Cf. Turner, V., "Symbolic Studies," in Siegel, B. (ed.), *Annual Review of Anthropology, Vol. 4,* Palo Alto (Calif.), 1975, pp. 145–61.

66. For a detailed example of this process, see Rosen, L., "The Negotiation of Reality: A Study of Male-Female Relations in Morocco," in Beck and Keddie, *op. cit.*

67. Additional support for many of the economic and social indicators cited in this chapter will be found in the thesis, unavailable before this book went to press, by Hassan Benhalima, *Sefrou: De la tradition du Dir à l'intégration economique moderne, etude de geographie urbaine,* These, Doctorat de zème cycle, Université Paul Valéry, Montpelier, 1977. See also Benhalima, H., "L'artisanat traditionnel Sefrioui: Son agonie et ses limites de sa renovation," *Revue de Géographie du Maroc* 41–51 (1977); and Chaoui, M., "Sefrou: De la tradition à l'integration, ce qu'est un petit centre d'aujourd'hui," *Lamalif,* 99:32–9 (1978).

111

Annex A: Irrigation in the Oasis of Sefrou and the Lower Aggai River

Structure of the Sefrou irrigation system

The water used to irrigate the gardens surrounding the city of Sefrou is derived entirely from the Aggai River, a narrow and rather shallow watercourse that begins in the hills to the west of the city and runs all the way down to the Sebou River. The river itself is formed by two branches: One begins in the rugged hills of the Haynajen territory, and the other bubbles up from several sources near the foot of Jbel Kandar. From the juncture of these two streams (at a place called Malaqil l-Widan), the river flows eastward, cascades down a waterfall some 20 meters high, continues down a long narrow valley (along which is located an electrical generating plant), cuts through the heart of the medina of Sefrou, and continues on through the rolling hills of Kouchata to its juncture with the Sebou. (From below the city the river is also referred to as the Yahudi River, perhaps because it passes by the reputed site of the first settlement of [Berberized?] Jews in that area.)

The supply of water in the Aggai River is reasonably plentiful and regular even during the hot summer months. Although the river comes nowhere near drying up in the summer, it has, in the past, been the source of major though irregular flooding in the late winter and early spring.

The irrigation of the Sefrou oasis is carried out through five canal systems, each of which leads off from the Aggai at a point above the city proper (Figure A.1). The first of these canals (sg. *sāqiya*) is Kenitra (also referred to as Saquia Sidi Ahmed Tadli), whose two main branches (Khayna and Shershara) water the gardens on the west side of the road that leads north from Sefrou to Fez. The second canal to depart from the river is Saquia Chouicha. Its four main subdivisions (described in detail below) irrigate the territory around the Qla^{c}a, the gardens and villas of the Ville Nouvelle, and the land that rims the   113

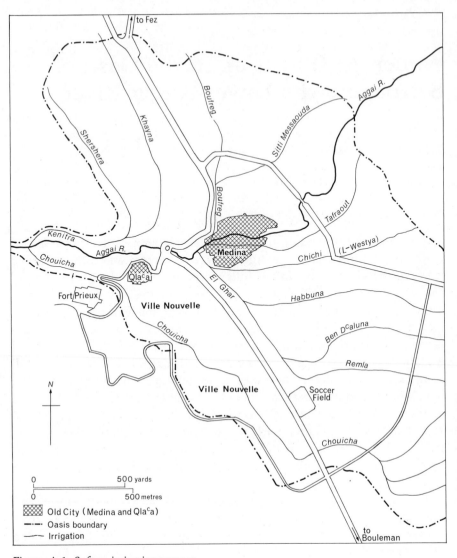

Figure A.1. Sefrou irrigation system.

border of the oasis south of the city along the base of Jbel l-Kebir. The third channel, Saquia Boufreg, taps the river just above the city at the main gate to the Fez road. One segment of the canal, Boufreg proper, waters the gardens along the east side of the Fez road; another segment, Saquia Sitti Messaouda, irrigates the gardens just north of the medina in the quarter of the same name.

The fourth irrigation canal is called Saquia Tafraout, and it, too, branches off from the river at the gate to the Fez road. The saquia flows beneath the quarters of the city lining the southern edge of the river and emerges near the Beni Medreg gate to irrigate a portion of the southeastern quadrant of the oasis. Because this saquia picks up a certain amount of waste as it passes through the medina, the government does not permit gardens irrigated by its waters to be planted in crops that are eaten uncooked (e.g., strawberries, salad greens). Finally, the saquia known as El Ghar, which leads off from the river at the city's western edge near the swimming pool, irrigates the land just south of the medina through a series of four main branches: Remla, Ben D^caluna (also called Kerrush), Habbuna, and Chichi (also called l-Westya).

Thus, each of the five canal systems waters a separate section of the oasis. However, the area watered by each, the amount of water flowing through each, and the systems of distribution among subsidiary channels of each vary significantly. In terms of area, an *arrêté viziriel* of July 27, 1955 (published in the *Bulletin officiel,* no. 2255, January 13, 1956) fixes the total area of irrigated land in the oasis of Sefrou at 623.47 hectares. Broken down by canal systems the figures are as follows: Kenitra, 86.82 hectares; Chouicha, 84.46 hectares; Boufreg, 215.67 hectares; Tafraout, 137.52 hectares; and El Ghar, 98.99 hectares.

The Sefrou irrigation network operates on the *mubiḥ* system, in which land and water are linked. Water cannot be sold independently of the land or moved around to water some other plot in the system. Moreover, in the mubih system water is not allotted to land on the basis of a fixed period of time. Although different branches of the canal system receive water for an allotted period, within each branch plots are irrigated in succession, each site receiving a full complement of water before the next garden gets its turn. A landowner thus possesses the right to use water for his specific plot, although the government retains the right to use whatever portion of the flow is deemed necessary for public purposes, and no compensation is paid for such a taking.

An irrigation channel in detail: Chouicha

In order to see how water is distributed, we will look at one of the five canal systems, Chouicha, in some detail. As Figure A.2 indicates, the Chouicha system irrigates the gardens above the Qla^ca, the entire Ville Nouvelle, and the most southern portion of the oasis of Sefrou, on the east side of the Bouleman road. For analytic purposes the Chouicha system can be divided into two main sections. The first section irrigates all the gardens along the Aggai, around the Qla^ca, throughout the Ville Nouvelle, and in that part of the oasis irrigated

115

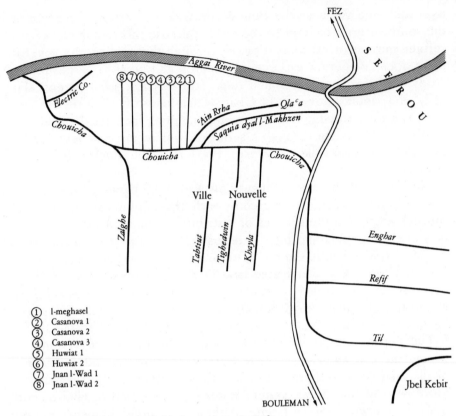

Figure A.2. The Chouicha irrigation system in Sefrou.

by the Enghar branch of the canal. All the plots irrigated by this section of the Chouicha canal can properly be called "gardens" (*jananat*), and all are watered on a seven-day cycle of irrigation. The two remaining segments of Chouicha, Refif and Til, irrigate the southernmost part of the oasis. They do not carry nearly as much water as the rest of the system because they receive water from 2200 hours until 1300 hours the following day only once every ten days. Much of the land along these two branches is not irrigated at all, and most of the water available is used for olive trees and small vegetable gardens. Because there is insufficient water to grow commercial garden crops, many people refer to these lands as bled ("countryside"), rather than irrigated garden lands.

Within the first part of the Chouicha system the distribution of water is roughly proportional to the size of the individual branches. (Saquia Rrha is perhaps a special case because the water it carries goes to the mosque of the Qla°a.) Because fully one half of the entire flow 116 of the Aggai goes into Chouicha–except from 1900 to 2200 hours, during which the entire river passes through the turbines of the electrical generating plant–there is never really any dearth of water in the whole first section of Chouicha.

Each time a new building has gone up in the Ville Nouvelle on former garden lands, the supply of water available for irrigation has increased. The jari, who oversees the daily operation of the system, freely cuts water on and off to gardens that do not need all the water to which they are entitled because he knows that should anyone complain he can easily arrange to give them all the water they need at a later time.

Within the very small channels along the Aggai there has been some subdivision of garden sites in recent years and a consequent subdivision of irrigation periods. For example, the gardens called "Casanova" were formerly part of a single garden that received water from 1300 to 1900 hours one day a week. Now the three subdivisions share a single period of time. The same applies for the two sections of Huwiat and the two sections of Jnan l-Wad. This last was split around 1956; the others quite a bit earlier.

Chouicha displays the typical characteristics of a mubih system: Although sections of Chouicha receive water during timed portions of the day, week, or (in the case of Refif and Til) ten-day cycle, within each branch the gardens are filled successively without any fixed period of time allotted each. Moreover, water and land are inseparable, and there is a relatively plentiful supply of water within the system as a whole.

Landholding patterns

It is possible, using the data from the *Bulletin officiel* article, to calculate the distribution, by size, of irrigated plots within the entire oasis, (Table A.1). Out of a total of 1,260 plots, only 9.4 percent are larger than 1 hectare. Although the average-sized plot is about 0.5 hectare, the mean is nearer to 0.25 hectare. Moreover, it is rare for a single individual to own more than about 3 hectares, for those sharing the same family name to own more than 4 hectares within a given irrigation system, or for such a family to own more than 6 hectares (exclusive of family habus). Out of a total of 623.47 hectares of irrigated land, 52.66 hectares were registered as habus (religious foundation property) in 1955. Of this, 39.64 hectares were *ḥabus kubrā* whose incomes are devoted to public religious works, and 13.02 hectares were *ḥabus ṣuḡrā,* whose incomes go mainly to private groups, in this case individual families. Thus, 8.4 percent of the oasis is habus (6.2 percent kubra, 2.2 percent sughra).

117

Table A.1. *Distribution of irrigated plots within Sefrou oasis, by size*

Size of plot (hectares)	Number of plots
Less than 0.01	1
0.01–0.10	108
0.10–0.25	420
0.25–0.50	396
0.50–0.75	144
0.75–1.0	72
1.0–1.5	59
1.5–2.0	30
2.0–2.5	14
2.5–3.0	2
3.0–3.5	2
3.5–4.0	2
4.0–4.5	3
4.5–5.0	0
5.0–7.5	3
7.5–10.0	2
10.0–20.0	2
Total	1,260

Source: Bulletin officiel, No. 2255, Jan. 13, 1956, pp. 23–35.

Not all the irrigated plots listed in the 1955 survey were gardens. Many of the gardens have been used for the construction of houses, stores, and public works. In recent years, land has changed hands mainly through purchase and sale. This has not always been the case. Consider, for example, some of the lands irrigated by the Chouicha canals. Virtually all the land in what is now the Ville Nouvelle was extorted by Qaid Umar al-Yusi from people living in the Qlaᶜa. After Umar's death the land passed to Umar's heirs, mainly his son, Qaid Mohammed. In an attempt to legitimize his title to some of the lands illegally obtained by his father, Qaid Mohammed made a deal with the government whereby he recieved clear title to certain properties in exchange for ceding to the government most of Umar's lands in the Ville Nouvelle. (By this tactic Mohammed also managed to cut his own mother out of her share of the inheritance.) The Qlaᶜa people were never able to regain their land, which was later auctioned off by the government to form the Ville Nouvelle.

A detailed survey of the Chouicha system in 1966 showed that there were only sixty-four commercial garden plots in the system. Of these gardens, twenty-five were worked by sharecroppers, but the actual number of sharecroppers is clearly less, because some men care for more than one garden. (Four other gardens, not included above,

were owned by the habus and rented out.) Thus, 61 percent of the
gardens that were farmed commercially were actually worked by their
owners; the remainder were worked by sharecroppers.

The survey also showed that of the sixty-four commercial gardens in
the Chouicha system in 1966, two were owned by Jews, two by
Frenchmen, four by people living in Fez, one by a Sefroui, and five by
other non-Qla^{c}a people. Thus 78 percent of these gardens were still
owned by people from the Qla^{c}a. It is clear that, with the exception of
the four Fassis and maybe two Frenchmen, all the garden owners were
indeed local people. Although the figures for all the above factors are
probably higher in the case of Chouicha than in some or all of the
other systems, the size of the holdings and the dearth of absentee
landlordism is broadly characteristic of the entire oasis.

Irrigation in the Lower Aggai

Between the oasis of Sefrou and the Sebou River, the Aggai turns
increasingly northward as it passes through a series of low, rolling hills
inhabited by various fractions of the Ait Yusi tribe. This territory,
referred to here as the Lower Aggai (also called the Yahudi River by
residents of the area), is itself divided into three main sections: Dar
Attar, Beni Mansour, and l-Glet. Each of these three regions is irrigated by the waters of the Lower Aggai according to the mubih system
(i.e., each garden is filled in succession during the period of time
water is present in any given branch of the system). The operation of
the mubih system in the Lower Aggai varies in some respects from its
application in the Sefrou oasis.

For purposes of irrigation, the Lower Aggai is divided into two
regions, each of which is entitled to water every other year. During
one year water flows only into the canals of the Beni Mansour and
Dar Attar areas. The following year, water is made available only to
the gardens of l-Glet. Unlike the Sefrou system, where all areas receive the same allotment every year, the people of Beni Mansour–Dar
Attar and l-Glet can legally refuse water to one another during the
year that it is their turn to use the river. In fact, as we shall see, the
full exercise of this right never seems to be either necessary or desirable. Given the yearly alternation of water, the gardens of each of
these two irrigation regions are used to raise irrigated crops one year
and unirrigated crops, mainly grain crops, the second year.

During each region's annual use of the river, the irrigation cycle
employed is a straightforward successive filling of gardens. There is an
internal division of water within each of the two regions, however. 119

During the year the Beni Mansour and Dar Attar areas are irrigated, the Dar Attar region receives water during two-thirds of each day, and the Beni Mansour gardeners use the river the remaining one-third. A similar division occurs between the two sections of l-Glet: l-Glet proper and Boujerou.

Thus in purely formal, and legally enforceable, terms the divisions of waters is quite simple. So, too, are certain consequences. It is obvious that in a system of successive filling of gardens, the greater the overall supply of water, the more often each garden will have a turn at the available supply, and the greater the likelihood of success for its crops. Conversely, the less the total volume of water the more infrequently each garden can be filled and the greater the chances of crop failure. Furthermore, the less the supply of water in the river as a whole during a very hot summer or following a winter of little rain and snow, the greater the likelihood of widespread reductions in garden production generally, the higher the prices of those crops that are produced, and the greater the likelihood that disputes will occur concerning the short supply of water. In characteristically Moroccan fashion, the people of the Lower Aggai have chosen to institute certain informal procedures as a hedge against the effects of a rigidly legalistic order.

Specifically, it is seldom the case that during any given year those who have rights to the river do in fact cut off the inhabitants of the other region from any use of the waters whatsoever. Usually there is enough water in the river so that neither region remains completely dry for an entire year. Thus, during the year that l-Glet has use of the river, the peole of that region usually irrigate their gardens only from sunup prayers to sundown prayers, allowing the Beni Mansour-Dar Attar area to use the river during the night. The reverse is then usually true on off-years. However, because one can never be certain about the level of the river during any given year, almost everyone in the region not formally endowed with water during a given year plants a grain crop, rather than a garden crop. The water in off-years is, therefore, not expected mainly for the planted crop, though its availability is, to say the least, welcome. Rather, nighttime waters are used mainly to irrigate olive trees.

There are, however, years when the supply of water as a whole is indeed very short, and at these times borrowing and stealing of water are common. Where stealing of water may be an individual or collective effort, borrowing is only done collectively. In a very dry year the people of the region that is formally without water borrow enough water from the people of the favored region to irrigate the crops in their gardens one time. For instance, in 1966 it was the turn of l-Glet to use the river, and because the water level was unusually low there was little water left over for the people of Beni Mansour – Dar Attar. The people of the latter area, therefore, borrowed some water from the farmers of l-Glet. It was a straightforward loan: No ritual sacrifice was involved and no written agreement prepared. The people of l-Glet could have refused the request, but informants insisted that no one would ever fully cut water off entirely from the people of the opposite region because the roles of each might easily be reversed at a later time.

There is always some additional room for maneuver before one crosses the line into the actual theft of water. For example, there was considerable tension during the period of fieldwork between the people of Dar Attar and those of Beni Mansour concerning the water contained in the swimming pool of Sefrou. The water in this pool is completely changed twice a week during the summer. A question arises, however, concerning what hour of the day the water should be released. The Beni Mansour gardeners wanted it let out during the evening when it was their turn for the water, and the Dar Attar people wanted it released during their daylight turn. At last count, the Beni Mansour people had bribed the government gardener in charge of releasing the water to pull the plug in the late afternoon – which is formally the period of Dar Attar's use – knowing that the rush of water does not actually reach the Lower Aggai until darkness has fallen and it is Beni Mansour's turn to use the river. This kind of maneuvering will continue in one form or another as long as there is water in the Aggai.

The formal pattern of irrigation in the Lower Aggai is a classic mubih system of distribution. The relative dearth of water (as compared with the Sefrou oasis proper) contributes a somewhat greater degree of uncertainty to successful garden farming in this region, and certain clear adaptations have been made accordingly. The farmers in this region make full use of collectively arranged, ad hoc contracts for the borrowing of water. Particularly in the past, but to a certain extent even now, a group of shurfa from the Beni Sadden area has been called in to settle disputes over water, and a person caught stealing his neighbor's water often enlists a go-between to make a ᶜar sacrifice to the offended party and seek his forgiveness. Most people just plant dry land crops on the off-years, even though some water is almost always let through to the unfavored region, but the main consideration is the survival in bad years of the olive trees. People are, therefore, quite eager to hedge against the environmental uncertainties

121

with a variety of tactics: varying the timing of irrigation within and between years, not enforcing the legal prerogative to the entire flow of the river during alternate years, regularized lending of water, and elaborate forms of deceit and theft. With the use of such devices, the basic mubih system can be accommodated to individual and collective goals.

Suq: the bazaar economy in Sefrou
Clifford Geertz

The bazaar as an object of study

Characterizing whole civilizations in terms of one or another of their leading institutions is a dubious procedure, but if one is going to indulge in it for the Middle East and North Africa, the bazaar is surely a prime candidate. Generations of observers, native and foreign, historical and ethnological, have seen in the bazaar's fat grocers and bent tailors, ingratiating rug sellers and elusive moneylenders, the image of life as it is lived in that part of the world. Goitein discerns a "large and powerful merchant class" rising "all over the Middle East" as early as the eighth and ninth centuries, a class that, by the tenth through twelfth "was the main bearer of Muslim civilization, including its Jewish and (Oriental) Christian enclaves."[1] What the mandarin bureaucracy was for classical China and the caste system for classical India – the part most evocative of the whole – the bazaar was for the more pragmatic societies of the classical Middle East.

Yet for all that, the intensity of scholarly attention directed toward the mandarin bureaucracy or the caste system, running to hundreds of titles in both cases, has not been even remotely approached with respect to the Middle Eastern bazaar. There are a few data-collection-type reports, usually brief, on this or that market; some discussion, usually general, on the role of the merchant class in this or that Islamic society; and a lot of travel literature, complete nowadays with color photographs, romanticizing about smells and sharp practices. But there is only a handful of extended analyses – such as Goitein's – seriously concerned to characterize the bazaar as a cultural form, a social institution, and an economic type.[2] Whatever the reason for this neglect (the fascination of Middle Eastern scholars with the phenomenon of Islam is surely one of them), the result has been that the   123 revisions forced on our concept of status by Indian studies, or of power by Chinese, have not, as they should have, been forced on our concept of exchange by Middle Eastern.

The bazaar is more than a place set aside where people are permitted to come each day to deceive one another, and more, too, than one more demonstration of the truth that, under whatever skies, men prefer to buy cheap and sell dear. It is a distinctive system of social relationships centering around the production and consumption of goods and services (i.e., a particular kind of economy), and it deserves analysis as such. Like an "industrial economy" or a "primitive economy," from both of which it markedly differs, a "bazaar economy" shows whatever general processes it shows in a particular and concrete form, and in so doing it reveals an aspect of those processes that alters, or should, our conception of their nature. *Bazaar,* that Persian word of uncertain origins which has come to stand in English for the oriental market, thus becomes, like the word *market* itself, as much an analytic idea as the name of an institution, and the study of it, like that of the market, as much a theoretical as a descriptive enterprise.

The search for information

Considered as a variety of economic system, the bazaar shows a number of distinctive characteristics, characteristics that center less around the processes that operate there than around the way those processes are shaped into a coherent form. The usual tautologies apply here as elsewhere, perhaps even more here than elsewhere: Sellers seek maximum profit, consumers maximum utility; price relates supply and demand; and factor proportions reflect factor costs. But the principles governing the organization of commercial life are less derivative from such truisms than one might imagine from reading standard economics textbooks, where the passage from axioms to actualities tends to be rather nonchalantly traversed. And those principles, matters less of utility balances than of information flows, give the bazaar both its particular character and its general interest.

To start with a dictum, in the bazaar information is generally poor, scarce, maldistributed, inefficiently communicated, and intensely valued. Neither the rich concreteness or reliable knowledge that the ritualized character of nonmarket economies makes possible, nor the elaborate mechanisms for information generation and transfer upon which industrial ones depend, are found in the bazaar – neither ceremonial distribution nor advertising; neither prescribed exchange partners nor product standardization.[3] The level of ignorance about everything from product quality and going prices to market possibilities and production costs is very high, and a great deal of the way in which the bazaar is organized and functions (and within it, the ways its various sorts of participants behave) can be interpreted as either an attempt to reduce such ignorance for someone, increase it for someone, or defend someone against it.

That is, these ignorances are *known* (or known about) ignorances, not simply matters concerning which information is lacking. Bazaar participants realize how difficult it is to know if the cow is sound or the price is right, and they realize also that it is impossible to prosper without knowing. The search for information one lacks and the protection of information one has is the name of the game. Capital, skill, and industriousness play, along with luck and privilege, as important a role in the bazaar as they do in any economic system. But they do so less by increasing efficiency or improving products than by securing for their possessor an advantaged place in an enormously complicated, poorly articulated, and extremely noisy communication network.

Looked at in this way, the institutional peculiarities of the bazaar seem less like mere accidents of custom and more like connected elements in a coherent system. A finely drawn division of labor and a sharp localization of markets, inhomogeneity of products and intensive price bargaining, extreme fractionalization of transactions and stable clientship ties between buyers and sellers, itinerant trading and extensive traditionalization of occupation in ascriptive terms do not just co-occur: They imply one another. The same is true for the personal nature of reputation and the preference for partnership arrangements over employer-employee ones; for the diversity of weights and measures and the primacy of buying skills over selling ones; and for item-by-item accountancy and the tendency to investigate possibilities in depth with single partners serially rather than to survey them broadly with several concurrently. The search for information – laborious, uncertain, complex, and irregular – is the central experience of life in the bazaar, an enfolding reality its institutions at once create and respond to. Virtually every aspect of the bazaar economy reflects the fact that the primary problem facing the farmer, artisan, merchant, or consumer is not balancing options but finding out what they are.

The bazaar of Sefrou

The term for both market and marketplace in Sefrou is, of course, the same as it is generally in the Arab world – *sūq*. The term can be applied   125 to a market center as a whole, as in *sūq Ṣ-Sefrū* ("the Sefrou market"); to a specialized marketplace, as in *sūq l-behāyim* ("the animal market"); to the part of a quarter that is commercial as opposed to residential (i.e., as a place name), as in Bistna Suq, Bistna being the name of a quarter; to a commodity market considered analytically, as in *sūq l-fūl* ("the bean trade"); for a market day, as in *suq l-ḵemīs* ("the Thursday market"). *Kaysūwweq* is to sell in the marketplace, *kaytsūwweq* is to go to market (or, of a girl, to have loose morals), a *sūwwāq* (or *suwwāq*) is a market seller, a *taswīqa* is something bought in the market, *meswāq* is the act of marketing, *sūwwāqī* is something "marketlike" (i.e., cheap, commercial, manufactured, vulgar), and so on.

At the most general level, however, Sefrouis divide the bazaar into three main sectors or, as we might better call them, realms: (1) the permanent trading quarters of the old town and its recent extensions; (2) the network of periodic markets, centered on the town but spreading out through the neighboring countryside; (3) the more Westernized business district of the so-called new town. Each of these realms is vaguely bounded. Not only is it not always possible to place a particular activity, much less a particular trader, firmly within one or another of them, but the interconnections between them are multiple, deep, and intricate. Yet, for all that, they do represent, in the eyes of the Sefrouis and in actual fact, distinguishable spheres of commercial activity, trading systems with somewhat different functions and somewhat different modes of operation.

The permanent bazaar in the old city and the newer quarters adjoining it consists, first, of more than 600 shops, representing about forty well-defined commercial trades, each specifically named in terms of the product handled. Second, in addition to the shops there are nearly 300 craft ateliers, representing about thirty distinct crafts. And third, there is a significant number of people whose activities seem to fall mainly within the realm of the permanent bazaar, but who are not housed in a shop or an atelier: auctioneers, brokers of various sorts, "footloose" craftsmen such as masons or tile layers, curers, scribes, musicians, porters, keepers of caravanserais, bath attendants, prostitutes, street peddlers, buttonmakers. Taken together these three categories of permanent bazaar occupations probably account for 40 to 50 percent of the town's employed labor force.[4]

The periodic market system consists of a cloud of open-air markets scattered more or less continuously across the whole of Morocco, each of which meets once a week.[5] Some of these markets are in towns; more are spread out on open plains or strung along narrow valleys. Some are rooted and have been in place for centuries; more are recent and responses to increasing commercialization. Some are large and focus the trading activities of extensive regions; more are small and focus the trade of ten or fifteen surrounding settlements.

The ties between these markets are loose and irregular, the product of the activities of those who move from one of them to the next. But within any general area market days tend to be arranged in such a way that locality-focusing markets do not conflict with one another, locality-focusing markets do not conflict with region-focusing ones, and region-focusing markets do not conflict with their equivalents in adjoining regions.[6] Sefrou town, whose market day is Thursday, is the region-focusing market for some 2,000 square kilometers and 90,000 or 100,000 people. Some 19 kilometers to the south, 10 kilometers to the north, 26 kilometers to the southeast, 27 kilometers to the east, and 21 kilometers to the southwest, five locality-focusing markets meet, respectively, on Tuesday, Wednesday, Saturday, Sunday, and Monday. Immediately adjoining the Sefrou region, large region-focusing markets meet on Sunday, Monday, Tuesday, and Wednesday. And 40 kilometers along the highroad north lies Fez, the premier bazaar of central Morocco (Figure 1).

The participants in the periodic market system are of three main sorts: (1) itinerant traders, who move through it in various routes, hardly any two the same, seeking a living from the difference something can be bought for in one place and sold for in another; (2) local traders, who are also usually part-time cultivators and/or pastoralists; (3) farmers and herdsmen, who come habitually into one or another market to offer their grains and animals and purchase what they need. On Thursday, the whole of the Sefrou countryside (or rather, this being the Arab world, the male half of it) seems to descend upon the town to buy and sell grain, wool, animals, rugs, fruits and vegetables, wickerwork, household equipment, and various sorts of secondhand objects in the locations specialized for trade in these commodities established at various points around the perimeter of the town, while from all directions of the compass (including, of course, from Sefrou itself) professional traders come to meet them there. Exact estimates of the number of people coming into Sefrou town for market day are impossible to make in the absence of extended survey research dedicated precisely to that question, but some idea of the scale is given by the fact that in 1965 about 50,000 animals (i.e., an average of almost 1,000 a week) changed hands in the Thursday market. Were comparable figures for the other major commodities available, the impression of intense, even feverish, activity would only be reinforced.[7]

Finally, the more Westernized business district is the Sefrou exten-   127

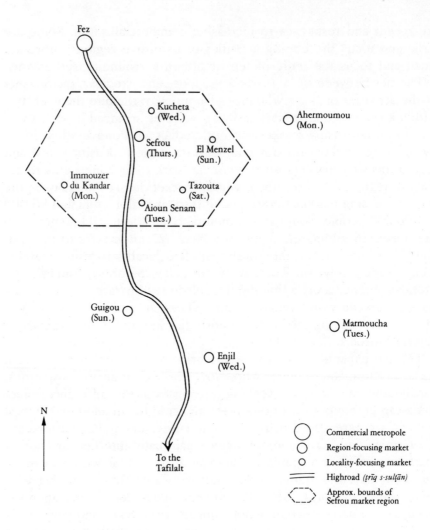

Figure 1. The Sefrou market system. Note that locality-focusing markets are shown only for Sefrou region.

sion, slight as it is, of the French-built industrial economy of Morocco, whose center of gravity is in Casablanca and the other half-developed cities—Tangiers, Safi, Rabat, Kenitra—of the Atlantic coast. In Sefrou, whose only proper factories are a couple of machine-driven olive-oil mills, a small cannery, and a building in which ten or fifteen people stuff mattresses with hassock grass, this sector consists of various glass-fronted stores selling electrical appliances, auto parts, packaged groceries, plumbing fixtures, bicycles, European furniture, and Bata shoes; some garages, several gas stations, a half dozen bars and French-style sidewalk cafés, a few seedy hotels, and a couple of photo studios; a pharmacy, a bank, a bus depot, a pinball parlor, and a cinema. Interspersed with the main government offices of the town – the city hall, the court, the tax bureau, the post office, the gendarmerie, the hospital – and strung ribbonlike along the Fez highroad as it passes west of the old city, these poor fragments of European capitalism constitute commercial modernity as it exists in Sefrou.

In any case, the boundaries of the *sūq l-medīna* ("the old city bazaar"), the *sūq l-ḵemīs* ("the Thursday bazaar"), and the *sūq l-betrīna* ("the show-window bazaar", from the French *vitrine*), though visible and recognized, are readily crossable. Tribesmen come to town on Thursday, haggle in the shops and ateliers of the old city, and sit gossiping in the cafés along the highroad. An old city cloth merchant deals in the wool market. A man who sells European furniture out of a highroad show window manufactures it (or has it manufactured) in a medina atelier. An itinerant grain buyer owns a taxi, a bath, and a business district garage. Structurally, the Sefrou bazaar is a partitioned system; behaviorally, it is an unbroken confusion.

The formation of the Sefrou bazaar

Though Sefrou is today essentially a regional market, a place where half-commercialized tribesmen meet supercommercialized shopkeepers on free if somewhat less than equal ground, it has not always been thus. Prior to the Protectorate (and especially prior to the French incursion into the Algerian Sahara around the turn of the century), the town's role in short-distance trade was distinctly secondary to its role in long-distance trade. It was out of the caravan traffic – south toward the Sahara and black Africa and north toward the Mediterranean and Latin Europe – that the Sefrou bazaar arose. For about the first millennium (900 to 1900) of its existence, the town was less a hub than a way station, a link between remote economies rather than a focus for adjacent ones. Its function was to connect.

Probably the most important, and certainly the most elaborately developed, of such connectings was that between Fez, then the political and cultural as well as the commercial capital of the country, and the Tafilalt, the great desert port of southeastern Morocco.[8] The first stopover (and the last town) on the way out, and the last stopover (and the first town) on the way in, Sefrou was both the jumping-off place and the landfall of this trade – the passage gate to 480 kilometers of winding mule trail, as accidented politically as it was physically.

This trail, the famous *ṭrīq s-sulṭān* ("The Royal Way," so-called because it linked the dynasty's capital with its ancestral shrine) ran from

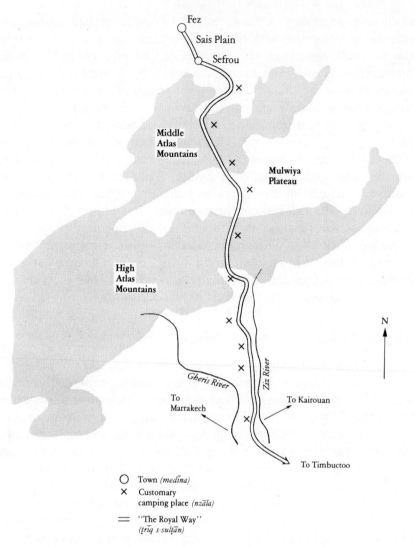

Figure 2. The Royal Way. (Based on J. Brignon et al., *Histoire du Maroc,* Paris, 1967.)

Fez across the Sais Plain into Sefrou, from which it climbed up into
the Middle Atlas, then down to cross the blank Mulwiya Plateau, then
up again, this time to 2,000 meters, through the High Atlas, finally
descending into the palm groves and camel tracts of the north
Sahara – an eleven- or twelve-day trek (Figure 2). Little circumstantial
can be said about Sefrou's involvement in the trade that passed along
this route prior to 1900. Except for the fact that the volume of trade
was not what it must once have been and that, by 1900, European
guns and cottons were beginning to appear in it, though the amber,

slaves, and civet cats of black Africa no longer did, there is no reason to believe that the essential form of the trade itself, and thus of the town's relationship to it, had changed for centuries.[9] Certainly the main institutions regulating the trade – the caravanserai (*funduq*), the commenda (*qirāḍ*), and the passage toll (*zeṭṭaṭa*) – had not.

The funduq

A combination depot, hostelry, emporium, artisinat, animal pen, whorehouse, and ecclesiastical benefice, the funduq was the social heart of the caravan economy. Its physical form was invariant: a narrow, two-story building constructed rectangularly around a broad open court, with a large gated passage cut into one end and an open gallery stretched along the whole length of the second floor. A series of extremely small, airless cubicles opened off this gallery, and beneath it, along the arcade it formed on the ground floor, were ranged a number of storerooms, workshops, and countinghouses. The passing caravaners picketed their mules and donkeys in the courtyard, bolted their merchandise inside the storerooms, and slept (as noted, not usually unattended) in the second-floor cubicles. There were eleven such funduqs, of varying size and significance, in the Sefrou of 1900; and in and immediately around them virtually the whole of the city's commercial life, then much more highly concentrated and much less various than it is now, was centered (Figure 3).

The funduqs were not privately owned, but were, insofar as one may use the term in a Muslim context, church holdings. More exactly, they were what Moroccans call *ḥabus* – properties deeded by their original owners (pious traders of the seventeenth and eighteenth, in one case apparently the sixteenth, centuries) to God's community of believing Muslims, the *umma*. Entrusted to the stewardship of a religious official known as a *nāḍir* (cl. *nāẓir*), they were auctioned by him to private merchants, usually several of them in partnership, to operate in their own way and for their own profit, the rents thus collected being distributed by the nadir for the construction and operation of mosques, the support of Quranic education, and so on.[10] They were, in short, pious foundations given wholly over to commercial activities themselves untrammeled by any sort of pious scruples. And, as we shall see, this curious symbiosis between the most headlong sort of merchant capitalism – business is business, and may God take pity on the both of us – and the established institutions of public Islam has remained, through all sorts of detailed changes, a central characteristic of the Sefrou economy to this day.

131

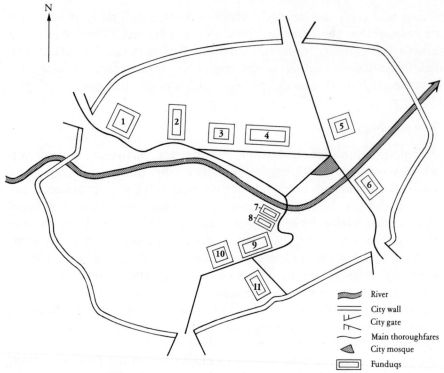

N

River
City wall
City gate
Main thoroughfares
City mosque
Funduqs

Figure 3. Location of the funduqs in Sefrou, ca. 1900.

This odd circumstance is all the more odd because, although, as Islamic law demands, the funduq holders themselves were inevitably Muslims, most of the Sefrouis involved in the funduq world – a quite restricted group in any case – were Jews. There has been an untypically large number of Jews in Sefrou for as long as we have record, and between about 1880 and 1948 (the year Israel was born), they seem consistently to have composed about 40 percent of the town's population and 80 percent of its commercial labor force. Of the perhaps 600 or 700 men involved in the swirl of activity around the funduqs in turn-of-the-century Sefrou, not more than 100 were Muslims; the rest were Jews. (For the general picture ca. 1900 compared with the strikingly different one in 1960, see Table 1.)[11]

In any case, Jewish or Muslim, large or small, the relationship of the funduq class to the Saharan trade is both critical to an understanding of the development of the bazaar economy and quite difficult to characterize. The funduq class was surely not the driving force of that trade: The grand merchants of Fez, seldom stirring from their countinghouses, but linked to agents in the Tafilalt (and indeed all over Morocco and into Europe) through a developed letter-of-credit sys-

Table 1. *Muslims and Jews in Sefrou commerce, ca. 1900 and in 1960 (1960 figures in parentheses)*

	Total population	Employed labor force	Employed in bazaar occupations		
			Number	% of group's employed labor force	% of total bazaar labor force
Muslims	3,000 (17,583)	1,000 (3,249)	100 (1,966)	10 (61)	14 (79)
Jews	2,000 (3,041)	700 (634)	600 (526)	86 (83)	86 (21)
Total	5,000 (20,624)	1,700 (3,883)	700 (2,492)	41 (64)	100 (100)

Note: Totals for 1960 exclude 337 foreigners, mostly French and Algerian. Unemployed and "inactive" men over fifteen composed 19% of the population in 1960; only 9% of the employed labor force was female, and that mostly in schools and government offices.

Source: Based on historical population figures for the town assembled from various sources in L. Rosen, "The Structure of Social Groups in a Moroccan City," doctoral dissertation, Department of Anthropology, University of Chicago, 1968, p. 40; a detailed computer analysis of the 1960 census data for Sefrou; and extensive interviews with aged informants concerning the social composition of the town during the decades immediately preceding the Protectorate.

tem, financed and organized virtually the whole of the trade. Nor did the funduq class have anything to do with the transport side of things: The caravaners were pre-Saharan Berber nomads whose sheikhs assembled them into companies, found them cargoes, and then piloted them through the tangle of tribal jealousies that separated the capital from the oasis. The Sefrou involvement was mostly ancillary, limited to providing the passing services of the funduq – food, lodging, women, various sorts of craftwork (blacksmithing, saddlemaking, tinsmithing, shoemaking, weaving) – and a certain amount of petty trading of sugar, tea, and cannabis with the caravaners. Yet, beyond this undynamic roadside commerce, there was a handful of men – around 1900, perhaps a dozen Muslims and twice that many Jews – who did contrive to buy into the caravan trade as such, to become what Moroccans call, still today with a touch of awe, *tājir.*[12] They, employing the second of the organizing institutions upon which that trade depended, the *qirāḍ,* laid the real foundations of the bazaar economy and turned the town from a mere service station or doorsill to Fez into a commercial center, minor but vigorous, in its own right.[13]

The qirad

The qirad, or what is called in the Western tradition, the commenda, combines, as Udovitch has remarked, the advantages of the loan with those of the partnership, without quite managing to be either one.[14]

133

Indeed, unless pressed, Sefrouis still refer to it, as they do to almost
any persisting commercial relationship, as a "partnership" (*šerka*). The
qirad is not precisely that because instead of risks being shared between the contracting parties they are borne wholly by the supplier of
the capital, who provides money or (despite some juridical opinions
opposing it) goods to a trader, who then trades on his own, in his own
way, and without answering to anyone but himself. If there is a profit,
the investor shares in it in some preagreed proportion; if there is not,
then not, and no debt remains to haunt the relationship. The trader's
liability (anyway, his financial liability) is not only limited, it is for all
intents and purposes nonexistent. And, contrariwise, the investor has
no responsibility for anything the trader does or says and is expected,
indeed, not to meddle. The qirad is a curious sort of contract, one that
so isolates the participants' commercial activities from one another as
to maximize the need for a personal bond between them.[15]

In turn-of-the-century Sefrou, the few merchants with resources
enough to launch qirad arrangements were, again, mostly Jews. They
made the arrangements with both Muslims and Jews, but the latter
formed the core of their operations.[16]

There was a large Jewish community, at least as ancient if not so
urbane as Sefrou's, in the Tafilalt, and small knots of Jews, also originating mainly from the Tafilalt, could be found huddled around most
of the camp stops along the route, doing a little selling here, a little
buying there.[17] It was between the urban *maḡārba* ("Moroccan," but
more generally "northern town-dwelling") Jews of Sefrou and the
filālī ("Tafilalt," but more generally "rural of the south and east") Jews
that quite extensive and usually highly stable investor-agent qirad relationships crystallized. And again, as we shall see, this not uninvidious
intracommunity contrast between the prosperous, settled, civilized
"sitting" (*gles*) merchant and the impoverished, itinerant, unlearned
"riding" (*rkeb*) peddler became, like the habus-funduq pattern, an enduring feature of the bazaar economy. It was across this city Jew–
country Jew synapse of class that the shopkeeper and artisan world of
the permanent bazaar was first linked with the shepherd and traveling-
man world of the periodic bazaar.

Yet, for all the prominence of Jewish qirad givers in Sefrou's penetration of the caravan trade – and their activities surely accounted for
vastly the greater part of it – the two most considerable of such buyers
into the passing traffic were Muslims: a kinetic Berber chieftain and a
descendant-of-the-Prophet munitions maker. What the Jews had in
volume, these men had in scale; and what the Jews had in skill, they
had in power.[18]

The Berber, Umar al-Yusi Buhadiwi, was the dominant political figure both in the town and in the countryside immediately around it from 1894 to 1904. A tribesman from the great Ait Yusi confederation that ranged the countryside south and east of town, he was recognized by the then sultan, Mulay Abdel Aziz, as the local *qā'id* ("chief," "commander," "governor," "administrator"). Unlike previous qaids, however, he installed himself, his family, and his entourage inside the town (the only Berbers then living there) to become, until lured to an ambush assassination by tribal rivals, a small sultan of the place.

So far as the caravan trade is concerned, he was, of course, himself neither a merchant nor possessed of extensive contacts with merchants. He was, as well, illiterate, and so he operated through two or three Sefrou Jews as his personal agents. The depth of his involvement in the caravan trade is now difficult to measure with any precision, but his investments, based on his ability to appropriate wool and hides from Berber herds and, as his grip grew tighter, on a similar ability with respect to the wheat and olives of the town itself, were clearly both large and far-flung. As he muscled into Sefrou's political life, he thrust himself (and, indirectly, his tribal followers) into its economic.

The munitions maker, Mulay Ali b-l-Hashimi Bu Bnitat l-Alawi, was something rather different: a classic urban type. He was, as noted, a descendant of Mohammed, what Muslims refer to as a *šerīf*. But, more than that, he was an Alawi sherif, which meant he was, in theory anyway, a distant relative of the sultan and the closest thing to a local patrician (what the French later called a "notable" and, even later, and more misleadingly, a "bourgeois") that the intensely plebian, most ungenteel Sefrou society was capable of producing.

His Alawi ancestors had come to Sefrou from the Tafilalt, probably shortly after the dynasty's capture of Fez in 1667, and his contacts with the large (Dunn says "several thousand") Alawi community still living and trading there at the end of the nineteenth century provided the social foundation for his activities. The economic foundation lay, as indicated, in the gun trade – after the 1890s, a very rapidly expanding affair.[19] In the funduq, of which first his father and then he held the lease (number 4 in Figure 3), Mulay Ali organized a fair-sized craft industry, some twelve or fifteen workers, in ammunition manufacture (i.e., cartridge stuffing). This industry not only projected him into the midst of the local traffic but gave him something of a monopoly hold on it and proved immensely profitable.

In time, Qaid Umar, jealous of the growing power of Mulay Ali and of the emerging class of funduq entrepreneurs, of which he was in a

135

sense the doyen, persuaded the sultan to remove the sherif from this
particular line of work. (The sultan's predecessor had given him the
right to drive arms in the first place.) This was done. The workers
were imprisoned and the funduq ransacked; Mulay Ali escaped, as
such men will, with a ransom. But by then he had built up an extensive network of qirad relations with Tafilalt sherifs and other traders,
Muslim and Jewish alike, to become a large-scale operator – almost of
Fez proportions – in the tea, sugar, wool, cloth, and olive trades, and
disentanglement from the not altogether healthy arms business may
have come as something of a relief. Himself literate in only a quran-
school sense, Mulay Ali had four secretaries, all Sefroui Muslims, in
his funduq, which was the most substantial commercial institution in
the town until about 1915, when rural security, calico tastes, and the
gasoline engine put an end to the caravan trade forever. No longer a
mere pause point for trade headed elsewhere, Mulay Ali's funduq had
become what Moroccans call a "commodity house" (*ḍār s-silʿa*), a
domicile of trade in itself.

It was not, however, the only one. By the turn of the century,
almost all the funduq lessees were qirad givers, some of them on a fair
scale, and their funduqs had become commodity houses too, each
specialized in one or another trade. Funduq number 6 in Figure 3,
headed by a pair of wealthy Meccan pilgrims, one of whom became
the dominant political figure in Sefrou after Umar's death, was the
center of the grain trade. The wool and lumber trades, separated in
different parts of the building, were concentrated in number 11,
whose director was another Alawi, but no immediate relation of Ali's.
Yet a third Alawi, unrelated to either of the other two, leased number
9 in partnership with an Arab-speaking migrant from northwest Morocco, the so-called Jbala, and made it the focus of the hide and
leather trade. The tea and sugar trade was centered in Mulay Ali's
funduq, number 4, after its munition days were over; the cloth trade
in the Fez-launched one, number 2; the olive and olive-oil trade,
under two wealthy local farmers (about the only example at this time
of significant trade involvement by large landowners) in number 7.
And so on.[20] All sorts of people – financiers, traders, millers, weavers,
tanners, blacksmiths, shoemakers, caravaners, Jews, Arabs, Berbers –
crowded in and around these miniemporiums (which were, of course,
public places not private firms). Shops, ateliers, and even small ad hoc
in-the-street markets in old clothes, bread, vegetables, mats sprang up
around them. Mule stops transformed into markets, they provided the
nucleus around which the developed region-focused bazaar economy
that emerged in full force after World War I crystallized.[21]

For that to happen, however, the hub had to be joined to its rim: The Sefrou-centered trade swirl the qirad induced had to be integrated with the local economy, and most especially with the rural economy of transhumant shepherds and olive grove farmers surrounding the town. And for this, the third of the caravan trade's enabling institutions, the *zeṭṭāṭa,* provided, suitably reworked, at once the means and the model.

In the narrow sense, a zettata (from the Berber *tazettat,* "a small piece of cloth") is a passage toll, a sum paid to a local power (the *zeṭṭāṭ*; Br. *azettat*) for protection when crossing localities where he is such a power. But in fact it is, or more properly was, rather more than a mere payment. It was part of a whole complex of moral rituals, customs with the force of law and the weight of sanctity – centering around guest-host, client-patron, petitioner-petitioned, exile-protector, suppliant-divinity relations – all of which are somehow of a package in rural Morocco.[22] Entering the tribal world physically, the outreaching trader (or at least his agents) had also to enter it culturally.

Despite the vast variety of particular forms through which they manifest themselves, the characteristics of protection in the Berber societies of the High and Middle Atlas are clear and constant. Protection is personal, unqualified, explicit, and conceived of as the dressing of one man in the reputation of another. The reputation may be political, moral, spiritual, or even idiosyncratic, or, often enough, all four at once. But the essential transaction is that a man who counts "stands up and says" (*qām wa qāl,* as the classical tag has it) to those to whom he counts: "This man is mine; harm him and you insult me; insult me and you will answer for it." Benediction (the famous *baraka*), hospitality, sanctuary, and safe passage are alike in this: They rest on the perhaps somewhat paradoxical notion that though personal identity is radically individual in both its roots and its expressions, it is not incapable of being stamped onto the self of someone else.

The zettata proper involved the establishment by the caravan sheikh of such a protective covering of borrowed personality at point after point along his route. The sheikh on the one side and the zettat on the other solemnly exchanged turbans, cloaks, saddle covers, or sections of tent material – "the little piece of cloth" – to create a symbolic fusion of their public selves. The basis thus laid (the rite usually took place in the local market with every man of local standing in attendance), each time the sheikh came through thereafter, his zettat provided him with a small band of men, again more as a symbolic indica-

137

tion of the fact of protection than as a literal guard. Meeting his caravan at one limit of the zettat's influence, this band conducted it, via a grand meal in the zettat's camp at which the toll (paid in currency and adjusted to the size and value of the caravan) was negotiated, to the other limit, where the next escort of the next protector waited to begin the process anew. From the Tafilalt to Fez there were long chains of such relationships, enclosing the caravan sheikh in a series of local identities – Moha's or Rahu's or Lahcen's – as he led his train through the turbulent countryside.[23]

When the Sefrou-centered economy moved, after around 1890, to reach out with some definitiveness to join its immediate hinterland to itself, to become, eventually, a region-focusing bazaar rather than an emporium-linking caravan stop, the zettata type of protection pattern provided the mechanism by which the connection was made.[24]

In the first instance the connection was made, as mentioned earlier, by the Jews, who for months at a time, located themselves in the villages, camps, and markets of the countryside under the protection of one or another tribal strong man. Here, the protection pact was signalized by a sheep sacrifice – again public, with all the local men assembled for a meal in the protector's tent – rather than a turban exchange (perhaps because *that* intimate a mingling of identity with a Jew was too much for a Berber to tolerate) and was called a *mezrāg* (literally, "a spear").[25]

It was as solemn an undertaking, and based on the same complex of ideas about hospitality, personal reputation, the bindingness of oral contract, and divine human retribution, as the zettata relation between two Berbers, and it was at least as resolutely observed.[26] Except for its focus and its cross-ethnic, indeed cross-religious, quality, it was the same institution.

The mezrag made, the protector, the *mūl l-mezrāg,* would send a small group of his men down to Sefrou town to pick up the Jew and escort him and his goods to their locality. There, usually by the side of a small market or set off a few hundred meters outside a settlement, the Jew would trade for several months and, his stock exhausted, be escorted back home with his wool, hides, grain, or whatever. By the early 1900s, the countryside behind Sefrou was laced with Jewish-Berber mezrag relations of this sort. There was hardly a tribesman who, through the courtesy of his local strong man, did not have a riding Jewish trader reasonably nearby, and hardly a sitting Sefroui Jew, whose agents these riding Jews were, who did not have extensive mezrag-based interests in the countryside.

A caravanserai transformed into a commercial house, a passage trade transformed into an investment business, and a protection pattern transformed into a market channel–these were the elements out of which the bazaar economy was built. In time, the commercial house dissolved into the hundreds of stores and ateliers of the permanent bazaar, the qirad disappeared in favor of the more familiar financial arrangements of central place hierarchies, and the mezrag gave way to the free market higgling of the cycling suq. But the general character, the cultural ground plan, of the commercial network in Sefrou was established by then. The sort of system it is, the way in which information gets around it (or does not get around it), the manner in which trade is conducted, and the assumptions in terms of which it is conducted are not only outcomes of the world of Umar, Mulay Ali, and the riding Jew; they are, for all the differences in scale, products, and personnel, continuations of it. A lot has changed in Sefrou since 1900, a time at least two epochs away. But the cultural framework within which the homely business of buying and selling proceeds, the conceptual structure that gives it point and form, has altered but in detail.

Once fairly launched, the metamorphosis of long-distance trade into short-distance trade rapidly accelerated. In place of the extended lines of commercial connection, twisting across large tracts of merely intervenient social structure, came a dense field of immediate exchanges gathered around Sefrou and centered directly on it. The world of the Sefroui merchant at once contracted and expanded. Contracted, for now the range of his operations was drawn in toward the symmetrical hexagon shown in Figure 1. Expanded, because, within that hexagon, the variety of his activities multiplied, their volume increased, and their social importance grew. By the onset of the Protectorate, the penetration of Sefroui Jews into the surrounding countryside, the linking, through them, of the isolated Berber markets to the town and to each other in an organized pattern, and the transformation of the town's Muslims from a population overwhelmingly agricultural to one overwhelmingly commercial had wrought an economic revolution that the French establishment of security and improvement of transport merely consolidated.[27]

This revolution had begun at least three decades earlier and had emerged out of a complex of ideas and institutions as old as, or older than, Sefrou itself. Stimulated by outside forces, imitative of outside forms, and integrated first into a colonial system and now into that

139

curious combination of capitalism and sultanism that has succeeded it, the bazaar economy is, nevertheless, neither an import nor an enclave. Its shape is as indigenous as its origins.[28]

The bazaar as a cultural form

There are bazaar economies all over the so-called underdeveloped world, as there were not so long ago over much of that now supposedly developed, and, in some difficult to articulate sense, they clearly form a coherent class. There are important similarities among them, as there are important differences between them taken as a group and the sorts of economies one finds in, say, Germany or New Zealand, New Guinea or the Kalahari desert. Yet, in another sense, one even more difficult to articulate, they all partake as well of the place where they are and the time in which they exist. And this is as true of the Moroccan bazaar as of any other. As a social institution, and even more as an economic type, it shares fundamental similarities with the Chinese, the Haitian, the Indonesian, the Yoruban, the Indian, the Guatemalan, the Mexican, and the Egyptian – to choose only some of the better described cases. But as a cultural expression, it has a character properly its own. And one of the advantages of looking in depth at so particular a case as Sefrou is that it is possible thereby to discern something of what that character is: what is Moroccan about Moroccan commerce, and what difference it makes.[29]

In these terms, terms at least implicitly comparative, three aspects of the Sefrou bazaar are worth more extended attention: (1) its enmeshment in a vast arabesque of what, lacking an English word that genuinely applies, one can only call ethnic-like distinctions; (2) its integration – interfusion, even – with some of the major institutions of popular Islam; and (3) the role of the Jewish community in its development and functioning.

Nisba: trade and cultural identity

The discussion of the formation of the bazaar economy has already demonstrated that the class, if it can properly be called that, which was formed with it was not religiously, linguistically, or culturally homogeneous. For all the prominence of the Jews in the bazaar economy and for all their tendency to concentrate in it, not only was the bazaar an all-sorts affair, but the interrelations among the various kinds of people within it – sitting Jews, riding Jews, Berber chiefs, Arab notables, Saharan mule skinners, and a number of other types not yet mentioned–were intricate, crosscutting, and anything but distant. *Suq: the bazaar* The bazaar economy was particolored from the start: Different vari- *economy in Sefrou* eties of people entered it in differing degrees, in different ways, and with not altogether complimentary views of one another. But the crystallization of a culturally encysted trading class, half intruder and half pariah, so common in other parts of the world (Southeast Asian Chinese, East African Indians, Medieval European Jews) never oc- curred in Sefrou.[30] Between those in commerce and those not, there has been, and is, essentially no line save that.

This promiscuous tumbling in the public realm of varieties of men kept carefully partitioned in the private one, cosmopolitanism in the streets and communalism in the home, is, of course, a general feature of Middle Eastern civilization. Often called a mosaic pattern of social organization – differently shaped and colored chips jammed in irregu- larly together to generate an overall design within which their distinc- tiveness remains nonetheless intact – it is made possible by a number of characteristic ideas: that religious truth is so little subject to argu- ment and so little responsive to temporal concerns that it ought not to hinder practical activities; that non-Muslim groups are not outside Muslim society but have a scripturally allocated place within it; that law is personal and determined by who one is, not territorial and determined by where one is; and that, though usually cruel and always capricious, the state is a machine less for the governing of men, who are anyway more or less ungovernable, than for the amassment and consumption of the material rewards of power. Nothing if not diverse, Middle Eastern society, and Moroccan society as a frontier variant of Middle Eastern society, does not cope with diversity by sealing it into castes, isolating it into tribes, or covering it over with some common denominator concept of nationality – though, fitfully, all have occa- sionally been tried. It copes with diversity by distinguishing with elaborate precision the contexts (marriage, diet, worship, education) within which men are separated by their dissimilitudes and those (work, friendship, politics, trade) where, however warily and however conditionally, men are connected by their differences.

In contemporary Sefrou, though the contrast between Jew and Muslim is perhaps the most vivid and obvious example of the way this concern for fitting differences together operates within the bazaar economy, it is hardly the only such contrast of importance.[31] Ascrip- tive distinctions – generated out of language, religion, residence, race, kinship, birthplace, ancestry – run through the whole of the bazaar, partitioning the Muslim community into literally dozens of categories. In 1968–9, there were 1,013 shops and ateliers in Sefrou's permanent 141

bazaar; among the "owners" of these establishments there were represented no less than sixty-six different locally recognized "ethnic-like"
categories.[32] Were a similar analysis of the periodic bazaar possible,
the number of different sorts of men – again different sorts in the eyes
of the Sefrouis themselves – would quite possibly double.[33]

This collective habit, not to say obsession, of classifying man into a
large number of essentialist categories – categories resting on the general premise that a person's provenance pervades his identity – is practically effected by the extensive use of a morphological process of the
Arabic language known as *nisba*. Deriving from the root (*n-s-b*) for
"ascription," "attribution," "imputation," "relationship," "affinity,"
"correlation," "connection," "kinship" (*nsīb* means "in-law"; *nsab*
means "to attribute or impute to"; *munāsaba* means "a relation," "an
analogy," "a correspondence"; and so on), nisba as a linguistic device
consists of changing a noun into what we would call a relative adjec-
tive, but what for Arabs is just another noun, by adding *ī* (fem. *īya*).
Examples are: *Ṣefrū*/Sefrou – *Ṣefrūwī*/native son of Sefrou; *Sūs*/region
of southwest Morocco – *Sūsī*/man coming from that region; *Beni
Yazġa*/a tribal group near Sefrou – *Yazġī*/a member of that group;
Yahūd/the Jews as a people, Jewry – *Yahūdī*/a Jew; *Adlūn*/surname of a
prominent Sefrou family – *Adlūnī*/a member of that family. As, once
formed, nisbas tend to be incorporated into personal names (Umar
al-Yusi Buhadiwi – Umar of the Buhadu fraction of the Ait Yusi confederation; Mulay Ali b-l-Hashimi Bu Bnitat al-Alawi – the sherif Ali,
son of the Hashim family, father of little girls [a sobriquet], of the
Alawite line), the ethnic-like classification is publicly stamped onto a
man's identity.[34] A few newcomers and marginal figures aside, there is
not a single case in the bazaar survey where an individual's nisba type
(if, dropping approximate glosses, we may now call it that) was not
generally known. Indeed, people, in the bazaar and out, are far more
likely to be ignorant of what a man does, how long he has been
around, what his personal character is, or where exactly he lives than
they are of where he fits – Sussi or Sefroui, Buhadiwi or Alawi, Yazghi
or Yahudi – in the perduring mosaic.

All this is important not only because the bazaar is extravagantly
heterogeneous with respect to nisba types, a profusion of peoples, but
because such types are correlated with trades and occupations within
it. This correlation is, of course, a statistical, not an absolute, matter;
but it is pronounced enough to be clear to the naked (and native) eye,
and to affect profoundly the organization of commercial life. The
distinct nonrandomness of the classification of individuals according to
142 background vis-à-vis their classification according to vocation leads to

the partial assimilation of the two ways of sorting men and thus to the view that there is an immanent, transaccidental connection between social origins and lines of work.[35] The mosaic quality of Moroccan society, and beyond it Middle Eastern civilization, not only penetrates the bazaar but finds there perhaps its most articulate and powerful expression, its paradigmatic form.

To gain a clearer picture of that form, of what, in concrete terms the mosaic principle comes to in the bazaar, we can begin with Table 2. In fact, the table does not deal with nisba types, which are cultural categorizations applied by the Moroccans themselves to themselves, but with externally invented sociological categorizations that are here called socioethnic.[36] Though notions like Sefrou Arab, rural Arab, Berber, and, of course, Jew have a certain general currency and application among Sefrouis, especially when they are regretting one another's existence, the effective everyday categorizations in terms of which people are actually perceived and reacted to are Adluni, Meghrawi, Yazghi or Bhaluli, Zaikumi or Zgani, Tobali or Robini; that is, nisbas.[37] Table 2 indicates few of the general sociological forces – rural-to-urban migration, linguistic integration (i.e., Arabization), and religious contrast – that engendered the particular mosaic found in Sefrou and that continue to maintain it. It does not reach, save indirectly, to the mosaic itself. Yet, for all that, some important aspects of the cultural shape of the bazaar are discernible in the pattern of its entries.

The first is that the traditional sector of the bazaar, still the heart of it, is the particular bailiwick of the two old urban groups, the town-born Arabs and the Jews. This is especially true for the crafts – the largest single occupational sector in the town, approached only by agriculture – but it extends to traditional commerce too. Until 1960 anyway, old Sefrouis, both Arab and Jewish, were not only heavily concentrated in the traditional bazaar, they clearly dominated it.

The second matter visible from the table is the formation by the immigrant Arabs and, to a lesser extent, the Berbers of a kind of bazaar rabble of marketplace peons – the flunkies, menials, and hangers-on of commercial life. Even the relatively high participation figures in traditional craft and, for the Berbers, traditional commerce categories do not modify this seriously. The line between being a casual laborer in the bazaar and a lowly assistant or apprentice (or, indeed, between being a casual laborer and outright unemployed) is far from sharp, and most of the rural Arabs and Berbers in these categories are in fact at the bottom edge of them.[38]

In short, there are at least two main clusters of socioethnic/occupation association: (1) the Jews and the "real Sefrouis" (as they some-

143

Table 2. *Percent of Sefrou town employed labor force of various socioethnic categories in different occupational categories, 1960*

	Traditional commerce[a]	Traditional craft[b]	Bazaar worker[c]	Nontraditional commerce and craft[d]	Total bazaar	"New middle-class" occupations[e]	Agriculture[f]
Sefrou-born Arabs[g]	18	39	6	7	70	10	20
Rural-born Arabs[h]	14	26	24	1	65	10	25
Arabs born in other towns[i]	10	21	3	8	35	46	19
Berbers[j]	17	17	17	8	59	21	20
Jews[k]	35	37	6	5	83	16	1
Overall[l]	19	30	8	7	64	16	20

[a] Arab-type shopkeepers, market peddlers, auctioneers, etc. dealing in food, clothing, craft goods, hardware, agricultural products. N = 738.
[b] Weavers, tailors, masons, butchers, saddlemakers, carpenters, blacksmiths, millers, potters, etc. N = 1,166.
[c] Manual workers in the bazaar, porters, bath employees, watchmen, etc. N = 311.
[d] Large- or medium-scale extralocal merchants, managers of commercial firms, Western-type storekeepers, bus and taxi owners, auto mechanics, plumbers, electricians, photographers, radio repairmen, etc. N = 272.
[e] Public officials, clerks, professionals, policemen, soldiers, schoolteachers, etc. N = 621.
[f] Farmers, sharecroppers, farm laborers. N = 777.
[g] Persons whose first language is Arabic and who were born in Sefrou town. N = 1,397.
[h] Persons whose first language is Arabic, who were born in a village and have moved to Sefrou town. N = 981.
[i] Persons whose first language is Arabic, who were born in another town and have moved to Sefrou town. N = 580.
[j] Persons whose first language is Berber (virtually all urban-dwelling Berber men are bilingual in Arabic). As the vast majority of Berbers living in Sefrou town are immigrant from the surrounding countryside, the category is not subdivided. N = 580.
[k] As almost all Jews living in Sefrou town were born there, the category is not subdivided. N = 634.
[l] N = 3,883.
Source: Data from official 1960 Census of Sefrou.

times call themselves) in the traditional commercial trades and the crafts, the heart of the classical bazaar; and (2) Arab and Berber ex-tribesmen in the ancillary, marginal, and, as population grows, out-right redundant jobs that surround this heart. But though this is a stratificatory difference and a systematic one, it is not, in the proper sense, a class one. Neither old Sefroui Arabs and Jews, nor rural-born Arabs and Berbers, form any group at all, or even a category, either in their own eyes or in those of others. Because they do not have any effective reality as collective social actors (the Jews are a partial exception, but only partial), they do not form units in the bazaar's stratification system. To explain that system and, in fact, the social organization of the bazaar generally, it is necessary to talk in terms, not of groups, classes, and other sociological constructions of the outside observer, but of trades and nisba types – the chips in the mosaic.

We can begin with Table 3, which summarizes what the bazaar survey has to say about the degree to which traditional trades pattern out in nisba terms. The table is arranged in accordance with a measure of *nisba compactness*, running from blacksmiths at the compact (i.e., nisba-homogeneous) end to grocers at the diffuse (i.e., nisba-hetero-geneous) end. The measure consists essentially of the degree to which the membership of the trade diverges from an equal-nisba percentage distribution, and thus can be read with zero as the nisba random, perfectly diffuse, base point.[39]

As is readily apparent, the established primary crafts are the most compact; the everyday consumption goods trades, the least; and various secondary crafts, less generalized trades, and service occupations spread out in between. (The anomalies – bakers, who should on this reasoning be somewhat higher; hardware and spice sellers, who should be somewhat lower, etc. – have as usual, special explanations.) About half the blacksmiths come, indeed, from a single old Sefroui family, and at least one of every sort of man found in Sefrou is engaged, if only in some marginal way, in the grocery business. But all the trades are reasonably well defined in nisba terms, as Table 4, in which concentration is measured by percent of the total membership in a given occupation accounted for by the four most numerously represented nisbas in it, makes even more clear. Not only is there no trade in which the top four nisba types do not account for a majority of the occupants, but in about 80 percent of the trades, these four nisba types account for more than three-quarters of the occupants.

Approaching the problem from the other direction, in terms of the degree to which a given nisba type is concentrated as to trade, poses

Table 3. *Traditional trades ranked (high to low) according to degree of compactness in nisba terms*

Trade[a]	Nisba compact-ness index[b]	Number of workers	Number of nisbas
High			
1. Blacksmith	43.0	15	2
2. Carpenter	36.7	18	3
3. Weaver	30.3	22	4
4. Butcher	21.4	22	5
5. Mason	20.4	31	5
Medium			
6. Hardware/spice seller	17.0	10	5
7. Silk merchant/spinner	16.4	22	6
8. Prepared-food seller	15.6	15	5
9. Cloth merchant	15.2	35	9
10. Coffee shop keeper	14.7	29	6
11. Baker	12.6	19	7
12. Tinsmith	12.5	10	4
13. Miller	10.5	12	7
14. Tobacconist	10.2	16	7
15. Barber/cupper	10.1	42	10
16. Wool/hide trader	10.0	11	5
Low			
17. Tailor	6.6	83	17
18. Shoemaker	6.5	31	13
19. Odds-and-ends seller	6.2	17	8
20. Ready-made clothes seller	5.4	36	11
21. Wheat/bean trader	4.0	13	9
22. Vegetable and fruit seller	3.4	90	25
23. Grocer	3.3	211	34

[a]Occupations with less than ten members or whose main locus is the periodic bazaar have been ignored. For a full list of bazaar occupations in Sefrou, see Annex A.
[b]Nisba compactness index:

$$X = \frac{\Sigma \, (P_E - P_1) + (P_E - P_2) + \ldots (P_E - P_n)}{N_{nsb}}$$

where P_E = expected percentage of workers with a particular nisba = $100/N_{nsb}$
$P_1 \ldots P_n$ = actual percentage of workers with a given nisba = $N_1/N_{nsb} \ldots N_n/N_{nsb}$
$N_1 \ldots N_n$ = number of workers with a given nisba in the trade
N_{nsb} = number of nisbas in the trade
All signs positive

146

Table 4. *Percent of total members of trade accounted for by top four nisbas*

Trade	Percent	Trade	Percent
Weaver	100	Café keeper	89
Carpenter	100	Cloth seller	86
Blacksmith	100	Baker	85
Tinsmith	100	Barber	84
Bathhouse keeper	100	Tobacconist	82
Saddlemaker	100	Tailor	79
Goldsmith	100	Odds-and-ends seller	77
Mason	97	Miller	66
Butcher	95	Wheat/bean trader	62
Silk merchant/spinner	95	Grocer	62
Prepared-food seller	93	Shoemaker	60
Hardware/spice seller	91	Vegetable and fruit seller	57
Wool/hide trader	91	Ready-to-wear clothes seller	55

more difficulties technically. First, the multiplicity of nisba types means that most nisbas embrace too small a number of persons for meaningful statistical treatment. Second, as already noted, nisba classification is fundamentally a relative matter. At one level, everyone in Sefrou has the same nisba: Sefroui. At another level, Sefrouis, Yazghis, Bhalulis, Zganis form a coordinate set; at another, Sefrouis, as one member of this set, divide into Alawis, Adlunis, Meghrawis, Ngadis, and similarly, with other divisions, do the other types. And so on. There are twelve different sorts of Alawis in Sefrou, and some of the larger of these groups further subdivide. The whole matter is far from regular: What level or sort of nisba is used and seems relevant and appropriate (relevant and appropriate, that is, to the users) strongly depends on the situation. A man who is a Sefroui to his acquaintances in Fez may be a Yazghi to his acquaintances in Sefrou town, and a Ydiri to other members of the Beni Yazgha tribe, a Taghuti to other members of the Wulad Ben Ydir fraction of the Beni Yazgha, a Himiwi to other members of the Taghut subfraction, and so on, if not ad infinitum, at least to quite striking lengths.[40] (Should he happen to journey to Egypt, he would, of course, become a Maghrebi.)

Looking at the matter from the trade end, one can operate at the "Sefrou" level of differentiation without excessive distortion, and this is what has been done in Tables 3 and 4. But this procedure has some consequences when one turns the matrix over, as in Table 5, and looks at the situation from the nisba end. The most important consequence is that a very large number of cases falls into the Sefroui (as opposed to Yazghi, Jebli, Fassi, etc.) category. That category can be further differentiated, of course, but at this next level down, the numbers tend to get quite small.[41] Nor can one simply aggregate these "lower level," or "finer grain" nisbas, because then the occupational concentrations cancel one another out. If the eight Bushamawi are, with one exception, blacksmiths, three of the four Busharebi are carpenters, and half of the eight Adluni are in weaving, then lumping them merely produces the false appearance of a scatter, as the wildly misleading figure of 0.13 in Table 5 for "other Sefroui" shows. In Table 5, then, those ten nisbas with more than ten representatives in the traditional trades are merely ranked, by the same sum-of-the-deviations index applied earlier to the trades as such, and the conglomerate Sefroui are left unranked. This is not entirely satisfactory. But even from such a procedure the fact that nisba types are markedly concentrated in certain trades as opposed to others is clear, as is the fact that this concentration varies in far from random ways.

Table 5. *Nisba types ranked (high to low) according to degree of traditional trade concentration*

Nisba type	Nisba compactness index	Number of workers in nisba in trade	Number of occupations represented in nisba
High			
1. Fassi[a]	12.53	12	6
2. Alawi[b]	9.66	43	13
3. Sussi[c]	6.21	23	7
4. Announceur[d]	5.71	25	6
5. Bhaluli[e]	5.08	30	12
6. L-Weta[f]	4.85	30	8
7. Jew[g]	3.47	30	14
Low			
8. Jebli[h]	1.63	71	15
9. Qlawi[i]	1.60	34	14
10. Yazghi[j]	1.54	69	14
Unranked (see text)			
11. Other Sefroui	0.13	297	24

[a]Fez-born. Very few of the Fassis in Sefrou (about 10% of their total employed labor force) are in traditional trade; most are white-collar workers and administrators. Of those in traditional trades, near half are grocers, and the only other trades represented, by a man or two each, are tailor, shoemaker, silk merchant/spinner, goldsmith, and hardware/spice seller.
[b]Sefrou-born descendants of the Prophet (sherifs of the Alawi line). These are strongly represented in three trades, grocer, vegetable seller, and silk merchant/spinner (about 20% of their total in each); moderately represented in the butcher trade (12%); with the rest thinly scattered in tailor, cloth seller, weaver, and other "light" trades.
[c]Berbers from the Sus, the southwestern part of Morocco. They are famed all over the country as especially aggressive traders, particularly in the grocery trade. About

148

The nisba system not only provides a classification scheme in whose terms men perceive one another and themselves, but a framework within which they organize certain of their transactions with one another – in the immediate case, certain economic ones. The mosaic is more than merely a Moroccan representation of what persons are and how society is composed, a specific conception *of* social reality, though it is that. It is also a set of principles by means of which to order the interaction of persons – in the bazaar, in politics, in the casual intercourse of everyday life – a guide *for* the construction of social reality.

The bazaar, which, as we shall see later in more detail, lacks much collective organization of any sort, has essentially only two axes along which to organize itself: (1) the division of labor, which gives rise to occupational types; and (2) the a-man-is-his-provenance discrimination

Suq: the bazaar economy in Sefrou

Table 5 (cont.)

70% in Sefrou are grocers. The only other trade of significance among the Sefrou Sussis is ready-made clothes seller (10%).

^{d}A lumped category of three immediately adjacent mountain Berber nisbas. They are strong in vegetable selling (30%); moderate in tailor and grocer (20% each) and in farm produce selling (10%).

^{e}From a developed village (or a near-town) a few miles north of Sefrou; Arab speaking. They are strong in grocer (30%) and tailor (20%); moderate in barber (10%); the rest scattered, mostly in marginal trades like odds-and-ends seller, ready-to-eat-food seller.

^{f}A lumped category of two immediately adjacent plains Berber nisbas. About 43% are grocers, 23% vegetable and fruit sellers, 13% café keepers, and of the small-scale variety in each case. The remainder are scattered.

^{g}All Sefrou-born. A third are cloth sellers. The only other significant category is produce seller (17%). Jewish occupations are "abnormally" scattered by the need to have one each of some major occupations as parallel, within-the-community trades owing to dietary and other religious considerations: butcher, grocer, baker, bathhouse keeper, tailor, shoemaker. Owing to the now-small total number, these "enclave" occupations lead the index to be misleadingly low, and a group that is actually very highly concentrated so far as bazaar occupations generally are concerned (besides cloth and produce, the only other occupation in the general sphere, is represented by the two Jewish goldsmiths) looks much more diffuse than it is.

^{h}Rural Arabs immigrant to Sefrou from the region (Jebel) north and east of Fez. Various nisbas (Branti, Ghewani, Tuli, etc.) are involved, but they are known generally in Sefrou as Jebli. They are strong in the grocer (26%) and tailor (18%) trades; moderate in cloth selling (13%) and vegetable and fruit selling (11%). The rest are scattered, mostly in marginal trades: prepared food, tobacconists, barbers, shoemakers.

^{i}Sefrou-born Arab speakers, but residing in a separate walled quarter (*l-Qlaᶜa*), originally a rather separate community. They are very heavily concentrated as (mostly quite small) grocers (47%). The rest are scattered widely over a large number of occupations, at one or two apiece. Thus, rather like the Jews, the group is in fact more concentrated than our measure suggests.

^{j}Members of the largest Arab tribe in the immediate Sefrou hinterland. Their main trades are grocer (26%) and tailor (22%), the smaller ones in both cases. They are moderately represented in vegetable and fruit selling (12%) and in ready-made clothes selling (7%). The rest are more or less randomly scattered.

149

of persons, which gives rise to nisba types. The development of these two classifications to extraordinary levels of differentiation, together with their partial but quite real interfusion, provides the bazaar with both map and mold, an image of its form that is also a matrix for its formation.

The Sefrou bazaar (and beyond it the Moroccan and, I suspect, the Middle Eastern) is a great heterogeneous collection of individuals sorted out partly by trade and partly by what one can only call, invoking again a grammatical term, attributive identity. As noted, the attribute involved can be quite various: Fassis are people from a particular town. Jeblis or Sussis are people from a particular region (and speaking a particular language: a Berber speaker from the Jebel is called a Riffi; an Arab speaker from the same region is called a Jebli; an Arab speaker from the Sus is called a Seharawi; a Berber speaker, a Sussi). Alawis are people descended from the Prophet; Adlunis are members of a particular patrilineage; Yahudis are adherents of a religious faith; Bhalulis are people from a large village a few kilometers from Sefrou; Qlawis are inhabitants of a quarter of Sefrou; Yazghis are members of a particular tribe. And so on. As has been noted, occupations themselves can form the basis of a nisba, as can allegiance to a religious brotherhood, a political commitment, or even individual circumstances. What is regular here is the attributive principle, the adjectival ascription to individuals of some dimension of their social setting and the use of such ascriptions as a framework, at once conceptual and institutional, of bazaar activity. Like all social systems, the Sefrou bazaar is but partly ordered; but the degree to which it is derives in no mean part from the habit of seeing men as named by their backgrounds.

Islam and the bazaar

Beyond the nisba and nisbalike categorization of individuals, the other cultural force with a shaping effect on the Sefrou bazaar is, as would be expected in a country notorious for a clamorous sort of piety, Islam. A good deal of this effect is diffuse, a general coloring of style and attitude in commercial relationships that only extended ethnographic description could capture, and then but obliquely. Some of it, also, is only skin deep – quranic prohibitions against interest taking, gambling, or trafficking in gold that seem to exist mainly to be circumvented. But some of it is both precise and powerful, built into specific institutional forms whose impact on commercial life is as readily visible as that of transport, taxation, or the rhythm of the seasons. Among the world religions, Islam has always been notable for its ability to sort

150

its utopian and its pragmatic aspects into distinct and only partially communicating spheres – the former left as ideals to be affirmed, explicated, codified, and taught; the latter cast into ingenious pieces of social machinery regulating the detailed processes of community life.

In Sefrou, the two most important such pieces of machinery have been the *ḥabus* and the *zāwia*. Habus, material property dedicated to the spiritual welfare of the Islamic community (mortmain, Muslim style) has already been mentioned in connection with the classical funduq, but it survived the caravan economy period to be an even more critical institution in the bazaar economy. Zawia, in Moroccan usage, refers to a Sufi brotherhood, and though the heyday of such brotherhoods has apparently passed, they played a central role in the formation of the bazaar economy in the first half of the century. Between them, the habus and the zawia provided the kind of organizational framework for locally centered, marketplace trade that the funduq, the qirad, and the zettata had played for long-distance, passage trade.

The habus

The economic importance of the habus institution in Sefrou can be gauged from a few preliminary statistics. A total of 183 shops and ateliers in the town is under one form or another of habus ownership. So are four ovens, four funduqs, three public baths, four grain warehouses, and a slaughterhouse. In addition to such commercial properties in the narrow sense, the habus owns forty houses, twenty-eight rooms within houses, and forty water-supply systems for houses. Beyond that, there are, in the countryside immediately around the town, 103 gardens (mostly irrigated), 305 fields (mainly in rainfall wheat), literally thousands of olive trees, and because, like rooms in houses, they can be separately dedicated, even branches of olive trees. The total income for 1965 from all these properties was about $20,000 and the expenditures about $17,000, the surplus being deposited in a bank for eventual use in acquiring new properties. Of the income, about three-quarters came from the urban properties (most of it from the commercial ones, because the houses, rooms, and water systems are rented for wholly nominal prices) and a quarter from agriculture.[42] Along with the government, which manages several former French farms now nationalized, and perhaps a half dozen private individuals, the habus is clearly one of the major landholders in the region. In the town – public facilities such as roads, parks, bureaus, and so on aside – it is *the* largest property owner by far. In the bazaar, it is the only one of any scale at all.[43]

151

Aside from lending a religious justification to commerce as a useful and praiseworthy activity – something not all the world religions have been able to do with such equanimity – the heavy involvement of the Islamic establishment in the bazaar in the form of the habus has exercised an effect on the economic life of the town in three quite specific ways: through monetary expenditure, through usufruct auctioning, and through fixing rents. In Sefrou, the religious institution (to use Gibb and Bowen's useful substitute for church in clergyless Islam) does not merely sanction trade: It engages in it.[44]

On the expenditure side, habus funds mainly go for the upkeep of religious properties (mosques, quranic schools, shrines, etc.) and to support various sorts of religious functionaries. The former provides employment for a certain number of people in the construction trades, such as painters, carpenters, masons, and tile layers; but the latter is the more important. The nadir's payroll runs to about 250 persons, including, besides the small staff of his own office, the prayer leaders (*imām*), prayer callers (*muaddin*), and sermon givers (*katīb*) of all the major mosques, as well as their janitors, timekeepers, plumbers, and so on. (In the main mosque, there is even a man hired to warm the lustral water on cold mornings.) Further, there is a large number of, as it were, piecework celebrants: men who hand out the Qurans on Friday; men who chant for a quarter hour on Monday and Friday afternoons before evening prayers; men (thirty altogether) who read a section of the Quran (*hizb*) in the morning and in the afternoon, getting through the sixty into which it is evenly divided in a month. And finally, many quranic schoolteachers, religious students, and so on receive small subsidies. As virtually all these people – known collectively, the janitors and such aside, as *tulba* (sq. *tāleb*), "religious scholars" (literally, "devoted, eternal students") – are also market traders, often prominent and influential ones, habus money not only mostly gets back into the bazaar economy from which, mostly, it originally comes, but acts to fuse the religious and economic elites of the town.[45]

The habus's activities in usufruct auctioning merely reinforce the connection. The main products involved are cereals (wheat, barley, occasionally maize) and olives. In the case of cereals, access to plots of land is auctioned; in the case of olives, rights to harvest particular trees. The land auctions take place in the late summer just before fall plowing, and the leases run for a growing season with right of renewal for a second season at the same price. In the case of olives, the auction takes place in midwinter, just before the harvest, the legal opening date for which is set by the government. The trees, in lots containing

152

from two or three up to 200 or 300, are bid upon, and the purchaser obtains the harvest from them for that year.

The auctions, in both cases completed in a single morning, are conducted by the nadir in a small square in the center of the old city; the bidders are mainly bazaar traders in cereals and olive oil. The traders then either hire sharecroppers for the land or pieceworkers for the olive drive and sell the product on site to millers' agents, who deliver it to the mills by hired truck, or, as is perfectly permissible, resell the leases to yet other traders. Details aside, the placing of a significant proportion of the area's cereal and olive production on the market in the form of short-term usufruct leases brings the bazaar trader far deeper into the rural economy than as a mere purchaser of agricultural products carried to market. Under the agency of the habus the bazaar not only capitalizes a significant part of that economy, but, in effect, manages it.

The most important contribution of the habus institution to the functioning of the bazaar economy comes through neither its expenditures nor its agricultural operations, but through its role in setting rents on urban commercial properties. The shops, ateliers, funduqs, and so on that the habus owns are also distributed to lessees through an auction system. But here the leases are not short term but long – in fact, lifelong. Once a trader has bid and won the right to use a vacant habus property, it is his for as long as he wishes to keep it, assuming he neither defaults on the rent, commits a crime, or moves away. If he retires or, as is very common, becomes engaged in other activities, he may sublet it freely. Indeed, it is for all intents and purposes heritable because, though his death necessitates a new auction, other traders do not normally bid against his heir. Finally, and most importantly, rents of commercial properties are almost never renegotiated, with the result that, given the general expansion of the Sefrou economy over the last fifty or sixty years, they are, in market terms, extremely low. Of all the subsidies the habus institution provides to the bazaar economy this letting of sites, buildings, and even in some cases certain sorts of equipment (e.g., forges, looms, mills) at extremely low and almost perfectly stable rents is surely the greatest.[46] Rent as a factor in bazaar calculations is reduced to virtual unimportance. Land is not precisely a free factor of production in the bazaar economy (though low, rents are, as the fact that they bring in about $15,000 a year demonstrates, not trivial), but it is a very cheap one.[47]

This stabilization of rents at abnormally low levels is not a result of any provision of Maliki law or of any general policy on the part of the Ministry of Habus. The law permits adjustments in response to market forces and the ministry, which is only just now beginning to organize itself into an effective force, still has little practical control over matters so traditionally regarded as local concerns. What holds habus rents down is simply the unified desire of the Sefrou trading community that they be held down. Here, as in so much else, the operation of the habus reflects the fact that the leaders of the religious institution and (if we may call it that) the commercial institution are the same people; that the main locus of the orthodox, sunni community in Sefrou, the *umma* in the strict sense of the term, is the bazaar. Normative Islam – as contrasted, on the one side, to the so-called saint worship or maraboutism characteristic of the countryside and the urban poor and, on the other, to the indifferentism of the Western-educated national elite – has emerged in direct association with the emergence of a recognizable commercial class that has both advanced the cause of scripturalist orthodoxy and benefited from its provisions.[48]

The habus's importance in the development of the bazaar was even greater in the early days of its formation, the first three or four decades of the century, than it is now. In the first place, an even greater proportion of commercial property was then in habus – indeed, virtually all of it – because the building of shops, ateliers, and the like outside the medina by the government and by various private parties has mostly taken place since the end of World War II. In the second place, the French encroachment upon habus properties, particularly agricultural ones, grew during the Protectorate period to fairly serious proportions, reducing the resources, and thus the power, of the institution quite significantly. And third, recent reforms, still minor but increasing in scope, on the part of the newly independent state have begun to limit the habus's role still further. But whatever the future of the habus as a factor in the bazaar economy, its role in that economy's development was of central importance, and the deep bond between commerce and orthodoxy it helped to forge will not soon be broken.

The zawia

In its dictionary definition, *zāwia* means "cubicle" or "corner of a room, especially in a mosque" (i.e., a prayer nook), but in Morocco it means about what *ikwān* ("brethren") or *tarīqa* ("path," "way") mean elsewhere: a sufi sect. Properly, the zawia is the building, a kind of small mosque or prayer house; the ikhwan is the social body, the sect as such; and the tariqa is the observance, what the members of the sect do in the building. But colloquially zawia is used for all three of these, whether taken separately or as a single whole.

The religious and organizational dimensions of the Sefrou zawias, which are essentially identical to those of Morocco and North Africa generally, need not be described here in any detail.[49] Massignon's (surely incomplete) list of brotherhoods in Islam mentions thirty-four, past and present, as existing in Morocco, though much depends in these matters on how you count.[50] The major zawias during the period with which we are concerned – that is, since 1910 – were (in order of estimated memberships), the *Tijānīya,* the *Darqāwa,* the *Naṣirīya,* the *Qādarīya,* the *Wazzānīya,* the *ᶜIsāwa,* and the *Kittānīya,* all of which, save the Wazzaniya, which had only a few isolated followers, were present in strength in Sefrou, as were several less prominent ones locally popular.[51]

Suq: the bazaar economy in Sefrou

Part of the importance of the zawia in the development of the bazaar economy lies in the simple fact that its members were, at least until the 1950s, almost all merchants and artisans, and almost all merchants and artisans were members.[52] Like the habus, the zawia drew piety and trade together into a single world. The darkened prayer house lined with men telling beads, and the cobbled alleyway thronged with men striking bargains, were separated only by a doorsill: Outside, one could hear the chants as one passed; inside, the clatter as one knelt. But a larger part was that, also like the habus, the zawia played an organizing role in that economy, lent it structure, gave it form. What the habus did for the property system, the zawia did for the occupational: outlined it, stabilized it, and, so doing, reinforced it.

To understand how this was so, and to avoid the misinterpretations that have arisen from a too-ready use of the word *guild* in the Moroccan context, we must become involved in yet a few more intra-Arabic ordinary language distinctions, that tiresome sorting of semisynonyms and partial contrasts necessary to make exotic social arrangements understandable. In Sefrou, at least, *zāwia* must be set beside two other terms, *ḥerfa* ("profession," "vocation") and *ḥenṭa* ("pious society," "mutual aid group"), in order to delineate a very complex interaction of conceptions underlying an equally complex set of social forms. Some of these conceptions were religious, some economic, and some moral; together they defined an unusual institutional pattern whose exact nature the application of standard terms from Western economic history has done more to obscure than to clarify.[53]

In themselves, the three terms are easily enough understood; it is their conjunction that raises the problems. Zawia, as indicated, refers to a religious group of, in Protectorate Sefrou, twenty or thirty to seventy or eighty men, following one or another style of Sufistic practice under the leadership of a religious adept, known as a *muqad-*

155

dem (a general word, meaning "leader," "overseer," "headman"), himself usually a disciple of a regional or all-Morocco tariqa leader called a *šaīḵ* ("chief," "patriarch," "master"). The group, as a body, possessed a prayer building, as well as some habus property deeded to it by deceased members to support it.[54]

The actual practices, all directed toward the attainment of some level of mystical experience, varied from sedate chanting of classical religious phrases over and over again to exalted dancing and drumming, playing with fire, handling of snakes, swallowing glass, self-mutilation with knives or hatchets. In more general terms, this variation in "way," from the ecstatics of order to those of frenzy, was expressed as a gradation between "clean" (*nqi*) sects and "dirty" (*mūssek*). Even small differences in practice, such as whether one stood or sat to chant (it was cleaner to sit, cleaner yet not to chant aloud but under one's breath) played a role in the classification that ran from the Malin Dalil, Mulay Ali Sherif, and Tijani at the clean pole, through the various Darqawa sects (b-l-Larbi, Kittani, b-l-Khadira, and l-Ghazi), to the Nasiriyins, Sadqiyins, and Qadariyins in the dirtier direction; the dionysian Aissawa and Hamadsha (the first eating fire and leaping about, the latter opening their heads with hatchets) held down the farther end.

The importance for the bazaar economy of this classification of zawias into clean and dirty was that the various trades and professions, the herfas, were similarly classified, and the classifications in the one domain were, in a broad but yet clearly outlined way, parallel to those in the other. That is, individuals pursuing cleaner occupations (e.g., cloth selling, wool trading, silk handling, tailoring, grocering) tended to belong to cleaner zawias, and those pursuing dirtier occupations (e.g., butchers, vegetable and fruit sellers, blacksmiths, odds-and-ends peddlers) tended to belong to dirtier zawias.

As with the nisba, it is important to understand the highly relative, even probabilistic, nature of this pattern and not to oversubstantivize it into a precise and stable structure. First, the classification, on both the sect side and the trade side, was only partly consensual. Whether Zawia b-l-Khadira was cleaner than Zawia b-l-Larbi, or whether tile making was a dirtier way to earn a living than wheat selling, was to some degree an arguable matter and often enough argued. Second, though in some vague moral and even metaphysical sense "clean" was a more estimable thing for either a profession or a sect to be than "dirty," the system was not in fact hierarchical. Clean trades and brotherhoods did not dominate dirtier ones, and whatever dispraise was involved (which, this being Morocco, was a great deal) flowed

156

freely in all directions. *Caste* is no more appropriate a characterization of occupational organization in the bazaar than *guild*. Third, though the membership correlation was real, recognized, approved, and encouraged, it was nowhere near perfect; nor was it expected to be. Most cloth traders belonged to Malin Dalil (and no butchers did); but some cloth traders belonged to Mohammed b-l-Larbi or Mulay Ali Sherif. Though grocers clearly dominated b-l-Khadira, there were a fair number of ready-made clothes sellers and hardware and spice merchants in that zawia also, as well as an odd barber or café keeper. And so on, down the line. Finally, some traders – especially footloose ones like musicians and auctioneers – were not specifically associated with any zawia, but were either scattered about fairly randomly or did not belong at all.

Yet, for all this, the match between the classification of sects according to their liturgical style and the trades according to their sort of work was reasonably systematic. And, being so, it was as critical in the evolution of the social form of the central place network of the bazaar economy from the point-to-point network of the caravan economy as were the nisba system, the habus, or, as we shall see, the florescence of Jewish paternalism.[55]

A partial list (partial because not all the correlations are recoverable from after-the-fact interviews, and so far as I have been able to discover, there are no written sources on the subject) of trade-sect connections in Sefrou around 1920 is given in Table 6.[56]

Given this clean-dirty interplay between bazaar vocations (herfas) and religious tendencies (zawias), the nature of the third, and most problematical, element in the complex, the henta, can be grasped without invoking external parallels. From one point of view, the henta was the herfa in its religious dimension; from another, it was the zawia in its secular dimension. In the henta the impulse of the trader to relate his career to the deeper reality Islam defined and the desire of the adept (in any case, the same man) to realize his piety in the practical world met and confirmed one another.

The hybrid nature of the henta as a social group was reflected in its membership, which consisted of those practitioners of a particular herfa who were also members of a particular zawia. As indicated, this was rarely, if ever, either all the practitioners of the vocation or all the adherents of the sect.[57] Rather the henta was but a part element in both the zawia and the herfa: a socially focused subgroup within the sect and a religiously focused subgroup within the trade. The cloth-seller henta, which was located in Malin Dalil, contained neither all the cloth sellers nor all the members of Malin Dalil. Similarly for the

157

Table 6. *Trades and sects in Sefrou, ca. 1920*

Trade (ḤERFA)[a,b]	Sect (ZĀWIA)[c]
Cloth seller	Malin Dalil, Abdelhayy l-Kittani, Sidi Ahmad l-Tijani, Mulay Ali Sherif
Silk merchant	Mulay Ali Sherif, Tijani, Kittani, Malin Dalil
Tailor	Mohammed b-l-Larbi, Mulay Ali Sherif, Kittani, Malin Dalil
Wool trader	b-l-Larbi, Kittani, Mulay Abdelqader l-Jillali
Ready-made clothes seller	b-l-Larbi, b-l-Khadira, Abdelqader l-Jillali
Grocer	b-l-Khadira, Abdelqader l-Jillali, Mohammed ben Nasser, Sidi Hamid b-l-Abdelsadeq
Wheat trader	b-l-Khadira, ben Nasser
Tobacconist	b-l-Khadira, b-l-Larbi
Hardware/spice seller	b-l-Khadira, Abdelqader l-Jillali, ben Nasser
Café keeper	b-l-Larbi, b-l-Khadira
Miller	Abdelqader l-Jillali
Funduq keeper	Abdelqader l-Jillali
Bathhouse keeper	Abdelqader l-Jillali
Weaver	ben Nasser, Abdelqader l-Jillali, Sidi l-Ghazi
Saddlepack maker	l-Ghazi
Cord maker	l-Ghazi
Carpenter	Abdelqader l-Jillali, b-l-Abdelsadeq, ben Nasser
Mason	b-l-Abdelsadeq, Abdelqader l-Jillali

158

Table 6 (*cont.*)

Baker	ben Nasser, Abdelqader l-Jillali, b-l-Abdelsadeq
Shoemaker	ben Nasser, Abdelqader l-Jillali
Barber	Abdelqader l-Jillali, ben Nasser, Sidi Lahcen Yusi
Vegetable and fruit seller	Aissawa, Sidi Lahcen Yusi, ben Nasser
Butcher	Aissawa, Abdelqader l-Jillali
Blacksmith	Aissawa
Cooked-food seller	Sidi Ali Hamdush, Aissawa
Odds-and-ends peddler	Aissawa, Sidi Ali Hamdush
Porter	Aissawa, Sidi Ali Hamdush

*a*Trades are listed in sequence from clean to dirty.
*b*Trades that had no, unknown, or scattered affiliations with zawias were musicians, auctioneers, charcoal sellers. Goldsmithing and tinsmithing were largely Jewish trades (as were significant parts of the shoemaker and butcher trades). Those government officials, teachers, etc., who belonged to local zawias (a number belonged to Fez ones) were mostly affiliated with the Tijaniya. Those farmers (i.e., a few, large, urban-dwelling ones) who were members, belonged to the Kittaniya, which, in Sefrou, was dominated by a single, powerful, landed family, the Adluns. For the Arabic names for these trades, see Annex A.
*c*Sects are listed, for each trade, in approximate order of popularity.
Source: Interviews with older informants who had been both traders and zawia members in the 1920s and earlier, some even before the Protectorate.

grocers in b-l-Khadira or the blacksmiths in Aissawa. The henta formed where the occupational structure and the devotional intersected, but it was an independent entity, with its own activities, purposes, and rationale.[58]

The particular activities involved were multiple and not identical from one instance to the next, but the majority fell into one or another of three broad categories: (1) general sociability, (2) mutual assistance, (3) collective participation in ritualized civic events. It is difficult to argue that any one of these was fundamental to the others, for they flowed into one another to give the henta the part private club, part protective society, part social faction quality that has made it so difficult for outsiders to comprehend.

The informal socializing aspect ought not, in any case, to be underestimated simply because of the natural difficulties of obtaining circumstantial reports about it decades after the fact. The common interest of the members, deriving from a single profession, promoted socializing, of course; like any business club, the henta was an excellent place to strike deals over drinks, even if the drinks were nonalcoholic. But the mere day-to-day routine of zawia life also promoted socializing: the five daily prayers, usually followed by tea and cakes for those who had time to tarry; a meal after the noon prayer on Friday (itself usually performed in one of the major mosques); major feasts on the religious holidays; and the special "nights" (*lilāt;* sg. *līla*) of mystical practice, also usually connected with conviviality. For those who belonged to one, the henta was their main home away from home. For their wives, meeting on Fridays in the house of one or another members, the henta provided, along with the bath, almost the only legitimate extrafamilial social life. "The henta," the saying said, "is better than the family."

It was better, too, because of its mutual assistance functions, a much more formalized matter.[59] Such assistance consisted of collective rallying around bereaved and mourning members; attendance with appropriate gifts and appropriate prayers at birth, marriage, and circumcision ceremonies; visiting the sick; as well as material help, whether in the form of individual donations, "contribution club" type insurance schemes, or whatever.

The funeral aspect was clearly the most important and the one most often pointed to in reminiscence. The henta usually undertook the whole of the burial expenses, dug the grave (which, for a particularly prominent figure, might be in the zawia floor rather than the public graveyard), provided monetary and moral support to the immediate survivors, and offered up a stream of prayers, sometimes continuing periodically for years, for the deceased's soul. But the obligation to present gifts, cook food, and the like at the happier rites of passage; to aid and comfort the ill (often with curative talismans from the zawia sheikh); and even at particular crises, including business crises, to lend money was also quite strong. The large and wealthy hentas were not only powerful solidary groups in Protectorate and immediate pre-Protectorate Sefrou (i.e., in roughly the first half of the twentieth century), they were virtually the only such groups in the entire bazaar context (to some degree in the entire society), otherwise a radically one-on-one, man-to-man affair.[60]

The third type of activity, group representation in the annual saint festivals, projected the henta, as socializing and mutual aid did not, out of the world of personal interrelations into the public arena; and it thus has been the activity most often noticed.[61] So far as the henta was concerned, there were two main sorts of such festivals (*mwāsim,* sg.

musīm – literally, "time of the year," "season," "harvest"): those honoring the saint associated with the henta particularly, and those honoring the saint associated with the town as a whole. The former connection was based on the zawia affiliation of the henta: The blacksmiths, being in Aissawa, participated in the musim for Sidi ben Aissa; the tailors in that for Sidi b-l-Larbi; the carpenters in that for Sidi Abdelqader; the weavers in that for Sidi Ali Hamdush. The latter connection, that for the town saint, Sidi Ali Buseghine, a legendary miracle worker migrant to Sefrou from some distant place at some distant time, was based on the mere fact of residence, and all the hentas participated, though they did so severally, not cooperatively, as distinct and independent units.

The zawia musims were each on different, traditionally fixed days of the year. As the shrine (*qubba*) of the brotherhood saint was, for Sefrouis, always elsewhere – ben Aissa's in Meknes, b-l-Larbi's in the Rharb, Hamdush's in Zerhun, ben Nasser's in the pre-Sahara – the henta usually held a celebration in Sefrou just prior to the musim proper, parading around town with the henta banners and music to signal the event, and then either went off in a body or sent a delegation to the festival itself. The musim for the local saint (his shrine, a small white cupola structure, sits atop a high hill rising directly behind the town) was held for two days in early October and, until the French suppressed it in the 1930s, was, along with the usual *ᶜid* celebrations, the main communal ritual of the city as a whole.[62]

The members of each henta, carrying banners and various sorts of insignia, marched in a body around the town and then up to the shrine, where they camped in a particular place on the knoll behind the structure. Most hentas endeavored to sacrifice a bull, or even two, or failing that at least several sheep. Some, for example, silk merchants and weavers, brought samples of their craftwork to adorn the shrine. Some chanted, sang, or danced, often to the point of trance. Some provided meat, couscous, soup, tea, cigarettes, and so on for invited guests from comparable hentas in other towns, for the "children of the siyyid" (i.e., the guardians of the shrine, considered to be the saint's descendants), or for the tribal peoples from the surrounding countryside who engaged in the riding and shooting displays that were the high point, in secular terms, of the festival. And they all prayed in turn, though, so far as one can now discover, in no fixed order, before the tomb of the saint. At no other point in the normal course of town life did the henta emerge so emphatically into public view, and in no other context were the foundations of that life in the workings of the bazaar asserted in so explicit a symbolism.

161

As has been suggested, if obliquely, the hentas are no more. The herfas, the occupational groupings, remain, more or less as they were and structured as they were, except that a few new ones – truck and bus drivers and garage mechanics, most notably – have been added.[63] Most of the zawias also remain, but as shadows of their former selves: mere prayer houses, to which a dwindling band of aging members, survivors from the institution's heyday, repair for chanting and conversation. Indeed, as the florescence of the zawia in effect created the henta, its retrogression has destroyed it – a retrogression caused less by economic or religious factors (though these played a role as well) than by political ones.[64] Nationalism destroyed the zawias and with them the interaction between the work-type classification of the trades and the liturgy-type classification of the sects, the clean-dirty correspondence, that made the henta possible.

The first indication that the zawias were beginning to be projected, or to project themselves, into the political arena came with the French prohibition of the town musim in 1931.[65] This prohibition was part of the general reaction of the Protectorate government to the upsurge of mass religiopolitical protests by the Moroccan urban population following the proclamation of the so-called Berber Decree in 1930, a policy that seemed designed to separate the Berber-speaking population from the Arab, and even from Islam. All over Morocco, mass prayers of supplication, called *laṭīf* (from *yā laṭīf*, "O, Kind One!," the shout that goes up at them), were held in protest, the first truly popular nationalist outcries.[66] The Sefrou saint musim was banned on the basis of the (correct) suspicion that the nationalist, anti–Berber Decree stalwarts were seeking to turn it into such a political latif and had indeed partly done so the year before.

The irony of the situation as it developed for the established zawias was that, initially suspected by the French (to some degree accurately) as seed grounds for rebellion, they became increasingly identified, and in part identified themselves, with the established order, sharing finally in the radical discrediting of that order when at length it fell. The reasons for this are complex, and not all of them are relevant to an understanding of the bazaar economy. But surely the most important reason was the rise, under the combined stimulus of religious reformism and radical nationalism, of a new sort of zawia: the Istiqlal (*istiqlāl*, "independence"), Morocco's first mass political party.[67]

The casting of the Istiqlal (formally founded in 1943 but preceded by a number of clandestine cadre organizations from 1930) into the zawia form has often been noted. Stimulated originally by the Islamic reform movement, *s-salafīya,* the Istiqlal was opposed to the existing

162

zawias, as indeed they tended to be to one another, and put itself forward, as they had before it, as an improved, more authentic version of the brotherhood tradition. The proto-Istiqlal group, the organization that grew out of the latif agitation, actually called itself the Zawia, and its head, later the leader of Istiqlal proper and Morocco's most prominent nationalist, Allal Al-Fassi, was considered its sheikh; the group was referred to, on the usual model, as the Allaliya, its adherents as Allaliyins. The chapters were called *ṭā'ifa* ("part," "portion"), in Morocco a synonym for zawia; the dues were called *ziāra,* on the pattern of contributions by the members to the sheikhs and muqqadems in the older zawias; the nationalist slogans were recited in the style of the traditional prayer chants; the members referred to one another as *ikwān* ("brethren"). And so on. As the movement developed, the zawia idiom weakened somewhat at the leadership levels in favor of the political party idiom. But in the countryside and in small towns like Sefrou – and, for that matter, among the urban masses – the zawia form remained strong. And in the revolution it, and the organizational pattern it reflected, served the movement and its cause well.

The earliest phases of the Istiqlal (i.e., those prior to its official foundation) seem to have had no formal representation in Sefrou, though from the latif agitation forward there were a number of sympathizers and even a dedicated adherent or two. The party itself was established in Sefrou in 1943, coincident with its national appearance, and of the original twenty-one members, all but three were bazaar traders or artisans.[68]

This bazaar economy aspect of the movement became crucial in the revolution. In 1946, a number of the leaders of the Istiqlal in Fez, including Allal Al-Fassi's brother, called the inner core of the Sefrou Istiqlal, together with a few militants from various smaller settlements in the area, to a midnight meeting at the house of a prominent Fez merchant living in Sefrou. At the meeting, the central leadership of the party offered to put up 100,000 rials (about $5,000) to each of eight men to set up grocery stores in various places in the Sefrou region to serve as centers for Istiqlal organization. The money, donated to the party by rich Fez merchants, was not turned over to the shopkeepers directly, but given as a credit to the most prominent of the Sefrou grocers, a man immigrant from the Sus in south Morocco, who then provided goods to the storekeepers, most of whom were themselves Sefrou townsmen. The storekeepers, who also traveled to rural markets, set up secondary satellite stores of their own, traded as usual, and prospered. But the main purpose was not commerce; it was the setting up of a nationalist network in the Sefrou area, a network that turned

Suq: the bazaar economy in Sefrou

163

out to be extraordinarily effective. The French never uncovered it, and Sefrou became one of the strongholds of the Istiqlal party.[69]

As the Istiqlal rose as the nationalist zawia as well as the bearer of Islamic reform, the older established zawias, led by the Kettaniyin, which was headed on the national level by a long-time Fez rival of Al-Fassi, Abdel Hayy Al-Kettani, became increasingly identified with the Protectorate. Except for the Kettaniyin, which grew more and more powerful in the countryside during this period, the older zawias do not seem to have actively cooperated with the French, but indeed to have been hostile to them, as to Christian domination of the Muslim world generally. But on the principle of "the enemy of my enemy is my friend," they generally supported, in a passive and even somewhat reluctant way (they would have really liked to find a way to be apolitical), Abdel Hayy's anti-Istiqlal, and eventually anti-king, activities. When Istiqlal, and even more clearly, the king, triumphed, they participated in Abdel Hayy's disgrace and have never fully recovered.[70] But though, at least for the moment, the zawia is no longer a central institution in Sefrou, it was critical in the formation of the bazaar economy and has left its stamp permanently on that economy. Indeed, as its spiritual style – a passionate devotionalism trained on charismatic figures – remains intense, the brotherhood pattern may again revive to give shape to the evolution not only of religious but of commercial and political life.

The Jewish community

The Jewish trading community provides, when set beside the Muslim, a model case in the delicacies of sociological comparison: From many points of view it looks exactly like the Muslim community; from as many others, totally different. The Jews were at once Sefrouis like any others and resoundingly themselves. Many of their institutions – in the bazaar setting, most of them – were direct counterparts to Muslim ones; often even the terminology was not changed. But the way those institutions were put together to form a pattern, the organizational whole they add to, was in such sharp contrast to the Muslim way as to be almost an answer to it. It is not possible to treat the Jews as just one more "tribe" in the Moroccan conglomerate, another nisba, though they were certainly that. Nor is it possible to treat them as a set-apart pariah community, deviant and self-contained, though they were as certainly that too. Moroccan to the core and Jewish to the same core, they were heritors of a tradition double and indivisible and in no way marginal.[71]

164

This curious just-the-same, utterly different image the Jews presented was made possible by the street cosmopolitanism, domestic communalism pattern of social integration mentioned earlier in connection with nisba classification. In public contexts, and most especially the bazaar (where, it will be recalled from Tables 1 and 2, nearly 90 percent of adult male Jews were in one way or another employed), Jews mixed with Muslims under uniform ground rules, which, to an extent difficult to credit for those whose ideas about Jews in traditional trade are based on the role they played in premodern Europe, were indifferent to religious status. There was, of course, some penetration of communal concerns into the bazaar setting (exclusively Jewish trades, like goldworking and tinsmithing, and such special phenomena as kosher butchers), but what is remarkable is not how much there was but how little. The cash nexus was here quite real; the Jew was cloth seller, peddler, shopkeeper, shoemaker, or porter before he was Jew, and dealt and was dealt with as such.[72] Contrariwise, there was some penetration of general Moroccan patterns of life into the communal area: Jewish kinship patterns were not all that unlike Muslim; Jews not only had saints of their own but often honored Muslim ones as well; and Arabic, not Hebrew, was the language of the home. But this penetration too was minor: As a community (Heb. *qahal*), the Jewish population formed a world very much its own.

Suq: the bazaar economy in Sefrou

The Jews in the mellah

That world was marked by three main characteristics: hyperorganization, thoroughgoing plutocracy, and intense piety. Pressed in behind the walls of their own quarter, the *mellāḥ,* where, until the Protectorate they were obliged to live, the Jews seem to have concentrated their social personality as the Muslims diffused theirs. Locked each night in their quarter (no non-Jew could enter after dark), an increasingly crowded and unexpandable ghetto, whose buildings raised up like miniskyscrapers to accommodate the pressure, the Jews developed a society whose closest counterpart, the religiosity perhaps somewhat aside, seems to be the merchant oligarchies of Renaissance Italy.[73]

Hyperorganization was the aspect in which the Jewish community was most strikingly different from the Muslim. The dominating institution was a small band of magnates called "the committee" (Heb. *ha-maᶜamad*).[74] In Sefrou, the committee had four members up until the 1940s, when a minirevolt by younger, "evolved" Jews forced it to expand to six. Nominally elected, the members were in fact inevitably

165

the richest mercantile figures in the community, and once in place they stayed there until it was time, through aging or death, to coopt their replacements. The plutocracy thus created was further extended by a formal division of the community into five classes of steeply increasing numbers and even more steeply declining wealth: (1) those who had to pay 1,000 rials (in the 1930s, about $50) every six months at the two holiday seasons, Passover and the High Holy Days; (2) those who had to pay 500 rials; (3) those who had to pay 250 rials; (4) those who had to pay 125 rials; and (5) those, the poor, who had to pay nothing and to whom the committee, whose job it was to organize the holidays, distributed this money on behalf of the community. The committee's monopolization of charity, at least of this sort, was official: It was explicitly forbidden for individuals to give private alms (or to beg), and few seem to have done so. This hierarchy of welfare obligations, which was at the same time an economic, a social, and a political hierarchy, was the general backbone of the social pattern I referred to earlier as plutocratic paternalism. "On peut," as Le Tourneau said with respect to the slightly larger Fez committee (it had ten members), "le considérer comme un conseil de gestion de la 'firme Mellah.' "[75]

As such a "conseil de gestion" of such a "firme," the committee faced in several directions: outward, toward the Muslim government, and later the French; downward, toward an enormously complex set of public sodalities controlled and regulated by it; and sideways, so to speak, toward a culturally powerful rabbinate standing moral guard over its, and everyone else's, behavior.

Of these, the connection with the state was perhaps the least important, because in the wider world of Moroccan society individual Jews defended their own interests on the same terms, and through the same maneuvers and institutions, as did the Muslims. A few formal matters aside, the general society and its rulers did not deal with the Jews as an undivided collectivity, but as just so many separate Jews scattered in among so many separate Muslims.[76] What was needed in the role of official representative to the state – the *šaīḵ l-Yahūd* (Heb. *nagīd*) – was someone nerveless enough to haggle with the established powers, Muslim or French, concerning Jewish rights, constraints, grievances, hopes, and obligations. In Sefrou, a single wealthy family, popularly regarded as "stubborn but not intelligent" provided the sheikh al-Yahud for several generations in the nineteenth and early twentieth centuries until an excess of stubbornness at the expense of intelligence led the sultan to inform Sefrou's Jews that he did not much care whom they had for their sheikh so long as he did not come from that family, a suggestion – it came in the form of a decree – to which the community instantly, and apparently with some enthusiasm, acceded. The sheikh, who was simultaneously chairman of the committee, was mainly concerned with relations to the authorities; the internal functions often ascribed, usually rather vaguely, to him in the literature (enforcement of committee decisions, collection of contributions, maintenance of peace) seem to have been reflexes of his formal leadership of the committee and not independent, personal powers. Externally of some consequence because of his contacts with the local qaids and pashas, and occasionally with the royal court itself, his role inside the community was about the same as that of his peers: one of the ruling clique of affluent merchants. As he was not even necessarily the most substantial of them, they could be counted on to contain any "king of the Jews" ambitions he might harbor.[77]

Of the public sodalities (Ar. *ribāᶜ*, sg. *rabᶜ*; Heb. *ḥebrah*) that were regulated by the committee and formed the internal structure of the community, the most important was one that embraced the entire population and was named after one of the saints venerated in a nearby cave, the Jewish equivalent of Sidi Ali Buseghine, Rabbi Simaun. The Simaun rebaa had three sections (also referred to as rebaa), each with its own chairman, vice chairman, and "messenger." Section membership for both men and women was by patrifiliation: One belonged to the section to which one's father belonged. The functions of the organization were broadly social. At burial, the relevant section prepared the corpse, conducted the funeral, and comforted the survivors. When Jews quarreled among themselves, the section officers sought to settle the matter before it exploded into a public dispute, in which case the committee settled it, usually with advice from the rabbinate. Indeed, all intra-Jewish issues, conflictual or not, were handled within the Simaun rebaa whenever possible.[78] But besides the Simaun rebaa there was a large number – informants speak, vaguely, of *bezzef* ("lots"), and I managed to elicit about a dozen – of less formal, voluntary sodalities, engaged in various social, religious, and philanthropic activities: making clothes for the poor, helping them get married, finding housing for them, supporting orphanages, financing synagogues, reading the Torah, founding schools.[79] In comparison with the Muslim community, where about the only corporate groups worthy of the name, and those but barely, were the zawias and hentas, the Jewish community was a maze of intensely solidary associations dominated in every case by members of the same small band – fifteen, twenty, or twenty-five at the most – of very rich merchants, a thoroughly interlocked directorate of which the committee was but the visible arm.[80]

167

Yet, for all the committee's power, there was another institution that constrained the oligarchy's behavior from within the community as the Muslim or French state constrained it from without: the rabbinical court (Heb. *bēth dīn*). The religious life of the community need not be described in any detail here. In its formal outlines it was not different from that of other maghrebi communities, and its tone, rigorous to the point of zealotry, would take a monograph to convey. The point is that, like the institutions of Islam in the wider society, Jewish institutions had more than spiritual consequences. As the Muslim community had its tolba (individuals claiming some degree of religious learning, skill, or piety beyond the normal run of men and regarding themselves as the spiritual conscience of the population), the Jewish had its *ḥazzānīn* (a Hebrew term strictly meaning "cantor[s]," but popularly extended by the general Muslim population, and in colloquial contexts by the Jews themselves, to apply to the religious class generally: scholars, ritual slaughterers, teachers in Talmudic schools, rabbis, judges, even just especially pious men). Of these, three, headed by the chief rabbi of the community, called *rāv* ("master") or *ḥakām* ("sage"), sat on the religious court and were known as *dayyānīn* ("judges"). The jurisdiction of the court extended, as did the differently organized qadi court among the Muslims, only to those aspects of social life explicitly covered by religious law: most especially marriage, divorce, and inheritance.[81] The main impact of the religious tribunal on the economic and political life of the community stemmed from its ability to criticize dominant figures from a spiritually secured moral base. The effectiveness with which the tribunal accomplished this and thus formed, with the hazzan class generally, a genuine counterweight to the merchant oligarchy, varied with individuals and circumstances. Depending upon the character of the judges, especially the rav, one could get a narrowly legalistic conception of the judge's office, the hazzan role, and indeed of religious life generally that left the plutocrats a largely free hand, or one could get a broadly moral conception that subjected the plutocrats to a drumfire of prophetlike criticism from the local agents of God's justice. But whatever the momentary situation, the rabbinical court was, aside from its particular judicial functions, a potential counterbalance to the power of the committee and its clientele.

The Jews in the bazaar

When one turns from this brief description of the internal structure of the Jewish community to the integration of its labor force into the bazaar, it is first necessary to forestall a common misconception, one

Table 7. *Comparative percent of Muslim and Jewish bazaar workers in large-, medium-, and small-scale activities, 1960[a]*

	Large scale	Medium scale	Small scale
Muslims			
(N = 1,966)	3	38	59
Jews			
(N = 526)	3	44	53

[a]The large-, medium-, and small-scale classifications are by occupational category and were made totally independently of ethnic considerations. Employment of alternative culting points does not alter the picture appreciably.
Source: Data from official 1960 Census of Sefrou.

Table 8. *Comparative percent of Muslim and Jewish bazaar workers in commerce and artisanry, 1960*

	Commerce	Artisanry
Muslims	28	72
Jews	46	54

Source: Data from official 1960 Census of Sefrou.

even many Moroccans (though none who have themselves spent any significant amount of time in bazaar occupations) hold: namely, that the Jews as a group had a specially privileged role within the bazaar. In Sefrou, at least, this was not the case. As Table 7 shows, the distribution of Jewish merchants and artisans across the economic class structure was, to the degree one can measure it, very similar to that of the Muslim.[82]

If, however, one looks at the situation in terms not of scale of operation but of types (Table 8), a striking difference between the two groups appears: Whereas the Jews are rather equally divided between commercial and artisanal occupations, the Muslims are heavily weighted toward the artisan side.[83] In part, this merely reflects certain value differences between the two groups, the Muslims regarding craft labor more highly than the Jews. In part, it reflects history, the Jews having been relatively more prominent in the 169 largely nonartisanal caravan trade in nineteenth-century Sefrou. But in the main it reflects the nature of the Jewish role as it developed, given those values and that history, in the evolving opportunity structure of the bazaar economy: The Jews became the intermediaries between the (largely) Arab-speaking population of the town and the (largely) Berber-speaking population of the countryside.[84]

As remarked above, the role of the Jews in connecting Sefrou's region-focusing bazaar to the cloud of locality-focusing bazaars growing up around it was crucial from the earliest stages of the transition from passage to central place trade and to some extent even preceded them. Just why this should have been so, why the Arabic speakers of Sais Plain Morocco and the Berber speakers of Middle Atlas should have needed a third element distinct from them both to relate them commercially, can only be a matter for speculation. The desire of intensely competitive groups – suspicious of each other's actions, jealous of each other's power, and frightened of each other's ambitions – to conduct their trade through politically impotent agents, individuals who could bring neither force nor authority to bear in the exchange process and could achieve nothing more than wealth by means of it, is perhaps part of the answer. A related desire to divest trading activities of any meaning beyond the cash and carry and so blunt their acculturative force may be another. But whatever the reason, the fact had a profound impact, virtually a determining one, on the shaping of Jewish activities in the bazaar economy.

In the first place, it meant that Jewish trade was heavily rural-oriented. Not only were many Jews engaged in itinerant petty commerce, but as artisans they were heavily concentrated in a very few light crafts, particularly shoemaking and tailoring, specifically oriented to a rural clientele.[85] In the second place, it meant that, within the town, the various strands of trade were drawn up into a very few hands, those again of the dominant figures of the community. In contrast to the Muslim pattern of long sequences of ad hoc two-person connections between traders of every size and description, running in diverse directions and crossing and recrossing one another in hopeless complexity, now and then converging momentarily on some more formidable figure emerging from the crowd and then immediately scattering again, the Jewish pattern consisted of a large mass of marginal and semimarginal operators directly and almost totally dependent on one or another of a dozen or two established financiers. The similar distribution of Muslim and Jewish traders across the very gross categories of large, small, and medium scale shown in Table 7 thus masks a sharp difference in the nature of the relations among individuals in those categories in the two groups. Among the Muslims, the leading traders stood out from the rest; among the Jews, they stood over the rest.

Each of the major figures – the "sitting" (*gles*) Jews referred to earlier – had attached exclusively and more or less permanently to him a number of itinerant merchants – "riding" (*rkeb*) Jews.[86] The riding Jews traveled about the countryside, often in twos and threes, their goods loaded onto donkeys. They camped in areas where their backers had established updated versions of the old mezrag trade-place arrangement with a local power (the major sitting Jews seem to have parceled out spheres of influence in the countryside in a conscious, precise, and systematic manner, to the point where exactly whose writ ran exactly where is still recallable today) at the edge of one or another Berber settlement. There they set up a makeshift shop out of which, as well as in the local periodic bazaar and even – only a Jew could approach a Berber woman in her home – door to door, they peddled cloth, ready-made clothes, shoes, domestic implements, soap, sugar, salt, tea, matches, perfumes, medicines, oil, spices, jewelry, talismans, and, increasingly, cheap imported manufactures such as combs, clocks, and mirrors. On the buying side they purchased, again both directly and more and more in the expanding local suqs, hides, wool, animals, olives, and grain, which the Berbers themselves then carried to the sitting Jews in town. They lent money, either outright or through taking pawns, and they arranged share contracts (oral, as all these arrangements) concerning animals or olives in which the Jews purchased beasts or trees, the Berbers raised and cared for them, and the returns were, by one or another elaborate formula, divided. After a month or six weeks of this the Jews moved on to another location of the same sort, repeated the process, and then moved on again.

The riding Jews were, in fact, riding, camp to camp, suq to suq, virtually the whole of the year, returning to Sefrou for any length of time only during the two main holiday seasons.[87] In town, the sitting Jews sat, sources not only of capital for the riding Jews, but of food and housing, and indeed of a whole range of welfare services, for the latter's families, including governance of their moral and religious life. Though not explicitly conceived as such, the riding Jews were almost as much the sitting Jews' servants as their agents. Toward the artisans, most of whom, especially in shoemaking and tailoring, were also dirt poor, the financiers had a similar relation, capitalizing them, engrossing their output, and providing for their subsistence almost as an extension of an expanded family economy. The welfare hierarchy that governed community life generally provided the framework for com-

171

mercial relations within the community as well. Outside the community, whether dealing with a Berber pastoralist, a town weaver, or a Fez importer, the Jews fitted, as mentioned, into the more general structure of the bazaar as a whole. Indeed, in Sefrou at least, tying town and country together, permanent suq and periodic, they helped create the bazaar.[88]

This done, they then turned, as the Protectorate period advanced, toward yet another form of commercial pioneering, the development of the modern business district, the show-window bazaar connecting the European community – by the 1930s some 700 or 800 people – commercially to the local economy. The first modern-type grocery stores, called épiceries rather than hanuts, along the highroad were opened by Jews, soon followed by other European-oriented businesses: bars, furniture stores, gas stations, garages, pharmacies, bicycle shops, (Western) tailors, and eventually a motion picture house. In time, some Muslims became involved in this expansion, but the formative phase (which ended, as did so much else, in 1940) seems to have been largely Jewish.[89] By 1969, when the European population had fallen to less than 100, and the Jewish to less than 400, about ten out of the thirty-five or forty business-district-type enterprises were still Jewish-owned. But the end of that development, like the end of the community generally, was drawing near. Having helped in turn to project Sefrou into the caravan trade, link it to the rural bazaar, and adjust it to enclave capitalism, the Jews disappeared from the scene to apply their practiced ability to change with change in another history.

The bazaar as an economic institution

Product of a transformation of long-distance caravan trade into short-distance central place trade, set in the context of Moroccan ideas of piety, community, and personal identity, and animated by a jumble of received practices, borrowed tastes, and changing possibilities, the bazaar is also, of course, a social mechanism for the production and exchange of goods and services: an economic system. It is not there, in the first instance, to express Moroccan religious conceptions or to exemplify Moroccan social arrangements, but to bring supply crowds and demand crowds usefully together. The institutional structures and practical procedures through which it does this (and changes them thus from mere crowds to formed webs of personal connection) are as distinctive a characteristic as nisba categorization, habus property law, or the moral impact of zawia mysticism.

172　　　Looked at in this light – as a ramifying pattern of material transactions, most of them face to face – the bazaar consists in the integration of physically separated marketplaces into a continuous system. In part, this integration is accomplished spatiotemporally, as one market-day area overlaps with the next, chain-mail fashion, across virtually the whole of Morocco. In part, it is accomplished hierarchically, as national emporiums, region-focusing markets, and locality-focusing markets reach out toward one another in a center and subcenter, headquarters and outpost fashion. And in part it is accomplished functionally, as the wheat-dominated markets of the plain, the wool-dominated ones of the steppe, the olive markets of the piedmont, and the manufactures ones of the coast balance off their specialties.

Suq: the bazaar economy in Sefrou

But it is not the marketplaces that do all this. It is those who frequent them: the *sūwwāqa*.

Sūwwāq (sg.) is a term for which no precise equivalent exists in English. It covers anyone who attends markets, of whatever size and for whatever purpose, with some regularity; an habitué of suqs. It includes the countryman bringing his two or three sheep or his basket of barley into a mountain bazaar in search of a little cash, together with the great Fez or Marrakech engrosser pyramiding deals in his urban warehouse. It includes buyer and seller, producer and consumer, master and apprentice, transporter, auctioneer, moneylender, and market official. It includes the man who squats on a carpet and tells sad stories of the death of kings, the man who wanders through the crowd with a zawia pennant collecting pious contributions, the man who sits behind a small table and writes whorled, grandiloquent letters to order; and it includes the gambler, the pickpocket, the snake charmer, the prostitute, even the idler just hanging around as part of the life (a secondary meaning of *sūwwāqa* is "rabble," "mob"), so long as they pursue their occupations in a place called a suq. What sets any one Moroccan marketplace off from any other one, and one section of such a marketplace from another section, is less where it is located, how it is housed, or even its size, than the types of suwwaqs characteristically found there.

This point is of some importance because of a tendency in what literature there is on Moroccan suqs to draw sharp contrasts between them along rural-urban lines, and in particular to characterize so-called tribal markets as a distinct economic type.[90] The fact is that, at least so far as Morocco is concerned, the rural or "tribal" market and the urban or "bourgeois" market are, in analytical terms, the same institution. Suqs may be developed or undeveloped, permanent or periodic, crowded alleyway quarters in built-up towns or sprawling tent camps set up for the day in an open field, and they may serve whole sections

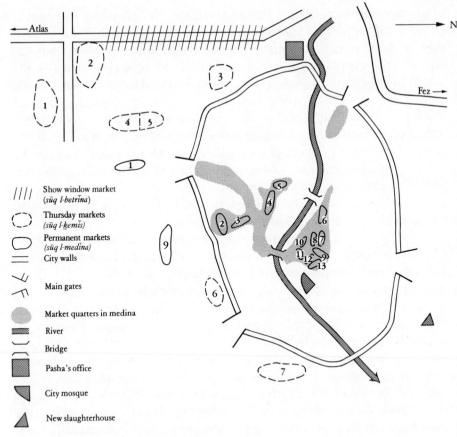

Figure 4. The markets of Sefrou, 1968–9.

Thursday markets
1 *Sūq l-koḍra*: vegetables, fruits, spices
2 *Sūq l-kṣiba (l-behayīm, l-begra)*: sheep, goats, cattle, donkeys
3 *Sūq s-sella*: baskets, woven mats, chickens, eggs, salt
4 *Sūq z-zraᶜ (l-gemeḥ)*: grain, beans
5 *Sūq ṣ-ṣūf*: wool
6 *Jutīya (kerīa)*: secondhand goods, flea market
7 *Sūq z-zrābī*: rugs, textiles, clothes, medicines, storytellers, odds and ends

Permanent markets
1 *Terrāfīn*: shoemakers, shoe repairers
2 *Šwiqa (keḍḍāra)*: vegetables, fruits
3 *Blaṣa (gezzāra)*: butchers
4 *Kiyyāṭa*: tailors
5 *Ḥarrāra*: silk
6 *Qīsarīya (bezzāziyīn)*: cloth, jewelry
7 *Bradᶜīya (semmārīn)*: saddlemakers, horseshoers
8 *Ḥaddādīn*: blacksmiths
9 *Ṅajjārīn*: carpenters (two locations)
10 *Qsādrīya*: tinsmiths
11 *Ṭiyyābīn (kiffitiyīn)*: cooked food
12 *Ṭḥīnīya (kebbāzīn)*: flour, baked bread, sweet rolls
13 *Ḥajjāmīn*: barbers, cuppers

174

of the country or a handful or nearby villages. But their basic organization and mode of functioning vary very little. A suq is a suq, in Fez or in the Atlas, in cloth or in camels. The players differ (and the stakes), but not the shape of the game.[91]

Ecology: the suq on the ground

Three aspects of a suq, as suq, need to be addressed in describing it: (1) its physical form – how it is laid out, populated, sectioned into parts; (2) its social form – how practical relationships (seller and buyer, lender and borrower, master and apprentice, professional and layman) are ordered and regulated with it; and (3) its dynamics, the characteristic patterns of activity it sustains – how bazaar actors behave and why. For convention's sake, we begin with the first; hard data give a place to stand, or seem to. But we might as well have started with either of the other two, for they are all, in actuality, interfused – part of a single reality suwwaqs inhabit.

To reprise an earlier discussion, the main sub-elements of the Sefrou bazaar are (1) "the old city bazaar" (*sūq l-medīna*), which during the past thirty years or so has spilled over into the newer quarters immediately outside the walls; (2) "the Thursday bazaar" (*sūq l-ḵemīs*), which connects Sefrou with the periodic market system of the region generally and thus integrates it into the wheat-sheep-and-olive economy of the countryside; and (3) "the show-window bazaar" (*sūq l-betrīna*) of the French-built new town, which integrates Sefrou into the cosmopolitan economy of developed Morocco – Fez, Rabat, Casablanca, and beyond. The layout of these various bazaars can be seen in detail in Annex A, where each established enterprise is mapped and classified. A general picture can be obtained from Figure 4, which summarizes in schematic form what is recounted in Annex A.[92] The figure shows the Sefrou market at its fullest extent, on market day, when the popula-

Note to Figure 4: Suqs are referred to in various ways, and I have given in each case what seems to me the most popular (and where two seem about equally current, an alternative in parenthesis) in Sefrou ca. 1968–9. Suqs named after occupations may be designated by either the masculine (*terrāfīn, nejjārīn, haddādīn*) or the feminine (*terrāfa, nejjāra, haddāda*) sound plural. I have again given what seems to me the more common usage in each case, but the alternative (*kiyyātin, hajjāma*) is almost always also current. It is usually possible, particularly when a sort of good (e.g., flour, silk) rather than a type of skill (e.g., tailoring, carpentry) is involved, to use the combining form, as with the Thursday markets – *sūq l-tḥin* ("flour market"), *sūq l-ḥrir* ("silk market") – or the "owners of" (*mwalin*; sg. *mūl*) form – *mwālin l-tḥin* ("flour owners"), *mwālin l-ḥrir* ("silk owners"). Finally, for almost all trades, not just the *tḥinīya, bradᶜīya*, etc. of the list, where it is preferred, the plural of the occupational nisba – *ḥrārīya* ("silk-merchantish or "silks area", a barbarous translation, but the closest I can get); *nejjārīya* ("carpenterish area") – is usually acceptable. It is possible that actual choices in these matters reflect subtle conceptual, and thus sociological, differences, rather than being mere free variants. If so, I cannot yet sort them out.

tion of the town probably doubles or more as, by foot, donkey, mule, bus, and truck, the countrymen (and suwwaqs from other towns) stream in to trade.

The first thing that leaps to notice from Figure 4 is that all the Thursday markets, each quite definitely specialized, are located outside the walls in the new quarters to the south. As reference to Annex B ("The Markets of Sefrou around 1910") will make apparent, this has not always been the case. Each of these markets was originally inside the medina amid the permanent ones, which latter were themselves then rather more periodic affairs, functioning with much force only on Thursdays, than they have since become. By 1936, when Le Tourneau made a brief survey of the periodic markets in Sefrou town (he paid only glancing attention to the permanent ones, which were just then beginning to become truly such), all save the flea market had moved out to a single location—the place where the wool and grain markets are today. At that time, the animal market immediately adjoined this "vaste enclos bordé de boutiques et de magasins," to which it was physically connected by an arcade. In addition to wool, wheat, barley, maize, and beans, such items as salt, rugs, charcoal, pots, baskets, mats, fruit, vegetables, chickens, and eggs were sold in this French-built (1931) *marsi (i.e., Fr. marché)*.[93] By 1951, when Si Bekkai, then pasha of Sefrou, made an even more cursory survey (though one that did distinguish the periodic and permanent aspects of the bazaar, a contrast it was no longer possible to miss), the animal market had been moved, "pour des raisons faciles a concevoir," to its present location. At the same time, the rug and basket traders had drifted, or been pushed, to their separate places, leaving the "vaste enclos" (it is only about 1,000 square meters) exclusively to wool at one end and cereals, legumes, fruits, and vegetables at the other.[94] The establishment of an external Thursday market in vegetables and fruits, separate both from a refurbished permanent vegetable market within the medina and from the wool-wheat extramural one, in the late 1960s completed the process; no periodic market remained within the old city.[95]

The reasons for this evolution, if that is what it should be called, are the obvious ones: expansion and solidification of commerce (including a sharpening differentiation of permanent bazaar trade from periodic); overcrowding of the medina, mainly as a result of rural in-migration; and French (and now Moroccan) attempts at more systematic, "functional" zoning.[96] There are government plans to rationalize further the Sefrou market layout to the point where all commercial and industrial activity will be located outside the medina, leaving the latter wholly residential – an archaic slum awaiting only the next lurch toward "modernity" to be razed altogether.

As for the permanent markets (of which only those more commonly referred to are indicated in Figure 4), perhaps the most striking thing about them is that they exist. Despite the enormous expansion in numbers of traders (since 1900, over 300 percent, as indicated in Table 1), trades (about a third of the trades of Sefrou postdate the establishment of the Protectorate), and volume of trade (difficult to estimate numerically, but universally attested to by knowledgeable informants), activity remains strongly localized in occupational terms, as demonstrated in Tables 9 through 11. It is still the case, as it was in 1910, 1935, and 1950, that most forms of commercial and artisanal activity cluster together in definite – usually quite small – sections of the town.[97]

The permanent, periodic, and show-window bazaars differ in physical appearance as well.

The last, with its glass-fronted stores, sidewalk cafés, and motion picture houses strung out along the main street (Boulevard Mohammed V), with signs proclaiming what they are and often the owner's name and telephone number, looks about like any small-town business district – complete with sidewalks, parking zones, a stoplight, and the inevitable *ronde pointe* – in provincial France.

The periodic marketplaces consist of large cleared areas, on a lively day packed beyond imagination with would-be buyers and sellers: a collection of small-scale medieval fairs. The animal marketplace is enclosed by walls, the sellers of goats, sheep, cattle, donkeys, and mules, occupying distinct regions within it. They stay put with their animal(s) while the buyers wander among them, inspecting, bargaining, choosing. The wool, grain, and bean marketplace is bordered, as Le Tourneau noted, with shoplike buildings, except that all of them now are used either to house motor-driven mills (sg. *ṭāḥūna*) or as storage houses (sg. *ḵzīn*). The grain, beans, and wool are piled by their vendors in large heaps around the open plaza, also according to established place, and a group of scale owners (sg. *mūl l-mīzān*) occupies a weighing shed at one end. The other periodic marketplaces show a similar pattern: The offerer of rugs or baskets or clothes or vegetables sits at his place, his *mūḍac*, as possible buyers wander by to look, haggle, and decide. Sellers (auctioneers, of whom more later, aside) virtually never wander about hawking their wares.

In the permanent marketplaces, the "sitting pattern," which is what selling there is commonly called (*gles f-l-ḥanūt,* "sitting in a shop") is even more pronounced. Each trader has a small, usually wooden cubi-

Table 9. *Distribution of strongly localized trades in Sefrou, 1968–9*

Trade	Number in suq area[a]	Total number	Percent in suq area
Blacksmith (*ḥaddād*)	15	15	100
Saddlemaker/horseshoer (*bradᶜī/semmār*)	7	7	100
Vegetable and fruit seller (*keddar*)	82	90	91
Butcher (*gezzār*)	20	22	91
Prepared-food seller (*ṭiyyāb*)	12	15	80
Cloth merchant (*mūl l-kettān, mūl t-tūb*)	25	35	71
Tinsmith (*qṣādrī*)	7	10	70
Tailor (*kiyyāt*)[b]	52	73	70
Weaver (*derrāz*)	15	22	68
Hardware/spice seller (*mūl l-ḥadīd*)[c]	6	10	60
Silk merchant (*ḥarrār, ḥrārī*)	13	33	59
Carpenter (*nejjār*)[d]	10	18	56
Odds-and-ends seller (*kordāwī*)	9	17	53
Shoemaker (*ṭerrāf*)	16	31	52
Barber/cupper (*ḥajjām*)[e]	20	42	48
Miller (*teḥḥān*)[f]	5	12	42
Ready-made clothes seller	16	36	41
Overall	330	488	68

[a] By suq area is meant the part of the town informants regard as the place where members of the trade are normally to be found, their *mūḍaᶜ* or *reḥba* ("place," "space"). Such areas, which are named, in various ways, after the trade concerned (see Figure 4), are admittedly fuzzy at the edges, necessitating some practical judgments on the part of the ethnographer about where to draw the line. But their overall location is perfectly consensual for all informants. All are quite small, never more than a few hundred square meters, most a good deal less.

[b] The tailors are in two locations, rather than one. Thirty-four (47%) are in the old khiyyata of Figure 4; eighteen more have clustered near the cloth market, the Qisariya, giving the composite 70% figure.

[c] All (six) of the traditional-type hardware/spice traders are in one region (*Reḥbt l-ᶜawed;* see Figure A.13, Annex A). The other four, somewhat more "modern" in form, are in the new quarter, Derb l-Miter (Sections A.5 and A.6 on Figure A.1 of Annex A).

[d] Only two carpenters remain in the old area of Annex B; the new carpenters' suq is outside the medina in Derb l-Miter.

[e] All old-fashioned barbers (those who also serve as cuppers) are in the old hajjama suq; the appearance of new-style barbers in the new quarters is quite recent.

[f] Four of the five millers run modern machine-driven grain mills located around the Thursday grain market. The scattered millers are the remnants, all outside the medina, of the water-driven-mill (*rḥa b-l-mā*) industry, once quite large, which the 1950 flood more or less wiped out.

Source: Based on data presented in Annex A plus informants' judgments about the location of the various suqs.

Table 10. *Distribution of moderately and weakly localized trades in Sefrou, 1968–9*

Trade	Location
Moderately localized trades	
Wheat and bean trader (*mūl z-zraʿ; mūl l-fūl*)	Operate mainly in Thursday market where many have storage houses and some own or share in mills. Also travel to rural markets.
Wool trader (*mūl ṣ-ṣuf*)	Operate in Thursday market and travel to rural ones.
Café keeper (*qehwājī*)	Mainly clustered along Fez road and near gates to medina.
Baker (*mūl l-ferrān; kebbāz*)	Distributed by quarter, theoretically (and for most part actually) one to each quarter.
Bathhouse keeper (*mūl l-ḥammām*)	As bakers. Bakers and bathhouse keepers are only trades not confined to properly suq areas of town, but commonly found in midst of residential areas. See separate listing in Annex B.
Lime kiln (*kūša*)	There are ten or so lime kilns for making whitewash located in the rocky hillsides just south of town in a definite cluster (not mapped in Annex A). Most are owned by old Sefroui townsmen and worked by rural in-migrants. Product is sold mainly by hardward/spice merchants.
Prostitute (*qaḥba*)	Prostitutes are difficult to census for obvious reasons, but most live in and around mellah, which has turned into a slum-cum-red-light district since departure of Jews to the new quarters. Ready-made clothes dealers, café keepers, etc., act as pimps.
Flour and bread seller (*mūl l-ṭḥīn wa l-kubz*)	The four or five who are left still in tihiniya. Flour is now mostly sold in grocery stores.
Porter (*ḥemmāl; zerzai*)	Hang out, waiting for jobs, just outside the major gates of town. Some have crude handcarts; some merely bear things on their backs.
Casual laborer (*keddām*)	Casual laborers, whose numbers fluctuate with season and circumstance between about ten and about a hundred, hang out, waiting for pickup work, around plaza in front of Mkam gates, along edge of park in front of pasha's office, and near public works and public welfare offices in Derb l-Miter (see Figures A.5 and A.11, Annex A).

179

Table 10. (*cont.*)

Scribe (*kātib*)	Sit at small tables in arcade in front of Merba^c gate and in various Thursday markets.

Weakly or nonlocalized trades

Grocer (*beqqāl*)	Small grocers are found almost everywhere in suq areas outside medina. However, the very largest ones (their stores are called *herī,* roughly "depot," "emporium"), who serve as suppliers to many of the others and to small shops in villages, are concentrated just outside Merba^c gate (see Figure A.5, Annex A).
Mason (*bennaāī*)	Masons have no business abode in most cases, though a few large ones have storage yards in the new quarters.
Tobacconist (*saka*)	Tobacconists are randomly scattered.
Auctioneer (*dellāl*), broker (*semsār*), arbitrager (*sebaībī*)	These are unlocalized by profession. They are discussed further in text.
Home spinner (*ḡezzāla*)	Home spinning is connected to the wool trade and carried out by women in their homes under a putting-out system, mediated by women engrossers, who then sell the produce in a special women's market. This is discussed in text.
Hashish seller (*mūl l-kīf*)	Hashish selling is at least formally illegal and is conducted semiclandestinely at various well-known points scattered around town. Most hashish comes into Sefrou area from Rif area of northeast Morocco.

Various marginal trades such as (traditional) plumber (*qwādsī*), musician (*šaik̲*), tile maker (*zellaiz̆ī*), cord maker (*šerrāt*) are not considered. What representatives of them still exist are scattered randomly about.

Source: Based on data presented in Annex A plus informants' judgments about the location of the various suqs.

cle (a hanut) a couple of meters wide, deep, and high in most cases, rarely more than 3 or 4 meters, where he squats with his goods about him as market goers stream by in front of him (see Figure 5). Craft ateliers, also called hanuts, are about the same, except that they are oriented toward the workplace inside the cubicle rather than toward the street, and, of course, the interior layout is adjusted to the particular demands of the craft.

The various bazaars of Sefrou thus are distinctive in layout, architecture, and the flow of traffic. Yet, because they all at base *are* bazaars of one sort or another, highly specialized areas set apart exclusively for craft and trade, the distinctions, though real, have not hardened into
180 divisions.[98] There is the boutiquier propriety of the business district;

Table 11. *Distribution of modern trades in Sefrou, 1968–9*[a]

Wholly new trades

Bicycle seller and repairman (*sīklist*)[b]
Radio repairman (*kehrabī*)[c]
Electrical supplies seller (radios, refrigerators, fans, lighting fixtures, etc.) (*mūl l-'ālāt
   l-kehrabā*)[c]
Watchmaker (*mūl l-mwāgen*)[b]
Gasoline station keeper (*pumpīst*)[e]
Garage mechanic, auto parts seller (*garājīst*)[d]
Transport worker: trucker (*mūl l-kamiūn*), bus owner or driver (*mūl l-kār*), taxi owner
   or driver (*mūl t-taksi*)[e]
Electrician (*mūl ḍ-ḍū*)[c]
Movie house owner (*mūl s-sinima*)[e]
Pharmacist (*mūl d-dwā*)[c]
Photographer (*ṣuwwūr*)[c]
Physician (*ṭabīb*)

Modern versions of older trades

Grocer (*pīserī*)[c]
Tailor (*taīyūr*)[c]
Barber (*kwāfūr*)[c]
Plumber (*plumbī*)[b]
Carpenter, sawmill owner (*menīsiwī*)
Innkeeper (*mūl l-uṭīl*)[c]

[a] Modern trades may be loosely divided (though Sefrouis do not) into those that are
wholly new, imported from the West, and those that are modernized versions of older
trades. Some modern trades have Arabic names (*suwwūr*, photographer), some have
Arabized French names (*menīsiwī*, carpenter, sawmill owner, from *menuisier*), and
some have a mixture of both (*mūl l-uṭīl*, innkeeper).
[b] Trades located in Derb l-Miter (see Figures A.5–A.7, Annex A).
[c] Trades located in show-window bazaar (see Figures A.2–A.4, Annex A).
[d] Clustered at upper end of Derb l-Miter (see Figures A.3 and A.5, Annex A).
[e] Vehicles garaged at, and buses and taxis operate out of, station in front of Mkam
Gate (see Figure A.11, Annex A).
Source: Based on data presented in Annex A plus informants' judgments about the
location of the various suqs.

there is the carnivalesque, country-fair hubbub of the animal, grain, or
rug markets; there is the casbah mysteriousness of the winding, cob-
blestone thoroughfares of the medina, some covered with lattices and
none wide or level enough to accommodate wheeled vehicles; and
there is the neither-this-nor-that, square-buildings, gridstreet attempt
at urban regularity of the new quarters (Derb l-Miter, "Metric
Street[s]") that the persistence of older styles of doing things has turned
into a medina housed in a bourgade. These are all discernible enough to
the eye of the suwwaq, as are the subareas and the sub-subareas within
them. But they are, to that same eye, also mere locales, various arenas
in a single, continuous, entangled whole: *Sūq Ṣ-Ṣefru.*

181

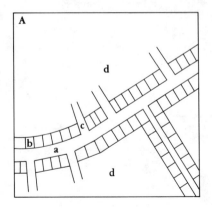
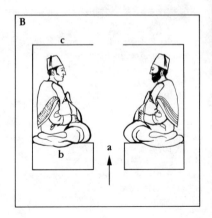

Figure 5. Permanent shops. *A.* Air view of shop layout in part of permanent market: *a,* street *(zenqa); b,* shop *(ḥānūt); c,* alley *(derb); d,* residential quarter (hūma). *B.* Cross section of shops: *a,* street; *b,* sitting platform; *c,* roof. *C.* Front view of shops: *a,* street; *b,* sitting platform; *c,* roof; *d,* alley. (Constructed after the mode of presentation used by Le Tourneau [*Fès avant le Protectorat,* Casablanca, 1949, p. 316] for Fez, which in this regard hardly differs from Sefrou.)

Organization: the structures of order

If, in describing the ecology of the suq, one begins, naturally, with the physical layout, one begins, equally naturally, with the division of labor in describing its social form. But, as with physical layout, such a description must be cast in terms of the perceptions of those caught up in bazaar life, not in terms of some conventional grid of occupational differentiation impressed upon that life from outside. The network of conceptual distinctions suwwaqs use to divide themselves into

182

general categories, those general categories into more focused component categories, and those more focused component categories into particular roles or role types needs to be uncovered. An attempt to do this, in a form still far too gross to be adequate to the enormous delicacy of discrimination that is actually there, is shown in Figure 6, a tree-diagram of suwwaq classification, the indigenous typology of work, as it exists in Sefrou.

The division of labor

Figure 6 presents the main types of bazaar roles (e.g., shopkeeper, arbitrager, craftmaster, target seller) as the Sefrouis see them, and indicates how the Sefrouis conceive of the relations among these roles.[99] Below, indicated by the dotted lines, the tree branches into the separate trades and crafts: cloth sellers, carpenters, wool traders, bathhouse keepers, sheep vendors, rug auctioneers, cattle brokers, and so on. Above, similarly indicated, the suwwaq 'market participant" category is in contrast with the other overall occupational domains in Sefrou, of which the main ones are *fellāh* ("farmer") and *mūḍḍaf* (strictly, "government clerical worker," but now applied to office workers generally), each of which has its own internal pattern of division. The middle-range categorizations shown in the figure, the ones we are concerned with here, bring the spectacular complexity of the division of labor at the level of particular activities – of which even the 110 trade abbreviations listed in Annex A represent a simplified picture – into a comprehensible order. They outline the overall structure of the bazaar economy as an occupational world for those who have, each day, to operate within it.[100]

The major contrast within the bazaar domain between "buyer-seller" and "artisan" is extremely sharp and completely consensual. Special cases aside, there are virtually no examples of artisans who themselves hawk their manufactures directly in the marketplace. Either they contract jobs with particular clients who seek them out, by far the more common pattern, or they sell their product to buyer-sellers who then sell them in turn to consumers (or, as commonly, to other buyer-sellers). Inversely, though buyer-sellers will put out special contract jobs, usually rather small-scale ones, to particular artisans, thus engrossing their output for a few weeks, I was unable to find a single case where an artisan was an employee of a buyer-seller (i.e., where a buyer-seller owned an atelier run for him by a craftmaster subordinate to him) or even a case where a master was so deeply in debt to a buyer-seller that it amounted to the same thing. (The explicit

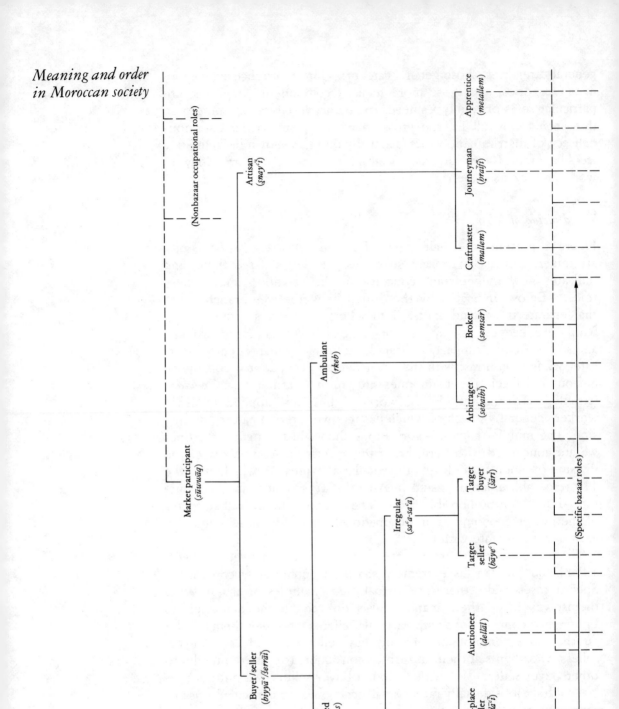

184

fear of precisely this on the part of many artisans, and their conscious effort to avoid contracting the bulk of their output to any one buyer-seller, suggests, however, that it does on occasion occur.) Except for one or two modern furniture enterprises, there are no integrated craft-commercial enterprises of significance in Sefrou, and there seem never to have been any.[101] One either makes (or repairs) things, or one vends them; almost never both.

On the buying and selling side, the absence of a single term (or at least one in common use) for *merchant* is itself indicative. Buying and selling are regarded as a unitary activity to be looked at simultaneously from the wholly interchangeable perspectives of the man who is passing goods to a trading partner and the man who is passing money, a difference in itself of no essential import. Both bi^c ("to sell") and *šri* ("to buy") have one another's primary meaning as their own secondary one, so that each really signifies something like "to make, or conclude, a deal, a bargain, a contract, an exchange." This implies, in turn, that even an ordinary customer – what is here glossed as a "target buyer" (and of whom more in a moment) – is viewed as himself a kind of trader, and there is no clear contrast between wholesale, in the sense of trader-to-trader, and retail, in the sense of trader-to-consumer, commerce.[102] In the universe of the suq, which *is* a universe, and, conceptually at least, a closed one, all are suwwaqs of one sort or another. There is no general public.

The next two levels of discrimination on the buyer-seller side (they have no application on the artisan side) are adjectival, not nominative; they are not themselves roles, but rather groupings of roles, genres of occupation. The "fixed"/"ambulant" distinction has already been mentioned several times, and is in any case fairly transparent in its meaning. The only remark still left to be made is that the distinction does not rest on whether the role occupant ever moves from his accustomed place. Almost no suwwaqs, a restless lot in a restless society, stay put all, or even most, of the time. On the contrary, they wander about constantly. Even shopkeepers, the most settled group, are half the time off somewhere up to something possibly profitable, their young sons or nephews left in place to inform inquirers innocent enough to believe them that father or uncle will "soon" be back. The distinction projected here is between those conceived, and who conceive themselves, to have a defined place – a shop, a customary selling spot, a particular market – where they, so to speak, belong and can at least normally be found, and those who, in the nature of the case, by virtue of their function, move among several such places. No one in the bazaar can afford to remain immobile; it's a scrambler's life.

("Move and you will confound your enemies," a Moroccan proverb runs, "sit and they will confound you; *fi l-ḥaraka, baraka,*" "there is blessing in movement," runs an even more famous one.) But some suwwaqs are footloose by profession, and some, by profession, are anchored.

The "regular"/"irregular" contrast within the fixed category (all "ambulant" roles are "regular") discriminates those suwwaqs who engage in trade day in and day out or, in periodic markets, week in and week out, from those who engage in it only when the impulse, need, or occasion takes them. On the regular side, shopkeepers and fixed-place sellers have already been discussed, and more detail about them can be found in Annexes A and C. It remains only to say something about auctioneers, a disappearing phenomenon in the bazaar economy, before turning to the irregular target seller and target buyer categories, whose crystallization is responsible for the disappearance.

Auctioneers (*dellāla;* sg. *dellāl,* from a root meaning "to show," "demonstrate," "display") were once a major element in the Sefrou suq. In the years before World War II, there were forty or fifty of them engaged in various sorts of trade; today (1968–9), there are but nine or ten marginal figures, dealing mainly in cheap cloth, yarn, and secondhand goods, the tattered remnants of a once flourishing and colorful profession.[103]

The main function of the auctioneers was to bridge the gap between buyer-sellers knowledgeable in commerce and those who, though wishing to trade in the suq, were not so knowledgeable. By shifting price making into the hands of buyers forced to compete among themselves for the right to purchase – which is what any form of auctioning does – both the farmer and the craftsman could avoid the direct bargaining pattern most of them felt gave all the advantage to the professional merchants and leave the latter to joust with one another. The dellal took an item of trade, most commonly but not exclusively, a craft item, on which its owner set a floor price, and walked about among the crowds of the suq carrying it, or a sample of it, with him, crying out for all to hear first the floor price and then, as individuals bid upward (usually in terms of customarily fixed intervals), the most recent offer until, bids ceasing to come, the last bidder was sought out and the item sold to him.[104] Clearly there was great room for chicanery in all this – misrepresentation, kickbacks, sheer embezzlement – and the dellal (who received a commission, usually 2 percent, on the sale) had to have an unmarked reputation for honesty, in the eyes both of his clients and of his potential bidders, something not that easy to come by in the suq and even harder to maintain. Of all the

186

trades in Sefrou, that of the auctioneer, inevitably a Muslim, was,
through mechanisms we will come to presently, among the most regulated, both internally and from the side of the government. (Only the
moneylender, inevitably a Jew, was more ambiguous and more
watched.) The uncertainty of the system and the aura of shadyness
surrounding it finally weakened it as, the bazaar economy firmly in
place, artisans and primary producers grew knowledgeable and confi-
dent enough to participate in the bazaar directly. The competence gap
between regular buyer-sellers and irregular ones narrowed, the irregular ones developed roles of their own, and the auctioneer, who had
been, so to speak, their commercial stand-in, was rendered less and
less necessary.

When they come to stand in for themselves, such irregular market
goers are no longer external to the suwwaq domain, but, in the form of
the target trader roles, an integral part of it. The term target seller –
someone who, in need of a certain amount of cash for some purpose or
other, brings something of his (a quantity of wheat or some animals) to
market to sell – has come to have a certain currency in recent anthropological work on "traditional markets."[105] The majority of grain and
animal sellers in Sefrou periodic markets, even those of the town, are
target sellers in this sense and are recognized to be such. They sell
sporadically in response to their need for cash (which is not to say they
are insensitive to price conjunctures, unaware of inventory issues, or
uninterested in accumulating balances) and, essentially farmers, do not
deal in commodities as such. Though there are, of course, also fully
commercial figures, the people with the money, in the throngs crowded
into a periodic grain or animal market (we shall come to them in a
moment), the *bāyeᶜ* is by far the most common type: a man who has
come to a particular, for him familiar, "known," suq to convert something he has himself produced into cash.[106]

The transfer of the "target" idea from sellers (or laborers) to buyers
is, so far as market studies go, an innovation, but one the suwwaq
buying-is-selling and selling-is-buying view of things demands. Individuals (still, as noted earlier, predominantly men, and twenty or
thirty years ago almost entirely so) concerned to purchase some item
or another, whether it be a basket or a cow, are not regarded as
members of some general external, residual class called "customers"
or "consumers," but of an internal class on a par with other sorts of
suwwaqs and distinguished only by the fact of a particular focus on a
particular end. Whether the purchased item is consumed or itself
target-sold in turn is a matter of no consequence (and quite often
indeterminable, so far as the seller is concerned); the *šārī* role is 187

regarded as fully a professional one as any other, and the occupant of it is treated as such. Not only is competence in "shopping" (a word, with its connotation of idle search, save for tourists a rare phenomenon in Morocco, that is precisely the wrong one here) something a target buyer is expected to have – and if he does not, so much the worse for him – but the instiutions of the market, from price bargaining and the intricate division of labor to the purposeful destandardization of quality and long-term clientelization, all ensure that the amateur will be at as great a disadvantage in the target buyer role as in any other. Some of the implications of this fact – perhaps the most important are that, a "fixed" activity, one "shops," as one "vends," only in specific, well-known environments and that target buyers and target sellers almost never confront one another directly – will be touched on later. The general point is that the noisy communication-network nature of the suq makes of even the consumer role, in advanced economies but an aspect of family roles and in "primitive" ones but a reflex of structural position, a commercial occupation.[107]

As a fixed or sitting buyer-seller, whether quotidian or occasional, is one associated, both in his own mind and those of others, with a particular suq or section of one, an ambulant or riding buyer-seller is one associated with at least two and most commonly several.[108] Of these, there are two main classes: arbitragers and brokers. Arbitragers are traders who gain their living out of the differential between what something sells for in one marketplace and what it sells for in another to which they can readily transport it. Brokers are those who act as the agents in one market of a trader (or traders) sitting in another. There are some other types of ambulant merchants – peddlers who travel around door to door in the countryside, for example – but these two are by far the most important.[109]

Most arbitragers (*sebaībīya*) have a more or less fixed itinerary, though what that itinerary is varies widely from individual to individual, to the point where one hardly encounters two that are precisely identical. As itineraries involving more than nine markets and less than four are relatively rare, and as almost all Sefrou arbitragers contrive to be there on Thursdays, the typical sebaibi trades in the Sefrou suq and anywhere from three or four to seven or eight others. The others may be nearby locality-focusing markets, relatively distant region-focusing ones, or even locality-focusing ones in other regions than Sefrou. Just which markets a given sebaibi operates in, as well as what he buys and sells in them, depend on his personal contacts and his familiarity with local situations, products, in turn, of his particular background and experience. His direct and detailed knowledge of

188

diverse bazaar environments, or rather of a definite, limited set of them, and his ability to move effectively among them capturing the profit of price discrepancies are the basis of his living–a living that can range from the extremely marginal to the quite considerable.[110]

Unlike other sorts of buyer-sellers, sebaibis deal in a variety of goods rather than focusing on one or two. The specializations of the markets they frequent shape their activities somewhat. Those who go to Guigou are likely to be looking for hides or cattle, to Marmoucha for rugs or wool, to El Menzel for wickerwork, to Immouzer for fruits, to Kucheta for wheat. But in general they trade in whatever seems profitable at the moment. One Sefrou sebaibi I traveled with to Marmoucha for the Tuesday market (he also works, in an intricate schedule, Missour, El Menzel, Guigou, and, of course, Sefrou) first bought two head of cattle. One he immediately resold locally to a sebaibi from Guigou; the other he contracted with another Sefrou sebaibi on a share arrangement to carry back in the latter's truck to Sefrou for sale there the following Thursday. Then he bought some chickens and a half a sack of wheat, which we carried back with us. And finally he bought some textiles, which he consigned, qirad fashion, to another Sefrou sebaibi, who took them off to Enjil by bus for the following day's market there. A series of such cases could be recounted, many of them far more complex than this. But the main point would emerge in them all – that sebaibis (who almost never hold goods for more than a few days) live by suq-to-suq trading, jobbing an income out of a sort of commercial cosmopolitanism.[111]

Semsār, which translates quite unproblematically as "broker," is a rather more familiar role in Western eyes, and less needs to be said therefore to describe it. Strictly, the term is used for real estate brokers, a function of minor importance in Sefrou, but generally it is extended to anyone who acts as a commission-paid agent for someone else in a commercial transaction. (Indeed, in any transaction: The feminine form, *semsīra,* means "matchmaker.")

In Sefrou, semsars are most prominent in the commodity trades, especially animals, wool, and wheat, where they are major actors, though they can appear in virtually any commercial context. In the commodity trades most of them are agents of large Fez merchants buying up local goods on behalf of their patron. Most animal sales, especially of cattle and sheep, are to semsars, rather than to butchers, arbitragers, or target buyers. Many of the largest transactions in wool and grain and virtually all in olives involve them as well.[112] Le Tourneau estimates for the 1933–6 period that about three-fifths of the cattle and about half the cereal sales in the Thursday market went, via

189

semsars, most of whom were local, to Fez. Having tried, over a much longer research period, to devise a way to estimate such matters with any precision and failed, I am unable to take Le Tourneau's figures as more than offhand guesses disguised as calculations. But the picture of the critical role of the semsar in connecting Sefrou to higher nodes (and not just Fez) in the bazaar hierarchy is clearly accurate.[113] As but an undocumented assertion, I would hazard that at least three-quarters, and quite possibly more, of the primary product flow from the Sefrou region toward the more developed regions of central Morocco, the Atlantic coast, and beyond, takes place through the agency of local semsars working on commission for engrossers in the superordinate bazaars of those regions. If the sebaibi connects suqs laterally, the semsar connects them hierarchically.

On the artisan side of the tree, the role pattern is either extremely simple or forbiddingly complex: simple, if one has the courage to leave details to themselves; complex, if one has not. The general discrimination of statuses into those who are acquiring a skill, those who have acquired it, and those who have conquered it applies more or less across the board; it is found in similar form in virtually every craft, save odd cases like watchman or curer.[114] But exactly how these statuses are defined and how the relations among them are organized vary markedly from one craft to the next depending on technical requirements and the work traditions that have grown up around the crafts. The integration of masters, journeymen, and apprentices into the productive process is clearly going to be rather different among tailors than among blacksmiths, weavers, butchers, or masons, because the process is different. Yet for all that, the critical feature of artisan roles from the point of view of bazaar economics is one that marks them all: their complete independence from any sort of corporate organization. Mallems, hraifis, and metallems alike are not employers or employees, bosses or workers, but rather so many tinsmiths or shoemakers more or less expert. However good they are or are not at what they do, and however dependent they may be in fact, they are free professionals, and their relations with one another are as contractual as with those who buy their products or hire their skills, and very nearly as fragile.

Which of the three statuses any particular artisan occupies is clear enough in the vast majority of cases. (A master craftsman is commonly referred to and addressed as such, "Mallem Mohammed"; and an established journeyman is frequently called by the nisba of his profession, "Khiyyati Mohammed.") But there is no formal process of movement, ritual or legal, from one such status to the next in any trade;

190

there is no public marking, save for the terms themselves, of the
occupants; and there are no collectively defined rules allotting duties,
rights, or powers to them. Any one who owns an atelier is in the
nature of the case a master and takes on whom he will as journeyman
or apprentice (which is not to say he does so randomly, as earlier
discussion should have made clear), and organizes his enterprise as
seems to him, and whomever he takes on, appropriate. There are, of
course, customs and precedents in these matters, a certain amount of
civil law, and even some guidance (not much) from the Sharia, which
provide Durkheim's "noncontractual bases of contract" and thus constrain the shapes such arrangements take. But – another nail in the
coffin of the guild stereotype – there are no tradewide regulations or,
for that matter, any body that could enforce them if there were.

An atelier, in whatever craft, is essentially a partnership (*šerka*) between artisans of varying skill, and whether one is master, journeyman, or apprentice depends upon what sort of partnership one has
contrived to make. At base, all partnerships in the bazaar, commercial
as well as industrial, are conceived of as between two persons, more
complex arrangements being regarded as compounds of these. One
variety of partnership is distinguished from another by the sort (and
size) of the contribution each participant makes to it and the reward
each in consequence draws from it. A craft atelier is a web of diverse
partnerships in this sense converging on the master (or masters, for
there may be more than one). And indeed, the diversity is greater
than the general threefold distinction is capable of expressing. Specific
outcomes of specific negotiations, hardly any two arrangements are
exactly the same. Though reflective of age, experience, and expertise,
and connected organizationally to technical function, at base the craft
role categories indicate types of dyadic contract prevalent between
artisans – forms of reltionships, not bundles of skills.[115]

The complexity of such contractual ties varies enormously, both
from craft to craft and from atelier to atelier within a given craft. A fair
number of smaller artisans, especially in the barbering, butchering, and
shoemaking trades, is not involved in them at all, but works alone. At
the other extreme there are ateliers with two or three masters locked in
an intricacy of arrangements probably no single participant completely
understands. There are master weavers with twenty looms, not all of
them in the same place, in contract with various sorts of masters,
journeymen, and apprentices up to nearly a hundred, and there are
master weavers with one loom and a boy to keep the yarn straight.
Blacksmithing demands a group of at least three for effective operation,
but it cannot really utilize more than five or six. Large-scale tailoring 191

establishments are uncommon, but most tailors have at least an apprentice or two to assist the master, and some have eight or nine, ranked
with three or four levels and including children as young as six.
Journeyman/apprentice contrasts are sharp in carpentry, blurred in baking; master/journeyman contrasts are sharp in milling, blurred in café
keeping. Family connections underpin contractual relations importantly in tailoring and blacksmithing, weakly in café keeping and silk
spinning. And so on. Only an extended, and rather wearisome, recount-
ing of concrete descriptions of work organization could capture the
variety. And even then not much more could be said as summary than
"other cases, other arrangements."[116]

The amin system

A universe of roles sorted into types and gathered into classes, the suq
is thus a structured domain of human activity, a bounded field of
meaningful goings-on. But like all such universes, domains, and fields,
it does not maintain itself; it takes more than a map of distinctions to
keep a world in order. The map must have a force neither its formal
beauties nor its functional convenience can themselves assure. Custom, the sheer weight of social habit, provides much of this force in
any society, and ritual, law, and government contribute most of the
rest. But in the suq world, an unusual institution, drawing somewhat
on the authority of each of these and yet not readily identifiable with
any of them, supplies most of the force: the amin system.

Amīn (pl. *umanā*, occasionally *amīnāt*), from the root for "faithful,"
"reliable," "trustworthy," "safe," means a "trustee," "guarantor," "cus-
todian," "superintendent," "guardian" – more or less. In Morocco, it is
applied to a selected member of an occupation, eminent, trusted, and
usually pious and elderly, as well as comfortably situated, whose function it is to mediate disputes both between practitioners of that occupation and between them and dissatisfied clients. There are (ca. 1965)
forty-eight amins in Sefrou, some of them of great weight in the life of
the market, others of essentially none, covering everything from
doughnut sellers to goldsmiths, quranic scholars to garage mechanics.
A list of them (or rather, as their personal names are of no significance
here, the occupations they serve) is given in Table 12.[117]

One thing is apparent from this list, merely from inspection: Whatever amins are, their distribution is no mere reflex of occupational
structure. Jewish cloth sellers and shoe repairmen are distinguished
from Muslim cloth sellers and shoe repairmen. Truck, taxi, and bus
operators are lumped together. Shoe repairmen and shoemakers are

192

Auctioneer	Jewish shoe repairman
Baker	Jewish slipper maker
Barber	Mason
Bathhouse keeper	Miller
Blacksmith	Musician/singer
Bread seller	Porter
Butcher	Plowmaker
Carpenter	Plumber
Charcoal seller	Religious scholar
Cloth seller	Saddlemaker
Coffeeshop keeper	Scribe
Cooked-food seller	Shoemaker
Cord maker	Shoe repairman
Farmer	Slipper maker
Floor layer/excavator	Stone cutter/quarry worker
Flour seller	Tailor of cloaks
Fried doughnut seller	Tailor of ready-made clothes
Funduq keeper	Tinsmith
Garage mechanic	Truck, taxi, bus operator
Goldsmith/jeweler	Vegetable and fruit seller
Grocer	Weaver
Horseshoer	Weigher/measurer
Jewish cloth seller	Wheat/bean trader
Jewish grocer	Wool/hide trader

Source: Sefrou municipality office (the Baladiya).

separated (even though the majority of the one are also the other), as are cloak tailors and ready-made clothes tailors (though few of the one are also the other). There are no amins for such major trades as silk merchant or hardware seller, whereas distinctly marginal trades such as scribe, musician, and quarry worker boast them. Farmer is not a bazaar occupation, and religious scholar not really an occupation at all, as its members, a few Quran teachers aside, actually earn their living at something else.

Nor do any of the by now familiar suq distinctions seem to apply with genuine strictness: modern/traditional: garage mechanics and horse-shoers have amins, bicycle repairmen and rug merchants do not; permanent market/periodic market: carpenters and charcoal sellers do, silk merchants and herbalists do not; large/small occupations: grocers and plowmakers versus ready-made clothes sellers and potters; skilled/un-skilled: goldsmiths and porters, tile makers and lime kiln workers. And, of course, the great merchant/artisan divide does not sort either: grocers, auctioneers, cord makers, and masons have amins; tobacconists, odds-and-ends sellers, glaziers, and buttonmakers do not.

The amin functions in the suq setting, and only there, but his socio-

193

logical foundations are elsewhere: in the culturewide Moroccan (and to some extent generally Mid-Eastern) idea that the possibility of effective settlement of public disputes between diversely interested individuals depends, at base, upon the existence of a single, splendid, and very hard to find figure – the reliable witness.

To trace out the reasons why the reliable witness is such a critical figure in Moroccan life would take us far afield into the intricacies of authority, morality, and public discourse in that life, as well as into peculiar corners of Islamic doctrine and North African history. But the uncertainty of information quality already attributed to the suq, and inferentially, to the society as a whole, clearly has something to do with it: Where fact is elusive, the man who can fix it is a prize resource. And that, not an imperious *Zunftmeister,* is what the amin is and, in Sefrou anyway, always has been.

"Amin" is actually one of a set of such reliable witness roles found throughout the society. In irrigation, there is the *jāri* (from the root for "to run," "flow," "stream"), who is not an oriental water bureaucrat managing matters, but a countryside water expert monitoring them. For descendants of the Prophet (Alawis, Idrissis, and so on, the so-called *šurfa*) and certain other special groups there is the *mezwār* (from the Berber *amzuaru,* "first"), who, whatever his personal influence, does not govern them but attests to the fact that they are what they say they are and serves as a kind of notary public for them. In the religious (qadi) court, the *ᶜadel* (from "to act justly," "equitably") fulfills a similar professional attestor function, and in the secular court (the *maḥkama*) an official called an *ᶜarīf* (from "to know," "be aware of," "recognize," "discover") or a *ḵebīr* (from "to know by experience," "be acquainted with") is sent out by the judge to visit the scene of the dispute and report back what the facts of the case "really" are.[118] At marriage, a woman must have a (male) *walī* to attest before the qadi to her status, her propriety, and her very desires. The justness of market scales are guaranteed by the sworn declaration of four religious scholars (*ṭolba*). Even lower-level, local administrative officials – the village or quarter muqqadems – serve more this reliable witness function than a decision-making and enforcing one.

From this point of view, the amin is merely the suq variant in a bracketed series of official, quasi-official, or as in the old tribal oath-swearing patterns, extraofficial reliable witnesses, specialized as to domain, upon which another, similar series of law- (or custom-) applying officials – the pasha, the qaid, the qadi, the hakim, and, in the suq, the *muḥtaseb* ("the market inspector," of whom more in a moment) – rely for the empirical foundations of their judgment. The amin system

194

is an expression of a distinctive style of social control, a dialectic of "fact legitimators" and "norm appliers," which, rooted in some of the most general concepts of Maghrebi culture, extends far beyond itself. No more than the zawia, the habus, or the nisba is it a simple product of the suq; no less than they is it a force there.

Amins are chosen (usually for indefinite terms, occasionally for set ones) by a process of negotiation between the members of the trade and the government—the royal bureaucracy in the pre- and post-Protectorate periods, the colonial bureaucracy during the Protectorate. As in all negotiational processes in Moroccan society, the weight of the two parties, and thus the balance of the outcome, varies with places, times, personalities, and situations. Sometimes amins are essentially elected functionaries of the traders they serve upon whom the government has passively placed its official imprimature. Sometimes they are essentially government appointees the traders have had necessarily to accept. Most often they are the result of a compromise between the sort of man the traders would prefer (one capable of spitting in a pasha's eye) and the sort the government feels it must have (one who does what he is damn well told).

As one would imagine, the general trend over the half century we are concerned with here has been toward the cat's-paw side of things as central rule has grown, consolidated, and come to think of itself in modern terms. But there is still much variation, not only from suq to suq—smaller or more far-flung ones having more autonomy—but even within a single suq, such as Sefrou, where some trades (cloth seller, blacksmith, porter, funduq keeper) maintain a fair degree of independence and others (tailor, grocer, mason, auctioneer) rather less. By now, however, all important Sefrou amins are at least as much arms of the government as they are agents of their colleagues.[119]

In any case, when a trader has a dispute with respect to workmanship, prices, debts, quality of material, contract provisions, and so forth, either with another trader or with a customer, which cannot be directly resolved through the usual exchange of insults, excuses, concessions, and promises, the dispute is taken to the amin (or if representatives of different trades are involved, amins) for determination. The amin, who has no formal judicial powers, simply endeavors to discover what the facts of the matter are, a task in which he seems inevitably to consider himself successful. Normally this ends the matter, because if the disgruntled disputant carries things to the muhtaseb, who does have formal judicial powers (and a court in which to exercise them), the amin will be called upon as the reliable witness and but repeat his conclusions. Moroccans being an argumentative and

195

headstrong lot, not much given to letting well enough alone, this does nonetheless happen with some frequency, the usual outcome being that the intransigent protester ends up with an even less favorable resolution than he had to begin with.

Whether the muhtaseb has formally to decide the case or it resolves itself at the amin level, the settlement is effected in terms of a combination of customary, religious, and civil commercial law, a kind of half-codified morality of the market, called the *hisba.* Strictly, the hisba (which is mentioned in connection with North Africa at least as early as Ibn Khaldun) is the authority to supervise markets, an authority vested ultimately in the caliph, and there is a fairly sizable classical literature, within Morocco and without, concerning it. Concretely, the hisba consists of the principles, some of them stemming from government edict (*dahīr*), some from Islamic law (*šraᶜ*), and some – in a place like Sefrou, a great many – from local practice (*ᶜurf*), that the amin, and if need be, the muhtaseb use in regulating suq activities.[120] The balance of importance among these three main sources of the hisba has also shifted toward the governmental pole in the past half century or so, and the muhtaseb, once, with the pasha (or qaid) and the qadi, "le seconde personnage de la trinité" of local government, the amin of amins, presiding over a separate realm of law, has been reduced to but another government functionary.[121]

In any case, whatever the recent, and far from definitive, weakening in favor of state power, the amins as "reliable commercial witnesses" and the muhtaseb as "commercial norm applier" were the main agents of social control in the bazaar, containing disruption in a society where enmities tend rather easily to become both intense and long lasting and to spread rapidly from their source to involve more and more people. In the marketplace, where individuals from all sorts of background, with all sorts of loyalties, and possessed of all sorts of intentions meet in an atmosphere of hectic interaction, the possibility of discord mounting to "explosion," to use Francisco Benet's only somewhat dramatized image, is clearly much enhanced.[122]

The fear of *nefra* (the "sudden, panicky 'snapping' which breaks the peace of the *suq,*" scattering its occupants in all directions and leaving it a pole of avoidance rather than a pole of attraction) is alive in even the best regulated of markets; and in the not-so-well-regulated ones it hangs in the air like a premonition.[123] Where the occupational structure is not developed enough or the population of the market not stable enough – in small markets, in remote ones, in new ones – to support an effective amin system, other reliable witnesses and norm appliers are brought into play: religious scholars (*tulba*); descendants of the Prophet

(*šurfa*); members of saintly lineages (*murābtīn;* Br. *igurramen*); generally
recognized "market masters" (*mwālīn s-sūq*, unofficial muhtasebs);
brotherhood muqaddems; local political leaders of one sort or another;
and, of course, nowadays, uniformed representatives of state standing
about with repeating rifles. Saint shrines cast a general beneficence
over the marketplace and provide sacred ground (where violence or
lying under oath bring supernatural disaster) for peaceful resolution of
conflict. Customary law forbids the carrying of firearms, the unsheath-
ing of knives, and so on, and is popularly enforced to the point of
lapidation or the gouging out of eyes. Adjacent tribes guarantee each
other's safety under zettata-like protection pacts. The marketplace is
physically and institutionally insulated from virtually all the other contexts of social life (normally one should not even discuss extracommer-
cial disputes there). All these ingenious cultural devices, and others,
work to protect the precious and delicate peace of the marketplace.

Behind the amin system and behind the hisba, what Benet well calls
"the covenant of the market," lies more than an abstract thirst for
justice. Behind them lies a quite unabstract fear of anarchy – *nefra, sība,
fitna, hāraž;* the Moroccan vocabulary of disorder is rich and nuanced –
rising in the bazaar, "*the* danger spot in the social structure," and raging
out from there across the whole landscape of collective life.[124]

Exchange: toward a communication model of the bazaar economy

To the foreign eye, a mid-Eastern bazaar, Sefrou's like any other, is a
tumbling chaos: hundreds of men, this one in rags, that one in silken
robe, the next in some outlandish mountain costume, jammed into
alleyways, squatting in cubicles, milling in plazas, shouting in each
others' faces, whispering in each others' ears, smothering each other in
cascades of gestures, grimaces, glares – the whole enveloped in a smell
of donkeys, a clatter of carts, and an accumulation of material objects
God himself could not inventory, and some of which He could probably not even identify . . . sensory confusion brought to a majestic pitch.
To an indigenous eye, it looks much the same; but with one essential
difference. Embodied in all this high commotion, and in fact actualized
by it, is, Revelation (maybe) aside, the most powerful organizing force
in social life: *mbādla* ("exchange"). What holds everything more or less
together in this knockabout world is that men want what others have
and find it, normally, easier to chaffer it out of them than force it.

In attempting to reduce the surface tumult of bazaar economies to
the deep calm of social theory, anthropologists who have turned their
attention to such economies have found themselves entangled in a   197

received idea they could neither escape nor make much of: Now that so much of the world is filled with corporation directors and advertising men, the bazaar is the nearest thing to be found in reality to the purely competitive market of neoclassical economics, the one place in the world where isolated, interest-rivalrous, profit-maximizing sellers still actually confront isolated, nonpropagandized, utility-maximizing consumers on equal ground, deterministic actors in the cosmic drama of supply and demand. Some have embraced the idea in the hope that, applied to exotics, it would somehow get them somewhere economists had not already been; some have angrily rejected it as just so much more Western ethnocentrism, an attempt to make all the world look like natural capitalists; more have striven to construct some "yes, but" middle way – "my people are rational, but in their own peculiar fashion."[125] But few have been able to turn entirely away from the idea with the unconcern it seems most to deserve. As a speculative instrument, the concept of "the perfect market" yields, when applied to a system like the Sefrou suq, mere banalities (surely we need no more demonstrations that, left to themselves, prices equilibrate wants to resources) or wanderings off in unhelpful directions (that trade localization functions to minimize travel costs is not so much false as obscurant of more interesting truths; e.g., that it focuses search). The tumult of the suq, all that goods crying and arm waving, must be approached directly. And the first step in approaching is to understand that, whatever the state of competition may be (and it is not, in fact, all that Marshallian), that of communication is a good deal less than pure, perfect, and undistorted.[126]

To say that is not to say, however, that one ought to turn from the distracting formalisms of market theory to the even more misleading ones of information theory, which accentuate the measurabilities of communication while washing out its import.[127] The need is for (1) a qualitative formulation of the information situation in the suq as the Moroccans themselves conceive it, followed by (2) an analysis of the relation of that situation thus conceived to the process of exchange as it actually takes place (or fails to take place) in the ordered muddle of bazaar encounter.

The information situation

A description of what the suq looks like in information and communication terms from within, from the point of view of those who have or are looking for the information and doing or not doing the communicating, takes us first into the realm of ideas, and that in turn entangles us once more in the arabesques of Arabic. Not only is what goes on in the suq mainly talk (*klām,* literally "words"; figuratively, as we shall see, very much more), but the meta-talk in which that talk is talked about defines the conceptual space in which the exchange process moves. "The linguistic turn" that has transformed so great a part of modern social though has, as yet, barely touched economics; but here it must, briefly, hesitantly, and more than a little elliptically, be made. In the suq, the flow of words and the flow of values are not two things; they are two aspects of the same thing.

There is no simple way (and possibly no complicated one either) to convey the exact shape of the conceptual world of the suq or to outline with any firmness or exhaustiveness the language games that sustain it. All that can be done is to work through a small catalogue of words relevant to that world in such a way that its general character will be at least broadly invoked. But though this is a limited aim, it is not a misdirected one. For it is just such a general sense of a diffuse situation, not a precise theory of a definite state of affairs, that the Moroccans, struggling like the rest of us to order indistinct experiences with inadequate ideas, themselves have. Wittgenstein's remark to the effect that an accurate picture of a vague object does not consist in a clear picture but a vague one applies here with a special force.

But prior even to discussing particular words, something must be said about Arabic in general, for even the word *word* does not translate easily between Arabic and English. The heart of the matter is, of course, the famous Semitic root system in which a (usually) triconsonantal cluster is worked out through a series of (mostly) vocalic modulations to yield a set of lexemes with (generally) related meanings. We have already seen something of this in connection with the discussions of *sūq* (*s-w-q*) and *nisba* (*n-s-b*), but it is a matter hard to formulate and impossible to ignore in any attempt beyond the most mechanical to gloss Arabic words in English. The Arabic root and modulation system connects – morphologically connects – a set of words in such a way as to set up an overall semantic field within which the particular meaning of a particular word has its being. Each word, to change the metaphor, is but a more or less defined semantic cloud in a diffuse and general, yet readily enough sensed, atmosphere of meaning projected by the root.[128]

As an orienting example, let us look at a word we shall find playing a role of some importance in the suq "information situation": *şdiq.* In itself, *şdiq* means "truth," "trueness," "sincerity," "candor," "honesty." One says of a man, *fī-h şdiq* ("he is honest," "there is *şdiq* in him"); or of an assertion, *kantkellem-mᶜa-k b-ş-şdiq* ("I tell you sincerely," "I   199 speak with you with *ṣdiq*"), or even *ma-kayn ma-ḥsen men ṣ-ṣdiq* ("honesty is the best policy," "there is nothing that is better than *ṣdiq*").

Here, in no particular order, are some other derivations of the same root (*ṣ-d-q*):

Ṣadīq	Friend, friendly, connected by bonds of friendship (pl. *aṣdiqā*)
Ṣdeq	To be right, to guess right, to succeed, to turn out well (a venture, a meal, etc.)
Ṣdāq	A dowry, a marriage contract
Ṣādiq	True, reliable, accurate, authentic
Ṣeddeq	To believe, to accept as truthful, to verify, to give alms, to donate to charity
Ṣedeq	To tell the truth, be candid with
Ṣiddīq	Strictly veracious, righteous, upright, loyal, saintly
Ṣadaqa	Alms, charitable gift, religious tax, offerings
Ṣedāqa	Friendship, loyalty, clientship
Taṣdīq	Belief, faith, consent, agreement, covenant
Meṣaddeq	Credible, believable, reliable, trustworthy[129]

One gets the picture, even if the picture is difficult to focus. The point is that there is nothing special about *ṣdiq* as an example: All the words we will consider are set in a similar field of root-conditioned meanings. In the discussion this field will be assumed rather than as here systematically displayed, and, largely ignoring the niceties of morphological class and grammatical function, absorbed into their definitions. Thus, in our example, the "friendship," "marriage contract," "alms," and "loyalty" intimations of *ṣdiq* – its "human relationship" penumbra – will be invoked in explicating what "truth" here means, without actually parading related forms and meanings justifying the interpretation or going, save glancingly, into the hardly unimportant matter of its place in the structure of Arabic *langue*.

The words to be thus treated – those that can lead us into some sense of how Moroccan suwwaqs conceive the bazaar in information terms – are: *zḥām* ("crowd"), *klām* ("words"), and *ḵbar* ("news"); *ṣdiq* ("honest"), *maᶜrūf* ("known"), and *shiḥ* ("unblemished"); and *maᶜqūl* ("reasonable"), *ḥaqq* ("right"), *kdūb* ("lying"), and *bāṭel* ("worthless"). These ten (the rationale for the subgrouping will be presented in a moment) are hardly the only such words that might have been chosen, and certainly they are not all that could be. But because they recur in both the rhetoric of bazaar exchange as such and in participants' attempts to represent to themselves (and to inquiring ethnographers) what goes on in such exchange, to unpack their meaning is to unpack as well a good deal of what the suq comes to as a cultural system.[130]

The first three words – *zḥām, klām,* and *ḵbar* – are mostly employed in characterizing the "phenomenal" aspects of the bazaar information situation: how it appears, if not quite unreflectively, at least more or less immediately, to someone caught up directly in it. They are describing terms. The second three – *ṣdiq, maᶜrūf,* and *šḥīḥ* – on the contrary, define considerations brought to bear on phenomenal information in estimating its worth. They are appraisive terms. And the last four – *maᶜqūl, ḥaqq, bāṭel,* and *kdūb* – are judgment terms: conclusions the appraisal of things seen and heard jostling about in the suq lead finally on to. This categorization, modeled, of course, on Austinian procedures, is admittedly not without a certain arbitrariness and makes the process of finding out what the devil is going on in the bazaar look far more mechanical and clear-cut than it in any way is. Nevertheless, the classification does outline reasonably well the logical (or, perhaps more exactly, the semiological) structure within which that process unfolds and can serve, therefore, as a useful frame for a general account of it.

Description: crowds, words, news. Zḥām, which means "crowd," "mob," "throng," "swarm," "crush," but connects to forms meaning to "push," "shove," "jostle," "elbow," "harass," or "beset" someone; to forms meaning "jammed," "packed in," "(over)stuffed," "teeming," or "crammed (with)"; to forms meaning "competition" and "rivalry," and "competitor" and "rival"; and, along more imaginative lines, to a form meaning "a convulsive fit" or "an acute attack of dysentery" is simply the word most commonly used to characterize the suq as a social setting: *Hiya zḥām* ("it's a shoving, pushing, elbowing crowd"). The competitiveness of the bazaar is imaged not as a set of isolated confrontations, hand-to-hand tests of strength, but as a mass of people jammed into a space too narrow to accommodate half of them, harassed individuals struggling to maintain their footing in a crush. For the suwwaq, the first thing about the bazaar is that it's a mob.[131]

The second thing is that it's a talkative mob. As noted, *klām* (like *zḥām* a collective noun – the singular is *kelma*), which means "words" and beyond that "language," "speech," "speaking," "utterance," "phrase," "statement," "trope," "proverb," "dialect," "discussion," "argument," "debate," and – the informing twist – "power" or "influence," is a word to conjure with in Arabic. The central conceptual node of the semantic field in which it is enclosed is quite clearly "talk." The verbal forms mean to "speak," "say," "utter," "express," "address (someone)," "converse with (someone)"; the nounal forms refer to a "speaker," "spokesman," "orator," "(good) conversationalist"; and the adjectival forms invoke such qualities as "talkative," "fluent," "loqua-

201

cious," "eloquent." But the peculiar status of "talk" in the Arab world, and especially the Muslim part of it, with its concept of the Quran as the direct speech of God (*klām allāh*), give to that core meaning an almost energic dimension. *Klām* is not just an attribute people have; it is a force they wield.[132]

For all the actual jostling that goes on in a bazaar mob, something most people take more or less in stride, the real pushing and shoving is done with talk. The varieties of *klām* Moroccans perceive and index with fixed idioms are virtually endless: *klām ǧādi u māji* ("words coming and going," "rumor"); *klām ḵāwi* ("empty words," "insipid, vapid speech"); *klām meblūz* ("words of a blunderer," "inappropriate, awkward, speech"); *klām merr* ("bitter talk"); *klām qāseḥ* ("hard, wounding talk"); *klām b-l-maᶜna* ("significant, serious words," "polite, polished, formal speech"); *klām fertek* ("words ripped apart at the seams," "disjointed, incoherent talk"); *klām qbīḥ* ("rotten, spoiled words," "distasteful, unpleasant talk"); *klām l-mḵasma* ("quarrel words," "invective"); *klām ṭiyyeb* ("pleasant, delicious words," a "compliment"); *klām siyāsa* ("political, diplomatic words," an "insinuation"). And there are more complex locutions constructed around *klām* to mean: "to speak in a boring manner" ("boring talk," "a bore"), "to digress," "to interrupt," "to contradict," "to deny," "to be speechless with rage," "to perseverate," "to turn a phrase," "to attack someone's reputation," "to compromise one's own reputation," and so on through a jungle of expressions constantly heard to the one most often heard – ᶜ*and-u klām* (or *kelma*) ("he has words [word]," "he has [the] power, the 'say' "). To "have words," to speak with carrying force in a given situation, is to be the one whose wishes count. And the hubbub in the market is in great part a scramble to gain just that: to have, as we would put it, the last word.

So the tumult of the marketplace is largely a tumult of words (and various paralinguistic signs, *išārāt,* a subject in itself), or anyway is seen as such. But for all the richness of classification of types of "words," "talk," "statements," and so on, and for all the judgmental quality of many of the characterizations involved in that classification, the attitude toward the particular things actually said in the marketplace, the *klām* in fact emitted there, is, in epistemological terms, radically agnostic. "Bitter," "wounding," "distasteful," even "insipid" or "disjointed" talk may be, for all that, well worth believing and acting on – truly informative; "polite," "pleasant," or "fluent" talk may equally well not be – stylishly deceptive. "Invective," "compliment," "rumor," and "insinuation" may be either clarifying or misleading with respect to the exchange process. The talk of the market is, like the crowd that populates it, merely

202

prodigiously there. How reasonable, creditable, veracious, or useful it is is altogether another question, separately asked, separately answered. "A tale," the proverb goes, "is a tale; talk is talk."

It is this sheer appearance view of what is heard (and seen) in the market that the word *kbar,* the term most commonly used to sum it up, projects. *Kbar* means "news," "report," "tidings," "message," "communication," "story," "indication," "notification," but it means these things in a manner that bleaches them of any implication beyond their simple phenomenal existence – pure, brute, received intelligence. Connected to forms for "direct experience of," "immediate awareness of," "knowledge-by-acquaintance of" on the one hand, and to forms for "empirical inquiry," "to seek information about" on the other (the man sent out by the judge to explore the facts in a dispute [see above] is called a *kebīr,* a *mukbīr* is a newspaper reporter or a detective, a *kebbār* is a police spy, a *mukebāra* is an interview or an investigation, a *bīt iktiber dwa* ["room for inspecting 'medicine' "] is a laboratory), *kbar* sums up the information situation the suwwaq confronts in the bazaar in resolutely noncommittal terms. There is no lack of messages; but one is as actual as the next.

Descriptively, then, the suwwaq's suq is a crowd of rivals, a clatter of words, and a vast collection of ponderable news. Pondering it (although the English word is much too contemplative, equable, and altogether passive in tone to characterize accurately what in fact goes on) and coming to decisions about what to make of it is the critical matter for the suwwaq and what distinguishes, in his eyes at least, the numberless failures of this world from the handful of successes. Keeping your feet in the bazaar mob is mainly a matter of deciding whom, what, and how much to believe and, believing (or half-believing), what and how much – and in whom – to confide.

Appraisal: candor, consensus, wholeness. A suwwaq faced with a particular piece of marketplace news – a price quotation, a wage offer, a representation concerning quality, a promise to do something or other – and obliged to decide what to make of it normally proceeds by placing the news simultaneously in three different contextual frames: the identity of its purveyor, the current state of bazaar opinion, and the accepted norms of credibility. *Ṣdiq, maᶜrūf,* and *shīh,* each of which should properly be written with a question mark following it ("is he being honest with me?" "does it square with the consensus?" "is it sound?"), set these frames. They point appraisal toward its appropriate concerns: personal relationships, community attitudes, and the defining feature of sane belief.

203

Ṣdiq has already been partly explicated. It has to do, as Smith has suggested, with "the truth of persons."[133] What holds together the "sincerity," "friendship," "alms," "marriage contract," "loyalty," and "faith" dimensions of *s-d-q* is that they all have to do with assertions, celebrations, demonstrations, promises, tokens of individual reliability, of being someone whose integrity empowers his words. Smith's summary of the meaning of *taṣdīq*, the "faith" derivative, though cast in the accents of the mosque rather than those of the bazaar, puts the matter exactly:

> [*Taṣdīq*] can mean, to regard as true, and this is indeed its most general connotation; but we must remember that "true" here is in the personalist sense. Its primary object is a person . . . so that *ṣaddaqahu* [the second, "causative" form of the verb plus a *hu* "him" object suffix], or "he gave him *taṣdīq*" may mean "he held him to be a speaker of the truth" – he believed him . . . because he trusted him . . . he held him to be *ṣādiq*, a speaker of truth on a particular occasion, "or held him to be *ṣiddīq*, an habitual teller of the truth by moral character. . ."

> Another standard usage, moreover, is that it mean, not "He found him to be a speaker of the truth," but rather, "He found him to be so." One may hear a man's statement, and only subsequently find reason or to know that the man was no liar.

> Thirdly, it may indicate this sort of notion but with a more active, resolute type of finding: that is, "he proved him to be a speaker of the truth," or confirmed or verified it. Thus the common phrase *ṣaddaqa al-khabara al-khabru*: "the experience verified the report" . . . [or better, given the personalist meaning of *s-d-q*] "the [experience] verified the report and the reporter."

> Fourthly . . . *taṣdīq* may mean "to render true," "to take steps to make come true" – for instance, one's own promise (a radically important matter), or another's promise, or another's remark . . .

> Throughout this *taṣdīq* form, the sincerity involved may be on the part of the subject of the secondary form, as well as or perhaps even rather than of the primary subject; so that if I *taṣdīq* some statement, I not merely establish its truth in the world outside me, but incorporate it into my own moral integrity as a person . . .

> *Taṣdīq* is to recognize a truth, to appropriate it, to affirm it, to actualize it. And the truth, in each case is personalist.[134]

There are many implications of this "personalist" view of truth so far as bazaar exchange is concerned, among them that candor is about as rare as saintliness. But by far the most important are that a reputation for speaking (relatively) honestly is a valuable resource for a suwwaq to have and that such a reputation (or lack thereof) is not a general, context-free, "characterological" quality of an individual, like his temperament, taste, or political orientation, but is embedded in

particular, concrete, person-to-person relationships from which it cannot be even conceptually disentangled. One is honest (or not honest
or not quite honest) *with* someone, *about* something, in a given instance, not as such. The "friendship," "marriage contract," "covenant,"
"alms giving" aspects of honesty are not mere secondary connotations,
metaphorical extensions, of the notion of "being (or, what is the same
thing, 'speaking') true"; they are part of its defining essence. Strictly, a
bazaar trader or artisan does not have a reputation, good or bad. He
has reputations, dozens of them.[135]

The very nature of the bazaar – the enormous multiplicity of participants, combined with the absence of advertising, brands, or even store
names – makes this inevitably the case, renders the establishment of a
general reputation next to impossible. The most the average suwwaq
can hope for is that those in his corner of the suq or (which, given
localization, may be the same thing) in his trade, may have some
overall opinion, preferably not too bad, of him. And even that opinion, so far as it exists, will be highly diffuse and not very important to
his actual day-to-day functioning. The people in whose eyes he really
has a reputation – "reputations" – in the proper sense of the term are
those with whom he actually conducts exchanges repeatedly. The clientelization of trade (which is marked, and of which more later)
means that a given suwwaq does not relate to the bazaar mob as an
undifferentiated whole. He relates to a more or less defined (though,
as relationships ripen and sour, changing) set of individuals within it.
And the issues raised by the question, *Waš kayṣedeq mᶜa-ya?* ("Is he
being honest with me?"), always, of course, a reciprocal one, crystallize and are at least tentatively resolved with respect to each particular case. Except for the most minor or passing transaction, or in
cases where advantage is so obvious as to override caution, people
deal largely with people they know; and the evolution of those dealings, the concrete exchange experience of particular pairs of individuals, forms the foundation for *ṣdiq* "truth-of-persons" type appraisals of
bazaar news. It is the state of the relationship between the two parties
that matters – men are true or false (or, most commonly, something
uncertainly in between) to each other, not in themselves.[136]

The relationship of oneself and the person whose news one is considering – are you or aren't you *aṣdiqā* (truth-telling "friends") – is not,
however, the only criterion one can employ in appraising it. The
degree to which the news conforms to the prevailing consensus about
what is "normal," "customary," "usual," "conventional," or "standard"
is another, no less important, criterion.

The word for this is *maᶜrūf,* which means (something) "known," "well known," "familiar," "widely recognized," "generally ac-knowledged," "universally accepted"; as well as (something) "fitting," "proper," "fair," or "equitable"; and, by extension from that, "a favor," "a courtesy," "a kindness," or a "good deed." In Quranic usage (where it is always *al-ma^{c}rūf*), and in the moral system that spreads out from it, *ma^{c}rūf* means "good," in the sense of acts in consonance with God's commands, and therefore "recommended." Thus, behind the notion lies the conviction that public consensus is a trustworthy guide for behavior because God commands only that which all unimpaired men (an unimpaired woman is a contradiction in terms) are capable of knowing and following and unless, as is, alas, too often the case, blinded by divisive lies and illusions, will in fact know and follow. "God's community," as the maxim has it, "cannot unite in error."

So far as the bazaar is concerned, this means that one way to decide the worth of what a particular suwwaq says or does is to measure it against settled social opinion: *^{c}urf* ("practice," "custom," "tradition," "mores," "customary law," or, considering the root, "the known," "the accepted," "the recognized," "the acknowledged"). There, too, cognition, consensus, and virtue are internally connected in such a way that though the community may divide in error, and chronically does, it can agree only in truth.[137]

The range of the *ma^{c}rūf*—the generally acknowledged, the equit-able, and the recommended—is as wide as the bazaar and as differenti-ated as its parts. There are established practices for virtually every trade, every marketplace, and every situation. The *^{c}urf* of the suq—its commonplace ethic—is a palpable presence at every point in it. Part of getting into a trade is learning the relevant details of it (and part of keeping people out is preventing them from doing so). It is what the amin and muhtaseb rely on, or should, in clarifying and settling dis-putes and the ultimate foundation of their authority. Everything from the day, hours, and place of a suq, through who has a right to be in which part of it doing what, to the rules governing bargaining, partnership, working conditions, clientship obligations, habus rights, craft standards, credit relations, and general public comportment—indeed, just about anything that goes on in the suq that has anything remotely to do with exchange—is governed by *^{c}urf*.[138] Appealing to what is "known" is central both to the rhetoric of the bazaar and to the process of determining what in that rhetoric should be credited and what not.

Yet despite its more public, collective status, the consensus of the suq concerning any particular matter, what really is considered fair and proper dealing, is not that much more easily determined than is

206

the honesty of personal intention. Such consensus varies from place to place, trade to trade, time to time, and issue to issue. And when you get down to it, individuals, more divided in error and interest than they are united in truth and obedience, in fact differ, even for one place, trade, time, and issue in their expressed views about what the consensus is. Finding out what the ground rules are with respect to having a cloak made, or buying raw wool, or patronizing a client butcher, or advancing a grocer credit, or selling mules in the Thursday market does not in general work out to be a set and straightforward task, but a vexed and problematic one. Like *ṣdiq, maᶜrūf* poses an appraisive question: *Waš ḥād ši maᶜrūf?* ("Does this thing [proposed, argued, reported, claimed, asserted, promised, insinuated, demanded] square with recognized practice?"). Answering—actually making the appraisal—is a more difficult matter.

In any case, besides personal relations and community perceptions, the worth of bazaar news can also be appraised in terms of what we would call more "objective" considerations: its inherent plausibility, its credibility as such. Plausibility and credibility are, however, not quite the right glosses. For the Arabic word that invokes this range of considerations, *ṣḥīḥ,* trails a stream of associations that connect it not with likelihood, probability, chance, logic, demonstration, argument, but with health, strength, vigor, wholesomeness, salubriousness, lack of impairment, absence of blemish, recuperation, healing, cure. The entire concept pivots around the notion either of being whole or of restoring wholeness—an almost medical view of truth as a state of disease-free well-being: scatheless, blotchless completeness.

The Arab, and especially the Muslim Arab, concern with bodily integrity, the tendency to identify physical imperfection with moral, has often been noted. (There is even a special morphological class for adjectives denoting defects—"mute," "blind," "deaf," "lame," "scabrous," "demented," "moronic," "pregnant.") So has the connection between that idea and the evaluation of statements, documents, traditions, reports, and the like. A chain of "healthy," "unblemished" witnesses to a purported fact, whole and intact in both the material and spiritual senses, is a guarantee of the fact's validity; the discovery of one "weak" or "damaged" link in such a chain undermines it. That which is worthy of belief is that which is sound in the most literal sense of the term, in which no hidden infirmity of the slightest sort can be uncovered. So far as matters seen or heard in the bazaar are concerned, none of which reach such immaculate levels, what one looks for (and looks for, and looks for) are defects, especially unobvious ones. Like most conceptions of health, *ṣḥīḥ* turns the attention toward a concern with signs of its absence – the symptoms of false-hood, not the evidences of truth.

Around the idea of *shīḥ* ("well," "strong," "whole," "valid," "credi-ble," "sound") is formed a whole doctrine of suspicion, a catalogue, though hardly a systematic one, of the pathologies of communication and their outward expressions. Like *sdiq* and *maᶜrūf, shiḥ* is more a sceptical question expecting a negative answer than an expression of confidence or an affirmation of belief. One searches for what may be wrong – a juggled measure, a product switch, a disguised cost – and for the false signals – an evasive response, an overready agreement, an excessive promise – that reveal its presence. In the message-saturated world of the bazaar, where everyone is trying to lead everyone else down the garden path, mistrust is an adaptive attitude and ethically a quite proper one. The credulous do not thrive. "The power of the people of the Sous is lying," the song of Al Hiba says of that quintes-sential suwwaq group. "All that comes from the Sous is [vegetable] oil, locusts, and a great deal of misinformation."[139] The development of a fine sense for the deceptive and devious hidden within the appar-ently *shīḥ* (the "not healthy" disguised as the "healthy") and the skill to correct for it, *sehheḥ* ("restore to health," "heal," "emend," "rec-tify," "repair"), is prerequisite to any sort of success in the market. Or in life generally: A person who hears some news he does not believe, Westermarck remarks in *Wit and Wisdom,* asks ironically: *Kull mā smaᶜt f-s-sūq shīḥ?* ("Everything heard in the market, is it true?").[140]

No. Nor are all the men one meets trustworthy or all the proposi-tions one is tendered proper. The information situation in the market is itself seriously defective – a hum of locusts. Coping with that fact, trying to filter out of all that outpouring of earnest declaration just what, whom, and how much even to begin to believe, is what *sdiq, maᶜrūf,* and *shīḥ* (trueness as friendship, trueness as consensus, and trueness as health) are all about. They are names for ways of weighing talk.

Judgment: reason, reality, deception, vanity. The judgments – verdicts, if you will – to which the appraisals of bazaar news, the weighings of talk, lead are extremely various and hardly to be captured in four isolated terms. Yet as a general classification of those judgments, or verdicts, an overall typology of them, the oft-heard and intricately deployed words, *maᶜqūl, ḥaqq, kdūb, bāṭel,* do well enough. The categories they evoke are ultimately metaphysical ones: The first two bespeak a movement toward God, the second two a movement away from Him; but brought down into the marketplace as concrete conclusions about mundane matters, they sort what happens there into what seem to

208

Moroccans natural varieties. In a sense, everything one confronts in the bazaar—persons, talk, and actions alike—is rational, authentic, fraudulent, or vacuous; and conclusions about which is which are as impossible to avoid as they are difficult to arrive at.

Maᶜqūl simply means "reasonable," "sensible," "understandable," in the sense of "restrained," "controlled," "unexcessive," "not carried away by passion," "prudent." Historically, the root seems to have referred (the joke is not wholly a joke) to the hobbling of a camel, and it still secondarily means to "confine," "control," "tie up," "fetter," "curb," "bind," even to "impound," "detain," or "arrest." How far this set of "constraint" meanings interworks with the "reason" set in the minds of contemporary speakers is not altogether clear. But that "the understanding" (*ᶜaql*) is conceived in terms of a bridle for "the appetites" (*nafs*) is beyond much question. Reason, here, is neither a mirror nor a lamp, but a tether, a holding in, a curbing, a hobbling—of desire, passion, vitality—in the interest of a moral, ordered life.[141] In the market, *maᶜqūl* is mainly heard in approval or, negated, in disapproval of a price, a contract, a proposal, as, in this sense, "within (or not within) bounds." Though the theological penumbra surrounding it is somewhat different, referring less to notions of natural law than to the necessary containment of the appetitive faculties by the intellectual in any redeemable world, a *taman maᶜqūl* is about what was known in the premodern West as a "just price," and is—as is a "just wage," "just rent," or "just partnership"—a powerful moral idea in bazaar exchange. And if, as in the Western case, no one can define very exactly what a "just price" is and precisely why it is just when a price half or twice its size is not, the sense for the contrary is, nevertheless, quite keen. *Mā ši maᶜqūl; wākka maᶜqūl* ("It isn't just"; "yes, it is so just") is probably the exchange of protestations most often heard in the higgling apologetics of the bazaar.

But where *maᶜqūl* is a fairly easy notion for English speakers to grasp, at least so long as subtleties are bypassed, *ḥaqq*, one of the Quran's most resonant words and one of colloquial speech's most idiomatic, is almost impossible to explain to someone who has never been faced with the problem of having actually to use it. The standard translation is "real," or in the nounal form (*ḥaqīqa*), "reality"; this is not incorrect, just rather unhelpful if one has no idea of what the concept of reality involved might be. "In Arabic, *ḥaqq*," Smith remarks, struggling heroically to summarize the matter in a paragraph,

refers to what is real, genuine, true in and of itself by dint of metaphysical or cosmic status. It is a term par excellence of God. In fact, it refers absolutely to Him, and indeed *al-Ḥaqq* is a name of God not merely in the sense of an

209

attribute but of a denotation. *Huwa al-Ḥaqq*: He is reality ["The Real"] as such. Yet every other thing that is genuine is also *ḥaqq* – and some of the mystics went on to say, is therefore divine. Yet it means reality first, and God only second, for those [i.e., Muslims] who equate Him with reality. It is somewhat interesting . . . that this in a sense makes it more realistic to talk about atheism in Arabic than in English, since in Arabic the question can become whether one believes in Reality, whether one trusts Reality, whether one commits oneself to Reality, and the like. But I let that pass. We simply note that *Ḥaqq* is truth in the sense of the real, with or without the capital R.[142]

The critical point, however, is that, like God, *ḥaqq* is a deeply moralized, active, demanding real, not a neutral, ontological "being" merely sitting there awaiting observation and reflection; a real of prophets not of philosophers. Thus besides "real," and more profoundly, *ḥaqq* means "right," "correct," "obligatory," "necessary," "just," "lawful," "legitimate," "merited," "authentic," and therefore "a right, title, or claim to something," "rightful possession," "property," "one's due," "one's duty, responsibility," "accountability," and a number of other things our notion of the "real," an affair of objects not imperatives, does not encompass. The play of prepositions around the term generates a whole series of judgmental categories constantly applied in the suq and out: *ʿand-ik l-ḥaqq* ("you are right," "right is on your side"); *fī-k l-ḥaqq* ("you are in the wrong"); *min ḥaqq-ek* ("you're entitled to it," "it's your due"); *ḥaqq ʿalī-k* ("it is your duty, responsibility," "you must," "you are obligated to").[143] And as with *klām,* the phrases run on *ḥaqq* seem endless: a beneficiary, a participant in a business deal, a legitimate share in something (a profit, a bundle of goods), a contracted duty, a general responsibility in some matter, a due bill, a fine or indemnity – all are indicated by idioms constructed around *ḥaqq.* And in its plural, the word means "jurisprudence."

Clearly, *ḥaqq* is a rather extreme example of the tendency we have been tracing of Arabic to link a set of disparate ideas into a single morphologically marked off conceptual field no one lexeme can even begin to sum up. (The listing in Wehr here runs to four full columns and dozens of entries and subentries.)[144] But concerning the information situation in the suq, what is important is that the term characterizes the distribution of rights and duties in the frame of conclusions about where (or with whom) reality lies. The rightful and the genuine are fused, and to determine the one is to determine the other. The metaphysical optimism and practical skepticism we have found already in *maʿruf* and *ṣḥīḥ* is here finally reinforced. The facts, in the bazaar or anywhere else, are normative; it is no more possible for them to diverge from the good than for God to lie. What is possible is for men, who can lie and inveterately do, to lose sight of what the facts really are.

210

That lying (*kdūb*) is not just one sin among many in Islam, but in many ways the premier sin, is apparent from the intense quranic imprecations against it: "Who does more wrong, or who is more unjust than he who forges against God a lie?" "Forge not a lie against God, lest He destroy you with punishment."[145] But the condemnation of lying is not less intense in everyday life, where, as prevalent as it is decried, it is seen as the main source of just about every sort of evil. "The Moors," Westermarck remarks with what sounds like prejudice but would not be thought so by Sefroui suwwaqs, "have a large number of proverbs condemning lying, although they cannot be called a truthful race."[146] Whether they are more given to falsehood than anybody else is, of course, both doubtful and beside the point. But that they are obsessed with its malignity, the way Greeks were with that of hubris or Calvinists with that of indolence, is very much to it.

It should be clear from what has already been said why this is so, for the deliberate purveying of falsehoods contravenes almost every norm we have reviewed. The liar is personally not reliable; lies divide opinion, dissolve consensus, and destroy community; lying blemishes, sickens, enfeebles communication. False words or other representations do not just conceal reality, they disown it—resist it, reject it, refuse to accept its demands. On the religious plane, contradictory of "the words of God," lying is quite simply unbelief:

[A] particular sacrosanctity is attributed in the Qur'ān to the word "Truth," *ḥaqq,* and consequently, all use of language which contradicts it in any way is considered to be glaring blasphemy against God and His religion. It is not at all surprising, then, that we find *kadhib,* "falsehood," or "lying," talked of in the *Qur'ān* as a heinous sin. it constitutes one of the most salient features of a *Kāfir.*[147]

On the secular plane lying, a willful undermining of trust in the words of men, is but marginally less serious. So far as the bazaar is concerned, lying—active, deliberate, systematic lying—is the main disruptive force, leading, if it is uncontained, to the feared "snapping of the market," the transformation of relations of exchange into ones of violence. "Greet a liar," says yet another proverb, grimly, "in arms."

Yet lying, though perhaps the most worrisome, is not the only sort of falsity that exists in the world: Ignorance, cant, prattle, slander, cajolery, boasting, inanity, imprudence, deviousness, venality, and that hard to define but easy to detect form of smoke blowing, moral cowardice, are others. The most general term for such things and for the ostensible "information" produced by them is *bāṭel* ("worthless," "vain," "futile," "vacuous," "baseless") or, as Moroccans say in one of their most settled idioms, *kif wālu* ("like nothing," "zeroesville"). Often directly con-

211

trasted with *ḥaqq* in the Quran ("The *ḥaqq* has come and the *bāṭil* has vanished," XVII 83/31), *bāṭel* is sometimes glossed as "unreality"; but its connections are not so much with "illusion," "fantasy," or "hallucination" as with "pointlessness," "uselessness," "inactiveness." *Bṭala* is "unemployment," "absence from school," "a vacation," "an interruption (of an action)"; *bṭel* is "to be canceled, called off," "to be omitted, left out," "to expire, become invalid," "to be dismissed" (a suit, claim, etc.); a *beṭṭāl* is a person out of work or simply "lazy"; *beṭṭel* is "to be absent," "to abolish," "to abrogate," and, with the word for "work" as object, "to go on strike"; *mebṭūl* is "amputated" (a hand, arm, etc.). In the suq context, *bāṭel* essentially means something not worth paying attention to – the vain and vacuous noise emitted more by the weak and foolish of the bazaar (the favorite image is the sound of an empty water jar when struck with the knuckles) than by its accomplished knaves.

Sorting lies and nonsense from the reasonable and the real is the information problem as it finally appears to the suwwaq. Beginning with the hodgepodge of people, words, and news he encounters in the suq (as well as, of course, adding his small bit of confusion to it), he tries to contextualize what he hears, sees, and thinks he understands in terms of his exchange experience with particular individuals, what he knows of general suq practice, and some sort of symptomatology of market deceit to divide it into that which perhaps can be somewhat relied upon (exceedingly the smaller part) and that which very likely cannot (enormously the greater). Three things are true about market information: It is luxuriant, it is unreliable, and there are more ways of getting lost in it than there are of finding paths through it. Virtually the whole institutional structure of the market is, in one way or another, a response to the problem of organizing exchange in such an unpromising situation. Even more remarkably, it is an effective response: Trade goes on, at great pace and some efficiency, in a moral climate that seems almost designed to prevent it.

The shape of trade

The cast of thought – *mentalité, Geisteshaltung, ēthos, ᶜaqalīya* – which the rhetoric of exchange projects is not, therefore, a bodiless subjectivity lodged somewhere in the darker reaches of "the Moroccan mind"; it is an overt, observable feature of a well-lit public arena in Moroccan society.[148] The intricate system of customs, rules, and practical arrangements that marks the suq is at once an adaptation to this cast of thought and the best example of it. More than mere instruments of commerce, the institutions of the bazaar give to trade a distinctive form.

To identify that form, to show that there is such a system and not a mere conglomerate of usages and devices inherited from a checkered past, it is necessary to establish that its elements, the parts of the system, in fact constrain one another; that taken together they constitute a whole within which their presence is logical, their interrelationships motivated, and their workings comprehensible. The terminology here ("constrain," "logical," "motivated," "comprehensible") derives less from a causal idiom, the worn formulas of social mechanics, than from a hermeneutical one, and the choice is deliberate. Extremely complex webs of causal connection cross and recross the whole field of bazaar life, but not only are they extremely difficult, if not impossible, to isolate, they are not germane (or, anyway, not immediately so) to what we here want to display: how the institutions of the suq combine to provide a coherent framework for the processes of exchange and how those processes, in turn, fit intelligibly within that framework. The constraints are partial, the logic approximate, the motivations incomplete, the comprehensibility limited – and the system, thus, as all social systems, far from fully coherent. But, however imperfect, the organization of bazaar institutions into an ordered whole with properties of its own is real. It can be described. And described, it can extend our understanding of how the suq operates and why; can clarify just what sort of animal the bazaar economy is. The deeper physiology of the beast, assuming it has one, will have to wait.

With this proposition as premise, Table 13 has been constructed. It attempts to list, in more or less systematic form, the leading characteristics of the institutional pattern of the bazaar as it has here been described in terms of the information perspective as it has here been defined.[149]

Most of these characteristics, as well as the subpoints extending them, modifying them, or spelling them out, have already been explicitly discussed; others have at least been alluded to, and others will be touched on shortly. It is clear that small enterprises, a finely drawn division of labor, person-to-person transactions, inhomogeneous goods, equivocal signaling systems, the predominance of trading skills, unitary exchange roles, a reliance on personal contract, and a broad dispersion of coordinating mechanisms are prominent features of the bazaar and that, from a communication systems point of view, they somehow go together. What is not so clear – hence the "somehow" – is just what "going together" means in this context.

Primarily it means that, taken together, these features create an exchange situation in which the first problems, and often the last, 213

Table 13. *The bazaar as a communication system: general characteristics*

A. There is a great multiplicity of *small-sized enterprises.*
  1. The commercial class is large in relation to the population as a whole.
  2. There are almost no multifunctional or multitrade enterprises.
  3. Most enterprises have very low fixed costs in terms of rents, machinery, housing, inventory, etc.
  4. There is a continuous gradation from very small, man-on-a-mat enterprises to quite moderately sized (two or three major partners) ones, with the overwhelming majority lying toward the smaller end.

B. There is a very *finely drawn division of labor* in technical, social, and spatial terms.
  1. Occupational specialization is extremely intensive.
  2. Trades are fairly clearly differentiated in ethnic-like (nisba) terms.
  3. There is a significant degree of trade-type localization, especially within bazaars, but also, to an extent, among them.
  4. Temporal coordination of trading sites by means of a periodic marketplace system is highly developed.

C. *Transactions are mostly interpersonal.* They take place between individuals as individuals, not as representatives of collective economic entities (e.g., firms, companies, cooperatives).
  1. There is an enormous plurality of small transactions, each more or less independent of the next.
  2. The overwhelming proportion of those transactions involves two persons, and hardly ever more than three or four persons.
  3. The overwhelming proportion of transactions is face-to-face.
  4. Initial-seller to final-buyer chains are often long and circuitous, involving a large number of intermediary transactions.

D. *Goods and services are inhomogeneous.* Those that flow through the bazaar are, for the most part, highly divisible, extremely various consumption items that are unstandardized, of mixed provenance, and very hard to evaluate.
  1. Trademarks and brand names are absent, and the qualitative classification of goods is markedly subjective and ad hoc.
  2. There is essentially no advertising, even in the form of artful display, and reputation is personal and changing, not corporate and stable. Differential educational attainment (which is not great) plays essentially no role in labor market signaling.
  3. There are no institutions specifically devoted to assembling and distributing market information (e.g., price quotations, production reports, employment agencies, consumer guides).

E. *Formal signaling systems are undeveloped,* both irregular and unreliable, and their outputs are consequently ambiguous and difficult to interpret.
  1. There are virtually no aggregate statistics generally available to market participants concerning any economic variable.
  2. Price dispersion is high, and price movements erratic.
  3. Accounting techniques are unsystematic, clumsy, and unanalytical.
  4. Weight and measure systems are intricate and incompletely standardized. The same is true of grading systems.
  5. Price feedback to production and inventory decisions is poor.

214

Table 13(*cont.*)
F. *Exchange skills predominate* over either managerial or technical ones.
   1. Both technical and managerial skills are but modestly developed, and within any one trade they are too evenly diffused to yield much in the way of competitive advantage.
   2. Exchange skills are very elaborately developed. Differential possession of them is marked and is the primary determinant of who prospers in the bazaar and who does not, as much among craftsmen and laborers as among storekeepers and commodity traders.
   3. Haggling, in the strict sense of arguing, wrangling, caviling over terms with respect to any aspect or condition of exchange (i.e., not just price bargaining), is pervasive, strenuous, and unremitting.

G. As general processes, *buying and selling are virtually undifferentiated.* Essentially a single activity, the assumptions and procedures governing the one are the same as for the other.
   1. Tastes are autonomous: They are still mainly traditionally set and the operation of the market has at best a marginal and/or very long-term impact upon them.
   2. Trading involves a serial search for specific partners, not the mere offering of goods to the general public.
   3. Intensive search (i.e., pursuing matters with a given partner) is primary; extensive search (surveying competing offers) is but ancillary to it.
   4. Clientship to and between specific merchants and craftsmen is very common. Free shopping in an anonymous market is avoided.

H. The (normally oral, sometimes written) *personal contract is the main legal form of relationship.*
   1. Partnerships are preferred to employer-employee organization.
   2. Socialization into trades and crafts is by an apprenticeship system considered as a special form of (unequal) partnership.
   3. The regulation of disputes involves the testimony by reliable witnesses to factual matters, not the weighing of competing juridical principles.

I. *Overall integrative institutions are diffuse,* informal, and generally weak.
   1. Governmental controls over marketplace activity are marginal, decentralized, and mostly rhetorical.
   2. There is virtually no hierarchical coordination of enterprises in wholesale/retail, headquarters/branch, supplier/distributor organization. Firm bureaucracy is extremely rare.
   3. There are no true guilds consolidating trades into corporate units, but rather an interaction of various crosscutting forms of trade classification. Functioning trade unions, business associations, consumer organizations are also absent.

facing would-be participants are to obtain reasonably reliable information of even the most elementary sort about the relevant economic variables (not all of which – e.g., whether the participants are *aṣdiqā* ["friends"] – are economic in the stricter sense) and having obtained such information, to use the knowledge differential it creates to advantage. The very difficulty of doing this in a diffuse, highly personal, highly fractionated setting without the aid of settled standards, unambiguous signals, or believable statistics raises the natural enough desire not to operate in the dark to the level of a ruling passion and heightens enormously the utility of even partially succeeding. When information is both widely scattered and poorly encoded, as well as transmitted along channels it would be flattery to call noisy, it takes on a special prominence. The usual vicissitudes of life and trade aside (and most suwwaqs regard them as wholly beyond the reach of man), the only thing that can really hurt you in the bazaar is what you don't know . . . and someone else does.

There are at least two consequences of this state of affairs: (1) any notion of attacking, altering, or systematically manipulating the general framework of economic life is absent; and (2) search is the paramount economic activity, the one upon which virtually everything else turns, and much of the apparatus of the marketplace is concerned with rendering it practicable.

Aside from sporadic protests concerning government regulations – usually those having to do with taxation or the attempt to fix prices – collective action in favor of one or another sort of economic policy simply does not appear.[150] Indeed, the very idea of policy (to say nothing of planning, a notion that has not managed to diffuse the few hundred meters from the city hall where, in the form of *planification,* it is, in a theoretical way, quite popular) is foreign in a context where what matters is capitalizing on dysfunctions, not correcting them. The nationalist activity of the Independence period already described, which comes as close to concerted effort by suwwaqs as suwwaqs as has ever occurred in Sefrou, was dedicated to a rather simple political aim, not an economic or even politicoeconomic one. And that half-exception half aside, what has been, and remains, remarkable about the bazaar class (and not merely in Sefrou) is that, given its large size, its great vigor, its enormous strategic importance, and its reputation for explosiveness, it has neither exercised nor made any effort to exercise any conscious, organized influence on the conditions of its existence. In commerce, as in the cosmos, parameters are parameters.[151]

The given being so flatly given, the energies of the suwwaq that are not absorbed in the more routine demands of his occupation are freed for what is, when all is said and done, the critical task: combing the suq for usable signs, clues to how particular matters at the immediate moment specifically stand. The matters investigated may include everything from the industriousness of a prospective co-worker or the reliability of a certain craftsman to regional variations in taste or the supply situation in agricultural products. But the two most persistent concerns, which more or less sum and enfold all the others, are with price and the

216

quality of goods. The overwhelming centrality of exchange skills – as
against those involved in production or coordination – puts tremendous
emphasis on knowing what particular things are actually selling for and
what sort of thing they precisely are. And it is toward gaining such
knowledge, or at least reducing one's ignorance somewhat, that search,
the really advanced art in the suq, is directed.[152]

From such a perspective, the various elements of the institutional
structure of the bazaar can be seen in terms of the degree to which
they, on the one hand, render search a high and difficult, thus costly,
enterprise or, on the other, serve to facilitate it and so bring its costs
(the main one of which is time) within practical limits. Not that all
those elements line up neatly on one side of the ledger or the other.
Most have effects in both directions, for suwwaqs are about as interested in making search bootless for others as they are in making it
effectual for themselves. The desire to know what is really going on is
matched by the desire to deal with people who do not but imagine
they do (in that direction profit lies), and so the structures enabling
search and those casting obstructions in its path are thoroughly intertwined. Indeed, they are often the same structures.

Some of the features of bazaar trade evoked in Table 13 seem, on
balance, to be fairly clearly search impeding: the multiplicity of units,
the inhomogeneity of goods, price dispersion (a measure, in part of
inhomogeneity and, beyond it, of the general difficulty "participants in
the market have [in] collecting information about their environments"),
the amorphousness of business reputation.[153] Others, on the same balance, seem to be as clearly search facilitating: the localization (and
"nisbazation") of markets, the elaboration of exchange skills, the perva-
siveness of clientship. Yet others – discriminatory (sliding) prices, the
interpersonal quality of exchange, the intensive division of labor – are
more ambiguous in their effects. But it is the overall pattern – the interaction of such institutions as they set the conditions for search – that
needs to be understood if we are to see how would-be exchangers find
their way through the jungle of prices and cacophony of goods the suq
represents to some commercial consummation. And for this, a brief
consideration of the two most important search procedures – clientelization and bargaining – can be of use. The one concerned with finding
an exchange partner, the other with what to do with him once you have
found him, the two procedures bring almost all aspects of the bazaar
system in some way within their ken.

Search: clientelization. Strictly, clientelization applies to the tendency,
very marked in the suq, for repetitive purchasers of certain goods and   217

services – whether consumption ones like vegetables or barbering, or intracommercial ones like bulk weaving or porterage – to establish continuing relationships with certain purveyors, occasionally one, much more often a half dozen or so, instead of searching widely through the market at each occasion of need. More broadly it applies to the establishment of relatively enduring exchange relations of any sort, for in essence the phenomenon is the same, whether the client is a household head buying his morning piece of lamb, a cloth seller laying in his weekly stock of jellaba materials, an adolescent apprenticing himself to a carpenter, or an arbitrager consigning his gathered-up goods to a carter or truck driver to be taken off to another market. Within what looks like Brownian movement of randomly colliding suwwaqs is concealed (concealed, at least, to casual observation) a definite and surprisingly resilient pattern of specific, if informal, personal connections. Whether or not "buyers and sellers, blindfolded by a lack of knowledge simply grop[ing] about until they bump into one another" is, as has been proposed, a reasonable description of modern labor markets (and anybody who has been in one would hardly think so), it certainly is not of the suq, whose buyers and sellers, moving along the grooved channels clientelization lays down, find their way again and again to the same adversaries.[154]

"Adversaries" is the correct word, for, some apprenticeship and some credit arrangements partially aside (and the vanished sitting Jew/ riding Jew systems wholly so), clientship relations are not, either in fact or in conception, dependency relations: They are competitive ones. Given the unitary view of buying and selling, the avoidance of explicitly hierarchical organizational forms, and the preference for face-to-face dealings, clientship is perceived as at once symmetrical, egalitarian, and oppositional. There are, a few half-exceptions again apart, no real patrons, in the master and man sense, here. Whatever the relative power (wealth, knowledge, skill, status) of the participants – and it can be spectacularly uneven – clientship is a reciprocal matter, and the butcher, wool seller, tailor, or coffeeshop keeper is tied to his regular customers in precisely the same terms as they are to him. By partitioning the bazaar crowd into those who, from the point of view of a man in the middle of it, are genuine candidates for his attention and those, infinitely the larger group, who are merely theoretically such, clientelization reduces search to manageable proportions, transforms a diffuse, anonymous mob into a reasonably stable collection of familiar antagonists.[155]

This use of repetitive exchange between acquainted partners as the main behavioral strategy for limiting the time costs of search (others,

218

such as the employment of agents, bulk purchasing and selling, formal *Suq: the bazaar*
subcontracting, collective pooling of information, do exist, but they *economy in Sefrou*
are much less important) is both a practical consequence of the overall
institutional structure of the suq and an element within that structure
itself—a reflex of the rules by which the game of trade is defined and
a procedural device that makes the game playable.

In the first place, the high degree of submarket specialization in
technical, spatial, and quasi-ethnic terms simplifies the process of finding plausible clients and stabilizes its achievements. If one wants a
kaftan or a mule pack made, one knows where, how, and for what
sorts of persons to look; and, as individuals do not move easily from
one line of work or one place to another, once you have found a cloth
seller, weaver, tailor, or saddler (or more often, several of each) in
whom you can have some faith and who seems to have some faith in
you, he is likely going to be there awhile. One is not constantly faced
with new faces in unaccustomed places and the consequent necessity
to seek out new clients. Search, in brief, is made accumulative.[156]

In the second place, clientelization itself lends form to the bazaar,
rather than merely relying on the form that is already there, for it
further partitions the bazaar in directly informational terms, dividing
the market into complexly overlapping subpopulations within which
more rational estimates of the quality of information, and thus of the
appropriate amount and type of search, can be made. Suwwaqs are not
projected, as for example tourists are, into foreign settings where
everything from the degree of price dispersion and the provenance of
goods to the stature of participants and the etiquette of contract are
unknown to them. They operate, as they have since the days of the
zettata and the qirad, in places where they are very much at home and
rarely stray very far from them. (Those places themselves may of
course be widely scattered: Moroccans are anything but geographically
immobile.)

Below the level of the gross institutional differentiation of the bazaar
economy—periodization, localization, specialization, hierarchicaliza-
tion—and lying athwart it, a fine structure of communication is formed
that has a high degree of stability and brings the problem of figuring out
what is what within manageable limits. The oft-noted tendency for
individuals to frequent particular bazaars when other markets, equally
(sometimes even more) accessible, would seem to offer a more competitive environment, a wider variety of goods, or a more efficiently
organized setting is but the most obvious indication of the reality of the
advantage this fine structure provides for someone who is even peripherally part of it. As Rothschild has remarked, "perfect competition will

219

not protect the imperfect consumer" (or, he might have added, the imperfect seller); but integration into a network of client relations, reducing the imperfection, can, at least to a degree.[157]

The preference of market goers for familiar suqs, however inefficient in terms of some ideal system of distribution, is evidence not of "traditional," "irrational," or "noneconomic" modes of thought, but of a clear understanding of how bazaars really work and what it takes to thrive in one. That an ordinary villager wishing to dispose of a few sheep prefers the arbitrager in his locality-focusing market to the broker in the Sefrou region-focusing one or, a steeper gradient yet, the Sefrou broker to the Fez exporter with whom the broker deals, despite the "obvious" advantages of the more developed settings is a reflex of his realization that those advantages are genuine only for persons with the clientship connections to exploit them.

Indeed, the enormous multiplication, not only of marketplaces and cycles of marketplaces, but of units within marketplaces, and the fractionization of exchange, the elongation of transaction chains, and the intensification of specialization that go with that multiplication ("l'hypertrophie des étalage et des négociants," as Troin, who has a rather overharsh view, puts it " . . . la pénurie . . . diffusée dans l'espace"), are not mere symptoms of "backwardness" or "lack of enterprise." They are related features of a system in which exchange is mediated across a thousand webs of informal personal contract.[158] When relations are so immediate in character, demand so much in nuanced response and detailed attention, the number any one individual can effectively manage is clearly very limited, and the proliferation of small bazaars, shops, traders and exchanges is a natural development. This has long been recognized in the area of credit, where the penalties of not knowing whom you are dealing with take on a peculiar force; but it applies to bazaar exchange all the way across the board.[159] Where the flow of economic transactions runs along channels of mutual knowledge, trust, and loyalty (or supposed such), the fractionization, miniaturization, specialization, and chain linking of trade units are unavoidable if that flow is to maintain any volume at all. Replication is a substitute for scale as direct acquaintance is for public repute; clientelization, complexification, and *"l'hypertrophie des négociants"* are all of a piece.

In the most general terms, clientelization represents an actor-level attempt to counteract, and indeed to profit from, the system-level deficencies of the bazaar as a communications network – its structural intricateness and irregularity, the absence of certain sorts of signaling systems and the undeveloped state of others, and the imprecision, scattering, and uneven distribution of knowledge concerning economic matters of fact – by improving the richness and reliability of information carried over elementary links within it. The rationality of this on the surface somewhat quixotic effort, rendering the clientship relation dependable as a communications channel, while its functional context remains unimproved, rests in turn on the presence within that relation of just the sort of effective mechanism for information transfer that seems so lacking elsewhere. And as that relation is adversary – men seeking gain at one another's expense – so too is the mechanism: intensive bargaining along virtually every dimension of commercial life. The central paradox of bazaar exchange is that advantage stems from surrounding oneself with relatively superior communications links, links that themselves are forged in a sharply agonistic interaction in which the existence of information imbalances is the driving force and their exploitation the end.

Search: bargaining. The proper understanding of bazaar bargaining has been somewhat hampered by the moral ambivalance that open, unapologetic jockeying for material advantage tends to arouse in the minds of those not habituated to it. The appreciation of its presumedly integrative economic effects – especially in price making, to which it is too often considered to be confined – goes hand in hand with fear and dislike of its supposedly disruptive effects on the social order. When the appreciation dominates, as it does among most economists, the alleged socially disruptive effects are written off as so many unpleasant but unavoidable social costs. When the dislike dominates, as it does among most anthropologists, the presumed economic functions are regarded as being less painfully performed by more cooperative forms of exchange in marketless societies. In either case, bargaining tends to be represented rather negatively – either a necessary evil or an avoidable one, but in any case an evil.[160]

A more positive characterization of bargaining begins and ends with the recognition that it is a particular mode of information search, not a means for integrating prices (which, given the system frailties of bazaar communication, it can hardly do and, by concealing transactions as private deals, may even hinder) or of exercising the instinct of sociability.[161] The relationships that clientelization (the search for vis-à-vis) produces, bargaining (the search for terms) actualizes. Bargaining's function is to provide men who, amid the suspicions that haunt the suq, have managed to develop enough confidence to imagine trading with one another, with a workable means of actually doing so.

As a process exploring the instant possibilities of face-to-face exchange, suq bargaining displays four critical characteristics:

221

1. Though price setting, in the narrow sense, is the most conspicuous aspect of bargaining, the higgling spirit penetrates the whole of the confrontation: Whatever is alterable is negotiable.
2. The competitors in a bargaining situation are a buyer and a seller – not two or more sellers, as in modern retail markets; two or more suppliers, as in bid-for-contract markets; or two or more buyers as in an auction.
3. Bargaining does not operate in purely pragmatic, utilitarian terms, but is hedged in by deeply felt rules of etiquette, tradition, and moral expectation.
4. The amount of bargaining involved in any one transaction is affected by a wide number of factors, the more important of which include: type and quantity of good, depth of clientelization, frequency of repetitive exchange, degree of information asymmetry, the shadow price of time, and the relative economic strength of the principals.

Regarding the first item, the most obvious method of manipulating the terms of trade, aside from altering (money) price while keeping quantity and quality constant, is to alter quantity and/or quality while keeping price constant; this is an extremely widespread practice in the suq. In some transactions, especially of ordinary foodstuffs, manipulation may simply consist in adding or subtracting items to the prepriced pile of fruit, vegetables, meats, or whatever. Or, rather commonly in cloth dealings, the buyer may first offer a price and then higgle with the seller over what it will buy.[162] In other transactions – wheat and wool sales, for example – the manipulation may consist in varying the size of supposedly established units, something the imperfect standardization of weights and measures not only facilitates, but actually encourages. A pint may be a pound the world around, but a *medd* (the reigning grain measure) certainly is not.[163] In yet others, it may consist in offering higher (or lower) quality goods from behind or under the counter.[164] Bulking and, much more significantly, bulk breaking – selling kitchen matches by the match, detergent by the cup – provide an important dimension of negotiation flexibility. Even labor contracts are highly manipulable, and highly manipulated, in work-condition terms. And so on. In a system where so little is packaged, not much more is regulated, and almost everything is approximative, it is almost always possible to do a deal in, so to speak, real rather than monetary terms.

Many other matters in the exchange confrontation are capable of manipulation, including aspects of the clientelization relationship itself. (For some examples of these, see Annex D, "The Song of the

222

Baker": "I bring him [the baker] any news or gossip I hear quickly/Yet he has sworn not to give my bread its due.") Probably the most important is credit, all but the most marginal of transactions being conducted in these terms. Despite appearances, the suq is anything but a cash-and-carry affair; the management of credit balances is a high and delicate art through a very large part of it, and the mechanism of such management is inevitably bargaining. The famous remark of Keynes to the effect that if you owe your banker a thousand dollars you are in his power but if you owe him a million he is in yours, applies – if in radically reduced figures – with great force to the bazaar, where the actual terms of trade as often lie hidden in debt relations as exposed in price quotations.[165]

Aside from the sheer amount of credit (the level of credit balance that is to be maintained between any two cliented suwwaqs) several other aspects of credit giving and taking enter into the bargaining sphere. Although the Islamic prohibition of usury normally removes an open interest rate as a possible item of negotiation, it certainly does not remove a concealed one, and the interaction of credit balances and money prices is an intricate matter, subject to a very high level of moral nuance and commercial artfulness.[166]

Similarly, repayment schedules, which can be extremely complicated and adjusted to all sorts of special situations (salary periods, festival rhythms, seasonal variations, personal conjunctures, acts of God), are often a prime object of negotiation. So are partial payment liquidations of debt, a phenomenon rather more common than one might imagine and, even more surprising, one that does not always dissolve clientship ties: *lli fāt māt* ("what is past is dead") the not very injured creditor says and starts the relationship up, on an even more favorable basis to himself, again. And so, too, is the giving of security, almost always in a pawn-type pattern, where the lender holds the collateral (jewelry, grain, rugs), rather than a mortgage-type one, where the borrower does. The role of credit in the exchange process is very great, and every dimension of it – amount, conditions, forms – is subject to higgling of the most thoroughgoing sort, rivaling at least and often actually dwarfing price higgling as such.

The second characteristic of suq bargaining aside from its intricately multidimensional character – higgling along several interactive gradients at once – is that it channels competitive stress across the exchange frontier rather than along it (i.e., between buyer and seller, rather than between seller and seller). This has a number of implications from an information-and-communications view of bazaar exchange, of which the most important is that search more readily takes the form of exploring matters in depth with particular partners than surveying widely through the market, a case approach rather than a sampling one, or what Rees has called an "intensive" as opposed to an "extensive" strategy:

The search for information in any market has both an extensive and an intensive margin. A buyer can search at the extensive margin by getting a quotation from one more seller. He can search at the intensive margin by getting additional information concerning an offer already received. Where the goods and services sold are highly standardized, the extensive margin is the more important; when there is great variation in quality, the intensive margin moves to the forefront. This point can be illustrated by considering the markets for new and used cars. Since there is relatively little variation in the quality of new cars of the same make and model and since the costs of variation are reduced by factory guarantees, the extensive margin of search is the important one. A rational buyer will get quotations from additional dealers until the probable reduction in price from one additional quotation is less than the cost of obtaining it.

In used cars of the same make, model, and year, much of the variation in asking prices reflects differences in the conditions of the cars, and this calls for a substantial change in the strategy of the rational buyer. He will invest less in obtaining large numbers of offers and much more in examining each car. For example, he may have each car he seriously considers inspected by a mechanic. He may want information on the history of the car as a substitute for the direct assessment of condition and will pass up a used taxi in favor of the car owned by the proverbial little old lady who drives only to church. It will not be irrational for him to pay a relatively high price for a car owned by a friend if he has favorable information about his friend's habits as a car owner.[167]

The prominence of bargaining is thus a measure of the degree to which the suq is more like a used car than a new car market: one in which the important information problems have to do with determining the realities of the particular case than the general distribution of comparable cases.[168] Further, and more important, bargaining is an expression of the fact that such a market rewards a clinical form of search (one that focuses on the diverging interests of concrete economic actors: individual suwwaqs wrangling an exchange) rather more than it does a survey form (one that focuses on the general interplay of functionally defined economic classes: anonymous crowds of vendors and customers integrating prices).[169] Search is intensive, in Rees's sense, or anyway primarily so, because the sort of information one most has to have cannot be acquired by asking a handful of index questions of a large number of people, but only by asking (and answering) a large number of diagnostic questions of a handful of people. It is this kind of questioning (and counterquestioning), exploring nuances rather than canvassing populations, that, for the most part, suq bargaining represents.

All this is not to say that extensive search plays no role in the bazaar, but rather that it is considered ancillary to intensive search, the true heart of the matter. Suwwaqs, in fact, make a clear distinction between bargaining to test the waters (*sāwem,* from a root meaning "to estimate the value of an object," "to appraise something") and bargaining to conclude an exchange (*tšeṭṭer,* from a root meaning "to divide, split, or share out something") and tend to conduct the two in different places: the first with people with whom they do not have clientship ties (or at most weak ones); the second with people with whom they do. This reduces the value of extensive search even further, of course, for bargaining is not likely to be serious when the participants know exchange is unlikely to eventuate, though the desire of suwwaqs to extend their clientele acts to correct this somewhat, and what begins as *sāwem,* an extensive bargaining relationship between mere acquaintances, can end as *tšeṭṭer,* an intensive one between suq "friends," if things go right. In general, extensive search tends to be desultory and to be considered an activity not worth large investments of time.[170] From the point of view of search (which, trying to sort the real and the reasonable from the lying and the vain in a swirl of news, is the suwwaq's point of view), the truly productive type of bargaining is that of the clientelized buyer and seller exploring the dimensions of a particular, likely-to-be-consummated transaction. Here, as elsewhere in the suq, everything rests finally on a personal confrontation between intimate antagonists.

The whole structure of bargaining as a social institution is determined by this fact: that bargaining is a communications channel evolved to serve the needs of men coupled and opposed at the same time. The rules governing it – some of them technical, some of them merely conventional, and many of them deeply moral – are a response to a situation in which (normally) two persons on opposite sides of some exchange possibility are at once struggling to make that possibility actual and to gain some (usually) very marginal advantage within it. Most bazaar price negotiation takes place to the right of the decimal point, a good deal of it several places to the right; but it is no less keen for that.

The technical rules are more or less given by the situation and thus are essentially universal, the same in Haiti or Oaxaca as in Nigeria or Morocco. "A tug of war between seller and buyer," bargaining as a formal procedure consists in a series of alternating, stepwise approaches toward an agreed price from separated initial offers. The

225

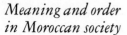

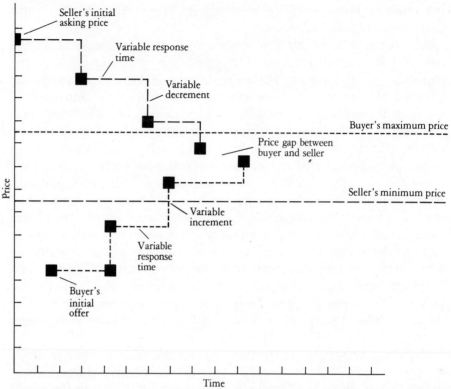

Figure 7. Bargaining: the basic model. (After R. Cassady, "Negotiated Price Making in Mexican Traditional Markets," *América indígena,* 28:51–79, 1968.)

most important variable factors are the spread between the initial offers, the size and number of the approaching steps, the distance each participant can be persuaded or can persuade himself to go, and the amount of time the process takes. Cassady has presented a use-fully simple model of the process (Figure 7).[171]

Within this frame, the course of bargaining mainly depends on the size of the settlement region – the overlap between the maximum price the buyer will pay and the minimum price the seller will accept. If the overlap is wide, agreement is virtually certain; if it is narrow, agreement is less so; if it is nonexistent (i.e., the buyer's maximum is below the seller's minimum), accord is impossible. Considered as a communications channel, bargaining consists of a system of conventionalized signals designed to reveal which of these situations obtains. Sluggishness on one side or the other, or on both, in moving toward consensus – long periods between bid changes and/or small magnitudes of change – indicates agreement will be difficult at best and per-

haps impossible; the inverse suggests the inverse. Bargaining gener-
large bid changes accelerate it toward consummation; slow and small
ones declerate it toward abortion. It is the way things move that
counts.

More precisely, there are three main phases of intensive bargaining: initial bidding, movement toward a settlement region, and, if
that region is in fact entered, settlement itself. The absolute separation of initial bids, almost never so great in bargaining between
clients as to preclude exchange from the start, suggests how wide the
settlement region is likely to be (the greater the separation, the
narrower) and the difficulty of reaching it.[172] The rapidity of movement toward the settlement region further specifies the situation (the
faster, the wider). And the settlement itself will be more protracted
the wider the region as each participant, more or less assured of
exchange, maneuvers to locate final price a few rial closer to his
boundary than to his antagonist's. (Where the region is narrow, the
final phase, if it is reached, hardly differs from the middle one.) The
interaction of these processual signals with price signals as such (i.e.,
how much is at stake) is, of course, complex, and the variation in the
temporal structure of bargaining is consequently extremely great.[173]
But so too, are the capacities of accomplished suwwaqs to discrimi-
nate the signals: A sense for the "music" of chaffering is one of the
primary (and one of the most unequally distributed) exchange skills
in the bazaar.[174]

This formal dimension of bargaining is, of course, supported by a
wide range of conventions: that the seller bids first, that bids alternate,
that backward moves are forbidden, that accepted bids must be honored, that one ought not break off an interchange that is moving
actively ahead, and so on. Like any conventions, these may sometimes
be breached – a buyer is sometimes forced to make the initial bid,
several consecutive moves are occasionally made by one side or
another, a buyer occasionally refuses to purchase at a price he has
already offered or walks away from a responsive seller – but hardly
ever without complaint from the injured party. The cry Cassady heard
from an Oaxaca vendor – "I *palabra* three times and you only *palabra*
once" – can be heard now and then (though there the term is *tkellem*)
in Sefrou as well, and suwwaqs have been known to strike people who
fail to exchange at a price they themselves have offered.[175] The conventions of bargaining thus slip into its etiquette and morality. This is
a vast subject, touching on everything from speech styles (which can
be very elaborate – the "I will give you kisses, I will give you hugs"   227

rhetoric of bazaar trading those foreign to it consistently misinterpret as hypocrisy) and hospitality patterns (hardly any large-scale exchange in the suq is consummated without drinking tea, and for clients tea may accompany even small-scale deals) to humor, flexibility, and patience. But the main principle animating bargaining is that participants should conduct themselves vis-à-vis one another so as to render the process successful. Both buyer and seller have more than a material desire to triumph over their functional opposition to effect an exchange: They have a moral obligation to do so. For only to the degree that they are able to do this over and over again, able to keep aborted encounters to the absolute minimum of those cases where there is no settlement region, can the bargaining relationship serve them as an effective communications channel, a useful device for intensive search:

Bargaining . . . serves an economic purpose, that is, to regulate prices in societies where suspicion and uncertainty of the value of commodities dominate. In the Middle East [and North Africa], bargaining is not for fun, nor merely for the sake of bargaining. Through the manipulation of cultural norms and symbols, a bargainer, whether seller or buyer, aims to eliminate suspicion of commodity and price and establish instead an atmosphere of trust often leading to client-relationships, and occasionally to friendship. True . . . "business tricks" . . . are used, but even these tricks cannot be carried out without the initial establishment of trust and through an idiom of trust: kinship terms, polite formulas, observance of good manners. In the Middle Eastern case, the failure of a bargainer to evoke and manipulate this idiom of trust leads eventually to a failure in successfully consummating the intended transaction. As long as the consummation of a transaction depends primarily on the establishment of trust in bargaining, trust necessarily takes precedence over the profit motive. Any act of discourtesy . . . inevitably puts an end to the bargain[ing] . . .

In bargaining, the social status of the bargaining partners is at stake. They attempt to neutralize this status by following the strict rules of bargaining etiquette. But bargaining is not used only to neutralize positions, but also to improve them. If either party to the bargain, seller or buyer, is unusually successful in his approach, he earns social recognition among his group by developing the reputation of knowing how to "handle" people and subsequently affect their choice of behavior. Since profit in bargaining is translated into social recognition, seller-bargainers in the Middle East resort to all sorts of polite formulas to affect the economic choice of their partners . . .

In the absence of [fixed prices], as in the sūqs of the Middle East, bargaining becomes essential to . . . sustained economic relationships between buyer and seller. Just as bargaining enables the buyer to distinguish reliable sellers from unreliable ones . . . it also enables the seller to eliminate distrustful buyers . . . and to establish lasting clientship with trustful ones . . . Hence, in a very intricate and sensitive way, bargaining brings order into an otherwise uncontrolled market system.[176]

Bargaining and clientelization are thus not so much two search processes, the one following after the other in the tracks laid down, as reinforcing aspects of a single search process. Through intensive bargaining, enclosed in an established cake of custom, clientship is formed and given substance; clientship, an institutionalized bazaar-friendship relation, with its own rules, obligations, and expectations, directs intensive bargaining and contains its powerful agonistic elements within an organizing moral code. The elaboration and stabilization of the two-person communication link that enables operation in the information cacophony of the suq can be seen equally as a social relationship within which an exchange pattern forms or an exchange pattern around which a social relationship forms. In either case, whether "clientelized bargaining" or "bargainized clientship," it is a good deal more than a war of opposed preferences.

Finally, the amount of bargaining that takes place in any given transaction is itself highly variable. *Ceteris paribus,* which they never are, higher price transactions normally take longer than lower price exchanges, strong clientship ties normally shorten bargaining time, repetitive exchanges (e.g., buying food) are normally completed more rapidly than occasional ones (e.g., buying a cow), and so on. Several even more incidental facts also influence the amount of bargaining: time of day; season of the year; inventory size, composition, and flexibility; the perishability of the goods; the "fullness" of the bazaar; and, not least, the relative social status, experience, astuteness, and the mere temperaments of the participants – the list, if not infinite, is surely very long.

The shadow price of time for a suwwaq may not be as high as for a modern corporation executive, but it is not so low as is often thought. The length of time bargaining takes is an important cost for suwwaqs, who could, after all, be higgling with someone else and who in any case are extremely busy men in their attempts to cumulate a large number of marginal gains into a decent living. Along with the ability to assess the quality of goods and the rationality of their prices, and the capacity to persuade others into profitable agreements, a sense for whether a particular effort to come to terms is worth the candle is a primary attribute of an effective suwwaq. One needs to know not only how to bargain, but how long.[177]

The information game: the large and the small. Looked at from the point of view of the observing ethnographer, *sūq Ṣ-Ṣefrū* is a distended complexity; looked at from the point of view of the acting suwwaq, it is a shrunken one. The individual shopkeeper, artisan, arbitrager, auctioneer, or target seller operates over a very narrow region of what, when it is projected onto the level of a comprehensive description, is a vast and multiplex system ramifying irregularly in diverse dimensions. From within, the whole, as a whole, is but a dim outline. It spreads away from the individual like a sea, its general form perceived in only the most abstract and simplified terms and regarded – the overall behavior of prices, flow of goods, location of marketplaces, distribution of wealth – as so much presented fact. It is the immediate environment, the surround of actual and potential exchange partners, particular men in particular places placing particular prices on particular goods, that is apprehended in concrete and differentiated form and toward which the energies of the struggle for advantage, immense, unremitting, and sensitive to microns, are directed. What in the large is beyond human control is, in the little, malleable to the ambitions of lilliput merchants.

Clearing a small space in the grand cacophony of the suq where one can interpret and evaluate information with at least some minimal confidence is thus the central strategy of any suwwaq. The multiplicity of enterprises, the intensive division of labor, the inhomogeneity of goods, the complexity of the flow of trade, the elaborate structure of religious, ethnic, and moral categorization are overcome, to the degree they are overcome, by constructing around oneself a personal network of exchange relations in which these matters can be given a reasonably determinate, stabilized form. The gross structure of the bazaar, considered as an institution – one of the great social formations of Moroccan (and, beyond it, Mideastern) civilization, on a par, at least, with the city, the state, the family, the clan, the village, or even *ummat l-Islām* – only sets the frame within which the fine structure, a virtual infinity of overlapping suwwaq-to-suwwaq connection clusters, develops. At the heart of the suq system, considered as an information game, lies a seeming paradox dissolved by a familiar principle. The paradox is that comprehensive ignorance promotes local knowledge. The principle is that in the country of the blind, the one-eyed man is king.

This can perhaps be most easily clarified with the aid of what may seem a rather curious model but is actually an apt one: horseracing.

As M. B. Scott has shown, horseracing revolves, like the suq, around the distribution of information, information being "defined simply as what a social actor knows about a situation."[178] Considered formally, horseracing consists of three main parts: the race as such, the betting on the race before it is run, and the payoffs to successful bettors after the race is run. The odds on the individual horses, and thus the payoffs, are pari-mutuel (i.e., they are determined by the distribution of bets: the greater the percentage of the entire pool wagered on a particular horse, the less, dollar for dollar, the return to the bettor if he wins, and vice versa). For the bettor, therefore, the road to maximization consists not just in picking winning horses, but in picking winning horses others do not pick; that is, in possessing (correct) information – knowledge – about a situation with respect to which those from whom he profits are either ignorant or misinformed. "There is," as the racing writer Joe Palmer once said, "nothing better around a track than a well-told lie except a truth that no one will believe."[179]

One has, then, a crowd of bettors out of which the actual race selects a much smaller crowd of winners; the larger crowd of losers is kept more or less in play by the fact that there is, save for those washed out entirely, always another race coming along. Although the role of luck, important in any game where information is less than perfect, plays a role in determining betting success, as does capital, enabling one to engage in more elaborate strategies, the main differentiating factor between the effective and the ineffective horseplayer is, as Scott demonstrates in fine detail, the amount of knowledge (or ignorance) they possess concerning the instant facts:

What is generated in the world of horse racing is an *information game.* The information game is a game of *strategy.* That is, each player in deciding on a course of action takes into account that other players are engaged in the same sort of accounting. The players in this game are concerned with *strategic information,* which is not shared by the players in interaction; if this information were shared, the nature of the interaction would be radically different. Since information is a crucial feature of this game, much activity will be devoted toward discovering, concealing, and using information. Taken together, these *patterns* of interaction make up the information game, and the *mode* of interaction characteristic of the information game [may] be called *strategic interaction.*

For [the] players, the object of this game is to obtain "reliable information," which will enable them to make winning bets. Each bet may be called a play, and the game generated event where the play occurs is the race. To make a successful play is to "beat the race." A continual pattern of beating the race gives rise to the much sought state of "beating the game" or "beating the system."[180]

Scott goes on to describe both the various sorts of players in this game (owners, trainers, jockeys, stewards, bookies, touts, regular bettors, occasional bettors, hustlers) and the devices they employ (form charts, paddock observation, personal contacts, a great deal of rumor chasing and rumor mongering) in their effort to gain an information edge over their fellows.

231

There are, obviously, substantial differences between playing horses and operating in the suq (that is why racing is only a model): Rival bettors do not bet against one another directly; the formal aids to search are very much more developed; action is well defined and discontinuous; a mass of unprofessional participants is thrown in together with a much smaller number of professionals. Yet the structure of the information game as such is the same (that is why racing is a model): a set of interest-opposed individuals pursuing the high art of local, intensive, qualitative search so as to capitalize on the ambiguity, scarcity, and maldistribution of knowledge generated by the system as a whole. Beating the game, either in the suq or in horseracing, something rather difficult in both cases, does not turn on how much you know as such. That rarely comes to a great deal anyway. It turns on how much more you know (i.e., how much less ignorant you are) about particular, given cases than others are – how many races (exchanges) you can beat. Whatever their other differences, which are vast, both the horseplayer and the suwwaq live, or fail to, from marginal information asymmetries they first detect and then exploit.

Leaving the model behind, its analogical force already a bit extended, this concept of the bazaar as an information game played out in piddling maneuvers casts a somewhat different light on its general structure. Rather than an ascending hierarchy of broader integrations, each one manned by more and more imposing entrepreneurs, it is a vast field of petty traders and craftsmen, amid which now and then a more consequential individual arises. Success in the bazaar – and there are those who succeed by any standard, though not very many, and usually not for very long – comes from accumulating small-scale advantages, not from coordinating large-scale activities. With modern developments, especially in such fields as construction and transport, a few such large-, or anyway larger-, scale managerial types have begun to appear. But, for the most part, the suq is still populated, indeed overpopulated, by scramblers, some a bit more adroit, a bit more lucky, or a bit more relentless than others.

The extreme difficulty, if not the impossibility, of seeing the suq steadily and whole, of gaining knowledge about its general workings sufficiently circumstantial to enable one to conceive large-scale operations or pursue long-term strategies – to say nothing of exercising any deliberate control over those workings – reduces the suwwaq's life to a continuing string of hand-to-hand combats in particular, intimately known corners of commercial life, a microworld of perfected tactics. The overall structure of the suq, a weakly joined system of multiple divisions, multiple units, multiple signals, and multiple activities, none of them either clearly outlined or well standardized, puts an enormous premium on interpersonal exchange skills, the developed apparatus of practical judgment, informal contract, and intensive search.[181] For all the apparent incoherence, the large and the small in the suq play into one another: The prismatic quality of the first and the focalizing quality of the second are reflexes of one another, aspects of a single, not very elegant, not very efficient, and not very rewarding, but nonetheless ordered, intensely active, and reasonably workable tradesman economy.

Conclusion: suq and society

The large/small question applies, of course, not only to the relation between the Sefrou suq as a system and Sefrou suwwaqs as individual actors within it, but to the relations between the suq as a system and the wider context within which it in turn is set. That wider context is, in the first instance, Moroccan, or, perhaps better, Maghrebian, society; but it stretches beyond to transregional, intercontinental, even global dimensions. One institution, if a formidable one, among others in North African society, the suq is also an element, if a marginal one, among others in the modern world order.

It is neither possible nor appropriate to describe these wider relations, removed or immediate, in any detail here. But much of what has been described here cannot properly be understood if they are not kept at least generally in mind. It is not necessary to comprehend everything to comprehend anything, and the megaanalyses of macrosociology – Marxist, Durkheimian, Spencerian, Weberian, or whatever – are all too often of more rhetorical than cognitive force, ideological efforts to direct the destiny of modern society rather than scientific inquiries into its dynamic. Yet modern society has such a dynamic, and microstudies of contemporary social phenomena that are not conducted with a sense for the nature of that dynamic and directed toward clarifying it are reduced to academic exercises.

Whatever the traditional forms it employs – *nisba, habūs, henta, hanūt, sedaqa* – the Sefrou bazaar was born and evolved in the twentieth century and represents as much a response to the social, political, and economic realities of that century as they have appeared on the local scene as it represents an emanation of Morocco's arabesque past. If the development of underdevelopment occurred anywhere, it occurred here, as an increasing number of increasingly marginal traders and artisans tried to crowd themselves into a slowly expanding economic niche, a niche whose size and nature were in good part reflexes of developments elsewhere. The immiseration that accompanies a form of economic change which consists in accentuating the struggle for the leftover rewards that appear at the edge of an industrial system as it connects up with a classical agrarian one – the leitmotif of Asian, African, and Latin American history from about 1870 – appears here in, if anything, hypertrophied form.[182] The development of the Sefrou bazaar from about 1900 to1970 represents at once the quantitative growth and structural complexification of local commercial activity as the region became peripherally integrated into the modern capitalist system and the parcelization of that activity in such a way that, save for a few fortunate moments (mainly around 1920) and a few well-placed individuals (mainly men with political connections), the gains of the whole, modest in any case, were dispersed in the parts.

This general situation remains intact despite the formal devolution of colonial power: The suq, in Sefrou and elsewhere, is still rather more in the world economy than of it. Changing that fact, assuming one wishes to see it change and the Sefrou economy to "develop" in the nonironic sense of the term, would seem, if what has been written above has any merit, to involve the reconstruction of the bazaar as a communications system, the creation of institutional forms within which the individual suwwaq's access to relevant information would be improved.

Whether such a change is possible at all (to say nothing of whether deliberate policy decisions can do anything to accelerate it) is simply not known, because theoretical understanding of bazaar economies is still so limited and because most development thinking has been concerned with replacing bazaar systems with supposedly more modern (read Western) forms, rather than with perfecting such systems – modernizing, if that is the word, what is already in place and in its own terms.

If "the bazaar economy" is seen as an economic type rather than an evolutionary step toward something more familiar to people used to other ways of doing things, and, more importantly, if a deeper understanding of its nature can be obtained, perhaps, just perhaps, some relevant and practicable suggestions for improving it, for increasing its capacity to inform its participants, might emerge and its power of growth be restored and strengthened. Even such an improvement, assuming it can be done at all, would not be costless and certainly would not lead to radical transformation of the suwwaq standard of living. But given the present levels of collective ignorance and the

234

standard of living that goes with them, the attempt should well be worthwhile:

> Ignorance is like subzero weather: by a sufficient expenditure its effects upon people can be kept within tolerable or even comfortable bounds, but it would be wholly uneconomic entirely to eliminate all its effects. And, just as an analysis of man's shelter and apparel would be somewhat incomplete if cold weather is ignored, so also our understanding of economic life will be incomplete if we do not systematically take account of the cold winds of ignorance.[183]

However that may be, the suq is also of importance in understanding Moroccan–Maghrebian, even, to an extent, Mideastern–society generally. Drawing on anthropological traditions of analysis, students of Moroccan social organization have tended to apply a kinship-derived model, the so-called segmentary system theory, to it.[184] That such a model fits the North African situation very well has been questioned with increasing frequency.[185] The pyramiding of corporate lineages into larger and larger solidary unilineal units, each in complementary opposition to one another at the appropriate level of organization, not only fails to account for the great part of Moroccan society, now and in the past, that cannot in any reasonable reading be called "tribal," but is not much more effective with respect to the section of society that, a bit more reasonably, can. And although no one model is adequate to such broad purposes, it is at least arguable that a model constructed out of an analysis of the bazaar will fit the surface facts better and reveal more accurately some of the deeper processes underlying them. Imperfect communication may be a better key to the distinctive features of Maghrebian social organization than lineage fission and recombination; information bargaining, than complementary opposition; clientship, than consanguinity.

Looking at the Moroccan sultanate, the social organization of Fez or Marrakech, or the nature of Berber "tribalism" (to say nothing of Algerian religious life or Tunisian village structure) in such terms lies in the future as but a beckoning possibility. But the great social formations of the Maghreb do bear a family resemblance to one another that the suq, as one of the most formidable and most distinctive of them, can, when properly understood, throw into more exact relief. This is not to suggest that Maghrebian society is a big bazaar, any more than it is a big tribe. Nevertheless, in the details of bazaar life something of the spirit that animates that society–an odd mixture of restlessness, practicality, contentiousness, eloquence, inclemency, and moralism–can be seen with a particular and revelatory vividness.

235

Notes

1. Goitein, S. D., *A Mediterranean Society,* Vol. I; *Economic Foundations,* Berkeley, 1967, p. 70.

2. For some other good ones, see Le Tourneau, R., *Fès avant le Protectorat,* Casablanca, 1949, pp. 271–452; Massignon, L., "Enquête sur les corporations musulmanes d'Artisans et Commercants au Maroc," *Revue du Monde Musulman,* 58:1–250 (1924); Waterbury, J., *North for the Trade,* Berkeley, 1972; Skinner, G. W., "Marketing and Social Structure in Rural China," *Journal of Asian Studies,* 24:2–43 (1964), 195–228 (1965); Davis, W. G., *Social Relations in a Philippine Market,* Berkeley, 1973; Dewey, A. G., *Peasant Marketing in Java,* Glencoe (Ill.), 1962; Bohannan, P. J., and G. Dalton (eds.), *Markets in Africa,* Evanston, 1962; Mintz, S., *Caribbean Transformations,* Chicago, 1974; Beals, R. L., *The Peasant Marketing System of Oaxaca, Mexico,* Berkeley, 1975; Tax, S., *Penny Capitalism,* Washington, D.C., 1953; Oster, A. "A Bazaar Narrated," (Bengal), forthcoming. Cornelius Osgood's Hong Kong study (*The Chinese, A Study of a Hongkong Community,* Tucson, 1975) is perhaps the fullest description of a developed bazaar economy but lacks much analytical interest. For an interesting series of studies from a central place theory point of view, see Smith, C. A. (ed.), *Regional Analysis,* Vol. I., New York, 1976. For a general descriptive review of Mideastern city bazaars from an urban geography point of view, see Wirth, E., "Zum Problem des Bazaars (Suq, Çarsi)," *Der Islam,* 52:1–46, 204–61 (1975). Cf. my earlier attempt for Indonesia, *Peddlers and Princes,* Chicago, 1963.

After the present study was essentially completed, a major work on Moroccan suqs from the point of view of economic geography appeared: Troin, J. F., *Les Souks Marocains,* Aix-en-Provence, 1975, 2 vols. Troin's study, conceived on entirely different lines than the present one, relies on government statistics, survey methods, computer manipulations, and mapping techniques to produce an essentially quantitative analysis of 384 bazaars in the northern half of Morocco. (The southernmost points of his dividing line are Skhirat, Tounfite, Midelt, Missour, and Berquent. Sefrou is thus included.) B. G. Hoffman's brief and inadequate treatment (*The Structure of Traditional Moroccan Rural Society,* The Hague, 1967, pp. 79–84) is, like the book as a whole, useful mainly for its references. A brief description of market activity in a town (Azemmour) about the size of Sefrou can be found

in Le Coeur, C., *Le Rite et l'outil,* Paris, 1939, pp. 129–50; an extended investigation of a single bazaar trade, tanners, in Marrakech, is presented in Jamma, D., *Les Tanneurs de Marrakech,* Algiers, 1971; and some interesting remarks about rural markets in northeastern Morocco can be found in Hart, D. M., *The Aith Waryaghar of the Moroccan Rif,* Tucson, 1976, pp. 69–88. A brief, general "state of the art" review of Mideastern bazaar studies appears in Bonine, M., "Urban Studies in the Middle East," *Middle East Studies Association Bulletin,* 10(3):1–37 (Oct. 1976). Other particular studies of Moroccan markets will be cited, as occasioned, below.

3. For nonmarket economies, see Polanyi, K., C. Arensberg, and H. Pearson, *Trade and Markets in the Early Empires,* Glencoe (Ill.), 1957; Mauss, M., *The Gift: Forms and Functions of Exchange in Archaic Societies,* London, 1954; Firth, R., *Primitive Polynesian Economy,* London, 1939; Sahlins, M., *Stone Age Economics,* Chicago and New York, 1972; Dalton, G. (ed.), *Tribal and Peasant Economies: Readings in Economic Anthropology,* Garden City (N.Y.), 1967; Dalton, G., "Aboriginal Economies in Stateless Societies," in *Exchange Systems in Prehistory,* New York, 1977, pp. 191–212; Belshaw, C. S., *Traditional Exchange and Modern Markets,* Englewood Cliffs (N.J.), 1965. For information mechanisms in modern economies, see Lamberton, D. H. (ed.), *Economics of Information and Knowledge,* Middlesex (Eng.), 1971; Spence, M., *Market Signalling,* Cambridge (Mass.), 1974. As the sequel will make clear, these matters are quite relative, and virtually any developed economy, and many not so developed ones, will display all three types of "information pattern" in one context or another. A contrast similar to the one drawn here is made briefly in Khuri, F., "The Etiquette of Bargaining in the Middle East," *American Anthropologist,* 70:698–706 (1968).

4. According to the 1960 census, bazaar-connected occupations accounted for about 64% of the employed labor force, as against about 16% for professionals, white-collar workers, government officials, etc., and about 20% for farmers and farmworkers (see Table 2). It is difficult, of course, to distribute these "bazaar workers" among the three realms because so many of them participate in more than one. But that the permanent bazaar is far and away the main occupational sector in the town economy, so far as numbers employed are concerned, is beyond all doubt.

5. There are some markets that meet twice a week and a few that meet three times. The very largest cities have only traditional peak days in what has become by now a more or less continuous meeting pattern. There are no periodic markets now that meet on Friday, the Muslim day of collective prayer, but this has not always been the case. Troin (*op. cit.,* t. 2, pl. 2) gives a total figure (excluding the very smallest markets) of about 850 markets in Morocco in 1968. There are actually some hiatuses in the market scatter across the countryside (*ibid.,* p. 361).

6. For a general discussion of market cycle patterns in northern Morocco, see Troin, *op. cit.,* t. I, pp. 81ff. A market cycle sketch for a region in north Morocco is given in Hart, *op. cit.,* p. 75. The simple division of market centers into two levels is something of a simplification. Both locality-focusing markets within a region and region-focusing markets within a section of the country differ among themselves in size and range. On this problem, see Berry, B. L., *Geography of Market Centers,* Englewood Cliffs (N.J.), 1967.

7. My figures for animals are from the Sefrou Cercle office. Troin (*op. cit.,* t. 2, pl. 10, p. 9) gives the following approximate figures (I have estimated them from his graphs) for the Sefrou periodic market, per year:

Sheep	32,000 head
Goats	5,000 head
Cattle	10,000 head
Mules, donkeys, etc.	2,500 head
Cereals, beans	4,000 metric tons
Fruits, vegetables	2,000 metric tons

These figures, gathered in a formal questionnaire survey with "autorités locales" by Troin and two young officials from the Ministries of Agriculture and Agrarian Reform sometime between 1963 and 1968, ought not, as Troin himself emphasizes, to be taken too exactly; but they seem the proper order of magnitude. Troin's estimate (t. 2, pl. 12) of the weekly value of goods and services of just under Dh 400,000 for Sefrou (Fez, Dh 1,610,000) is even more tremulously based (for the method, see t.1, p. 133), but again the order of magnitude – it puts Sefrou in about the sixtieth percentile of the markets surveyed – appears about right.

8. The Tafilalt, a very large (about 311 square kilometers) "mesopotamian"-type alluvial oasis lying between the Gheris and Ziz rivers at the edge of the Sahara, was the major entrepôt of the Moroccan trans-Saharan trade – both south toward Timbuctoo and east toward Kairouan, Cairo, and Mecca – from the tenth century forward. Until the end of the fifteenth century, the oasis was the site of the famous city of Sijilmasa, the capital of "the golden trade of the Moors" and most especially of the slave trade north from the Sudan. After the sixteenth century, trans-Saharan trade gradually declined, essentially disappearing by 1894, the year the French finally took Timbuctoo, but the Tafilalt (whence, in the seventeenth century, the present Moroccan dynasty – the Alawites – arose and moved north to capture Fez) remained an important trade center, and caravans to and from Fez continued, if with diminished frequency and shrunken size, up to the eve of World War I. For an excellent description of the Tafilalt in the nineteenth century (when there was, in fact, something of a brief recovery of the trans-Saharan trade), see Dunn, R., "The Trade of the Tafilalt," *African Historical Studies,* 4:271–302 (1971), and the same author's *Resistance in the Desert,* Madison (Wis.), 1977. On Sijilmasa, see George Colin's entry under that title in *The Encyclopaedia of Islam,* and Brignon, J., et al., *Histoire du Maroc,* Paris and Casablanca, 1967, pp. 78, 83, 88–9, 121ff., 155, 190–1, 218–21, 236, 239. For the Fez end of things, see Le Tourneau, *op. cit.,* pp. 405–37. On the North African caravan trade generally, see Bovill, E. W., *The Golden Trade of the Moors,* London, 1958.

9. During the nine months or so the route was passable, perhaps twenty-five or thirty caravans (*qwāfel;* sg. *qāfla*), some as large as a 100 mules, came through Sefrou each year in the first decades of this century. Toward the Tafilalt (whose population, ca. 1900, was some 100,000), they carried cotton goods, sugar, tea, firearms, cannabis, and various sorts of craftwork; toward Fez, dates, skins, leather, figs, raisins, perfume, and henna. Sefrouis also called this trail *s-sbᶜa l-ᶜaqabi* ("the seven climbs upward"). See also Le Tourneau, *op. cit.,* p. 471. Stopovers varied in length and number, but six or seven hours was considered a fair day's travel. An itinerary of caravans between the Tafilalt and Fez can be found in *Renseignements coloniaux, supplément au "bulletin du comité de l'Afrique française" de Juin 1905,* 6:220 (1905).

10. *Habus* (pl. *hubus*) is the Malikite term; elsewhere the institution is known as *waqf.* See Schacht, J., *An Introduction to Islamic Law,* Oxford, 1964; and entry under *waqf* in *The Shorter Encyclopedia of Islam.* Cf. Stillman, N. A., "Charity and Social Service in Medieval Islam," *Societas,* 5:105–15 (1975).

11. Sefrou's Jewish population, which had risen steadily since at least 1880, and espe-

237

cially readily in the French period, dropped 40% between 1947 and 1960 (see Voinot, L., *Pèlerinages judeo-musulmans du Maroc,* Paris, 1940, pp. 9–10). Voinot's estimate for the Sefrou Jewish population in 1900 – 1,000 – is, however, almost certainly much too low. *La Vie juive au Maroc* [in Hebrew], Jerusalem, 1973, p. 18, gives 2,500 for 1904; 4,046 for 1931; 5,757 for 1947; and 3,118 for 1960. Since 1960 the decline has been even more precipitous. By 1972 less than 200 out of a community that by 1947 was approaching 6,000 remained (Stillman, N., "The Sefrou Remnant," *Jewish Social Studies,* 35:255–63 [1973]); by 1976, less than 50. In 1960, the Muslim population of Sefrou was 0.7% of the total Moroccan Muslim population; the Jewish was 2.3% of the total Moroccan Jewish population (Benyoussef, A., *Populations du Maghreb,* Paris, 1967, p. 111). The foreign→largely French–population was 0.1% of the whole foreign population.

12. Roughly "long distance trader." The term is never used in Sefrou for ordinary merchants, no matter how large. (It also means "rich," plain and simple.) The estimate of a dozen Muslims and two dozen Jews is derived from interview material, obtained from aged informants, which is particularly circumstantial in this regard.

13. Again, it is impossible to say anything very exact, or even very positive, about the situation prior to 1900; but what evidence exists suggests that this entrance by Sefrouis into the body of the caravan trade is quite recent. Al-Bakri in the eleventh century, al-Idrisi in the twelfth, Leo Africanus in the sixteenth, and Charles de Foucauld in the nineteenth all remark that, though a stop on the caravan trail, Sefrou is essentially an agricultural, not a commercial, town. Al-Bakrī, *Description de l'Afrique septentrionale,* de Slane (ed. and trans.), 2 vols., Algiers, 1911–13, Vol. 1, p. 146; al-Idrīsī, *Description de l'Afrique et de l'Espagne,* R. Dozy and M. J. de Goeje (eds. and trans.), Leiden, 1866, p. 87; Leo Africanus, *Description de l'Afrique,* Ch. Schefer, ed. and annotated, 2 vols., Paris, 1896–8, Vol. 2, p. 359; de Foucauld, C., *Reconnaissance du Maroc,* 2 vols., Paris, 1888, Vol. 1, pp. 37ff. Scattered but interesting descriptions of bazaar and caravan activities in and around Sefrou during the first decade of the present century can be found in *The Gospel Message,* the publication of the Gospel Missionary Union in London, from 1904 to 12, which had (and still has) a mission station in Sefrou (see especially Apr. 1904, Jan. 1906, Feb. 1906, Mar. 1906, Feb. 1907, Dec. 1908, Aug. 1909, Nov. 1909, Dec. 1909, June 1912).

14. Udovitch, A. L., "At the Origins of the Western *Commenda:* Islam, Israel, Byzantium?" *Speculum,* 37:198–207 (1962). Udovitch traces the various forms of this sort of contract in the Jewish, Byzantine, and Islamic traditions, concluding that the Islamic and the European (i.e., Italian Renaissance) forms are virtually identical. Cf. Udovitch, A. L., *Partnership and Profit in Medieval Islam,* Princeton, 1970. For the operation of the qirad in medieval Egypt, see Goitein, *op. cit.,* pp. 171ff.

15. Regarding amounts advanced, the terms of agreement, and so on, qirad contracts seem to have always been written and officially witnessed, but their operation clearly depended most heavily on the personal relation between the parties, and especially on the confidence of the financier (*muqriḍ*) in the trader (*muqāriḍ*). Such contracts were often, however, not between individuals, but between groups of capital suppliers and/or groups of traders, operating, each on his own side of the line, in genuine partnerships. The highest development of the qirad was in maritime rather than caravan trade, but the similarities between the two sorts of long-distance commerce – including the dangers faced, the goods carried, and the organization required – made the institution equally suitable to both. For the qirad in North African maritime trade, mainly that going in and out of Kairouan, see Idris, H.R., "Commerce maritime et Kirād en Berbérie orientale," *Journal of the Economic and Social History of the Orient,* 4:225–39 (1961). For its probable origins in Meccan overland trade, see Udovitch, *Partnership and Profit,* pp. 170–6.

16. In intra-Jewish contracts, Talmudic commercial forms, setting a two-thirds/one-third, agent/investor return and saddling the agent with a certain degree of liability, seem mainly to have been used; in Jewish-Muslim contracts, the liability-free and normally half/half qirad pattern was employed. On the Jewish form, called *ᶜisqā,* and its similarities to and differences from the Muslim qirad, see Udovitch, "At the Origins." For the *ᶜisqā* in Morocco, see Zafrani, H., *Les Juifs du Maroc,* Paris, 1972, pp. 181–8.

17. Dunn (*Resistance,* p. 87) estimates the Jewish community in the Tafilalt as ca. 6,000 in 1900, which would make it about three times the size of Sefrou's, three-quarters the size of Fez's (Dunn, *Morocco's Crisis,* p. 159). There seems to have been a fairly sizable group of Tafilalt Jews (informants' estimates run as high as a fifth of the whole) in Sefrou itself around the turn of the century.

18. One other element, Fez merchants temporarily resident in Sefrou (about a dozen of them rented one of Sefrou's larger funduqs,

number 2 in Figure 3, for a while toward the end of the nineteenth century as a base for their cloth trade operations), should be mentioned in connection with qirad operations. But they were never numerous and their relations to the Sefrouis were always quite distant, not to say hostile. Fez-Sefrou commercial alliances were (and are) extremely rare, and this was as true for the Jews—whose connections with the Meknes Jewish community, about 80 kilometers away, were always closer than with the Fez, only 40 kilometers distant—as for the Muslims.

19. The gun trade developed with increasing intensity after the fall of Mulay Hasan in 1894 and the rise of various self-promoted claimants to the throne, the most important one in the Sefrou region being Bou Hamara. On this whole period, see Burke, E., III, *Prelude to Protectorate in Morocco,* Chicago, 1976, and Dunn, *Resistance.* The guns were made in Fez, Meknes, Marrakech, or Tetuan or, increasingly, brought into the country from Europe. They were mostly single-shot muzzle loaders, though some German and Italian craftsmen produced some breach loaders in the royal workshop, the famous *makina* in Fez (see Le Tourneau, *op. cit.,* pp. 353–5).

20. Funduq number 5 was the center of trade concerning animals, but there most of the activity was in the area surrounding it, rather than the funduq itself: blacksmiths, saddlemakers, sellers of animal feed, and animal brokers all collected around it. (Owner-to-owner selling of animals was virtually nonexistent then; both seller and purchaser were represented by brokers. This tended to be the pattern in the lumber and olive-oil trades as well.) Funduqs 3, 8, and 10 seem to have remained in the more traditional pattern—mere caravanserais rather than commodity houses. For Sefrou markets around 1910 and the funduq role in them, see Annex B.

21. Only Funduqs 2, 3, 4, 5, 7, 8, and 9 still stand (1969), and they are either reduced to parking lots for donkeys and mules or house various craft workplaces, in either case but faint images of what they once were. For their present uses, see Annex A.

22. For more ethnographic detail (and there is a great deal) on all this than can be given here, see Westermarck, E. A., *Ritual and Belief in Morocco,* London, 1926, Vol. I, pp. 518–69; Brunot, H., and G.-H. Bousquet, "Contribution a l'étude des pactes de protection et d'alliance chez les Berbères du Maroc central," *Hespéris,* 33:353–70 (1946). The latter paper, however, formulates the matter in "tribe-and-territory" terms rather than as here, in "person-to-person" ones. A (rather schematized) summary of types of "alliance-relationships" is given in Hoffman, *op. cit.,* p. 101. For some brief comments on these pacts among Berber groups at the southern end of the caravan trail, see Hammoudi, A., "Segmentarité, stratification sociale, pouvoir politique et sainteté: réflexions sur les thèses de Gellner," *Hespéris,* 15:147–80 (1974).

23. How many links the chains contained is difficult to determine, but it can hardly have been fewer than the number of days involved in the journey. Also the chains were not necessarily identical for all the caravan chiefs, for there were normally alternative local powers among whom one could bargain. Nor did a caravan sheikh's zettat relations in one area have to be confined to a single man, and such relations were not insusceptible of shifting, dissolving, broadening, and so on. To attempt to formalize the zettata pattern in some systematic way—by tribe, by territory, by institutionalized political role—is inevitably to misrepresent it, for power relationships in the Berber highlands were neither stable nor clear-cut. Rather, a constantly rearranging kaleidoscope of political constellations centering around rising and falling strong men was the pattern, and to this sort of mobile complexity the caravan sheikhs (whose own positions were not all that fixed) had to adjust as best they could. For all that, the zettata system seems, from all reports, to have worked exceedingly well. Actual attacks upon caravans, even in the more than usually disordered period after 1894, seem to have been rare. At the same time, the zettata system is not entirely responsible for that: The caravaners themselves were well enough armed.

24. This is not to deny that there were such connections earlier, but merely that they were very developed or played a very important role in either town or countryside. The tendency to assume that a system of social relationships (which, like the caravan economy before it, is what the bazaar economy is) that operates in terms of traditional forms is, historically speaking, old is based on the mistaken premise that traditional societies are incapable of reorganizing their institutions into novel patterns, that persistence of cultural forms implies fixity in their social use. Though most "development" theorizing in the social sciences is based on this premise, nothing could be further from the truth—and not only in Morocco.

25. The usual practice was for the Jew to make the first sacrifice, binding "the man who knew how to shoot" (the Berber) under the "conditional curse" (*ᶜar*) pattern (for this, see Westermarck, *op. cit.,* pp. 518–69), though the actual relationship had been personally ne-

Suq: the bazaar economy in Sefrou

239

gotiated before all this ritual sealing took place. The Berber word most often used in this context was *amur* ("neck") in the sense of "by my neck, I will protect you." But the (probably) Arabic term, mezrag, seems, despite the fact that virtually all riding Jews spoke Berber, to have been far more common.

26. For some specific examples of vigorous reactions to breaches of mezrag protection (which, in themselves, seem again to have been quite rare), see Geertz, C., *The Interpretation of Cultures,* New York, 1973, pp. 6–30.

27. Another important factor was the increasing involvement after 1900 of Sefroui merchants, especially Muslims, in the caravan trade to the northeast – Tetouan, Tangiers, Ksar El Kebir, Ceuta – with which previously the town, away from its main routes, had not been directly connected. The northward caravans, which carried mainly wool outbound and pepper, tea, cannabis, and Spanish cloth inbound, differed from the Saharan ones in that they (1) were more frequent; (2) had much shorter and less arduous routes to traverse; (3) were not composed of professional Berber porters but of Arabic (and some Jewish) traders grouping themselves into ad hoc bands of five or six for company and security (which, as there were towns more or less all along the route, was much less of a problem here); (4) were financed either by the traders involved or by other traders on a simple consignment-and-commission basis (qirad arrangements occurred, but they were rare). All in all, the northeast trade – which continued to flourish well into the Protectorate period, when the creation of an international border just north of Fez turned it into a contraband operation – was more like itinerant trading than it was like the classical Atlas and Saharan type of caravaning. Indeed it gradually evolved into such itinerant trading.

28. On the general question of the role of endogenous and exogenous economic factors in the development of bazaar systems, see Schwimmer, B., "Periodic Markets and Urban Development in Southern Ghana," in Smith, *op. cit.,* pp. 123–44.

29. For a comparable microsociological attempt to discuss a bazaar economy in its cultural setting – the Islamic/Javanese – see Geertz, *Peddlers and Princes.*

30. In addition to ethnic-like diversity, another "demographic" characteristic of the Sefrou (and the Moroccan) bazaar sets it apart from most such economies in Asia, Black Africa, the Caribbean, etc.: the virtual absence of women in it. For Morocco as a whole the number of men in "commerce" (i.e., merchants) in 1950 was about 62,000: the number of women,

1,400 (i.e., about 45:1). Though there is a noticeably higher degree of female participation in the Jewish than in the Muslim community (about 15:1 vs. about 70:1), the male predominance is overwhelming in both cases (Bensimon-Donath, D., *Evolution du Judaisme marocain,* Paris and The Hague, 1968, p. 134). For Sefrou (1960) the comparable proportions were Muslims 46:1, Jews 10:1, overall 29:1, suggesting either (or, more likely, both) that Sefrou is not at the extreme in these matters and that the situation evolved somewhat between 1950 and 1960. There are some specialized, and not unimportant, modes of participation of women in the bazaar, which will be touched on below; cf. Troin, *op. cit.,* t.1, pp. 113–88. But overall, the bazaar is an emphatically male realm, and so far as Sefrou is concerned there is not a single woman of any real importance in either the trade or artisan worlds (see Annex A). Though the pattern is changing, even most of the everyday household shopping in the bazaar is still done by men. Elsewhere in Morocco, especially in the Northwest, female participation in market activities has apparently become much more significant in recent years (see Troin, *op. cit.,* t.1, pp. 63–4). For some brief and generalized comments about women (or paucity thereof) in rural markets in Morocco, see Fogg, W., "Changes in the Layout, Characteristics, and Function of a Moroccan Tribal Market, Consequent on European Control," *Man,* 72:104–8 (1941), and "A Tribal Market in Spanish Morocco, *Africa,* 11:428–58 (1938). Cf. Montagne, R., *Les Berbères et le makhzen dans le sud du Maroc,* Paris, 1930, pp. 251ff. Hart, *op. cit.,* pp. 86–8, briefly describes some of the few rural women's markets in Morocco. For useful discussion of women's economic role overall in a Middle Atlas region south of Sefrou, see Maher, V., *Women and Property in Morocco,* Cambridge (Eng.), 1974. For the generally very great prominence of women in bazaar activities, amounting occasionally to outright dominance, outside the Middle East, see Mintz, S., "Men, Women and Trade," *Comparative Studies in Society and History,* 13:247–69 (1971).

31. Today (1972), when there are perhaps only forty or fifty Jews still active in the bazaar, it is no longer of much importance at all. In describing the bazaar as a cultural form, the sixty-year period, 1910–70, a line in time not a point, will be treated as a unit. Changes occurring during (and, in a few cases, after) that time which it would be misleading to ignore will, of course, be remarked on as well. But unless otherwise specified, present tense references refer in a general way to the period as a whole.

32. These figures, which should have the appropriate *approximatelys* and *abouts* prefixed to them, are drawn from a systematic census of all permanent bazaar establishments carried out during 1968–9 in the course of fieldwork (see Annex A). This census, which we shall refer to as the bazaar survey, is, along with the computer analysis of the 1960 government census of Sefrou, the source of all the quantitative material – and much of the qualitative – on the Sefrou bazaar that follows. For some brief and highly general impressions of ethnic division of labor in other Moroccan towns ca. 1924, see Massignon, *Enquête*, pp. 25ff.

33. To survey the periodic bazaar, especially that of Sefrou town, in the same manner as the permanent would be a bit like trying to census a swarm of bees. Theoretically it could be done, but practically it is beyond a lone ethnographer's power, at least if he is going to do anything else. A census of one rural periodic suq (Aioun Senam in Figure 1; see Annex B) found that, in sixty-one in-place traders (as opposed to the general populace moving as casual buyers and sellers through the bazaar), twenty-one locally recognized ethnic-like categorizations were represented.

34. The nisba is not confined to the above more or less straightforward "ethnicizing" uses, but is employed in a wide range of domains to attribute relational properties to persons: e.g., occupational role (*ḥrār*/silks – *ḥrārī*/silk merchant); religious sect membership (*Darqāwa*/a Sufi brotherhood – *Darqāwī*/a member of that brotherhood); abstract relations (*madīna*/city – *madanī*/civil, civilized, civic; cf. *sūq*/*sūwwāqī*, above); even ad hoc characteristics (Ben Barka/ a martyred political leader – *Barkāwī*/a follower of his). The effect of this extensive use of nisba (apparently more extensive than elsewhere in the Arab world, though it is common everywhere) is to turn all sorts of social statuses into ethnic-like properties and extend this way of perceiving people as carrying their backgrounds with them through the whole of life. But a discussion of this, crucial to an understanding of Moroccan culture generally, and Moroccan concepts of personhood particularly, would take us too far afield. For the beginnings of such a discussion, see Geertz, C., " 'From the Native's Point of View,' On the Nature of Anthropological Understanding," in Basso, K., and H. Selby (eds.), *Meaning in Anthropology*, Albuquerque, 1976, pp. 221–37.

35. The causal language should not mislead. The nonrandomness could as easily be said to derive from the view as the view from the nonrandomness. What is being defined here is not a sequence of products, *A* determines *B*, and *B*, *C*, but a culturally conventional way of looking

at things: *A* implies *B*, *B* implies *C*, and *C* implies *A* – *for Moroccans*. For the general methodological position, which derives from Weber's concept of *sinnzusammenhang*, see Geertz, *Interpretation of Cultures*, pp. 3–30.

36. For a full discussion of the construction of these categories (which are not themselves those of the census), their methodological basis, and their sociological import, see H. Geertz's "Appendix: A Statistical Profile of the Population of the Town of Sefrou in 1960," in the hardcover edition of this volume. For a simpler (twofold) classification of traders of this same sort for a coastal city, see Brown, K., *People of Salé, Tradition and Change in a Moroccan City, 1830–1930*, Cambridge (Mass.), 1976, pp. 152–3.

37. Adluni and Meghrawi are old Sefrou names. Yazghi and Bhaluli refer to nearby rural places; Zaikumi and Zgani refer to certain Berber-speaking villages; Tobali and Robini are Sefrou Jewish names.

38. Unemployment figures (which here include those merely "inactive") reinforce the picture: Sefrou-born Arabs, 19% (of men over fifteen years of age); Jews, 15%; rural Arabs, 37%; Berbers, 35%. This contrast is even greater than it looks, because if one takes the critical age group (thirty-one to forty-five) alone, the figures are 15%, 3%, 34%, and 37%. That socioethnic category, however externally constructed and inadequately named, is a genuine variable is further supported by the fact that breakdowns according to length of time in town (i.e., for in-migrants) show no clear pattern, either for employment categorization or unemployment rate.

39. The measure is quite conservative, for two reasons. First, no within-trade divisions, by size, type, scale, technical development (e.g., hand tailors vs. machine tailors), etc., have been made. Narrowing the universe to the larger, more substantial enterprises would, in any of the trades, markedly raise the degree of compactness. This is especially important for such categories as grocers, ready-made clothes sellers, tailors, shoemakers, and café keepers, all of which are surely underrated in comparison with other trades in Table 3 because of the larger number of marginal operators in them. Second, the measure was constructed by using not all the nisbas that could possibly be represented in the trade (i.e., all those found in Sefrou, weighted by their proportion in the population – a parameter whose value is not known), but merely those actually represented. This, of course, eliminates the zeros and so greatly reduces the deviation sum and with it the index.

In short, the degree of nisba concentration

241

is, from a stricter null hypothesis point of view, even higher than here displayed, and the range of the scale is somewhat exaggerated on the downward end. Also, it should be noted that this survey is, in the nature of the case, only of men with fixed permanent-bazaar places of work (and thus is much more complete for occupations like miller, barber, grocer, tobacconist, or blacksmith, than for ready-to-eat-food seller, odds-and-ends seller, or even silk merchant); includes only the owners among them, not apprentices, employees, and assistants (surely more than half the whole); and includes only traditional trades, not "modern" ones. The modern trades are also strongly nisba-bound, but the number of people in any one trade, like plumber or radio seller, is too small for statistical handling.

40. The terms *tribe, fraction, subfraction* are used here merely for momentary convenience. It should not be assumed that they, and the nisbas deriving from them, point to an underlying segmentary type of social organization. Though it is not possible to go into the problem here, they do not.

41. The two exceptions, the Alawi sherifs and the residents of a separate walled quarter in the town, the Qlawis, are included in Table 5. All other nisbas fall below ten. After the Alawis and Qlawis, the next eight nisbas (the so-called, and like tribal, miscalled, family categories) yield only 35 cases, or an average of 4.4 per nisba. Beyond them the mosaic gets differentiated indeed: For the entire "all other Sefroui" category, the average number of persons per nisba *in the survey* is 3.8.

42. These data come from the records of the Sefrou habus office. There are two basic compilations, one of separate deeds of gift (*ḥawāla,* literally "transfer of obligation") stretching from the mid-seventeenth to the early nineteenth centuries, and one (*l-mujallad l-mubarak,* "the blessed bound book") a systematization of these, produced in the early nineteenth century at the behest of Sultan Mulay Sliman, who, in response to the reform movement in Islam, wished a more rational ordering. The original habus gifts seem to have been essentially completed by the time of the *Mujallad,* the overwhelming proportion of later additions to the habus being purchased out of profits, though there is an original gift recorded as late as 1920. In the late nineteenth century, another reforming Sultan, Mulay Hassan, unified the Sefrou habus, which had previously been scattered among a large number of nadirs (i.e., habus stewards) according to the particular mosque, quranic school, or whatever concerned, under the nadir in Fez. After the establishment of the Protectorate, which set up a central Direction des Habous, a separate nadir was placed in Sefrou. Since Independence, he has been transformed into a civil service official under the minister of habus in Rabat, but for all intents and purposes he still operates autonomously.

43. The extent of the agricultural property the habus owns could only be recovered from an exhaustive examination of the records mentioned in note 42. The largest single parcel, now exploited as a modern olive-tree plantation, runs 170 hectares, and it is not the only sizable holding. The percentage of the town's shops and ateliers owned by the habus is also difficult to determine because of multiple occupancy (running to a dozen or more in the funduqs), but I would estimate that about a third, including a majority of those in the heart of the old city, are habus-owned. If habus-owned sites on which individuals have erected their own shops are added, the total goes even higher. The situation is further complicated by the fact that habus holdings – agricultural or urban – take a variety of rather elaborate legal forms, many of which give the habus a part share in an individual property, rights to shares of output, fixed payments, and so on. Finally, a distinction must be made between the "public habus" discussed in the text, called in Sefrou *ḥabus kubrā* ("greater habus"), and habus properties whose income goes to private groups, mainly families and religious brotherhoods, and which is not under the nadir's control, called *ḥabus ṣuḡrā* ("lesser habus"). So far as its bazaar role goes, however, the "lesser" habus acted about as the "greater," if on not so broad a scale (see note 54).

44. Gibb, H. A. R., and H. Bowen, *Islamic Society and the West in the XVIIIth Century,* 2 vols., London, 1950-7.

45. In the 1965 budget mentioned above, about 80% of the $17,000 or so expenditure went for personnel costs and about 20% for property maintenance. It is more difficult to determine the proportion of the total spent in the town, but, given the generally low level of activity of the habus in the countryside, it is probable that more than three-quarters is spent in the town. Indeed, it seems likely that the activities of the habus provide a subsidy of several thousand dollars a year to the bazaar economy from the agricultural. This is certainly the rural view of the matter and the reason for the limited spread of the institution beyond the town. Berber groups, in particular, almost never make use of the habus.

46. There have been *some* increases, both through new auctions and in the course of running leases, but they are extremely rare.

Of a large number of habus rents for different trades checked through interview in 1965, only a handful were found to have changed at all, and they quite moderately, in thirty or forty years, and the general opinion was that such rents not only would not, but should not, change in the future. The practice also keeps government taxes on commercial property low, of course. There is no significant trade in subleases because it is considered immoral to earn a profit on habus properties, and one can lose one's right to a habus property for doing so. If a habus property is improved by its holder, the improvements are the private property of the lessee and can be added to the price of a sublease. If an improved habus is surrendered, the improvements are charged to the habus institution. The whole system is thus arranged for the benefit of the lessee, the market trader, not the lessor, the community.

47. This applies especially to fixed enterprises in what has been called above the permanent bazaar (the *sūq l-medīna*). "Rent" in the Thursday bazaar (the *sūq l-ḵemīs*) and the periodic markets connected with it comes in the form of tickets purchased (from the government market administration) for a one-time right to sell goods. These tickets (which can be resold, so that there is something of a brokerage trade in them) are more responsive to market changes, but still tend to remain, for political reasons, fairly low. Stores and sites in the *sūq l-betrina* (the business district bazaar) rent on a more or less free-market basis and are thus, comparatively, both high and unstable.

48. On varieties of Islam in Morocco, see Geertz, C., *Islam Observed*, New Haven, 1968.

49. On zawias in Morocco, see Drague, G., *Esquisse d'histoire religieuse du Maroc, confréries et zaouias*, Paris, 1951; Michaux-Bellaire, E., *Essai sur l'histoire du confréries marocaines*, Paris, 1921; Brunel, R., *Essai sur la confrérie des aissaoua au Maroc*, Paris, 1926; Abun-Nasser, J. M., *The Tijaniyya*, London, 1965; Crapanzano, V., *The Hamadsha*, Berkeley, 1973; Gellner, E., *The Saints of the Atlas*, London, 1961; Eickelman, D., *Moroccan Islam*, Austin, 1976; Depont, O., and X. Coppolani, *Les Confréries religieuses musulmanes*, Algiers, 1897; and the article under that title in *Shorter Encyclopaedia of Islam*. For a general sociological view of their role, see Geertz, *Islam Observed*, pp. 48–54. A good bibliographical review is given in Hoffman, *op. cit.*, pp. 120–9, whose own comments should be ignored.

50. At entry, Ṭarīka, in *Shorter Encyclopaedia of Islam*. The real problem in censusing brotherhoods is deciding which are properly branches of others and which autonomous entities, something even their members do not always agree upon. Overall brotherhood integration is commonly quite weak in any case.

51. The size figures (surely far too low, as Moroccans did not like to admit zawia membership to French authorities) are from Drague, *op. cit.*, p. 121, who estimates about 4% (also too low) of the entire Moroccan population ca., 1939 belonged to zawias. (For the city of Fez, the estimated rate was 13%, the highest in the country.) In Sefrou, the leading zawias ca. 1920 seem to have been, also in roughly estimated order of size, the following (I give the names they were colloquially known by, usually names of famous sheikhs or founders, with their general, all-Morocco tariqa affiliations in parentheses): B-l-Khadira (Darqawa); Mulay Abdelqader l-Jillali (Qadariyya); Mohammed ben Nasser (Nasiriyya); Sidi ben Aissa (Aissawa); Sidi Ahmad l-Tijani (Tijaniyya); Mohammed b-l Larbi (Darqawa); Malin Dalil (Malin Dalil); Abdelhayy l-Kittani (Kittaniyya); Sidi Hamid b-l-Abdelsadeq (Sadqiyya); Sidi l-Ghazi (Darqawa); Mulay Ali Sherif (Alawiyya); Sidi Lahcen Yusi (Nasiriyya); and Sidi Ali Hamdush (Hamadsha). This list, too, is incomplete, for a number of small, often evanescent zawias also existed. For another list, for the whole Sefrou region and dating from 1952, see Si Bekkai ben Embarek Lahbib, "Sefrou," *Bulletin économique et social du Maroc* 15:230–42 (1952).

Similarly membership sizes are very hard to estimate. The largest, the "green turban" Darqawa of Zawia B-l-Khadira, had upward of seventy members at its peak (i.e., men: many of the zawias also had "women's auxiliaries" that met in members' houses, not in the zawia proper); but size estimates of the others vary too widely to report. A significant number of individuals in the town also belonged to zawias located elsewhere, most especially in Fez. All the zawias, save the one in the Qlaᶜa, were in the medina, in the heart of the permanent bazaar areas. For the ten still (1969) functioning, at a much reduced level, see Annex A. There was also a large number of, generally very small, zawias in the countryside, entirely separate from the urban ones and functioning quite differently, though often affiliated with the same tariqas (Nasiriyya, Kittaniyya, Qadariyya, Aissawa, and so on). Unconnected to the bazaar economy – they played no role in the periodic market system – they are not considered here. Zawia membership ca. 1939 for all Morocco is summarized in Hoffman, *op. cit.*, pp. 127–9.

52. Hard statistics are again hard to establish, but in a series of detailed interviews with older informants I could not find a leading

243

trader or artisan of the interwar period not known to have been a zawia member, and most minor ones seen to have belonged also. Not very many nonbazaar types were involved, at least in the Sefrou town zawias. Partial exceptions were the Tijaniyya, which, founded by the son of Qaid Umar al-Yusi, himself later qaid under the French, attracted a number of civil servants, and the Kittaniyya, which was closely connected in Sefrou with one of the town's leading families, the Adluns, only some of whom were traders.

53. The main studies of Moroccan "guilds" (called, in even less suitable terminology, *corporations*) are Massignon, "Enquête" (cf. his "Complément à l'enquête de 1923–1924, sur les corporations musulmanes," *Revue des études islamiques,* 2:273–93 (1928), and Le Tourneau, *op. cit.,* pp. 295–306. Unlike Massignon, whose study was conducted by an officially circulated questionnaire, Le Tourneau seems well aware of the problem, even if he does little more than throw up his hands at it:

"Ce mot [corporations–*ḥnaṭi,* plural of *henṭa*] évoque aussitôt, dans nos esprits européens, des souvenirs de notre Moyen Age; nous songeons à des groupements de travailleurs d'un même métier étroitment réglementés, fortement hiérarchisés, jalousement fermés à l'étranger, où l'on ne peut pénétrer que grâce à des répondants et où l'on ne peut faire un chemin que dans la mesure où a donné la preuve de solides capacités professionelles. Peut-être cette représentation ne traduit-elle pas très fidèlement la réalité à laquelle elle s'appliquait jadis; en tout cas, elle n'a que peu de rapports avec l'organisation corporative de Fès.

"Quand on examine la corporation fasie, on est étonné d'y trouver si peu de cohésion, si peu d'efficience. Certes, l'institution, telle qu'il m'a été donné de l'étudier à partir de 1934, avait perdu de sa vigueur depuis l'établissement du Protectorate, mais tous les témoignages que j'ai recueillis auprès de vieux artisans qui avaient connu l'ancien régime me permettent d'affirmer qu'elle n'en avait pas tellement plus au temps des Sultans indépendants. Cette organisation apparente recouvrait un réalité très anarchique: la corporation fasie n'était pas un faisceau de forces solidement cordonnées, mais bien plutôt un agglomérat de forces seulement juxtaposées et qui répugnaient à s'appuyer les unes sur les autres" [*ibid.,* p. 295].

That the perception of exotic social arrangements as "anarchic" is almost always the result of the analyst's misconception of their nature is perhaps the one proposition anthropology can confidently be said to have established. The

244

reason "la corporation fasie" seemed to Le Tourneau, who was a thorough, careful, and honest, if somewhat flat-footed, observer, a mere "agglomérat de forces seulement juxtaposées" was, or at least so on the basis of the Sefrou evidence one could argue, that it did not exist. The sense of disorder arises from aggregating separate social institutions into a supposedly unitary one; discovering the order that in fact was there demands disaggregating the imaginary "corporation" back into the particular institutions and reconceptualizing their relationships to one another. This is especially evident in Massignon, where simple headings his market officials gave their "corporation lists" display it: *Bayān al ḥiraf wal ṣanā'i bi Fās* [Fez]; *Taqyīd iḥṣā arbāb al tijara wal ḥanātī wal ḥiraf bi hadhihi'l hadrat al Marrākoshiya* [Marrakech]; *Bayān asmā al ḥiraf* [Rabat]; *Fihrist konnāshat al ḥisba* [Salé]; *Taqyid al omanā* [Taroudant] (transcriptions Massignon's). For a brief, rather generalized, recent discussion of Moroccan "guilds" (*ḥanṭa*) closer to the present one, see Brown, *op. cit.,* pp. 135–49.

On the absence of guilds in medieval Egypt, see Goitein, *op. cit.,* pp. 82–3. For an excellent survey of corporate trade organization in ancien régime France, see Sewell, W., Jr., *Corporate Community to Social Revolution: French Workers from the Old Regime to 1848,* forthcoming, especially Chap. 2.

54. Zawia habus, some of which was considerable in scope, was considered lesser habus, not greater, and thus was not under the town nadir's control but was managed independently by a nadir of the zawia itself. The general policies of management were, however, about the same. Zawia muqqadems were usually elected by the local group, though occasionally appointed by the tariqa sheikh.

55. The principles upon which trades were ranked from clean to dirty are even less precise than for the sects. In general, dealing in cloth or clothing, commercial trading (mainly in wool or wheat) on a "large" scale, and light artisanry were cleaner than ordinary peddling, heavy artisanry, and manual labor, with common grocery, café keeping, etc. in between. Certain behavioral traits (e.g., hashish consumption, considered by many of the heavier trades as essential to their work) also were involved. Cf. Jamma, *op. cit.,* pp. 83–5. A ranking of traditional occupations in Salé in "noble/ignoble" terms by a single older trader is given in Brown, *op. cit.,* pp. 140–8.

56. Massignon (Enquête, pp. 140ff) gives a series of brief and unsystematic lists of trade-zawia "affiliations" (ca. 1924) in various Moroccan towns and cities, though he says nothing

People of Sefrou and the Middle Atlas

Photographs by Paul Hyman
Design by Bea Feitler

Most photographs in anthropological works are intended to illustrate something, to prove something, or to beautify something. These are not. They are intended to say something. They are a view and a comment, visual notations of Sefroui life.

Paul Hyman, a professional photographer, took these pictures over a period of four months in 1969 at our invitation, mainly as a kind of experiment to see what someone innocent of academic social science who approaches the world through a lens rather than a typewriter would see. We anthropologists who were in the field at that time–Clifford and Hildred Geertz and Paul Rabinow–discussed our work and that of the study as a whole with him, but offered him no thesis to document nor findings to illustrate. We just introduced him to our acquaintances. Hyman learned enough conversational Arabic to become welcome in their homes on his own. We were impressed by his ability to gain access and to mingle freely.

The selection of the photographs presented here was a difficult task. We wanted to provide examples from a wide range of Sefroui activities, to include all of the major social groups, and still remain true to Hyman's own visual sensibilities–to allow the larger, ordered view of life in Sefrou that he found to stand forth.

The nature of that view is best known through an unimpeded study of the pictures themselves and so the captions we have provided at the end of this section are merely description, designed only to connect the images to our written texts.

This is what, to a mindful eye, Sefrou looks like.

2

3

10

16

19

21

24

26

29

33

37

40

41

46

49

51

54

60

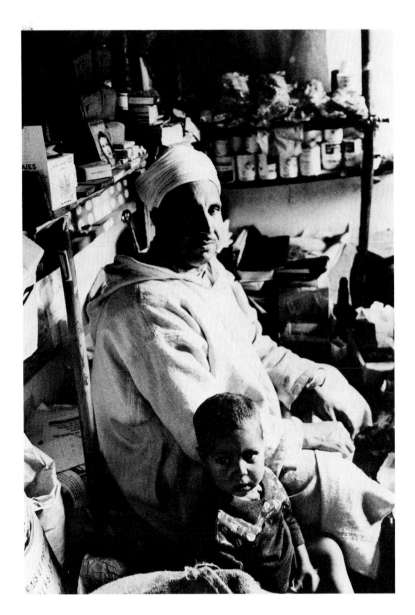

List of illustrations

about the basis of rationale of the affiliations. Jamma (*op. cit.*, pp. 92–5) discusses the role of zawias among the Marrakech tanners, most of them belonging, as would be expected, to the hyperecstatic Hamadsha and Gnawa sects.

57. There were nearly 100 herfas (see Annex A) in Sefrou, but only a minority were involved in the henta system, the most important being (in no particular order): blacksmiths, carpenters, weavers, butchers, silk merchants, cloth merchants, café keepers, bakers, barbers, wheat traders, wool traders, tailors, shoemakers, vegetable and fruit sellers, grocers, saddlepack makers, masons, porters.

58. There could be more than one henta in a zawia (e.g., blacksmiths, butchers, and porters in Aissawa; tailors, wool sellers, and café keepers in b-l-Larbi), but not, apparently, more than one in a trade. This is one of the reasons the guild image has sometimes seemed to apply, though there does not, in fact, seem to have been a henta in Sefrou to which all members of the trade concerned belonged. Also it should be remarked that there were not hentas in all zawias: There were apparently none in Tijaniya, Kittani, or Sidi Lahcen Yusi, for example.

59. That is, among members. Some hentas also indulged in a certain amount of general "charity" (*ṣadaqa*) work for the population at large (orphans, poor, sick), but this seems generally to have been minor.

60. In particular, neither the zawias nor the herfas were in themselves such groups. The zawias were very loosely organized: a small crowd of adepts clustered around a spiritual leader, the whole representing a religious "path" to be followed, whether in company or alone, by each person individually. The herfas were somewhat less invertebrate, but were not groups at all or even composed of groups, but categories of men (butchers, grocers) composed of subcategories of them (masters, apprentices; suppliers, peddlers) multiply connected in an involuted network. The internal organization of the trades–including the so-called *amīn* system, usually conflated with the henta in the guild interpretation–will be discussed below in the context of the role structure of the bazaar, where it properly belongs.

61. For example, by Le Tourneau, *op. cit.*, pp. 301–4. For descriptions of saints' festivals, see Brunel, *op. cit.;* Rabinow, P., *Symbolic Domination,* Chicago, 1975. On saints and saint worship generally, see Bel, A., *La Religion musulman en Berbérie,* Paris, 1938; and Geertz, *Islam Observed.*

62. This was just the most prominent of a number of local saints, not a patron saint in the Christian sense. The use of Christian vo-

cabulary–"saint" (*siyyid, sīd*); "shrine," "sect," one even sees "cathedral mosque" for *l-jamiᶜ l-kebir*–is unfortunate, but not always avoidable. Hentas played no role in the Aids (i.e., the Day of the Sacrifice and the Day of the Breaking of the Fast), which involved mass open-air praying, a public sermon "from the throne" by the Khatib, official sheep sacrifice by the qadi, etc. On the French suppression of musim, see later in this essay.

63. Of emerging modern occupations actually very few have been absorbed into the herfa system, mainly because they tend to be represented by only two or three occupants each. Only those brought into being by the automobile have grown large enough to develop an apprentice system, elect amins, and so on.

64. For a review of the religious (and some of the political) factors leading to the enfeeblement of the zawias in Morocco generally, see the discussion of "scripturalism" in Geertz, *Islam Observed,* Chap. 3. Cf. 'Alāl al-Fāsi, *Independence Movements in North Africa,* New York, 1970, pp. 111–18; Eickelman, *op. cit.*

65. The entire cult was not banned, only the musim, the collective side of it. Individual worship at the shrine continued, but the social heart was cut out of it by prohibiting henta participation. At first, people stayed away altogether, fearful of French reprisals, but in time they drifted back. Today, the shrine is moderately important again, but the worship pattern is almost wholly individual, and the cult appeals mainly to women, countrymen, and the poor. The bazaar class as such no longer has anything particular to do with it.

66. Latifs are an old tradition in Morocco, considered to be very powerful, even dangerous, and so invoked only in times of great public calamity–droughts, earthquakes, locust plagues. In Sefrou, hentas participated as units in these too. For the latif movement generally, see Halstead, J. P., *Rebirth of a Nation: The Origins and Rise of Moroccan Nationalism, 1912–1944,* Cambridge (Mass.), 1967, pp. 181–4; Brown, *op. cit.*, pp. 198–205. On the Berber decree, see Halstead, *op. cit.*, pp. 178ff; Al-Fāsi, *op. cit.*, pp. 118ff; and Berque, J., *Le Maghreb entre deux guerres,* Paris, 1962.

67. For a general description of the rise of Moroccan nationalism and the formation of the Istiqlal, see Ashford, D. C., *Political Change in Morocco,* Princeton, 1961; Halstead, *op. cit.;* Rézette, R., *Les Partis politiques marocains,* Paris, 1955. An adequate history of the role of the zawias in the rise and triumph of the nationalist movement has yet to be written. When, aided perhaps by in-depth local

studies such as this and Eickelman's (*op. cit.*), one is finally written, the now-standard view (e.g., Bidwell, R., *Morocco Under Colonial Rule*, London, 1973, pp. 144–52) of a "good guys/ bad guys" opposition between "progressive" nationalists and "reactionary" brotherhoods is in for serious revision. Bidwell's straight-faced quotation (*ibid.*, p. 146) of a French captain's report that the number of Derqawis in Sefrou had declined from 750 to 10 between 1921 and 1937 only demonstrates the naiveté of both of them.

68. The specific occupations were as follows: grocers, 4; barbers, 2; periodic market sellers, 2; hardware/spice sellers, 2; masons, 2; coffeeshop keeper, 1; porter, 1; bathhouse keeper, 1; tobacco seller, 1; cloth seller, 1; wool trader, 1; clerk in the religious (qadi) court, 1; farmer, 1; soldier, 1. This material and that in the text derive mainly from interviews with two of these men, the coffeeshop keeper and the wool trader, the first a participant in the movement from the latif days, the second a younger man who emerged as the main leader of Istiqlal in Sefrou during the revolution.

69. The stores were set up mainly at the other region-focusing markets in the area, such as Guigou, Enjil, Marmoucha (see Figure 1), plus a few other small towns (e.g., El Menzel, Boulemane, Bhalil). In the 1963 elections, the last reasonably free ones held in Morocco, Sefrou was one of the twelve circumscriptions (out of 144) in the country in which the Istiqlal vote exceeded 35% (national Istiqlal average, 21%), electing an Istiqlal candidate over one of the king's closest, best known, and most vigorously promoted aides. See Marais, O. [R. Leveau], "L'élection de la Chambre des Représentants du Maroc," *Annuaire d'Afrique du Nord*, 2:85–106 (1963); cf. Leveau, R., *Le Fellah marocain défenseur du trône*, Paris, 1976, pp. 150–1. For a description of similar activities among tradesmen in Casablanca during the revolution, see Waterbury, *op. cit.*, pp. 68, 122–31.

70. On the role of Abdel Hayy Al-Kittani, whose hostility to both the royal family and that of Al-Fassi was of very long standing, in the revolutionary period, see Le Tourneau, R., *Evolution politique de l'Afrique du Nord musulmane, 1920–1961*, Paris, 1962, pp. 180–1, 225–6, 234–5, 246; Burke, E., III, *Prelude to Protectorate in Morocco*, Chicago, 1976, pp. 121–2, 129–30, 133–5.

71. In the following discussion I am concerned with the Jewish community only so far as it relates to understanding the bazaar economy and shall describe just so much of it as seems essential to that end. For general dis-

cussions of the Sefrou Jewish community, see Rosen, L., "North African Jewish Studies," *Judaism*, 17:425–29 (1968); Rosen, L., "A Moroccan Jewish Community During the Middle Eastern Crisis," *American Scholar*, 37:435–51 (1968); Stillman, "The Sefrou Remnant." The last Rabbi of Sefrou, David Ovadiah, has compiled a collection of documents relating to the Jewish community there: *The Community of Sefrou*, Jerusalem, 1974–5, 3 vols., in Hebrew.

Some material on Jewish economic activities in 1938 in Sefrou, which rather exaggerates them, can be found in Le Tourneau, R., "L'activité économique de Sefrou," *Hespéris*, 25:269–86 (1938).

The main works on Jewish life in Morocco include: Zafrani, H., *Les Juifs du Maroc*, Paris, 1972; Bénech, J., *Essai d'explication d'un mellah*, Baden-Baden, 1949; Bensimon-Donath, D., *Evolution du Judaisme marocain sous le Protectorat français, 1912–1956*, Paris and The Hague, 1968; Chouraqui, A., *La Condition juridique de l'Israélite marocain*, Paris, 1950; Chouraqui, A., *Between East and West: A History of the Jews of North Africa*, Philadelphia, 1968; Chouraqui, A., *La Saga des Juifs en Afrique du Nord*, Paris, 1972; Flamand, P., *Un Mellah en pays berbère: Demnate*, Paris, 1952; Flamand, P., *Diaspora en terre Islam*, Casablanca, n.d. (ca. 1948–58); Slouschz, N., "Etude sur l'histoire des Juifs et du Judaisme au Maroc." *Archives marocaines*, Paris, 1905–6; Slouschz, N., *Travels in North Africa*, Philadelphia, 1927; Voinot, *op. cit.*; Brunot, L., and E. Malka, *Textes judéo-arabes de Fès*, Rabat, 1939; Foucauld, *op. cit.*; Marty, P., "Les Institutions israélites au Maroc," *Revue des études islamiques*, 4:297–302 (1930); Goulvin, J., *Les Mellahs de Rabat-Salé*, Paris, 1927; *La Vie juive au Maroc*, Jerusalem, 1973, in Hebrew. For a full bibliography, see Attal, R., *Les Juifs d'Afrique du Nord, bibliographie*, Jerusalem, 1972, pp. 145–222. For the earlier history of the Jewish community in North Africa, see Hirschberg, H. Z., *A History of the Jews in North Africa*, Vol. I, *From Antiquity to the Sixteenth Century*, Leiden, 1974. Some remarks on Jewish-Muslim relations in traditional Salé are given in Brown, *op. cit.*, esp. pp. 151ff.

72. All this refers to the urban setting, for there were, unlike the case in many parts of Morocco, virtually no permanent Jewish settlements in the countryside in the immediate Sefrou region. (The 1960 census does not list a single Jew as living outside the town, and 90% of the town's Jewish population—as against 56% of the Muslim—was born there.) The role of the itinerant Jew was rather another matter. Sefrou has long had a general reputation in Morocco of being a place where Muslim-Jew-

ish relations were unusually good, a reputation it seems to deserve. Though there have been occasional raids on the Jewish community by rural tribesmen during periods of political turmoil, there seems never to have been an urban pogrom of any sort – at least there is no memory of one in either community. Since the foundation of Israel, and especially since the Six Day and the Yom Kippur (or Ramadhan) wars, relations have, of course, worsened, but even then they have been marked by a surprisingly high level of civility and a complete lack of violence. (On Sefrou during the Six Day War, see Rosen, "A Moroccan Jewish Community.")

It is worth noting, in accord with the argument in the text, that Muslim negative stereotypes of Jews in Sefrou are largely not economic in content (cheats, misers, usurers, etc.) but social (they don't take care of their old people; they marry their nieces; even, they aren't circumcised). Comments about Jewish commercial abilities tend to be positive and admiring, their fairness more affirmed than doubted.

73. The origin of the word *mellāh* is disputed, but the most common folk theory is that it derives from *milḥ* ("salt") because it was the duty of the Jews in the old imperial capitals to salt the heads of the king's fallen enemies and hang them on the city gates. In the 1920s and 1930s, when almost all Jews still lived in the mellah, its density (about 4,000 persons per hectare) was more than twice that of the surrounding Muslim quarters and was the densest by far of any in Morocco (Stillman, "The Sefrou Remnant"). Despite the Protectorate's abolition of obligatory residence, in 1960, 55% of the Sefrou community (i.e., about 1,600 people) was still living there; by 1965, none of the 400 or 500 Jews still in the town resided in the mellah. Except for soap making and a couple of kosher butcher shops and grocery stores, the Sefrou mellah was entirely residential; Jewish bazaar activities, both commercial and artisinal, took place outside it, scattered more or less randomly among the Muslims. This virtual absence of bazaar activities in the mellah is not general for Morocco, however (for the suq section in the Fez mellah, which was quite elaborate, see Le Tourneau, *Fès avant*, pp. 379–80). One final peculiarity of the Sefrou mellah should be noted: The overwhelming proportion of residential land and housing was Muslim-owned (much of it in habus) and rented to the Jews. The reason for this seems to have been not a Muslim regulation but a Jewish preference, a disinclination to hold capital in the form of land or buildings.

74. On the *maʿamad*, detailed references to which are found in responsa at least as early as the mid-sixteenth century, more generally, see Zafrani, *op. cit.*, pp. 104ff; Bensimon-Donath, *op. cit.*, pp. 87–8; cf. Chouraqui, *La Condition juridique*, pp. 180ff. After the French arrival, the more common term for it in Sefrou generally was *l-komiṭī*.

75. Le Tourneau, *Fès avant*, p. 369. Virtually every work on Moroccan Jewish communities, including those by Moroccan Jews, stresses their near total domination by rich merchants. Zafrani (*op. cit.*, p. 105): "Les notables qui peuvent être, eux aussi, de fins lettrés, représentent, en quelque sorte, une oligarchie ploutocratique qui, en règle générale, sert le bien public avec zèle et dévouement mais il lui arrive aussi parfoir de se prévaloir de sa fortune et de son influence pour 'régenter durement la communauté' pour réclamer des priviléges et commettre des abus que le rabbinat est obligé de condamner." Bénech (*op. cit.*, p. 71): "Cependant il existe dans le mellah une classe riche et puissante. Elle est formé par le petit nombre de Juifs 'indispensables' auquels les [Muslim]puissants réservent leurs faveurs." Bensimon-Donath (*op. cit.*, p. 19): "Ainsi s'est créée une caste qui, sans être vraiment riche au sens occidental du terme, vivait à l'aise et jouissait d'une certain influence auprès des [Muslim] pouvoirs. Son aisance était d'autant plus remarquée que la masse du peuple végétait dans une indescriptible misère." Le Tourneau (*Fès avant*, p. 369): "[The committee's] membres étaient théoriquement élus, mais dans la réalité le recrutement se faisait par cooptation; les membres du conseil appartenaient tous à l'aristocratie d'argent du Mellah et la communauté était soumise à une petite oligarchie." Even as late as 1953, Flamand refers (*Un Mellah*, p. 229), for Demnate, to an "oligarchie ploutocratique."

Of course, there were rich Muslims too, but they did not form a solidary class, much less a committee. They were, rather, a collection of mutually rivalrous and antagonistic big men connected personally to the less rich by ad hoc patron-client arrangements, and they did not concern themselves much with issues of community welfare.

76. There were, of course, the *dimmī* (cl. *dimmī*) ("protection" rules): the capitation tax; the obligation to wear distinctive clothing (in Morocco, black), live in the mellah, and remove one's shoes when passing a mosque; the prohibition against carrying guns and riding horses, some of which persisted, as custom if not law, even after French rule. There were also obligatory gifts to the sultan and various local officials of his, raised by the committee

from the community generally on the same sliding scale described for charity, on Muslim holidays, royal entries, and so on. Though symbolically important in defining the dominance of Islam over Judaism in the society and thus Jews as wards of a state not their own, the rules do not seem (certainly not in Sefrou) to have led to either Jewish or Muslim communalism beyond the domains of the religious and the domestic, where it was absolute. (No record of an interfaith marriage was uncovered in either the statistical or qualitative data.)

77. The role of the sheikh l-Yahud varied somewhat from community to community, though his power has, in my opinion, tended to be much overestimated by external observers anxious to find "someone in charge" and unaware of the strong checks upon him by the plutocrats whose creature he was. For a Marrakech sheikh l-Yahud who does seem to have achieved a certain independent power (though more on his own than as a result of his role) in the early part of this century, see, but with a good deal of caution, Bénech, *op. cit.*, pp. 256–70. For a situation where a sheikh is claimed (by his grandson!) to have acted as a protector of the populace against the "aristocratie de l'argent," see Zafrani, *op. cit.*, p. 106, note 23.

78. When Jews quarreled with Muslims – almost inevitably in the bazaar context – regulation took place through the same mechanisms as intra-Muslim disputes, the so-called amin system or, for some matters, the qadi and, later, French courts. Intra-Jewish disputes occasionally were also taken to Muslim (or French) authorities, but this was generally considered something assiduously to be avoided. The authorities usually sent the disputes back to the committee anyway for resolution. On the Sefrou rebaas, see Ovadiah, *op. cit.* (Eng.), 1974, pp. 102–8, who gives the formal name of the Simaun rebaa as *Ḥevrat Gōmelē Ḥasādīm*. I am grateful to Professor Norman Stillman for this information.

79. Synagogues (at one time there were as many as sixteen) were built by rich men, whose names they usually bore, and membership, though theoretically voluntary, was in fact more or less fixed: Men joined the synagogue of their fathers; women (who, in any case, were less involved) could choose that of either their fathers or their husbands. The school system was equally complex, including both religious and secular schools of various sorts. The intrusion of the Alliance Israélite, which founded a modern French-type elementary school in 1911, further complicated the situation, for it tended to divide the commu-

nity, at times quite bitterly, along traditionalist vs. modernist lines. On the Jewish educational system in Morocco in general, see Bensimon-Donath, *op. cit.*, pp. 21–40.

Another division found in many Moroccan Jewish communities – that between descendants of exiles from fifteenth-century Andalusia (Heb. *megorāshīm*) and supposed "autochthons" (Heb. *toshābīm*) – was, however, absent in Sefrou, as, a few odd cases aside, there were no Andalusians. Until the 1940s, when a large number of rural Jews from southeast Morocco moved into Sefrou (by the 1960s most had moved out again, either to Israel or the Atlantic coast), to the intense displeasure of the Sefroui Jews, the meghrarba/fillali ("citified"/ "rustic") distinction mentioned above as critical in the caravan period was reflected in the town population composition, only, so to speak, retrospectively. Nor were there more than a handful (less than 1% in 1960) of meghrarba Jews immigrant from other urban communities. In general, the Sefrou community seems to have been one of the more culturally homogeneous internally, in Morocco, as well as dating back to at least the thirteenth century (Stillman, "The Sefrou Remnant"), one of the oldest and the most stable. Except for Tangiers, a rather special case, the Sefrou Jewish population fluctuated less than that of any urban Jewish community in Morocco between 1904 and 1960 (*La Vie juive*, p. 18).

80. All these public properties – synagogues, religious schools, orphanages, funds for charity or holiday celebrations, sacred objects, the Jewish graveyard, the cave shrine – were part of what the Jews called *heqdeš* (from Heb. ha-qōdeš, "the Holy"). Usually compared to the Muslim habus (e.g., Zafrani, *op. cit.*, p. 127; Le Tourneau, *Fès avant*, p. 269), the heqdesh was, in fact, a somewhat different institution. Aside from the fact that, in Sefrou anyway, only a handful of secular properties (stores, ateliers) seem to have been involved, the institution was conceived more in terms of a "community chest" public appeal notion than a mortmain "church foundation" one – a continuing religious-cum-moral obligation of the community to itself (not of individuals to the community), an obligation defined, organized, and administered by the committee. On Jewish philanthropy in medieval (950–1250) Cairo, see Goitein, *op. cit.*, Vol. II, pp. 99ff; in twentieth-century Marrakech, Benech, *op. cit.*, pp. 207–17. Cf., now, Gil M., *Documents of the Jewish Pious Foundations from the Cairo Geniza*, Leiden, 1976.

81. As with the qadi court for Muslims, commercial disputes (i.e., intra-Jewish ones) could be submitted to the court for advisory

opinions. But, as with the qadi court, this seems to have been very infrequently done.

82. The data in Table 7 are for 1960. As emigration from the Sefrou Jewish community has generally been from the bottom up – the poor leaving first, the rich last – these figures may slightly exaggerate the Jewish advantage over the half century or so considered here, whereas increased upward Muslim mobility in the bazaar sector since Independence may slightly obscure it. All in all, there is no reason to believe the 1960 picture much different (except in numbers) from the prewar one, a view supported by Sefroui informants, Jewish and Muslim alike, who say that *so far as the bazaar is concerned* there has never been sharp economic stratification between the two groups. On the other hand, it must also be remembered that until quite recently an enormously greater proportion of Jews than of Muslims was traders and artisans (see Table 1), so that *so far as the society as a whole was concerned,* the Jews did form, and were perceived as, a relatively advantaged group. For the country as a whole, of every 10,000 Jews in the all-Morocco labor force in 1951, about 9,100 were in bazaar-type occupations; of every 10,000 Muslims, about 2,600 were (Bensimon-Donath, *op. cit.,* p. 138). Even here, however, one should keep in mind that a great many Jewish peddlers and craftsmen were indescribably poor, and at least a certain number of Muslim farmers were spectacularly wealthy. For some assorted data on Jewish bazaar occupations in various Moroccan towns ca. 1924, see Massignon, *Enqête,* pp. 149–58 (Sefrou, p. 154).

83. Another, and sociologically more precise, way of putting the general point is to narrow the universe to only "traditional commerce" and "traditional craft" occupations, and to the "old urban" social groups, town-born Arabs and Jews, as defining the heart of the permanent bazaar, in which case the phenomenon is even more striking. The proportion of bazaar workers in traditional commerce and in traditional craft occupations is, respectively, 24% and 76% for Sefrou-born Arabs (N = 1,074) and 52% and 48% for Jews (N = 441).

84. In 1960, after a significant postwar migration of Berbers from the countryside to the town was well underway, the town was still about 85% Arab speaking, the countryside about 60% Berber speaking. If the two main Arab concentrations – Bhalil, a small town-village just north of Sefrou and something of a satellite to it, and the Beni Yazgha, the main Arab-speaking tribe in the region – are put aside (and Jews have played virtually no role among either group), the countryside was nearly 80% Berber speaking. In the 1920s and 1930s there were only a few dozen Berbers living permanently in the town, and urban Arabs (except for a few religious figures, government officials, and large landowners) scarcely ventured into the countryside.

85. Though a fact any Sefroui trader will quite spontaneously affirm (it is almost always the first distinction between traditional Muslim and Jewish trade one is offered, and quite commonly the last), this is very hard to measure precisely. Census categories are not readily disaggregated along such lines, and the effect was much more pronounced in the period preceding World War II, for which there are no exact figures, than for that following, for which there are. However, even in 1960, when the pattern was coming to an end (by 1969 it had virtually disappeared), about 70% of the Jewish traditional craft workers were in tailoring and shoemaking – both largely of the cheap rural product sort – alone. Only about 15% of the Muslim traditional craft workers were in these occupations, and they concentrated on the better-made, urban product side. In contrast, if one takes only the very clearly urban-oriented crafts – masonry, carpentry, baking, butchering, barbering – about 50% of the Muslim craft workers were in them as against about 10% of the Jewish.

The commercial side is even harder to divide into urban- and rural-oriented components on the basis of census data. But even under very weak assumptions, only about a fifth, if that, of the traditional Muslim merchants of the town were predominantly rural-oriented in 1960 (and they to rural Arab, rather than rural Berber, settlements), whereas more than three-fifths of the Jewish were. For 1938, Le Tourneau reports ("L'Activité économique") the Jews as extremely prominent in the animal, hides, wool, and wheat trades.

Of the major traditional crafts in Sefrou, the only one in which the Jews were not represented was the masons, though there were very few Jews among the weavers and bakers. Gold- and silversmithing (always small trades in Sefrou) tinsmithing (a trade hard to classify in rural-urban terms), and soap making (a home industry wholly directed to the rural market) were entirely Jewish.

Yet another index of the Jews' rural orientation is language: Virtually no urban Arabs were bilingual in Berber (and until the 1940s, very few Berbers in Arabic); the majority of male Jews seem to have spoken Berber as well as their native Arabic.

249

86. Other terms for such ambulant traders were *sefārin* (sg. *sāfer;* "traveler," "stranger," "guest") and *duwwāsa* (sg. *duwwās,* apparently from a Hebrew root meaning "to walk about"): cf. Zafrani, *op. cit.,* p. 160; Stillman (personal communication) regards the word as properly *duwwāz,* from an Arabic, not a Hebrew, root, meaning "to go about." The sitting Jews, sometimes called *škā'ir* (sg. *škāra,* a kind of "purse," "moneybag"), provided capital on the two-thirds/one-third, agent/investor *ʿisqa* pattern prescribed by Jewish law, though, as always, circumstances were altered to fit cases. Numbers here are hard to recover, but the largest Jewish financier of Sefrou—head of one of the Simaun sections—in the 1930s was said by informants, perhaps exaggeratedly, to have "about a hundred" riding Jews connected to him. For some comments on Jewish activities in a rural market in northern Morocco ca. 1937, see Fogg, W., "A Tribal Market in the Spanish Zone of Morocco," *Africa,* 11:428–58 (1938).

87. The usual pattern was for the riding Jews to leave town on the morrow of Passover, return the eve of Rosh Hashanah, leave again immediately after Succoth, and return on the eve of Passover. For the same pattern in a rural south Moroccan settlement, see Zafrani, *op. cit.,* p. 215.

88. The siting Jews were, of course, the apex of only the local hierarchy and dealt in turn with even more formidable figures, Jewish and Muslim both, higher up at the city levels. However, it was mainly in tying the locality-focusing levels of the central place structure that the Jews seem to have been especially critical; Sefrou-Fez commercial ties were as much mediated by Arabs as by Jews, or more exactly, by Arabs and Jews intermixed (see, in this regard, Le Tourneau, "L'Activité économique"). Indeed, the ties between the Jewish communities of Sefrou and Fez seem not to have been especially close, even somewhat antagonistic. As mentioned earlier, their pole was Meknes.

89. There were some European stores—French and Spanish—as well by the mid-1930s. Again, language—or more specifically literacy—is an excellent, if indirect, index of the greater involvement of Jews than Muslims in this sector of the bazaar. If one takes, from the 1960 census, men over forty-five years of age (i.e., those who would have been at least twenty years old in 1935), 5% of the Muslims were literate in French, 14% of the Jews.

90. For this view, see the (otherwise quite useful) series of papers by Walter Fogg: "Villages and *Suqs* in the High Atlas Mountains of Morocco," *Scottish Geographical Magazine,* 51:144–51 (1935); "The Economic Revolution in the Countryside of French Morocco;" *Journal of the Royal African Society,* 35:123–39 (1936); "The Importance of Tribal Markets in the Commercial Life of the Countryside of North-West Morocco," *Africa,* 12:445–79 (1939); "A Tribal Market in the Spanish Zone of Morocco," *Africa,* 11:428–58 (1938); "Beliefs and Practices to a Nearby Tribal Market," *Folklore,* 51:132–8 (1940); "Villages Tribal Markets, and Towns: Some Considerations Concerning Urban Development in the Spanish and International Zones of Morocco," *Sociological Review,* 32:85–107 (1940); "A Moroccan Tribal Shrine and Its Relation to a Nearby Tribal Market," *Man,* 124:100–4 (1940); "Changes in the Lay-Out, Characteristics, and Functions of a Moroccan Tribal Market, Consequent on European Control," *Man,* 72:104–8 (1941); "The Organization of a Moroccan Tribal Market," *American Anthropologist,* 44:47–61 (1942). A similar view can be found in Mikesell, M. W., "The Role of Tribal Markets in Morocco," *Geographical Review,* 48:494–511 (1958), and, much less critically, in Benet, F., "Explosive Markets: The Berber Highlands," in Polanyi, K., et al. (eds.), *Trade and Market in the Early Empires,* Glencoe (Ill.), 1957, pp. 188–217.

For a view closer to mine (though one that still seems to regard the suq as an essentially rural phenomenon—"une ville à la campagne et pour la campagne . . . enraciné au plus profond de la vie rurale marocain"), see Troin, *op. cit.,* t.1, pp. 38–9: "Néanmoins, malgré la variété de ses visages, le souk conserve dans son principe son fonctionnement, son organisation interne, son rôle, une réele unité. Qu'ils soient situés en pays bebérophone ou arabophone, en plaine ou en montagne, dans des zones céréalières, fruitières ou pastorales, près des villes ou loin d'elles, les souks du Nord Marocain connaissent le même déroulement, semaine après semaine, et ont les mêmes fonctions." Except that it is as profoundly enraciné in la vie urbaine marocaine as in la vie rurale and that the gulf between ville and campagne is (and from Ibn Khaldun forward, characteristically has been) easily exaggerated for Morocco, this seems exact.

91. Rural markets may not only be larger and more complex than urban ones, but as high or higher in any central place hierarchy one might want to fit to the Moroccan situation. One of Walter Fogg's Spanish Zone "tribal markets" contained (1930–5) no less than 1,100 regular suwwaqs (thirty of them Jews) representing, in Fogg's classification, about 100 occupational categories ("A Tribal Market"). Dwarfing ur-

ban markets in Asilah, Larache, and Ksar Al-Kebir, it was the commercial hub of the whole western sector of the northern zone, frequented by individuals from more than twenty different major tribal groups spread over some 3,000 square kilometers. Rural markets in the immediate Sefrou region (i.e., those within the hexagon of Figure 1) are not very large, ranging from 50 to 250 regular suwwaqs (and 300 to 1,500 visitors – also suwwaqs, but not purchasing tickets giving rights to a particular selling place) per market day, but the region-focusing markets in the Atlas to the south (Guigou, Marmoucha, Enjil) run upward of 500 or 600 regular suwwaqs (and 3,000 to 4,000 visitors) (Records, Bureau de Cercle, Sefrou, 1968). The population, regular and visitor, of any particular marketplace varies importantly with season, current economic situation, and various other matters, including the state of local political stability (for the latter, see, though rather overdrawn, Benet, *op. cit.*). For a map and census of a small rural market near Sefrou, see Annex C. Plans of large, medium, and small rural markets are given in Troin, *op. cit.*, t.2, pl. 3; see also t.1, pp. 355–9. Hart (*op. cit.*, pp. 72–86) describes some rural markets in northeast Morocco.

92. Figure 4 should be compared with Figure 3, showing the funduq distribution ca. 1900; with Figure B.1 (in Annex B), showing the layout of markets in immediate pre-Protectorate Sefrou; and especially with Figures A.1, A.13, and A.19 (in Annex A), depicting the present (i.e., 1968–9) pattern. A very schematized map of Sefrou's extramural markets, apparently ca. 1964, can be found in Troin, *op. cit.*, t.1, p. 415. The easy sociological generalizations appended to Troin's map – the product apparently of a few elite interviews and a walk around the town – need to be taken with a very large grain of salt. The most recent (1976) disposition of Sefrou's markets can be found in Annex E. For another cultural setting in which an indigenous distinction is made between a permanent "shop" market (*mercado*) and an open-air periodic (*plaza*), see Beals, *op. cit.*, pp. 8–9.

93. Le Tourneau, "L'Activité économique."

94. Si Bekkai, *op. cit.* The third staple of the Sefrou region, olives, had already by Le Tourneau's time become, as now, a crop sold on site (i.e., in the groves surrounding the town and in the countryside) and carted away to mills by truck; there was no longer a specific olive bazaar in Sefrou. Except for local consumption milling, oil sold retail in grocery shops, and the auctioning of habus-owned trees for harvest, the olive trade in Sefrou no longer passes through either the periodic or the permanent bazaar; the crop is bought up (ostensibly at prices fixed by the government, which, as noted, also establishes the opening of harvest season) directly by agents of large-scale entrepreneurs, almost all of them from Fez. (There are four motor-driven oilmills in Sefrou town, only one of them of any size.) As Annex B indicates, olives is not the only trade to have disappeared from the Sefrou bazaar in the last half century: Tanning is another. Cord making, goldsmithing, and plow-making also used to be more important than their few scattered remnants now indicate, and shoemaking – mainly by Jews of *belġa,* a form of leather slipper once the almost universal footware – was in the 1920s and 1930s the largest craft. On the other hand, neither potting nor dyeing, important trades elsewhere, seems ever to have been significant in Sefrou. For a salutary warning against the easy assumption that all commodities flow through a given hierarchy in similar ways, see Jones, W. O., "Some Economic Dimensions of Agricultural Marketing Research," in Smith, *op. cit.*, pp. 303–26.

95. In the mid-1970s (after the completion of our fieldwork) a process of spatial unification of the Thursday markets in a government-built suq area at the southern edge of town was begun, which by 1976 was nearing completion. For this, see Annex E.

96. About 56% of the adult Muslims living in the medina in 1960 were rural-born (non-medina quarters; 40%), as against virtually none (certainly well under 5%) before 1930. Well over 80% of these in-migrants derive from the immediate countryside around Sefrou.

97. The distribution described in these tables is based on the data in Annex A plus informants' judgments about the location of the various suqs. This involves a certain amount of judgment concerning boundaries, but the general pattern is beyond question. If only the more well established enterprises in each trade were taken into account, the effect would be markedly stronger. Permanent markets remain in the old city, shoemakers and carpenters being the major exceptions (for their original locations, see Annex B). The shoemaker trade shifted to the new quarter as Muslims began to replace Jews in it; the carpenters, as increased mechanization (motor-driven saws, lathes, grinders) became important. For some general comments on trade localization in other Moroccan towns, see Massignon, *Enquête.*

98. Virtually no one in Sefrou lives in, above, or behind his shop or workplace or, in general, anywhere near it. As Figure 4 (and the figures of Annex A on which it is based) clearly

Suq: the bazaar economy in Sefrou

251

shows, residential and commercial areas are sharply discriminated, and Weber's supposedly modern separation of "home" and "office" is, in line with the "mosaic pattern" of integration discussed earlier, as complete here, and not just spatially, as perhaps anywhere in the world.

99. As always, usage varies, and there is no simple consensus on such matters. I have merely given the distinctions and the terms for them that seem in most common use in Sefrou. Also, it must be understood that the tree form of the diagram is intended solely as a presentational device: It depicts the distinctions – and connections – Sefrouis make, but not their concept (so far as I can discover, they don't have one) of how the total system of such distinctions should be abstractly represented. A Venn diagram could probably catch the suwwaq overall image better than a tree (though Sefrouis don't draw those either), but I do not feel certain enough of the nuances involved – how large to make the circles, how to overlap or space them – to construct one.

100. The total number of terms, or modifications of terms, for commercial and craft occupations in the raw data of the bazaar survey is over 150, and I could doubtless have gathered more were my patience for fine detail equal to the task. This extraordinarily intensive division of labor (remembering a total bazaar labor force of slightly over 2,000) is apparently characteristic of Middle Eastern bazaars everywhere and always: "While scanning the Geniza records [of tenth to twelfth-century Cairo] for the arts and crafts mentioned in them, the modern observer is impressed by the great number of occupations and by the high degree of specialization and division of labor apparent in them. The terms for about 265 manual occupations have been identified thus far, as against 90 types of persons engaged in commerce and banking and approximately the same number of professionals, officials, religious functionaries, and educators. With this total of about 450 professions compare the 150 or so professional corporations traced in ancient Rome by J. T. Waltzing . . . and the 278 *corporations de métier* listed by André Raymond for Cairo in 1801 . . . The collection of 435 colorful descriptions of Damascene occupations begun by Muhammad Sa'īd Qāsimi . . . also includes agricultural laborers of different types, long lists of shopkeepers selling specialties, as well as musicians and other persons engaged in the entertainment business" (Goitein, *op. cit.*, p. 99). On the intense division of labor in other Moroccan towns, see, with caution, Massignon, *Enquête;* cf. Brown, *op. cit.*, pp. 152–3.

101. The nearest exception is prewar Jewish shoemaking, whose practitioners were under the thumb of one or another of the large sitting merchants. But even those in fact wholly dependent craftsmen were conceived of as formally independent, their output being merely more or less completely engrossed. The modern furniture enterprises, in which a single entrepreneur presides over both the craft and sales aspects, are also Jewish. For a counterexample of a bazaar economy in which integrated craft-commercial enterprises are of importance, see Geertz, *Peddlers and Princes,* pp. 28–81.

102. The wholesale/retail contrast in English has two meanings – gross vs. detail selling and intratrade sale vs. sale to the general public. This produces a great deal of confusion when the terms are used with respect to bazaar economies. Though the first, scale-based opposition (in fact, more a gradation than an opposition) exists and is of importance, the second, functionally based opposition, by and large does not. Thus, though there are Moroccan expressions for selling *en gros* (*b-ž-žumla*) as against *au détail* (*b-t-tefrād*), they are not applied to merchant-merchant, as opposed to merchant-consumer, trade, a distinction that is simply not made. On the difficulty of consistently applying the wholesaler/retailer distinction in eleventh-century Egypt, see Goitein, *op. cit.*, pp. 150–2. On the complementary meaning relations of *bi* and *šri* (the first originally means "to shake hands," the latter the "busy activity of the market"), see under *bai* in *Shorter Encyclopaedia of Islam,* p. 56. For a popular proverb expressing the equivalence ("O buyer, remember the day when you will sell"), see Westermarck, E., *Wit and Wisdom in Morocco,* London, 1930, p. 170.

103. On the importance of the *dellāl* (an occupation mentioned by Ibn Khaldun) in traditional Fez, where there were 140 of them in hides and 70 in cloth alone (they were, as in Sefrou, specialized by market area), see Le Tourneau, *Fès avant,* pp. 310–14, 347, 349, and Bousquet, G. G., and J. Berque, "La Criée publique à Fès," *Revue d'économie,* pp. 320–45, May 1940. Popular critical proverbs concerning them (that they are friendless, thieves, shameless, etc.) can be found in Westermarck, *op. cit.,* p. 174. For a theoretical-empirical treatment of auctioneering in general, see Cassady, R., Jr., *Auctions and Auctioneering,* Berkeley and Los Angeles, 1967.

104. The dellal pattern was especially used for rural crafts, such as rugs, blankets, and baskets; certain secondary rural products, such as rock salt, eggs, hides, and firewood; secondhand goods of all sorts; and certain urban light

manufactures, such as cloth, shoes, rope, and farm implements, and because of the women's role in it, yarn. Smaller quantities of grain, wool, and even vegetables were occasionally sold this way, and a certain number of live animals were "dellal-ed" in the animal market rather than sold directly. Dellals were particularly active on the day of the periodic market, though permanent market traders – shopkeepers and place sellers – would give them goods to hawk about the various appropriate market areas as well. A few dellals could also be found, and still can, in the country markets, but the gap between the suwwaq and the non-suwwaq being less formidable there, they were never as important in the town. Finally, in the prewar period there was a handful of female auctioneers who went about from house to house in town taking bids from women on household items. This practice has now virtually disappeared.

105. On "target marketers," see Bohannan and Dalton, *op. cit.,* p. 7, and, in the same volume, E. Colson, "Trade and Wealth Among the Tonga," p. 615. Bohannan and Dalton tie target selling to target buying more closely than I, or the Moroccans, do (" 'target marketers' engage in marketing sporadically to acquire a specific amount of cash income for a specific expenditure, such as a bicycle or tax payment") and seem to think they are confined to minor, "peripheral" markets, and minor, peripheral transactions. Whatever the case in sub-Saharan Africa this surely does not hold for Morocco. But the essential notion (which can apply as well to labor – e.g., in South Africa) of seeking a more or less discrete and immediate economic end, rather than engaging in a continuous, cumulative enterprise, is the same.

106. The *bāyeᶜ* pattern is not confined to grain and animals. Among the Berbers especially, rugs, blankets, and cloak material, woven by the women and carried to market by the men, serve as a reserve to be drawn on as the need arises. In many Berber farmhouses one sees piles of rugs, fluctuating in size, to be used for target selling and quite explicitly regarded as a homemade bank account, as well as, like animal herds and granary stocks, prime public symbols of family wealth and status. To a lesser extent, wickerwork and rock salt, as well as minor farm products (chickens, condiments) serve in the same way. In the market described in Annex C, a rather small one, upward of 80% of those present (excluding target buyers, who, as they neither rent spaces nor purchase tickets, cannot readily be counted) were target sellers. Even most of the fruit and vegetable sellers were *bāyeᶜ* – i.e., people selling their own produce (and only in this mar-

ket) in occasional fashion – rather than regular *keddāra* greengrocers. Town artisans, on the other hand, now sell most of their products via client systems (including putting out contracts from merchants) of one sort or another, and almost never target sell.

107. It should be understood that "sitting" is applied not just to sellers but to buyers as well, so that even what we would call a customer is regarded as sitting in the market he customarily buys in. This too is, apparently, a very old and widespread pattern: "The term 'sitting' applied [in Medieval Egypt] to both the vendor and the buyer. 'I arrived in Alexandria on the Muslim holiday and did not find him sitting' that is, his store was closed. 'I shall sit with these goods in a store,' that is, sell them locally, 'or travel with them to Syria.' 'Let there be no other business to you on Sunday morning except sitting in the bazaar of the clothiers and picking up all you need,' that is, while shopping the buyer would sit down in the stores where he intended to make his purchase" (Goitein, *op. cit.,* Vol. I, p. 192). Unless the essential identity in Moroccan eyes of the buyer and the seller functions and the precise, rather than apparent, meaning of the sitting (fixed)/riding (traveling, ambulant) contrast are grasped, the suq division of labor cannot be properly understood.

108. There *are* some fixed merchants who are established in two different settings, and some target sellers and buyers operate equally in more than one nearby market. In fact, and rather in opposition to the appearance of fluidity and randomness the bazaar often gives to foreign observers, this is quite rare.

109. In the Protectorate period such door-to-door countryside peddling, of household implements, spices, cosmetics, medicines, charms was mainly a Jewish specialty, because only a Jew could approach a Muslim woman easily. The trade was mostly barter, the peddler (called a *duwwās,* "trudger," a term used only for Jews) receiving eggs, secondhand clothes, sheep skins, and so on in exchange for his goods. This sort of trade has now entirely disappeared, though a few Muslim peddlers (called, to distinguish them from the Jews, *ᶜaṭṭar;* see Annex B) and knife sharpeners are still occasionally seen in villages. Even in Protectorate times, however, most Jewish riding merchants operated in or at the edge of marketplaces, and in 1936 the French, pressured by pious town Muslims, actually forbade duwwas trading in the Sefrou region as exploitative of rural female credulity and contrary to local mores (Le Tourneau, "L'Activité économique"). In the countryside, as in the town, trade and women – or anyway, trade and decent women – do not mix (but see, for the

253

exception proving the rule, note 116), and the home and business realms are sharply separated. Aside from the marginal and carefully insulated exceptions already mentioned, no bazaar activities take place (and, at least for the proximate past, apparently never have) in the villages, and suqs are always located a significant distance from the nearest settlement. This too is general in the Maghreb (see Benet, *op. cit.,* p. 196). For some general remarks on the role of itinerant peddlers in laying the groundwork for the development of periodic markets, see Plattner, S. M., "Periodic Trade in Developing Areas Without Markets," in Smith, *op. cit.,* pp. 69–88.

110. Only a minority of Sefrou-based sebaibis limit themselves to the locality-focusing markets of the immediate Sefrou area (for which see Figure 1). Of those who roam more widely, the largest number moves southward toward Almis du Guigou, Enjil des Ikhatarn, Ksabi, and even Boumia and Midelt. But significant numbers go southeastward toward Imouzzer des Marmoucha, Outat Oulad el Haj, and Missour; eastward toward El Menzel, Ahermoumou, and Sidi Brahim; northeastward toward Arhbalou Arkane, Ras Tabouda, and Outa Bouabane; northward toward Ain Aicha, Taounate, and Sidi El Mokhfi; northwestward toward Ain Cheggag, Sebaa Aioun, Ain Chkef, and Mikkes; westward toward Immouzer du Kandar, El Hajeb, and Agourai; and southwestward toward Ifrane, Azrou, Timhadite, and even Khenifra – thus more or less boxing the compass so far as Sefrou is concerned. Very few go to Fez (though some Fez sebaibis come to Sefrou) or any other large cities, or indeed to higher-order markets than Sefrou of any sort. I am at a loss how to estimate the numbers of sebaibis working out of Sefrou or the number of markets in which they are to be found, save to say that both numbers are quite large. Even in the small (and, when the census was taken, but moderately active) rural market of Annex C, there were ten sebaibis, two of them residents of nearby villages, one from Fez, and seven from Sefrou town; and Sefrou sebaibis may be encountered in rural and small town markets almost anywhere within the rough hexagon formed by Midelt, Khemmiset, Ouezzane, Ketama, Taourirt, and Outat Oulad el Haj. For the locations of these various markets and places, see Troin, *op. cit.,* t.2, pl. 1.

111. Today, most sebaibis travel by bus between suqs, which are well served by lines. (For the suq-related bus network centered on Sefrou – from which about 1,000 "bus places" to other suqs are available per week – see Troin, *op. cit.,* t.2, pl. 22.) Some of the more substantial sebaibis own or hire (often in groups of two

or three) automobiles or trucks, space in which they often sell or lease to others. Though sebaibis may remain several days at a time on the road (and earlier, when transport was less rapid, somewhat longer), they do not engage in the extensive stays in distant markets described earlier for the riding Jews, and most return to Sefrou weekly, or at the very least biweekly. Sebaibi itineraries do not require, and the larger ones preclude, attendance at any particular market every week; some markets are visited only every three, four, or even five weeks. As in everything else, much depends upon season, the state of the market in various commodities, the ceremonial calendar, and so on, including, not least, the condition of the sebaibi's personal finances.

112. As noted above, the bulk of semsar buying of olives is conducted in the groves at harvest time, and the olives are immediately carted away to non-Sefroui processers, so that the trade really does not pass through the local suq system.

113. Le Tourneau, "L'Activité économique." Le Tourneau (who, it should be noted, has an excessively Fez-eye view of Sefrou) mentions semsars as important in the hide, charcoal, wool, and rug trades. There are also semsars for Sefrou town merchants operating, usually on a quite moderate scale, in the country markets about. The term more often used for them, however, is *mulāqī* (a word that also means "pimp") rather than semsar.

114. Which occupations are considered by Sefrouis to fall on the artisan side and which on the buyer-seller side (something not entirely predictable on the basis of Western conceptions) is indicated in Annex A. Some remarks on masters, workers, and apprentices in Moroccan towns generally can be found in Massignon, *Enquête*, pp. 80–1, where the term for journeyman is given as "*sonnàᶜ*" (i.e., *ṣunnàᶜ*; sg. *ṣānāᶜ*), a term also common in Sefrou. Cf. Jamma, *op. cit.,* pp. 79–80; Brown, *op. cit.,* p. 136.

115. Goitein, *op. cit.,* Vol. I, p. 172, remarks with respect to medieval Egypt, that although "muslim lawyers usually envisage partnerships only between two persons, ... "this should be viewed merely as legal idiom." Even on his own evidence (*ibid.,* pp. 87ff.) this seems too constricted a view; and so far as Sefrou is concerned, the radically dyadic concept of the nature of contract is a popular, virtually universal one, not a property of the jurists. The "idiom" is thus a powerful and pervasive cultural, not a narrowly legal, one.

116. The organization of one rather special craft – special, in that it is the only one that significantly involves women and that it takes

a household industry form not otherwise developed in Sefrou – may be briefly described, both for its intrinsic interest and for its usefulness in indicating the limits of the artisan work structure. It is the yarn trade.

Yarn is made by women, called *ğezzāla,* in their homes. Most of these women are urban, though some are found in Arabic-speaking villages as well, in a sort of complementary contrast to the rug, blanket, and cloak-cloth weaving of the Berber-speaking women mentioned earlier. The woman's husband may buy the wool and market the yarn, but this is quite uncommon and indeed is felt as a male intrusion into female affairs. Instead, professional entrepreneurs (also called *ğezzāla*), themselves women, commonly take the wool on consignment from a wool trader, more often than not a relative, and then, having washed and carded it, put it out to anywhere from a half dozen to thirty or forty women to twine in the privacy of their homes. (The latter may put the work out further to various relatives and neighbors.) When the yarn is finished, the entrepreneurs, of whom there are perhaps a dozen of any significance in Sefrou, carry it to the "yarn market" (*sūq l-ğzal*), which is held very early in the morning in front of the Funduq L-Habus L-Kebir in the Bradᶜaiya (see Figure A.11 of Annex A) on Wednesdays and Sundays, where they consign it to dellals to sell. The dellals walk about the market taking bids in the usual manner and the women leave the scene. (The purchasers are town weavers, sebaibis intending to resell in rural markets to the husbands of those Berber rug and blanket makers, and semsars representing Fez yarn merchants.) The yarn sold, the entrepreneur collects from the dellal and gives him his commission, distributes their shares to the workers, returns to the wool merchant his price, and retains what is left, enough in some cases to make her markedly well-off by Sefrou standards.

The only other, and much less important, putting-out craft of any note is the making of knotted silk buttons (*ᶜuqad;* sg. *ᶜuqda*), also by women at home. In this case, the silk merchants/spinners are the putter-outers and engross the product directly, but the yarn entrepreneurs act, on a commission basis, as go-betweens here as well.

117. For the Arabic names of the trades, see Table A.2, Annex A. Both Le Tourneau (*Fès avant,* esp. pp. 299–301) and Massignon (*Enquête,* es. pp. 99ff.) treat extensively of amins, though both discussions, and particularly the latter, which wobbles factually besides, are seriously marred by the earlier mentioned confusion of socioreligious organizations, occupational categories, and dispute settlement arrangements under the single, unexamined, but nonetheless reified, rubric of "corporation." (Most of Massignon's diversely organized lists seem – that for Taroudant, by far the shortest, notably aside – to be of occupational types, *ḥerfa,* not of amins. His Sefrou list [pp. 48–49] more confusedly presented than most, seems to indicate 43 amins in 1924, almost certainly much too low a figure.) Leo Africanus's references to amins as "consuls" and his insistence on their purely economic role (quoted, quizzically, in Le Tourneau, *Fèz avant,* pp. 78, 294) was closer to the mark than later descriptions of them as diffuse, multifunctional *chefs de corporation.* Le Tourneau says the *umanā* plural is used for certain state officials (fiscal officers, etc.) and the *amīnāt* one for the commercial figures here being discussed, but that is not true in Sefrou, where the *umanā* plural is the usual one in all contexts. Cf. Brown, *op. cit.,* p. 137.

118. *ᶜArif* is probably the most general term applied to this class (or, more strictly, paradigmatic set) of roles; each term, including *amīn,* is sometimes denoted by it, as is the class as a whole. For similar "expert" roles (the French derivative, *ekspir,* is now often applied to them as well) in the countryside, see Hoffman, *op. cit.,* p. 141.

119. It would be incorrect, however, or at the very least premature, to see in this any intrinsic evolutionary development rather than the most recent state of a very long-term, and as yet unended, bargaining relationship between *ahl s-sūq* ("people of the market") and *ahl l-makzen* ("people of the state") eventuating in the usual mixture of *sība* ("fractiousness," "recalcitrance," "dissidence") and *ṭāᶜa* ("submissiveness," "compliance," "obedience"). In medieval Cairo, "the *ᶜarīf,* or head of a profession – as far as such an office existed – was not a leader elected by members of his group, but a supervisor appointed by the market police in order to assist it in its fight against fraudulent practices" (Goitein, *op. cit.,* p. 84). The porters of Fez, following Berber models, traditionally elected four amins for six-month terms whom the government automatically recognized (Le Tourneau, *Fès avant,* p. 196). There have been, and are, certain amins, those of the prostitutes for example (called *ᶜarīfa,* the feminine of *ᶜarīf*), with no official standing at all but nonetheless of some significance. Even more "nonimmoral" but unofficial amins exist in Sefrou – those of mule skinners (*ḥammāra, ḥammāla*), hornblowers (*ğiyyāṭa*), and soup dispensers (*mwālin l-ḥarīra*), for example. Nisba-based amins such as Le Tourneau found in Fez (*ibid.,* p. 193) – Soussi cooks, Touat charcoal sellers, and the like – do not, the Jewish case and con-

255

ceivably (the facts are unclear) Fassi cloth sellers in the 1920s aside, seem to have existed in Sefrou. It should also be noted that it is possible, though uncommon (the only cases I know of for Sefrou involve porters and wheat sellers, and no longer obtain), for there to be more than one amin in a profession.

120. Massignon (*Enquête,* pp. 129–30) gives a few casebook-type examples of the application of hisba principles in Sefrou during the 1920s, which, save that more tailors and carpenters are involved than millers or bakers, reflect as well present practice. Three examples are:

1. A man gives a quantity of wheat over to a miller to be milled. After delivery, the man claims the flour is impure. The amin of the millers examines the stock of wheat from which that given to the miller was drawn to see if it is of good quality. If it is, the miller is responsible and must reimburse the plaintiff.

2. A man buys a loaf of bread from a baker. He claims the merchandise is of inferior quality and does not attain the asserted weight. The amin of the bakers determines the weight question, for which the baker is held responsible. The amin of the millers then examines the flour from which the loaf was made to see if it is adulterated, in which case the miller who milled it is responsible to the baker.

3. Two butchers buy a sheep in partnership. The purchase effected, one of the butchers wishes to slaughter the sheep immediately; the other wishes to grow it for a month first. The amin of the butchers auctions the animal between the two. The higher bidder gains the sheep to slaughter or conserve as he will, the other collects from him the bid price.

Massignon also has (*ibid.,* pp. 192–224) a set of governmental documents detailing formal cases of muhtaseb decisions from the same period, but none, alas, are from Sefrou. For a poem addressing a complaint to the amin of the bakers, see Annex D. The notion of ʿurf is further discussed below.

Aside from dispute settlement (*ṣulḥ*), for which they usually receive a small gift from the winner, the amins, backed when need be by the muhtaseb, are responsible for collecting ceremonial presents (sg. *hedīa*) offered to the king on behalf of the trades on various royal occasions, though this custom, once powerful, is now much less so. The amins also witness the guarantors (sg. *ḍāmen*) who swear to make good any defaults of entrants (usually apprentices of theirs or in-migrants from elsewhere with whom they are acquainted or otherwise connected) into certain trades–especially butchers, bathhouse keepers, porters, and bakers, but often tailors, carpenters, cof-

feeshop keepers, and shoemakers as well– though the amins have no actual control of entry as such. In some cases, for example, goldsmiths (who are usually moneylenders as well) and auctioneers, the guarantee takes the form of a cash bond (also called *ḍāmen*), which the amin holds. Finally, in an attempt to control speculation and fraud, the muhtaseb, with the assistance of the relevant amins, posts "official" maximum price lists (sg. *sʿar*) at irregular intervals for certain basic necessities, especially flour, sugar, charcoal, and meat, an effort fitfully effective at best.

121. The phrase is Le Tourneau's (*Fès avant,* p. 211) and pertains to pre-Protectorate Fez. He also calls the muhtaseb (p. 214), reflecting on his powers (he could order traders fined, whipped, imprisoned, or merely paraded about the market with their crime loudly proclaimed) and his possibilities for graft, "un personnage redouté et impopulaire." And elsewhere (*ibid.,* p. 294) he says of the muhtaseb, with a subtle accuracy missing from accounts that represent him as an administrator rather than a judge, "il ne donnait pas d'impulsion à la machine économique de Fès, il n'était pas le cerveau qui s'efforce de prévoir et de diriger; il apparaissait surtout comme une force d'inertie qui fixait au sol l'échafaudage de l'économie fasie et l'empêchait de vaciller et de se désagreger." For a general review of the hisba and the muhtaseb role, see Massignon (*Enquête,* pp. 107–10), who sees strong Andalusian influence on its formation in Morocco (cf. Cahen, C., and M. Talbi, "Hisba," *Enyclopaedia of Islam,* Vol. III, pp. 486–89, London, 1971; Chalmata, P., *El Señor del Zoco,* Madrid, 1973). In 1917, the muhtaseb was formally made a state official by the French with the result that "actuellement le Mohtassib n'est plus qu'un fonctionnaire municipal chargé de la surveillance des corporations de métiers et de celles qui vivent du commerce" (Massignon, *Enquête,* p. 110). Some of the aura of his former eminence still clings to him, however, at least in Sefrou. On the decline of the muhtaseb role in Salé, see Brown, *op. cit.,* p. 138.

122. Benet, *op. cit.* Benet's pioneering essay relies too heavily on the "Land of Government" (*Bled l-Makzen*) vs. "Land of Insolence" (*Bled s-Sība*) dichotomy so favored by French colonial ethnographers, anxious, for romantic reasons or political, to contrast Arabs and Berbers, and treats the subject too briefly and in too unshaded a manner to be of more than suggestive value. But his central point, that keeping the suq safe for trade and society safe from the suq has long been a central concern, amounting indeed to something of an obses-

sion, of Maghrebian (not just Berber) social, political, and even religious organization, is beyond question.

123. The internal quotation is from Benet, *ibid.,* who remarks: "It is not surprising that the *nefra'a* breeds xenophobia. Strangers and foreigners are sometimes inclined to take the law into their own hands; they have no part in the policing of the market and do not suffer from the long-range consequences of a *nefra'a.* *Nefra'as* will discredit a *suq* and people will stop coming to it. Besides, if a murder has been committed in the suq the market is closed for a period of purification, generally one year." *Nefra* derives from the root "to bolt," "stampede," "run away." The importance in the popular mind of the peace of the market can be seen in two proverbs given by Hart (*op. cit.,* p. 71): "market day is a day of respect (*ḥurma*)" and "market day is a day of peace (*sulḥ*)."

124. The internal quotations are from Benet, *op. cit.;* stress original. Cf. Montagne, R., *Les Berbères et le makhzen dans le sud du Maroc,* pp. 252ff., and "Une Tribu berbère du Sud-Marocaine: Massat," *Hespéris,* 4:357–403 (1924). On the insulation of the market and village spheres in another part of North Africa, see Bourdieu P., *Outline of a Theory of Practice,* Cambridge (Eng.), 1977, pp. 185–6.

125. For the first approach, see Tax, *op. cit.;* for the second, Polanyi et al., *op. cit.;* for the third, Beals, *op. cit.*

126. For a (rather schematic) discussion of imperfect competition in a bazaar, see Swetnam, J., "Oligopolistic Prices in a Free Market – Antigua, Guatemala," *American Anthropologist,* 75:1504–10 (1973).

127. For some acute comments on the limitations of Shannon-type, quantitative communication approaches to economic issues, see Marshak, J., "Economics of Inquiring, Communicating, Deciding," in Lamberton, D. M., (ed.), *Economics of Information and Knowledge,* Harmondsworth (Eng.), 1971, pp. 37–58; cf. Lamberton, D. M., "Introduction," *ibid.,* pp. 7–15, and Arrow, K. J., *The Limits of Organization,* New York, 1974, esp. Chap. 1.

128. Whether one sees the clouds as local crystallizations of the atmosphere or the atmosphere as the summary resultant of the clouds, is, as in all field conceptualizations, more or less a matter of convenience. What is very difficult for a speaker of English, where roots are buried and etymology all too often a notional archeology for digging them up, fully to appreciate, and what most needs to be so appreciated, however, is the degree to which, for a speaker of Arabic, pure, lexically unrealized roots, mere clusters of paradigm consonants,

trail with them a palpable aura of meaning, an aura that in turn envelops, more obviously or less, any actually generated lexical item. As Arabic writing, which normally omits most of the vocalic elements, further accentuates the roots (which, of course, here are not buried, but available to immediate perception), the effect is quite pervasive, extending to some of the most developed dimensions of Arab thought. On this, see (with caution), Massignon, L., *Essai sur les origines du Lexique technique de la mystique musulmane,* Paris, 1954. Cf. Izutsu, T., *Ethico-Religious Concepts in the Qur'an,* Montreal, 1966.

129. I have given only derivations that seem to appear (and as they appear) in Moroccan coloquial, though with no claim that these are all that do so. The full classical list can be found in Wehr, H., *A Dictionary of Modern Written Arabic,* ed. by J. M. Cowan, Ithaca (N.Y.), 1961, pp. 508–9, where it covers two full-page columns, and upward of thirty entries, including *miṣdāq* – "touchstone," "criterion"; *taṣadūq* – "legalization," "authentication"; and *muṣādaqa* – "consent," "assent," "concurrence." For a fascinating discussion of the religious meaning of *ṣdiq,* and some of the other words discussed below, to which the following analysis is much indebted, see Smith, W. C., "Orientalism and Truth," The T. Cuyler Young lecture, Program in Near Eastern Studies, Princeton, 1969; and Smith, W. C., "A Human View of Truth," *Studies in Religion,* 1:6–24 (1971).

130. For this concept of "culture," see Geertz *Interpretation of Cultures.* Of course, and as will become, at least in passing, evident, these words play roles in other rhetorics and meta-languages – moral, political, domestic, aesthetic, religious than those connected with bazaar exchange. It is impossible not to requote here yet once more the old wheeze: "Every Arabic word has five meanings – its proper meaning, the opposite of its proper meaning, a poetic meaning, an obscene meaning, and the name for a part of a camel."

131. As noted above, *sūwwāqa,* the plural of *sūwwāq,* itself has "mob" and "rabble" as part of its meaning. An active, and thus prosperous and attractive, suq is said to be *ᶜāmer* ("populous," "peopled," "full"); the opposite, *ḳāwi* ("desolate," "deserted," "empty").

132. For a brief discussion of the Moroccan concept of the role of speech in social life and the connection of that concept with their religious and aesthetic views, see Geertz, C., "Art as a Cultural System," *MLN,* 91:1473–99 (1976). On the *k-l-m* root in higher Islamic thought, see Wolfson, H. *The Philosophy of the Kalam,* Cambridge (Mass.), 1976, esp. pp. 1–111.

257

133. Smith, "Orientalism and Truth."

134. *Ibid.* Some quotation marks have been added for clarification; brackets indicate interpolations. The syntax of *"ṣaddaqa al-khabara al-khabru,"* which might most literally be translated "the (further) news (or experience) caused to be regarded as true (the previous) news (or experience)," is: causative verb, object, subject. *Taṣdīq* is, of course, not a verb; its gloss as one is merely a stylistic convenience of Smith's. For a similar discussion of *ṣdiq* as it appears in the Quran which comes to similar conclusions (*"Ṣdiq* [possesses] obvious implications of sincerity, steadfastness, honesty, and trustworthyness ... For a given statement to be *ṣdiq* ... it is not enough that the words used conform to reality; they should also conform to the idea of reality in the mind of the speaker. It is the existence of the intention or determination to be true that constitutes the most decisive element in the semantic structure of *ṣdiq*"), see Izutsu, *op. cit.,* pp. 89–94, who also adverts (p. 91) to the Quran as eternal Divine Speech side of all this, quoting VI, 115 ("Perfect are the words of thy Lord in *ṣdiq* and *ʿadl* [justice]. Naught can change His words") and remarking: "Here we see *ṣdiq* used in reference to the words of God. This means simply that God as an active participant in the 'covenant' remains true to His own words. And this is nothing other than a particular way of expressing the thought that God's words once uttered cannot be changed with fickleness, that, in other words, they are absolutely trustworthy." And, it needs be added, absolutely powerful.

135. Smith's representation of *ṣiddīq* as someone held to be "an habitual teller of truth by moral character" may seem to count against this argument. But Smith here is perhaps a bit misled by his own "inner light," Protestant conscience view of things, for the term *ṣiddīq* is applied to someone whose specific reputations for honesty, normally attested by a string of concrete examples (the paradigmatic one being Abu Bakr's response to Mohammed's account of the night journey), are, so to speak, very many. It points to a history of social encounters, not a settled, much less "habitual," psychic state. On the relational nature of Moroccan conceptions of selfhood and personal identity, see Geertz, " 'From the Native's Point of View,' " *Islam Observed,* and above.

136. As with the other appraisal terms, *ṣdiq* has no true antonym. Its opposite is indicated by its negation, *ma-ši-ṣdiq* ("not *ṣdiq*"). The normal, mixed situation is indicated by the addition of that all-purpose skepticising term, without which no Moroccan could talk at all, *šwīya* ("somewhat," "a little bit," "to a certain

258

extent," "yes and no") to either the positive or the negated form.

137. The connection is developed across the whole field: *ʿaref* is "to perceive," "to distinguish," "to be aware of," "to discover"; *maʿrifa* is "learning," "lore," "knowledge," "gnosis"; *tʿāref* is "to become mutually acquainted," "to get to know one another," "to associate with one another"; *ʿurfi* is "correct," "conventional," "socially acceptable." The quranic antonym for *maʿrūf, munkar* ("unacknowledged," "denied," "evil," "forbidden"–from a root having to do with "ignorance," "obliviousness," "estrangement," "foreignness," "deviance," "rejection") does not seem to appear in the bazaar context, or indeed in any secular contexts at all, where the opposite of *maʿrūf* is, again, merely its negation. On *maʿrūf* in the Quran, see Izutsu, *op. cit.,* pp. 213–17.

138. Descriptions of bazaar *ʿurf,* even for as limited a field as Sefrou, could run to volumes. For some typical examples concerning everything from tailors' thread and dyers' dyes to masters' responsibility for the insulting language of their apprentices and the rights of perfumers to sell the work of braidmakers (*majādlīya*), see Massignon, *Enquête.* For a popular poem that projects the "generally accepted" expectations surrounding an important trade–baking–with some vividness, see Annex D.

139. Cited in Waterbury, *op. cit.,* p. 35. A J'ha trickster tale Waterbury quotes also communicates well the bazaar mentality to which the *šīḥ* (or, better, *šīḥ??*) concern for whether things are what they seem to be is appropriate. J'ha was dying. He promised his neighbors that if they prayed for him and he recuperated he would sell his donkey and divide the proceeds among them. They did, and he did. He then went to the bazaar and said, "who wants to buy my donkey for a dirham and my stick for 500 dirham?" The two sold for 501 dirham, he returned and gave one dirham to his neighbors: "May peace be on you. Know that the donkey was sold for one dirham. As for the rest, it is not yours; it is the price of the stick." As Waterbury well remarks, "the people have been had, but they curse their own stupidity [better, their unwariness] rather than the man who had them" (*ibid.,* p. 95). In Sefrou, similar stories, all with the same moral–think about what is really being "said"–are legion: A man wants to borrow four dirham from a moneylender, but has no security. But he is carrying another man's purse for him. The moneylender takes the purse for security and lends four dirham of the fifty in it.

140. Westermarck, *op. cit.,* p. 267. The transcription has been altered.

141. For an excellent discussion of the constraining function of *ᶜaql* ("reason," "the faculty by which one knows God's commands") over *nafs* ("everything that arises from within man – hunger and sexual yearning, as well as love for the world") and the relation of such a concept of things to bazaar trading ("each successful act of exchange maintains the dominance of [*ᶜaql*] over [*nafs*] and affirms the rationality of the trader" in a Muslim society (Acheh), physically very distant from Morocco, but in this regard at least, spiritually very close, see Siegel, J., *The Rope of God,* Berkeley and Los Angeles, 1969, pp. 98–133, 242–50.

142. Smith, "Orientalism, and Truth." Cf. Izutsu, *op. cit.,* pp. 89, 97–9.

143. These constructions can, of course, take any object-pronoun ending: *ᶜand-u l-ḥaqq* ("he is right"); *fī-hum l-ḥaqq* ("they are in the wrong"); *ḥaqq ᶜalī-na* ("it is our duty").

144. Wehr, *op. cit.,* pp. 191–3. Others include "essence"; "real meaning"; "to test, verify, check"; "to make come true, implement, realize"; "worthy"; "deserving"; "legal"; "assertion, affirmation"; "conviction, certitude"; and "legitimate exploiter of a habus property."

145. Cited in Izutsu, *op. cit.,* pp. 40, 101. There are dozens of examples. The classical root is *k-ḍ-b,* but the *ḍ* changes to *d* in colloquial Moroccan. *Kdūb,* a verbal noun, can mean either "lying" or, in the abstract collective sense, "lies."

146. Westermarck, *op. cit.,* p. 53. Some examples, from among many: "Truth [*l-ḥaqq*] is a lion and lies [*l-kdūb*] are a hyena." "Lies are a stinking dead worm and truth is a clean thing." "Lies are the weapon of the rascal." "The liar is cursed, even though he is a learned man he is cast off by God." "Everything is useful, except that lies and slander bring no profit." "The breaking of wind will not save [a liar] from death." "The cause of death in the world is lies and fornication" (*ibid.,* pp. 264–5). Cf. comments on oaths and perjury – "the most dangerous form of falsehood" (*ibid.,* pp. 269–71). For a fascinating discussion of the concept of falsehood – there rendered as *kzib* – in an Arabic-speaking community in North Lebanon, see Gilsenan, M., "Lying, Honor, and Contradiction," in Kapferer, B. (ed.), *Transactions and Meaning,* Philadelphia, 1976, pp. 191–219.

147. Izutsu, *op. cit.,* p. 99. It should perhaps be added that as *tasdiq* means "faith," the same form built on *k-ḍ-b* means "skepticism". "*Takdhīb* . . . is a flat denial of the divine revelation, refusal to accept the Truth when it is sent down, with an additional element of mockery and scorn. In other words, *takdhīb* in the Qur'anic context denotes the characteristic attitude of those stubborn unbelievers who persist in their refusal to accept the revelation as really coming from God, and never cease to laugh at it as mere old folks' tales" (*ibid.,* p. 100).

148. As the imagery suggests, this view of what thinking is and where it takes place descends from Ryle, G., *The Concept of Mind,* New York, 1959; for a discussion of its implications for anthropological analysis, see Geertz, *Interpretation of Cultures,* pp. 32–54, 55–83, 360–1.

149. It should be unnecessary, but alas probably is not, to note that the table is, however primitive, a model, and that "of course" there *are* some standardized goods, some impersonal exchanges, some bureaucratized relationships, some demarcation of vendor roles from purchasing ones, etc. The suq is no more a perfect "bazaar" than it is a perfect "market."

150. In the course of the research period a decree by the muhtaseb lowering advisory meat prices led to a spontaneous one-day work stoppage by most of the butchers. This led, in turn – more because of the fear of violence than the solidarity of the butchers, which had already begun to dissolve – to the withdrawal of the decree.

151. Insofar as it has any meaning at all (and it has very little), this is what the supposed Islamic fatalism comes to: the conviction that the equations governing human life are "written," and what maneuvers are possible must take place within the space these equations define. The maneuvers, however, are, at least in Morocco, manifold, and most individuals, men and women alike, are about as far from being passive as one can get and not expire from nervous exhaustion. So far as the suq is concerned, this ultimately metaphysical view of how things "really" are does not in itself prevent a collective policy approach to economic matters; it merely prevents the absence of one from seeming conspicuous, worrisome, unnatural, or scandalous. On the nature of the relation of religious concepts and social practices generally, see Geertz, *Interpretation of Cultures,* pp. 126–41, and *Islam Observed,* pp. 90–117.

152. On search in general, see Stigler, G., "The Economics of Information," in Lamberton, *op. cit.,* pp. 61–82, upon which much of the following rather unrigorously depends. Cf. Akerlof, G. A., "The Market for 'Lemons': Quality, Uncertainty and the Market Mechanism," *Quarterly Journal of Economics,* 84:488–500 (1970); Spence, A. M., "Time and Communication in Economic and Social Interac-

tion," *Quarterly Journal of Economics,* 87:651–60 (1973); and, for a general review, Rothschild, M., "Models of Market Organization with Imperfect Information: *Journal of Political Economy,* 81:1283–308 (1973). The usual automatic "and services" should, of course, be appended to all general references to "goods" in this discussion.

153. The internal quotation is from Rothschild, *op. cit.* Cf. Stigler, *op. cit.:* "Price dispersion is a manifestation – and indeed, it is a measure – of ignorance in the market."

154. The quotation is from Cohen, S., *Labor in the United States,* as given in Rees, A., "Information Networks in Labor Markets," in Lamberton, *op. cit.,* pp. 109–18. Rees goes on to deny the applicability of such an image to industrial labor markets, commenting: "The effectiveness and advantages of informal networks of information [in labor markets] have been too little appreciated." In bazaar economies, where they are of paramount importance throughout, they have been perhaps a bit more appreciated, but that's about all. Clientelization has been more often ascribed to the supposed greater "embedding" of economic life in the wider society in traditional cultures – the hedging in of narrowly "material" concerns by more broadly "humane" ones – than to the characteristics of bazaar-type exchange as such. For exceptions, see Mintz, S., "Pratik: Haitian Personal Economic Relations," *Proceedings, American Ethnological Society,* Seattle, 1961, pp. 54–63; cf. Davis, *op. cit.,* pp. 211–59; and for the Middle East, Khuri, *op. cit.;* for India, Oster, *op. cit.*

155. Though clearly recognized, and even celebrated, there is in line with its informal nature, no firmly established term for clientship. The word probably most often used to refer to the relation is, again, an ṣ-d-q derivative, ṣedāqa ("friendship," "loyalty"; see above). Given the oppositional, even agonistic quality of such ties, this may seem odd, but the oddness arises from the highly un-Moroccan assumption that friendship and loyalty (as opposed to "love," ḥubb, a wholly other thing) have mainly to do with affection and absence of conflict rather than veracity and straightforwardness in necessarily conflictual relationships. The Euro-American and North African conceptions of what "friendship" (ṣedāqa) is (a sublimated form of romantic attachment, "warmth," on the one side, and generalized form of contractual probity, "trustworthiness" on the other) simply do not match very well; and nowhere is this clearer than in the suq. Finally, it must be explicitly noted that, in itself, clientship is a wholly economic, functionally specific tie. Broadly social, functionally

diffuse relationships may, of course, form around it once it has been created or may precede and lay the basis for it; but this is not normally, or even very commonly, the case. Khuri (*op. cit.*) argues that diffuse ties are often consciously avoided in Middle Eastern bazaars because of the fear they will be used exploitatively – to delay delivery, pass off shoddy goods, pressure terms, etc. An excellent general discussion of Moroccan conceptions of interpersonal ties under the general rubric of "closeness" (qarāba) can be found in Eickelman, *op. cit.,* pp. 95–105, 206–10.

156. Reliable statistics on interoccupation mobility are hard to come by, but several dozen occupational history interviews with representatives of the major categories of trader in the bazaar survey revealed almost no occupational shifts, except at the very beginnings of careers. Once a man has his stall in the cloth market or his blacksmith forge, he tends to stay there. This even holds in the periodic markets, where some suwwaqs return to the same spot over extended periods of time, and arbitrager itineraries tend, as mentioned, to be highly fixed. It is less true, of course, for marginal figures; but even among them stability of occupation and even of place seems to be high. On accumulative search, and its relation to market localization and repetitive exchange generally, see Stigler, *op. cit.*

157. Rothschild, *op. cit.*

158. The quotations are from Troin, *op. cit.,* t.1, pp. 219, 222. That transport costs and "the friction of distance" have precious little to do with all this is evidenced by the fact that the radical improvement in transport in the past fifty years has not reversed this involutional pattern and has not even slowed its growth. Improved transport spreads out the webs somewhat, but it does not simplify them or change their nature.

159. "There is no doubt that . . . the numbers of small-scale middlemen in the societies under consideration [Sarawak, Hong Kong, Malaya, Uganda, Ghana] are large. So are those of retailers . . . My suggestion is that such a state of affairs is at least partly to be accounted for by the fact that . . . a large proportion of the everyday commercial transactions . . . is carried on by means of some form of credit arrangement. In the vast majority of cases the creditor parties to such arrangements themselves have very little capital, the number of debtors they can serve is closely restricted. Furthermore, these are nearly always arrangements of personal trust made between individuals who are well acquainted with each other, and there is a limit to the number of individuals any one creditor can know well

enough to trust in this way . . . If credit is to be advanced only to personal acquaintances, then there is a limit – and a fairly low limit – to the number of clients any one creditor can have . . . [and there must be] a large number of creditors" (Ward, B. E., "Cash or Credit Crops? An Examination of Some Implications of Peasant Commercial Production with Special Reference to the Multiplicity of Traders and Middlemen," *Economic Development and Cultural Change*, 8:148–63 [1960]). It is not, however, the amount of capital one has that limits the number of clients one can service, but, for the most part anyway, the number of clients one can service that limits the capital one can effectively deploy. This, too, is true for bazaar trade generally, not just for the credit market: Fixed costs are low because scale is small, not (or not mainly) the other way around. My own earlier discussion of the bazaar economy (*Peddlers and Princes*) now seems to me to have underestimated the importance of clientelization outside the area of credit manipulation and overemphasized what I there called (pp. 35–6) "an essentially speculative, *carpe diem*, approach to commerce." For a more balanced view, cf. Waterbury, *op. cit.*, pp. 178–9.

160. For a general discussion of this problem, to which the present one is much indebted, despite a somewhat different tack in avoiding it, see Khuri, *op. cit.*

161. For an interesting, if rather formal, discussion of the maintenance of "perpetual price variability" in information-imperfect markets, see Rothschild, *op. cit.* Cf. Shalop, S., "Information and Monopolistic Competition," *American Economic Review*, 66:2, 240–45 (1976). For a balanced judgment on the oft-invoked "social enjoyment" aspect of bargaining – that it is real, but secondary – see Cassady R., Jr., "Negotiated Price-Making in Mexican Traditional Markets: A Conceptual Analysis," *América indígena*, 28:51–79 (1968).

162. Such bargaining modes as these give rise to what may be called "fixed-price illusion" with respect to certain bazaars that sometimes appears in the literature. This is especially common with respect to perishables, where price negotiation is hidden beneath delicate manipulations, invisible to the innocent observer, of the great inhomogeneity of goods. It also occurs with respect to the apparently take-it-or-leave-it approach of modern, or anyway modern-looking, businessmen, such as those of Sefrou's show-window bazaar, where the fact that money prices are not, or not usually, bargained does not in itself imply that real ones are not. In fact, totally unbargained exchange, though it occurs, remains

quite rare in any part of the suq. For goods bargaining of the add-a-radish, subtract-a-radish sort in Mexican bazaars, see Beals, *op. cit.*, pp. 194–5, who discusses it under the rubric of "quasi-negotiated prices," though just what is "quasi-" about it – especially from the point of view of those who engage in it – is not clear. For the "packaged to price" approach in Philippine bazaars, see Davis, *op. cit.*, p. 166.

163. For a discussion of bazaar weights and measures and their variability in both Fez and Sefrou, see Le Tourneau, *Fès avant*, pp. 276–82. In addition to facilitating goods bargaining, variable weight and measure systems also function to control entry into trades (because one cannot learn to operate as a cloth trader or a carpenter until, through apprenticeship, one has learned how to use the particular scales involved) and, of course, to increase information asymmetry between those inside a trade and those outside.

164. Lowering quality often includes rather frank adulteration, which can on occasion be dangerous. In 1959, a number of grocers, including prominently a number from Sefrou, mixed surplus fuel oil bought from American authorities closing down a Casablanca airbase with cooking oil, leading to paralysis and even death for a large number of people. (Some also mixed it with hair tonic, causing baldness.) Most of the grocers, who were eventually brought to trial, claimed they did not know the adulteration would be dangerous in any serious way and were merely following normal practice in adjusting quality to price. This view – that they had made an honest, if serious, technological mistake in the pursuit of a quite legitimate, pervasive, and indeed often quite open activity – seems to have been rather general; and in fact the king eventually pardoned them all. For a description of this event and some characteristic suwwaq attitudes toward it, see Waterbury, *op. cit.*, pp. 99–102. Cf. Feruel, J., "Etude sur une intoxication par l'huile frelatée au Maroc," CHEAM, 1960, pp. 3372ff. Most adulteration procedures (e.g., of coffee, spices, construction materials, metals) are more careful, tested, and undramatic.

165. I have quoted this remark of Keynes's before (another version of the same idea is the aphorism attributed to a Zurich gnome: "once you owe enough you own the bank") in the course of a fuller discussion of the maintenance of credit balances in a bazaar economy than can be given here (see *Peddlers and Princes*, pp. 36–40). For a fine empirical study of the phenomenon, see Ju-Kang T'ien, *The Chinese of Sarawak*, London School of Economics and Political Science Monographs on Social Anthropology, No. 12, London, n.d. Cf. Firth, R., and B.

261

S. Yamey (eds.), *Capital, Saving and Credit in Peasant Societies*, London, 1964. For medieval Egyptian practices, see Goitein, *op. cit.*, pp. 197–200, 250–62.

166. Simple moneylending, still (in 1968) mostly by Jews, is also frequently disguised as goods transaction. Commercial borrowing from banks and elaborated legal instruments with respect to credit are virtually absent in the bazaar–even the qirad has largely disappeared, though something like it is sometimes found in arbitrager activities. Some small intrafamilial loans aside (and even those are rare), the advancement of credit for direct investment purposes–to finance someone else's enterprise–seems to be rather uncommon. The role of credit is confined to more or less direct exchange processes.

167. Rees, *op. cit.* I have discussed this matter, too, in *Peddlers and Princes* (pp. 33–5), if in less technical terms. Cf. Spence, M., "Job Market Signaling," *Quarterly Journal of Economics*, August 1973, pp. 355–74.

168. The new and used car markets are far from the only examples of the contrast in our economy: "Organized commodity and security exchanges deal in highly standardized or perfectly uniform contracts, where the intensive margin of search is effectively eliminated. One is entirely indifferent as to whether one buys a hundred shares of General Motors from a taxi company, a little old lady, or Alfred P. Sloan, though much search may enter into the decision to buy General Motors rather than some other security. Organized exchanges perform a highly effective job of widening the extensive margin of search and need to transmit only a few bits of information (the name of the contract, the quantity, and the price) to conclude a transaction. Labor markets lie as far from this pole as used car markets, and a grain exchange for labor is about as possible as a contract on the Chicago Board of Trade for 1960 Chevrolet sedans" (Rees, *op. cit.*). Rees then goes on to describe the elaborated institutions for intensive search in labor markets. All this merely demonstrates once again that, as used here, "bazaar" is an analytic notion, and indeed one that fits some of our so-called markets rather better (domestic housing is perhaps another example) than the neoclassical concept of market does. Cf. Khouri, *op. cit.*

169. Cf. Cassady, *op. cit.*: "[Inter-vendor] competition in a negotiated price market is not likely to be as sharp as that found in a one-price market . . . The main reason for this is that knowledge of competitors' prices is much more difficult to obtain, and indeed to interpret, in a market where prices for each sale are individually negotiated. Price warfare,

for example, which occasionally develops out of [vigorous] price competitive efforts in a fixed price system, would be inconceivable in a negotiated price situation.

170. "Many buyers test prices (bargain) in one shop and buy their goods in another [and] this behavior is repeated so frequently . . . that shops situated at the entrance of a market [area] are considered less profitable than those situated in the center. These shops, a shopkeeper in Rabat . . . complained, are 'rich in bargaining but poor in selling'" (Khuri, *op. cit.*). Actually, outsiders often overestimate the amount of price testing that goes on, confounding it with genuine bargaining. There are other modes of extensive search in the market as well, of course–exchange of information along various sorts of seller and buyer grapevines, mere overhearing of the higgling of other suwwaqs, etc.–but their importance also can easily be overestimated. Even extensive (*sāwem*) bargaining tends to be confined to suwwaqs one at least knows, rather than conducted with strangers; true sample shopping is, in Sefrou anyway, quite rare. Indeed, asking the price of something from someone you have no acquaintance with at all may not even bring a response. If you don't know anyone in a particular trade, you usually will find someone who does to introduce you before discussing prices, etc. with him.

The terms for bargaining in Sefrou are actually interrelated along a gradient of markedness, rather than categorically, as the text may seem to suggest. The most general, unmarked, term is again merely *bᶜ u šri* ("to buy and sell"). *Sāwem* is a somewhat more marked form, perhaps best glossed as "looking at prices" (*kayšuf t-tamanat*); and *tšetter* is the most marked: well-launched, "four-eyes" bargaining with intent to commit an exchange. Thus even intensive bargaining may be generally described merely as *bᶜ u šri* or even (especially the opening phases) as *sāwem;* the inverse (use of the more specific terms more generally) rarely, if ever, occurs.

171. Cassady, *op. cit.*, from which the "tug-of-war" quotation also comes. Cassady goes on to complicate the model for situations of unequal vendor-buyer strength, aborted transactions where the price gap is not closed and either vendor or buyer withdraws, and so on. It must be remembered that money price bargaining is but the most straightforward example of the process, not the whole of it, and though Cassady's model represents the general form of buyer-seller interaction well enough, it does so at the usual expense of realism.

172. Normally, and especially in significant exchanges, initial bidding includes not just the

very first offers, but the first several, as the buyer and seller maneuver to establish starting positions, and thus has an internal temporal structure of its own. How suwwaqs determine their initial bids is a complex and ill-understood subject involving a wide variety of factors: whether the seller has a prior price to guide him (as is usually not the case for artisans or target sellers), the social characteristics of the bargainers, the time of day, the nature of the good or service at issue, inventory sizes, the distance the buyer (or seller) has come, the depth of clientship, and so on almost *ad infinitum*. But, for all this, and for all their importance, initial offers are usually quite quickly established and the movement toward consensus promptly begun. A systematic study of this matter – a difficult and delicate enterprise – would reveal a very great deal about the structure of bazaar judgments and expectations in general.

173. For a general discussion of the relations between price and time signaling, see Spence, "Time and Communication." Cf. Khuri (*op. cit.*), who for Beirut found the average bargaining time for very expensive carpets was about 54 minutes (range 100–9); for cheaper, but still expensive carpets, 36 minutes (range 45–10); for clothes, 5 minutes (range 7–2); and for everyday foodstuffs, 40 seconds (range 3 minutes–12 seconds).

174. For an interesting distinction between "adventurous" and "nonadventurous" bargaining, depending upon whether, after having reached their seller-minimum or buyer-maximum price, exchangers tend immediately to settle or to press on beyond it to wrangle the price gap – a matter depending, *inter alia*, on the durability and homogeneity of the good (or service) at issue, amount of markup, relative economic strength of the participants, and individual variations in willingness to be perceived as hard traders, see Swetnam, *op. cit.*, some of whose other comments on bazaar price formation are less persuasive.

175. Cassady, *op. cit.* There are also many conventions for special trades and markets: the palm-to-palm hand touch to conclude a deal in the animal market, provision of eleven pieces of fruit when the bargaining has been for ten, and so on. Also conventions may differ with situations: A professional wool trader bargaining with a rural target seller is expected to bid first.

176. Khuri, *op. cit.* Again, to deny that bargaining is for fun is not to deny that proficient practitioners do not hugely enjoy it; merely that enjoyment is not the central motivation for bargaining.

177. In addition to a cost (and *because* it is a cost) time is also, of course, a signal, indicating how serious the intensive bargainer really is: "The value of time as a signal is its unavoidable cost. It is difficult to counterfeit" (Spence, "Time and Communication"). The notion that the supply elasticities of time are very high in the bazaar – that suwwaqs' willingness to bargain is a result of the fact that they are sitting around with time on their hands, or lacking wristwatches, have no sense of its value – could hardly be more wrong. A suq is not a scene of limp indolence but of high impatience.

178. Scott, M. B., *The Racing Game,* Chicago, 1968, p. 1. What follows is stimulated by and depends heavily on Scott's fascinating study, but I have added some formulations of my own and simplified a good many of his. Of these latter, the most important are that I assume the betting pool is wholly distributed to bettors (ignoring track takeout, taxes, etc.) and that there is one payoff horse, not three.

179. Formally, the difference between being ignorant and misinformed (or for that matter irrational) is trivial, because it does not matter why people bet on the wrong horse so long as they do so. Practically, however, because misinformation may be a positive stimulus to wrong bets, it is not trivial. The matter is not very different in the suq.

180. Scott, *op. cit.*, p. 4; italics original. On the concept of "strategic interaction," see Goffman, E., *Strategic Interaction,* Philadelphia, 1969.

181. This is as true for artisans as for buyer/sellers. The craftsman's ascendancy comes but marginally at best from any edge he may have in technique. The range of variation in such matters is minute in the plebian artisanry of a suq such as Sefrou's, and what there is goes largely unappreciated. (The one exception, and that partial, is rugs.) Nor does industriousness differentiate much, being uniformly high. It is in their ability to handle the commercial ties – the acquisition of materials, the disposal of products, the contracting of labor – in which their activity is set that separates the more successful artisans in any trade from the less successful.

182. For an extended discussion of this general thesis concerning the Europe and non-Europe confrontation in the late nineteenth and early twentieth centuries, but for agriculture and Indonesia, see Geertz, C., *Agricultural Involution,* Berkeley, 1963. An economic geography study based on 1970 census materials, of Sefrou which appeared while this book was in press, and so could not be utilized, Benhalima, H., "Sefrou, de la tradition du dir à l'integration economique – Etude de géographie urbaine," Thesis, Université Paul Valery, Montpelier, 1977,

develops this point further. Cf. Chaoui, M., "Sefrou: de la tradition à l'integration, ce qu'est un petit centre d'aujourd'hui" *Lamalif*, July–August, 1978, pp. 32–9.

183. Stigler, *op. cit.* Cf. Demsetz, H., "Information and Efficiency: Another Viewpoint," in Lamberton, *op. cit.*, pp. 160–86: "The view that now pervades much public policy economics implicitly presents the relevant choice as between an ideal norm and an existing 'imperfect' institutional arrangement. This *nirvana* approach differs considerably from a comparative institution approach in which the relevant choice is between alternative real institutional arrangements. In practice, those who adopt the nirvana viewpoint seek to discover discrepancies between the ideal and the real and if discrepancies are found, they deduce that the real is inefficient. Users of the comparative institution approach attempt to assess which alternative real institutional arrangement seems best able to cope with the economic problem; practitioners of this approach may use an ideal norm to provide standards from which divergences are assessed for all practical alternatives of interest and select as efficient that alternative which seems most likely to minimize the divergence." If the primary (but not, of course, the sole) "economic problem" of the bazaar is socially organized ignorance, than a comparative institution approach will judge proposed reforms in terms of the relation between their cost, broadly conceived, and their capacity to reduce it.

184. For an all-out effort in this direction with respect to a southeast Moroccan group, see Gellner, E., *The Saints of the Atlas*, London, 1969; cf., more carefully and circumstantially, Vinogradov, A. *The Ait Ndhir of Morocco*, Ann Arbor, 1974.

For a (rather strained) attempt to extend this sort of analysis to the level of the national polity, see Vinogradov, A., and J. Waterbury, "Situations of Contested Legitimacy: Morocco–An Alternative Framework," *Comparative Studies in Society and History*, 13:1 (Jan. 1971). For a fine discussion of the problem in general, see Meeker, M., *Literature and Violence in North Arabia*, Cambridge (Eng.), (forthcoming).

185. See, for example, Peters, E., "Some Structural Aspects of the Feud Among the Camel-Herding Bedouin of Cyrenaica," *Africa*, 32:261–82 (1967); Hammoudi, *op. cit.*; Eickelman, *op. cit.*; Rabinow, *op. cit.*; Geertz, C., "In Search of North Africa," *New York Review of Books*, April 22, 1971, pp. 20–4; and Meeker, *op. cit.*

Annex A: The bazaar survey, 1968–9

The bazaar survey was conducted during 1968–9, in several stages, by a single investigator – the author of the present study. First a mapping of each suq area was undertaken, with the assistance of several market people, according to trade or craft, the name of the owner or manager, his nisba, and (less reliably) his place of origin and approximate length of time in Sefrou. This was done first through the agency of a knowledgeable informant overall; then separately with such an informant in each identified area and sometimes subarea. Finally the information was checked directly door to door, at least in regard to trade or craft type and nisba. Very little failure to cooperate was encountered, and in the few cases where it was a neighboring suwwaq could always be found to check the material. Finally, several responsive informants in each of the major trades were interviewed at some length, in part to recheck the survey data, but more particularly to investigate the nature and organization of the trade and various matters concerning the bazaar in general.

For all that, the methodological difficulties of this sort of work should not be underestimated: Kinship, language, political process, even art and religion, are, in a practical sense, much easier to research in a non-Western society than is the bazaar because, given the fractioning quality of the suq discussed in the text, no single person can inform you about more than a very small aspect of it.

Beyond the general difficulties, some specific limitations of the survey must be kept in mind in interpreting it:

1. It is concerned only with the owners of the stores (*mwālīn l-ḥawānut*) or the masters of the ateliers (*mᶜāllemin ṣ-ṣnaᶜ*), not with all those at work in them, which would simply have been too great a task for a lone investigator to carry out.

2. It includes only sitting merchants or craftsmen (i.e., those with established stores or ateliers). Completely ambulant suwwaqs, those selling only in the Thursday markets, and craftsmen working out of their homes on a contract basis – masons, tile 265

layers, prostitutes – are not included. The survey thus represents the heart of the Sefrou suq, but far from the whole of it.
Certain critical sorts of suwwaqs discussed in the text (e.g.,
auctioneers and arbitragers) do not enter into it at all, nor do
mere handymen, marginal peddlers, colporteurs, and so on.

3. The maps, although generally in proportion within themselves, are not to exact scale and are not all on the same
approximate scale (the medina ones are magnified with respect
to the extramedina ones, for clarity's sake, because the medina
is enormously more crowded than the new quarters). This is
why the illustrations are called figures rather than maps. Nor
is variation in size of establishment (of which there is, in fact,
not all that much) indicated. Major institutions relative to the
market, but not themselves commercial or craft enterprises
(e.g., zawias, administrative offices), are indicated.

4. The results of the bazaar survey and of the census study compiled by Hildred Geertz and presented as the Appendix to the
hardcover edition of this volume are, though mutually reinforcing in their implications, incapable of direct comparison.
Not only do they refer to different times (1960 vs. 1968–9),
but one is a census of the whole population, the other of only
the more established merchants and craftsmen within it, and
different sorts of characteristics (e.g., birth place vs. nisbas,
employment vs. trade type) are counted.

This presentation of the bazaar survey is organized into four tables
and twenty-four figures.

Table A.1 is a general key to the symbols used in the figures to
indicate physical features, regional designations, and market elements.

Table A.2 lists the Arabic terms and English glosses for the various
trades found in the Sefrou market, together with the abbreviations for
these terms that are used in the keys to the figures.

Table A.3 lists the nisba classes of the various owners and masters
of bazaar enterprises, together with the abbreviations of these nisba
classes that are used in the keys to the figures. For the purposes of the
bazaar survey, the nisbas are classified into general types because
actual nisbas are meaningless to anyone unfamiliar with the detailed
structure of Moroccan, or anyway Sefrou, society. Personal names
(three-fourths would be some variation on Mohammed, Umar, or Ali)
are not given because they are not significant in the context. Only two
women, both widows whose sons operated their enterprises, appeared
in the bazaar survey. It is important to note that these are nisba
266 classifications, *not* birth-place classifications.

Table A.4 lists each public bath and public oven in the Sefrou market area, together with the number of the figure that shows its location, the nisba class of the bathhouse keeper or baker, and, where relevant, a descriptive comment.

Figures A.1 through A.24 chart the establishments that make up the Sefrou market areas surveyed. The areas are divided into three main sections: the extramedina area, the southern half (right bank) of the medina, and the northern half (left bank) of the medina. Figures A.13 and A.19 show the general layout of, respectively, the southern and northern halves of the medina. Figures A.1, A.14, and A.20 show the disposition of the areas charted in the remaining figures in the three main sections of the bazaar area.

In Figures A.2 to A.12, A.15 to A.18, and A.21 to A. 24 the location of each of the establishments is indicated by an identifying number, and the accompanying key explains for each establishment the nisba class of the owner and the type of trade practiced. For example, in the legend to Figure A.21, the entry *30 SRA hrr* should be interpreted as follows: *30* indicates the number locating the shop (i.e., on the right side of the street, just inside Mkam Gate): *SRA* (Sefrou Rural Arab) indicates the owner's nisba is one connecting him to an Arabic-speaking group within the immediate area around Sefrou; *hrr* indicates this person's trade (silk merchant, *ḥarrār*).

Table A.1 *General key to symbols in figures A.1–A.24*

Major physical features

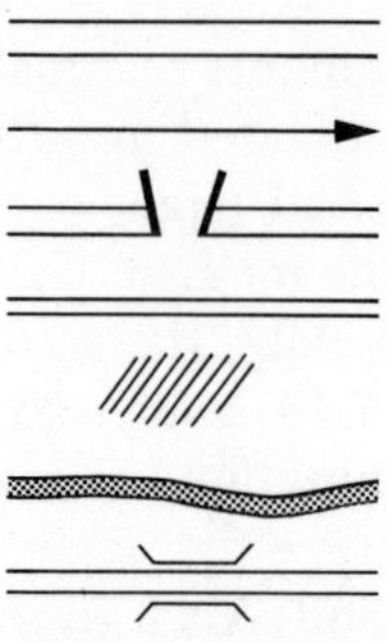

────────	Street (*ṭriq*)
────────►	Alley (*derb*)
─┤ ┝─	Gate (*bab*)
════════	City wall (*ṣoṛ*)
/////////	Public space
∿∿∿∿∿	River (*wad*)
════⌒════	Bridge (*qenṭra*)

Other physical features

□	Point of interest (e.g., Semarin mosque)
▲	Public fountain (*seqqāya*)
○	Traffic circle
≡	Stairs

Regional designations

EL MENZEL	Town or distant area
ZEMGHILA	Quarter or neighborhood (*ḥūma*)
Qisariya	Specialized market area (*sūq*)

Market elements

1, 2, 3	Shops and ateliers (*ḥānūt*)
△, ⚠, △	Public baths (*ḥammām*)[a]
1, 2, 3 (boxed)	Traditional public ovens (*ferrān*)[a]
①, ②, ③	Modern public ovens (*ferrān jdid*)[a]

Incidental market elements

✕✕✕✕✕	Pottery sellers
○○○○○	Sellers of chickens, eggs, etc.
 ⋰⋰⋰	Basket sellers
□□□□□	Melon sellers
△△△△△	Sellers of secondhand items

268 [a]For a brief description of each public bath and public oven, see Table A.4.

Abbreviation	Approximate English gloss	Arabic term
asa	†Watchman	ᶜAssās
ashb	†Herbalist[a]	ᶜAššāb
att	*Small grocer[b]	ᶜAṬṬār (see bql)
awd	*Wood seller	ᶜAwwād
awwd	†Curer[e]	ᶜAwwūḍ
bgr	*Cattle raiser/seller	Mūl l-bger
blg	†Slipper maker[d]	Blaḡī (see trf, krz)
bny	†Mason	Bennāy
bql	*Grocer[e]	Beqqāl
brd	†Saddle maker[f]	Bradᶜī (see smr)
dll	*Auctioneer	Dellāl
drz	†Weaver	Derrāz
dwa	†Pharmacist	Mūl d-dwā
epc	*Modern grocer	Pīserī (see bql)
fkkr	†Potter	Fekkār
fkr	*Charcoal seller	Mūl l-fāker
fndq	†Funduq keeper	Fnādqī, mūl l-funduq
fqh	†Quranic school teacher[g]	Fqīh
frn	†Baker	Mūl l-ferrān, frārnī, ḵebbāz
ful	*Bean trader	Mūl l-fūl
gbl	*Seller of grain-sifting screens	Mūl l-ḡorbāl
grj	†Garage mechanic/autoparts seller	Garājīst
gss	†Floor layer/excavator	Gessās
gyt	†Horn blower	Ḡiyyāṭa
gzr	†Butcher	Gezzār
hdd	†Blacksmith	Ḥaddād
hdid	*Hardware/spice seller[h]	Mūl l-ḥadīd
hjm	†Barber/cupper[i]	Ḥajjām
hjr	†Stone cutter/quarry worker	Hejjār, maᶜden d-l-ḥjer
hlb	*Milk seller	Mūl l-ḥalīb
hlf	*Esparto grass seller	Mūl l-ḥelfa (see mkn dum)
hlw	*Candy seller	Mūl l-ḥelwa
hml	†Porter	Ḥammāl (see zrz, hmr
hmm	†Bathhouse keeper[j]	Mūl l-ḥammām, ḥmaīmī
hmr	†Mule skinner	Ḥammār, ḥammāl (see zrz, hml)
hri	*Large wholesale retail grocer[k]	Mūl l-herī (see bql)
hrir	†Soup dispenser	Mūl l-ḥarīra
hrr	†Silk merchant/spinner	Ḥarrār, ḥrārī
hut	*Fish seller	Mūl l-ḥūt
hwj	*Ready-made clothes seller	Ḥwaijī
jlb	*Ready-made jellaba seller[l]	Mūl j-jlāleb
jld	*Hide seller	Mūl j-jild
kar	†Bus owner/driver	Mūl l-kār
kbz	*Bread seller[m]	Mūl l-ḵubz

Table A.2 (*cont.*)

Abbreviation	Approximate English gloss	Arabic term
kdr	*Vegetable/fruit seller	*Keddār*
kft	†Cooked ground-meat seller	*Kefaitī* (see tyb)
khb	†Radio (and other electrical appliances) repairman	*Kahrabī*
kif	*Hashish seller	*Mūl l-kīf*
kmn	†Truck owner/driver	*Mūl l-kamiūn*
krd	*Odds-and-ends seller	*Kordāwī*
krz	†Shoemaker	*Kerrazī* (see trf, blg)
ktb	†Scribe	*Kātib*
ktb mkn	†Typing teacher, typist	*Kātib b-l-makina*
ktn	*Cloth seller	*Mūl l-kettān* (see tub)
kwf	†Modern barber	*Kwāfūr*
kyt	†Tailor[n]	*Kiyyāt*
kyt hwj	Tailor of ready-made Western clothes	*Kiyyāt hwaīj*
kyt jlb	Tailor of cloaks (jellabas and selhams[l])	*Kiyyāt jlāleb*
kyt mkn	Sewing machine tailor	*Kiyyāt makina*
kyt qft	Kaftan tailor	*Kiyyāt qfāṭan*
kzn	Storage place[o]	*Kzīn*
kzn suf	Wool warehouse	*Kzīn d-ṣ-ṣūf*
kzn zit	Olive-oil warehouse	*Kzīn d-z-zīt*
kzn zra	Grain warehouse	*Kzīn d-z-zra[c]*
lqm	*Mint seller	*Mūl-l-liqāma*
mgn	†Watchmaker	*Mūl l-mwāgen*
mht	†Plowmaker	*Mhārtī*
mkn dum	Mattress factory[p]	*Makina d-dūm*
mkn sbn	Soap factory	*Makina d-ṣ-ṣābun*
mkn thn	Motor-driven flour mill	*Makina d-ṭ-ṭhīn*
mkn zit	Motor-driven olive-oil mill	*Makina d-z-zīt*
mns	†Modern carpenter, sawmill owner	*Menīsiwī*
mshrb	*Soft drink seller	*Mūl l-mešrūb*
mul khb	*Electrical supplies, appliances	*Mūl l-'ālāt l-kehrabā*
mzn	†Weigher/measurer	*Mūl l-mizān, ᶜabbār*
nhs	*Seller of tea equipment, trays, etc.	*Mūl n-nhās*
njr	†Carpenter	*Nejjār*
pmp	†Gasoline station man	*Pumpīst*
gds	†Traditional plumber	*Qwādsī*
qhw	†Café keeper	*Qehwājī*
qsdr	†Tinsmith	*Qsādrī*
rha	Water-driven grain mill	*Rhā b-l-mā*
sdf	†Button maker[q]	*Sedaīf*
sfz	†Fried doughnut seller	*Šfāž* (see tyb)
shik	†Singer/musician	*Sīk, ḡiyyāt, ṭebbāl*
shrb	*Barkeep, liquor seller	*Mūl š-šrāb*

Abbreviation	Approximate English gloss	Arabic term
shrt	Cord maker	*Šerrāṭ*
ska	*Tobacconist	*Ṣaka*
skl	†Bicycle seller/repairman	*Sīklist*
smr	†Horseshoer	*Semmār* (see brd)
snm	Movie house owner	*Mūl s-sinima*
suf	*Wool/hide trader	*Mūl ṣ-ṣūf*
swr	†Photographer	*Suwwur*
syg	†Goldsmith/jeweler	*Ṣiyyāǧ, deḥḥāb*
tbl	†Drummer	*Ṭebbāl*
tbn	*Fodder seller	*Mūl t-tbin*
thn	*Flour seller	*Mūl ṭ-ṭḥin*
tks	†Taxi owner/driver	*Mūl t-tāksi*
trf	†Shoemaker	*Ṭerrāf* (see blg, krz)
tsbn mkn	†Machine launderer	*Teṣbīn b-l-makina*
tub	*Cloth seller	*Mūl t-tūb* (see ktn)
twj	*Pottery seller	*Mūl t-ṭwājen*
tyb	†Prepared food seller⁵	*Ṭiyyāb*
tyr	†Western-style tailor	*Ṭaiyūr*
utl	†Innkeeper	*Mūl l-uṭīl*
zaj	†Glazier	*Zajjāj*
zra	*Grain seller	*Mūl z-zra^c*
zrb	*Rug seller	*Mūl z-zrābī*
zrz^t	†Porter	*Zerzaī, ḥummāl*
zyt	*Olive oil dealer	*Ziyyāt*

*Commercial trader (*biyyā^c/serrāī*); see text Figure 6.
†Artisan (*ṣnay^cī*); see text Figure 6.
[a] Herbalists sell various medicinal herbs as well as diagnosing the illness for which the herbs are appropriate. They are a combination of traditional doctor and pharmacist. Nowadays, some sell various cooking spices as well, but most of the permanent market spice trade (herbalists are even more prominent in the periodic market) remains in the hands of the hardware/spice sellers. See note h.
[b] ^cAṭṭār, which derives from the word "perfume," was traditionally used in Morocco for someone who sold sugar, tea, candles, soap, scent, etc., particularly wandering peddlers; now it has come to mean any very small grocer, as opposed to *beqqāl*, by now the overwhelmingly most common name for grocer.
^cAwwūḍ, which comes from a root meaning "to restore," "come back," "revive," and in noun form "the normal, customary, usual state of affairs" is the most common word for a traditional curer, as opposed to a Western doctor, *ṭabīb*. In Sefrou, the most common types of curers are people who suck illness from a patient's throat and those who irritate his skin at appropriate points with burning cotton wadding.
[d] *Blāǧī* make traditional slippers, called *belǧa*, a once flourishing Jewish trade now almost wholly disappeared. Almost all shoemakers are now called *ṭerrāf*, a word that also means, in Morocco, "a faithless friend," "an untrustworthy person," and "a habitual thief."
[e] *Beqqāl* strictly means, in Morocco, "someone who sells butter, oil, or milk," but has come to be the standard term for a grocer of any sort (except greengrocer, as it means in some other parts of the Arabic world), with ^caṭṭār being reserved for particularly

271

Table A.2 (*cont.*)

small grocers (see note *b*) and *mūl l-herī* for particularly large ones (see note *k*), though both these are frequently merely referred to as *beqqāl* as well. For some representative inventories (not from Sefrou) of traditional grocers, see Troin, *op. cit.*, p. 150. Another form of grocer, selling only tea and sugar, called *skākrī,* and important in many places in Morocco, is apparently not found in Sefrou, where tea and sugar are sold by regular beqqals.

[f] "Saddlemaker" is a poor gloss, because these men make, not leather riding saddles but cloth pack-saddle bags for mules and donkeys. Although once separate trades, and much larger than now, saddlemakers and horse (mule) shoers have now essentially fused into a single occupation.

[g] A *fqīh* teaches young children, for a fee, to chant the Quran in a special school, called a *msid.* Not all are listed in the survey, for many of the msids are in residential areas.

[h] For reasons not wholly clear, hardware (knives, tools, nails) and cooking spices are fused into a single trade in Sefrou. Each *hadīd* has a special trade-secret mixture of seasoning spices called *rās l-ḥanut* ("head of the shop"), which Moroccans use in cooking and upon which his reputation as a spice seller mainly rests, though the actual variation in the mixtures does not seem very great.

[i] Traditional barbers in Morocco are all also cuppers (i.e., they drain blood, usually from the back of the neck, for curative purposes). Many are also circumcision experts.

[j] Most bathhouses are habus-owned (see text) and rented to the keepers.

[k] *Mūl l-herī* are large grocers (*herī* means "warehouse," "granary"). They are discussed in the text. See also note *e.*

[l] A *jellāba* is a long cloak, with a hood, worn as traditional male dress. A jellaba seller sells very cheap or secondhand cloaks only to very poor people. A man with any means at all buys the cloth from a cloth seller and has his jellaba made by a tailor specializing in their manufacture. A *selhām,* also traditional male dress, is a light satin overrobe with a hood and no sleeves.

[m] Bread sellers serve only the very poor. Almost everyone else makes the dough at home and sends it, usually via a child who carries it on a board on his head, to the baker to be baked. In the main the clientele of the bread sellers was, like that of the jellaba sellers (see note *l*) and the blaghi (see note *d*), the rural Berbers, unused to town facilities. But nowadays these persons too have their bread baked, and the bread-selling trade has contracted, like jellaba selling and blaghi selling, virtually to disappearance.

[n] The tailoring trade is highly subspecialized – even more than is indicated here. Yet all form a single trade in their own eyes, even if certain specialties (e.g., kaftan tailoring) are considered more prestigious than others.

[o] Almost anything may be stored in a *k̲zīn.* Only the major sorts, connected with important trades, are indicated here.

[p] Palmetto (*dūm*) and esparto grass (*ḥelfa*) are used to stuff mattresses, pillows, saddlebags, etc. The gathering of these materials, which grow wild, is a valuable income adjunct for the rural poor, and there are a couple of such factories in the countryside as well as the one in Sefrou town proper.

[q] A *ṣedaīf,* of which there are hardly any left in Sefrou and never seem to have been very many, makes and/or trades in shell, mother-of-pearl, and plastic buttons, as opposed to the thread made by silk merchants through the putting-out system (see text).

[r] *Tūb* is used mainly for sellers of traditional hand-woven fabrics, *kettān* for those of manufactured textiles, but the distinction is not clear-cut and many cloth sellers sell both.

[s] Prepared-food sellers, include sellers of soup (*ḥrīra*), fried doughnuts (*sfinž*), ground meat (*kifta*), and broiled mutton (*mešwī*), often all together. They are sharply distinguished, however, from café keepers.

Table A.2 (*cont.*)

ᵗ In Fez (see Le Tourneau, *Fés avant,* p. 385), a distinction between *zerzaī* as Berber porters and *ḥāmmāla* as Arab porters seems to have existed, but it does not in Sefrou. *Hāmmāl* also sometimes meant a mule skinner, and so is a synonym for *ḥammār.*
General Note: A few trade abbreviations are listed but not represented in the figures because no permanent establishments of them were found, though representatives of them exist in Sefrou. They are included for the sake of completeness. For an assuredly incomplete (it totals but forty-three) list of trades in Sefrou in 1924, see Massignon, *Enquête,* Appendix III. His lists also give the following number of trades for other towns at that time: Fez, 164; Marrakech, 89; Salé, 93, Meknes, 106; Casablanca, 64; Mogador, 39; Mazagan, 23; Wezzan, 36; Taza, 10 (an impossible figure); Boujad, 18; Taroudant, 19. The method by which the data were gathered makes these figures not strictly comparable, but in rank-size terms, the high position for Sefrou among the smaller towns is probably about right.

Table A.3 *Nisba class of owners and masters of Sefrou bazaar enterprises*

Abbreviation	Gloss and explanation	Number	Percent of total
SA	Sefrou Arabs. Nisbas indicating long-time, Arabic-speaking residence in Sefrou town (including the Qlaᶜa). There is a list of the more eminent of such families in the city records, and the others are relatively easily determined by questioning informants.	435	44
SRA	Sefrou rural Arabs. Nisbas indicating membership in Arabic-speaking tribes within the Sefrou Cercle. The main ones are a large confederation to the east of town, called the Beni Yazgha, and a group gathered into a large-village/small-town north of it called Bhalil. But various Arabic-speaking groups are scattered in villages, even sections of villages, all along the piedmont from Sefrou to El Menzel.	150	15
SB	Sefrou Berber speakers. Nisbas of old urban Berber-speaking (though, like all town-dwelling Berber men and most women, bilingual in Arabic) families. There are very few of these, most of them descendants of the people around Qaid Umar, the Berber chief of the town ca. 1900 (see text).	14	1
SRB	Sefrou rural Berber speakers. The two main confederations in the area are the Ait Yusi and the Ait Seghoushen, but there are several minor groups as well.	102	10
F	Fassis. Nisbas from the city of Fez.	22	2
UA	Urban Arabs. Nisbas of Arab speakers from other towns (except Fez). They are scattered, Marrakech, Meknes, and Taza being among the leading sources.	16	2
J	Jews. Virtually all Jews are old Sefrou families.	29	3
SS	Sussis. Nisbas of rural Berbers from southwest Morocco.	26	3
RA	Rural Arabs. Nisbas of Arabic speakers from outside the Cercle of Sefrou. Most are from the Jebel area northwest of Fez, a fair number from the pre-Sahara (i.e., the ex-	126	13

Abbreviation	Gloss and explanation	Number	Percent of total
	treme South and Southeast), and some from the Fez-Meknes plain, the Sais.		
R3	Rural Berbers. Nisbas of Berber speakers (except Sussis) from outside the Cercle of Sefrou. Most are from the Rif, the mountainous area north of Fez, but some are from the Marrakech region.	52	10
E	Europeans. Almost all French, save for a couple of Spaniards.	9	1
X	Nisba unknown. These are mostly either very recent newcomers at the time of the survey or very marginal figures.	10	1
Total		991	

Table A.4. *Public ovens and public baths in Sefrou market area*

Identi-fication	Nisba class of baker or bath-house keeper	Description	Location
Modern ovens (○)[a]			
1	Owned since 1961 by Sefrou Arab; managed for him by Spaniard; originally French-owned	Once electrified; this proved uneconomic and use of wood fuel was resumed	Fig. A.2
2	Owned by rural Arab from northwest Morocco		Fig. A.5
3	Owned since 1960 by rural Arab from south of Fez; originally Jewish owned		Fig. A.6
Traditional ovens in medina (□) [b]			
1	Managed by Sefrou rural Arab	The original oven for the Qlaᶜa	Fig. A.12
2	Managed by two Sefrou Arabs from the Qlaᶜa	Established in 1954, after factional fight in Qlaᶜa, just out-side walls	Fig. A.12
3	Managed cooperatively by several Sefrou Arabs	Originally built by Qaid Umar	Fig. A.13
4	Managed by Sefrou Arab		Fig. A.13
5	Managed by Sefrou rural Arab		Fig. A.13
6	Managed by Sefrou Arab	Supposedly oldest of medina ovens; referred to as Ferran l-Habus	Fig. A.19
7	Managed by Sefrou Arab		Fig. A.19
8	Managed by Sefrou rural Arab; formerly Jewish-owned, sold ca. 1960		Fig. A.18
9	Heqdesh-owned, Jewish-managed	Original Jewish oven	Fig. A.18
Traditional ovens in new quarters (□) [c]			
10	Owned and run by Sefrou Arab	Built ca. 1960	Fig. A.7
11	Owned and run by Sefrou Arab	Built shortly after oven number 10	Fig. A.7
12	Owned by two Sefrou Arabs (brothers);	Built ca. 1963	Fig. A.7

276

Table A.4. (*cont.*)

Identi-fication	Nisba class of baker or bath-house keeper	Description	Location
	leased to Sefrou rural Arab		
13	Owned by Sefrou Arab family habus; leased to Sefrou rural Arab	Built in 1967	Fig. A.10
14	Owned by Sefrou Arab family habus; leased to family member	Built ca. 1965	Fig. A.10
15	Built and run by urban Arab from Marrakech		Fig. A.11
16	Built and run by Fassi	Built in 1968	Fig. A.11
17	Owned by Sefrou family habus; leased to family member	Despite extra-mural location (in the olive gardens), oven is quite old	Fig. A.8
Public baths (▲) [d]			
1	Habus-owned; leased to Sefrou Arab	Called the "lower" bath	Fig. A.19
2	Originally habus-owned; now family habus and leased to family member, a Sefrou Arab	Called the "upper" bath	Fig. A.13
3	Owned by two Sefrou Arabs; leased to Sefrou rural Arab	Built (as private [enterprise] ca. 1920 for Jews in mellah by former pasha	Fig. A.13
4	Owned by partnership of six Sefrou Arabs from Qla^c a; run by one of them	Built in 1940s to replace original Qla^c a bath, which collapsed	Fig. A.12
5	Built by Sefrou Arab; run by his son	Built ca. 1912, first building in new quarters	Fig. A.6
6	Built by habus; leased to Sefrou Arab	Built in 1968, in modern style, with separate buildings for men and women[e]	Fig. A.9

[a] These ovens–all of which date from after World War II–make both French-style long loaves and flat, round Moroccan loaves. The bakers sell the bread to modern grocers and to peddlers, who then retail it. The modern ovens buy flour, have a staff of workers, and are larger than the traditional ovens. All are privately owned.

[b] These ovens (except the formerly Jewish ones) are habus-owned and auctioned by the nadir to the bakers who run them. In addition to the nine ovens listed, two others in the medina (in Shebbak and Nas Adlun) were destroyed in the 1950 flood.

[c] These ovens are all privately owned.

[d] There were originally two baths, called "upper" and "lower," in the medina. Later, after the Protectorate, the Moroccan pasha of Sefrou built a bath in the mellah, which had not before been permitted to have one.

[e] At the other baths men and women use the same facilities at different times.

277

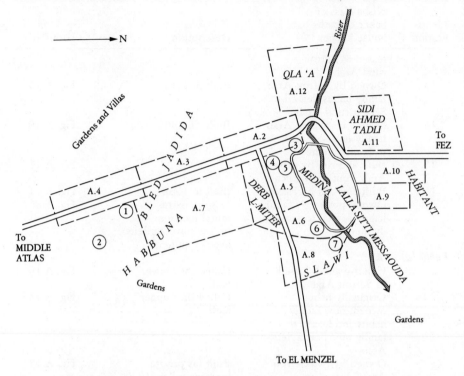

Figure A.1. Locality key to figures (A.2–A.12) charting the extramedina areas.
Circled numbers indicate Thursday markets: *1,* animals; *2,* vegetables; *3,* baskets; *4,*
wheat and beans; *5,* wool; *6,* flea market (jutia); *7,* rugs.

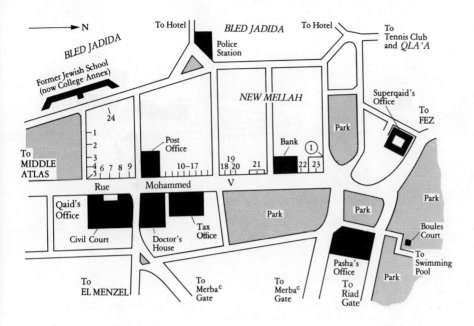

Figure A.2. Bled Jadida and Rue Mohammed V.
Key: nisba class of owner and type of trade practiced

1	SA kyt	7	SA qhw	13	J qhw (and shrb)	19	SRB hlb
2	SA tyr	8	SS epc	14	SA grj	20	E shrb
3	SA (two partners) hdid	9	SS pmp	15	SA kwf	21	SA snm
4	SA swr	10	J ska	16	J mul khb	22	E epc
5	SA bql	11	SA epc	17	SA mns	23	E utl
6	SRB qhw	12	Vacant	18	J epc	24	J shrb

279

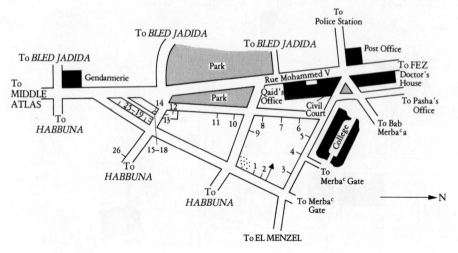

Figure A.3. New cinema area.
Key: nisba class of owner and type of trade practiced

1	SA hdid	11	SA skl
2	RA bql	12	SA qhw
3	SA grj	13	SA snm
4	SA grj	14	SA hlw
5	Government youth and sports bureau	15–18	Vacant
6	SA mns	19	RA bql
7	SRB kzn zra	20	SS grj
8	Government transport office	21	RA fqh
9	SA grj	22	SA grj
10	SA grj	23	SA bql
		24–25	Vacant
		26	SA grj

280

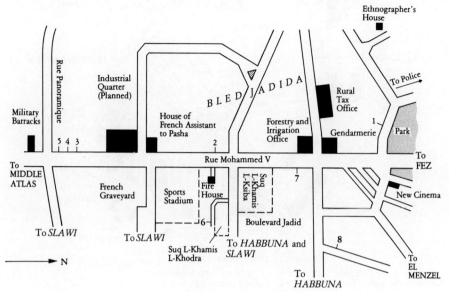

Figure A.4. Rue Mohammed V, southern end.
Key: nisba class of owner and type of trade practiced

1 SA pmp
2 SA pmp
3 SA mns
4 E mkn dum
5 J mkn zit
6 E small canning factory for olives
7 SS mkn zit
8 RA grj (also skl)

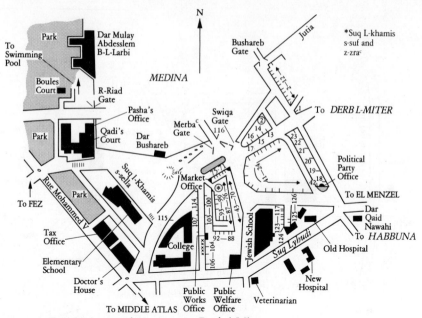

Figure A.5. Rue Mohammed V to upper Derb l-Miter.
Key: nisba class of owner and type of trade practiced

1 SA bql	41 SRA grj	84 SA zra
2 RA bql	42 RA qds	85 SA zra
3 RA bql	43–45 Vacant	86 J zra
4 SA ska	46 RA trf	87 SRB zra
5 J kyt mkn	47, 48 Vacant	88 RA zra
6 SRA kyt mkn	49 RA trf	89–92 Vacant
7 SA njr	50 SRA trf	93 SA zra
8 SA hjm	51 SRA trf	94 J zra
9 SA njr	52 Vacant	95 SA kzn zra
10 SA kyt jlb	53 SRA trf	96 SRB zra
11 SA kyt mkn	54 Vacant	97 J zra
12 SA njr	55 SA trf	98 SRB zra
13 SA ktn	56 Vacant	99 RB zra
14 SA swr	57 RA trf	100 RA kdr
15 SA mns	58 SRA trf	101 SA kdr
16 E kar	59 RA trf	102 UA kmn
17 SA qhw	60 SRA hjm	103 SA khb
18 SA hdid	61 SA trf	104 RA kdr
19 SA hdid	62 J trf	105 SRA ktb
20 SA kwf	63 RB trf	106 J mns
21 SRA qhw	64 SA trf	107 SRB mkn thn
22 SA mgn	65 SRA trf	108 SRB grj
23 SA kar	66 SA trf	109 SRB kdr
24 Vacant	67 RB trf	110 SRA grj
25 J mgn	68 SA trf	111 SRB bql
26 SRA skl	69 SRB trf	112 SA kwf
27 SRA hwj	70 SRB qhw	113 SB dwa
28 Vacant	71 SS ska	114 SS hri
29 SS hri	72 SA bql	115 J pmp
30 SS hri	73 F hlb	116 SA kar
31 SS kar	74 SS hri	117 RA zra
32 RA tyb	75 J grj	118 SA drz
33 SA kar (also kmn)	76 SA mkn thn	119 SA drz
34 J zra	77 RB fkr	120 SA drz
35 J kzn zra	78 SRA fkr	121 J zra
36 J zra	79 SA mkn thn	122 SA drz
37 SS hri	80 SA mkn thn	123 SA drz
38 SA fkr	81 SRB mkn thn	124 RA kzn suf
39 RA grj	82 SA mkn thn	125 J zra
40 SA grj	83 SRB kzn zra	126 Storage place for Jewish ritual equipment:

116–126 are all part of the *heqdeš*, Jewish public property, and known generally as *sūq l-yhūdī* ("Jewish market"), which until recently (and after the Jewish exodus from the Mellah) it was.

282

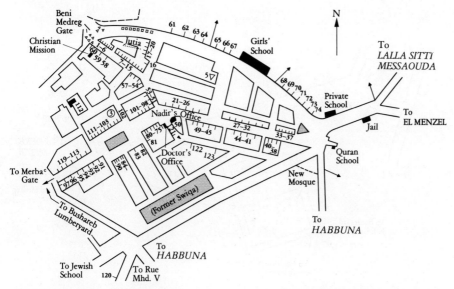

Figure A.6. Lower Derb l-Miter.
Key: nisba class of owner and type of trade practiced

1	SRA hjm			82	J mns		
2	RA khb	42	SA bql	83	SA qhw		
3	RA khb	43	SA bql	84	SRB ktn		
4	RA khb	44	RB bql	85	SA ktn		
5	RA ashb	45	SRB bql	86	SA ktn		
6	RA hjm	46	SS zra	87	SA ktn		
7	RB bql	47	SRA bql	88	SA ktn		
8	Vacant	48	SRA bql	89	STA ktn		
9	SA hjm	49	RA kyt	90	SA ktn		
10	RA hjm	50	Office of religious properties	91	F kyt jlb		
11	Vacant	51	RA ska	(habus)	92	SRA ktn	
12	RA bql	52	RA bql	93	SA kzn zra		
13	Vacant	53	RB bql	94	Vacant		
14	SA mul khb	54	Vacant	95	SRA hwj		
15	SA hwj	55	SA mns	96	SA kyt jlb		
16	SA njr	56	SA hwj	97	SS hri		
17	Vacant	57	RA skl	98	RA ska		
18	SA drz	58	SA mns	99	SA swr		
19	SA hdid	59	RA skl	100	SA skl		
20	SA hdid	60	SA bql	101	SA bql		
21	Vacant	61	RA krd	102	SS hri		
22	SA tyb (sfz)	62	SA fkr	103	SA hwj		
23	SRB kyt mkn	63	SRA krd	104	J hwj		
24	SRA bql	64	SA krd	105	UA kwf		
25	RA bql	65	SA fkr	106	SA ktn		
26	SRB bql	66	SA grj	107	SA khb		
27	SA bql	67	SA njr	108	SA kyt mkn		
28	RB bql	68	SA njr	109	SRA qhw		
29	SRB bql	69	SRA ska	110	SA kwf		
30	SA kyt mkn	70	Vacant	111	SA kwf		
31	UA tyb (sfz)	71	SRA bql	112	SA, SA, SA (3 partners) mns		
32	SRB hjm	72	SRB bql	113	SA ktn		
33	RB bql	73	SRA bql	114	SA hjm		
34	SRA bql	74	SRA bql	115	SA njr		
35	SA qhw	75	SRB kwf	116	RA ktn		
36	F tsbn mkn	76	SA trf	117	Vacant		
37	SA bql	77	SRA skl	118	Vacant		
38	SA ktb mkn	78	RA hlb	119	J hdid		
39	SA ktb mkn	79	SA mns	120	SA pmp		
40	UA bql	80	SA zaj	121	SA hdid		
41	SA gzr	81	RA skl	122	SA njr		
				123	SRA drz		

283

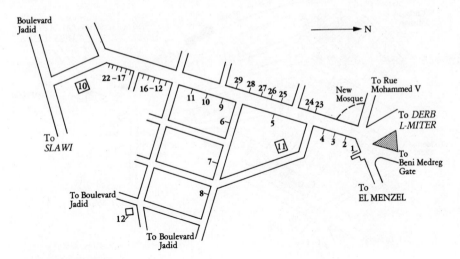

Figure A.7. Habbuna.
Key: nisba class of owner and type of trade practiced

1   SRB fqh
2   SRA bql
3   RB bql
4   RA bql
5   RB grj
6   SRA bql
7   SA bql
8   SRB tks
9   E hlb (French farm owner; his agent sells milk here)
10 SRA kdr

11 Vacant	20–22 Vacant
12 SA bql	23 SA grj
13–16 Vacant	24 SA grj
17 RB bql	25 SRB bql
18 RB bql	26–28 Vacant
19 RB bql	29 RA fqh

284

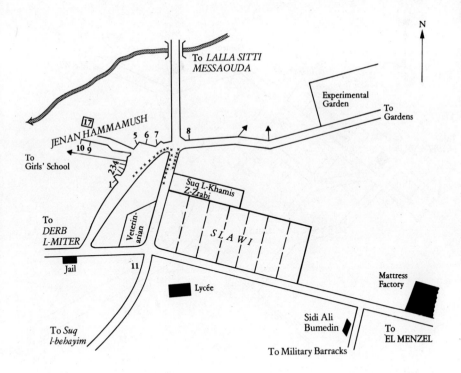

Figure A.8. Slawi.
Key: nisba class of owner and type of trade practiced

1	SA tbn	4	SA ska	7	SA grj	10	SA kzn zit
2	RB kzn zit	5	RA bql	8	SA grj	11	RB pmp
3	SA bgr	6	SRB bql	9	SA bql		

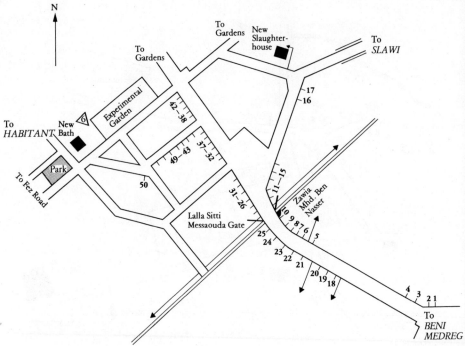

Figure A.9. Lalla Sitti Messaouda.
Key: nisba class of owner and type of trade practiced

1	SA bql	16	SRB bql	31	RA bql
2	Labor union/political party office	17	SA bql	32	SRA bql
3	Government clinic	18	SA bql	33	SS bql
4	SRA drz	19	SA bql	34	Vacant
5	SRA bql	20	SA bql	35	UA bql
6	SA drz	21	SA trf	36–40	Vacant
7	RA bql	22	RB bql	41	SB fkr
8	RA bql	23	Vacant	42	SB fkr
9	RB bql	24	SA bql	43	SA drz
10	Vacant	25	SA bql	44, 45	Vacant
11	RA tyb (sfz)	26	SA bql	46	SA drz
12	SA bql	27	SA ska	47	SA drz
13	Vacant	28	SRB bql	48	SA bql
14	Vacant	29	UA bql	49	Vacant
15	SRB grj	30	SRA bql	50	SRB att

286

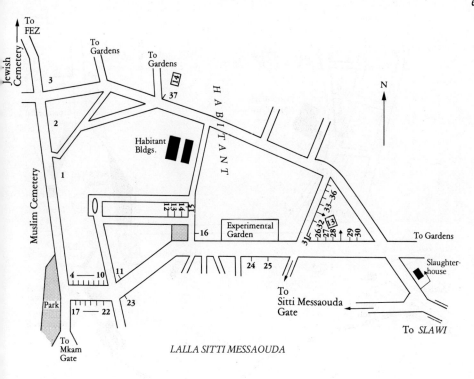

Figure A.10. Habitant.
Key: nisba class of owner and type of trade practiced

1	E utl (shrb)	11	SRB bql	23	SRA zra
2	SA, F, E (partners) mkn zit	12, 13	Vacant	24	SA fkr
3	SA pmp	14	SRB bql	25	SA tbn
4	SA pmp	15	SA bql	26	X kyt
5	Vacant	16	SA hmm	27	X bql
6	SA njr	17	SB grj	28–30	Vacant
7–9	Vacant	18	Vacant	31	SA frn
10	SRA bql	19	RA fkr	32	SA grj
		20, 21	Vacant	33–36	Vacant
		22	SA hlb	37	SA frn

287

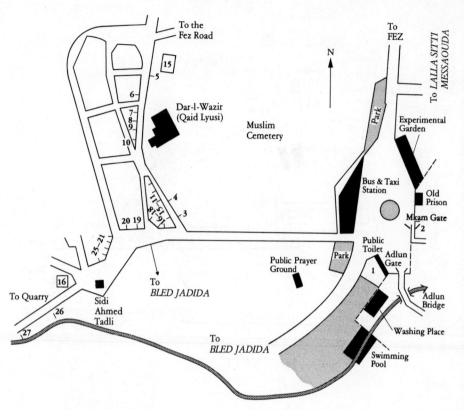

Figure A.11. Sidi Ahmed Tadli.
Key: nisba class of owner and type of trade practiced

1	SA qhw	6	SA bql	16	SA bql	21–23	Vacant
2	SRA ska	7–10	Vacant	17	RB ska	24	SA bql
3	Closed	11	SRB grj	18	SA bql	25	SA drz
4	SA bql	12	SRB grj	19	RB bql	26	SRA rha
5	SRA frn	13–15	Vacant	20	RA njr	27	SRA rha

288

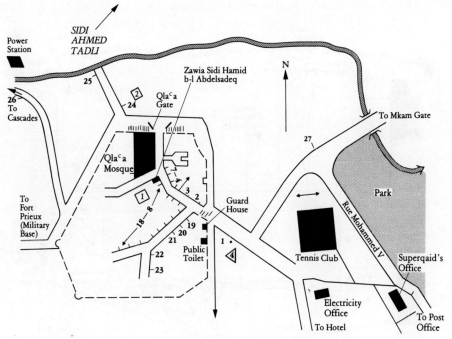

Figure A.12. L-Qla^{c}a.
Key: nisba class of owner and type of trade practiced

1	SA hmm					21	SA bql
2	SA bql					22	SA bql
3	SRA bql	9	SA bql	15	SA bql	23	RA bql
4	SRA bql	10	SA bql	16	SA bql	24	SA frn
5	SRA bql	11	SA ska	17	SA bql	25	SA rha
6	F bql	12	SA bql	18	SRA bql	26	J utl
7	Vacant	13	SA bql	19	SA asa	27	SA grj
8	SA krd	14	SA bql	20	SA bql		

289

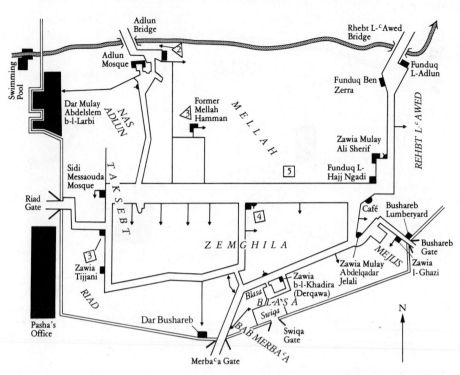

Figure A.13. General layout of southern half (right bank) of the medina.

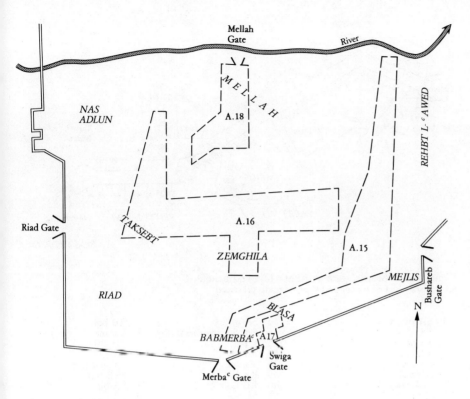

Figure A.14. Locality key to figures (A.15–A.18) charting the right bank of the
medina.

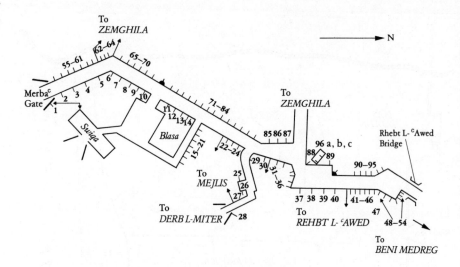

Figure A.15. Merba^c gate to Rehbt l-^cAwed bridge.
Key: nisba class of owner and type of trade practiced

1 SA tyb (kft)	34 SA mshrb	67 RB bql
2 SA qhw	35 SA, SA (partners) qhw	68 Vacant
3 SA gzr	36 F bql	69 RB bql
4 SRB bql	37 SA gzr	70 SA ska
5 SA gzr	38 Vacant	71 SA mul khb
6 RB bql	39 RA bql	72 SRB bql
7 SRB hwj	40 RB fkkr	73 SA bql
8 RB hwj	41 SS bql	74 SA bql
9 RB hwj	42 RA gzr	75 F hwj
10 RB hwj	43 SA kdr	76 SA hwj
11 SA gzr	44 SS bql	77 SS hwj
12 RA mgn	45 RA gzr	78 SS bql
13 X bql	46 SA gbl	79 RA att
14 Derqawa zawia (B-l-Khedira)	47 SA jld	80 Vacant
15 SA gzr	48 Vacant	81 SA hwj
16 SA gzr	49 SRA bql	82 SA hwj
17 X bql	50 SRA bql	83 SRA hwj
18 SA gzr	51 SA fndq	84 SRA drz
19 SA gzr	52 SA rha	85 RA att
20 RA gzr	53 X tyb (sfz)	86 J hwj
21 Vacant	54 SRB kbz	87 J hwj
22 SRA hwj	55 RB kdr	88 SA fndq (see 96a,b,c)
23 SRB hwj	56 SS ashb	89 Zawia Mulay Ali Sherif
24 SA hwj	57 SRA bql	90 RA zyt
25 RA bql	58 SA bql	91 F bql
26 SRA hwj	59 Vacant	92 SA fndq
27 SRB hjm	60 RA bql	93 RB zyt
28 SA mns	61 SRB bql	94 SRA att
29 Mulay Abdel Qader Jillali zawia	62 SA gzr	95 SA ktb
30 SRA bql	63 SA qhw (tyb)	96 Second floor of 88
31 SA njr	64 SA bql	a. SA drz
32 SA hwj	65 SS hri	b. SA drz
33 SRA qhw	66 SA gzr	c. SA drz

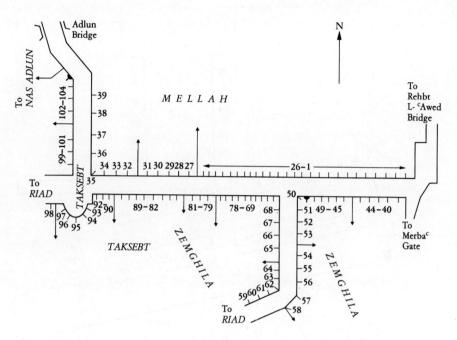

Figure A.16. Zemghila-Taksebt.
Key: nisba class of owner and type of trade practiced

1	SS bql		69	RA kyt mkn
2	J ktn		70	RA kyt mkn
3	SS hwj	36 RA bql	71	SRB kyt mkn
4	SA hjm	37 SRA att	72	Vacant
5	SRB hjm	38 SRB att	73	SRA kyt mkn
6	SRA hjm	39 SRB hrr	74	RA hjm
7	SRA kyt jlb	40 SRA kyt qft	75	RA att
8	RA bql	41 RB ska	76	SA kyt jlb
9	SA kyt jlb	42 UA kyt hwj	77	RA bql
10	SRA frn	43 SRA kyt hwj	78	SRB kyt mkn
11	SRA kyt qft	44 SA kyt hwj	79	Vacant
12	Vacant	45 RA kyt qft	80	SRA kyt mkn
13	RA kyt mkn	46 RA kyt qft	81, 82	Vacant
14	SRA sdf	47 RA kyt qft	83	SA hrr
15	Vacant	48 RA kyt qft	84	SA kyt mkn
16	SRA kyt mkn	49 Vacant	85	RA kyt mkn
17	SRA kyt mkn	50 SA frn	86	Vacant
18	SRA kyt jlb	51 SA trf	87	SA hrr
19	SRA kyt qft	52 F blg	88	SRB bql
20	UA khb	53 SA kyt jlb	89, 90	Vacant
21, 22	Vacant	54–56 Closed	91	SA blg
23	SRB suf	57 SA thn	92	SA bql
24, 25	Vacant	58 RA bql	93	Vacant
26	SRA hrr	59 SA bql	94	SRA kyt jlb
27	SA kyt jlb	60 SRA att	95	SRA bql
28	SA bql	61 SRB fkr	96	RA bql
29	SA kyt jlb	62 SRB att	97	SRA bql
30	SA kyt jlb	63 SA bql	98	SA kyt jlb
31	SA kyt jlb	64 RB att	99	RA bql
32	F fkr	65 SRA kyt mkn	100	SRA bql
33	RA kyt jlb	66 SRA kyt mkn	101	SRB hrr
34	Vacant	67 SA, SA (partners) kyt jlb	102	SRA kyt jlb
35	SRB hlb	68 RA kyt mkn	103	SRA bql
			104	SRA bql

293

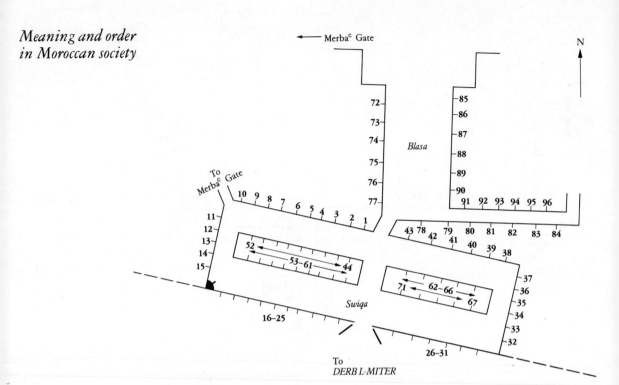

Figure A.17. Swiga and Blasa.
Key: nisba class of owner and type of trade practiced

1	SRA kdr					
2	SRB kdr					
3	SRA kdr	34	SRB kdr	65	SRB kdr
4	SA kdr	35	RB kdr	66	SRA kdr
5	SRB kdr	36	RA kdr	67	RA kdr
6	RB kdr	37	SRB kdr	68	SA kdr
7	SRA kdr	38	SRB kdr	69	SRB kdr
8	RB kdr	39	RA kdr	70	RB kdr
9	UA kdr	40	SB kdr	71	RB kdr
10	SRB kdr	41	SB kdr	72	SRA gzr
11	RB kdr	42	SRA kdr	73	SA kdr
12	SA kdr	43	SRA kdr	74	SA kdr
13	SRB kdr	44	SB kdr	75	SA kdr
14	RB kdr	45	SB kdr	76	SA kdr
15	SRB kdr	46	SRB kdr	77	SRA gzr
16	RA kdr	47	SA kdr	78	SA gzr
17	SA kdr	48	SA kdr	79	SA kdr
18	SRA kdr	49	SRB kdr	80	SRA lqm
19	RA kdr	50	SRB kdr	81	RB kdr
20	SA kdr	51	SRB kdr	82	SRB kdr
21	SRB kdr	52	SRB kdr	83	SA kdr
22	SRA kdr	53	SRB kdr	84	Vacant
23	RA kdr	54	SRB kdr	85	SA gzr
24	SA kdr	55	RA kdr	86	SA gzr
25	SRA kdr	56	RA kdr	87	SA gzr
26	SA kdr	57	SRB kdr	88	SA gzr
27	SRA kdr	58	SRB kdr	89	SRA kdr
28	SRA kdr	59	SB kdr	90	SA hut
29	SRB kdr	60	RA kdr	91	SRA lqm
30	SA kdr	61	SA kdr	92	SRA kdr
31	SRB (partner of 30) kdr	62	SRB kdr	93	RB kdr
32	SRB kdr	63	SRA kdr	94–96	Vacant
33	SRB kdr	64	RB kdr		

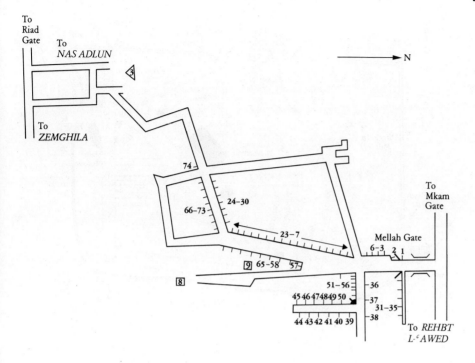

Figure A.18. Mellah.
Key: nisba class of owner and type of trade practiced

1	SA asa					
2	Vacant					
3	UA ska					
4	SRB kdr	30	J bql	51	RB kdr
5	SRB kdr	31	Meeting place for quarter chiefs	52	SRB kdr
6	RA kdr	32	RA hlf	53	SA att
7	RB att	33	SA kyt mkn	54	SRB kdr
8	RA kdr	34	Vacant	55, 56	Vacant
9	RB att	35	SA hrr	57	RA bql
10	RB bql	36	RB bql	58	RA fkr
11	RA ashb	37	RA fkr	59	RA fkr
12	RB fkr	38	RA bql	60	RA fkr
13	RA krd	39	SA qsdr	61, 62	Vacant
14	RA qsdr	40–44	Vacant	63	SS blg
15	SA ashb	45	SRB awd	64	Vacant
16, 17	Vacant	46	SRA blg	65	RA bql
18	RA trf	47	SRA blg	66	RA bql
19–27	Vacant	48	J gzr	67–72	Vacant
28	RA zrz	49	RA hut	73	RB blg
29	Vacant	50	F bql	74	RA blg

295

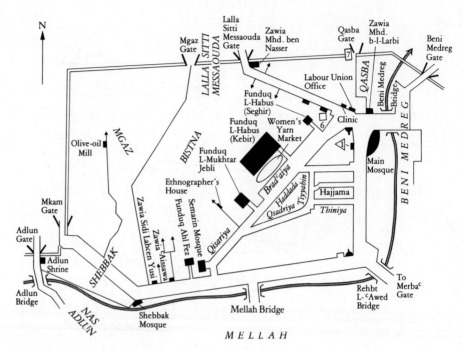

Figure A.19. General layout of northern half (left bank) of the medina.

296

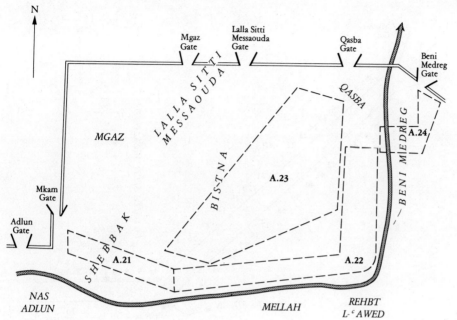

Figure A.20. Locality key to figures (A.21–A.24) charting the left bank of the medina.

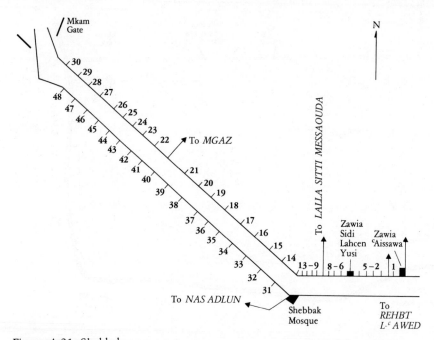

Figure A.21. Shebbak
Key: nisba class of owner and type of trade practiced

1 SA hlb	13 SA hrr	25 SRA hrr	37 SA bql
2 SRA hrr	14 RA bql	26 SA bql	38 Vacant
3 SRA hrr	15 SRA hwj	27 SRA hrr	39 SS tyb
4 SA hrr	16 SA bql	28 SA hrr	40 SA bql
5 SRB bql	17 Vacant	29 RA fkr	41 SA bql
6 SA hjm	18 SRA bql	30 SRA hrr	42 SA hjm
7 SRB bql	19 SRA qsdr	31 SB hwj	43 SA kyt jlb
8 RA qhw	20 F hrr	32 SA kdr	44 SA hjm
9 SRA mul khb	21 SRA awwd	33 SA hrr	45 SRA mul khb
10 SA bql	22 SRA hrr	34 Vacant	46 SA hjm
11 RA bql	23 SA bql	35 SRB hwj	47 SRA utl
12 SA hrr	24 SA kdr	36 F bql	48 Political party office

298

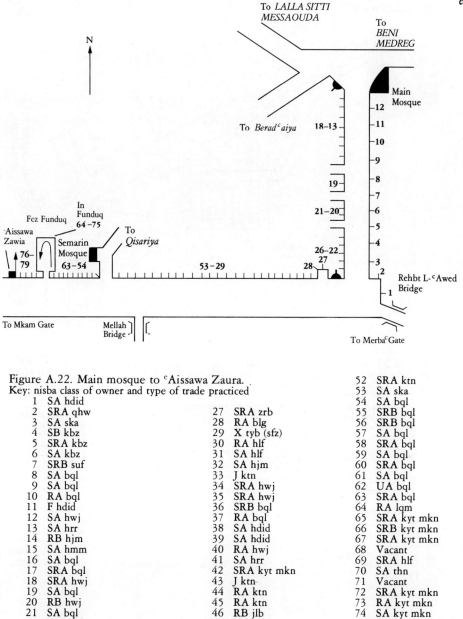

Figure A.22. Main mosque to ᶜAissawa Zaura.
Key: nisba class of owner and type of trade practiced

1	SA hdid			52	SRA ktn
2	SRA qhw	27	SRA zrb	53	SA ska
3	SA ska	28	RA blg	54	SA bql
4	SB kbz	29	X tyb (sfz)	55	SRB bql
5	SRA kbz	30	RA hlf	56	SRB bql
6	SA kbz	31	SA hlf	57	SA bql
7	SRB suf	32	SA hjm	58	SRA bql
8	SA bql	33	J ktn	59	SA bql
9	SA bql	34	SRA hwj	60	SRA bql
10	RA bql	35	SRA hwj	61	SA bql
11	F hdid	36	SRB bql	62	UA bql
12	SA hwj	37	RA bql	63	SRA bql
13	SA hrr	38	SA hdid	64	RA lqm
14	RB hjm	39	SA hdid	65	SRA kyt mkn
15	SA hmm	40	RA hwj	66	SRB kyt mkn
16	SA bql	41	SA hrr	67	SRA kyt mkn
17	SRA bql	42	SRA kyt mkn	68	Vacant
18	SRA hwj	43	J ktn	69	SRA hlf
19	SA bql	44	RA ktn	70	SA thn
20	RB hwj	45	RA ktn	71	Vacant
21	SA bql	46	RB jlb	72	SRA kyt mkn
22	SA hdid	47	SA kyt	73	RA kyt mkn
23	SRA bql	48	J ktn	74	SA kyt mkn
24	SRB kbz	49	X ktn	75	SRA kyt mkn
25	SA kdr	50	UA ktn	76	SA bql
26	SRA bql	51	SRA ktn	77	SA bql
				78	SA bql
				79	SA bql

Note: Establishments 64–75 are in the funduq, indicated by arrow. The funduq is owned by the heirs of its original owners; there are a dozen or more of them and they all live in Fez.

299

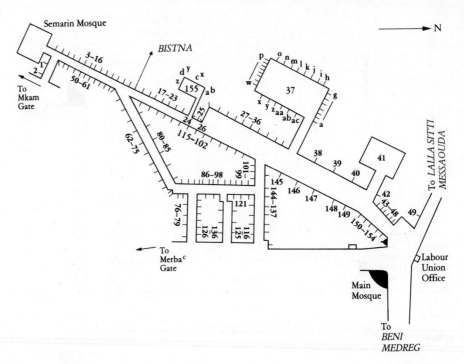

Figure A.23. Semarin mosque to main mosque area.
Key: nisba class of owner and type of trade practiced

1	SA hlb					37	x Vacant
2	Public washroom						y SA krd
3	Entrance area, for ablutions, to Semarin mosque						z SRB krd
4	SRA kyt mkn						aa F zrb
5	RA tub						ab J blg
6	J tub	32	SA hdd				ac SA asa
7	SA tub	33	SA brd			38	SA brd
8	SRB kyt mkn	34	SA smr			39	SA brd
9	SA ktn	35	SA smr			40	SA brd
10	RA tub	36	SA tyb			41	SA fndq
11	SA tub	37	Funduq l-habus kebir			42	Vacant
12	RA kyt mkn		a SA kzn			43	SB trf
13	SA ktn		b SA kyt jlb			44	SA hrr
14	SRB tub		c SA krd			45	SA dll
15	SA tub		d SRA krd			46	SA hrr
16	J ktn		e SA drz			47	SA hjm
17	RB kyt (also ktn)		f SA drz			48	SA hjm
18	SA tub		g Storage place for mosque equipment			49	SA frn
19	J syg		h SA hrr			50	RA kyt mkn
20	Vacant		i SA kyt jlb			51	SA kyt mkn
21	SRA hjm		j SA kyt jlb			52	RA tub
22	F syg		k SA zrb			53	RA tub
23	SA hjm		l SRB krd			54	RA tub
24	RA fndq		m F hrr			55	RB tub
25	SA hjm		n–p Vacant			56	SRB tub
26	SA brd		q F krd			57, 58	Vacant
27	SA smr		r F krd			59	RA tub
28	SA hdd		s SA krd			60	Vacant
29	SA smr		t SA krd			61	SRB kyt mkn
30	SA qhw		u, v Vacant			62	J ktn
31	SA smr		w SA blg			63	RA kyt mkn
						64	SRB kyt mkn
						65	SA awd

300

66	SRA kyt mkn	98	SA tbn
67	SA hjm	99	Vacant
68	SA hjm	100	SA bql
69	SRA bql	101	SA hdd
70	RA tyb (sfz)	102	RA hdd
71	UA qsdr	103	Vacant
72	RA hjm	104	SA hjm
73	SA qhw	105	SA qhw
74	SA qhw	106	SA smr
75	SA hrr	107	SA hdd
76	SRA hjm	108	SA ghw
77	Vacant	109	SA hdd
78	RA hjm	110	SA awd
79	SA hjm	111	SA qsdr
80	SA kyt mkn	112, 113	Vacant
81	SA hrr	114	J syg
82	RA qsdr	115	SRB kyt mkn
83	SA qsdr	116	SA bql
84	SA qsdr	117	SA bql
85	UA qsdr	118	UA bql
86	SA kyt jlb	119	SRA tyb
87	SA hjm	120	SA bql
88	SA hjm	121	SRA tyb (kft)
89	SA thn	122	SRA tyb (kft)
90	SA twj	123	SRA tyb
91	SRB bql	124	SRA krd
92	SRB hjm	125	UA awd
93	SA hjm	126	SA bql
94	SA tyb	127	SA bql
95	RA tyb	128	SA bql
96	SA tyb	129, 130	Vacant
97	SRA tyb (kft)	131	SA tyb (kft)

132	Vacant
133	SA tyb
134	SRA tyb
135	SA krd
136	SA nhs
137	SA bql
138	Closed
139	SS bql
140	SRA hjm
141	SS ful
142	SA tyb (kft)
143	SA tyb (kft)
144	SA tyb (sfz)
145	SA hdd
146	SA brd
147	Vacant
148	SA njr
149	SA njr
150	SA bql
151	RA qsdr
152	SS bql
153	SA bql
154	Public toilet
155	Funduq l-Mukhtar Jebli

First floor:

a	SA hdd
b	SA drz
c	SA drz
d	SA drz

Second floor:

x	Vacant
y	SA drz
z	SA drz

301

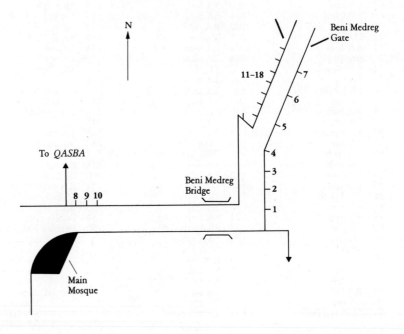

Figure A.24. Beni Medreg.
Key: nisba class of owner and type of trade practiced

1	SA krd	4	SRA mgn	7	SA hjm	10	RA att	13	SA att	16	RA kyt jlb
2	SA krd	5	SRA swr	8	SA bql	11	SA qhw	14	SA ska	17	SRB att
3	RA hlf	6	Vacant	9	RA att	12	Vacant	15	F blg	18	Vacant

302

Annex B: The markets of Sefrou around 1910

The market area of Sefrou was somewhat differently arranged around 1910 than at the time of the bazaar survey described in Annex A. The layout shown in Figure B.1 is based on information obtained during 1964–6 from extended interviews with aged informants. The locations of the various enterprises are, therefore, only approximate.

This is especially true of the nine olive-oil mills and thirteen flour mills stretched along the river. None of these is now in existence. In 1910 all were habus-owned and rented to private entrepreneurs. In the 1930s they began to be replaced by motor-driven mills, and the 1950 flood wiped out all that remained in operation.

In 1910 kosher butchers, grocers, shoemakers, and tinsmiths (enterprises 9, 18, and 19 on Figure B.1) were largely (in the kosher cases, exclusively) Jewish. Now (1968) both tinsmithing and shoemaking are largely Muslim, though a few Jews remain in these trades.

303

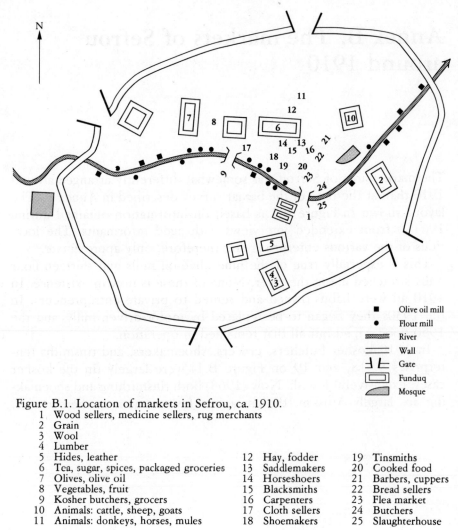

Figure B.1. Location of markets in Sefrou, ca. 1910.

1	Wood sellers, medicine sellers, rug merchants				
2	Grain				
3	Wool				
4	Lumber				
5	Hides, leather	12	Hay, fodder	19	Tinsmiths
6	Tea, sugar, spices, packaged groceries	13	Saddlemakers	20	Cooked food
7	Olives, olive oil	14	Horseshoers	21	Barbers, cuppers
8	Vegetables, fruit	15	Blacksmiths	22	Bread sellers
9	Kosher butchers, grocers	16	Carpenters	23	Flea market
10	Animals: cattle, sheep, goats	17	Cloth sellers	24	Butchers
11	Animals: donkeys, horses, mules	18	Shoemakers	25	Slaughterhouse

Annex C: The Tuesday locality-focusing market, 1967, at Aioun Senam

The market opens about seven in the morning and is largely closed by the early afternoon, a typical pattern for periodic suqs, including that of Sefrou town. It is served by a bus from Sefrou town, which can carry about thirty people with merchandise on top. Also, anywhere from one or two to ten or so trucks and autos, depending on the season, travel from the town to the market. This suq has been at its present location (see Figure 1 of text) only three years, having moved (or more accurately having been moved, under government stimulation) from another, less suitable site at Annonceur, 4 or 5 kilometers away. Rural markets frequently, indeed almost characteristically, show such minor spatial instability, changing sites to adjust to minor local changes in residence patterns, transport routes, water supply, and so on.

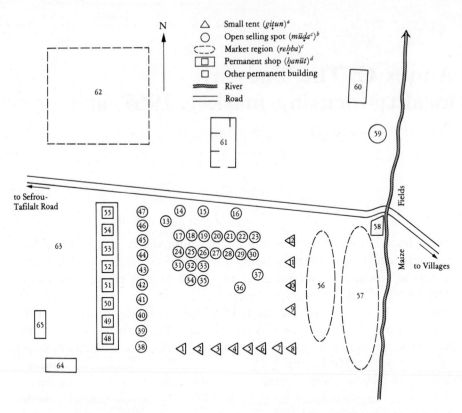

Figure C.1. The Tuesday locality-focusing market at Aioun Senam, 1967.
Key: Inside the market (*dakel ṣ-ṣūq*)

1–8	Small grocer (*beqqāl*)[a]
9	Fried fritter seller (*seffāj*)
10	Small grocer
11	Cooked-food seller (*ṭiyyāb*)
12	Small grocer
13, 14	Bread seller (*mūl l-kubz*)
15	Pottery seller (*fekkār*)
16	Olive-oil seller (*mūl z-zit*)
17–20	Fruit seller (*ğellāl*)
21–30	Vegetable seller (*keddār*)
31–35	Ready-made-clothes seller (*mūl l-ḥwāyj*)
36	Salt seller (*mūl l-mleḥ*)
37	Dish seller (*mūl t-ṭwājen*)
38–47	Butcher (*gezzār*)

The border of the market (*ṭarf ṣ-ṣūq*)

48–51	Small grocer
52, 53	Hardware seller (*mūl l-ḥadīd*)
54	Coffee shop (*qehwa*)
55	Unoccupied

Outside the market (*berra min ṣ-ṣūq*)

56	Grain market (*reḥbt z-zra*ᶜ)[e]
57	Animal market (*reḥbt l-behāyim*)[e]
58	Office of market inspector (*š-šaik ṣ-ṣūq*)[f]
59	Spring
60	Religious shrine
61	Slaughterhouse (*gūrna*)[g]
62	Corral (*ksiba*)[h]
63	Parking place for motor vehicles
64	School
65	Commune council house

[a]These are small, lean-to type canvas tents, hardly more than 20–25 square meters.

[b]The "place" usually consists of a rug or cloth spread on the ground, plus sometimes a small table or two and various display boxes. Butchers have hanging racks and cutting blocks. The same "place" tends to be occupied by the same person each week so that quasi-property rights are acquired, at least by the more regular traders.

[c]Any specialized region of the market may be called a rehba; sometimes muda is extended to such a use: *mūda*ᶜ *dyal l-gezzāra* ("place of the butchers"). When the space involved is a trading area, the word suq itself is frequently used: *ṣ-ṣuq z-zra*ᶜ ("the grain market").

[d]These are built of wood and concrete, owned by the commune (as are the school, the commune meeting house, and the suq as a whole).

[e]The grain and animal markets vary extremely widely in size week to week, by season, temporary economic conditions, etc. The qaidal office in Sefrou estimates that about 3,000 sheep and 4,000 goats are sold during the year; 1,000 quintals of barley, 250 of maize, and 50 of wheat.

*f*The main function of the sheikh is to sell tickets to vendors and collect rents. (Two or three policemen sent out from the Sefrou qaidal office maintain order.) A tent location cost about 75 cents in 1966; a spot, 30 cents. To sell a goat or sheep cost 50 cents; a chicken, 10 cents; a donkey load of grain 20 cents; a mule load, 30 cents. (Animals and grain brought to market but not sold are untaxed.) The permanent stores rented for $5 a month, the ksiba corral for $100 a year. A butcher paid $1 to slaughter a sheep or goat in the slaughterhouse. These taxes go to the treasury of the communal council, but the market is generally regulated by the qaid's office in Sefrou, the local sheikh being as much his representative as the council's—given Moroccan political realities, far more so.

*g*The slaughterhouse is owned by the commune; the butchers do their own slaughtering there.

*h*Strictly, ksiba means animal market, but in the Sefrou area it is used for the place where the donkeys and mules of suq attenders are "parked," on the model of the urban funduqs, a term also sometimes used for these corrals. Occasionally a donkey or mule will be sold there, and there is a blacksmith (*haddād*) in residence, but basically it is merely a pen.

307

Annex D: The song of the baker

Oral recitation of poetry remains a live art in the Moroccan country-side. Such recitations are given by local folk poets, who sing either their own compositions or those of others in a metallic falsetto, usually accompanied by a chorus, tambourines, and lines of male dancers. Most of the poems (for some other examples, see Geertz, C., "Art as a Cultural System," *MLN* 91:1473–99 [1976]) express popular concerns in a popular idiom, and indeed the individuals to whom they refer are often present. "The Song of the Baker," which was collected in Sefrou, depicts a criticism addressed to the amin of that trade concerning a particular baker by an aggrieved client. It exemplifies the complex of moral expectations (*ᶜurf*) surrounding an important bazaar trade, as well as the seriousness with which those expectations are taken. The translation makes no attempt to reproduce the poetic devices of the original and is quite free.

Chorus:
O God! O bakers! I come to you[1] to complain about the baker
My bread is always treated as his enemy in his bakery
O God! O bakers! I come to you to complain about the baker
My bread is always treated as his enemy in his bakery.

Verses:
He said [the man who is complaining about the baker]:
   O by God, O bakers, what shall I do?
Our baker came to our quarter and swore never to serve us first
He doesn't want our tips and he is always contrary with us
And the dough that we have kneaded always makes him angry, la! la! la!

And I am tired of pleading with him, and I am tired of urging him to
   a good job
And I give him his pay promptly every week
And I bring him any news or gossip I hear quickly
Yet he has sworn not to give my bread its due.

[Chorus]

And the plaintiff said: O sir! Sometimes the baker lets my bread get
308   hard[2]

Sometimes he puts it in too soon; sometimes he loses it.[3]
He doesn't put the cloth[4] back on the bread; anything that comes near him he takes
I try to be patient with him so that he will deign to look for my bread tray.

May God bring some relief from this faithless one, this man of little religion
He has even lost our covering cloth and he makes us go without our dinner
Our bread is cooked too fast and it becomes hard and is black with smoke
And yet my sugar is never absent from his bakery.[5]

[Chorus]

And the plaintiff said: O we have had a birth feast[6]
A new little baby was born
And the women of the family decided to have a small party
They have made a few little butter cookies and almond crescents.

I took the cookies to the baker myself[7]
So that, God willing, he would see my face and do me a kindness
And the baker said to me: O kinsman, take care of me on the holiday
Give me my share of the
    dry meat, and bring me my share of the eve-of-Ramadhan gifts.[8]

[Chorus]

And prepare for me the soup of Ramadhan[9]
And if you bring cookies to be baked bring the money for them too
The plaintiff said: O sirs! We made cookies on the day of the end of the fast
My mother's sister made them and my neighbor counted them
And I took them to the baker myself
In hopes that when he saw my face he would do me a kindness
That he would bake them carefully in the best part of the oven
And they would come out with the right texture.

[Chorus]

And that he would put them into the oven gently
And that all my household would be happy
And that the baker would be our friend by heart and by completeness[10]
But despite all that we still quarreled in his bakery.

The plaintiff said: O sirs! We made cookies on the Day of the Sacrifice
My mother's sister made them, and my neighbor counted them
And Marjana [a young girl of the house] took them to the baker's oven
And she found the baker annoyed and troubled, la! la! la!

[Chorus]

The baker's mind was empty due to hashish
And he was confused by the cookies and lost track of them
She [Marjana] told the baker: 'I am in a hurry, do it quickly for us."

309

Upon hearing this the baker chased her from the bakery and swore
after her, the bad and irreligious man.

The plaintiff said: O sirs! I say only good things about bakers[11]
There are capable ones among them
There are brave and noble men
Bakers do good on the earth.

[Chorus]

And their profession is a good one
In all respects its dignity is great, la! la! la!
And I am ashamed to speak badly of one of them
Some of them I keep company with as a friend.[12]

Notes

1. The amin of the bakers.
2. If the baker doesn't let the bread sit for a
certain amount of time before putting it in the
oven, so that it has a chance to rise, it becomes hard upon baking.
3. That is, he gives it to someone else out of
carelessness.
4. A piece of toweling or tablecloth covers
the bread when it is brought to the oven. If it
is left off afterward, the soot of the oven and
other dirt will collect on the finished loaf.
5. Usually people give a gift of sugar to the
baker as a gesture of goodwill and so that he
will cook their bread well.
6. *Sbūᶜ*, a naming celebration held by the
family on the seventh day after the birth of a
child.
7. That is, he didn't just send a small girl
from the family, as people normally do, but
went himself so as to shame the baker into
doing a good job.
8. Meat salted and dried during the fast
month (Ramadhan, *Ramḍan*) is distributed to
various people – friends, neighbors, clients –

on the holiday ending that month. Immediately preceding the fast month other gifts –
wheat and so on – are similarly distributed.
9. During Ramadhan the fast is broken in
the evening by sipping a soup called *ḥrīra*.
10. That is, he would complete the family;
the family would not be complete without him.
This is a reference to the fact that the baker's
activity, like the bathhouse keeper's, is ideally
viewed as part of domestic life, and thus he is,
so to speak, an honorary family member.
11. That is, about bakers in general. He doesn't slander the whole profession, just this
one member.
12. This "some of my best friends are
bakers" plaint ends the body of the poem.
Several versus follow praising poets and their
ability to put men in the balance and judge
between them. The poet protests that he has
told the story of the errant baker only so that
other bakers will act differently and not in
order to slander the trade. He also calls on the
bakers to give gifts to the poets and to honor
the sultan.

Annex E: The integrated Thursday market, 1976

Beginning in the mid-1970s the Moroccan government began construction of a marketplace for all the Thursday markets, previously scattered at various points in the new quarters of the town. By 1976 this market, though still unfinished was in full operation, and the scattered marketplaces had all been absorbed into it. The grain mills remained in the old grain market, but housing for them was in process of construction at the new site.

The new market is located at the extreme southern edge of town and thus is even more clearly separated from the permanent medina market, about 1.5 kilometers to the north, than were the earlier scattered markets. The new market consists of a large walled area divided into three main sections: a general market and two animal markets, one of which is not yet in operation. Hanuts are being constructed in the general market, but are not yet occupied. A covered market area in the central part of the general market is also as yet incomplete, though the space is filled with traders.

The construction of the integrated market completes the differentiation of the periodic market from the permanent market traced in the text. This differentiation has occurred in three main stages:

1. Around 1900–25: both periodic and permanent markets inside the medina with only partial separation of the two (see Annex B)
2. Around 1925–75: movement of the periodic elements to various sites immediately outside the walls of the medina, the animal market (ca. 1935) and the vegetable market (1970) eventually moving to more peripheral locations southward (see Annex A)
3. 1975–present: concentration of the periodic markets at a single site at the extreme southern edge of town.

311

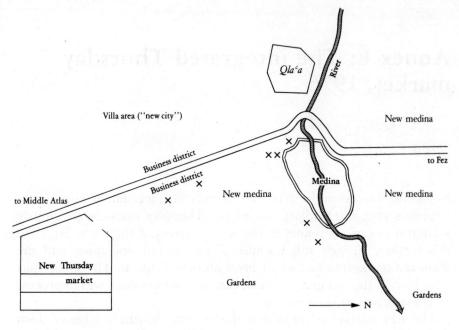

Figure E.1. Location of new (1976) integrated periodic market (*suq l-ḵemīs*). X, former scattered market locations.

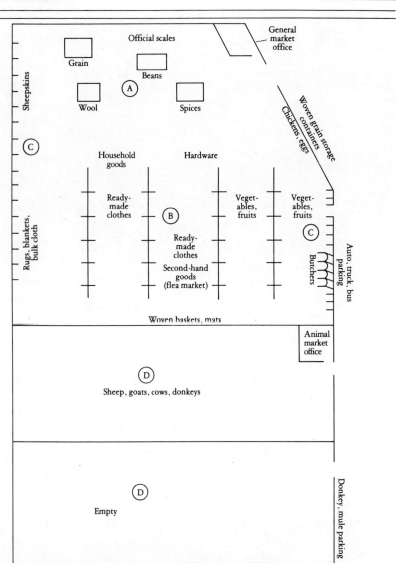

Figure E.2. Layout of integrated Thursday market (*suq l-ḵemīs*). *A*, open plaza with low concrete platforms for grain, beans, etc. Housing for mills is in process of construction. *B*, covered market (incomplete). *C*, shops (incomplete and unoccupied). *D*, animal markets (only one as yet operative).

313

The meanings of family ties
Hildred Geertz

Family, friendship, and patronage

A first, rough approximation of Moroccan views of "family ties" can be gained by presenting the idea of "family" as set within a semantic context that also includes what Americans call "friendship" and "patronage." All three forms of affiliation are understood by Moroccans to be fundamentally dyadic, all three can be seen as expanding into broad networks, and all three are to a large extent known to be contingent on personal action. Everyone in Morocco is viewed as building up throughout life various webs of reliable relationships that include friendship and patronage links as well as those of family. Although distinctions are made in Moroccan speech between what we would call "kinsman" and what we would consider "non-kin" on essentially biogenetic grounds, the operative, everyday, acted-upon premises do not rely on sharp and simple distinctions among family, friend, and patron.

Ties between parent and child, of course, are recognized to entail greater emotional commitment than do other kinds of links. In the first place, it is within a circle of close kinsmen that each child is first nurtured and protected, although in many cases that circle of intimacy and domesticity includes members who are not kinsmen. Second, the economic dependency of a son on his father is often extended far into adulthood through the delay of the transfer of land or other goods from parent to child until after the parent's death. But even this economic dependency between son and father is understood, in part, as a patron-client relationship.

Another way to state the matter is to say that all three – family, friendship, and patronage – are ordered by the same cultural principles. In American culture the three are viewed as contrasting or even conflicting forms of personal relationships. That is, the norms governing them are felt to be qualitatively different. For many Moroccans, however, the social ties of friendship and patronage intergrade with 315 family, and many of the same norms apply to any of them. Individual family members may or may not be reliable allies, depending not on biogenetic distance or on membership in a genealogically defined group, but on the summation of personal debts and obligations that has historically been built up between them. The general form of personal relationships is, as Rosen has described them, one of "a running imbalance of competitive advantage" and of contextual claims, and this basic culturally established concept holds for "familial" relations as well.

The terms "family" and "familial" as used in this essay are given no special definition, but are employed as in colloquial American to indicate a wide variety of disparate referents, including what otherwise might be termed "conjugal family," "personal kindred," "affines," "lineage," "sublineage," "clan," and "relatives." As will become clearer analyzing Moroccan conceptualizations of this aspect of their life should not start with an attempt to define component social units. In fact, to approach the subject with an assumption that Moroccan society is successively "built up" out of component "families," whether these are assumed to be domestic groups or descent groups, can lead only to error.[1]

Throughout the first stages of field research, an effort was made to uncover Moroccan concepts of and about "family groups," and some of these futile attempts are chronicled below. I was at first deaf to an informant's statement, made to me very early in our stay in Sefrou, that his family was *mustabik* ("tangled," "interwoven," "interlaced")–a remark that was accompanied by a graphic gesture of twisting together the fingers of both hands into a constantly moving but tightly bound knot. The significance of this image escaped me as long as I continued to search for cultural concepts of groups that were assumed to be clearly bounded and ordered according to distinct principles that in some simple way could distinguish members from nonmembers, in accordance with recognition or nonrecognition of specific "kinship" ties.[2]

How the people of Sefrou actually speak of these matters, and how they organize their lives, emerged gradually as I accumulated the complex and ambiguous details of those lives. This essay will, in a way, retrace this research process and slowly give the above general and preliminary remarks about family, friendship, and patronage, and about groups and tangles, some circumstantial content.

Throughout, I use as illustration a particular Sefrou family–a large, urban, Arabic-speaking aggregate of some 250 people, all with the same surname. They are by no means to be understood as typical, for many of their ways of relating to one another are extreme by Moroccan standards.[3] But the consistency of development of this particular case makes certain underlying cultural concepts easier to grasp than they would be in other kinds of families. My account of the external specifics of the lives of the people of the example – the shape of their home and neighborhood, who lives with whom, how they make their living, who has married whom – is accompanied by a description of the main explicit institutional frameworks that govern those lives – the rules of inheritance, the religious rituals that take place in domestic settings, the terms used to designate groupings and persons, the procedures for choosing a spouse and for getting married and divorced. I set forth some of the implicit cultural constructs that shape Sefrouis' interpretations of their familial experiences and the manner in which these constructs are given specific content in everyday interaction. The conventions for the naming of persons are shown to be central to the process by which cultural categories become integral elements of social action.

There is a danger of my being misunderstood when I say that Moroccans conceive of familial relationships similarly to the way they view friendship and patronage, and when I state that the calculation of mutual advantage is an essential element in all three. It might seem that I am describing behavioral and attitudinal patterns alone and that I am arguing that Moroccan social structure reduces to an intricate field of competing interests. I am not content with a simple description of how people behave toward one another; rather, I want to show what the cultural guiding principles are that define for Moroccans the nature of their actions, their relationships, their interests, and the means they recognize by which they can adjust conflicting interests. I do not mean to suggest that Moroccans are without norms (which would be absurd), but that their most important norms are personalistic and highly sensitive to subtle situational conditions. This person-centered ethic needs to be explicated if we are to understand how Moroccans themselves make sense of the behavior of others around them. It forms part of a more general world view, a Moroccan conception of the nature of society and man in which every person is seen as an active agent creating a meaningful life within an essentially arbitrary world.

The organization of space

The houses of the town of Sefrou were, until the early 1920s all confined to the small area within the walls of the town. Crowded up against one another, with little room for additions except by building new on top of old, they were reached by winding narrow alleyways that were themselves frequently roofed over by extensions of the buildings on either side. From these cobblestoned canyons all that is visible of the houses are high dirty-white walls, broken by closed wooden doors and, above the street level, a few small, barred windows. An aerial view reveals a checkerboard of open courts, hidden from the street. Most of these medina dwellings are two or three stories high, some as many as seven, and most contain two or more households. Today, all but a few of these houses are dilapidated and in many cases actually falling down. But in the past, as is evident from the quality of the carving of the doors and their frames, from the interior tiling, and from the spaciousness of the inner courts, many of these houses had a certain elegance and presence. Most were built at least two or three centuries ago, many even earlier, but over the course of time there has been a continuing process of renovation, partial tearing down and replacement of rooms, and addition of smaller structures in the interstices of the larger ones. The result is an intricate jumble of rooms of various sizes, usually opening onto central courts or connected by small back stairways and dark corridors.

One small set of twisted, branching alleyways in Sefrou is called Derb Adlun. This is the quarter or neighborhood bearing the name of the family I shall describe as the major example. The group as a whole is usually referred to as the Nas Adlun ("the Adlun people"): individuals are given the name el Adluni.[4] They are sherifs of the Idrisiyyin category and have been a prominent element in Sefrou's social world since at least the fifteenth century. The Nas Adlun have a family tradition of religious scholarship and have in the past produced several judges (*qadis*) and notaries (*aduls*). For the most part, however, the Adluns are farmers and landowners, and some of them have been and are wealthy by Sefrou standards. As a family, they are very conscious of their high status vis-à-vis the other people of Sefrou, and they take considerable care to maintain it. They keep themselves somewhat aloof from others and pay special attention to protecting the reputation of their women by confining them within their houses and quarters and by marrying most of their daughters to Adlun men. (We will see, however, that all branches of the Adlun family do not follow these standards equally faithfully.)

You enter Derb Adlun through a small archway and find yourself at an open space where two alleys cross. A tiled public fountain stands at one corner. At the side of the space is a wall concealing a small yard; the top of an olive tree is visible above the wall, and from the court-

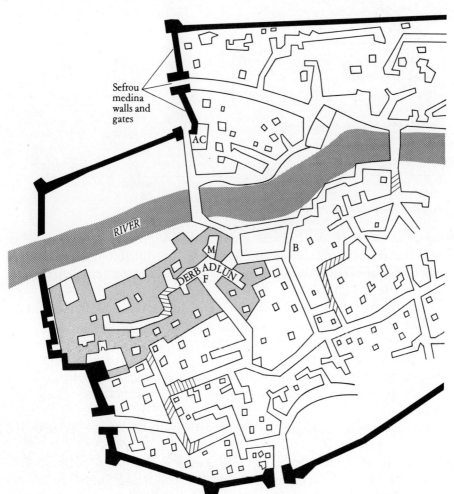

Figure 1. Portion of Sefrou medina showing Derb Adlun. Gray area is approximate extent of buildings surrounding Derb Adlun. White squares are larger courtyards. Cross-hatching indicates covered passageways. *M,* Adlun mosque; *AC,* Adlun cemetery; *B,* Adlun bath; *F,* fountain.

yard you hear the sound of children chanting the Quran. This is the mosque and children's religious school of the Nas Adlun, built several hundred years ago by the family and still maintained by it. There is also a public bath (*ḥammām*) around the corner, owned by and in the past monopolized by Adlun families (see Figure 1). Fifty years ago there were only a few outsiders living here, mainly the sharecroppers, servants, and other dependents of the Adluns. Today the majority of the residents of the neighborhood are neither Adluns nor their cli- 319

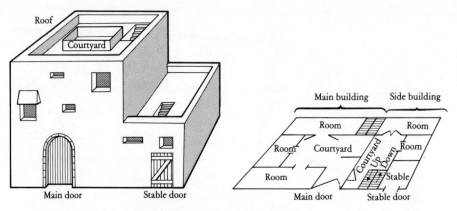

Figure 2. Sketches of exterior and first floor of Dar Hamid.

ents, but newcomers, mostly rural-born and poverty-stricken, who rent the rooms and houses the former Adlun inhabitants left behind when they moved to newer, brighter homes in the gardens outside the wall of the old city.

There are today (1968) about 145 adult members of the entire Adlun family. Of these only thirty-six still live in Derb Adlun, together with approximately thirty children. This group of conservative stay-behinds is not, however, poor and powerless, for it includes one man of great wealth, who lives in a luxurious house he built in Derb Adlun, surrounded by his wives, sons-in-law, assistants, servants, and dependents. Despite the dispersal of many to the suburbs of Sefrou, the Adlun family continues to dominate socially, if not numerically, its ancestral quarter.

One of the oldest houses in Derb Adlun is called Dar Hamid ("the house of Hamid"). It is named after the paternal grandfather of the older residents of the house, Mulay Hamid bel Hassan el Adluni.[5] Mulay Hamid's living adult descendants, sometimes referred to as Nas Hamid ("the Hamid people") are more numerous than could be fitted into his house, and most of them have moved elsewhere in Sefrou or to other towns. Hamid today comprises thirty-six adults, of whom twelve have remained in the old house (Figure 2). The people of Dar Hamid form the center of our descriptive example. They are deeply conservative persons and their living arrangements are, like their houses, very old-fashioned.

The house is large and rather run-down, but its spaciousness conveys a kind of dignity. It has three floors, with a great square court, open to the sky, down their center, lined by about fourteen rooms. There is a similar, but smaller, building immediately adjacent, which

320

forms an annex and contains about six more rooms and a central *The meanings of* court. That this side building is only an annex is clear from the fact *family ties* that it is entered by a door in the wall of the larger house, not directly from the street.

Most of the life of the house is carried on in the courtyards and their adjacent rooms. There is also a basement level below, with access to an ancient underground water conduit used for toilet facilities. Today, drinking water is piped in from the springs above Sefrou, but in the past it was necessary to go out to the street fountain for water. Many houses in Sefrou's old city are still today without internal toilet facilities or drinking water, and those who live in them must use the public lavatories, the municipal fountains, and the river. The rooftop is an important additional living space where the women and the children of the house relax, where meats, wool, and laundry are dried, and where cages of pigeons and rabbits are sometimes kept. Opening into the outer wall of the building, onto the alley, is a stable where a donkey and two mules are kept.

The main part of the Dar Hamid has three large rooms on the ground floor around the inner court and five or six on the floor above, connected by a balcony running around the four sides. The rooms on the third floor are unused, for their roofs are falling in and it has been a long time since they were repaired. Each of these rooms is long and narrow, with a wooden door that can be shut and barred in the center of the long wall. If the door is left open, as is usually the case, a curtain conceals the interior. In many other houses of this style in contemporary Sefrou such side rooms are used as separate apartments for families of highly heterogeneous origins, with the central court becoming a neutral, often empty, public area. But for Dar Hamid, the court and its activities stand for the unity of the entire house because all the inhabitants are linked in one way or another. In the past, some of the members of this house were not kinsmen, but they were servants, clients, or dependents of the dominant man or men of the house.

Two of the largest rooms on the ground floor are more ornately decorated. The doorway of one is strung with varicolored electric lights, like Christmas decorations, and the room is furnished with velvet-covered divans and bolsters, a large portrait of the king on the wall, and a picture of a young man of the family on another. These are the rooms used for entertaining important guests, for the long dinners and ceremonial serving of tea that are demanded by the Moroccan code of hospitality. Larger festivals, with musicians and dancing, overflow into the central court itself. At other times, when no strangers are present, the court becomes a place for the women and children, 321 for husking and grinding corn, for carding and spinning wool. There, on the great holy day, ʿid l-Kebir, the ceremonial sacrifice of several sheep or goats, one in the name of each married woman of the house, is performed.

Every room in such a house can be separately owned, inherited, even rented or sold. Given the fragmenting character of Islamic inheritance laws, by which every immediate heir is given a specified fraction of the estate, these large houses commonly have many owners who are related to one another in complex ways, each with a deed to a particular part of the building. The law also provides that a kinsman has the right to rent or buy a piece of family property before it is given to an outsider, thus permitting the members of the family to keep the house to themselves if they desire.

Generally, the rooms in dwelling houses are given in inheritance settlements to the male heirs, with the women being granted their shares of the estate in some other form. A woman, at marriage, usually leaves her father's home to go to that of her husband. The result is that each woman lives in a room owned by a man, usually her husband or one of his kin, though sometimes her father or other paternal kind. To balance this, the contents of the room – the divans, bolsters, blankets, dishes, cooking equipment, and the like – are the property of the woman. At marriage, the groom's payment to the bride's father (the *ṣdāq,* pl. *ṣdāqāt,* on which more below) is used to buy domestic equipment that remains the property of the woman the rest of her life, whether she stays married or not. Should she divorce and not remarry, she could return to the house of her father or brothers, bringing her furnishings with her.[6]

Each of the rooms around the courtyard is thus the domain of a particular woman and of a particular man. The men who own the various rooms in the house, and on whom the women are dependent economically, are usually related patrilaterally.

The house as a whole is termed a *ḍar* (pl. *ḍyūr*), a room in the house, a *bit* (pl. *byut*). The courtyard is *wusṭ ḍ-ḍar* (the center of the house"). Fifty years ago, when most of the inhabitants of Sefrou lived in houses of this type, each house was known by the name of a single man. For instance, there were Dar Mulay Ali, Dar Cheikh Tahar, and Dar l-Haj Ali l-Baghdadi, each named after a person of prominence identified with the house.[7] Normally a house is named after the most prominent or oldest man living in it, but Dar Hamid happens to be referred to by the name of a man long since dead, for reasons that will become clear as the relationships among those who dwell in this par-

ticular house are described.

If there is a single dominant man living in the house, he is referred to as *mūl ḍ-ḍar* (the "owner" or "master" of the house). These terms are in quotation marks, for as translations of the term *mūl* they are rather misleading. Obviously, given the property system described above, no one person is likely to be the sole "owner" of the house. "Master" of the house as a gloss is perhaps least wrong, so long as it is not taken as indicating an institutionalized authority role. The women of the house are conventionally referred to – as a group, never in the singular – as *mwālīn ḍ-ḍar*. Mwalin is the plural of mul. Thus, the women, too, are considered the "masters" of the house.

The important thing to note in all these linguistic forms, such as mul d-dar and mwalin d-dar, is the implicit assumption that the house (the dar) is the most significant unit. In Moroccan eyes, the dar has a social integrity of greater significance than the room (the bit), despite the fact that each room serves as the place of orientation of a woman, her husband, and their children. What this means concerning the social position and functions of what is usually called the conjugal family will be discussed below.

I have spoken in these first few pages of description of four specific residential spaces: the town of Sefrou, the derb of Adlun, the dar of Hamid, and the rooms within Dar Hamid. These spaces are of decreasing inclusiveness, the large areas enclosing the smaller ones. In an apparently parallel way, I have mentioned three specific aggregates of people that appear to be also of decreasing inclusiveness: the Nas Adlun, the Nas Hamid, and the people who live in Dar Hamid, the Nas Dar Hamid.

It is tempting to view these three aggregates as examples of three culturally standard ways of grouping people that are systematically related to one another along a dimension of decreasing inclusiveness, parallel to the arrangements of spaces. This, however, would be a serious mistake. What the basis is of the attribution of proper names to such groups, what ways they form part of the social environment of their members, what other forms of groupings exist, and what the cultural conceptualizations underlying all these phenomena might be will become clear only as I inquire deeper into the life of the Nas Adlun.

Tangled relationships

What are the essential characteristics of life within this crowded quarter and this many-roomed house? Given the architectural forms – the central court and its overlooking rooms, the number and closeness of houses along the alley, the sharing of water sources and bathing

323

facilities – the group of daily interaction can be very large. Relationships among these people who share the domestic aspects of their lives can be extremely intricate.

In the next sections I will describe (1) the tangled network of familial relationships that is created by the successive practice of intermarriage and the continued close residence of family members; (2) the custom of the seclusion of women, its basis in cultural concepts of sexuality and its effect on domestic life; (3) the great amount of moving around from house to house and town to town as people visit one another for extended periods and the degree to which continued and important contact between geographically distant family members strengthens and further complicates the web of personal relationships; (4) how the activities usually associated with the conjugal family are dispersed within a wider network of relatives; and (5) how patron-client clusters crosscut in a significant way all these familial, domestic, residential, and personal networks.

The Nas Adlun, compared with other family groups in Sefrou, more frequently marry among their own group. Their family name is a noble one, their status within the town and region is high, and they are at pains to preserve their unity vis-à-vis the rest of their society. Repeated marriages among kinsmen over generations have produced a complexly interwoven net of multiple consanguineal ties.

Many other Sefrou family groups, however, do not value intermarriage to this degree, and some, in fact, have consciously pursued a policy of bringing in wives for their sons from outside sources and attaching their daughters to nonrelated families. In consequence, their domestic networks are extensive and widespread rather than intensive and reticulate. In fact, even within the Nas Adlun as a whole, there can be found certain subgroups who have followed such an out-marrying policy. For example, one highly educated Adlun judge made sure his sons received French educations and sent them into the civil service with positions scattered over the towns of Morocco, and married off his daughters to men of similar social status: the next generation's marriages followed again the same pattern, even further stretching out the range of connections. A statistical comparison of marriage practices of the Nas Adlun as a whole and of its subsections with several other similarly large families in the Sefrou area is given in Annex B. For the moment, however, I want to describe the effects on a family network of a steadily followed pattern of endogamous marital choices. The very consistency of development of this pattern among the Nas Adlun presents a clearer picture of certain characteristics that remain only potentials in other Moroccan families.

324

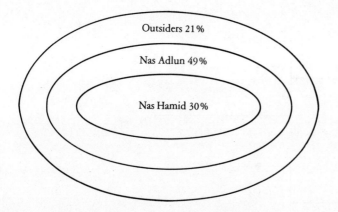

Figure 3. Marital concentration of descendants of Mulay Hamid: origins of women
who married men of Nas Hamid. N = 33 marriages.

Islamic law prohibits marriage with a specified list of close kin.[8]
Polygamy is permitted. Divorce and remarriage are relatively simple.[9]
It has often been stated in the anthropological literature that in
Arabic-speaking or Islamic societies, there is an institutionalized preference for marriage with the father's brother's daughter.[10] I found no
unanimity among Moroccans about this "rule." Although some felt
that any marriage between cousins, and especially between those who
are the offspring of two brothers, was a wise practice (provided the
two sets of parents were on good terms), others expressed the opinion
that such a marriage was just asking for trouble. The reasons given, on
either side, were pragmatic rather than normative.

Within Dar Hamid alone, among its twelve adult members there
have been two marriages between the children of two brothers, and
two other marriages between the grandchildren of two brothers.
Among the Nas Hamid as a whole, out of thirty-three marriages four
(12 percent) were with the father's brother's daughter. But when the
marriages of the entire Nas Adlun are examined, the proportion of
father's brother's daughter marriages reaches only 9 percent.[11]

To center attention on this particular form of cousin marriage de-
tracts from the much more important and pervasive pattern: marriage
between close kinsmen of any sort. Of the thirty-three marriages entered by the men of Nas Hamid over the last three generations, nearly
one-third were with women of Nas Hamid, an additional half were
with women from other branches of the Nas Adlun, leaving only
about one-fifth of the women coming into the group from outside
families. Of these, several were already related to their husbands
through maternal connections (Figure 3).

325

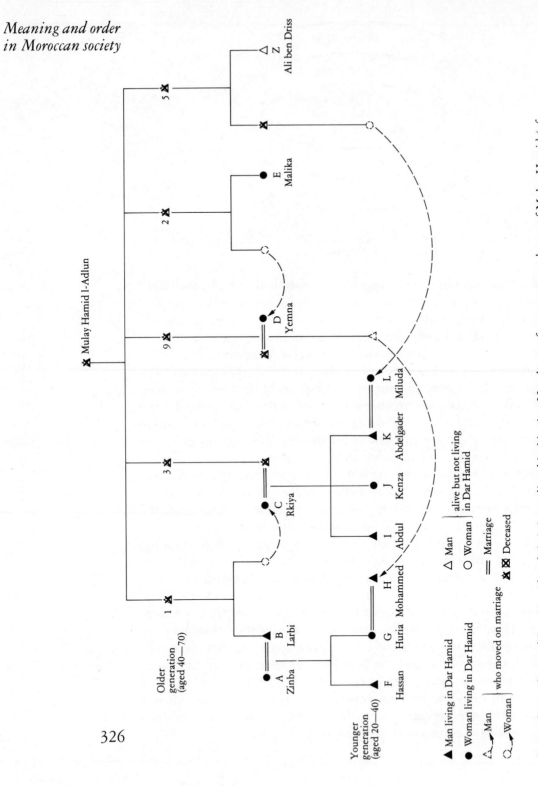

Figure 4. Residents of Dar Hamid and their immediate kinship ties. Numbers refer to purported sons of Mulay Hamid (of which there were nine or ten) who have living descendants. The man labeled Z is Mulay Ali ben Driss, who is not a resident of Dar Hamid; his relationship to others on the chart is described later.

What this means in terms of actual people's lives requires a specific The meanings of illustration from the people of Dar Hamid. Figure 4 is an attempt to family ties depict the kinship web that binds together the twelve adults of Dar Hamid. Despite its apparent complexity, the chart has been drastically simplified by including only those persons needed to demonstrate the main links among those actually living in the house and by omitting many siblings, former spouses, and grown children.

All but one of the people living in Dar Hamid are descended from the same man. The one "outsider," Lalla Zinba (A), came from another branch of the Nas Adlun, one that has numerous marital ties with Nas Hamid. She was born in and grew up in Derb Adlun, and her husband is her mother's brother's son.

Inspection of Figure 4 shows that the Dar Hamid group consists of two generations. The older generation contains one man, Mulay Larbi (B), together with his wife, Lalla Zinba (A), and three old women. Mulay Larbi is about sixty, a fairly well-to-do farmer. Then there is Mulay Larbi's aged and widowed sister, Lalla Rkiya (C), who had been married to her father's brother's son. Finally in the older generation, the two other old women are sisters, Lalla Yemna (D) and Lalla Malika (E). The first had been married to her father's brother's son, who is deceased. The second is the Moroccan equivalent of a spinster, a woman who had been married briefly as a young girl (also to a paternal cousin living in Dar Hamid now deceased) but was divorced within a year and never remarried. With the exception of the outsider, Lalla Zinba, all the members of both generations grew up in this very house.

The younger generation of Dar Hamid is made up of two married couples and three single adults. One of these latter, Mulay Hassan (F), is a young man who has not yet married. The other two, Mulay Abdul (I) and Lalla Kenza (J), had tried marriage several times with people from other Adlun families, divorced, and now live with their mother, Lalla Rkiya (C), and brother, Mulay Abdelkader (K), who is married to Lalla Mulida (L), his grandfather's brother's granddaughter. The other married couple is Lalla Huria (G) and Sidi Mohammed (H), who are also paternal cousins.

This is a ramifying thicket of ties in which no one person is linked to anyone else in a simple, one-dimensional way. But even as presented here, the relationships are already misleadingly oversimplified. By stripping it down to the web of connections existing within the house group, we lose sight of the equally important tangle of connections extending to people outside the house, who in turn are linked back in multiple ways to other house members. Figure 5 is another 327

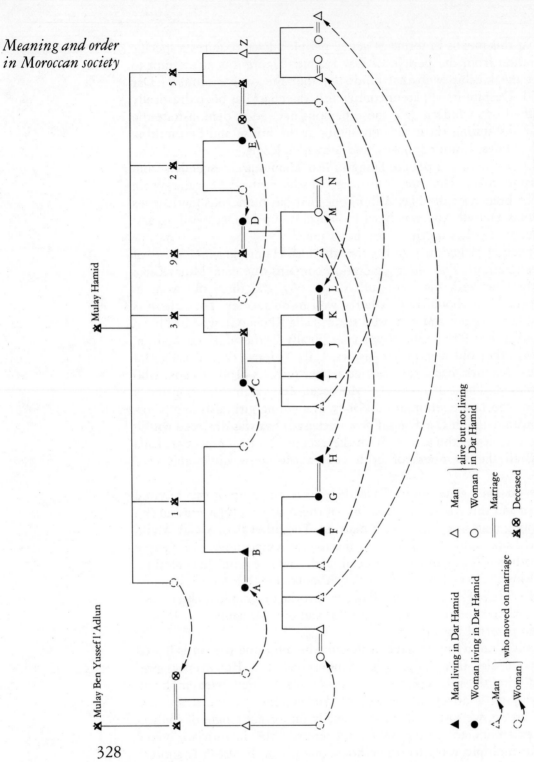

Figure 5. Residents of Dar Hamid: additional kinship connections. This is only a partial account of the kinship ties of the people of Dar Hamid. Note that of the eleven marriages shown, two are with a mother's brother's daughter and one with a father's sister's daughter.

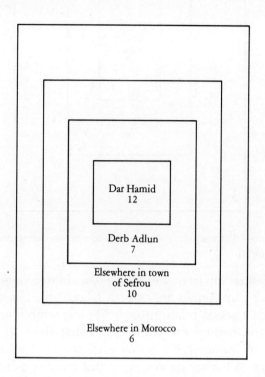

Figure 6. Residential distribution of Nas Hamid adults. N = 35.

attempt to graph these relationships through marriage and genealogy via outsiders, another try at illustrating visually the intricacies of involvement these people have with one another.

The density of the broader networks within which the lives of the people of the house are embedded may be further suggested by analyzing the residence patterns of the Nas Adlun as a whole. Figure 6 indicates where the present-day living members of the Nas Hamid reside; according to whether they live in Dar Hamid, Derb Adlun, elsewhere in the town of Sefrou, or in other parts of Morocco. More than half of the living descendants of Mulay Hamid live within Derb Adlun.

Figure 7 considers the Nas Adlun as a whole according to their residential distribution and shows how the members of Dar Hamid are surrounded by genealogically more distant kinsmen. Within Derb Adlun alone, including those who dwell in Dar Hamid, there live thirty-six related adults who are all closely bound together, much more tightly than the descent lines alone would show, through repeated intermarriage.

329

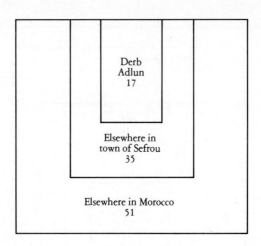

Figure 7. Residential distribution of Nas Adlun adults (excluding those of Nas Hamid). N = 103.

These residential, marital, and genealogical interconnections among the members of Dar Hamid are externally available clues to the nature of these people's social relationships. They resemble ecological characteristics of the natural environment in that although they may be consequences of innumerable social acts, they are also the determinants of others. Whether or not these ties are given cultural recognition, they constitute some of the fundamental parameters of life for these people.

Nonetheless, it should be recognized that such charts and calculations to which we anthropologists cling mainly because we know how to make them, may not provide an adequate and complete picture of our subjects' life situations as actually experienced. Significant linkages may be formed on other foundations, linkages that themselves generate ramifying connections among a number of people. An earlier marriage that ended in divorce, for instance may have left behind enduring ties and cleavages that cannot show up on a chart that stresses stable marriages. A period of common residence in the past, a time of temporary or long-term fosterage, involves more people than those immediately concerned and, like a dissolved marriage, may leave behind a fairly firm structure of personal links. These are just as real as those I have charted, but they escape the crude techniques.

Women's worlds and men's escapes

This tangled social world of home and neighborhood, the dar and the derb, is above all a women's world. The men who live there in among

330

their women come and go with circumspection: the women are at ease. This is a direct result of the Muslim custom of concealment of the family's women from the sight of "outside" men. This custom is perceived by westerners as one that limits the freedom of women, but the equally important converse fact is often overlooked: Men's lives are also sharply circumscribed by these rules. Although women cannot come and go easily in public places, or engage comfortably in public activities, they can do so within their own homes and neighborhoods. They may relate freely to any of their female companions, and because the intricacies of personal relations are constantly being discussed among them, most women have a detailed knowledge of everything that is going on. Men, on the other hand, find the domestic sphere a complexly structured place where many of their actions are limited by rules of avoidance and by their lack of sufficient information about current situations.

The seclusion of the family's women is a moral imperative taken seriously by people in all segments of Moroccan society, but in a variety of ways. The Adlun women follow the traditional urban conventions in a more developed form than many other Sefrouis, and certainly much more than rural women. A woman never appears outside the house unless she is veiled and wearing the cloaklike jellaba: if she ventures out of the neighborhood she is usually accompanied by a man of the family or at least by a group of women. Few, if any, Adlun women do the daily marketing. There are significant variations in these practices among the branches of the Adlun family. Those of highest status, notably the three polygamous wives of the wealthy Mulay Ali ben Driss, leave their homes no more than several times a year, aside from trips to the public bath, which is only a short distance away.

Some of the other urban women of Sefrou are as strict in their observance of the seclusion customs, but many are not. None, however, appears in public, as do the younger women of Rabat and Fez, in Western dress and unveiled. A few schoolgirls adopt this modern manner, but at marriage take on the jellaba and veil. Sefrou is a very small town and its manners are provincial in this regard. Rural women, especially Berber speakers, do not wear veils or jellabas, but they always have shawls on their heads. They have somewhat greater freedom of movement than their urban counterparts, but still remain at home most of the time.

These variations (which are such not only in practice, but also in the interpretations of the norms) are an important characteristic of the whole seclusion pattern in Morocco. The existence of a graded range of variation (from what kind of veil is worn, how it is worn, who must wear it and when, to which girls may go to school and for how long, and whether or not they may take a job) converts the custom into a language for assertion of social identity and status.

The inner meaning of the custom, however, and the source of emotional force behind it lie in Moroccan conceptions of sexuality and concern for containing its force within tightly limited bounds. A large part of the Islamic moral-legal code, the Shari'a, can be seen as a set of protective regulations aiming to preserve the stability of marital relationships and to protect the weakest members of families – the children and the older women – from neglect resulting from broken marriage, whether by death or divorce. The greatest threat to the stability of marital relationships is seen to be the sexual attraction, whose explosive potential is said to be present in any contact between any man and any woman. Women are cosidered to be as sexually assertive as, if not more so than, men, and in the eyes of the men at any rate, women's impulses are thought not to be tempered by a reasonable sense for social realities. Sexuality is considered to be a natural, God-given drive. It is not felt to be matter for inner control, but rather for exterior regulation, mainly on the part of the social community, but with the aid of the sanction of fear of the judgment of Allah and eternal damnation to hell.[12]

Given this conception of the sensual and passionate nature of human beings, and the need for social constraints on them, the cloistering of women and their veiling and chaperoning makes sense. The ramifying effects are considerable. Relationships between men and women, with certain crucial exceptions discussed below, are sharply restricted, both in their content and in their intensity. Even long-married couples spend little time together, seem to have limited areas of common interest and small capacity for enjoying one another's company. For most Moroccans, relaxed, intimate, and satisfying personal relationships appear possible only with persons of the same sex. For a woman, given the structure of the family, this means her mother, sisters, cousins, aunts, and the women of her husband's family. A man's closest friendships appear to be not with his father, brothers, or cousins, but with peers outside the immediate family.

The important exceptions to this pattern are the close, trusting relationships sometimes found between mother and son and occasionally between brother and sister or between aunt and nephew. Among the Nas Hamid, there were a number of such comfortable cross-sex pairs, the young men of the family who often sat around bantering with mother or aunt or sister, and turned to these women in times of trouble.

A boy spends the first four or five years of his life exclusively within this lively and meddlesome women's world. He is at home there, but only some of this original ease remains with him as an adult. An adolescent boy is permitted to attend the women's parties in his own home, parties at which the women sing erotic songs and dance explicitly sexual dances before one another. Most boys are adept at performing these sensual feminine dances and join in with great pleasure. At maturity, and especially after he has brought a wife into the family, a man becomes much more circumspect toward all the women of his family. Fathers and sons often are very formal with one another, even to the point of avoidance. The explanation given me was that the son feels a great deal of embarrassment toward his father in regard to sex matters, which are epitomized in the person of his wife. Older men of the family keep themselves aloof from nearly everyone, often sleeping and eating by themselves. Not so long ago, perhaps only twenty years ago, the men of the Adlun family always ate separately from the women, but this custom has been gradually changing.

From the time a boy is six years of age or so, he leads a life out in the streets that is quite independent of his family. The men and the boys enter the home mainly to eat and sleep, and spend their waking hours with their friends in school, coffee shops, workplaces, the market, the mosque, and the street. Sefrou has a lively prostitution quarter, located today in the old Jewish mellah, and it appears that for men this institution plays a significant compensating role for the frustration of family life.

Within the women's world of house and neighborhood, this intermeshed network of relationships, where one's cousin is also one's brother-in-law, one's ex-husband has married a woman next door, one's uncle is one's father-in-law, one's husband is a former playmate, and one's child seemingly is shared by everyone, there is little personal privacy. Everyone is well known to everyone else. Few of one's activities and feelings can be kept secret. There is a constant conversation going on among the women, a continual probing into and commenting on everyone's affairs. The comment is in turn good-natured, hostile, sympathetic, irritable, ironic,and frank – but it is always forthcoming. Once a week the women go to the public bath, a large steamy hall where they sit around for hours in seminudity with their children, other relatives, and neighbors, talking and laughing, scrubbing and sweating. The give-and-take of mutual review and appraisal continues at all times, sometimes desultory and trivial, sometimes intense and agonistic, often touching on their men's lives as well as their own.

The way domestic work is organized, the taking or giving up of a new job, movements to other localities, purchases of any sort, selection of a new daughter-in-law – all these matters come under open discussion. No conflicts or differences among the members of the house are permitted to fester unnoticed or to fade away unremarked, but instead are forced out into the open. A serious quarrel, for instance between sisters-in-law or between husband and wife, is allowed – or, more exactly, is encouraged – to erupt into public view, public at least in terms of the family, but it may also overflow into the street, with the neighbors and other kinsmen serving as judges, arbitrators, and allies.

Decisions and choices, the acts whereby social roles are given their sharpest expression and definition, are, in these circumstances, products of multiple social appraisals and pressures, rather than individual. This is not to suggest that individuals have no impact on this process. On the contrary, a strong personality has an enormous influence on the course of events within such a system. Nor is it to suggest that for Moroccans the regulation of behavior is entirely a matter of open argument and explicit social pressure. But the nature of social relationships within the Moroccan family, within any aspect of Moroccan life, cannot be understood without adequate accounting for the role of publicity. Efforts to conceal one's actions, motives, and plans take on heightened meaning in circumstances where privacy is not automatically granted.

Long-distance relations

Another important characteristic of the family life of the Nas Adlun is that, despite the fact that members of the family are scattered not only over the town of Sefrou, but over the whole of Morocco (and a few younger members are even in Europe), these people are not forgotten or truly isolated. There is always a great deal of traveling about and visiting one another, over long distances as well as short.

Men are more mobile than women and move more frequently as individuals than women do, but their patterns of travel are to a striking degree determined by the location of family connections, for wherever they go they try to stay with people they consider related to them. A trading trip can be seen from this point of view as a string of family visits. Women do not engage in trade, yet they visit one another frequently, traveling even to other towns, in the course of various familial festivities and emergencies, bringing their children with them.

334   I have no systematic data on this travel pattern or its variation

among differing socioeconomic groups. My impression, however, is that the general visiting pattern is the same for most Moroccans even though there are differences in the reasons for the physical dispersal of families as well as in the distances involved, the nature of the occasions for reunion, the length of stay, and the intervals between visits. The members of Dar Hamid had family members living in Casablanca, Meknes, and Oujda, among other places, largely because several of their men were teachers and civil servants who were frequently relocated. They all considered Sefrou their home, and they often visited and were visited by one another.

Other families, more involved in commerce, have different patterns of going apart and coming together, determined by the form of their markets. Rural people are no less active and no less dispersed than urban people, for most of them have relatives working in all the major cities as well as in Sefrou. I should stress that what I am describing is not a modern version of nomadism with entire familial groups on the move, but rather a custom of intermittent visiting over geographically dispersed networks.

The effects this pattern of visiting has on the nature of Moroccan familial relationships are complex. The most important is the reinforcement of the more distant ties, the strengthening of closer ones, and above all the amplification of public comment on these ties. Discussion of personal affairs continues uninterrupted by spatial scatter. Relationships are not permitted to weaken through disuse, as more distant outposts are continually drawn back into the effective web of obligations, expectations, aid, and criticism. Much of this activity is given form through the processes involved in the arranging and celebrating of marriages, which both create new ties and exercise old ones.

Groups within the network

These customs involving personal movement do not only facilitate the tightening of social connections; they also permit the breaking of ties. Careful study of the familial networks with which I am acquainted showed that some individuals and some subgroups in each family had all but vanished, socially speaking. Nearly everyone turned out to have a cousin or an uncle apparently living alone in Casablanca or elsewhere. If relationships within a familial web become too demanding, too confining, a man can always go elsewhere, and many do, at least for short periods in their lives. Although a few live alone, most of these people either live near other kin or frequently visit and are visited by their family.[13]

The conjugal family

I have stressed both the spread and the tightness of Moroccan familial networks, the intricate extension and interlacing of personal ties through repeated intermarriage, residential proximity, and continual visiting. I have suggested that the house – the dar with its central courtyard – is an important orienting space that singles out its inhabitants as a smaller portion of a larger network identified as members of that particular house. But although "the house" as a social group has considerable substance, both in the Moroccan view of it and in terms of the organization of activities, it has no corporate character and cannot act as a social entity. Are there any institutionalized smaller or larger familial groupings that do have such recognized social unity?

In particular, it is important to examine the conjugal family – the unit of a married couple and their children. What meaningful salience does this set of people have in Moroccan eyes? Does it form an important culturally recognized group in Moroccan theory and practice?

I start with the inhabitants of a "room" (*bit*) in a house. Each room in a house is, as I have said, usually felt to be the domain of a particular woman and a particular man, because she owns the furnishings and domestic utensils and he owns the room. The association of persons with rooms is by no means simple, however. Two women, sisters for instance, may share a single room, or one woman may be identified with several rooms. A woman can also own the room she lives in. And a wealthy man may have an extra room used only for entertaining his men friends. However, the general pattern remains: A room is the domain of a woman, her children, and a man.

But the arrangements for using these rooms, how they are actually lived in, have no prescribed forms. If the patterns of living in particular cases are closely studied, it can be seen that financial responsibility, domestic tasks, commensality, and day-to-day sociability are not always distributed in the same ways. A set of people who pool their food budget and who eat together regularly is referred to as being "of one table" (*mida waheda*), and this is probably the most stable way of identifying a Moroccan "household." But eating patterns are by no means congruent with their activity patterns. There is no feeling that a married couple and their immature children should be together always for sleeping, eating, and recreation. Children are moved from relative to relative for periods of long or short duration, according to necessity, convenience, or affection. Boys, especially, often sleep or eat with nearby kinsmen.

336   Some further material from Dar Hamid may help to clarify the

nature of these arrangements. Look again at Figure 4 showing the genealogical and marital connections among the adult residents of the house. There are two married couples who live more or less together in the smaller wing of the building. These are the old man and his wife, Mulay Larbi (B) and Lalla Zinba (A), and their daughter, Lilla Huria (G), and her husband Sidi Mohammed (H). The daughter spends most of her daytime hours with her mother, and they share cooking and laundry chores. The older woman helps care for the four young children and usually sleeps with them. However, the younger couple, Lalla Huria and Sidi Mohammed, do not wholly confine their life to that wing of Dar Hamid, for the husband owns two rooms in the main building, which he inherited from his deceased father, where all his wife's domestic furnishings (the bedding, dishes, etc. that she received at the wedding) are kept. They entertain there on formal occasions, and their guests sleep there. Sidi Mohammed was born and raised in these rooms. His mother, Lalla Yemna (D), lives in a room upstairs. If virilocality were a rigidly applied rule, the young couple would have been living in these rooms of Sidi Mohammed's and his mother would have been a part of the household and in a position of authority over Lalla Huria. But this was not the case, for Lalla Huria and her mother-in-law cannot get along and by mutual consent keep out of each other's way.

Another example of the disjunction of eating from other living arrangements, this one spilling over to people who actually live out-side the house, is provided by Lalla Yemna (D). She has, in addition to her son, Sidi Mohammed, an adult daughter who lives with her husband and children in rented rooms several doors away. This family (M and N on Figure 5) spends all its waking hours in Dar Hamid with the old woman, Lalla Yemna, cooking and eating with her but going back to the other place to sleep. The husband (N) is the oldest son of Mulay Larbi (B) and works as a sharecropper on his father's land.

Another kind of arrangement is illustrated by the set of people labeled on Figures 4 and 5 as C, I, J, K, and L. Poverty-stricken, unemployed, and some of them ill, they are all dependent on their wealthy cousin, Mulay Ali ben Driss (Z). They sleep and spend much of their time in Dar Hamid, where they own two rooms, but they eat many of their meals at Mulay Ali's house, where they all perform a variety of domestic chores for him and his wives.

These living patterns, in which various kinds of cooperation and sharing are spread among diversely composed sets of people, rather than focused in on a single multifunctional "family" unit, conjugal or otherwise, are made possible by the residential clustering of large numbers of relatives, closely packed within the great house and the urban neighborhood. The cultural conception that illuminates these patterns is one that sees familial relationships not in terms of the conjugal family as their basic and autonomous unit, but rather in terms of unbounded and interwined networks of kinsmen, affines, and even neighbors.[14]

The Nas Adlun have unusually large and tightly knit domestic networks. Many Moroccan families, of course, do not have so many members, and some people find themelves in rather isolated social situations, either as individuals or as conjugal families. Usually other relationships of neighborhood and patronage are developed to take the place of the missing ties of kinship. In other cases, antagonisms or a refusal of reciprocity among certain kin, especially between siblings or a father and son, result in mutual alienation, with consequent social isolation. A person without a strong network of family, neighbors, or patronage is at a considerable political and social disadvantage. A girl without such support (e.g., if she marries into a cohesive family or, as the wife of a civil servant, is required to live in a city distant from her home) can be extremely lonely and vulnerable.[15] Such separation and personal powerlessness are all the more difficult to bear because they are interpreted by everyone in terms of a cultural counterimage of the normal familial situation – an image that is both valued and a part of most people's early experience – of intricate and manifold ties and frequent interaction and of the agonistic pressing of personal interests within a large group. A somewhat similar situation surrounds a man who breaks the usual pattern and marries uxorilocally. The motives for such a marriage, normally, are the groom's poverty and the need of the father-in-law for extra labor power in farmwork or shop in the absence of sons of his own. In rural areas in particular, a man who consents to such a marriage is pitied and considered barely adult, for he has relinquished the basis of his own autonomy, authority, and influence within his domestic group. As with a girl who marries into a different family, if a man has behind him a strong network of relatives his position vis-à-vis his in-laws is strengthened. Similarly, he or she can, over some years, gradually build up a new constellation of allies within the domestic circles of house and neighborhood.

Patronage clusters

The organization of domestic life is to some extent determined by the manner in which family income is produced and distributed. Men own

most of the property, have the wage-earning skills and the opportunities to use them, and make most of the purchases for the family. Their wives and children, even their adult sons and daughters, if they have no external source of income, must bend to the authority that comes from control of the purse strings. But not all men are equally well-off, and this fact has direct effects on the internal structure of the networks of relationships described so far.

Most of the older generation of the Nas Adlun are farmers, as were their fathers before them. They own plots of irrigated garden land immediately outside the town or wheat land on the plains toward Fez, keep their donkeys and mules in stables in Sefrou, and go out each day to farm. As long as they are alive, this land is theirs alone, and their sons, as in one example above, must be sharecroppers to their fathers or seek other employment. Most of the younger generation of the Nas Adlun have done the latter, in part because with one exception most of the Adluns do not have sufficient land to support all their sons and their families. Some of the men of the younger generation have had a modern education, have gone through elementary school or even through secondary school to the equivalent of about the eighth grade, and have become minor office workers or teachers. None in either generation are merchants or craftsmen.

Taking the Nas Adlun as a whole, the variation in economic worth is extraordinary, ranging from great wealth to grinding poverty. A very crude survey of the sixty-one living men of Nas Adlun showed that one was wealthy, nine were well-off, twenty-eight were of average income, and twenty-three were very poor or even with no means of support.[16] A similar spread was found among the twenty men of Nas Hamid.

This striking heterogeneity of social status was found among members of nearly every particular family studied, whether small domestic group or large dispersed network. People of quite disparate incomes and occupations are found living under the same roof. An unemployed man can be seen waiting on the table of his rich brother. When distant kinsmen are gathered together, at a wedding, for instance, the variety of clothes worn–from expensive imported suits to ragged jellabas–is always striking. Whether one examines the composition of a large, far-flung group whose members bear the same patronym, or a small houseful of close relatives, the same heterogeneity is likely to be present, and it must be considered an important characteristic of Moroccan family life.

One reason for this heterogeneity is that economic and political achievement in Morocco is almost entirely an individual matter. An ambitious man may use the help of kinsmen in his climb, and in return may help them, but these exchanges are personally arranged and by no means obligatory. In addition, at a man's death his property is divided among a large number of kin, and his social reputation does not automatically transfer to his heirs. Another reason for status heterogeneity within family groups is that, by and large, kinsmen are not disregarded or neglected after poverty or disabling sickness hits them, but remain active members of the family. There seems to be little feeling that the economic status of one's family defines one's own social place in the outer world, or that the presence of poorer family members within the home or at public gatherings might somehow be embarrassing or degrading. In fact, a powerful and wealthy man often welcomes the dependent presence of poorer kinsmen, who then take the role of retainer, running errands, overseeing the affairs of their patron, helping to serve food at feasts, and the like.

These features – the specificity of status attribution to individuals and the range of variation in status that is found within any familial group – have important effects on the structure of relationships within the family. Any prominent or powerful person exerts an influence on familial affairs that cuts across the effect of other principles of association or obligation such as residence, generation, or even filiation.

Dar Hamid provides yet another illuminating example. The five adult men who live in Dar Hamid have quite different economic statuses, with incomes ranging from substantial to nothing, and occupations from farmer to civil servant to unemployed mason. Although the oldest man among them, Mulay Larbi, has the highest income and the greatest amount of status within the house, his authority – even over his own sons – is clearly undermined by that of a man who does not even live within the house, his cousin Mulay Ali ben Driss. The latter's home is several doors away, from the outside indistinguishable from Dar Hamid but inside a much more spacious and elegant residence equipped with many modern conveniences. Despite the fact that he rarely enters Dar Hamid, its inhabitants are dominated by his invisible presence.

The oldest man in Dar Hamid, Mulay Larbi, is a quiet and unassuming farmer who has always worked himself on some of his land and supervised the work of sharecroppers on the rest. Of his four sons, three live in other houses within Derb Adlun. The eldest, mentioned above, works on some of his father's fields. The next, also renting a room within the quarter, runs a gas station, the franchise for which was obtained through the influence of Mulay Ali. The third son is a civil servant who married one of Mulay Ali's daughters and lives in his father-in-law's house. He obtained his job through the efforts of Mu-

340

lay Ali. The fourth son, the only one still living at home, is unmarried, a teacher. Besides the married daughter described above who still lives at home, Mulay Larbi has two other daughters, both of whom have married civil servants and live in other cities.

The two other adult men in Dar Hamid are extremely poor. Neither has had a steady job for a long time and neither owns any land. They live together with three women closely related to them and several children. This group (on Figures 4 and 5 they are C, I, J, K, and L) is entirely dependent on Mulay Ali. He provides their food and clothing, and they are his servants, waiting on his table, helping with his marketing and laundry, taking care of his children. The oldest of this sibling group, however, has done much better. He has married one of Mulay Ali's daughters, lives in a fine house provided by his father-in-law, and is the manager of Mulay Ali's olive-oil mill.

Nearly every member of Nas Adlun is a client of Mulay Ali in one way or another. Within Dar Hamid there is no one who has not at one time or another been obliged to beg a favor of him, no one who is not in some way beholden to him. In countless small and large ways his net of transactions, debts, and obligations covers the entire house.

In consequence he is the de facto head of the house of Hamid. His authority binds together the people in it, even though he is not a resident. Seen from the vantage point of Mulay Ali, the house itself is not a unit but merely a shelter for part of his network of client-kinsmen that extends throughout the town. Even in the view of outsiders of Sefrou, this group of people is often perceived and called not Nas Hamid, but Nas Mulay Ali ben Driss.

Patronyms in action

Nas Adlun, Nas Hamid, and *Nas Mulay Ali ben Driss* are names that identify distinguishable sets of actual people in Sefrou. What are the criteria, explicit and implicit, by which Moroccans see these sets of people as distinct from other sets? Do the three names stand for three different kinds of Moroccan groupings?

The Nas Adlun is broader than the Nas Hamid, which is to say that the latter persons can and do carry both names. For both the Nas Adlun and the Nas Hamid the name is thought to be that of an ancestor, but in the first case he is very far removed in time, and in the second he is (or is thought to be) a fairly recent progenitor of the living group. In the third example, Nas Mulay Ali ben Driss, the name stands for the living central person, and its members are kinsmen and clients.

What is similar in all three cases is that a proper name is trans- 341 formed into a classificatory device, and as such it becomes an indication that the person who carries the name may belong within the classification. To the extent that these classifications are also social groups, the use of the name indicates group membership.

Adlun and *Hamid* are patronyms. That is, a person may be called Adlun if his or her father was an Adlun. In certain cases, a person may be called an Adlun or a Hamid if he has been closely associated with the group over a long period of time, as in the case of clientship or marrying into the family. Are these latter kinds of relationships conceived of as exceptions to a patrifiliative rule? Are the resultant groupings thought of by Moroccans as patrilineal descent groups? Is there a cultural concept of patrilineage as defining the boundaries of a group and its internal structure? Are these groups patrilineal descent groups in effect, regardless of the native concepts of them?

I will first take up the conventions of naming in order to clarify what is meant by a patronym and introduce the concepts of patrifiliative name chain and patronymic association. Following that I will describe the ways in which Moroccans talk about patronymic associations and the ways in which they view their internal differentiation, and put forth a third concept—the name cluster. Then I will describe the various ways in which the field of familial relationships is culturally mapped from the point of view of a central ego.

Every Moroccan has a number of names, and he is called different ones by different people in different contexts. These come to him at different points in his life, often in accidental and informal ways. He has a personal name given him soon after birth, such as Mohammed or Ali, Fatima or Khadija. These personal names are, at least among old-fashioned people, drawn from a sharply limited list of the names of the Islamic heroes and saints. Because there are very few of these names, they do not differentiate very well (in one list, out of 982 men, 156 were called Mohammed). These names are always used within the family and among close friends. In a face-to-face group the duplication presents no problem, for the context usually indicates which Mohammed is referred to. But as soon as the setting enlarges, some other name must be added to avoid ambiguity.

This can be a nickname. These, in contrast to the personal names, are highly idiosyncratic. They usually refer to some peculiar personal characteristic, such as a limp, skin color, a habit of speech, or a particular enthusiasm. They are often acquired in early childhood, and some are baby names. Related to nicknames are two other sorts of names: those derived from occupations and those indicating locality of origin. The latter always refer to some place other than the present

342

locality, and either the person named or one of his forebears is considered to have come from there.

But the personal name, the nickname, the occupational term, and the
origin locality tag do not identify a person as relating to certain other
persons. This is the effect of two naming conventions: patrifiliative
name chains and the names connected with patronymic associations.

By *patrifiliative name chain* I mean the list of names a man can
recite of his father, his father's father, his father's father's father, and
so on. For instance, Ali ben Driss ben Hamid ben Hassan. Each
person knows this name chain for himself going back at least three or
four generations, and some shurfa know it even further. But people
rarely know other persons' name chains past the grandfather link.

By *patronymic association* I mean to indicate the entire aggregation
of persons who can be called by the same patronym, such as the Nas
Adlun and the Nas Hamid. The group may or may not have any other
socially recognized features.[17] Moroccans do not reify or personify
such aggregates as the Nas Adlun and the Nas Hamid. That is, they
do not talk about them as if they were corporate persons with person-
like attributes such as the capacity to will and to act. We too should be
careful not to see patronymic associations in substantive terms. For
the moment we should look at them as aspects of the naming process
and recognize that the making of a bridge to other persons, whether
antecedent or contemporary, by means of a name, can be neither
simple nor unambiguous.

To summarize so far, each person has a set of different names as a
stock on which he and those around him can draw. In addition, new
names can be given him in terms of his current activities and associations. For example, one particular man might be called by any and all
of the following arrangements:

Hassan ben Larbi ben Mohammed	Hassan, son of Larbi, son of Mohammed
Hassan ben Larbi el Adlun	Hassan, son of Larbi of the Adlun family
Hassan ben Larbi el Hamidi	Hassan, son of Larbi of the Hamid family, which is known to be part of the Adluns
Hassan es-Sefroui	Hassan, the man from Sefrou
es-Sefroui	The man from Sefrou

343

Weld Larbi	The son of Larbi
el Hamidi el Gezzar	The Hamid man who is a butcher
Hassan ben Larbi el Gezzar	Hassan, son of Larbi, the butcher
Hassan ben Larbi el ᶜArez	Hassan, son of Larbi, the cripple
Hassan el ᶜAissawi	Hassan, of the Aissawa brotherhood[18]

In addition to the name forms listed above, there are an array of kin terms that can be analogically extended to anyone (brother, paternal uncle, mother, father, and maternal aunt are especially common) and a range of honorific titles (Sidi, Mulay, Mᶜalem, Sherif, to give only a few).

Addressing someone, where there is a broad choice of names, as here, is an act of singling out a context in which to place the person and requires a knowledge of the nature of that context. It is similar to the daily decision Americans have to make about whether to address someone by his first or surname, but in Morocco there are more alternatives, and some of these alternatives are systematically related to one another. Of course, in everyday life the context itself is already clear, and the number of names that could be appropriate has already been limited. Further, most interaction occurs in contexts that have been long established, such as a family, where choices about how to address a certain well-known person have already been made in previous situations.

What is of interest here, however, is not the phenomenon of choice in context, but that some of these names carry information about the social relationships of the person. What or who a person is named *for* (i.e., what his name is the name *of*) besides the person himself can have considerable, though implicit, significance.

For instance, referring to the names of Hassan listed above, to call a man "Sefroui" indicates that he is "not from around here." If the speaker and the named person were both in Sefrou at the time of speaking, the name "Sefroui" would not distinguish Hassan from anyone else around and a more precise name would have to be chosen.

The name "el-Adluni" would distinguish Hassan from all those who do not have that patronym. But if one wanted to be more precise and to indicate *which* Adlun is meant, one could name him "the Butcher

344

Adlun" or "the Sefrou Adlun" or "the Crippled Adlun" *or* one could invoke his immediate patronymic association. In the last case, still in the example above, the speaker might call him "el Hamidi." The hearer already knows Hassan is an Adlun, and now he knows he belongs to the Nas Hamid, who are within the Adlun patronymic category. The Hamid family might be one of various sizes, ranging from a small circle around a man named Hamid (who might be Hassan's father or his father's brother or his father's father – or even his patron or master) to a larger, vaguer segment referring to a now-dead Hamid, who formerly held the group together. The use of the name indicates that, in someone's eyes at any rate, there is a set of people who all have significant relationships with someone named Hamid and that Hassan is or was one of them.

Identification by one's father's name, as in "Hassan, son of Larbi," takes its meaningful place here as location in a context. When the conversation occurs within a localized community whose members are to a large extent kinsmen of one another, to indicate whose son a person is gives immediate information about where he fits socially. If the father is or was a man of substance, the "son of" name also signals that fact of close connection to a man of influence. I had the impression that the "son of" naming style was used most often in the latter case – that is, where the father or grandfather was a man of importance and something significant was conveyed by invoking his name.

A variation of the "son-of-father's-name" style appears occasionally, when a man is known by his mother's name. In one particular case, in the Nas Adlun, a man was known by his mother's region of origin. She came from the Beni Yazghra area, had married into the family polygamously, and had always herself been called, as an outsider, by her locality term "el-Yazghria." Her son was called Mulay Abdul ben Bushta el-Yazghri, to distinguish him from his half siblings, whose mother was an Adlun woman. This name was normally used only within the family, and outside the family he was called "el-Adluni." Another type of case is one in which a boy's father dies when he is an infant and his mother returns to her paternal family and attaches the boy to her patronymic association. In this case, he may retain his mother's name throughout his life, and if he becomes a well-known man, his sons and even his grandsons may retain this female name, along with their others.

Women are given names in a similar, but simpler, manner. In almost all cases I encountered, a woman was called by her personal name with or without one of her father's names (usually his personal name, but sometimes a patronym) or sometimes by her husband's personal name.

Thus a woman might be called Aisha bent Hamid ("Aisha daughter of Hamid") or Aisha Hamidia ("Aisha the [female] Hamid one") or bent Hamid ("Hamid's daughter") or if she had married into another patronymic association, Aisha el-Adlunia. To the best of my knowledge, women are not given nicknames. Nor are they often given names that refer to occupational terms, despite the fact that some do indeed have occupations (midwife, seamstress, bath attendant, wool processing jobber, singer, teacher, wedding specialist). This context of extrafamilial work roles seems to be thought inappropriate or unimportant in determining the identity of particular women. In general, this much more limited range of naming contexts reflects the family-bound character of the women's world. The absence or rarity of nicknaming suggest culturally defined limitation on assertion of individuality.

The patrifiliative name chain can be seen as a pedigree of male ascendants. The Arabic term for this is *ta'assul,* for which the root is *asl* (pl. *usūl*), which has a range of meanings: "root," "trunk of a tree," "origin," "foundation," "noble stock."[19] Like the English word *pedigree,* it is associated in everyday talk with the idea of noble descent, for only those whose ancestry is thought to infuse them with honor or baraka concern themselves with such matters. The sherifs, as descendants of the daughter of the Prophet Mohammed, generally have patronyms that indicate either a prominent saint as an ancestor or the geographical location where their line branched off from a line leading directly to the Prophet, or both.

For such persons, the patronym is a kind of condensed pedigree, a marker indicating a claim to noble descent. Nonsherifs (*ammī,* "commoners") have patronyms too, but the referents of their patronyms are not often clear – the name can indicate a locality of origin, a tribe, a title that some particular ancestor has achieved in his lifetime such as el-haj or sheikh, and even a nickname some ancestor once had. In the case of the Nas Adlun, a patronym indicates possession of a noble pedigree; therefore, it is no accident that there are many Adluns in Sefrou, that this patronym is retained by large numbers of people.

A patronym, even that of Adlun, however, is more than an end point in a pedigree. It is often an index of membership in a group of people who have the same patronym, a group that at the minimum is a classification and at the maximum can be a solidary, structured, and socially recognized organization. This is in both forms the patronymic association. To understand its nature, composition, and effects on personal lives, we need to explore more deeply how the Sefrou people speak about it and how they visualize its internal structure.

346   The difficulty is that there is no specific term in Moroccan Arabic

that clearly and definitely denotes the patronymic association as a noun. In everyday interaction, the normal way of speaking of a particular group or relationship is simply by means of the patronym itself, as in "So-and-So the Adluni" or as in "Nas Adlun."

Generic terms in Sefrou speech that might be translated "patronymic association" can be found, but they are not frequently heard. Some of the terms usually accompanied by a patronym are:

nas	people	Nas Adlun
wlād	sons, children, or descendants	Wulad Adlun
benī	sons, children, or descendants	Beni Adlun
ait	sons, children, or descendants (Berber term, but used by Arabic speakers; not usually employed to speak of families with long urban histories)	Ait Adlun
ᶜā'ila	family	ᶜa'ila Adlun

Reference can also be made to a group by pluralizing the patronym, as in el-Adluniyyin ("the Adluns").

Other terms for the patronymic association that are more abstract and context-free include:

fekẹda	thigh
ferqa (pl. *feraq*)	part or section, team, group
ᶜāreq	root, nerve, tendon
qbila	tribe, local region, to face directly; to accept; to guarantee
ᶜā'ila	family; that which is supported, sustained; domestic group

These last five ways of referring to the patronymic association are used with sliding reference (i.e., the same location can refer sometimes to a broadly inclusive grouping of kinsmen and sometimes to a narrowly defined set of kinsmen related through lines only two or three generations in depth). The context indicates which of these references is meant. For instance, the term fekheda could be applied to both the Nas Adlun and its constituent, the Nas Hamid.

Another way to indicate that several persons belong to the same patronymic association, aside from using the proper name itself, is by means of various phrases that include the term *ᶜamm* ("father's brother"). If you want to refer vaguely to a man as a member of your own patronymic association, you say he is *ᶜammī* ("my father's brother") or *weld ᶜammī* ("the son of my father's brother"). These terms can be taken to refer either to your own literal father's brother and his son or, in a classificatory way, to any collateral male agnate of roughly your father's generation or of your own, or even more inclusively, to anyone bearing your patronym. Although *ᶜamm* is the singular form of the word, it can be used in plural constructions, as in *wlad l-ᶜamm* ("the sons or descendants of fathers' brothers"). This last phrase is the commonest way to refer to a patronymic association as a whole and to the relationship among members of the same patronymic association.

Thus the conventional ways for speaking about the patronymic association, both in the fekheda, ferqa, etc. series of terms and in the uled l-ᶜamm constructions, have an important characteristic: the same term or phrase can be applied both to larger inclusive groupings and to smaller included ones. Only the specific action context of a particular utterance can reveal what the speaker actually means to refer to. This built-in ambiguity makes it possible to speak in identical terms of a range of different actual aggregates of people who may be united by a variety of social ties.

However, despite the facts that patronyms are the markers for the groups and that in many cases patrifiliative name chains or pedigrees are also conceptually involved, it would be a mistake to assume that these native conceptions imply what is usually called an "ideology of patrilinearity." By *patrilineal ideology* I mean a cultural model for group formation that is based on a systematic elaboration of the chain of father-son links into a branching tree form, with group segmentation programmed to occur at each forking point. Such a frame, as given in the anthropological literature, is often seen as a map of social statuses genealogically defined as successive relationships of parentage, siblingship, and marriage, and consequently as a primary mode for anchoring the norms that govern cooperation and opposition among kinsmen. Each fork serves as a unifying rallying point in the model, such that it defines the unity of a whole fan of descendants extending beyond it. Although this can be conceived of as a purely cognitive map, it is usually considered to have normative power generating the rule: "myself against my brother, my brother and I against my cousin, my brother and my cousin and I against the outsider."

My explorations of the ways in which the Nas Adlun view the internal structure of their patronymic association shed some light on this presumed ideology of patrilinearity. On the face of it, the Nas Adlun seemed to be an urban patrilineage, with maximal and minimum segments, genealogically defined. It has corporate attributes that further support such an interpretation. The Nas Adlun own a mosque and they have two special family graveyards. No other single family in Sefrou owns such special spaces. In addition, the Nas Adlun as a

348

group own considerable common farmland, held as a family foundation (*ḥabus kāṣṣ* or *ḥabus dyal l-ᶜā'ila*). This land is annually rented out
to poorer members of the family, who farm it, and the rents are
distributed equally to every man, woman, and child bearing the patronym Adlun. The members have a high sense of their identity as a
group, and outsiders, too, tend to perceive them as a unit. Early in my
fieldwork, the family was pointed out to me by other Sefrouis as a
grand famille (a French notion that was as highly misleading as the
similar ones of *tribu* and *fraction*). With all these attributes, the Nas
Adlun provides an excellent test case for the appropriateness of the
segmentary model to their kinship ideology.

The evidence is best presented in the form of a detailed account of
field interviews. I began the work of compiling the list of the members of the Nas Adlun with a young schoolteacher. It must be
stressed, in the light of the following narrative, that he was highly
intelligent, willing, and knowledgeable. I immediately found myself in
difficulties, both in my understanding him and in his comprehending
what I wanted to know. Not until a long time later did I realize that
the basis of our mutual confusion was that I had unwittingly begun
with the suggestion that he use a genealogical model. I asked first:
"Name the oldest ancestor you know of, then give me the names of
his sons and daughters and then their sons and daughters." And then,
to "help" him, I sketched a small downward-branching kin diagram
with circles and triangles. For all his cooperativeness, he had a very
hard time giving me answers. He could think of an ancestor, but could
not recall all his sons, let alone his daughters, and as we proceeded,
kept having to backtrack and insert additional names in earlier generations as he thought of them. That is, the informant kept having to add
"brothers" alongside various ancestral figures. He tried taking the
problem home and interviewing his grandmothers and great aunts.
The task was clearly extremely foreign to all of them.

Meanwhile, conversations with other people had revealed that some
of the members of this large family carried secondary patronyms that
somehow stood for smaller groups. This fitted my tree image. These
must be the branches. So then I tried a new task: "Name the sections
of the Adlun, and tell me how they are related to one another." At
this the informant quickly said: "Oh yes, the Nas Adlun have four
parts (*ferqat*)" and he named them, apparently by the apical ancestor
of each one. I thought he meant that these four names stood for four
brothers. Then, as he had learned from me, he drew a downward-
branching tree, showing the four "brothers," and inventing a father for
them; then we attempted together to list the descendants of the four

349

"brothers." I had assumed that he conceived of the four parts as partitions of the whole, but to my surprise he later found he had to add a fifth "brother," whose relationship to the others was quite unclear. Was he a full brother, a half brother, or some more distant collateral? Further research among his older kin produced contradictory opinions. In the end, it became clear that in his mind the first four names were not brothers at all, nor were these "parts" in complimentary opposition in any way.

It became increasingly evident to me through this fumbling attempt to map out the internal structure of the Nas Adlun that the anthropoligical notion of progressive subdivision of a whole (segmentation) was far different from the Moroccan view of kinship. The genealogical tree was a failure, both as a guide for making a census inventory and as a first approximation of the native kinship model.

How, then, did Sefrou people go about listing their relatives? I learned later to phrase the question better and, although it remained a strange request to them, they usually went about answering in the following way. The informant first thought of a list of older, dominant men living today and named them, selecting the patrifiliative chain – "Ali, son of Mohammed, son of Hassan." The informant then mentally examined this list with its chains of names and grouped them where he could, first by common fathers' names into sets of brothers, and then further by common grandfathers' names. Some of the men on the original list remained independent, unlinked to brothers or cousins; yet it was always evident that they were thought of as more closely "related" to certain men than to others. These residual men were then linked to the key men not by traced agnatic kin ties, but by ties that often turned out to be those of patron and client. Frequently, younger men – brothers and adult sons – were overlooked until probed for and then were added to the growing clusters. Daughters, mothers, and wives were never mentioned until I insisted, for the women were irrelevant to this mode of conceiving of the family. This was true for women informants as well as men.

This exercise usually exhausted a person's knowledge of the connections among living people, and the informant ended with an overall picture of a collection of separate clusters of people within which the genealogical or patronage ties were fairly clear and among which they were unclear. Each cluster was identified by the name of the prominent man at its center or by the name of a recently central, now deceased predecessor. Most of their members were attached by agnatic kin ties, but some appeared to be associated mainly by patronage, or patronage ties moved a person to a closer position than was explained by simple genealogy. Each informant, even when he followed this psychologically familiar manner of grouping his kinsmen, was always left with a miscellaneous set of unaccounted-for families or individuals whose kinship location remained unclear, but who had a right to use the same overall patronym. To some extent, each informant's difficulties in answering my genealogical questions were a result of simple ignorance of some relevant connection, but even the best informed had the same fundamental difficulty, which arose from the alienness of the segmentary model I had provided.

What is foreign to Moroccan culture is not the notion of biological ties of parenthood, but the idea of a position in a structure of categories of people sorted out solely according to biogenetic links. Both the idea of such a structure as an inclusive whole that is progressively partitioned and the alternative idea of a structure of strings of kinsmen knit together into a tree of branching and connecting lines are hard for a Moroccan to visualize. Social identity for Moroccans could never be built on such a unidimensional scheme. Kinship obligations and privileges cannot, in Moroccan cultural formulations be separated from all other types of ties, such as patronage, as somehow qualitatively and jurally different.

A model for subgroups within the patronmyic association that is psychologically more real to Moroccans, closer to their own modes of thinking, is that which I have called the name cluster. It differs from the lineage segment model in that it is not visualized as a subdivision of a whole but rather as an accumulation of persons into a progressively larger and larger complex.

These name clusters are held together from within, so to speak, by virtue of the links connecting their members to central persons, rather than from without, by imaginary boundaries around their outer edges created through the mental act of the progressive cutting up of a larger body. When the informant said, "the Nas Adlun have four parts," he did not mean that the Nas Adlun is constructed by putting together these four parts nor that it is systematically cut up into four parts, but rather that he knew of four major name clusters into which most of the Adluns fell.

The patronymic association and the name cluster are products of Moroccan procedures for identifying and sorting persons according to their most important affiliations.

The patronymic association is a complex Moroccan cultural concept that, like an unspecialized, all-purpose tool, can be adapted to many special situations. It can be applied to very large, tightly organized groups such as the Nas Adlun, or to small and scattered sets of elementary families linked only by a common surname. In rural areas in the past, and in a few cases in the present in the mountains, fairly large groups with a common patronym held communal tenure over large tracts of land that were farmed in minute plots by hundreds of individual farmers who, however, could not sell the land to someone outside the name group. The patronymic association is the concept for speaking about this style of land tenure. It is a rather vague umbrella concept that can be put to many different uses, that can fit the needs of quite different individual families and the persons in them, and that can be used in different contexts.

The name cluster, on the other hand, refers to a specific set of individuals who are socially recognized as belonging together by virtue of links of patrifiliation, marriage, and patronage, and who are frequently referred to by the name of the dominant central man. Neither the patronymic association nor the name cluster are ego-centered arrangements of persons.

Despite their differences, the name cluster and the patronymic association are spoken of in identical ways: the use of the terms *nas, ferqat,* and *wlad l-ᶜamm* is appropriate to both. The logic of this conception of name cluster and patronymic association as being essentially the same becomes apparent when it is realized that either one can be transformed in time into the other. How this happens is best illustrated by further details from the field interviews with the Nas Adlun. In this example there were three different informants, of different generations and positions, whose accounts contained a number of contradictions. Resolution of these contradictions throws light on the relationship between name cluster and patronymic association.

When my first informant, the young teacher mentioned above, stated confidently that "the Nas Adlun have four parts," he named them. "There are the Nas Hamid [which includes himself], the Nas bel Yussef, the Nas Bel Abes, and the Nas Messaoud." These were the names of four brothers, I guessed and he agreed, perhaps the sons of some one man, who lived at some indefinite time in the past. The young teacher then proceeded to try to fit his various kinsmen into these four categories. Very soon he found, however, that certain people he knew did not fit into any of these sections, so he improvised another section, the Nas Abdellah. There must have really been five brothers, he said.

Soon after that conversation, I went to see the informant's mother, a woman of about sixty who came originally from the Nas Bel Yussef. She said: 'Oh, no. There had been indeed a man named Mulay Abdel-

352 lah, but he was not a brother of any of the others; he was more closely

related to Mulay Hamid than to anyone else [apparently through this mother, but it may have been through patronage], so we always considered him part of Nas Hamid." And furthermore, she said, the Nas Bel Yussef do not stand alone, but are part of the Nas Bel Abes. When she was a child in her father's home, she knew her grandfather, Mulay Ben Yussef, to be a cousin of people called Bel Abes. So, in her mind, there are three main sections: Nas Hamid, Nas Bel Abes, and Nas Bel Messaoud.

A third informant gave a different picture. This was a man in his eighties who was not from the Nas Adlun, but who knew them all well. We had been interviewing him for some months about another matter, the population of Sefrou at the turn of the century. When he came to some men from the Nas Adlun, he remarked that at that time there were four sections: Nas Hamid, Nas Ben Messaoud, Nas Bel Mekki, and Nas le-Bet ᶜai. As he went along in his account of Sefrou of the 1900s, he was able to recall about thirty men who were named el-Adluni and was able to assign one of these four names to every man. There were doubtless a few inaccuracies, but the point is that these assignations were felt by the informant to be natural and proper.

It became clear as he talked about these thirty Adluns that he was visualizing them in terms of several networks of influence and domination. At the turn of the century, as he recalled it, the two most prominent Adlun men were Mulay Larbi ben Hamid and Qadi Abdeslem ben Messaoud. The first was a wealthy farmer and titular if not actual leader of the Sefrou town population because he was the khalifa (representative) of the powerful Berber Qaid Omar, who controlled the Sefrou region at that time. Mulay Larbi's father had been Mulay Hamid; the Nas Hamid were grouped around him and, today, are clustered around his son (called Z on Figure 4). The second man, Qadi Abdeslem ben Messaoud, was a wealthy land owner and for many years was qadi of Sefrou. His father, apparently, had not actually been named Messaoud, for there were at that time some other men with the Messaoud name who were not his actual brothers. But it is clear that all of today's Bel Messaoud group are direct descendants of Qadi Abdeslem, who died about twenty-five years ago, and it is he to whom the name Messaoud now refers.

As the eighty-year-old informant continued his account of the Adlun men of around 1900 and their relationships with one another, these two groups – the Nas Hamid and the Nas Messaoud – seemed as distinctly defined as that time as they are today. There were, however, many other men whom he called either Bel Mekki or le-Betᶜai. Among the former were a number of successful long-distance traders, 353 but no single one of these was especially prominent. A fairly affluent one was a man named ben Yussef Bel Bekki, who was the grandfather of the present-day Bel Yussef group. Apparently, those whom the eighty-year-old informant called Bel Mekki, the sixty-year-old woman called Bel Abes, and the young teacher called Bel Abes and Bel Yussef, were all the same people.

This Bel Mekki/Bel Abes/Bel Yussef aggregate did not have the stability of name that the first two groups, the Nas Hamid and the Nas Messaoud, had. Who the men Bel Mekki and Bel Abes might have been is lost to us. Perhaps this ignorance is because they were not very notable people. More likely, they had once been important, but had lived too long ago, and the power of their names had not been reinforced by becoming attached to an important descendant. Today, most of the Bel Abes men are poor and without claim to prominence, with the exception of some in the Bel Yussef group, who are substantial farmers.

As for the fourth section of Nas Adlun mentioned by the eighty-year-old informant, the le-Bet^{c}ai, the specific people so named by the old man had dropped out of sight for both the younger informants. What happened to these people, the le-Bet^{c}ai, I cold not find out. One possibility is that descendants of the persons he labeled le-Bet^{c}ai are living in Sefrou today today, but no longer identify themselves, or are identified by others, as Adluns. Another possibility is that they died off. The eighty-year-old listed only three men as le-Bet^{c}ai, a father and two sons, who lived around the turn of the century. They were poor people, butchers by trade. It may be that they were the tail end of a once-prominent and populous grouping. I was told that the name le-Bet^{c}ai is actually a nickname meaning "a weakling," and also meaning its opposite, ironically, "a strong, assertive man." It may be that once there had been such a man, whose nickname reflected his dominance over his network, and that this name had become adopted as a patronym by his descendants.

The transformation of a nickname into a patronym is common and I knew of several such sequences in contemporary Sefrou. The father becomes well known under his sobriquet, and his sons then become known likewise as "ben Whatever-it-is." Then his grandsons may continue to be referred to by the same distinctive name. How widespread a group such a nickname-turned-patronym finally embraces depends, in part, on accidents of birth rates, but mainly on the fortunes of the members, and consequently on the degree to which the name remains memorable. The same process of conversion into a patronym goes on for personal names as well.

Any patrifiliative name chain that a particular man carries has a built-in ambiguity. It is always unclear unless you know the man whether Hassan ben Hamid means "Hassan son of Hamid" or "Hassan of the ben Hamid crowd." This ambiguity provides the needed flexibility to the entire system, for it enables the name to be transferred from person to person without necessarily giving it a permanent objective existence of its own. A name is always first and foremost a name of a person, an actual being, and only by extension is it the name of an aggregate of persons.

This long discussion of the naming conventions and their effects has been necessary to support my contention that within Moroccan culture, there is no *kinship* ideology taken in its literal sense, no culturally patterned genealogical or "organizational" chart by means of which Moroccans grant group memberships in any simple way to the people around them, either directly or analogically. What counts to Moroccans are actual social ties, obligations, attachments, and loyalties, and the networks built up out of these. Names, too, are joined to specific real persons and refer first to those persons. But they need constant revivification or their attachment to specific referents decays. A group cannot exist long only as the bearer of a revered name. Its networks of relationships must continuously be exercised to give genuine significance in action to the possession of a common name.

This is a concrete and practical matter. A name belongs to a physical, actual person, but it can also indicate indirectly that he is one of a known group—of physical, actual people. These proper names are not the names of groups; that is, the name bearers are not seen metonymically as representative parts of objectified wholes. They are duplicated names, and the name bearer is seen as one among an aggregate of concrete people who all bear the same name. The boundaries and composition of each particular name set are used. The cultural principle of formation of such a group is not some abstract rule of association, such as patrilineal descent or residence, but the recognition of highly specific interdependence of its members, often centering on a central powerful man who is presently living or is alive in people's memories. At times his name is also attached to a house or neighborhood and thus to the people in it, but in that case, the name continues to indicate a complex set of personal interconnections among people, not their common abode.

Personal names, of course, do not always direct attention to specific interpersonal clusters: The use of nicknames and of regional, craft, or other attributional names operates, on the contrary, to distinguish the individual from others. And the converse is also true: An important interpersonal network built up out of patronage, kinship, and other specific personal ties may not be given the recognition of a name. Women in particular often participate in such unnamed sets – if the center is a woman, no patronym could serve to sort it out. The fact that the naming convention employed here is a patrifiliatively transmitted chain of patronyms works to give this system of grouping the deceptive look of one based on systematic employment of a principle of association of kinship alone. A too-hasty conclusion that these named groupings, such as the Nas Adlun and the Nas Hamid, are patrilineal units, neglects the complexities and subtleties of their actual organization and misses the crucial importance to them of the complicated operation of a very specific sociolinguistic act – naming.

Categories of kinsmen

Name cluster, patronymic association, and patrifiliative name chain are various constructs within Moroccan culture that serve as alternative modes for conceptually ordering relationships. All refer to ways of grouping people, and all are based on inferences from the patronym. They need to be understood, however, within another cultural context: that of the Moroccan ways of categorizing persons within the bilaterally extending kinship network centering on ego.

When a Moroccan wants to invoke or refer to those family members who are of primary social importance to him, he uses the phrase *ḥbāb u nsāb*. This phrase appears in many standard linguistic routines, in greetings, prayers, and songs. It signifies those people with whom a person spends most of his time, toward whom he has the strongest obligations, and from whom he can expect the surest loyalty. Economically, ritually, and emotionally, these are the people who make the most demands on a person and provide him with the most support. These are the people with whom he must discuss any major decision. These are the people he cannot easily turn away from his door.

As a phrase, hbab u nsab can best be translated as "one's familial network." Its two elements, however, can be used alone, and when they are, they have contrasting meanings. Hbab is a very complex word semantically. In this phrase it refers to the speaker's agnatic kinsmen, in contrast to his nsab, who are his affines.

Still, some other important family members are excluded by the phrase hbab u nsab. Maternal kinsmen are neither hbab nor nsab. Many informants were quite definite in stating that one's mother's brother is not in the group of hbab u nsab. Neither is one's own

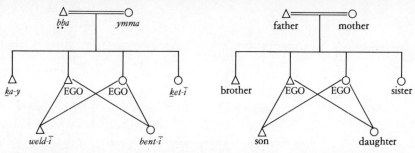

Figure 8. Basic terms for primary relatives of a man and a woman speaker.

mother or her parents. "What is your mother's brother, then?" "He's my father's nsab." Maternal kinsmen, despite their emotional importance and their genealogical proximity, are not often thought of as a homogeneous category of persons in the same way as are the paternal kinsmen who form the core of the patronymic association.

The formula hbab u nsab is a way of recognizing the intricacies of kin relations that result when there is no rule of exogamy and there is a positive preference for marriage to close kin. One's kinsmen through a marriage (nsab) are often also one's hbab, reckoned by a slightly longer series of links.

Despite this doubling, or perhaps because of it, the lexicon for referring to persons according to their kinship relationship makes meticulous distinctions between affines and consanguines and rather elaborate distinctions within each of these categories. Some (but not all) of the Moroccan concepts about kinship can be derived from a study of this lexicon.[20]

Starting with consanguine relations, a set of basic terms can be singled out for analysis. These are distinguishable from derived terms in that the latter are linguistically constructed by making compounds from two of the former. For instance, the child of one's brother is not called by a basic term, but rather by a term derived from those for brother and son, thus, brother's son.

The basic terms for primary relatives for both a man and a woman speaker can be charted as follows in Figure 8. These terms refer exclusively to these primary relatives. They are not extended in a classificatory way.

The chart of primary relatives can be augmented in a lineal dimension (Figure 9). The chart of ascendant and descendant kin terms, reckoned from ego, shows that no lexical distinction is made between maternal and paternal kin at the levels of grandparents and above and of grandchildren and below. A sharp distinction, however, is made in the parental generation between the siblings of one's father and the siblings of one's mother (Figure 10).

These are all the basic terms for consanguineal kin. All others are 357

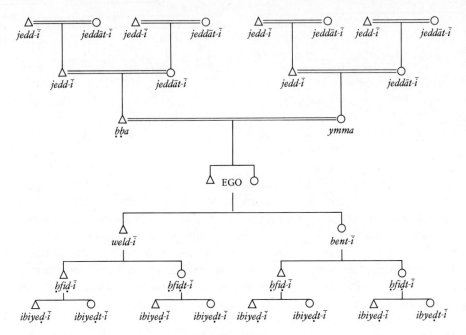

Figure 9. Terms for ascendant and descendant kin.

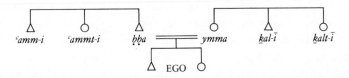

Figure 10. Terms for siblings of father and siblings of mother.

derived from them through the use of compounds. For example, "my brother's son" is *weld ka-y,* "my sister's son" is *weld ket-i,* "my father's sister's son" is *weld ᶜammt-i,* "my father's brother's son" is *weld ᶜamm-i,* "my mother's brother's son" is *weld kal-i,* "my mother's sister's son" is *weld kalt-i.*

For the most part these terms are not classificatory; that is, their reference is restricted to a specific kinship position or kin type. The most important exceptions are the terms for father's brother and father's sister.[21] These two terms, *ᶜamm-i* and *ᶜammt-i,* may be used to refer to anyone within one's patronymic association who is older than oneself.

The term hbab has a similar dual or sliding reference. One informant, an elderly urban sherif, used the term hbab habitually and confusingly in two quite different ways. One sense referred to those closest kinsmen toward whom he had the fullest social obligation of

358

support, from whom he could claim support, or, in more precise
Moroccan terms, those with whom he was in serious competition for
the means of material support. These were his father, grandfather,
brothers, cousins, sons, and their sisters and daughters. At other
times, he used the same term and concept (hbab) to indicate all the
members of the three name clusters nearest to him (which included
the descendants of his grandfather's brothers) within his very large
patronymic association (but he did not extend the term to include all
members of his patronymic association). For him, this latter, larger
group of the three name clusters was, for instance, the people he felt
he must invite to his son's wedding and who would then be obliged to
contribute substantial wedding gifts.

Other informants tended to think of the matter in jural terms, referring to Islamic laws of inheritance and of responsibility for maintenance. One man made a distinction between ᶜasab and hbab, saying that
the former comprises such kin as one's brother's grandchildren, one's
father's brother's grandchildren, and even conceivably others of greater
distance. These are the agnatic relatives who in Islamic law stand to
inherit if there are no living hbab, which he then listed as including
one's son, one's brother, his children, one's father's brothers, and their
children.[22] Asab for him was an unbounded category of "not-likely-to-
be-inheriting agnates." In other words, for this informant, the group of
kinsmen, including cognatic kin and spouses, who are united by the
possibility of inheritance from a particular living man were hbab.

Another informant introduced the term *quṛaba* (alternative forms:
qaṛaba, qarib), the "near ones." These are the people, he said, whom
one has the duty (*ferḍ* is the term he used) of helping when in trouble.
For him, as for some other speakers, the term quraba meant "all close
relatives," including maternal kin and, probably, some affines or even
nonrelatives who have long been household members. One woman,
using quraba, said that these are the people who give wedding presents of some substance to a newly married couple.

It can be seen that Moroccans make a distinction between close and
distant relatives, but that this distinction is not clearly marked lexically. When the term hbab is used to indicate close relatives, it singles
out those who are closest to one emotionally and juridically, while the
term may also be used in a broader sense to comprise all those within
one's recognized patronymic association.

The boundary line between close and distant kin is ambiguous in
another way. Even when a speaker makes a sharp distinction between
close and distant hbab, he may at different times include kinsmen in
the close category whom he excludes in other contexts. The percep-

tion of the location of the boundary between close and distant shifts according to the various situations in which the speaker finds himself.

To complicate the matter further, there is considerable disagreement among speakers about the maximum scope to which they will extend the category of hbab, and their stances in this regard are traceable to differing locations in the social structure. The same people who restrict use of the term ᶜamm-i to the literal "father's brother," also have a much more limited interpretation of hbab. These are likely to be younger, more modern, or urban people, whose patronymic association is not locally organized in any way. Those who take the broader classificatory view are older or rural or old-fashioned people who, like the Adluns, are (or were until recently) bound into socially important relationships with many members of their patronymic association.

All these different terms – from those for the father's brother, the categorical terms of hbab and quraba, to the term fekheda and its synonyms – have the same sliding characteristic, the capacity to shift referent from a restricted cluster of kin to a much larger grouping. Fekheda is usually used to refer to a larger name cluster, but it can also be used in the narrow sense of a man and his sons and their wives and children. The main difference between fekheda and hbab is that the latter refers to those groupings from the point of view of a person within them, whereas the former sees them from an outside vantage point. Hbab means "all those people related to x in a certain way"; fekheda means "all those people related to one another in a certain way." The concrete group of people may be the same in both cases.

This characteristic of sliding reference that is apparent in all the words – fekheda, hbab, ᶜasab, ᶜamm-i, and the like – must be understood in terms of the underlying ideas of the name cluster and the patronymic association. The imprecision and contradictory elements are essential to their flexibility, their adaptability to the special situations of quite different individual families and the persons in them. Consequently, their uses vary with different economic and social conditions, with different regions, and with different historical eras. Where cooperation of large numbers of persons is required, the patronymic association can provide the rationale, as, for instance, it did in nineteenth-century rural Morocco where warfare was waged between fekheda and alliances of fekheda as fighting units. At that period the fedheda as a concept was very inclusive and it was accompanied by corporate institutions. But where the fragmentation of families and the autonomy of individual men are desirable and there is a consequent need not for united action of a solidary group but rather for dependable networks of kinsmen, as, for instance, in some strata of

360

modern urban Morocco, the narrower meaning can take precedence.
The use of jural considerations in distinguishing close from distant
hbab (i.e., the possibility of claiming access to property,) reflects this
close tie-in with socioeconomic life. If land is to be held in common
by a large group of persons, as with the Berber-speaking mountain
groups, the patronymic association may be one of the cultural instruments used in organizing that ownership. On the other hand, modern
urban Moroccans tend to confine the scope of the concept to the
small group of siblings and cousins competing for a share in a father's
land, in response to the accelerating occupational differentiation and
consequent demand for free capital that creates pressure for the rapid
conversion of land claims into currency. Much of the observed variation in the use of the terms fekheda and hbab comes from the social
differences that have arisen from uneven rates of change in different
parts of Moroccan society over the past century.

The terms within the category of nsab, those persons to whom one is
related through a marriage, exhibit several revealing patterns. First, the
affinal terms contrast with the hsab and asab series in that there is very
little ambiguity about how far away from ego these affinal terms are felt
to be still appropriately applicable. They do not designate persons in
any positions other than those indicated in Figures 11 through 14. The
affinal relationship is never conceived of as a tie between two groups of
people, or between a person and a group, but always as a sharply
limited sequence of ego-centered links reckoned in terms of a particular marriage. Second, there is one rather general category of "my
relative-in-law" (*nsīb-ī,* fem. *nsībt-ī*) that contrasts with a heterogeneous
set of specific terms that indicate certain highly particular positions.

Figure 11 shows the terms employed by a parent with married
children (the terms here are the same whether the speaker is male or
female). Note that the only position singled out for a special term is
that of the woman who marries one's son (i.e., the woman is marrying
into the family). The term *ᶜarust-i* means "bride," but it is used for
many years after marriage by the women of the older generation of
the family. Sometimes it is used in the form, *ᶜarust-na* ("our bride") to
indicate that she has joined "us" – a whole group of people.

The reverse terms, used by a woman who has married into a family,
are shown in Figure 12. The terms for father-in-law and mother-in-law
are terms of respect that one might use to address any important older
man or woman. A man, however, when speaking of his wife's parents
does not use these respectful terms, but rather the unmarked nsib-i
and nsibt-i. In a similar way the woman marrying into a family has
special terms for those persons in that family who are of the same 361

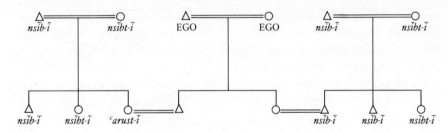

Figure 11. Terms employed by parent with married children.

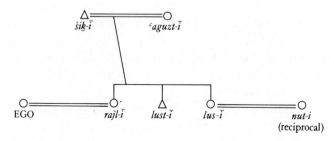

Figure 12. Terms employed by a woman to refer to her husband's family.

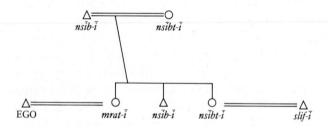

Figure 13. Terms employed by a man to refer to his wife's family.

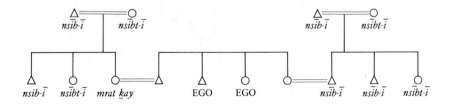

Figure 14. Terms for affinal connections through one's siblings.

generation with her, her husband's brother and sister. She refers to another woman who has married into the family by the reciprocal term, nut-i, the symmetry indicating that they are in the same boat. In contrast, the terms a man uses to refer to his wife's family are not

362

special terms, with one exception (Figure 13). The exception is the
term for the man who has married one's wife's sister, and here again
the term is reciprocal, suggesting symmetry of status.

The terms for affinal connections through one's siblings are the
same whether a man or a woman is speaking (Figure 14). The
brother's wife is never referred to as nsib-i, but rather by the derived
term, mrat khay, which means "my brother's wife."

Taken as a whole these affinal terms make sense when it is recognized that the special terms all center on relationships with an in-marrying woman, and particularly on those relationships she has with members of her new domestic group. A large house with rooms for a group
of brothers or even cousins and their fathers sets the stage for an
incoming wife in which relationships between the woman and her
mother-in-law, her father-in-law, her husband's brothers, and wives are
all quite different in feeling tone and obligations from those affinal
relationships that are not ones of day-to-day coresidence. These latter
positions of affines outside the house are all referred to by the general
terms nsib-i and nsibt-i. Because this pattern of affinal terms is present
even in those situations when the in-marrying woman is a close cousin,
it suggests that the position is, even then, a special and probably difficult one for all involved.

The making of marital choices

"Arranging marriages is a highly serious matter, like waging war or
making big business deals," said one young man. "The stakes are high
in all three cases, and a man must have good sense (*i-kun maᶜqūl*) and
virile forcefulness (*rujūla qwiya*)," he went on. This particular young
man, an Adlun, had poignant inner doubts about his own possession
of such attributes, but in any case he was in the worst possible position to find out. Youngest of four brothers and three sisters, all of
whom were already married, youngest adult in Dar Hamid (he is the
man marked F on Figure 4) he found himself powerless against an
increasing barrage of admonitions, advice, and complaints from his
siblings, their spouses, his parents, and their siblings, all of whom had
a painfully low opinion of his capacity to make a sensible choice on his
own. There was a girl he wanted to marry, but his mother, sisters,
cousins, and aunts unanimously turned her down, and the men in the
family backed up the feminine faction. After all, the women said, they
would have to live with her, and the reasons they gave for her unsuit-
ability were that she was not an Adlun and was too different from
them in other ways. (She was a highly educated, modern school 363

teacher from a rural, Berber-speaking background.) The women themselves suggested a number of candidates from within the Nas Adlun,
but the younger man either despised or was afraid of these girls. He was
incapable of taking any action on his own, not entirely from want of
personal forcefulness, but also from his lack of economic and political
leverage within the family. A marriage requires a large financial investment, and he was still economically dependent on his family.

In fact, when he made the statement about the need for virile
forcefulness in the arranging of marriages, he was not referring to
himself or his role at all, but to the role of the father. It is the father's
responsibility to select, negotiate for, and pay the bridewealth for the
mates of his children. This young man, and most of the other young
men I spoke with, assumed that to be a self-evident reality. He
wanted only, as do most of the others, a louder voice in the decision.

His assumption that the choice of a spouse is not the responsibility
of the marriageable person alone would be accepted by most Sefrou
people of all ages. Where many might differ with this young man's
view of the matter would be in regard to his other assumption that the
men of the family were responsible and that the qualities needed for
handling marriage negotiations were masculine characteristics (such as
maᶜqula, which women are considered to lack, and rujula, which literally means "masculinity"). The women of his family had a different
conception of the situation. They believed marriages should never be
left to the men to settle. In actuality, in most of the choice cases I
studied, both the men and the women of the families were actively
involved, and in hardly any of these did the young people themselves
have much to say.

In order to discuss how the processes of marital choice and negotiation reveal characteristic patterns of personal relationships and their
guiding norms, I need first to recount briefly the series of steps customarily entailed in bringing about a new marriage. As will be seen, the
process is lengthy and expensive, and it becomes the focus for various
personal and group interests and efforts.

Private, discreet, and indirect feelers usually precede public acts,
often via informal go-betweens, sometimes through direct though
quiet conversations between members of the two families. Usually a
tentative private agreement is in hand before steps are openly taken.
Initiative in these private negotiations comes from either side, although most of the time the man's family makes the first move. If,
however, the two families are closely connected, especially if there are
previous marriages between them, so that their women are intimates,
the initiative can come from the bride's side.

The agreement involves more than the betrothal of the two people; *The meanings of*
it also covers the probable date of the wedding and, most important of *family ties*
all, the size of the marriage payment. This last, the *ṣḍāq,* is of central
importance to everyone. Because it will be used to buy the domestic
furnishings that will remain the personal property of the bride, it is
related directly to the standard of living she will expect to lead and in
that sense is a direct measure of the value placed on the girl and her
family. The actual sum varies considerably, depending on the economic status of the families involved, and during the last fifteen years
has undergone considerable inflation. At the time of this first agreement, the sdaq is not paid, but the date for its payment is set. Normally, this date is around a year away, but it can be much sooner or, as
is very often the case, several years later.

This agreement, in all its detail, is formally sealed by the two fathers
with a written contract witnessed by a notary in the court (*ᶜadel*). The
signing of this legally binding document may precede, but often
comes just after, a more public formal request for the girl's hand at a
ceremonial dinner at her home (the *ḳiṭba*). Sometimes this formal
request is the actual opener in negotiations, and sometimes the discussions in regard to the amount of the sdaq and the date of the wedding
are held at the khitba itself.

The first step in the khitba ceremony is a gift of a large quantity of
sugar from the man's family to the woman's. This signifies that the
man's relations are planning to request the hand of the girl and that
they will be coming the next day to do so. Sometimes this gift of sugar
is the first sign the girl's family has of the marriage proposal, and it can
be returned wordlessly to indicate rejection.

If the sugar is not returned, the next day the women of the man's
family bring large supplies of ingredients for a dinner (in Sefrou this
customarily consists of fresh meat, sugar, and olive oil; in rural areas it
may be wheat flour and oil). The girl's family furnishes the remaining
elements and prepares a feast. At noon the men of the man's family
arrive and share the meal with the men of the women's family. After
the dinner formal speeches are made in which the girl's hand is requested. Often these speeches are made by friends of each of the two
families, kinsmen or inlaws, who serve as spokesmen. Usually a prayer
is said, led by a religious scholar brought in for the occasion.

An engagement party is held at the girl's house, at some point
between the khitba and the wedding. Called *l-mlāk* (from the stem
meaning "possession"), it is the public, social acknowledgment of the
agreement. The man's family sends gifts, consisting customarily of
clothes for the girl or the materials with which to make them, henna, 365

milk, and dates. The last three have symbolic, ritual significance: The henna is purifying and protective against evil spirits, the milk brings "whiteness" or good fortune, the dates bring happiness and wealth. The mlak is primarily a women's party, with dancing and singing, both in the girl's home and at the public bath, where she is taken and ritually hennaed and bathed. All the guests give their blessings to the girl.

The next step, which may be combined with the mlak, is a legal closing of the marriage contract (*ᶜaqed nikāh*), together with payment of the sdaq ("brideprice"). It takes place before a notary of the court, either at his office or in the girl's home. The girl must be present, and usually the man; their parents or guardians and other relatives are also there. The contract is prepared and usually includes a statement about the sum of the sdaq, as well as any stipulations the bride's family wishes to put on the marriage. These stipulations are optional and might include provisions that the man may not take another polygamous wife without granting the first wife a divorce, that the wife may not be required to move away from her family's neighborhood or town, and that she may have the right to divorce her husband if she wishes. A popular stipulation states that the entirety of the sdaq is not being paid at the time of wedding, but is held out to be given to the wife at the time of divorce or at any time she demands it. This condition, when adopted, gives the woman greater control over her husband's impulses to divorce her. The notary must formally ask both the bride and the groom if they are willing to marry, and each of them responds, "*qbelt*" ("I accept"). Anyone who objects to the marriage may speak up at this time.

A day or two before the actual wedding, the girl's family delivers to the man's home all the clothes, mattresses, blankets, kitchen goods, dinnerware, and so on, that have been purchased with the sdaq money. This act is called the *šhūra* ("display," "announcement," "show"), and it is indeed a public showing and celebration of the good fortune of the young people. The goods (which are also referred to as the *šhūra* or the *'attat l-bit,* "furnishings of the room") are carried all around the town, either on the heads and in the arms of the bride's family members, on donkeyback, or (among the affluent townsmen), on the open back of a truck, to the accompaniment of drums and woodwinds and the clapping and dancing of the girl's relatives. This spectacle is watched mainly by women and children, and the goods are then displayed further at the home of the groom. The sdaq money is generally supplemented with an equal or larger amount from the bride's father, and it is this cumulative total, or rather the actual goods bought with it, that is the focus of public attention. Status competition centers not on the actual sum of the sdaq, but on the value of the shura and the expenses of the wedding feasts that follow it.[23]

The wedding takes place primarily at the man's house, although there may be some lesser celebration at the bride's house before she is taken away. It begins with a long evening of feasting and talking, sometimes with professional musicians playing at the groom's house. Around two or three in the morning, the entire wedding party, including all the relatives of the groom except the groom and his father, set out to get the bride and bring her back. If she lives at a distance, they ride mules and donkeys, or if they can afford it they rent or borrow cars and trucks. The procession is noisy, with much blowing of horns and drumming. As they approach the girl's house, they chant the opening chapter of the Quran (*fatḥa*), and shout, "*ᶜaṭina dyal-na, matbqāš dyal-kum!*" ("Give us that which is ours, she's not yours any more!"). The groom's party enters the girl's house and engages the bride's party in a sort of drumming contest, an aggressive play-clash, until the groom's side is finally given the girl to take back. She is almost always weeping and sobbing, and most of the women with her are upset too. She is accompanied to the groom's house by two of her girlfriends, who stay with her for the next week.

When the bride arrives at the groom's house, she is ceremonially dressed in wedding clothes. These are heavy layers of finery and jewels, and they are usually rented from a marriage specialist, the *neggafa,* a woman who supervises the entire ritual over the next few days. Some of these specialists ask very high fees and provide wedding finery whose elaborateness depends on the level of ostentation the family is trying to achieve.

Dressing the bride takes several hours, at the end of which she looks like a huge, overdressed doll, who stands heavily veiled waiting patiently for her groom. The neggafa and her assistants then chant a series of blessings, sing songs about the wedding, and call in the groom. Before he comes in, however, the groom's mother enters, lifts the veil, kisses the bride, and ceremoniously drinks from a bowl of milk and eats a date. She then gives the neggafa some money. She is followed by other women relatives of the groom, who do the same. This money, referred to as *ḡrama,* goes in part to the neggafa and her helpers, and partly to the costs of the wedding. Finally the groom comes in. He lifts the veil, drinks milk with the bride, and shares a date with her. For a while they sit together on display and receive the blessings of their kinsmen and friends before retiring to a secluded room. The wedding party continues on through the night, and in the morning the neggafa and her helpers examine the sheets of the wedding bed for proof of the bride's virginity.

The morning after is also the occasion for another party, the wedding breakfast (*ftūr ṣ-ṣbāḥ*), for which the women of the girl's family come, bringing gifts of clothing for the groom and his family. The bride and groom may also exchange personal presents at this time. During the next few days, in rural areas, the bride and groom do not emerge from the wedding chamber; however, in town, they do come out, separately, to while away the days singing and listening to music with their friends. The girl has several young friends with her most of the time. Traditionally, these friends were titled the *wazirat* ("ministers"), who waited on her "like a princess" and on the groom "like a king."

There follows (ideally) seven days of feasting. In traditional Sefrou families a special dinner is given to the poor, who are brought in from the street for the occasion or for whom food is sent to the mosque. Other dinners are prepared for the religious students and scholars. In addition, several feasts are held for various categories of wedding guests, with the men and women eating separately.

A final and very important gift remains to be mentioned. On the occasion of the birth of her first child, the girl's father sends over several bags of flour, a sheep, some olive oil, and new clothes for the girl and her child. This is called *l-hdīya d-ḵluq u terbīya* ("the gift of the birth and the rearing").

The payments, gifts, and entertaining costs can be enormous, and may place a heavy burden on both sides of the marriage. Table 1 shows some of the payments in an Adlun wedding that occurred in 1968. The marriage involved the daughter of a taxi driver and a young office worker whose father had been dead for some time. Neither the girl's father nor the young man had an income of more than about $100 per month. The cost of the wedding feasts themselves have been omitted.

Table 1. *Distribution of wedding payments*

Groom's share	
Sdaq	$ 400.00
Clothes and jewelry given at mlak engagement	210.00
Clothes given morning after wedding	160.00
Groom's share, exclusive of food	$ 770.00
Bride's father's contribution to domestic furnishings	$1,000.00

From the point of view of a young man, the sdaq and other wedding costs are an enormous burden. During the period of field work in Sefrou, sdaq payments varied from $2,000 for a wealthy man's daughter, down to $40 for the daughter of a poor urban laborer. Because the sdaq is less than half of the entire cost of the wedding, when the expense of gifts, dinners, and entertainment is considered, the whole can be overwhelming and must be the product of years of saving or entail substantial indebtedness. This burden is carried almost entirely by the young man and his father. Further relatives contribute only in special cases, as when a prominent man helps a nephew or grandson or a servant in order to ensure his loyalty and support in other enterprises.

The expenses of getting married and the delicacy of the preceding negotiations are the focus of troubled attention by everyone, especially the young man involved. This is because the situation embodies in a frustrating and enraging way his entire subordination to his father, his powerlessness in a society that values personal autonomy and force. He can do little more than suggest a candidate and then wait until his father is ready and willing to embark on the enterprise. In the end he must accept the girl his family chooses, if he cannot persuade them otherwise. Because the one who is in control of the situation is the father (and the mother, through him), any advantages to be gained by the marriage (either in terms of alliance with someone in the girl's family or in terms of the girl's capacity to work) are more likely to go to the parents than to their son. Of course, sometimes the calculations of the parents are in terms of their child's own needs; that is, they look for a spouse for their son or daughter who will give their child a secure, satisfying married life. But even in those cases, it is the judgment of the parents about what is best for their child that counts.

Young girls are in a similar, but even more helpless position. They do not usually fight against it or resent it because there is little use. They are married soon after reaching maturity, and in the past commonly several years prior to puberty, whereas men are not married until they are capable of supporting a family. Girls, therefore, do not have to face the long period of waiting before marriage that confronts young men. Unlike a young man, a girl does not have any opportunity to build an alternative basis of power, nor is she taught, even indirectly, the desire for autonomy. There is, of course, considerable variation among families about the degree to which the young people are consulted on marriage choices and the vigor with which they express their feelings in the matter. The modernization of the occupational and educational systems, which give men, and to a much lesser extent women, both a different view of themselves and the economic means to oppose conventional authority, is affecting a large number of families. Marriages in which the couple themselves reached agreement without the interference of anyone else occur occasionally, and their number is increasing, even in Sefrou. Older men who have wealth and power within their familial network choose their own brides and may even initiate their own negotiations. Older women who have been married before also have much more to say about their own marital fate. The divorce rate is fairly high,[24] and in the past the mortality rate was high too, so that successive marriages are fairly common. Arrangements for later marriages are not quite so full of the strain and effort that accompany the first ones.

But for almost all the marriages I studied or heard about during the fieldwork period in Sefrou, the final decisions were not made by the couple themselves. Because the largest part of all the payments is made by the immediate households of the bride and groom, and because the heads of those households control the economic resources, the final decision is usually made by two men. Normatively these are the fathers of the bride and groom, but given the exigencies of mortality, divorce, and remarriage, or the economic fraility of the head of household and his (or, occasionally, her) dependence on a more powerful person, the actual sponsor of a marriage can be some other relative – a father's brother, or grandfather, or mother's brother, or even a sister's husband.

But in nearly every case of a marriage choice I knew of, the head of the household was besieged with advice from many sides. Usually there were lengthy familial discussions in which everyone in the vicinity expressed an opinion on the matter. The form of these discussions within the family, and the communications networks that support them, have important effects on the direction of choice. Whose voice has the most weight in the selection and who actually carries out the substantive negotiations directly determine the final outcome. For this reason, those underlying norms that are accepted as a self-evident framework for the acts of all those involved in each marriage arrangement are abstract and general, rather than concrete and specific. The anthropological favorite, the so-called preference for patrilateral parallel cousin marriage, is a minor alternative strategy, rather than a response to, or evidence of, a deeply held Moroccan conviction about the structure of the social world.

Accounts of these decision-making processes are often strongly slanted by the sex of the informant. When a man describes his own or other marital arrangements, male figures, especially the narrator himself, figure predominantly in the account. When a woman describes *The meanings of* the same event, female protagonists, especially the speaker, hold the *family ties* stage. The truth in most cases appears to be that discussions go on simultaneously within several separate communications networks, one made up mainly of men, the other of women. But at crucial points in the process, certain key members of each network must be approached from the other. If the men have reached a decision, they then have to inform the women of it and persuade the women either of its rightness or of their authority to put it into effect. If the women have reached a decision, they must demonstrate its merits to the sponsor of the person to be married. The influence of the women in these decisions must not be underestimated. Even though they cannot promote their candidates in the open but must, at least in the final stages, operate through a man, nonetheless their opinions carry considerable weight.

To suggest that the family is internally divided into men's and women's communications networks, however, is imprecise. There may be a number of women within a large family who speak to one another freely and openly, so that a fairly definite women's consensus may develop. But the network of men involved is cut up by marked intergenerational restraints and sharply competing interests. A man and his father observe strong rules of reserve in regard to the mention of sexually tinged subjects. This pattern of mutual delicacy extends to the father's brother and grandfather and is even more marked between a man and his father-in-law and his brother. A man does not go into the public bath if he knows some of these relatives are there, and he avoids all situations in which off-color talk or even sentimental love songs might be heard by both of them at the same time. For a man to speak with certain men of his family about the marital hopes, plans, or situation of someone in his family, and especially about his own desires, is, therefore, very embarrassing. A common solution for a man is to employ his mother, paternal aunt, or wife as a go-between in speaking his mind on these matters, to send messages via the women to the other men of the family.

Negotiations *between* families, however, follow marked lines of sexual division, the men dealing with the men, and the women with women. Most of the initial moves are made by women from the different families. Even for marriages between families who are unacquainted with one another, the go-between is often a woman – for instance, a seamstress who goes from family to family or a neighbor who carries information about potential spouses and evaluations of them. After the first openings, the women of the man's family find 371 some pretext to visit the women of the girl's family and look over the potential bride.

When the interfamilial contacts are between men, on the other hand, set as they are in the contexts of commercial and political arenas, the reverberations from any specific marital union are likely to be greater and to spread further. Because of the public weight of such a marriage, the key men may not get openly involved in negotiations until preliminary agreements have been reached by women on both sides.

The considerations that arise in discussions within the family, the motives entertained for choosing one girl over another or for accepting one suitor over another are incredibly varied. Those that appeal to the men of the family, of course, may be quite different from those the women consider important.[25] Seldom is there any appeal to, much less agreement on, a conventional ideology that would guide the choice. Rather, everyone seems to be making pragmatic assessments of the potential gains and losses that might be entailed by the union.

The primary recipe, mentioned and stressed repeatedly by all informants, is that above all one should look very hard at the characters of the father and mother of a potential spouse and at their other relatives. The familial context of the person, the network of personal ties, benefits, and claims that could be created by the marriage, are of far greater importance in everyone's mind than the personal attributes of the candidate alone. Of course, such qualities as a girl's probable fecundity, her sexual attractions, her capacity for domestic work, her docility and fidelity, or a man's economic prospects, his dependability, and his generosity were often mentioned. But more frequently the talk centered around their other relatives and what profit a new marital connection with that network might bring.

This calculation of various advantages in each possible match and the balancing of differing interests go on whether the marriage under consideration is within the family circle or outside it. A marriage between close cousins may be arranged for a variety of different reasons: the cementing of profitable relationships with the central man of the patronymic association, the provision of care for a disabled or otherwise undesirable person, as well as the comfort and ease of old acquaintance. Whether or not the participants are close relatives, the negotiation process is almost always difficult.

A normative preference for marriage with the father's brother's daughter, or even more broadly, for a marriage within the patronymic association, was rarely if ever expressed to me unsolicited. When

372 questioned directly about such a norm, some informants denied out-

right that this was a good policy; others asserted that when possible – other considerations such as those listed above being equal – such a marriage was a good idea. Interestingly, the arguments raised by informants both for and against endogamous marriage centered on the same issues. One was the quarrelsomeness or harmony that was to be feared or expected among kinsmen. Some informants claimed that trouble between a man and a wife would be eased or cushioned by appeals from their relatives, whereas others insisted that marital quarrels would only be exacerbated if the in-laws were also consanguineal kin. Another argument for the benefits of a patrilateral parallel cousin marriage revolved around the woman's inheritance of a portion of her father's estate. Those in favor of a marriage to the father's brother's daughter said that this prevents the fragmenting of any property shared by the two brothers who were the fathers of the marrying pair. Those opposed to it pointed to the possibility that an in-marrying girl might bring some new property with her. As in the case of quarrelsomeness, this line of reasoning can be made to back up either position. What is more important about these informants' statements is that they refer to considerations that are pragmatic rather than conventional or moral.

Some people when directly questioned about the preference rule recalled a proverb: *"weld ᶜamm-ha sabeq,"* ("a girl's father's brother's son has priority"). By this they meant that if a man wanted her as his wife, he could make a stronger claim if he were her father's brother's son than if he were an outsider. These same people sometimes spoke in terms of a *ḥaqq* or "rightful share" of the weld ᶜamm. No informant appeared to feel that such a haqq was an easily defensible one, and most remarked that it all depended on the nature of the relationship between the brothers – whether or not they were amicable, what forms of cooperation existed between them. In other words, where appeal is made to this form of prior claim to the hand of a woman, it is not to a jurally enforceable rule, but rather to a traditional practice that must also be defended in terms of its present pragmatic application, and by persons who have other claims to be able to influence the decision.

An important principle emerged, however, during my probings into the preference for the father's brother's daughter. This is that when there is any prescription, or any assertion of a prior claim, the holder of the right or claim is not the marrying man himself, but his father. In other words, the claim a man might have to a woman on the basis of kinship is not to his father's brother's daughter, but to his brother's daughter, to marry off to his son. The person who has the preferences, 373 rights, claims, or whatever, is the man who makes the decision – the father of the groom or the father of the bride. Any study of the patterns of actual marital choices made must be centered not on the marrying couple, but on their parents and their parents' situations, concepts of their social world, and interests.

Attempts were made to measure the strength of preference for marriage to the father's brother's daughter by means of statistical surveys of several large patronymic associations within the Sefrou area. The technical difficulties in making such censuses and in drawing conclusions from them are discussed in Annex B, where the material is presented in full. My best estimates for the frequency with which actual marriages have been contracted with the father's brother's daughter, narrowly and literally reckoned, are shown in Table 2.

My best estimates for frequency of marriges contracted with a classificatory father's brother's daughter (i.e., with a girl of the same patronym) in selected large patronymic associations are shown in Table 3.

Table 2. *Percent of marriages contracted with father's brother's daughter*

Nas Adlun as a whole (N = 66 marriages)	9.0
Patronymic subgroups of Nas Adlun	
Nas Hamid (N = 16 marriages)	25.0
Nas Bel Abes (N = 41 marriages)	11.0
Nas Messaoud (N = 9 marriages)	10.0
Ait Sidi Lahcen Lyusi (rural, sherifian; N = 111)	4.5
Nas Britel (urban, nonsherifian) (N = 110)	3.6
Ait Arawi (rural, nonsherifian) (N = 56)	8.9

Note: These percentages are based on totals of all marriages contracted within the last two generations for which information was available concerning the parents' siblings.

Table 3. *Percent of marriages contracted with the classificatory father's brother's daughter (including the father's brother's daughter)*

Nas Adlun as a whole (N = 107)	29.0
Patronymic subgroups of Nas Adlun	
Nas Hamid (N = 33)	30.0
Nas Bel Abes (N = 52)	38.0
Nas Messaoud (N = 22)	4.0
Ait Sidi Lahcen Lyusi (N = 223)	21.0
Nas Britel (N = 110)	25.4
Ait Arawi (N = 56)	10.7

Note: These percentages are based on totals of all marriages reported going back about four generations.

The major obstacle to a valid interpretation of such statistics is the lack of an estimate of the probability that the same pattern might appear by chance in any marriage population where there are no rules against cousin marriage.[26] If this drawback is ignored, Tables 2 and 3 show that the proportion of women marrying within the Adlun patronymic association is very low, lower than one might expect from the earlier qualitative description of the Adlun family as being tightly crisscrossed with a web of marital ties. With less than a third of these women coming from within the circle of immediate paternal kinsmen, the picture seems false to both the enthnographer's impression and the views of the informants themselves.

The explanation for this incongruity is that the drawing of the circle that separates women into insiders and outsiders cannot be made according to a model based solely on paternal genealogical lines and the counting of links. The discussion above made the point that Moroccan maps of kin and non-kin are more complex than that.

A convincing alternative mode of classifying marriages, suggested by Pierre Bourdieu, sorts them into those reached by "well-trodden paths" as against "extraordinary routes."[27] In his study of marriage practices in a similar North African society, the Algerian Kabyle villages, he rejects the usual distinctions among paternal, maternal, and affinal kinsmen and proposes to group together those marriages that are brought about by persons who know one another well and who have numerous daily ties with each other including the ties brought about by earlier marriages, as against those marriages that are arranged by and between persons with more tenuous and unusual connections (e.g., persons who live far apart, who have no prior kinship or affinal ties, or who have greatly differing lifestyles). This distinction between marriages reached via a well-used social road and those reached via a newly constructed and longer one cuts across the traditional anthropological framework of descent groupings or lines.

The category of "well-trodden paths" includes not only kin-group endogamous marriages but also those contracted with groups who have intermarried in the past and those contracted within the neighborhood. All these, says Bourdieu, belong properly within a single classification, culturally unmarked and taken for granted, but nevertheless a single domain.[28]

Dale Eickelman, who studied a Moroccan town somewhat similar to Sefrou, gives us a valuable alternative way of looking at the Moroccan images of their domestic world. He suggests that the general cultural construct under which all these relationships fall is as follows:

375

qaraba, a key concept which literally means "closeness." As used by urban and rural Moroccans, qaraba carries contextual meanings which range imperceptibly from asserted and recognized ties of kinship, to participation in factional alliances, ties of patronage and clientship and . . . common bonds developed out of residential propinquity. "Closeness" is acting *as if* ties of obligation exist with another person which are so compelling that they are generally expressed in the idiom of kinship. This is because kinship ties, especially those of blood, symbolize bonds which, however they are valorized, are considered permanent and cannot be broken. Most quarters have a cluster of households which claim relations to each other in this way.

In many respects "closeness" in present-day Morocco resembles the concept of "group feeling" (ʿasabiya) presented over five hundred years earlier by the North African philosopher and sociologist, Ibn Khaldun. In his exposition of the concept Ibn Khaldun indicates the multiple bases on which "group feeling" can be asserted among both townsmen and tribesmen, but ultimately opts for the ideological position that the "naturalness" of blood ties makes them superior to all other modalities as a basis for "group feeling" . . . Present-day urban and rural Moroccans make the same claim. Such a position does not distinguish between "closeness" using kinship as an idiom in which social relations can be expressed and as the presence of "actual" ties of kinship.[29]

Under this formulation "actual" kinship ties are a subset of other stable personal relationships. A term for "close relatives" given above is quraba, a nominative plural form of qaraba. As was pointed out earlier, this term is sometimes used to include people who have become part of the group in other ways than by birth or marriage. Ties by birth and marriage are felt to epitomize, and to be the most intense form of, qaraba, but they do not define it. For a phenomenologically valid statistical census of marital choice patterns, the perceived circle of qorabin is the central region of the actual in-marrying population and should be identified for each marriage. It should be kept in mind that qaraba is a gradable attribute, not a disjunctive one, and that it cannot have clear, stable lines around it, so that the membership within the quraba group is always debatable.

It is important, however, to recognize the forward-looking quality of the construct. Relationships of closeness are never fully stable and unalterable, but must be constantly tended. They can be generated, also, and many of the out-marriages must be seen as attempts to convert a lightly traveled road into a well-trodden one. The reason the arrangement of marriages is felt to be so fraught with potential embarrassment or conflict is that many delicate and highly valued social bonds are being tested, reinforced, or fabricated with each new contract. The high level of the sdaq is also related to this fact. It performs many functions simultaneously, but the greatest is the sealing of the contract, the act of giving an earnest of good intentions in regard to a whole range of future relationships. In the complex and shifting social world of Morocco, a well-placed marriage is an opportunity to build a zone of predictability and control, a framework of obligations and expectations that will provide slightly surer footing in the quicksand of personal relationships.

Notes

1. The literature on kinship and family relationships in North Africa and the Middle East has been unnecessarily burdened with a model of opposing descent groups whose internal segments are structured genealogically, together with an inordinate stress on the structural or functional importance of a so-called preference rule for marriage to the father's brother's daughter (see Evans-Pritchard, E.E., *The Sanusi of Cyrenaica*, London, 1949; and Gellner, *Saints of the Atlas*, London, 1969). For criticisms of this model, see Peters, "Some Structural Aspects of the Feud Among the Camel-Herding Bedouin of Cyrenaica," *Africa*, 37:261–82 (1967), and Berque, J. "Qu'est-ce qu'une 'tribu' Nord-Africaine?" *Eventail de l'histoire vivant*, 1:261–71 (1953). A few of the most important articles on father's brother's daughter marriage are: Murphy, R. F., and L. Kasdan, "The Structure of Parallel Cousin Marriage," *American Anthropologist*, 61:17–79; (1959); Patai, R., "The Structure of Endogamous Unilineal Descent Groups," *Southwestern Journal of Anthropology*, 21:325–50 (1965); Cuisinier, J., "Endogamie et exogamie dans le marriage Arabe," *L'Homme*, 4:71–89 (1962); Bourdieu, P., *Esquisse d'une théorie de la pratique*, Geneva, 1973, Chap. 3; and Keyser, "The Middle Eastern Case: Is There a Marriage Rule?" *Ethnology*, 8:293–309, (1974).

Given this literature, it is necessary to evaluate this model, and if, as is abundantly clear, it proves inadequate, we must indicate what a more valid model might look like. Although in certain contexts Moroccans employ an idiom that appears to be one of lineage segments and genealogical trees, I shall try to show that their more fundamental concepts of intergroup and interpersonal relationships are really quite otherwise.

2. My debt to David M. Schneider is obvious. In his critiques of the theoretical foundations of kinship studies he has radically recast the research questions in a way that makes it now possible to begin to understand Moroccan social life. His insight that most anthropologists have begun research with the assumption that there is to be found in every culture a version of a universal and logically fundamental system of categorization of social units and roles, based on biogenetic relationships of parentage, siblingship, and their extensions, and his assertion that this need not always be the case, provided the starting point for this analysis. See Schneider. D.M., *American Kinship: A Cultural Account*, Englewood Cliffs, (N.J.), 1967; "What is Kinship All About?" in Reining, P. (ed.), *Kinship Studies in the Morgan Centenial Year*, Washington, 1972, pp. 32–63; "Notes Toward a Theory of Culture," in Basso, K., and H. Selby (eds.), *Meaning in Anthropology*, Albuquirque, 1976, pp. 197–220. See also Leach, E. *Rethinking Anthropology*, London, 1962; Needham, R. *Rethinking Kinship*, London, 1973, Introduction; and Geertz, H. and C. Geertz, *Kinship in Bali*, Chicago, 1976.

3. For other circumstantial descriptions of family life in Morocco, see Fernea, E. *A Street in Marrakech*, New York, 1975; Goichon, A.-M., *La Femme de la moyenne bourgeoisie fasiya*, Paris, 1929; le Tourneau, R. *Fès avant le Protectorat*, Casablanca, 1949; Maher, V., *Women and Property in Morocco: Their Changing Relation to the Process of Social Stratification in the Middle Atlas*, London, 1974; and Mernissi, F. *Beyond the Veil: Male-Female Dynamics in a Modern Muslim Society*, New York, 1976.

4. This is a nisba. See Geertz, C., " 'From the Native's Point of View': On the Nature of Anthropological Understanding," in Basso and Selby, *op. cit.*, pp. 221–37. Properly, the plural of Adluni is Adluniyyin, but I will use the English plural form: Adluns.

5. Mulay is a title indicating that the person is a sherif. The name Mulay Hamid is a pseudonym, as are the names of all of his descendants discussed below.

6. For further details and analysis of the rules and practices of divorce, see Rosen, L., "I Divorce Thee," *Trans-action*, 7:34–7 (1970).

7. Sheikh and l-Haj are titles indicating, respectively, that the personage is a leader or a singer, and a man who has gone on the pil

grimage to Mecca and who is by inference wealthy.

8. The Islamic regulations regarding prohibited marriages state that a man may not marry his female ascendants and descendants, the former wives of his ascendants and descendants, his sister, and female descendants of his sister and brother, his paternal and maternal aunts, the sisters and aunts of ascendants, his mother-in-law, his wife's other female ascendants, his stepdaughter, his wife's other female descendants, a woman who as an infant nursed at the same breast he did, the sister of the woman who nursed him, or a woman related to his current wife within the forbidden degrees of consanguinity, affinity, and fosterage above (Schacht, J., *An Introduction to Islamic Law,* Oxford; 1964, p. 162). For Moroccan laws of prohibited marriages, see Colomer, A. *Droit musulman,* Vol. 1, Rabat, 1963. See also Goode, W. J., *World Revolution and Family Patterns,* New York, 1963.

9. For laws regarding marriage and divorce, see Schacht, *op. cit.,* pp. 161–8; Colomer, *op. cit.,* For details on Sefrou usage, see Rosen, *op. cit.*

10. See note 2 above.

11. Annex B gives details on the methods employed in collecting these marital statistics and further comparative materials.

12. See Mernissi, *op. cit.*

13. In the 1960 census 5.5% of households of the Sefrou-born, Arabic-speaking population were single-person households. Those population groups who were rural immigrants into town showed higher proportions of single-person households, the range being 10% to 11%.

14. On the other hand, the census interviewers had apparently little difficulty in conducting interviews concerning the household (*foyer*) as defined by international census conventions. A summary of household size and household composition based on the 1960 census is given in the appendix to the hardcover edition of this volume. These statistics ought to be interpreted in the light of the material presented here: What may appear to be a small isolated household centered on a conjugal family, or even consisting of a single adult, may be an artifact of the interview schedule. The members of the apparently "small" household may actually be parts of complex networks of personal arrangements of the type described here.

15. For a number of vivid case histories of husband-wife relationships and how they are affected by the pulls and pressures from familial networks see Maher, *op. cit.,* and *op. cit.*

16. These estimates of economic worth were made in the simplest and roughest manner. Several reliable informants, each of whom knew many members of the Adlun family, were asked to indicate their levels of income. The categories were common Sefrou ones, ranging from *wālu* ("nothing") to *la-bas bezzaf bezzaf* ("nothing wrong at all at all"). Though admittedly crude and certainly not quantifiable, the survey confirmed the main finding of the extent of differences in income within this family, which had been derived from personal observation. Other families were surveyed in the same manner, and the same spread was revealed.

17. This term is borrowed from Abner Cohen, "The Politics of Marriage in Changing Middle Eastern Stratification Systems," in Plotnicov, L., and A. Tuden (eds.), *Essays in Comparative Social Stratification,* Pittsburgh, 1970.

18. The length of such a list is by no means extraordinary. The legal documents of the first half of this century usually refer to individuals by several alternative names. Some Moroccans, during that period in which many land transactions with the French were being made while at the same time the Westernized civil law concerning property was still being developed in Morocco, obtained "letters of identity" that provided a list almost as long as that given above, officially establishing that all the names on the list signified the same man.

With the introduction of municipal registers (*l'état civil*), the naming system has been rationalized for some of the population. A person who registers must select a permanent surname (called in Sefrou, *kuniya*), which is then passed down to his sons in the Western manner. The registrants select their own official surnames out of the whole range of identifying and locational terms. It is of interest that in this process of deliberate selection of a surname, the patronym is not always or even often chosen. See also Gellner, *op. cit.,* pp. 36–7.

19. Another term for pedigree is *silsila n-nasab* ("chain of relations"). The word *nasab* is from the same root as nisba and *nsīb* ("affine"), but its burden in the above phrase is "agnatic ancestor."

20. Annex A gives a systematic list of the kin terms of one Sefrou dialect and a brief discussion of variation.

21. As can be seen in Figure 9, the term jedd-i also has a classificatory spread, in that it can be used for both the grandfather and the great-grandfather. Some speakers restrict the term to the parent's parents and refer to the great-grandfather by a derivative compound (e.g., my father's grandfather). Address forms can also introduce distinctions not provided in

the lexicon; for instance, the paternal grandparents may be differently addressed than the maternal ones. The uses of kin terms and other terms in address ae highly complex, too much so to go into here.

22. Actually, in Islamic law, according to Schacht (*op. cit.*, pp. 169–74), the term *ᶜasaba* has a much broader coverage and includes one's son, one's son's son, brother, father, father's brother, as well as more distant agnates. The inheritance rule is that sons and successively after them son's sons, brothers, and brothers' sons inherit the estate with the provision that the wife and the following cognatic kin be given specified fractional shares (*farḍ*) in specific sequence so that they will not be deprived of support: the daughter, sister, half sister, and mother. The details of the law are very complex, but come down to a protection of the members of the immediate family, which is conceptually distinguished from the agnatic kin.

23. See also Rosen, *op. cit.*

24. In 1965, in the qadi's court in Sefrou 423 marriages and 149 divorces were registered. Thus, the ratio of divorces to marriages was 35.2% (See Annex B, Tables B.4 and B.5).

25. See Rosen, L. "Bargaining for Reality: A Study of Male-Female Relations in Morocco," in Beck, L. and Keddie, N. (eds.), *Women in the Muslim World,* Cambridge (Mass.), 1979, pp. 561–84.

26. See Geertz and Geertz, *Kinship in Bali,* where a statistical index of marital choices is set forth which is appropriate where the total marrying population is known and the marriage pool has distinct boundaries. These conditions do not obtain in Morocco.

27. Bourdieu, *op. cit.*

28. Bourdieu (*op. cit.*) says that the use of a genealogical grid to estimate statistically the proportion of endogamous marriages ignores the exigencies of age differences because it imposes an assumption that any collaterals of the same generation are of marriageable age. This is only one of a number of similar assumptions imposed by such a model. Bourdieu further points out that the "rate of endogamy" can be raised or lowered by the simple shifting of the boundary between in-marriages and out-marriages and that there is no extrinsic way (such as number of collateral lines) to determine the location of that line.

29. Eickelman, D., *Moroccan Islam: Tradition and Society in a Pilgrimage Center,* Austin, 1976, p. 96. The work by Ibn Khaldun that Eickelman cites is *The Muqaddimah* (trans. by F. Rosenthal), Princeton, 1967, pp. 249–310, especially p. 264.

Annex A: Moroccan kinship terms of reference

The terms listed in Tables A.1 and A.2 are given in the possessive form. The suffix -*i* or -*y* means "my." Note that the terms for mother and father, *ymma* and *bba,* are what Harrell[1] calls "inherently possessed" (i.e., the terms in their unmodified forms mean "my mother" and "my father").

The terms given represent usage of one urban Arabic-speaking informant from an old Sefrou family, the Nas Adlun. Only some of the many alternative forms are given. In a town such as Sefrou with a heterogeneous population from all over Morocco and many residents who are bilingual in Arabic and in one of the various Berber languages, considerable variation is to be expected. Much of the variation is a matter of synonyms, with different words referring to the same category of kinsmen. Some of these alternative conventions appear to reflect differences in formality of life in various families, much in the same way that American choices between father, dad, and daddy are responses to situational or life-style differences. So, for instance, the term for "grandfather" can be a flat, homey *jedd-ī,* an affectionate *ḥennan-ī,* or a highly respectful *bba sid-ī.* Variation in address is even greater. There is another dimension of variation, which is a matter not of alternative lexical forms relating to life style or region, but of alternative views of the structure itself. This dimension appears most distinctly in the variant interpretations of the term *ᶜamm-ī* ("father's brother"). This is discussed in the text.

Note

1. Harrell, R.S., *A Short Reference Grammar of Moroccan Arabic,* Washington, D.C., 1962, p. 141.

Table A.1. *Consanguineal terms of reference*

	Term	Gloss	Kin type
Basic terms			
Primary relatives	*ymma*	my mother	Mo
	bba	my father	Fa
	ḵa-y (ḵuya)	my brother	Br
	ḵet-ī	my sister	Si
	bent-ī	my daughter	Da
	weld-ī	my son	So
Parents' siblings	*ʿammī*	my father's brother (some: also any male older than ego)	FaBr (FaFaBr, FaFaBrSo, FaFaFaBr, FaFaFaBrSo)
	ʿammt-ī	my father's sister (some: also my father's father's sister)	FaSi (FaFaSi)
	ḵal-ī (ḫbīb-ī)	my mother's brother	MoBr
	ḵalt-ī	my mother's sister	MoSi
Lineal ascendant and descendant	*jeddī (bennan-ī, bba sīd-ī)*	my grandfather (some: also my great-grandfather)	FaFa, MoFa (FaFaFa, FaMoFa, MoFaFa, MoMoFa)
	jeddat-ī (lalla)	my grandmother (some: also my great-grandmother)	FaMo, MoMo (FaFaMo, FaMoMo, MoFaMo, MoMoMo)
	ḫfīd-ī	my grandson	SoSo, DaSo
	ḫfīdt-ī	my granddaughter	SoDa, DaDa
	ibiyed-ī	my great-grandson	SoSoSo, SoDaSo, DaSoSo, DaDaSo
	ibiyedt-ī	my great-granddaughter	SoSoDa, SoDaDa, DaSoDa, DaDaDa

Table A.1. (*cont.*)

Term	Gloss	Kin type
Derived terms		
Cousins		
weld ʿamm-ī	my father's brother's son (some: also any male collateral agnate same age as ego)	FaBrSo FaFaBrSoSo, FaFaFaBrSoSoSo
bent ʿamm-ī	my father's brother's daughter (some: also any female collateral agnate same age as ego)	FaBrDa (FaFaBrSoDa, FaFaFaBrSoSoDa)
weld ʿammt-ī	my father's sister's son (some: son of any woman I call ʿammt-i)	FaSiSo
bent ʿammt-ī	my father's sister's daughter (some: daughter of any woman I call ʿammt-i)	FaSiDa
weld ḵal-ī	my mother's brother's son	MoBrSo
bent ḵal-ī	my mother's brother's daughter	MoBrDa
weld ḵalt-ī	my mother's sister's son	MoSiSo
bent ḵalt-ī	my mother's sister's daughter	MoSiDa
Sibling's children		
weld ḵa-y	my brother's son	BrSo
bent ḵa-y	my brother's daughter	BrDa
weld ḵet-i	my sister's son	SiSo
bent ḵet-i	my sister's daughter	SiDa
Half siblings		
ḵa-y d-ness	half brother (ness-half)	FaWiSo, MoHuSo
ḵet-i d-ness	half sister	FaWiDa, MoHuDa
ḵa-y šqīq, (pl. ḵut šqayq)	my full brother (šqayq-true)	Br
ḵet-i šqīqa	my full sister	Si

Table A.2. *Affinal terms of reference*

	Term	Gloss	Kin-type
Terms used by parents of a married child	*nsīb-ī*	my male in-law	DaHu, DaHuFa, DaHuBr, SoWiFa, SoWiBr
	nsībt-ī	my female in-law	DaHuMo, DaHuSi, SoWiMo, SoWiSi
	ᶜarust-ī	my son's wife (sometimes my brother's son's wife; the term nsibt-i is never used here)	SoWi (BrSoWi)
Terms used by a married woman	*rajl-ī*	my husband	Hu
	šik̲-ī	my husband's father	HuFa
	ᶜaguzt-ī (lalla)	my husband's mother	HuMo
	lus-ī	my husband's brother	HuBr
	lust-ī	my husband's sister	HuSi
	nut-ī (pl. nu yet)	my husband's brother's wife (reciprocal)	HuBrWi
Terms used by a married man	*mrat-ī*	my wife	Wi
	nsīb-ī	my wife's father	WiFa
		my wife's brother	WiBr
		my wife's brother's son	WiBrSo
		(my wife's brother son's son (my wife's father's brother)	(WiBrSoSo WiFaBr)
	nsībt-ī	my wife's mother	WiMo
		my wife's sister	WiSi
	slīf-ī (pl.)	my wife's sister's husband (reciprocal)	WiSiHu

383

Table A.2. (*cont.*)

	Term	Gloss	Kin-type
Terms used about sibling's spouses and affines	nsīb-ī	my sister's husband	SiHu
		my sister's husband's father	SiHuFa
	nsīb-ī	my sister's husband's brother (my sister's husband's brother's son)	SiHuBr (SiHuBrSo)
		my brother's wife's father	BrWiFa
		my brother's wife's brother (my brother's wife's brother's son)	BrWiBr (BrWiBrSo)
	nsībt-ī	my sister's husband's mother	SiHuMo
		my sister's husband's sister	SiHuSi
		my brother's wife's mother	BrWiMo
		my brother's wife's sister	BrWiSi
	mrat ḵay	my brother's wife (nsibt-i is never used here)	BrWi
Terms involved in the plural marriage situation	šrīḵa (pl. šrayḵ, šrīḵat)	plural wife	HuWi
	mrat bba	my father's wife (not my mother)	FaWi
	rbīb-ī	my husband's son by another wife, stepson	HuSo, WiSo
	rbībt-ī	my husand's daughter by another wife, stepdaughter	HuDa, WiDa,

Table A.2. (*cont.*)

Terms for kinsmen's spouses who are not considered to be affinal relatives		
rajil ḵalt-i[a]	my mother's sister's husband	MoSiHu
mrat ḵal-i- (*mrat ḫbibi*)[a]	my mother's brother's wife	MoBrWi
rajl ᶜammt-i[a]	my father's sister's husband	FaSiHu
mrat ᶜammi-i[a]	my father's brother's wife	FaBrWi
mrat weld ḵet-i[a]	my sister's son's wife	SiSoWi
rajl bent ḵet-i[b]	my sister's daughter's husband	SiDaHu
mrat weld ḵa-y[a]	my brother's son's wife	BrSoWi
rajl bent ḵa-y[b]	my brother's daughter's husband	BrDaHu

[a] These persons are never called nsib-i.
[b] Some speakers use the term nsib-i for these two persons.

Annex B: Statistics on marital choice patterns and divorce

The following materials, compiled by Hildred Geertz, Lawrence Rosen, and Paul Rabinow, are summaries of marriages contracted within four large patronymic associations in the Sefrou region. Complete genealogies of all known members of the group were drawn up with the help of several key informants, going back in generations as far as the oldest member could recall. In most cases the generational spread is four or five, including the living ones. The materials in each group were checked by several informants in consultation with other members of their families. For each person appearing in the tables, the following data were collected: name, names and family origin of all spouses including divorced and deceased ones, names of all offspring, current place of residence, and employment. From these data a tabulation of all marriages of the men of each group was made. (A tabulation of the marriages of the women of the groups was also made, but has been omitted here for simplicity.) Similar materials were collected for small patronymic groups that have only a few members, but because of their small size these are not susceptible to statistical summary.

Several difficulties are encountered in drawing up and interpreting a census of this sort. First, informants are liable systematically to omit certain kinds of data, notably daughters of a family and brief transitory marriages that ended quickly in divorce or death and left no children. Second, any one informant has only limited knowledge about many of the members of his patronymic association, and it is necessary to check and augment his accounts by consulting people in different positions in the system. Older women, generally, had the broadest range of kinship knowledge, even those who had married into the family from outside. Third, it was not always possible to decide which kinsmen were to be considered within a minor patronymic group and which were to be excluded. Even the identification of a woman as father's brother's daughter was sometimes difficult to ascertain, for informants would sometimes use the term in a very vague way. The

only way to ascertain the precise kinship relation between spouses was
to trace the lines out on the anthropologist's constructed genealogy.

A serious difficulty in the interpretation of the statistical data is the problem of finding a way to test for significance. The availability of a spouse within a certain category (e.g., father's brother's daughter, minor patronymic group) directly affects the exercise of choice. Demographic fluctuations make the size of any availability pool unstable. In very large patronymic associations these variations are statistically leveled off, but then the same difficulty of interpretation appears when one tries to compare subgroups within them. If one is studying a population that is almost entirely endogamous within the local community, a weighted index of marital choices can be calculated that takes into account the number of available women within any subgroup and the number of available women in the total pool.[1] But even this cannot take into account stochastic shifts at successive points in time.

Another problem must be given thoughtful consideration in regard to statistics on marriages collected by means of a genealogical grid. The assumption behind such a census procedure is that consanguineal links, chains, or networks can be taken as important elements in the definitions of social realities guiding the exercising of marital choice. It is assumed that some construct built up out of consanguineal links is the basic covert cognitive map of the actors themselves. In the light of some of the data and arguments put forth in the main essay, this assumption can seriously be questioned in regard to Morocco. The argument is made that the more strongly the tables produced by this method exhibit patterns in the direction of choices toward genetically defined kinsmen, or toward certain kinds of such kinsmen, the closer our model is to theirs. Certainly, the nearer our categorizing schemes are to those culturally defined frameworks that actually guide the actors, the clearer the statistical patterns ought to be. But in the absence of tests of significance that can evaluate the null hypothesis (i.e., that marriages within the total marrying population pool are distributed randomly in regard to kinship), it is difficult to know what a "strong" pattern might be.

Despite these recognized shortcomings in our data, we present below statistical tables giving simple, unweighted frequency distributions, with no attempt at testing for significance. The differences between groups appear large enough for us to feel that the figures are worth publishing, even though their value is primarily illustrative. The tables are based on a count of all known marriages, including those ending in divorce and death, to all known men, living and dead, of the patronymic association.

The four groups compared in Tables B.1 and B.2 were selected to contrast on two dimensions, urban versus rural, and shurfa versus nonshurfa. It is evident that nonshurfas, especially urban ones, do not marry close kinsmen to the degree that shurfas do. It is also probably that nonshurfa patronymic associations are much smaller than, and fragment much more easily than, their shurfa counterparts. In fact, it was difficult to find a nonshurfa urban patronymic association large enough to satisfy our statistical requirement. The smallness of non-shurfa patronymic groups is probably attributable to the fact that a relatively small amount of social utility or prestige is attached to non-shurfa patronyms. A nonshurfa name does not normally carry as much meaning as does a shurfa name. Nonshurfa, in fact, is an unmarked category in Moroccan classifications, further bearing this out.

On the other hand, the fact of possession of a shurfa patronym does not necessarily entail high endogamy, for a closer examination of sub-groups within the shurfa patronymic associations shows that certain ones have very low endogamy rates. In Table B.3 the subpatronymic groups within the two shurfa families studied are indicated. Despite their small numbers, it is quite evident that there can be great differences. Our interviews indicated that some subgroups that intermarry a great deal seem to have been following an endogamy policy for several generations, whereas others appear to have changed their policy from in- to out-marriage in a generation.

Divorce rates for the city and region of Sefrou, as calculated from the court records, are given in Table B.4. These figures are for all types of divorces, revocable as well as irrevocable. For purposes of comparison, divorce rates for all of the provinces of Morocco are given in Table B.5.

Note

1. See Geertz, H., and C. Geertz, *Kinship
in Bali,* Chicago, 1976.

Table B.1. *Marital choice patterns: father's brother's daughter marriage: four patronymic associations compared*

Patronymic association	Percent married to father's brother's daughter	Total marriages
Nas Adlun (urban, shurfa)	9.0	66
Nas Britel (urban, nonshurfa)	3.6	110
Nas Sidi Lahcen Lyusi (rural, shurfa)	4.5	111
Nas Iawen (rural, nonshurfa)	8.9	56

Origin of wives of men with same patronym within last two generations. Marriages tabulated here are only those about which accurate information was available as to the married couple's parents' siblings.

Table B.2. *Marital choice patterns: patronymic association versus outsiders: four patronymic associations compared*

Patronymic association	Percent married within same patronymic association	Percent married from outside	Total marriages
Nas Adlun (urban, shurfa)	69.0	31.0	107
Nas Britel (urban, nonshurfa	25.4	74.6	110
Nas Sidi Lahcen Lyusi (rural, shurfa)	73.0	27.0	223
Nas Iawen (rural, nonshurfa)	10.7	89.3	56

Origins of wives of men with same patronym within last three generations.

389

Table B.3. *Marital choice patterns: proximate patronymic association versus larger patronymic association.*

Patronymic association	Percent from same proximate patronymic association	Percent from same larger patronymic association (includes those in col. 1	Percent from outside larger patronymic association	Total marriages
Nas Adlun				
Nas Hamid	30	79	21	33
Nas bel Abes	38	76	24	52
Nas Messaoud	4	36	64	22
Nas Adlun as a whole	29	69	31	107
Ait Sidi Lahcen Lyusi				
Ait Yazi ben Allal	38	88	12	73
Ait Ben Sedli	11	55	45	46
Wlad Sidi Mohammed ben Nasr	0	43	57	14
Ait Bel Larbi	9	79	21	33
Ait Sidi Lahcen Lyusi as a whole	22	73	27	166

Origin of wives of men with same patronym within last three generations.

Table B.4. *Divorce rates in the city and region of Sefrou*[a]

Year	Total marriages	Total divorces	Percent divorces of marriages
1915	60	51	85.0
1919	160	118	73.8
1926	69	51	73.9
1931	67	57	85.1
1936	216	139	63.4
1939	438	198	45.2
1945	691	357	51.7
1955	1,194	430	36.0
1960	559	226	40.4
1962	545	180	33.0
1963	512	189	36.9
1965	423	149	35.2
1966[b]	271	107	39.5

[a] After Independence in 1956, several additional courts were established in the region, thereby reducing the jurisdiction of the qadi's court in Sefrou.
[b] Figures only for the eight months of March, April, May, July, August, September, October, and December.

Table B.5. *Divorce rates by provinces of Morocco (in percent divorces of marriages)*

Province	1960	1962	1963	1965
Fez (city)	54.2	54.9	45.6	46.9
Fez (province)	45.6	44.7	39.5	43.9
Agadir	22.5	28.6	23.2	27.8
Marrakech	45.3	45.3	30.7	34.2
Beni Mellal	56.5	46.8	42.3	51.1
Casablanca	40.2	33.2	30.2	39.8
Rabat	51.7	42.8	39.0	39.2
Meknes	52.5	48.8	42.9	
Oujda	30.9	24.8	23.2	29.7
Ksar Souk	51.3	46.8	49.6	31.5
Tangiers	50.2	53.0	44.6	
Tetouan	35.0	31.5	30.2	
Nador	15.7	14.8	12.3	
Taza[a]		41.8	38.3	43.5

[a] Taza was part of the province of Fez until 1960.

391

Appendix: A statistical profile of the population of the town of Sefrou in 1960: analysis of the census

Hildred Geertz

Contents

Introduction: the construction of the social group (Table 1)

This is an analysis of the information contained in the raw interview sheets of the official 1960 Census of Sefrou. The data were obtained through the courtesy of the Service Central des Statistiques, Royaume du Maroc, in Rabat, which kindly gave permission to copy in coded form the original interview sheets for Sefrou. The codes represent a detailed sorting of answers to the questionnaire that follows the international conventions adopted by the United Nations. In consequence, I had for each individual within the entire population of Sefrou (20,961 people) data concerning personal characteristics (ethnic category, sex, age, birthplace, years of urban experience, marital status, language spoken, language read, occupation, and level of responsibility in a job); characteristics of the dwelling occupied (location, building type, home tenure, number of dwelling rooms, and presence or absence of kitchen, workrooms, running water, electricity, bath, toilet, telephone); and characteristics of the household (the interviewee's place within it and the number of persons living together).

A critical attitude concerning the reliability of the original data must be maintained in regard to the statistics presented here, as with any census data. I give two examples drawn from experience in other countries. First, it is very likely that many persons of low income, uncertain residence, and irregular employment are not adequately enumerated, for the interviewers may have been unaware of their presence. Within certain age groups, this overlooked portion of the population can be significantly large. Second, there may be a systematic bias in the reporting of ages, notably of women, where ten- to fifteen-year-olds are reported as older than they are and women over thirty are reported as younger.

This material was processed with the aid of a computer, enabling me to sort the raw data into almost every imaginable arrangement and to explore virtually all possible interconnections among them. It was also possible to search for internal inconsistencies that indicate interviewing or copying error (e.g., instances of infants listed as "speaking Arabic"). All such cases were corrected or dropped from the final data base. Another check was made to see whether there were any systematic biases in the distribution of "no response" or "blank" answers to certain questions. The computer was asked, for instance, whether there were more blank answers on occupation among illiterate people than among literate, or whether there were more blanks in certain census tracts than others, or more blanks on literacy from Berber speakers than from Arabic speakers. It was found that for the town population the proportions of blanks were generally negligible and in any case were not systematically biasing. An exception was certain questions regarding the conditions of housing, where information about the presence of running water, toilet, and bath and kitchen facilities was often omitted. Because the distribution of blank answers was different for different questions on the schedule, many of the totals in the following tables differ by small numbers: The computer dropped out those individual answers on which a blank was drawn. Percentages were computed on the available filled-in answers, rather than on the total interviewed.

The rural interview schedules had far too many blanks and internal inconsistencies to permit the sort of detailed analysis that was possible for the town population. For this reason no report on the rural population of the region around the town has been drawn up. *Rural* in most of the tables means rural-born but at the time of census living in the town.

As a further assurance of the validity of the generalizations, I decided not to base the statistical analysis on a random sample of the available data, as is usual, but to employ all the interview schedules in my calculations. An exception was made, however, in the analysis of household composition and marriage patterns: For technical reasons I was obliged to base these calculations on a random sample of 60 percent of the population.

I have attempted to provide neither a simple statistical summation of the answers given to the questions on the schedules nor a blind exercise in correlations among these answers. Instead, I have tried to build up a reasonably complex picture of the population of Sefrou that accords with the social realities of

the town. Throughout each step in the data analysis, therefore, I constantly checked the findings against the more qualitative sociological image of the town's composition derived from field research.

The most important step was the sorting of the population into subgroupings whose social characteristics could be compared. The obvious first solution was the one apparently held by the designers of the census questionnaire: the answer to the question whether the individual was a Muslim, a Jew, or a citizen of a foreign nation. But for my purposes, this was too coarse a division because the Muslim population is 84 percent of the town's. I considered a number of other ways of distinguishing important subgroupings – such as residential location, economic status, and occupation – but on the basis of field experience I decided that all these were, in the eyes of the Sefrou population at any rate, secondary to two other personal attributes: the language a person speaks in the home and whether he or she was born in an urban or in a rural place. These two, combined with the first one, which the interview schedule lists as "ethnic category or nationality," were used to produce a basic sorting into what I have called the *social group*.

Because many people of Sefrou are bilingual or even trilingual, the following conventions were established for determining a person's primary language: An *Arabic speaker* was defined as a person who spoke Arabic and no Berber; a *Berber speaker* was defined as a person who spoke Berber whether or not he could also speak Arabic or other languages, for field research showed that those who spoke Arabic as children virtually never subsequently learn to speak Berber, whereas many people whose childhood language was Berber are also fluent in Arabic. The listed birthplaces were classified into the following categories: the town of Sefrou, other towns in Morocco, rural areas of Morocco, France and other foreign countries.

Thus the classification by *social group* was made on the basis of the three questions in the original interview schedule: ethnic category, primary language spoken, and birthplace. It soon became apparent that one further criterion was necessary. I found that the census interviewers classified young children of Berber speakers living in town simply as "Arabic speakers" and, of course, as "born in Sefrou," with the consequence that the number of Arabic-speaking urban-born Muslims was over-inflated, and the proportion of Berber-speaking rural-born Muslims was unrealistically reduced. For this reason, the population sorted into social groups was confined to those aged fifteen years and over.

Table 1 lists the resultant sixteen social groups together with each one's component ethnic category, birthplace category, and languages.

Classifying the population of Sefrou in this manner means that a few persons have been omitted from the tables. Twenty Moroccan Muslims who were born abroad are omitted, and nine Jews who were born abroad are classified among "other urban Jews." The category "North-Africa-born foreigners" consists mainly, but not entirely, of Algerians. For most of the analysis all three French groups have been merged

into one, and the other foreigners have been omitted. Highly detailed analyses were justified only for the four largest social groups: the Sefrou-born Arabic speakers, the rural-born Arabic speakers, the rural-born Berber speakers, and the Sefrou-born Jews. Together, the first three groups make up 84 percent of Sefrou's adult Muslim population, and the Sefrou-born Jews represent 89 percent of the adult Jewish population. These four groups are the main objects of the study, with occasional side comments on the other smaller groups, notably the Fez-born Arabic speakers and the Bhalil-born Arabic speakers (who make a neat contrast with one another, the former entering Sefrou mainly at the top of the social ladder, the latter at the bottom), the rural-born Jews, and the French.

These composite classifications, the social groups, have served as the basic matrix for most of the statistical analysis reported below. Unless otherwise noted, the percentages are calculated in such a way as to compare the composition of each social group with each of the others. An alternative matrix, for example, might have used socioeconomic status as the independent variable and compared high-, medium-, and low-status slices of the population in regard to their composition into social groups, literacy, possession of running water, and so on. Almost all the tables give the original numerical data, so that a reader can recalculate the comparisons in different ways. In fact, in the basic study, from which these tables are only a selection, nearly every conceivable direction of comparison was carried out.

The reader of the three essays in this

volume will be well aware that what I
term social groups in this statistical
analysis should not be assumed to have
substantiality, homogeneity, or sharp
social recognition. They form, nonetheless, sociologically useful general categories within which the quantitative
census data can be arranged without un-
due violence to cultural reality.

Table 1. *Social groups of Sefrou constructed from the census categories*

Social group	Ethnic category	Birthplace	Languages
Sefrou Arabs	Muslim	Sefrou	Arabic or Arabic plus French, Arabic plus Spanish.
Rural Arabs	Muslim	Rural areas	Arabic or Arabic plus French, Arabic plus Spanish.
Rural Berbers	Muslim	Rural areas	Berber or Berber plus Arabic, Berber plus Arabic plus French, Berber plus Spanish, Berber plus Arabic plus Spanish
Fez Arabs	Muslim	Fez	Arabic as above
Bhalil Arabs	Muslim	Bhalil	Arabic as above
Other urban Arabs	Muslim	Other urban centers in Morocco	Arabic as above
Other urban Berbers	Muslim	Other urban centers in Morocco	Berber as above
Sefrou-born Berbers	Muslim	Sefrou	Berber as above
Sefrou Jews	Jewish	Sefrou	Not applicable
Rural Jews	Jewish	Rural areas	Not applicable
Other urban Jews	Jewish	Other urban centers in Morocco	Not applicable
France-born French	French	France	Not applicable
North-Africa-born French	French	Morocco and Algeria	Not applicable
Europe-born French	French	Europe outside of France	Not applicable
Europeans, non-French	Foreign(ex-cluding French)	Europe and America	Not applicable
North-Africa-born foreigners	Foreign (ex-cluding French)	Morocco and Algeria	Not applicable

Basic demographic characteristics
(Tables 2–13; Figures 1–3)

Tables 2 and 3 give the general composition of the town according to ethnic category (Muslim, Jew, and foreign nationality) and according to the constructed social groups. Table 2 depicts the total population of 20,961; Table 3 is based solely on the adult population fifteen years of age and over. In both cases the Muslim sector comes to 83.9 percent of the whole.

Table 4 traces the distribution of birthplace according to ethnic category, showing that whereas 56.2 percent of the Muslims had been born in Sefrou, a massive 90.1 percent of the Jews living there in 1960 had been born there, and a minuscule 5.8 percent of the French living in Sefrou had been born there. (These last are all children.) Where those people born elsewhere originally came from is displayed in Tables 5 and 6. Of the Muslim adults born outside of Sefrou a larger proportion of the Arabic speakers comes from urban rather than rural backgrounds (1,169 urban-born, 2,635 rural-born) than the Berber speakers (135 urban-born, 1,362 rural-born). Sefrou draws people from towns all over the country, as indicated in Table 6, but an analysis of that table shows that 76.1 percent of all Muslims born in other Moroccan cities come from towns lying within a 100-kilometer radius of Sefrou. Of the French adults 72 were born in France, 15 were born in Morocco, and 26 were born elsewhere in North Africa.

The complexity of the linguistic situation in Sefrou is shown in Table 7. Although there are large numbers of monolingual Arabic-speaking Muslims, most Berber-speaking Muslims also speak Arabic. The Arabic speakers include a higher proportion who also speak French. The Jews of Sefrou speak Arabic in their homes, but a good proportion also speak Berber. (This proportion is increased when only adult men are considered.) About half of the French who live in Sefrou are monolingual in French, but a good 36 percent also speak Arabic.

Figures 1 through 3 and Tables 8 and 9 deal with the distribution by age and sex of the population of the town. The analyses by ethnic category include children; those by social group exclude everyone under 15 years of age, but allow a more detailed analysis of differences among the Muslim groups. Comparison can be made between the age-sex pyramids of Sefrou and those of the general Moroccan population in Figures 1 and 2, but the differences are extremely difficult to interpret owing to the complexities of the in- and out-migration patterns. If place of birth is taken into account, as in the analyses by social group, some tentative conclusions can be reached.

For instance, if sex ratios according to age are computed, as in Table 8, it can be seen that the general Moroccan pattern is replicated in Sefrou: There is a higher proportion of women to men up until about age thirty-nine, when the ratios reverse and there are increasingly more men than women as age goes up. The differences among Sefrou's social groups lie mainly in the age point at which this reversal occurs: The rural-born groups show the shift occurring at a much earlier age and the ratio reach-

Appendix: A statistical profile   401

ing a much greater imbalance in the ages above forty; the Sefrou-born people make the shift later and do not reach so great an imbalance. The Sefrou-born Jews closely resemble the Sefrou-born Arab speakers. These changes in sex ratios probably reflect differential health conditions for men and women, with the high loss of life in maternity accounting for most of the differences. Better health care in the urban environment may account for the differences among the social groups.

The Sefrou Jewish population as a whole shows a marked surplus of women over men, possibly indicating differential emigration patterns already in effect in 1960.

The higher proportion of children ten to nineteen years of age in both the Muslim and Jewish groups probably represents school-age children from outside Sefrou who board in town while attending the many schools there.

Another area in which Sefrou apparently varies from the general Moroccan pattern is a lower-than-expected proportion of young Muslim men between twenty and twenty-nine years of age. Two phenomena could account for this, aside from errors in the census itself. One is a movement of Sefrou's young men to other towns, and the other is a low level of migration by rural-born young men into Sefrou. Closer analysis suggests that the latter may be a more important factor than the former. If one takes the group of men over twenty years of age alone, and compares the age distribution within it by social group, the distribution shown in Table 10 appears. These figures suggest that, relative to the pool of young

men for each social group, the rural-born men are underrepresented in Sefrou. My statistics on the rural areas are not reliable enough to indicate whether young men of this age remain in the village or whether they tend to pass Sefrou by in looking for work away from the village and go directly to the large coastal urban centers or to Europe. Ethnographic experience suggests that the latter is the case.

The French population of Sefrou has much smaller proportions of persons under the age of nineteen and over the age of seventy than the two indigenous groups. The French population is highly overrepresented in the ages from twenty to sixty-nine – the working years.

Table 11 examines the Muslim population that has moved into Sefrou from rural areas. The question on the census asked how long the person had lived in a town. The table shows that more of the Berber speakers than of the Arabic speakers living in town have moved there recently. About 34 percent of the Berber speakers arrived during the last five years before the census (i.e., after 1955), whereas only 22 percent of the Arabic speakers did the same. Table 12 examines the relation of age to time spent in a town. Taking men only aged between twenty and fifty-nine, and comparing the groups within each decade of age, the same pattern continues to hold: The Berbers have much higher proportions of newly urban men, no matter what the age. The difference between Arabic speakers and Berber speakers is greatest in the youngest group, where 71 percent of the Berbers have arrived during the last ten years compared with 48 percent of the Arabs.

The patterns of rural-born women (Table 13) are the same, except that both groups have even larger proportions of newly urban women than men, most especially in the groups under thirty-nine years old.

Table 2. *Composition of Sefrou: ethnic categories*

Ethnic category	Number	Percent of total population
Muslims	17,583	83.9
Jews	3,041	14.5
French	172	0.8
Algerians[a]	126	0.6
Other foreigners[b]	39	0.2
Total Sefrou population	20,961	100.0

[a] Includes 25 Algerian refugees.
[b] Includes Spanish, Italian, American, "others."

Table 3. *Composition of Sefrou: social groups (adults only)[u]*

Social group	Number	Percent of total adult population
Main Muslim groups		
Sefrou Arabs	3,936	34.9
Rural Arabs	2,635	23.4
Rural Berbers	1,362	12.1
Fez Arabs	310	2.8
Bhalil Arabs	451	4.0
Minor Muslim groups		
Other urban Arabs	499	4.4
Other urban Berbers	144	1.3
Sefrou-born Berbers	117	1.0
Total Muslim adults	9,454	83.9
Jews		
Sefrou Jews	1,434	12.7
Rural Jews	108	1.0
Other urban Jews	70	0.6
Total Jewish adults	1,612	14.3

Table 3 (*cont.*)

French		
France-born French	72	0.6
North-Africa-born French	41	0.4
Europe-born French	9	0.1
Total French adults	122	1.1
Other foreigners		
Europeans, non-French	6	0.1
North-Africa-born foreigners	69	0.6
Total other foreigners	75	0.7
Total all Sefrou adults	11,263	100.0

[a] See Introduction for the construction of social group categories according to ethnic category, birthplace, language spoken. Adults are persons aged 15 years and older.

Table 4. *Composition of Sefrou: birthplaces and ethnic categories[a]*

Birthplace, ethnic category	Number	Percent within ethnic category
Muslims		
Sefrou-born	9,889	56.2
Rural-born	5,476	31.1
Fez-born	587	3.3
Bhalil-born	570	3.2
Other large towns in Morocco	692	4.0
Small towns in Morocco	215	1.2
Foreign-born	20	0.1
Blank	134	0.8
Total	17,583	99.9
Jews		
Sefrou-born	2,739	90.1
Rural-born (in Morocco)	142	4.7
Other Moroccan towns	148	4.8
Foreign-born	9	0.3
Blank	3	0.1
Total	3,041	100.0

Appendix: A statistical profile 403

Table 4 (*cont.*)

Birthplace, ethnic category	Number	Percent within ethnic category
French		
Sefrou-born	10	5.8
Rural-born (Morocco)	6	3.5
Other Moroccan towns	39	22.6
Algeria	20	11.6
France	86	50.0
Other foreign countries	10	5.8
Blank	1	0.6
Total	172	99.9

a Omitted from this table are 126 Algerians and 39 other foreigners.

Table 5. *Birthplace details by ethnic category and language group (Muslim and Jewish adults only)*

Birthplace	Arabic-speaking Muslims		Berber-speaking Muslims		Jews	
	No.	Percent within ethnic-linguistic group	No.	Percent within ethnic-linguistic group	No.	Percent within ethnic group
Sefrou	3,936	50.9	117	7.2	1,434	89.4
Rural Morocco	2,635	34.0	1,362	84.4	108	6.7
Large towns and cities	451	5.8	38	2.4	45	2.8
Small towns	591	7.6	73	4.5	13	0.8
Small urban centers	127	1.6	24	1.5	4	0.2
Total	7,740	99.9	1,614	100.0	1,604	99.9

Table 6. *Birthplaces in other towns in Morocco by ethnic category and language group (Muslim and Jewish adults only)*

Town	Arabic-speaking Muslims	Berber-speaking Muslims	Jews
Large towns and cities			
Agadir	2	2	0
Al Hoceima	1	1	0
Asilah	1	0	1
Azzemour	2	2	0
Casablanca	15	1	6
El Jadida	4	0	0
Essouira	3	0	1
Fez	310	13	21
Ifrane	0	2	0
Kenitra	3	0	0
Khouribga	1	0	0
Larache	2	0	0
Marrakech	14	3	2
Meknes	25	1	9
Nador	2	4	0
Ouezzane	24	4	0
Oujda	19	0	1
Rabat	18	1	1
Safi	2	1	0
Salé	2	1	0
Settat	3	0	1
Tanger	5	2	2
Taza	24	1	0
Tetuan	1	0	0
Small towns			
Ahfir	5	0	0
Azrou	4	2	0
Ben Ahmed	2	0	0
Beni Mellal	7	3	0
Beni Sliman	2	0	0
Berkane	13	4	0
Bhalil	451	9	0
Demnat	1	0	0
El Gara	2	0	0
El Hajeb	2	2	0
El Kelaa du Sraghna	9	2	0
Erfoud	4	0	0
Fqih ben Saleh	2	0	0
Goulmina	0	5	0
Guercif	2	1	0
Immouzer du Kandar	20	11	2

Table 6 (*cont.*)

Town	Arabic-speaking Muslims	Berber-speaking Muslims	Jews
Jemaa Shaim	1	0	0
Kasba Tadla	4	1	0
Khemmisset	5	8	0
Khenifra	2	4	0
Ksar es Souk	16	2	1
Mechra bel Ksiri	2	0	0
Midelt	4	2	7
Moulay Idriss Zerhoun	11	0	0
Ouarzazate	0	0	1
Oued Zem	1	0	0
Rich	0	2	2
Saidia	1	0	0
Sidi Kacem	5	0	0
Souk el Arba du Gharb	2	0	0
Tamanar	1	0	0
Taourirt	8	3	0
Taroudant	2	6	0
Tiznit	0	6	0

Table 7. *Composition of Sefrou: languages by ethnic category*

Ethnic category, language	Number	Percent within ethnic category
Muslims		
Arabic only	10,736	61.1
Arabic plus French	2,759	15.7
Arabic plus Spanish	5	0.0
Total Arabic speakers	13,500	76.8
Berber only	38	0.2
Berber plus Arabic	1,733	9.9
Berber plus Arabic plus French	319	1.8
Berber plus Spanish	0	0.0
Berber plus Arabic plus Spanish	2	0.0
Total Berber speakers	2,092	11.9
None (children under one)	1,558	8.9
Blank	428	2.4
Total Muslims	17,578	100.0

Appendix: A statistical profile 405

Table 7 (*cont.*)

Ethnic category, language	Number	Percent within ethnic category
Jews		
Arabic only	1,376	45.4
Arabic plus French	1,093	36.0
Arabic plus Spanish	1	0.0
Berber only	1	0.0
Berber plus Arabic	89	2.9
Berber plus Arabic plus French	19	0.6
French only	14	0.5
None (children under one)	378	12.5
Blank	62	2.0
Total Jews	3,033	99.9
French		
French only	78	49.7
French plus Spanish	6	3.8
French plus Spanish plus Arabic	1	0.6
Arabic only	1	0.6
Arabic plus French	58	36.9
Berber only	0	0.0
Arabic plus Berber plus French	3	1.9
None (children under one)	8	5.1
Blank	2	1.3
Total French	157	99.9

Table 8. *Male/female ratios: social groups compared by age (Muslim adults)*

Age(yr)	Sefrou Arabs			Rural Arabs			Rural Berbers			All Morocco Muslims[a] (ratio M/F)
	M	F	Ratio M/F	M	F	Ratio M/F	M	F	Ratio M/F	
15–19	328	325	1.01	143	107	1.33	54	54	1.00	
20–29	495	593	0.83	292	367	0.80	124	174	0.71	0.81
30–39	391	467	0.84	309	328	0.94	168	200	0.84	0.93
40–49	261	286	0.91	246	216	1.14	147	127	1.16	1.05
50–59	201	161	1.24	155	136	1.14	100	63	1.59	1.07
60–69	138	118	1.17	107	75	1.43	46	44	1.04	1.04
70+	83	84	0.99	84	65	1.29	37	24	1.54	1.20
Total	1,897	2,034	0.93	1,336	1,295	1.03	676	686	0.98	

[a] Royaume du Maroc, *Annuaire statistique du Maroc,* Rabat, 1960, p. 64.

406 *Meaning and order in Moroccan society*

Table 9. *Male/female ratios: Jews of Sefrou and Morocco compared by age (adults)*

| Age (yr) | Sefrou Jews | | | National Jewish population[a] |
	M	F	Ratio M/F	Ratio M/F
15–19	99	152	0.65	
20–29	122	193	0.63	0.68
30–39	107	162	0.66	0.92
40–49	107	118	0.91	0.85
50–59	83	70	1.18	1.26
60–69	67	55	1.22	1.27
70+	53	46	1.15	0.82
Total	638	796	0.80	

[a] Royaume du Maroc, *Annuaire statistique du Maroc,* Rabat, 1960, p. 63.

Table 10. *Proportions of young men: social groups compared*

Social group	No. of men over 20	Men aged 20–29 (% of total over 20)	Men aged over 30 (% of total over 20)
National Muslim population	2,634,600	30.2	69.8
Sefrou-born Arabic speakers	1,569	31.5	68.5
Rural-born Arabic speakers	1,193	24.4	75.6
Rural-born Berber speakers	622	19.9	80.1

Table 11. *Composition of rural-born Muslim population of Sefrou: years of urban experience and language spoken (percent based on number of persons in each social group)*

Years of urban experience	Rural-born Arabic speakers (N = 2,635)	Rural-born Berber speakers (N = 1,362)
0–5	21.6 } 36.2	34.1 } 52.7
5–9	14.6	18.6
10–14	14.8	11.7
15–19	13.9	7.9
Over 20	22.2	14.7
Blank	12.8	12.9
	99.9	99.9

Table 12. *Composition of rural-born Muslim population of Sefrou: years of urban experience, language spoken, and age: men twenty to fifty-nine years old (percents based on total within each age cohort of each social group)*

Years of urban life	Age 20–29		Age 30–39		Age 40–49		Age 50–59		Age 20–59	
	Arabic	Berber	Arabic	Berber	Arabic	Berber	Arabic	Berber	Arabic	Berber
0–5	31.5	42.2	28.2	34.6	20.8	43.1	17.6	31.6	25.1	38.0
5–9	16.9	28.4	19.3	21.8	15.0	16.0	11.2	19.9	16.3	21.3
0–9 (1950+)	48.4	70.6	47.5	56.4	35.8	59.1	28.8	51.5	41.9	59.3
10–19 (1940+)	34.2	21.1	32.4	25.6	31.0	26.2	33.8	17.8	32.8	23.3
20+ (before 1940)	17.3	8.2	20.0	17.9	33.2	14.6	37.3	30.5	25.2	17.3
Total number in each age group	254	109	284	156	226	137	142	95	906	497

Table 13. *Composition of rural-born Muslim population of Sefrou: years of urban experience, language spoken, and age: women twenty to fifty-nine years old (percents based on total within each age cohort of each social group)*

Years of urban life	Age 20–29		Age 30–39		Age 40–49		Age 50–59		Age 20–59	
	Arabic	Berber	Arabic	Berber	Arabic	Berber	Arabic	Berber	Arabic	Berber
0–5	31.3	51.0	26.3	39.4	20.4	38.2	12.2	32.6	25.0	42.0
5–9	19.8	24.9	22.0	20.0	17.4	26.5	15.9	23.2	17.3	23.1
0–9 (1950+)	51.1	75.9	41.5	59.4	37.8	64.7	28.1	55.8	42.3	65.1
10–19 (1940+)	35.4	19.3	31.8	28.6	30.8	20.5	35.1	15.4	33.2	22.6
20+ (before 1940)	13.4	4.8	26.7	12.0	31.4	14.7	36.8	28.8	25.0	12.2
Total number in each age group	313	145	277	175	191	102	114	52	895	474

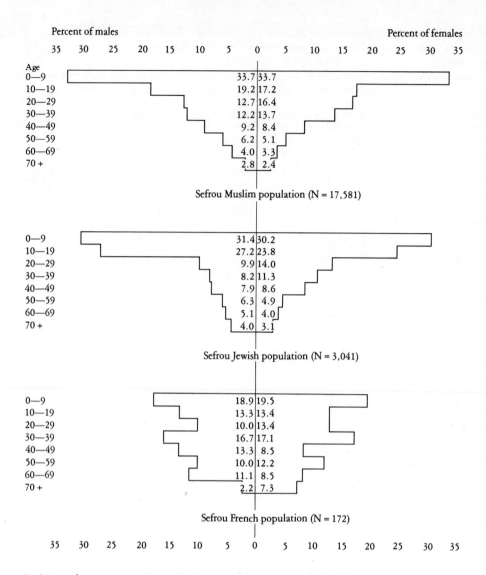

Figure 1. Age and sex composition: ethnic categories compared: Muslims, Jews, and French.

410 *Meaning and order in Moroccan society*

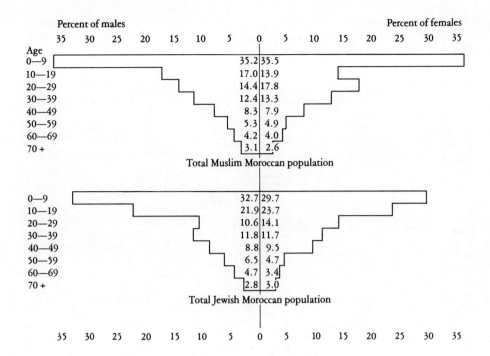

Figure 2. Age and sex composition of whole of Morocco: Muslims and Jews. (From Royaume de Maroc, *Annuaire statistique du Maroc,* Rabat, 1960, pp. 63, 64.)

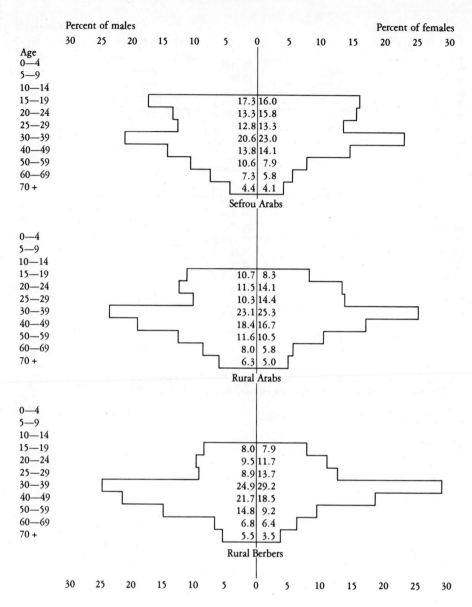

Figure 3. Age and sex composition: social groups compared: Muslim and Jewish adults.

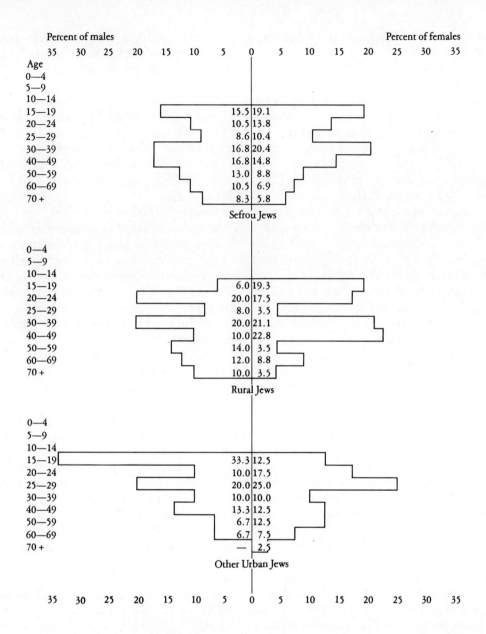

Percent of males								Percent of females						
35	30	25	20	15	10	5	0	5	10	15	20	25	30	35

Age

Age	Male	Female
0—4		
5—9		
10—14		
15—19	15.5	19.1
20—24	10.5	13.8
25—29	8.6	10.4
30—39	16.8	20.4
40—49	16.8	14.8
50—59	13.0	8.8
60—69	10.5	6.9
70 +	8.3	5.8

Sefrou Jews

Age	Male	Female
0—4		
5—9		
10—14		
15—19	6.0	19.3
20—24	20.0	17.5
25—29	8.0	3.5
30—39	20.0	21.1
40—49	10.0	22.8
50—59	14.0	3.5
60—69	12.0	8.8
70 +	10.0	3.5

Rural Jews

Age	Male	Female
0—4		
5—9		
10—14		
15—19	33.3	12.5
20—24	10.0	17.5
25—29	20.0	25.0
30—39	10.0	10.0
40—49	13.3	12.5
50—59	6.7	12.5
60—69	6.7	7.5
70 +	—	2.5

Other Urban Jews

35	30	25	20	15	10	5	0	5	10	15	20	25	30	35

Appendix: A statistical profile 413

Occupational composition of Sefrou (Tables 14–26)

The information provided in the census concerning occupation is of two sorts. The first kind, which I have called simply *occupation,* is a designation of the main occupation of the person, such as farmer, carpenter, shopkeeper. The original code manual of the census lists some 300 possible coded categories for locating the particular work. The second kind of information given I have called *job status* ("situation dans la profession principale"). This is coded by the census manual into the following scale:

> Employer of more than ten people
> Employer of one to ten people
> Employer of an unspecified number of people
> Independent, self-employed
> Employed or salaried person, private employ
> Employed or salaried person, public employ
> Domestic (anyone who works without monetary compensation, as for a kinsman)

I will deal first, in this section, with the material derived from the first interview question: occupation. I will describe the occupational composition of Sefrou and the participation of the various social groups in differing kinds of occupations. In the first run through the census data, I found that of the 300 possible codes for occupations given in the manual, the Sefrou interviewers actually used only about 75. These 75 occupational categories were already rather broad and inclusive (e.g., all sorts of teachers, religious and secular, were grouped under one rubric, *teacher,* and all sorts of legal practitioners, from judges to law clerks, were labeled *legal specialists*). I then revised this list slightly, combining closely related categories, to reach 55 occupations. This 55-item list is used in Tables 14 and 15. A further condensation of these 55 occupations into eight groupings, referred to as *occupational sectors,* is the basis of the analysis given in Tables 16 through 20.

Another, rather different, way of treating occupation is to use it as an indicator of social status and to compare social groups on their occupational achievements. This is the subject of the next section (Tables 27–43), in which job status is combined with occupation to produce what I have called *"occupational status."*

Tables 14 and 15 show that the numerically large occupations in Sefrou are teaching; white-collar office employment; taxi, truck, and bus driving; farming; farm labor; shopkeeping; itinerant peddling; tailoring; masonry; police work; and domestic work.

The rearrangement of these materials into the eight occupational sectors (Table 16) shows that the largest of these, artisan, takes up 28.6 percent of Sefrou's working population, with commerce (19.6 percent) and agriculture (17.7 percent) following. The "other" category is also quite large (16.9 percent) and consists mainly of domestic and other service occupations.

Table 17 provides a breakdown of the occupational sector list according to social group, with an indication of the percentage within each occupational sector that is taken up by members of each social group. At the bottom of the table are given the percentage within the total working population that is taken up by members of each social group, so that the reader can estimate the degree to which certain social groups are over- or underrepresented within each occupational sector.

It can be seen that the professions and managerial occupations are oversupplied with Sefrou-born Arabic speakers, Fez-born Arabic speakers, and Jews. The groups weakly represented in this sector are the rural-born Arabic speakers and the Bhalil-born Arabic speakers, but rural-born Berber speakers more than hold their own within this category of elite occupations.

The group of teachers is markedly lacking in Sefrou-born Arabic speakers and is oversupplied with people from Fez and other Moroccan towns. This pattern, as for soldiers and policemen, does not reflect an aversion on the part of Sefrou-born Arabic speakers to these particular occupations, but is a direct result of the policy of the Moroccan government to move teachers, soldiers, and policemen away from their home towns. The disproportion of Jewish teachers is a consequence of the presence of a large Jewish high school in Sefrou.

The white-collar workers (e.g., clerks, secretaries, messengers) show a similar pattern to the professions, with rural-born people underrepresented and townspeople from other towns, notably Fez, overrepresented. The Jews of Sefrou again are very numerous proportionately among the white-collar occupations.

Commercial occupations (shopkeeping, wholesale commerce, market peddling) draw a large proportion of Jews, at the expense of all the Muslim social groups except the Sefrou-born Arabic speakers.

Farming, on the other hand, is almost exclusively the province of the Muslims as against the Jews, and as might be expected, the rural-born groups dominate here, again with the exception of the Sefrou-born Arabic speakers, many of whom are farmers.

The artisan occupations are dominated by Sefrou-born Arabic speakers, with a strong representation of Jews. Certain specific crafts have different social group compositions. These are analyzed in Table 21. Weaving, blacksmithing, and meat butchering are all strongly dominated by Sefrou-born Arabic speakers, who make up about 75 percent of these groups. More than 50 percent of masonry and baking (i.e., operating a wood-burning oven to which individual housewives each day bring loaves of bread they have themselves made to be baked) is performed by Sefrou-born Arabic speakers; 27 percent is done by rural-born Arabic speakers, and the remaining members of these two occupational groups are spread among the other Muslim groups. Tailoring, carpentry, and shoemaking are all crafts that have Jews performing them, although in differing proportions. Some 27 percent of Sefrou's tailors are Jews, but the kind of tailoring they do—of modern Western men's suits—is sharply different from the kind of tailoring done by the Muslims, who make traditional jellabas and the like. The Muslim tailors are, in almost equal proportions, Sefrou-born Arabic speakers and rural-born Arabic speakers, with only a small scattering from the other Muslim groups. About

Appendix: A statistical profile 415

29 percent of carpenters are Jews and 51 percent are Sefrou-born Arabic speakers, with hardly any representation from the other groups. Shoemakers are almost entirely (73 percent) Jews, with Sefrou-born Arabic speakers making up most of the remainder.

The social composition of the modern skilled occupations (a very small category that includes such workers as automobile mechanics and electricians) fairly faithfully reflects the social composition of Sefrou as a whole, having drawn people from all groups.

Regarding Sefrou's occupational structure in general, the main axes of differentiation appear to be those between Muslims and Jews and, within the Muslim population, between those Muslims born in Sefrou and those born elsewhere. In the same way that Sefrou-born Muslims are scattered quite evenly spatially around the town, and those groups born elsewhere display more selective patterns, so also in regard to occupation, the Sefrou-born Muslims are distributed among most occupations in much the same proportions as they are found in the population at large, whereas the other Muslims show much greater selectivity.

Table 22 examines the differential participation of persons of the major ethnic categories in the active labor force. Of the total labor force, 8.2 percent of the Muslims are women and 13.8 percent of the Jews are women. For most of the ensuing tables on the active labor force, women have been included with the men.

There is a problem concerning the composition of the residual group that makes up the category *inactive*. These are the persons of Sefrou who responded to the question on occupation, not with the name of some sort of work or with the term student or housewife, but with some other response that the interviewer then transcribed as "inactive." Although there was a specific question in the interview about whether a person was unemployed in the sense of looking for a job, this blank was rarely filled in. Apparently, therefore, the unemployed persons of Sefrou were listed as inactive. In studying this group I set aside all the women and focused on the men.

Tables 23 and 24 show that the inactive men of Sefrou were unequally distributed among the social groups of Sefrou, with the largest proportions of inactive men coming from the rural-born groups. This information is congruent with data from fieldwork, which suggested that there was a larger reservoir of unemployed among the rural people come to town than among the townspeople themselves.

A further breakdown of the inactive population, this time according to age groups, appears in Tables 25 and 26. For the Sefrou-born Muslim Arabic speakers, inactivity is higher in the group aged sixteen to thirty; for both the rural-born Muslim groups, these younger men have the lowest rate of inactivity. The more important pattern revealed in these tables is that rural-born Muslim groups contain more inactive persons, regardless of age. The Jews have strikingly lower rates of inactivity.

Table 14. *Occupations (detailed list): Muslims and Jews by social group (numbers)*

Occupation	Sefrou-born Arabic speakers	Rural-born Arabic speakers	Rural-born Berber speakers	Other Muslims	All Muslims	Jews
1. Public official	2	0	0	3	5	0
2. Administrator or manager, government and private	7	0	5	2	14	4
3. Miscellaneous professional (engineer, veterinary, botanist)	5	2	0	0	7	2
4. Medical doctor	0	0	0	0	0	0
5. Teacher	37	50	9	54	150	54
6. Religious specialist (priest, fqih, mosque personnel)	4	7	1	0	12	2
7. Legal specialist (judge, court clerk, lawyer, etc.)	4	4	3	6	17	3
8. White-collar office employee	62	10	7	41	120	30
9. Trained nurse	3	4	1	6	14	7
10. Untrained nurse	3	2	1	1	7	2
11. Taxi, truck, and bus driver	41	34	26	25	126	6
12. Photographer	3	1	0	0	4	0
13. Miscellaneous trained occupations	5	1	0	3	9	2
14. Auto mechanic	19	3	2	1	25	4
15. Other mechanic	3	4	6	2	15	0
16. Plumber	0	0	0	1	1	2
17. Radio repairman	1	0	0	0	1	3
18. Electrician	13	3	0	1	17	2
19. Farmer	176	75	66	28	345	5
20. Farm laborer	84	115	75	63	337	1
21. Wholesale commerce	15	2	12	1	30	35
22. Shopkeeper	162	64	38	41	305	106
23. Petty commerce	40	20	13	4	77	73
24. Itinerant peddler	42	40	21	15	118	16
25. Wool worker, vegetable fiber worker	3	8	12	13	36	1
26. Yarn spinner	51	10	19	13	93	0
27. Weaver	46	4	3	6	59	2
28. Tailor	64	61	14	14	153	57
29. Burlap saddlemaker	6	1	1	2	10	0
30. Shoemaker	14	1	4	8	27	75
31. Babouche maker	3	1	2	2	8	4
32. Blacksmith	35	1	0	3	39	3

Appendix: A statistical profile 417

Table 14 (*cont.*)

Occupation	Sefrou-born Arabic speakers	Rural-born Arabic speakers	Rural-born Berber speakers	Other Muslims	All Muslims	Jews
33. Jeweler	2	2	0	0	4	6
34. Tinsmith	1	1	0	1	3	5
35. Miscellaneous artisans	3	5	2	1	11	5
36. Potter	3	2	0	0	5	0
37. Mason	83	52	5	22	162	0
38. Carpenter	59	11	6	5	81	34
39. House painter	3	3	3	0	9	6
40. Other building trades	28	14	3	14	59	0
41. Miller	11	4	0	1	16	4
42. Baker	36	19	4	9	68	1
43. Butcher	46	3	2	4	55	8
44. Miscellaneous manual labor	4	2	2	1	9	3
45. Policeman	13	43	41	53	150	1
46. Fireman	3	1	2	0	6	0
47. Soldier	0	9	6	3	18	0
48. Veteran	6	19	6	5	36	0
49. Watchman	8	9	6	7	30	1
50. Woodcutter	3	6	3	1	13	0
51. Hotel and restaurant manager, dormitory manager	3	3	1	1	8	3
52. Concierge	12	4	3	8	27	1
53. Hotel and café staff	22	23	15	17	77	7
54. Domestic	54	65	14	24	157	30
55. Barber, bath personnel	42	3	3	5	53	18
Total	1,398	831	468	541	3,238	634

Table 15. *Occupations (detailed list): French and other foreigners (numbers)*

Occupation	French	Other foreigners (mostly Algerians)	All foreigners
1. Public official	0	0	0
2. Administrator or manager, government and private	1	2	3
3. Miscellaneous professionals	3	0	3
4. Medical doctor	2	0	2
5. Teacher	30	6	36
6. Religious specialist	1	0	1
7. Legal specialist	0	0	0
8. White-collar office employee	10	3	13
9. Trained nurse	2	0	2
10. Untrained nurse	0	0	0
11. Taxi, truck, and bus driver	1	3	4
12. Photographer	0	0	0
13. Miscellaneous trained occupations	0	0	0
14. Auto mechanic	1	1	2
15. Other mechanic	0	0	0
16. Plumber	0	0	0
17. Radio repairman	0	0	0
18. Electrician	0	0	0
19. Farmer	4	0	4
20. Farm laborer	0	1	1
21. Wholesale commerce	0	0	0
22. Shopkeeper	1	1	2
23. Petty commerce	0	1	1
24. Itinerant peddler	0	0	0
25. Wool worker	0	0	0
26. Yarn spinner	0	0	0
27. Weaver	0	0	0
28. Tailor	0	0	0
29. Saddlemaker	0	0	0
30. Shoemaker	0	0	0
31. Babouche maker	0	0	0
32. Blacksmith	1	0	1
33. Jeweler	0	0	0
34. Tinsmith	0	0	0
35. Miscellaneous artisans	0	0	0
36. Potter	0	0	0
37. Mason	0	1	1
38. Carpenter	0	1	1
39. House painter	0	0	0
40. Other building trades	0	0	0
41. Miller	0	0	0
42. Baker	0	0	0
43. Butcher	0	0	0

Table 15 (*cont.*)

Occupation	French	Other foreigners (mostly Algerians)	All foreigners
44. Miscellaneous manual labor	0	1	1
45. Policeman	1	0	1
46. Fireman	0	0	0
47. Soldier	1	0	1
48. Veteran	0	1	1
49. Watchman	0	0	0
50. Woodcutter	2	1	3
51. Hotel and restaurant manager	1	0	1
52. Concierge	0	0	0
53. Hotel and café staff	0	1	1
54. Domestic	0	1	1
55. Barber, bath personnel	0	0	0
Total	62	25	87

Table 16. *Occupational sectors: Muslims and Jews aggregated*

Occupational sector	Number	Percent
Professional managerial occupations (1–4)[a]	32	0.8
Teaching (5)	204	5.2
White-collar (6–9)	205	5.3
Commerce (21–24)	760	19.6
Farming (19, 20)	688	17.7
Artisans (25–28)	1,109	28.6
Modern skills (11–18)	217	5.6
Other (10,44–55)	657	16.9
Total	3,872	99.8

[a] Numbers refer to occupation numbers in Table 14.

420 *Meaning and order in Moroccan society*

Table 17. *Occupational sectors compared: Muslims and Jews by social group (percents within each occupational sector)*

Occupational sector	Social groups								
	Sefrou-born Arabic speakers	Rural-born Arabic speakers	Rural-born Berber speakers	Fez-born Arabic speakers	Bhalil-born Arabic speakers	Other Muslims	All Muslims	Jews	Total
Professional, managerial occupations (1–4)[a]	43.7	6.2	15.6	6.2	0.0	9.4	81.2	18.7	99.9
Teaching (5)	18.1	24.5	14.4	11.3	3.9	11.3	73.5	26.4	99.9
White-collar (6–9)	35.6	12.2	5.8	9.2	1.0	15.6	79.5	20.5	100.0
Commerce (21–24)	34.4	16.8	11.2	1.3	1.8	4.9	69.7	30.6	100.0
Farming (19, 20)	37.8	27.6	20.5	0.4	6.8	5.9	99.1	0.9	100.0
Artisans (25–43)	44.8	18.3	7.2	2.7	4.1	3.8	81.0	19.0	100.0
Modern skills (11–18)	39.2	21.2	15.6	3.6	2.7	8.7	91.2	98.7	99.9
Other (10,44–55)	26.0	28.4	15.4	3.9	4.2	10.8	89.9	9.9	100.0
Social group's proportion in total population (excluding foreigners)	35.5	23.8	12.3	2.8	4.0	6.8	85.3	14.4	99.7

[a] Numbers refer to occupation numbers in Table 14.

Appendix: A statistical profile 421

Table 18. *Occupational sectors compared: Muslims and Jews by social group (numbers for Table 17)*

Occupational sector	Social groups								Total in working population, except foreign
	Sefrou-born Arabic speakers	Rural-born Arabic speakers	Rural-born Berber speakers	Fez-born Arabic speakers	Bhalil-born Arabic speakers	Other Muslims	All Muslims	Jews	
Professional, managerial occupations (1–4)[a]	14	2	5	2	0	3	26	6	32
Teaching (5)	37	50	9	23	8	23	150	54	204
White-collar (6–9)	73	25	12	19	2	32	163	42	205
Commerce (21–24)	259	126	84	10	14	37	530	230	760
Farming (19–20)	260	190	141	3	47	41	682	6	688
Artisans (25–43)	497	203	80	30	46	42	898	211	1,109
Modern skills (11–18)	85	46	34	8	6	19	198	19	217
Other (10,44–55)	173	189	103	26	28	72	591	66	657
Total	1,398	831	468	121	151	269	3,238	634	3,872

[a] Numbers refer to occupation numbers in Table 14.

Table 19. *Occupational sectors compared: French and other foreign-born (percents within each occupational sector; see Table 20 for numbers)*

Occupational sector	French	Other foreigners	All foreigners	Muslims and Jews	Total in Sefrou working population
Professional, managerial (1–4)[a]	15.0	5.0	20.0	80.0	100.0
Teaching (5)	12.5	2.5	15.0	85.0	100.0
White-collar (6–9)	5.9	1.3	7.2	92.8	100.0
Commerce (21–24)	0.1	0.2	0.4	99.6	100.0
Farming (19, 20)	0.6	0.1	0.7	99.3	100.0

422 *Meaning and order in Moroccan society*

Table 19 (cont.)

Occupational sector	French	Other foreigners	All foreigners	Muslims and Jews	Total in Sefrou working population
Artisans (25–43)	0.1	0.2	0.3	99.7	100.0
Modern skills (11–18)	0.9	1.8	2.7	97.3	100.0
Other (10,44–55)	0.7	0.7	1.5	98.5	100.0
Social group's proportion in total population	1.1	0.7	1.7	98.3	100.0

[a] Numbers refer to occupation numbers in Table 14.

Table 20. *Occupational sectors compared: French and other foreign-born (numbers for Table 19)*

Occupational sector	French	Other foreigners	All foreigners	Muslims and Jews	Total in Sefrou working population
Professional managerial (1–4)[a]	6	2	8	32	40
Teaching (5)	30	6	36	204	240
White-collar (6–9)	13	3	16	205	221
Commerce (21–24)	1	2	3	760	763
Farming (19, 20)	4	1	5	688	693
Artisans (25–43)	1	2	3	1,109	1,112
Modern skills (11–18)	2	4	6	217	223
Other (10,44–55)	5	5	10	657	667
Total	62	25	77	3,872	3,959

[a] Numbers refer to occupation numbers in Table 14.

Appendix: A statistical profile 423

Table 21. *Selected crafts compared: Muslims and Jews by social group (percents by group and craft; numbers from Table 14)*

Social group	Craft								Social group's proportion in total population (excluding foreigners)
	Weaver	Tailor	Shoe-maker	Black-smith	Mason	Carpenter	Baker	Butcher	
Sefrou-born									
Arabic speakers	75.4	30.5	13.7	83.3	51.2	51.3	52.1	73.0	35.5
Rural-born									
Arabic speakers	6.5	29.0	1.0	2.4	32.1	9.5	27.5	4.7	23.8
Rural-born									
Berber speakers	4.9	6.6	3.9	0.0	3.1	5.2	5.8	3.1	12.3
Fez-born									
Arabic speakers	3.2	2.4	6.8	0.0	0.6	1.7	4.3	1.6	2.8
Bhalil-born									
Arabic speakers	6.5	1.9	0.0	2.4	9.9	0.0	4.3	0.0	4.0
Other Muslims	0.0	2.4	1.0	4.7	3.1	2.6	4.3	4.7	6.8
All Muslims	96.5	72.8	26.4	92.8	100.0	70.4	98.6	87.3	85.3
Jews	3.2	27.1	73.5	7.1	0.0	29.5	1.4	12.7	14.4
Total number	61	210	102	42	162	115	69	63	

Table 22. *Women in the active labor force, by ethnic category*

Ethnic category	Number			Percent of women in active labor force
	Men	Women	Total	
Muslims	2,983	266	3,249	8.2
Jews	546	88	634	13.8
French	41	21	62	33.8
Other foreigners	22	2	24	8.3

Table 23. *Inactive or unemployed men fifteen years old and over, by social group (percents within adult men of each social group; see Table 24 for numbers)*

Social group	Percent inactive
Sefrou-born Arabic speakers	19.2
Rural-born Arabic speakers	37.6
Rural-born Berber speakers	35.2
Fez-born Arabic speakers	19.5
Bhalil-born Arabic speakers	31.7
Other Muslims	24.0
All Muslims	27.8
Jews	15.6

Table 24. *Inactive or unemployed men fifteen years old and over, by social group (numbers for Table 23)*

Social group	Active	Student	Inactive	Total men in group
Sefrou-born Arabic speakers	1,323	151	351	1,825
Rural-born Arabic speakers	749	60	488	1,297
Rural-born Berber speakers	410	17	232	659
Fez-born Arabic speakers	102	1	25	128
Bhalil-born Arabic speakers	125	6	61	192
Other Muslims	255	21	87	363
All Muslims	2,964	256	1,244	4,464
Jews	539	32	106	677

Table 25. *Age and inactive status, by social group (percent inactive men in each age group of each social group; see Table 26 for numbers)*

Social group	Young	Middle-aged	Older	Total men aged 16–60
Sefrou-born Arabic speakers	18.7	15.0	14.3	16.7
Rural-born Arabic speakers	31.3	33.9	43.6	35.0
Rural-born Berber speakers	28.6	37.2	35.3	33.8
Sefrou Jews	9.9	3.0	7.9	7.1

Table 26. *Age and inactive status, by social group (numbers for Table 25)*

Social group	Young		Middle-aged		Older		Total men aged 16–60	
	Number inactive	No. in age-group	Number inactive	No. in age-group	Number inactive	No. in age-group	Number inactive	No. in age-group
Sefrou-born								
Arabic speakers	160	854	73	486	49	342	282	1,682
Rural-born								
Arabic speakers	136	434	133	392	103	236	372	1,062
Rural-born								
Berber speakers	53	185	81	218	53	150	187	553
Sefrou Jews	21	213	5	168	10	126	36	507

Occupational status (Tables 27–43)

To a certain extent, occupation is an indicator of a man's social status. What level of work a man has reached shows, partially, his social rank. Other factors, such as influence, prestige of his family, or style of life, also enter into judgments people make of his social standing. If the information we have from the census could be arranged in such a way as to form a ranked scale of occupations, this could form a measure of occupational achievement for comparing the different social groups.

But occupational category alone is a very crude index of work achievement; for instance, whereas farmers are generally lower status than teachers in Morocco, a wealthy farmer who does not actually work in the fields is much higher than a poor teacher who has no other source of income. The census provided no measure of income, but it did provide data on whether a man employed others, was employed, or worked independently. This information on job status was combined with the fifty-five-item occupational list, and the resulting list was considerably condensed to form a series of fifteen ranked occupational categories. These rankings involved a number of subjective judgments about which of two particular occupations was higher, judgments based mainly on fieldwork in Sefrou. The whole procedure was somewhat crude, and the particular ranking of some of the specific categories remains questionable. This constructed, ranked occupational listing I have called *occupational status.*

An example of how I arrived at particular categories in the occupational status listing can be seen in what was done with the original categories of "farmer" and "farm labor," which were broken up and reassembled into a three-level ranked series, as shown in the unnumbered table preceding Table 27.

To simplify comparisons among social groups, the fifteen levels of occupational status were then sorted into a three-category scale called *occupational status levels* or *status levels,* with the categories of high-status occupations, medium-status occupations, and low-status occupations. This condensation gains in simplicity and ease of visualization, but loses in precision. I have included tables reporting the same data in both the long form of fifteen occupational statuses and the short form of three status levels because each form reveals different things about the data.

Table 27 gives the categories of both these dimensions, together with an indication of their content.

Tables 28–33 represent an exploration of characteristics of the population within each of these occupational status classifications, as a partial test of their sociological validity. My fieldwork had shown that persons of higher socioeconomic status usually lived in larger, better equipped houses, which were very often single-family dwellings, and had higher levels of literacy. Tables 28 and 29 calculate the proportion of persons within each occupational status category who lived in single-household dwellings. Tables 30 and 31 do the same for running water, and Tables 32 and 33 for literacy.

The association among these attributes is very rough, but definite. The most discriminating index is the one-family house, but even the association between such a house and higher status can be only partial, for many of the poorest people in Sefrou live in simple one-family rural houses or huts. Presence of running water also varies with occupational status in a fairly regular way. These two factors are, of course, directly responsive to income. The third dimension tested, literacy, does not fit so well with occupational status, for it varies more with the kind of occupation than with its status.

An examination of the six tables suggests that the category "modern, skilled worker," which consists of taxi drivers, auto mechanics, electricians, plumbers, and the like, who are employed by someone, should have been placed in a higher rank, perhaps among the occupations of medium status, despite the fact that these are workers rather than employers. This discovery was made too late in the study to allow the necessary changes.

Tables 34 through 41 provide a detailed comparison of the composition of the main social groups of the town with regard to these occupational status classifications. In these, an estimate can be made of the degree to which a particular social group's representation in a particular occupational status category is over or under what might be expected, by comparing it with the general distribution for all Muslims or all Jews. Thus it can be seen that the three major Muslim groups are generally similar one to another in their general pattern of distribution, but differ in small ways. The Sefrou-born Arabic speakers are overrepresented in the traditional crafts at all three status levels, and the two rural-born groups are overrepresented in the agricultural occupations, especially at the lowest level. Both Arabic-speaking groups have a higher proportion working in white-collar occupations than do the Berber speakers. Sefrou-born Arabs are markedly low in police and military occupations, a reflection of the government's policy of bringing in police from other localities. The rural-born Berber speakers have proportionately more people in commerce, especially the large- and medium-scale commercial occupations. Many of these people may be Berbers from the Sous in southern Morocco, who are predominant in the grocery trade all over the country, rather than Berbers from the Middle Atlas, but the census is silent on distinctions among Berber languages.

A striking contrast appears between these three most populous Muslim groups and the set of minor Muslim groups shown in Tables 36 and 37. The smaller Muslim groups have much greater occupational specialization. Fez-born Arabic speakers are concentrated in the professional and administrative positions, in white-collar work, in the police, and in the traditional skills especially at their upper levels. Bhalil-born Arabic speakers, in contrast have a higher proportion of their numbers engaged in low-status occupations, especially in farm labor and the traditional crafts. The Jews, as portrayed in Tables 38 and 39, are heavily represented in white-collar jobs, commerce, and traditional skills, and are virtually lacking in the agricultural sector. The French and other foreign-born persons are strongly bunched in the upper-status occupations. This is shown in Table 40, and, in greater detail, in Table 41.

Table 42 is a rearrangement of the data from Tables 32 to 41. The fifteen occupational statuses have been sorted into three status levels – high, medium, and low – and the social groups are compared to see whether there are sharper contrasts among the social groups when each is arranged into a simple three-level hierarchy. The same patterns that appear in the more detailed tables can be seen again. The three major Muslim groups basically resemble one another

more than they differ, although the Sefrou-born Arabic speakers have proportionately fewer people in high-status occupations. The Fez-born group has the highest proportion of high-status occupations of all the Muslims and Jews, the Bhalil-born group has the lowest, and the French have by far the most of all.

Table 43 takes the same data again, but this time the comparison is within the status levels themselves. It answers the question: What is the social composition of each status level taken by itself? French and other foreign-born have been omitted. It shows that the high-status level is composed primarily of Sefrou-born and rural-born Arabic speakers, but that these are underrepresented according to their numbers in the total Sefrou population. The medium-status level is dominated by Sefrou-born Arabic speakers, Sefrou-born Jews, and rural-born Arabic speakers, with the Jews being overrepresented according to their numbers in the total indigenous population. The low-status level is again dominated by Sefrou-born and rural-born Arabic speakers, and to a lesser degree by rural-born Berber speakers and Sefrou-born Jews. All four of these groups are represented in the low-status level almost precisely in proportion to their numbers in the total population.

New categories of *occupational status*	Census categories	
	Occupations (detailed list)	Job status
Big farmers	Farmer	Employing 10 or more workers
Medium and independent farmers	Farmer or farm labor	Independent or employing 1–10 workers
Farm laborers	Farmer or farm labor	Salaried or domestic help

Table 27. *Occupational status: content of the categories*

High-status occupations
1. Professional, administrator
   Public official
   Engineer
   Veterinary
   Botanist
   Medical doctor
2. Large-scale commerce
   Manager of firms
   Wholesaler employing more than 10 persons
   Shopkeeper employing more than 10 persons
   Contractor employing more than 10 persons
   Carpenter employing more than 10 persons
3. Large-scale farmer
   Farmer employing more than 10 persons
4. White-collar employee
   Priest, fqih, other religious specialties
   Legal specialist, lawyer, judge, law clerk
   Teacher
   Clerk, typist
   Mailman, telephone operator
   Accountant
   Trained nurse
5. Medium-scale commerce
   Wholesaler employing 1–10 persons

Table 27 (*cont.*)

   Shopkeeper employing 1–10 persons
   Hotel manager employing 1 person or more
   Bath owner employing 1 person or more
6. Medium- and small-scale farmers
   Independent farmer
   Farmer employing 1–10 persons
7. Police, military
   Policeman
   Fireman
   Soldier
   Veteran
   Watchman

Medium-status occupations
8. Petty commerce
   Independent wholesaler who employs no one
   Independent shopkeeper
   Independent auctioneer, market peddler
   Independent itinerant peddler
9. Modern skilled worker (independently employed) (includes any of the following who is independent or who employs others)
   Taxi owner
   Bus owner
   Performing artist, athlete, airplane mechanic
   Auto mechanic

Appendix: A statistical profile 429

Table 27 (*cont.*)   Table 27 (*cont.*)

Plumber
Electrician
Radio repairman
Other mechanics
Photographer

10. Master craftsman: traditional skills (includes any of the following who is independent or who employs others)
Jeweler
Tailor
Weaver
Barber
Carpenter
Mason
House painter
Plasterer
Butcher
Miller
Baker
Potter
Shoemaker
Babouche maker
Saddlemaker
Wool worker (cleaning, spinning)
Vegetable fiber worker
Blacksmith
Tinsmith
Rope maker
Tanner
Basket maker
Untrained nurse

Low-status occupations

11. Commercial worker (includes any of the following who is employed by someone else)
Petty commerce
Wholesaler
Peddler
Shopkeeper

12. Modern skilled worker (includes any of the following who is employed by someone else)
Taxi driver
Bus or truck driver
Auto mechanic
Plumber
Electrician
Radio repairman

Other mechanic
Photographer

13. Traditional skilled worker (includes any of the following who is employed by someone else)
Jeweler
Tailor
Weaver
Barber
Bath employee
Carpenter
Mason
Painter
Other building trades laborer
Butcher
Miller
Baker
Potter
Shoemaker
Babouche maker
Wool worker
Vegetable fiber worker
Yarn spinner
Blacksmith
Tinsmith
Untrained nurse

14. Service occupations
Hotel staff
Restaurant staff
Waiter, cook
Domestic
Concierge
Porter
Barber
Bath employee

15. Manual laborer, farm laborer (includes any of the following employed by someone else)
Farmer
Woodcutter
Other manual laborer

Table 28. *Occupational status categories compared: proportions living in one-family houses: Muslims by social group and aggregated, (percent living in one-family houses, within each occupational status category; see Table 29 for numbers)*

Occupational status category	Sefrou-born Arabic speakers	Rural-born Arabic speakers	Rural-born Berber speakers	All Muslims
High-status occupations				
1. Professional, administrator	71.4	100.0	100.0	76.9
2. Large-scale commerce	100.0	100.0	50.0	80.0
3. Large-scale farmer	100.0	0.0	0.0	100.0
4. White-collar employee	74.5	54.6	52.3	70.6
5. Medium-scale commerce	66.6	100.0	100.0	69.5
6. Medium- and small-scale farmers	62.3	38.4	43.7	52.9
7. Police, military	66.6	58.0	45.9	60.4
Medium-status occupations				
8. Petty commerce	48.4	31.5	52.3	44.4
9. Modern skilled worker (independently employed)	42.8	33.3	50.0	39.4
10. Master craftsman (traditional skills)	41.7	20.8	24.2	34.9
Low-status occupations				
11. Commercial worker	44.2	45.5	61.1	49.1
12. Modern skilled worker	50.0	25.5	32.1	40.9
13. Traditional skilled worker	36.7	30.6	29.4	34.8
14. Service occupations	43.3	46.6	48.4	47.5
15. Farm laborer and other manual laborers	30.7	30.8	24.4	28.3
Percent of one-family houses for social group as a whole.	46.5	37.6	39.4	44.4

Appendix: A statistical profile 431

Table 29. *Occupational status categories compared: proportions living in one-family houses: Muslims by social group and aggregated, (numbers for Table 28)*

Occupational status category	Sefrou-born Arabic speakers		Rural-born Arabic speakers		Rural-born Berber speakers		All Muslims	
	A	B	A	B	A	B	A	B
High-status occupations								
1. Professional, administrator	5	7	2	2	1	1	10	13
2. Large-scale commerce	8	8	1	1	2	4	12	15
3. Large-scale farmers	2	2	0	0	0	0	2	2
4. White-collar employee	82	110	41	75	11	21	221	313
5. Medium-scale commerce	6	10	0	2	2	2	16	23
6. Medium- and small-scale farmers	76	122	20	52	21	48	127	240
7. Police, military	20	30	47	81	28	61	151	250
Medium-status occupations								
8. Petty commerce	92	190	29	92	33	63	177	398
9. Modern skilled worker (independently employed)	6	14	1	3	3	6	13	33
10. Master craftsman (traditional skills)	81	194	15	72	8	33	120	343
Low-status occupations								
11. Commercial worker	27	61	15	33	11	18	59	120
12. Modern skilled worker	35	70	11	43	9	28	70	171
13. Traditional skilled worker	127	346	41	134	15	51	213	611
14. Service occupation	39	90	44	94	16	33	127	267
15. Farm laborer and other manual laborers	44	143	45	146	24	98	132	465
Total	650	1,397	312	830	184	467	1,450	3,264

A, number in one-family house.
B, total in occupational status category.

432 *Meaning and order in Moroccan society*

Table 30. *Occupational status categories compared: proportions with running water: Muslims by social group and aggregated (percent with running water within each occupational status category; see Table 31 for numbers)*

Occupational status category	Sefrou-born Arabic speakers	Rural-born Arabic speakers	Rural-born Berber speakers	All Muslims
High-status occupations				
1. Professional, and administrator	85.7	100.0	100.0	84.6
2. Large-scale commerce	100.0	100.0	75.0	100.0
3. Large-scale farmer	100.0	0.0	0.0	100.0
4. White-collar employer	73.6	62.6	80.9	75.4
5. Medium-scale commerce	90.0	50.0	100.0	56.5
6. Medium- and small-scale farmers	65.5	50.0	80.9	60.8
7. Police, military	76.6	80.2	73.7	77.6
Medium-status occupations				
8. Petty commerce	65.7	55.4	73.0	63.8
9. Modern skilled worker (independently employed)	64.3	33.3	100.0	57.5
10. Master craftsman (traditional skills)	64.4	48.6	51.5	57.1
Low-status occupations				
11. Commercial worker	78.7	51.5	66.6	68.3
12. Modern skilled worker	65.7	74.4	78.5	73.6
13. Traditional skilled worker	47.7	43.2	62.7	48.6
14. Service occupations	51.1	63.8	75.5	59.5
15. Farm laborer and other manual laborers	51.0	32.2	37.7	41.5
Percent with running water for social group as a whole	51.0	32.2	37.8	41.5

Table 31. *Occupational status categories compared: proportions with running water: Muslims by social group and aggregated (numbers for Table 31)*

Occupational status category	Sefrou-born Arabic speakers		Rural-born Arabic speakers		Rural-born Berber speakers		All Muslims	
	A	B	A	B	A	B	A	B
High-status occupations								
1. Professional, administrator	6	7	2	2	1	1	11	13
2. Large-scale commerce	8	8	1	1	3	4	14	15
3. Large-scale farmer	2	2	0	0	0	0	2	2
4. White-collar employee	81	110	47	75	17	21	236	313
5. Medium-scale commerce	9	10	1	2	2	2	13	23
6. Medium- and small-scale farmers	80	122	26	52	27	48	146	240
7. Police, military	23	30	65	81	45	61	194	250
Medium-status occupations								
8. Petty commerce	125	190	51	92	46	63	254	398
9. Modern skilled worker (independently employed)	9	14	1	3	6	6	19	33
10. Master craftsman (traditional skills)	125	194	35	72	17	33	196	343
Low-status occupations								
11. Commercial worker	48	61	17	33	12	18	82	120
12. Modern skilled worker	46	70	32	43	22	28	126	171
13. Traditional skilled worker	165	346	58	134	32	51	297	611
14. Service occupations	46	90	60	94	25	33	159	267
15. Farm laborer and other manual laborers	73	143	47	146	37	98	193	465
Total	846	1,397	501	830	292	467	1,942	3,264

A, number with running water.
B, total in occupational status category.

Table 32. *Occupational status categories compared: proportions of illiterates: Muslims by social group and aggregated, men only, (percent of illiterates within each occupational status category; see Table 33 for numbers)*

Occupational status category	Sefrou-born Arabic speakers	Rural-born Arabic speakers	Rural-born Berber speakers	Total (cols 1 + 2 + 3)
High-status occupations				
1. Professional, administrator	57.1	50.0	0.0	55.5
2. Large-scale commerce	12.5	0.0	25.0	15.4
3. Large-scale farmer	50.0	0.0	0.0	50.0
4. White-collar employee	4.8	8.1	9.5	6.6
5. Medium-scale commerce	80.0	100.0	0.0	71.4
6. Medium- and small-scale farmers	58.7	84.3	80.8	69.4
7. Police, military	46.7	58.0	70.0	60.2
Medium-status occupations				
8. Petty commerce	50.8	66.3	54.0	55.5
9. Modern skilled worker (independently employed)	21.4	33.3	50.0	30.4
10. Master craftsman (traditional skills)	61.0	50.0	50.0	57.7
Low-status occupations				
11. Commercial worker	68.4	63.6	29.4	54.0
12. Modern skilled worker	42.0	65.1	67.8	54.3
13. Traditional skilled worker	60.3	68.4	76.2	63.6
14. Service occupations	72.0	79.3	82.3	76.0
15. Farm laborer and other manual laborers	74.3	86.9	80.2	76.4
Percent illiterate for each social group	53.6	64.2	65.2	58.7

Table 33. *Occupational status categories compared: proportions of illiterates: Muslims by social group and aggregated, men only, (numbers for Table 32)*

Occupational status category	Sefrou-born Arabic speakers		Rural-born Arabic speakers		Rural-born Berber speakers		Total (cols 1 + 2 + 3)	
	A	B	A	B	A	B	A	B
High-status occupations								
1. Professional, administrator	4	7	1	2	0	0	5	9
2. Large-scale commerce	1	8	0	1	1	4	2	13
3. Large-scale farmer	1	2	0	0	0	0	1	2
4. White-collar employee	5	103	6	74	2	21	13	198
5. Medium-scale commerce	8	10	2	2	0	2	10	14
6. Medium- and small-scale farmers	71	121	43	51	38	47	152	219
7. Police, military	14	30	47	81	42	60	103	171
Medium-status occupations								
8. Petty commerce	96	189	61	92	34	63	191	344
9. Modern skilled worker (independently employed)	3	14	1	3	3	6	7	23
10. Master craftsman (traditional skills)	105	172	28	56	9	18	142	246
Low-status occupations								
11. Commercial worker	34	61	21	33	5	17	60	111
12. Modern skilled worker	29	69	28	43	19	28	76	140
13. Traditional skilled worker	198	329	89	130	32	42	319	501
14. Service occupations	54	75	46	58	14	17	114	150
15. Farm laborer and other manual laborers	90	140	113	130	69	86	272	356
Total	713	1,330	486	756	268	411	1,467	2,497

A, number of illiterates.
B, total in occupational status category.

Table 34. *Occupational status: major Muslim social groups compared (percent within each social group; see Table 35 for numbers)*

Occupational status category	Sefrou-born Arabic speakers	Rural-born Arabic speakers	Rural-born Berber speakers	Other Muslims[a]	Total All Muslims
High-status occupations					
1. Professional, and administrator	0.5	0.2	0.2	0.5	0.4
2. Large-scale commerce	0.6	0.1	0.9	0.4	0.5
3. Large-scale farmer	0.1	0.0	0.0	0.0	0.1
4. White-collar employee	7.9	9.0	4.5	19.3	9.6
5. Medium-scale commerce	0.7	0.2	0.4	0.2	0.5
6. Medium- and small-scale farmers	8.7	6.3	10.3	3.2	7.3
7. Police, military	2.1	9.8	13.1	14.0	7.7
Medium-status occupations					
8. Petty commerce	13.6	11.1	13.5	9.5	12.2
9. Modern skilled worker (independently employed)	1.0	0.4	1.3	0.5	0.8
10. Master craftsman (traditional skills)	13.9	8.7	7.1	7.9	10.5
Low-status occupations					
11. Commercial worker	4.4	4.0	3.9	1.4	3.7
12. Modern skilled worker	5.0	5.2	6.0	5.4	5.2
13. Traditional skilled worker	24.8	16.1	10.9	14.4	18.8
14. Service occupations	6.4	11.3	7.1	9.0	8.2
15. Farm laborer and other manual laborers	10.2	17.6	21.0	14.0	14.3
Total	99.9	100.0	100.2	99.7	99.8

[a] This category is the aggregate of Fez-born Arabic speakers, urban-born Berber speakers, other urban Arabic speakers, and Bhalil-born Arabic speakers, which are presented separately in Table 36.

Table 35. *Occupational status: major Muslim social groups compared (numbers for table 34)*

Occupational status category	Sefrou-born Arabic speakers	Rural-born Arabic speakers	Rural-born Berber speakers	Other Muslims	Total All Muslims
High-status occupations					
1. Professional, administrator	7	2	1	3	13
2. Large-scale commerce	8	1	4	2	15
3. Large-scale farmer	2	0	0	0	2
4. White-collar employee	110	75	21	107	313
5. Medium-scale commerce	10	2	2	1	15
6. Medium- and small-scale farmers	122	52	48	18	240
7. Police, military	30	81	61	78	250
Medium-status occupations					
8. Petty commerce	190	92	63	53	398
9. Modern skilled worker (independently employed)	14	3	6	3	26
10. Master craftsman (traditional skills)	194	72	33	44	343
Low-status occupations					
11. Commercial worker	61	33	18	8	120
12. Modern skilled worker	70	43	28	30	171
13. Traditional skilled worker	346	134	51	80	611
14. Service occupations	90	94	33	50	267
15. Farm laborer and other manual laborers	143	146	98	78	465
Total	1,397	830	467	555	3,249

Table 36. *Occupational status: minor Muslim social groups compared (percent within each social group; see Table 37 for numbers)*

Occupational status category	Fez-born Arabic speaker	Urban-born Berber speaker	Other urban Arabic speaker	Bhalil-born Arabic speaker	Other Muslims (cols. 1 + 2 + 3 + 4)
High-status occupations					
1. Professional, administrator	1.7	0.9	0.0	0.0	0.5
2. Large-scale commerce	0.0	0.0	1.2	0.0	0.4
3. Large-scale farmer	0.0	0.0	0.0	0.0	0.0
4. White-collar employee	34.7	15.4	22.4	6.6	19.3
5. Medium-scale commerce	0.0	0.9	0.0	0.0	0.2
6. Medium- and small-scale farmers	1.7	8.8	1.2	2.6	3.2
7. Police, military	16.5	18.6	18.8	3.3	14.0
Medium-status occupations					
8. Petty commerce	7.4	15.0	10.0	6.6	9.5
9. Modern skilled worker (independently employed)	1.7	0.9	0.0	0.0	0.5
10. Master craftsman (traditional skills)	10.7	6.2	4.7	10.6	7.9
Low-status occupations					
11. Commercial worker	0.8	0.9	1.2	2.6	1.4
12. Modern skilled worker	5.0	4.4	7.6	4.0	5.4
13. Traditional skilled worker	14.9	6.2	12.4	22.5	14.4
14. Service occupations	4.1	6.2	11.8	11.9	9.0
15. Farm laborer and other manual laborers	0.8	15.9	8.8	29.1	14.0
Total	100.0	100.3	100.1	99.8	99.7

Table 37. *Occupational status: minor Muslim social groups compared (numbers for Table 36)*

Occupational status category	Fez-born Arabic speaker	Urban-born Berber speaker	Other urban Arabic speaker	Bhalil-born Arabic speaker	Other Muslims (cols. 1 + 2 + 3 + 4)
High-status occupations					
1. Professional, and administrator	2	1	0	0	3
2. Large-scale commerce	0	0	2	0	2
3. Large-scale farmer	0	0	0	0	0
4. White-collar employee	42	17	38	10	107
5. Medium-scale commerce	0	1	0	0	1
6. Medium- and small-scale farmers	2	10	2	4	18
7. Police, military	20	21	32	5	78
Medium-status occupations					
8. Petty commerce	9	17	17	10	53
9. Modern skilled worker (independently employed)	2	1	0	0	3
10. Master craftsman (traditional skills)	13	7	8	16	44
Low-status occupations					
11. Commercial worker	1	1	2	4	8
12. Modern skilled worker	6	5	13	6	30
13. Traditional skilled worker	18	7	21	34	80
14. Service occupations	5	7	20	18	50
15. Farm laborer and other manual laborers	1	18	15	44	78
Total	121	113	170	151	555

440   *Meaning and order in Moroccan society*

Table 38. *Occupational status: Jewish social groups compared (percent within each social group; see Table 39 for numbers)*

Occupational status category	Sefrou-born Jews	Rural-born Jews	Jews born in other towns	All Jews
High-status occupations				
1. Professional, administrator	0.4	0.0	0.0	0.3
2. Large-scale commerce	0.7	0.0	3.7	0.8
3. Large-scale farmer	0.0	0.0	0.0	0.0
4. White-collar employee	13.7	9.3	55.6	15.1
5. Medium-scale commerce	1.4	0.0	0.0	1.2
6. Medium- and small-scale farmers	0.9	0.0	0.0	0.8
7. Police, military	0.4	0.0	0.0	0.3
Medium-status occupations				
8. Petty commerce	24.8	23.3	11.1	24.1
9. Modern skilled worker (independently employed)	1.2	0.0	0.0	1.1
10. Master craftsman (traditional skills)	16.1	16.3	7.4	15.8
Low-status occupations				
11. Commercial worker	11.3	16.3	0.0	11.2
12. Modern skilled worker	1.8	2.3	3.7	1.9
13. Traditional skilled worker	21.5	14.0	11.1	20.5
14. Service occupations	5.1	18.6	7.4	6.1
15. Farm laborer and other manual laborers	0.7	0.0	0.0	0.6
Total	100.0	100.1	100.0	99.8

Table 39. *Occupational status: Jewish social groups compared (numbers for Table 38)*

Occupational status category	Sefrou-born Jews	Rural-born Jews	Other urban-born Jews	All Jews (cols. 1+2+3)
High-status occupations				
1. Professional, administrator	2	0	0	2
2. Large-scale commerce	4	0	1	5
3. Large-scale farmer	0	0	0	0
4. White-collar employee	77	4	15	96
5. Medium-scale commerce	8	0	0	8
6. Medium- and small-scale farmers	5	0	0	5
7. Police, military	2	0	0	2
Medium-status occupations				
8. Petty commerce	140	10	3	153
9. Modern skilled worker (independently employed)	7	0	0	7
10. Master craftsman (traditional skills)	91	7	2	100
Low-status occupations				
11. Commercial worker	64	7	0	71
12. Modern skilled worker	10	1	1	12
13. Traditional skilled worker	121	6	3	130
14. Service occupations	29	8	2	39
15. Farm laborer and other manual laborers	4	0	0	4
Total	564	43	27	634

Table 40. *Occupational status: French and other foreign social groups compared (percent within each social group; see Table 41 for numbers)*

Occupational status category	French	Other foreigners
High-status occupations		
1. Professional, administrator	8.1	0.0
2. Large-scale commerce	3.2	8.3
3. Large-scale farmer	0.0	0.0
4. White-collar employee	69.3	37.5
5. Medium-scale commerce	1.6	0.0
6. Medium- and small-scale farmers	4.8	0.0
7. Police, military	3.2	4.2
Medium-status occupations		
8. Petty commerce	0.0	4.2
9. Modern skilled workers (independently employed)	3.2	4.2
10. Master craftsman (traditional skills)	0.0	0.0
Low-status occupations		
11. Commercial worker	0.0	4.2
12. Modern skilled worker	0.0	12.5
13. Traditional skilled worker	1.6	8.3
14. Service occupations	0.0	4.2
15. Farm laborer and other manual laborers	4.8	12.5
Total	99.8	99.9

Table 41. *Occupational status: French and other foreign groups compared (numbers for Table 40)*

Occupational status category	French Born in France	French Born in North Africa	French Born else-where	Total French	Other foreigners Other Euro-peans	Other foreigners North Africans (Algeri-ans, etc.)
High-status occupations						
1. Professional, administrator	4	1	0	5	0	0
2. Large-scale commerce	2	0	0	2	1	1
3. Large-scale farmer	0	0	0	0	0	0
4. White-collar employee	29	12	2	43	0	9
5. Medium-scale commerce	1	0	0	1	0	0
6. Medium- and small-scale farmers	1	2	0	3	0	0
7. Police, military	1	1	0	2	0	1
Medium-status occupations						
8. Petty commerce	0	0	0	0	0	1
9. Modern skilled worker (independently employed)	1	1	0	2	1	0
10. Master craftsman (traditional skills)	0	0	0	0	0	0
Low-status occupations						
11. Commercial worker	0	0	0	0	0	1
12. Modern skilled worker	0	0	0	0	0	3
13. Traditional skilled worker	1	0	0	1	0	2
14. Service occupations	0	0	0	0	0	1
15. Farm laborer and other manual laborers	2	0	1	3	0	3
Total	42	17	3	62	2	22

Table 42. *Status level composition: social groups compared (percents within each social group; see Tables 35, 37, 39, and 41 for numbers)*

	Muslims							Jews			
Status levels	Sefrou-born Arabic speakers	Rural-born Arabic speakers	Rural-born Berber speakers	Urban-born Berber speakers	Fez born Arabic speakers	Bhalil-born Arabic speakers	Other urban-born Arabic speakers	Sefrou-born Jews	Rural-born Jews	Other urban Jews	French
High	20.7	25.7	29.4	44.2	54.6	12.6	43.6	17.4	9.3	59.3	90.2
Medium	28.5	20.1	21.8	22.1	19.8	17.2	14.7	42.2	39.5	18.5	3.2
Low	50.8	54.2	48.8	33.6	25.6	70.2	41.8	40.4	51.2	22.2	6.4
Total	100.0	100.0	99.0	99.9	100.0	100.0	99.1	100.0	100.0	100.0	99.8

Table 43. *Status levels compared: Muslim and Jewish social groups (percents within each status level; see Tables 35, 37, and 39 for numbers)*

	Status levels				Social groups proportion in total adult population (excluding foreigners)
Social group	High	Medium	Low	Inactive	
Major Muslim groups					
Sefrou-born Arabic speakers	29.9	38.7	37.6	24.6	35.5
Rural-born Arabic speakers	22.0	16.2	23.8	37.0	23.9
Rural-born Berber speakers	14.8	9.9	12.1	17.7	12.3
Minor Muslim groups					
Fez-born Arabic speakers	6.8	2.3	1.6	1.9	2.8
Bhalil-born Arabic speakers	1.9	2.5	5.6	4.8	4.0
Other urban Arabic speakers	7.6	2.4	3.9	3.6	4.5
Sefrou-born Berber speakers	3.1	0.8	1.2	0.8	1.0
Other urban Berber speakers	2.0	1.4	0.8	1.9	1.3
Jews					
Sefrou-born Jews	10.1	23.2	12.1	6.3	12.9
Rural-born Jews	0.4	1.6	1.2	1.0	0.9
Other urban Jews	1.6	0.5	0.3	0.3	0.6
Total	100.0	99.5	100.2	99.9	
Total number	966	1,027	1,890	1,640	

Appendix: A statistical profile 445

Agriculture, commerce, and traditional crafts (Tables 44–49)

In the tables of this section three major occupational sectors are analyzed for their social composition.

The agricultural sector (Tables 44 and 45) is shown to include proportionately more of the locally born population (including in this at the moment the rural-born Arabic speakers and rural-born Berber speakers, many of whom came from the nearby countryside) than their overall position in the population would indicate. At the same time, these groups are not evenly distributed within the agricultural sector when job status (i.e., primarily, the difference between employer and employed) is taken into account. There are relatively more Sefrou-born Arabs in the group of medium- to small-scale farmers who are self-employed, and conversely there are relatively more rural-born Arabic speakers and Berber speakers among the farm laborers, than a random distribution would produce.

The market and shop sector (Tables 46 and 47) shows a complementary configuration: Large-scale commerce is shared among Sefrou-born Arabic speakers (40 percent), rural-born Berber speakers (20 percent; these are merchants from the Sous in the south of Morocco), and Sefrou-born Jews (20 percent). Medium-scale commerce has a similar pattern, except that there are fewer Berber speakers involved. The lower levels of the commercial world – the small peddlers, shopkeepers, assistants, and the like – have a configuration less divergent from the general distribution of social groups in the overall population of Sefrou, although rural-born people are somewhat underrepresented and the Jews are overrepresented.

The traditional crafts (Tables 48 and 49) are dominated by Sefrou-born Arabs (46 percent) with Sefrou-born Jews holding 18 percent of these jobs. In this field, unlike agriculture and commerce, there is no important difference in social composition between the employer and the employee categories.

Table 44. *Composition of agricultural sector: Muslims and Jews by social group (percents within each job status level; see Table 45 for numbers)*

Social group	Large-scale farmers	Medium- and small scale farmers	Farm laborers	Total farmers	Social group's pro-portion in total adult population (excluding foreigners)
Sefrou-born					
Arabic speakers	100.0	47.8	30.5	37.3	35.3
Rural-born					
Arabic speakers	0.0	21.2	31.1	27.6	23.8
Rural-born					
Berber speakers	0.0	19.6	20.9	20.4	12.3
Fez-born Arabic speakers	0.0	0.8	0.2	0.4	2.8
Bhalil-born					
Arabic speakers	0.0	1.6	9.3	6.7	4.0
Other urban-born					
Arabic speakers	0.0	0.8	3.9	2.3	4.5
Sefrou-born					
Berber speakers	0.0	3.6	2.9	3.2	1.0
Other urban-born					
Berber speakers	0.0	0.4	0.8	0.7	1.3
Sefrou-born Jews	0.0	2.0	0.8	1.2	12.9
Rural-born Jews	0.0	0.0	0.0	0.0	0.9
Other urban-born Jews	0.0	0.0	0.0	0.0	0.6
Total	100.0	97.8	100.4	99.8	99.4

Table 45. *Composition of agricultural sector: Muslims and Jews by social group (numbers for Table 44)*

Social group	Large-scale farmers	Medium- and small-scale farmers	Farm laborers	Total farmers
Sefrou-born Arabic speakers	2	122	143	267
Rural-born Arabic speakers	0	52	146	198
Rural-born Berber speakers	0	48	98	146
Fez-born Arabic speakers	0	2	1	3
Bhalil-born Arabic speakers	0	4	44	48
Other urban-born Arabic speakers	0	2	15	17
Sefrou-born Berber speakers	0	9	14	23
Other urban-born Berber speakers	0	1	4	5
Sefrou-born Jews	0	5	4	9
Rural-born Jews	0	0	0	0
Other urban-born Jews	0	0	0	0
Total	2	245	469	716

Appendix: A statistical profile 447

Table 46. *Composition of market and shop sector: Muslims and Jews by social group (percent within each job status level; see Table 47 for numbers)*

Social group	Large-scale commerce	Medium-scale commerce	Petty commerce	Com-mercial worker	Total commerce	Social group's proportion in total adult population (excluding foreigners)
Sefrou-born						
Arabic speakers	40.0	43.4	34.4	31.9	34.2	35.5
Rural-born						
Arabic speakers	5.0	8.7	16.7	17.2	16.3	23.8
Rural-born						
Berber speakers	20.0	8.7	11.4	9.4	11.1	12.3
Fez-born						
Arabic speakers	0.0	0.0	1.6	0.5	1.2	2.8
Bhalil-born						
Arabic speakers	0.0	0.0	1.8	2.1	1.8	4.0
Other urban-born						
Arabic speakers	10.0	0.0	3.1	1.0	2.6	4.5
Sefrou-born						
Berber speakers	0.0	0.0	1.0	0.0	0.7	1.0
Other urban-born						
Berber speakers	0.0	4.3	2.0	0.5	1.6	1.3
Sefrou-born Jews	20.0	34.8	25.4	33.5	27.5	12.9
Rural-born Jews	0.0	0.0	1.8	3.6	2.1	0.9
Other urban-born						
Jews	5.0	0.0	0.5	0.0	0.5	0.6
Total	100.0	99.9	99.7	99.7	99.6	99.6

Table 47. *Composition of market and shop sector: Muslims and Jews by social group (numbers for Table 46)*

Social group	Large-scale commerce	Medium-scale commerce	Petty commerce	Commercial worker	Total commerce
Sefrou-born					
Arabic speakers	8	10	190	61	269
Rural-born					
Arabic speakers	1	2	92	33	128
Rural-born					
Berber speakers	4	2	63	18	87
Fez-born					
Arabic speakers	0	0	9	1	10
Bhalil-born					
Arabic speakers	0	0	10	4	14
Other urban-born					
Arabic speakers	2	0	17	2	21
Sefrou-born					
Berber speakers	0	0	6	0	6
Other urban-born					
Berber speakers	0	1	11	1	13
Sefrou-born Jews	4	8	140	64	216
Rural-born Jews	0	0	10	7	17
Other urban-born					
Jews	1	0	3	0	4
Total	20	23	551	191	785

Table 48. *Composition of artisan group: Muslims and Jews by social group (percents within each job status level; see Table 49 for numbers)*

Social group	Traditional skills			Social group's proportion in total adult population (excluding foreigners)
	Master craftsman[a]	Worker	Total	
Sefrou-born Arabic speakers	43.8	46.7	45.6	35.5
Rural-born Arabic speakers	16.2	18.0	17.4	23.8
Rural-born Berber speakers	7.4	6.8	7.0	12.3
Fez-born Arabic speakers	2.9	2.4	2.6	2.8
Bhalil-born Arabic speakers	3.6	4.5	4.2	4.0
Other urban-born Arabic speakers	1.8	2.8	2.4	4.5
Sefrou-born Berber speakers	0.6	0.4	0.5	1.0
Other urban-born Berber speakers	0.9	0.5	0.6	1.3
Sefrou-born Jews	20.5	16.3	17.9	12.9
Rural-born Jews	1.5	0.8	1.1	0.9
Other urban-born Jews	0.4	0.4	0.4	0.6
Total	99.6	99.6	99.7	99.6

[a] Employers and independent artisans.

Appendix: A statistical profile   449

Table 49. *Composition of artisan group: Muslims and Jews by social group (numbers for Table 48)*

Social group	Traditional skills		
	Master craftsman[a]	Worker	Total
Sefrou-born Arabic speakers	194	346	540
Rural-born Arabic speakers	72	134	206
Rural-born Berber speakers	33	51	84
Fez-born Arabic speakers	13	18	31
Bhalil-born Arabic speakers	16	34	50
Other urban-born Arabic speakers	8	21	29
Sefrou-born Berber speakers	3	3	6
Other urban-born Berber speakers	4	4	8
Sefrou-born Jews	91	121	212
Rural-born Jews	7	6	13
Other urban-born Jews	2	3	5
Total	443	741	1,184

[a] Employers and independent artisans.

Residential patterns (Tables 50–56; Figures 4–7)

Physically, the urban dwelling areas of Sefrou differ widely among themselves in regard to street layout, population density, and architecture. Each has its own distinctive character deriving from its particular history and from the uses it is put to by its contemporary inhabitants. However, with the exception of the walled old city areas (the Medina; the Mellah, and the Qla^c^a), most neighborhoods or quarters have indefinite boundaries and internal variation in kinds of housing, and their social identity shifts with the point of view of the speaker. The boundaries of the census tracts, in contrast, although to some extent conforming to local concepts of neighborhood and so on, nonetheless divide the town's geography in a rather arbitrary way. In an attempt to order the census material according to a socially relevant geography, I have made two kinds of groupings of the census tracts, on the basis of knowledge derived from fieldwork. The first groups the twenty-four tracts into nine *residential areas,* each labeled with a local name that pertains to at least part of that area. The second is a further grouping of these nine residential areas into three general *residential types:* Old City, New Medina, and Ville Nouvelle.

This section is concerned mainly with various comparisons and contrasts among the nine residential areas and the three residential types. The next section presents a comparison among Sefrou's social groups for their distribution among the residential types, taking into account occupational status level. It provides a tentative answer to the question: In what ways is socioeconomic status related to type of dwelling area, taking into ac-

450 *Meaning and order in Moroccan society*

count birthplace, ethnic category, and language spoken? The section after that compares social groups for their housing condition (e.g., plumbing and electricity) and for forms of home tenure (e.g., ownership or rental).

Figures 4 through 6 show the distribution of social groups among the census tracts. The various Muslim social groups are fairly evenly scattered throughout the town. This is perhaps the single most important social fact documented by these statistics: The Muslim population, regardless of its internal differentiation by language and place of birth, is fairly evenly distributed in Sefrou. There are no residential areas that are not heterogeneous regarding Muslim social group and, as I will show in the next section, also regarding occupational status, which may be interpreted as a rough indicator of socioeconomic class. Fieldwork bears out this conclusion, for I found that, by and large, not only the large areas defined by census boundaries, but also smaller alleyways (derbs) and neighborhoods (humas) were diversified in regard to social group and class. However, minor subtle exceptions to this general evenness are to be found, and the tables following explore these variations.

Table 50 examines the distribution of the rural-born Muslims, including the people of Bhalil. It shows that more of the people moving into Sefrou from the countryside have settled in three residential areas: the Medina, the Qla^ca, and Slawi. Areas where they are underrepresented are Derb l-Miter and the Ville Nouvelle. There are a few differences between the Arabic speakers and the Berber speakers in this rural-born

population distribution, with the Arabic speakers tending to live in the Qla^ca and Slawi, where comparatively few Berber speakers are to be found. The Arabic-speaking rural-born seem to avoid Derb l-Miter; the Berber speakers are fairly well represented there. The Berber speakers, in contrast to the rural-born Arabic speakers, are fairly evenly distributed around Sefrou with two exceptions: an overrepresentation in Sidi Ahmed Tadli and a marked underrepresentation in Slawi.

The Jews and the French, in contrast, show markedly selective residential distributions (Figure 6). The Jews are concentrated in three areas: the Mellah (tracts 5–7), the Derb l-Miter area (tracts 19 and 20), and certain parts of the Ville Nouvelle (tracts 23 and 24). The French live primarily in the Ville Nouvelle.

The nine residential areas, as defined in this study, are shown in Figure 7 and described in Tables 51 to 56. The first of these, the old city residential areas, consisting of the Medina, the Mellah, and the Qla^ca, are all very similar in architecture and population density. The Mellah, Sefrou's Jewish ghetto until the mid-1960s, is an enclosed quarter in the center of the Medina. The Qla^ca is a separate quarter with its own high walls, situated about 400 meters south of the Medina. These three quarters differ in social composition. There are few areas within their walls that are not fully built up, few gardens or open courtyards, and their densities are all over 1,100 persons per hectare. The proportions of persons per building range between 9 and 11. Electricity has been installed in 85 percent of the Medina buildings, 92 percent of the Mellah buildings, but only 77 percent of buildings in the Qla^ca. The Qla^ca and the Mellah are similar in having very insufficient sanitary facilities, with less than 40 percent of their buildings supplied with toilets.

The Medina contains 42 percent Sefrou-born Arabic speakers, 26 percent rural-born Arabic speakers, and 16 percent rural-born Berber speakers, thus fairly well approximating the proportions found for the whole city, but only 4 percent of its population are Jews. The Qla^ca, with no Jews at all, has a slightly larger proportion of rural-born people than the Medina, especially if the Bhalil-born are counted as rural (Medina: 46 percent rural, including Bhalil-born; Qla^ca: 52 percent). About 30 percent of all Bhalil-born adults live in the Qla^ca. The occupational composition reflects this more rural character of the Qla^ca, with the Qla^ca having a greater proportion of persons of low-status occupations (i.e., manual laborers who are in the employ of others). Both areas are heavily low status, in terms of occupation, compared with the other parts of Sefrou.

The Mellah in 1960 is 84 percent Jewish. I suspect that most of the Sefrou-born Muslims (6 percent of the Mellah population) listed as living in the Mellah are there simply because the boundaries of census tract 7 include parts of quarters that are, strictly speaking, outside the Mellah. About 55 percent of Sefrou's Jewish population is living within its confines. Its occupational composition too is sharply skewed toward lower statuses. Almost all its Muslims are of low occupational status, and the same is true of the Jews. Jews with high-status occupations (i.e., white-collar occupations in commerce administration) live either in Derb l-Miter or in the Ville Nouvelle. About 60 percent of the buildings in the Mellah are rented rather than owned by the occupant, as against only 52 percent and 48 percent for the Medina and Qla^ca.

The New Medina areas include four residential areas – Sidi Ahmed Tadli, Lalla Sitti Messaouda, Derb l-Miter, and Slawi – plus the catch-all category of "others." All were built after the French Protectorate began, on lands that had formerly been gardens and orchards surrounding Sefrou. The streets are wide enough for automobiles and are arranged in a gridlike pattern; nonetheless, within many of the built-up blocks, something of the crowded quality of the Medina areas has been reproduced. The density ratio of persons to buildings is the most precise indicator of crowding, and the range for the four most representative areas (Sidi Ahmed Tadli, Lalla Sitti Messaouda, Derb l-Miter, and Slawi) goes from 8.5 to 5.4 persons per building. The census tract boundaries for Sidi Ahmed Tadli and Slawi include large segments of still-existing gardens so that the figures of persons per hectare for these two areas are misleadingly low.

Sidi Ahmed Tadli, the most densely populated of the New Medina areas, is also the newest. Built entirely since 1956, and still expanding, it has the highest person per building ratio (8.5). It also has the largest proportion of multihousehold buildings (6.8 percent), which are almost absent from the other three. And it has the highest proportion of buildings owned by one of the occupants, with 74 percent in this category. The social composition is 38 percent Sefrou-born Arabic speakers, 21 percent rural-born Arabic speakers, 21 percent rural-born Berber speakers (who are thus slightly overrepresented in comparison with only 12 percent in the overall Sefrou population), and no Jews. It is largely low status in occupational composition.

Derb l-Miter is the oldest of the New Medina areas, with almost all its structures dating from the 1920s and 1930s. It is actually more densely populated than its statistics indicate, because many commercial structures, market areas, and governmental buildings such as the hospital are included within its boundaries. Many of its buildings are three stories high, but contain only one household, with the remainder of the building given over to a store, workroom, or warehouse. Although it is almost entirely electrified, more than 20 percent of its buildings have no toilet on the premises. Its population is highly heterogeneous, with a large segment of Jews making up 28 percent of its population. Rural-born Arabic speakers are slightly underrepresented, but the other Muslims are distributed much as they are in the general population. There are a few Frenchmen. There are proportionately more people with high-status occupations living in Derb l-Miter than in Sidi Ahmed Tadli, making up about 29 percent of the working population. Only 50 percent of its buildings are owned by one of their occupants.

Lalla Sitti Messaouda has some sections almost as old as those in Derb l-Miter, but it also has large sectors in which buildings are still going up. These are all well provided with electricity and toilets (more than 90 percent of the buildings have both). The distribution of social groups shows a high overrepresentation of Sefrou-born Arabic speakers and an underrepresentation of Jews. It has about the same proportion of high-status occupations as Derb l-Miter, but this varies considerably by social group. Only 18 percent of the Sefrou-born Arabic speakers have high-status occupations, as against 39 percent of the rural-born Arabic speakers and 40 percent of the rural-born Berber speakers who live in this area.

Slawi is the last of the New Medina areas to be discussed. It is not very homogeneous in regard to housing characteristics, with only 44 percent of its units having toilets and only 49 percent electricity. There is in it a large "temporary" municipal housing project, which is without electricity or toilets; at the same time there is also a number of modern middle-class single-family houses of an adapted Moroccan style. The density of persons per building is quite low, only 5.4. Slawi has higher proportions of people with high-status occupations than the other New Medina areas and has a very similar occupational composition to the Muslim population of the French and elite quarter of the city, the Ville Nouvelle. On the other hand, Slawi has a higher proportion of rural-born Arabic speakers than any other section of the city, with 52 percent of its entire population falling in this category.

Five census tracts (13, 14, 15, 21, and 22) have been grouped as "others." This categorization was mainly required by the fact that the data on them are all very poor. All have more than 15 percent blank responses on questions concerning housing conditions and relatively high proportions of blanks on other questions. It is fairly reasonable to group them together, however, because they are all geographically peripheral to the town proper and all rather lightly settled. Two are adjacent to the quarter of Sidi Ahmed Tadli, and carry that name too, so I have indicated the central part of that quarter as *A* and the other two as *B* and *C*. For the summary comparison in the next section these "other" areas are included in the category New Medina.

The Ville Nouvelle, the French-style villa area, lies on the slopes above the Medina, on lands that were formerly orchards and gardens belonging to residents of the Qlaᶜa. The houses are almost all modern, single-family European-style villas, set back in gardens. Recently, a few single-family houses have been built by well-to-do Muslims along a modified Arabic pattern with an enclosed central court. At the base of the Ville Nouvelle runs the main thoroughfare of the town, Boulevard Mohammed V, which is lined by three-story arcaded buildings with shops on the ground floor and apartments above. And just behind this street is a more densely built up quarter where most of the Jews of the Ville Nouvelle live together in a kind of new Mellah. About 50 percent of these Jews hold high-status occupations.

Some 24 percent of the population of the Ville Nouvelle are Sefrou-born Jews, and an additional 3 percent are Jews who were born elsewhere. About 11 percent are French (representing 64 percent of all Sefrou's French popula-tion) and another 4 percent are other foreigners. Although small, this 15 percent foreign population of the Ville Nouvelle gives its tone to the entire quarter. As for the Muslims who live in this villa area, 18 percent of the total Ville Nouvelle population are Sefrou-born Arabic speakers, 11 percent are rural-born Arabic speakers, 10 percent are rural-born Berber speakers, and 20 percent are Muslims born in other Moroccan towns. This latter group is over-represented in the area, whereas the other three Muslim groups are underrepresented. Of the Sefrou-born Arabs who live in the Ville Nouvelle, 20 percent have high-status occupations; of the rural-born Arabic speakers, 25 percent; and of the rural-born Berber speakers, 30 percent.

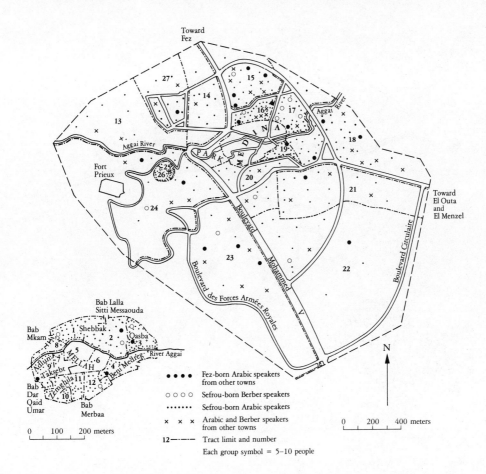

Figure 4. Distribution of members of urban-born Muslim social groups in Sefrou.

Map labels:

Toward Fez

27

15

14

16 17

13

Aggai River

P A R K

M E D I N A

Aggai River

18

Fort Prieux

19

25 26

20

21

Toward El Outa and El Menzel

24

Boulevard Mohammed V

23

22

Boulevard Circulaire

Boulevard des Forces Armées Royales

Bab Lalla Sitti Messaouda

Bab Mkam

Shebbak

Qasba

MELLAH

Adlun

Taksebt

Zenghla

Bab Dar Qaid Umar

Bab Merbaa

Ben Medreg

River Aggai

N

Legend:

• • • • Fez-born Arabic speakers from other towns

○ ○ ○ ○ Sefrou-born Berber speakers

• • • • • • Sefrou-born Arabic speakers

× × × Arabic and Berber speakers from other towns

12 —·—·— Tract limit and number

Each group symbol = 5–10 people

0 100 200 meters

0 200 400 meters

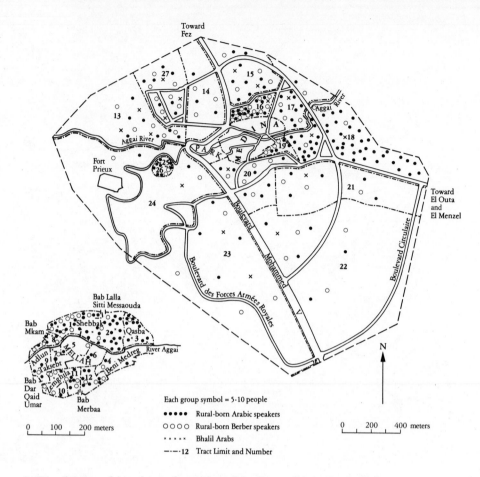

Figure 5. Distribution of members of rural-born Muslim social groups in Sefrou.

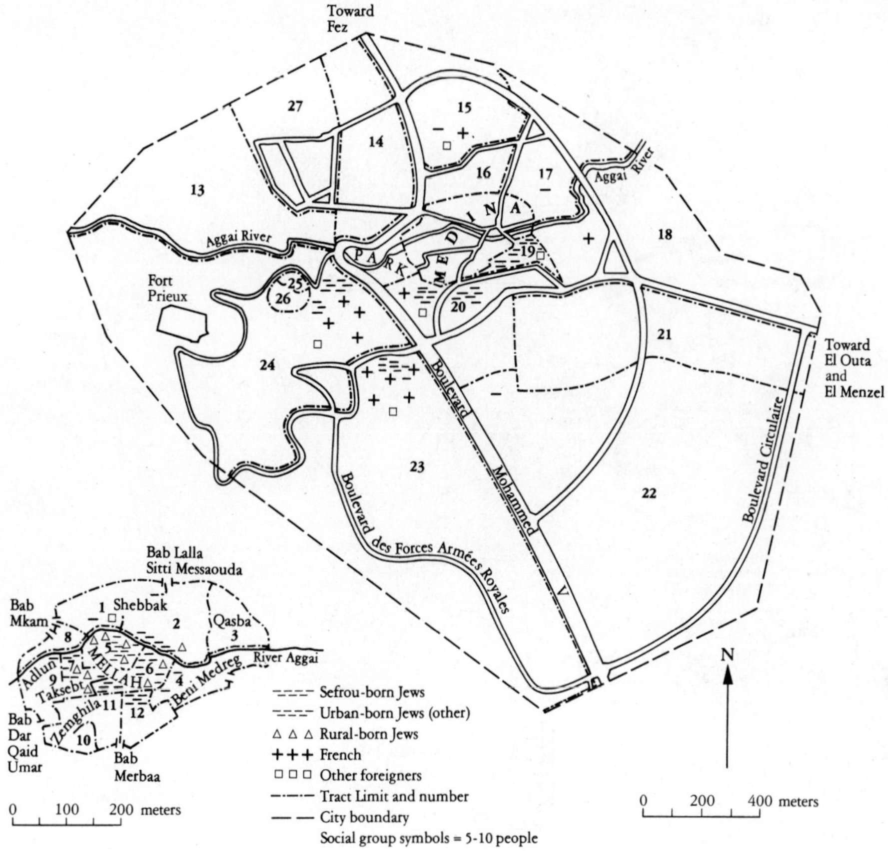
Toward
Fez
Toward
El Outa
and
El Menzel
Aggai River
Aggai River
Fort
Prieux
PARK
MEDINA
Boulevard
Mohammed
V
Boulevard des Forces Armées Royales
Boulevard Circulaire
27
15
14
16
17
13
18
19
25
26
20
21
24
23
22
Bab Lalla
Sitti Messaouda
Bab
Mkam
Shebbak
Qasba
River Aggai
Adlun
MELLAH
Taksebt
Zemghila
Beni Medreg
Bab
Dar
Qaid
Umar
Bab
Merbaa
1
2
3
4
5
6
7
8
9
10
11
12
0 100 200 meters
Sefrou-born Jews
Urban-born Jews (other)
△ △ △ Rural-born Jews
+++ French
□ □ □ Other foreigners
Tract Limit and number
City boundary
Social group symbols = 5-10 people
N
0 200 400 meters

Figure 6. Distribution of members of Jewish and foreign-born social groups in Sefrou.

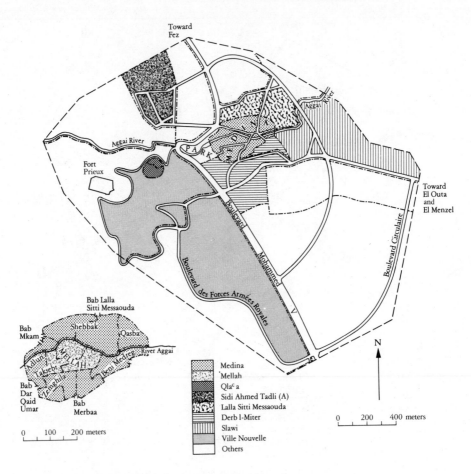

Figure 7. Major residential areas of Sefrou: classification of census tracts.

Legend:
- Medina
- Mellah
- Qlaᶜa
- Sidi Ahmed Tadli (A)
- Lalla Sitti Messaouda
- Derb l-Miter
- Slawi
- Ville Nouvelle
- Others

458 *Meaning and order in Moroccan society*

Table 50. *Rural-born Muslims: spatial distribution in Sefrou*

| Area | Rural-born Arabs + Berbers | | Bhalil-born | | 1 + 2 | | |
	Number	Percent of total rural-born population	Number	Percent of Bhalil-born population	Number	Percent of total rural population including Bhalil	Percent of total Sefrou population in each area
Medina	1,598	40.0	156	34.7	1,754	39.4	32.9
Mellah	71	1.7	7	1.5	78	1.7	9.5
Qla^c a	393	9.8	97	21.5	490	11.0	8.2
Sidi Ahmed Tadli	136	3.4	33	7.3	169	3.8	3.0
Lalla Sitti Messaouda	377	9.4	26	5.8	403	9.0	9.8
Derb l-Miter	259	6.5	17	3.8	276	6.2	9.2
Slawi	548	13.7	19	4.2	567	12.7	9.4
Ville Nouvelle	157	3.9	24	5.3	181	4.1	6.8
Other areas	458	11.4	71	1.6	529	11.9	11.0
Total	3,997	99.8	450	85.7	4,447	99.8	

Table 51. *Residential areas compared: population and housing density*

Area	Census tract	Population	Percent of total population	Number of buildings	People/ hectare	Bldgs./ hectare	People/ bldg.
Medina	1–4, 8–12	6,909	32.9	629	1,117	100.8	11.0
Mellah	5, 6, 7	1,988	9.5	218	1,155	126.7	9.1
Qla^c a	25, 26	1,715	8.2	174	1,361	138.1	9.8
Sidi Ahmed Tadli (A)	27	623	3.0	73	56.5	6.6	8.5
Lalla Sitti Messaouda	16, 17	2,067	9.8	311	152	22.8	6.6
Derb l-Miter	19, 20	1,940	9.2	296	203	30.6	6.5
Slawi	18	1,986	9.4	367	83.8	15.4	5.4
Ville Nouvelle	23, 24	1,428	6.8	283	12.2	2.4	5.0
Other							
Sidi Ahmed Tadli (B)	13	413 ⎫		68	15.6	2.5	6.1
Sidi Ahmed Tadli (C)	14	269 ⎪		45	19.6	3.2	6.0
Trek Fes	15	716 ⎬ 11.0		126	52.6	9.2	5.7
Habbuna	21	532 ⎪		89	19.9	3.3	6.0
Sidi Boumedienne	22	379 ⎭		76	4.5	0.8	5.0
Total		20,965	99.8	2,755	60.3	7.9	7.6

Appendix: A statistical profile 459

Table 52. *Residential areas compared: housing characteristics*

Area	Percent buildings 1 household	Percent buildings 6+ household	Percent buildings 5+ household	Percent Non-masonry buildings	Percent rented	Percent with toilet	Percent with electricity
Medina	41.6	10.5	17.4	6.0	52.2	81.4	84.9
Mellah	51.8	2.3	5.7	0.0	79.3	39.9	91.7
Qla‵a	36.8	3.4	5.7	6.3	48.2	36.2	77.0
Sidi Ahmed Tadli (A)	57.5	2.7	6.8	2.7	26.4	88.9	82.2
Lalla Sitti Messaouda	76.2	0.0	0.0	0.3	42.7	90.6	92.3
Derb l-Miter	84.1	0.0	0.3	0.0	49.6	78.6	95.6
Slawi	85.6	0.6	0.9	0.3	69.1	43.6	48.8
Ville Nouvelle	87.6	0.3	0.6	6.7	37.9	76.1	82.6
Other [a]							
Sidi Ahmed Tadli (B)	69.1	1.5	3.0	14.7	36.8	47.8	47.1
Sidi Ahmed Tadli (C)	73.3	0.0	0.0	13.3	11.1	73.3	46.7
Trek Fes	77.8	2.4	3.2	3.1	57.1	81.6	18.6
Habbuna	74.2	1.1	1.1	6.7	21.3	71.9	71.9
Sidi Boumedienne	65.8	0.0	0.0	26.3	28.9	53.3	51.3

[a] These are lightly settled areas, peripheral to town. All were poorly covered by the census, having 15% or more blank answers on housing variables.

Table 53. *Residential areas compared: composition by social group (percents within each area: see Table 54 for numbers)*

| Area | Social group | | | | | | | | |
	Sefrou-born Arabs	Rural-born Arabs	Rural-born Berbers	Other Muslims	Sefrou-born Jews	Other Jews	French	Other for-eigners	Total
Medina	41.8	26.0	15.8	11.7	3.7	0.5	0.02	0.5	100.0
Mellah	5.8	2.8	3.6	2.9	74.2	10.3	0.0	0.2	99.8
Qla°a	40.5	31.8	10.2	17.4	0.0	0.0	0.0	0.0	99.9
Sidi Ahmed Tadli (A)	37.6	21.1	20.5	19.2	0.0	0.0	1.2	0.3	99.9
Lalla Sitti Messaouda	48.4	21.7	13.2	15.0	1.2	0.0	0.2	0.1	99.8
Derb l-Miter	32.4	12.6	13.3	10.1	27.5	1.5	1.1	1.5	100.0
Slawi	31.2	52.0	1.7	14.2	0.0	0.2	0.6	0.0	99.9
Ville Nouvelle	18.1	10.6	10.0	20.0	23.7	2.6	11.2	3.7	99.9
Other Sidi Ahmed Tadli (B)	27.9	26.0	20.5	25.6	0.0	0.0	0.0	0.0	100.0
Sidi Ahmed Tadli (C)	49.3	21.7	21.7	6.6	0.0	0.0	0.6	0.0	99.9
Trek Fes	30.9	22.7	11.3	28.1	0.0	2.8	1.8	2.3	99.9
Habbuna	50.6	18.3	10.6	19.4	0.0	0.0	1.1	0.0	100.0
Sidi Bou-medienne	38.1	23.3	17.3	14.8	5.9	0.0	0.0	0.5	99.9
Percent in Sefrou population	34.9	23.4	12.1	13.5	12.7	1.6	1.1	0.7	100.0

Table 54. *Residential areas compared: composition by social group (numbers for Table 53)*

Area	Social group								
	Sefrou-born Arabs	Rural-born Arabs	Rural-born Berbers	Other Muslims	Sefrou-born Jews	Other Jews	French	Other for-eigners	Total
Medina	1,601	993	605	447	142	18	1	18	3,825
Mellah	64	31	40	32	810	112	0	2	1,091
Qlaᶜa	379	297	96	163	0	0	0	0	935
Sidi Ahmed Tadli (A)	123	69	67	63	0	0	4	1	327
Lalla Sitti Messaouda	521	234	143	161	13	0	3	1	1,076
Derb l-Miter	325	126	133	101	276	15	11	15	1,002
Slawi	319	531	17	146	0	2	7	0	1,022
Ville Nouvelle	138	81	76	152	181	20	85	28	761
Other Sidi Ahmed Tadli (B)	61	57	45	56	0	0	0	0	219
Sidi Ahmed Tadli (C)	75	33	10	0	0	0	1	0	152
Trek Fes	120	88	44	109	0	11	7	9	388
Habbuna	133	48	28	51	0	0	3	0	263
Sidi Bou-medienne	77	47	35	30	12	0	0	1	202
Total	3,936	2,635	1,362	1,521	1,434	178	122	75	11,263

Table 55. *Residential areas compared: composition by occupational status level: Muslims only (percents based on total employed persons in each residential area; (see Table 56 for numbers)*

Area	Low-status occupations (manual labor)	Medium-status occupations (independent artisan, petty commerce)	High-status occupations (administration, white-collar, commerce, independent farmer)	Total number in employed labor force
Medina	52.5	27.1	20.4	1,123
Mellah	50.8	40.4	8.8	57
Qlaᶜa	71.1	15.0	13.9	439
Sidi Ahmed Tadli (A)	51.8	27.3	20.9	110
Lalla Sitti Messaouda	42.3	27.7	30.0	376
Derb l-Miter	43.7	27.8	28.5	277
Slawi	41.7	21.7	36.6	254
Ville Nouvelle	51.0	7.0	42.0	200
Other				
Sidi Ahmed Tadli (B)	32.7	36.5	30.8	52
Sidi Ahmed Tadli (C)	49.1	14.2	36.7	49
Trek Fes	29.4	19.0	51.6	126
Habbuna	35.6	28.8	35.6	104
Sidi Boumedienne	51.2	20.2	28.6	84
All Sefrou	50.5	23.6	26.0	3,251

Table 56. *Residential areas compared: composition by occupational status level: Muslims only (numbers for Table 55)*

Area	Low-status occupations	Medium-status occupations	High-status occupations	Total number in employed labor force
Medina	590	304	229	1,123
Mellah	29	23	5	57
Qlaᶜa	312	66	61	439
Sidi Ahmed Tadli (A)	57	30	23	110
Lalla Sitti Messaouda	159	104	113	376
Derb l-Miter	121	77	79	277
Slawi	106	55	93	254
Ville Nouvelle	102	14	84	200
Other				
Sidi Ahmed Tadli (B)	17	19	16	52
Sidi Ahmed Tadli (C)	24	7	18	49
Trek Fes	37	24	65	126
Habbuna	37	30	37	104
Sidi Boumedienne	43	17	24	84
Total	1,634	770	847	3,251

Residence and occupational status (Tables 57–59)

The tables in this section display some interesting patterns. They enable a comparison of the internal makeup of nine major social groups, according to occupational level and residential area simultaneously. Each bloc of percentages is to be read as a compartmentalization of the population of the social group into high-status people living in the Old City, high-status people living in the New Medina, high-status people living in the Ville Nouvelle, and so on. The percentages thus are based on the table total of each bloc (i.e., the total at the bottom right side).

As is true of the information presented in the preceding section, the most important pattern for the Muslims is the evenness with which each social group and each occupational status category within it are distributed among the different residential types. The rural-born Berbers are the most evenly distributed around town and among status categories, but the Sefrou-born Arabic speakers are close behind. The most unevenly distributed are the Fez-born Arabic speakers, 55 percent of whom are in the high-status category, and of these 34.7 percent are living in New Medina-type areas. The Bhalil-born Arabic speakers show a reverse pattern, with the largest percentage in the low-status category (72.2 percent), and of these 39.1 percent are living in an Old City-type environment.

The Jews are very unevenly distributed around town, but they show a relatively even sorting into status levels. However, if rural-born Jews are separately examined, their pattern is seen to be quite different from that of those Jews born in Sefrou. The former are largely low status (51.2 percent) and primarily resident in the Mellah. Most Sefrou-born Jews live in the Mellah, but a sizable percentage has residence elsewhere. For these Sefrou-born Jews, there is a marked relationship between status level and residence: High-status people live in the Ville Nouvelle, medium-status people largely in the New Medina areas, and low-status people mainly in the Old City.

The relationship between occupational status and residential pattern is marked for the French as well. However, this reflects two independent characteristics of the French population: (1) no French live in a Medina-type area, and (2) 90 percent of French are in high-status occupations.

Table 57. *Residence and occupational status: social groups compared: major Muslim groups (percents of total in each social group)*

SEFROU-BORN ARABIC SPEAKERS

Occupational status level	Percent				Occupational status level	Number			
	Old City	New Medina	Ville Nouvelle	Total		Old City	New Medina	Ville Nouvelle	Total
High	8.1	11.1	1.4	20.6	High	113	155	20	288
Medium	14.2	13.9	0.4	28.5	Medium	199	194	6	399
Low	30.1	18.8	1.9	50.8	Low	421	263	26	710
Total	52.4	43.8	3.7	99.9	Total	733	612	52	1,397

RURAL-BORN ARABIC SPEAKERS

Occupational status level	Percent				Occupational status level	Number			
	Old City	New Medina	Ville Nouvelle	Total		Old City	New Medina	Ville Nouvelle	Total
High	10.0	14.3	1.2	25.5	High	83	119	10	212
Medium	10.2	8.4	0.4	19.0	Medium	95	70	3	168
Low	31.8	19.2	3.2	54.2	Low	264	159	27	450
Total	52.0	41.9	4.8	98.7	Total	442	348	40	830

RURAL-BORN ARABIC SPEAKERS

Occupational status level	Percent				Occupational status level	Number			
	Old City	New Medina	Ville Nouvelle	Total		Old City	New Medina	Ville Nouvelle	Total
High	11.5	15.0	2.5	29.0	High	55	71	12	138
Medium	11.5	9.7	1.3	22.5	Medium	55	46	6	107
Low	25.2	17.3	4.7	47.2	Low	124	82	22	228
Total	48.2	42.0	8.5	98.7	Total	234	199	40	473

Table 58. *Residence and occupational status: social groups compared: minor Muslim groups (percents based on total in each social group)*

FEZ-BORN ARABIC SPEAKERS

Occupa-tional status level	Percent				Occupa-tional status level	Number			
	Old City	New Medina	Ville Nouvelle	Total		Old City	New Medina	Ville Nouvelle	Total
High	4.1	34.7	15.7	54.5	High	5	42	19	66
Medium	8.2	11.6	0.0	19.8	Medium	10	14	0	24
Low	11.6	9.9	4.1	25.5	Low	14	12	5	31
Total	23.9	56.2	19.8	99.8	Total	29	68	24	121

BHALIL-BORN ARABIC SPEAKERS

Occupa-tional status level	Percent				Occupa-tional status level	Number			
	Old City	New Medina	Ville Nouvelle	Total		Old City	New Medina	Ville Nouvelle	Total
High	4.0	7.9	0.7	12.6	High	6	12	1	19
Medium	10.6	4.0	0.7	15.3	Medium	16	6	1	23
Low	39.1	25.2	7.9	72.2	Low	59	38	12	109
Total	53.7	37.1	9.3	100.1	Total	81	56	14	151

OTHER URBAN-BORN MUSLIMS

Occupa-tional status level	Percent				Occupa-tional status level	Number			
	Old City	New Medina	Ville Nouvelle	Total		Old City	New Medina	Ville Nouvelle	Total
High	11.7	24.4	7.8	43.9	High	33	69	22	124
Medium	6.4	10.5	0.7	17.6	Medium	18	30	2	50
Low	17.3	17.7	3.5	38.5	Low	49	50	10	109
Total	35.4	52.6	12.0	100.0	Total	100	149	34	283

Table 59. *Residence and occupational status: social groups compared: Jews and French (percents based on totals in each social group)*

SEFROU-BORN JEWS

Occupational status level	Percent				Occupational status level	Number			
	Old City	New Medina	Ville Nouvelle	Total		Old City	New Medina	Ville Nouvelle	Total
High	4.4	6.1	6.6	17.1	High	25	35	38	98
Medium	25.2	13.3	4.5	43.0	Medium	144	76	26	246
Low	31.3	6.5	2.1	39.9	Low	179	37	12	228
Total	60.9	25.9	13.2	100.0	Total	348	148	76	572

RURAL-BORN JEWS

Occupational status level	Percent				Occupational status level	Number			
	Old City	New Medina	Ville Nouvelle	Total		Old City	New Medina	Ville Nouvelle	Total
High	2.3	2.3	4.7	9.3	High	1	1	2	4
Medium	40.0	0.0	0.0	40.0	Medium	17	0	0	17
Low	51.2	0.0	0.0	51.2	Low	22	0	0	22
Total	93.5	2.3	4.7	100.5	Total	40	1	2	43

FRENCH

Occupational status level	Percent				Occupational status level	Number			
	Old City	New Medina	Ville Nouvelle	Total		Old City	New Medina	Ville Nouvelle	Total
High	0.0	30.6	59.7	90.3	High	0	19	37	56
Medium	0.0	1.6	1.6	3.2	Medium	0	1	1	2
Low	0.0	0.0	6.4	6.4	Low	0	0	4	4
Total	0.0	32.2	67.7	99.9	Total	0	20	42	62

Housing (Tables 60–62)

The housing characteristics for which we have relatively reliable data are electricity, toilet facilities, telephone, home tenure, and number of households per building. These are summarized in Table 60. These five characteristics are highly intercorrelated, and the social groups can be fairly clearly ranked regarding their housing conditions. The French are far above the other groups, and the Jews (not including the rural-born Jews) and the Fez-born Arabic-speaking Muslims are the best housed of the indigenous social groups. The social group labeled other urban Muslims, which stands below the Fez-born Muslims, consists for the most part of persons who have moved to Sefrou from other towns and includes a large proportion of civil servants. The rural-born Muslims, with those from Bhalil at the very bottom, are the most poorly housed.

The variable of home tenure (Table 61) indicates whether the person lives in a dwelling owned by one of the occupants, as against one in which all occupants are renters. The Sefrou-born Arabic-speaking Muslims, as might be expected, have the lowest proportion of persons living in wholly rented buildings. The groups with the highest proportions of rentals are the Jews, reflecting a traditional preference for rental over outright ownership.

Table 62 summarizes what the census shows about the dwellers in nonmasonry houses. Sefrou has no shantytown (*bidonville*). It has only a few dwellings that were classified by the census as not of masonry construction. These include shacks made of portions of wrecked automobiles, rural peasant houses of uncemented dry rock, traditional Berber tents made of black goat hair, and even a few inhabited caves in the limestone cliffs overlooking Sefrou. The total number of these dwellings is 84, 3 percent of the 2,750 Sefrou homes. They are not clustered together into a single shantytown, but are scattered individually or in very small groups over all but a few of the census tracts.

A total of 220 adults live in these shacks, 2 percent of the total Sefrou adult population. There are no Jews and no foreigners among them. This shack-dwelling group is dominated by rural-born persons (71 percent), and within this rural-born group the proportion between Arabic speakers and Berber speakers is about the same as in the general rural-born population.

A rural village, Cher Ben Safar, just outside the town line was not included in this survey.

Table 60. *Housing conditions: social groups compared (percents based on total in each social group)*

Social group	Percent living Westernized housing[a]	Percent living in multifamily rented buildings[b]	Percent having electricity	Percent having private toilet	Percent having telephone	Numbers in social group
Muslim (ranked by housing conditions)						
Fez-born Arabs	49.0	12.6	84.8	81.8	12.6	310
Other Muslims	31.4	21.7	80.5	73.1	6.4	760
Sefrou-born Arabs	29.6	17.8	88.3	79.3	4.2	3,936
Rural-born Berbers	19.0	28.1	78.3	70.8	3.2	1,362
Rural-born Arabs	14.8	25.2	71.5	61.8	2.3	2,635
Bhalil-born Arabs	14.6	28.5	72.5	62.0	3.8	451
Jewish						
Jews from other towns	58.6	12.8	98.9	65.7	11.4	70
Sefrou-born Jews	42.7	24.9	96.7	59.4	4.2	1,434
Rural-born Jews	14.8	38.0	96.3	30.6	1.9	108
French	93.8	0.0	91.0	92.6	45.9	122

[a] Single family houses, with running water and kitchen facilities.
[b] Multifamily means three or more households per dwelling.

Table 61. *Home tenure: social groups compared (percents based on total in each social group)*

Social group	Percent living in wholly rented dwellings[a]
Muslim (ranked by percent renting)	
Sefrou-born Arabs	37.8
Bhalil-born Arabs	51.4
Rural-born Berbers	55.5
Rural-born Arabs	57.8
Other Muslims	57.8
Fez-born Arabs	63.3
Jewish	
Jews from other towns	62.9
Sefrou-born Jews	76.3
Rural-born Jews	94.4
French	44.2

Note to Table 61

[a] This percentage excludes those people renting a portion of a house in which the owner also resides. This fact distorts these percentages of the renting population in an unknowable way. This omission of perhaps a large portion of the renting population is an unavoidable effect of the manner in which the interview schedule was drawn up: The question on home tenure was asked about the building, not about each person living in it.

Table 62. *The shack population: percent and number within each dwelling type, according to place of birth.*

Type of dwelling	Urban-born persons	Rural-born Muslims			
		Arab	Berber	Arab plus Berber	Total
Percent					
Nonmasonry (shack)	29.1	45.0	25.7	70.9	100.0
Masonry	58.6	27.4	14.0	41.4	100.0
Modern structure	60.4	27.1	12.5	39.6	100.0
Proportion of each social group within Muslim population	64.5	23.4	12.1		
Numbers					
Nonmasonry (shack)	64	99	57	156	220
Masonry	5,259	2,458	1,259	3,717	8,976
Modern structure	29	13	6	19	48
Total	5,352	2,570	1,322	3,892	9,244

Literacy and education (Tables 63–87)

The question on the census concerning literacy asked whether the person interviewed could read Arabic, French, Spanish, other foreign languages, or any of various combinations of these. For this analysis I grouped these answers into the following categories:

Literate in Arabic only

Literate in French (includes those literate in French alone as well as those literate in both French and Arabic)

Illiterate

Those literate in Spanish were very few and were omitted from the tabulations. Much of the analysis below focuses on those who are unable to read any language – the illiterates.

Tables 63 through 67 show the general rates of illiteracy for Muslims, Jews, and French, broken down by age and sex. The differences between men and women are very great for Muslims, but minor for the Jews and the French. When age is taken into consideration, it appears that all but two of the French illiterates are small children. The lowest rates of illiteracy for both the Muslims and the Jews are in the groups under twenty-nine years.

The category of Muslim is too broad to supply much information about social distribution of illiteracy, so the next step is to examine the variation by social group (Tables 68–87). This coding of the census data, it must be remembered, entails the omission of those members of the town population who are fourteen years old and under.

Tables 68 through 84 explore the association of age, birthplace, language spoken, and, for the rural-born population, years of urban experience.

Aside from sex, the rural-urban distinction appears to be the characteristic most closely related to variation in illiteracy. Of the Muslim men, the Fez-born Arabic speakers have by far the fewest illiterates (29 percent); the Sefrou-born follow, with 46 percent. The rural-born groups, in contrast, all have about 70 to 73 percent illiterates. The Bhalil-born, in this characteristic, follow the rural pattern rather than the urban.

Table 73 addresses the question: Which is the stronger factor related to illiteracy, rural birth or speaking a Berber language? By grouping all the urban-born Muslim groups, we find that they have a general rate of 47 percent illiterates, as against 71 percent for the rural-born. Grouping all the Arabic speakers, whether or not they are urban-born, gives a rate of 68 percent illiterate as against 56 percent for the Berber speakers. The importance of urban birth in literacy is still apparent when age is held constant (Table 74).

Tables 75 and 76 explore the relationship, for the rural-born men, between the number of years they have spent in a town and the rate of illiteracy. For men over forty-five years of age, the length of urban experience appears to make little difference. For those under forty-five, those who are newly urban are less likely to be illiterate. This is particularly true for men under thirty, a portion of whom are high school boys from rural homes. Although I do not give the figures here, the actual dividing line in length of urban experience comes not between those who have been in town five years or less as against the others, but between those who have been in town ten years or less as against the others.

Tables 77 and 78 reveal a difference in pattern between rural-born Berber speakers and Arabic speakers. Among the Arabic speakers rates of illiteracy are lower for those who are more newly urbanized than for those who have lived in town longer, with the young men who have come to town within the last five years having the lowest rate. But the Berber speakers with the lowest rate of illiteracy are those who have been in town for more than five years, and especially those young men who have been in town for fifteen to nineteen years, who have essentially been brought up in town.

In other words, the length of urban experience does affect the acquisition of literacy for the Berber speakers, for they must move into town to get their education; it apparently does not affect the Arabic speakers, who have had some education in Quranic Arabic in their rural villages. On the contrary, it may be the more educated young Arabic-speaking men who move into town, leaving behind the less educated.

Ability to read French (and in most cases, this is in addition to ability to read Arabic) is an index of modernity. Tables 79 through 84 show that the urban-born Muslims are far ahead of the rural-born in this characteristic, most especially those from Fez. When rural-born residents of Sefrou are literate, they are much more likely to be literate in Arabic only than in Arabic plus French.

After urban birth, age is the most important factor, with the youngest groups having by far the highest proportions of men who are literate in French. The factor of speaking Berber rather than Arabic has very little effect on literacy, except that if a rural-born Berber speaker learns to read, he is slightly less likely to learn Arabic than the Arabic speakers, and consequently slightly more likely to learn French.

The length of urban experience does not increase the likelihood of literacy in French. In fact, the relationship is the opposite: Those who are literate in French among the rural-born groups are also those who are more newly urban, even when age and language are held constant.

The Jews and the French, when they are literate, are literate in French. Some are also literate in Arabic (12 percent of the Jewish men, and 19 percent of the French men).

Do the different social groups send differing proportions of their children to school? Because of the manner in which the social group categories were constructed, I am able to answer this question only for those students aged fifteen and over, but this has the advantage of indicating the proportions within each social group who attain more than six or seven years of schooling.

Table 85 uses the total number of persons recorded as "students" over the age of fifteen as the base for computing percentages. It shows the proportion of students that are of each social group compared with the social group composition of the Sefrou population as a whole. More than half the male students over fifteen in Sefrou are Sefrou-born Arabic speakers; the rural-born Muslims are sharply underrepresented, the Berbers more than the Arabic speakers. The female students show a different pattern: The Jews send a much higher proportion of their girls to school than do the Muslim groups. Among the Muslim groups, the Sefrou-born Arabic speakers have a much higher proportion of girls in school than do the rural-born groups.

Tables 86 and 87 use the same data, but the percentages are calculated from the number of students against the number of persons in the age group fifteen to thirty, by sex and by social group. The same pattern appears: The Sefrou-born Arabic speakers, both male and female, are more likely to be in school than the rural-born Muslims, and of the rural-born Muslims, the Arabic speakers send more young people, both male and female, to school than do the Berber speakers. The Fez-born Arabic speakers have a low proportion of young people in school in this age group, because they usually send them to Fez schools rather than to Sefrou schools. The Jews and French both have considerably higher proportions of their young people in school than do the Muslims.

Table 63. *Illiteracy: ethnic categories compared by sex (percents of illiterates within each ethnic category; see Table 64 for numbers)*

Ethnic category	Male	Female
Muslims	62.1	86.0
Jews	61.4	63.2
French	15.6	17.1

Table 64. *Illiteracy: ethnic categories compared by sex (numbers for Table 63)*

Ethnic category	Male		Female	
	Illiterate	Total	Illiterate	Total
Muslims	5,370	8,646	7,680	8,935
Jews	897	1,462	998	1,579
French	14	90	14	82

Table 65. *Illiteracy: association with age and sex by ethnic category: males (percents of illiterates within each age cohort of each ethnic category; see Table 67 for numbers)*

Ethnic category	Children (0–14)	Young (15–29)	Middle (30–44)	Older (45–59)	Aged (60+)	Total
Muslims	63.0	48.9	64.2	73.3	82.0	62.1
Jews	61.2	41.5	57.5	76.9	94.3	61.4
French	45.2	0.0	0.0	0.0	0.0	15.6

Table 66. *Illiteracy: association with age and sex by ethnic category: females (percents of illiterates within each age cohort of each ethnic category; see Table 67 for numbers)*

Ethnic category	Children (0–14)	Young (15–29)	Middle (30–44)	Older (45–59)	Aged (60+)	Total
Muslims	75.2	91.1	97.8	99.3	99.3	85.9
Jews	50.7	53.9	83.3	98.6	100.0	63.2
French	52.2	5.9	0.0	7.7	0.0	17.1

Table 67. *Illiteracy: association with age and sex by ethnic category: males and females (numbers for Tables 65 and 66)*

Ethnic category	Children (0–14) M	F	Young (15–29) M	F	Middle (30–44) M	F	Older (45–59) M	F	Aged (60+) M	F	Total M	F
Muslims												
Number illiterate	2,569	3,051	910	2,192	903	1,404	652	742	327	286	5,361	7,675
Total number	4,081	4,055	1,860	2,405	1,407	1,435	890	747	399	288	8,637	8,930
Jews												
Number illiterate	478	364	102	214	107	210	110	139	100	70	897	997
Total number	781	718	246	397	186	252	143	141	106	70	1,462	1,578
French												
Number illiterate	14	12	0	1	0	0	0	1	0	0	14	14
Total number	31	23	12	17	20	17	18	13	9	12	90	82

Table 68. *Illiteracy: social groups compared by sex (percents of illiterates within each social group by sex; see Table 69 for numbers)*

Social group	Male	Female
Major Muslim groups		
Sefrou-born Arabic speakers	45.8	93.0
Rural-born Arabic speakers	70.1	98.7
Rural-born Berber speakers	72.1	98.4
Minor Muslim groups		
Fez-born Arabic speakers	28.9	74.3
Bhalil-born Arabic speakers	73.4	96.8
Other Muslims	57.7	92.4
Jews		
Sefrou-born Jews	60.5	73.2
Other urban Jews	43.5	61.5
Rural-born Jews	88.9	87.8
French	0.0	3.5

Table 69. *Illiteracy: social groups compared by sex (numbers)*

Social group	Male		Female	
	Illiterate	Total	Illiterate	Total
Major Muslim groups				
Sefrou-born Arabic speakers	837	1,826	1,823	1,959
Rural-born Arabic speakers	827	1,179	1,067	1,081
Rural-born Berber speakers	435	603	563	572
Minor Muslim groups				
Fez-born Arabic speakers	37	128	130	175
Bhalil-born Arabic speakers	141	192	243	251
Other Muslims	194	336	304	329
Jews				
Sefrou-born Jews	366	605	561	766
Other urban Jews	10	23	24	39
Rural-born Jews	40	45	43	49
French	0	55	2	57

Table 70. *Illiteracy: association with age and sex by social group: men (percents of illiterates within each age cohort of each social group; see Table 72 for numbers)*

Social group	Young (15–29)	Middle (30–44)	Older (45–59)	Aged (60+)
Major Muslim groups				
Sefrou-born Arabic speakers	40.9	56.0	63.2	77.8
Rural-born Arabic speakers	59.7	69.4	83.0	85.5
Rural-born Berber speakers	59.4	74.8	78.0	90.0
Minor Muslim groups				
Fez-born Arabic speakers	17.2	38.6	33.3	50.0
Bhalil-born Arabic speakers	58.1	81.7	88.9	77.3
Other Muslims	46.5	55.7	76.9	72.4
Jews				
Sefrou-born Jews	40.4	55.4	75.4	93.9

Table 71. *Illiteracy: association with age and sex by social group: women (percents of illiterates within each age cohort of each social group; see Table 72 for numbers)*

Social group	Young (15–29)	Middle (30–44)	Older (45–59)	Aged (60+)
Major Muslim groups				
Sefrou-born Arabic speakers	88.1	97.8	99.3	98.3
Rural-born Arabic speakers	98.0	99.1	99.5	100.0
Rural-born Berber speakers	97.6	98.5	100.0	100.0
Minor Muslim groups				
Fez-born Arabic speakers	63.0	86.3	94.4	100.0
Bhalil-born Arabic speakers	94.5	97.3	100.0	100.0
Other Muslims	83.4	96.7	97.6	100.0
Jews				
Sefrou-born Jews	53.2	82.8	98.4	100.0

Table 72. *Illiteracy: association with age and sex by social group: men and women (numbers for Tables 70 and 71)*

Social group	Young (15–29) M	F	Middle (30–44) M	F	Older (45–59) M	F	Aged (60+) M	F	Total M	F
Major Muslim Groups										
Sefrou-born Arabic speakers										
Number illiterate	349	886	272	541	216	280	112	116	949	1,823
Total number	854	1,006	486	553	342	282	144	118	1,826	1,959
Rural-born Arabic speakers										
Number illiterate	259	487	272	326	196	185	100	69	827	1,067
Total number	434	497	392	329	236	186	117	69	1,179	1,081
Rural-born Berber speakers										
Number illiterate	110	244	163	198	117	93	45	28	435	563
Total number	185	250	218	201	150	93	50	28	603	572
Minor Muslim groups										
Fez-born Arabic speakers										
Number illiterate	10	63	17	44	6	17	4	6	37	130
Total number	58	100	44	51	18	18	8	6	128	175
Bhalil-born Arabic speakers										
Number illiterate	43	103	49	73	32	46	17	21	141	243
Total number	74	109	60	75	36	46	22	21	192	251
Other Muslims										
Number illiterate	60	160	63	87	50	41	21	16	194	304
Total number	129	181	113	90	65	42	29	16	336	329
Jews										
Sefrou-born Jews										
Number illiterate	86	188	93	183	95	125	92	65	366	561
Total number	213	353	168	221	126	127	98	65	605	766
Other urban-born Jews										
Number illiterate	4	9	3	6	3	8	0	1	10	24
Total number	13	21	5	9	5	8	0	1	23	39
Rural-born Jews										
Number illiterate	11	16	11	18	12	6	6	3	40	43
Total number	16	22	11	18	12	6	6	3	45	49
French										
Number illiterate	0	1	0	0	0	1	0	0	0	2
Total number	11	16	20	16	18	13	9	12	58	57
Other foreigners										
Number illiterate	2	4	1	5	5	4	2	2	10	15
Total number	14	14	13	7	7	6	6	3	40	30

Appendix: A statistical profile 477

Table 73. *Illiteracy: Muslim men: urban- and rural-born compared, Arabic and Berber speakers compared*

	Percent illiterates within each social group	Number of illiterates	Total in social group
Urban-born			
Fez Arabic speakers	28.9	37	128
Sefrou Arabic speakers	45.8	837	1,826
Sefrou Berber speakers	39.7	29	73
Other urban Berber speakers	64.6	53	82
Other urban Arabic speakers	61.9	112	181
Total	46.6	1,068	2,290
Rural-born			
Rural-born Arabic speakers	70.1	827	1,179
Rural-born Berber speakers	72.1	435	603
Bhalil-born Arabic speakers	73.4	141	192
Total	71.1	1,403	1,974
Berber speakers			
Rural-born	72.1	435	603
Sefrou-born	39.7	29	73
Other urban-born	64.6	53	82
Total	68.2	517	758
Arabic speakers			
Fez-born	28.9	37	128
Sefrou-born	45.8	837	1,826
Rural-born	70.1	827	1,179
Bhalil-born	73.8	141	192
Other urban-born	64.6	112	181
Total	55.7	1,954	3,506

Table 74. *Illiteracy: Muslim men under forty-five years old: urban- and rural-born compared, Arabic and Berber speakers compared (percents of illiterates in each age cohort of each birthplace and language category)*

	Young (15–29)	Middle-aged (30–45)	Total (15–45)
Urban-born Muslims	40.2	55.3	46.0
Rural-born Muslims	60.7	72.3	65.7
Berber speakers	56.0	69.6	63.0
Arabic speakers	46.6	62.6	53.2

Table 75. *Illiteracy: rural-born men: variation by age and length of urban experience (percents of illiterates in each age cohort by length of urban experience; see Table 76 for numbers)*

Length of urban experience	Young (15–29)	Middle (30–44)	Older (45–59)	Aged (60+)	Total
Newly urban (under 5 yr)	50.7	69.7	82.4	89.6	65.1
Medium (5–19 yr)	64.4	71.7	84.5	90.4	72.6
Long urban (over 20 yr)	64.1	72.4	75.9	83.7	74.2
Total	59.6	71.3	81.1	86.8	70.8

Table 76. *Illiteracy: rural-born men: variation by age and length of urban experience (numbers for Table 75)*

Length of urban experience	Young (15–29) Number illiterate	Total number	Middle (30–44) Number illiterate	Total number	Older (45–59) Number illiterate	Total number	Aged (60+) Number illiterate	Total number	Total Number illiterate	Total number
Newly urban (under 5 yr)	110	217	127	182	75	91	26	29	338	519
Medium (5–19 yr)	207	321	211	294	137	162	47	52	602	829
Long urban (over 20 yr)	52	81	97	134	101	133	72	86	322	434
Total	369	619	435	610	313	386	145	167	1,262	1,782

Table 77. *Illiteracy: rural-born Muslim men: variation by language spoken, age, and length of urban experience (percents based on number of illiterates within each age-cohort and social group by length of urban experience: see Table 78 for numbers)*

Length of urban experience	Young (15–29)		Middle (30–44)		Older (49–59)		Aged (60+)		Total	
	Arabic	Berber	Arabic	Berber	Arabic	Berber	Arabic	Berber	Arabic	Berber
Newly urban (under 5 yr)	42.4	63.5	60.2	82.3	82.5	82.4	81.2	100.0	56.4	76.3
Medium (5–19 yr)	67.5	55.9	71.6	72.1	82.5	81.1	94.4	92.8	73.2	69.8
Long urban (over 20 yr)	66.2	56.2	74.7	65.7	79.3	69.6	84.1	82.6	76.1	69.2
Percentages for each age group	59.7	59.4	69.4	74.8	81.3	78.0	85.4	90.0	69.8	72.1

Table 78. *Illiteracy: rural-born Muslim men: variation by language spoken, age,ᵃ and length of urban experience (numbers for Table 77)*

Length of urban experience	Young Arabic		Young Berber		Middle-aged Arabic		Middle-aged Berber		Older Arabic		Older Berber		Aged Arabic		Aged Berber		Total Arabic		Total Berber	
	Illit-erate	Total	Illit-erate	Total	Illit-erate	Total	Illit-erate	Total	Illit-erate	Total	Illit-erate	Total	Illit-erate	Total	Illit-erate	Total	Illit-erate	Total	Illit-erate	Total
Newly urban (under 5 yr)	56	132	54	85	62	103	65	79	33	40	42	51	13	16	13	13	164	291	174	228
Medium (5–19 yr)	160	237	47	84	136	190	75	104	90	109	43	53	34	38	13	14	420	594	178	255
Long urban (over 20 yr)	43	65	9	16	74	99	23	35	69	87	32	46	53	63	19	23	239	314	83	120
Total	259	434	110	185	272	392	163	218	192	236	117	150	100	117	45	50	823	1,179	435	603

ᵃ Young, 15–29; middle-aged, 30–44; older, 45–59; aged, 60 and over.

Table 79. *Literacy in French and Arabic: men: social groups compared (percents within each social group;)*

Social group	Percent illiterate	Percent literate in Arabic only	Percent literate in French only or French and Arabic	Total number
Major Muslim groups				
Sefrou-born Arabic speakers	45.8	27.0	27.2	1,826
Rural-born Arabic speakers	70.1	21.3	8.6	1,179
Rural-born Berber speakers	72.1	17.2	10.7	603
Minor Muslim groups				
Fez-born Arabic speakers	28.9	32.1	39.0	128
Bhalil-born Arabic speakers	73.4	15.7	10.9	192
Other Muslims	57.7	20.8	21.5	409
Jews				
Sefrou-born Jews	60.5	3.0	36.5[a]	608
Other urban Jews	43.5	6.5	50.0	24
Rural-born Jews	88.9	1.1	12.2	49
French	0.0	0.0	100.0[b]	59

[a] There are 71 Sefrou-born Jews who can read Arabic in addition to French (11.7% of Sefrou-born Jewish men).
[b] There are 11 Frenchmen (18.6%) who can read Arabic in addition to French.

482 *Meaning and order in Moroccan society*

Table 80. *Literacy in French: Muslim and Jewish men: association with age by social group (percents of literates within each age cohort and social group; see Table 81 for numbers)*

Social group	Young (15–29)	Middle (30–44)	Older (45–59)	Aged (60+)
Major Muslim groups				
Sefrou-born Arabic speakers	37.9	26.3	12.5	1.3
Rural-born Arabic speaker	18.4	4.0	2.5	0.0
Rural-born Berber speakers	23.2	8.2	2.6	0.0
Minor Muslim groups				
Fez-born Arabic speakers	50.0	40.9	16.6	0.0
Bhalil-born Arabic speakers	21.6	6.6	0.0	4.5
Other Muslims	38.7	27.4	7.7	6.9
Jews				
Sefrou-born Jews	56.5	40.8	23.0	3.0

Table 81. *Literacy in French: Muslim and Jewish men: association with age by social group (numbers for Table 80)*

Social group	Young (15–29) Literate	Young (15–29) Total	Middle (30–44) Literate	Middle (30–44) Total	Older (45–59) Literate	Older (45–59) Total	Aged (60+) Literate	Aged (60+) Total
Major Muslim groups								
Sefrou-born Arabic speakers	324	854	128	486	43	342	2	144
Rural-born Arabic speakers	80	434	16	392	6	236	0	117
Rural-born Berber speakers	43	185	18	218	4	150	0	50
Minor Muslim groups								
Fez-born Arabic speakers	29	58	18	44	3	18	0	8
Bhalil-born Arabic speakers	16	74	4	60	0	36	1	22
Other Muslims	50	129	31	113	5	65	2	29
Jews								
Sefrou-born Jews	121	214	69	169	29	126	3	99

Table 82. *Literacy in French: Muslim men: urban- and rural-born compared, Arabic and Berber speakers compared*

	Percent literate in French	Number literate in French	Total number in group
Urban-born			
Fez-born Arabic speakers	39.0	50	128
Sefrou-born Arabic speakers	27.2	497	1,826
Sefrou-born Berber speakers	42.5	33	73
Other urban Arabic speakers	19.3	35	181
Other urban Berber speakers	12.9	20	155
Total	26.9	635	2,363
Rural-born			
Rural-born Arabic speakers	8.6	102	1,179
Rural-born Berber speakers	10.7	65	603
Bhalil-born Arabic speakers	10.9	21	192
Total	9.5	188	1,974
Berber speakers			
Rural-born	10.7	65	603
Sefrou-born	42.5	33	73
Other urban-born	12.9	20	155
Total	14.2	118	831
Arabic speakers			
Fez-born	39.0	50	28
Sefrou-born	27.2	497	1,826
Rural-born	8.6	102	1,179
Bhalil-born	10.9	65	603
Other urban-born	19.3	35	181
Total	19.6	749	3,817

484   *Meaning and order in Moroccan society*

Table 83. *Literacy in French: rural-born Muslim men: variation by age, language spoken, and length of urban experience (percents based on total within each cell; see Table 84 for numbers)*

Length of urban experience	Young (15–29)		Middle (30–44)		Older (45–59)		Aged (60+)		Total	
	Arabic	Berber	Arabic	Berber	Arabic	Berber	Arabic	Berber	Arabic	Berber
Newly urban (under 5 yr)	29.5	24.0	4.8	8.8	2.5	5.8	0.0	0.0	15.4	13.6
Medium (5–19 yr)	16.4	21.4	3.6	6.7	1.8	1.8	0.0	0.0	5.7	10.2
Long urban (over 20 yr)	3.0	25.0	4.0	11.4	2.2	0.0	0.0	0.0	2.8	6.6
Total	18.4	23.2	4.0	8.2	2.5	2.6	0.0	0.0	8.6	10.7

Table 84. *Literacy in French: rural-born Muslim men: variation by age,[a] language spoken, and length of urban experience (numbers for Table 83)*

Length of urban experience	Young Arabic		Young Berber		Middle-aged Arabic		Middle-aged Berber		Older Arabic		Older Berber		Aged Arabic		Aged Berber		Total Arabic		Total Berber	
	Literate in French	Total	Literate in French	Total	Literate in French	Total	Literate in French	Total	Literate in French	Total	Literate in French	Total	Literate in French	Total	Literate in French	Total	Literate in French	Total	Literate in French	Total
Newly urban (under 5 yr)	39	132	21	85	5	103	7	79	1	40	3	51	0	16	0	16	45	291	31	231
Medium (5–19 yr)	39	237	18	84	7	190	7	104	2	109	1	53	0	38	0	14	48	574	26	255
Long (over 20 yr)	2	65	4	16	4	99	4	35	3	87	0	46	0	63	0	23	9	314	8	120
Total	80	434	43	185	16	392	18	218	6	236	4	150	0	117	0	53	102	1,179	65	606

[a] Young, 15–29; middle-aged, 30–44; older, 45–59; aged, 60 and over.

Table 85. *Higher education: school population fifteen years of age and over: composition by social group* (*percents of males, of females in school, excluding French; see Table 87 for numbers*)

Social group	Percent of males (15–30)	Percent of females (15–30)	Proportion of social group in total population[a]
Major Muslim groups			
Sefrou-born Arabic speakers	51.1	33.1	34.9
Rural-born Arabic speakers	18.9	5.1	23.4
Rural-born Berber speakers	6.3	1.5	12.1
Minor Muslim groups	10.9	9.6	13.5
Jews (Sefrou-born)	12.8	50.7	12.7
Total school population	100.0	100.0	

[a] Foreigners excluded.

Table 86. *Higher education: proportion of young people each social group sends to school (percents within each cell that are enrolled in school; see Table 87 for numbers)*

Social group	Males (15–30)	Females (15–30)
Major Muslim groups		
Sefrou-born Arabic speakers	21.1	4.2
Rural-born Arabic speakers	14.4	1.1
Rural-born Berber speakers	11.2	0.7
Minor Muslim groups		
Fez-born Arabic speakers	5.0	4.9
Bhalil-born Arabic speakers	7.9	0.0
Other Muslims	22.4	3.9
Jews (Sefrou-born)	20.9	18.1
French	42.8	25.0

Table 87. *Higher education: proportion of young people each social group sends to school (numbers for Tables 85 and 86)*

Social group	Males (15–30)		Females (15–30)	
	In school	Total	In school	Total
Major Muslim groups				
Sefrou-born Arabic speakers	203	920	45	1,076
Rural-born Arabic speakers	75	520	7	614
Rural-born Berber speakers	25	224	2	301
Minor Muslim groups				
Fez-born Arabic speakers	3	60	5	102
Bhalil-born Arabic speakers	6	76	0	110
Other Muslims	34	152	8	206
Jews (Sefrou-born)	51	244	69	382
French	6	15	5	18
Total	403	2,211	141	2,809

Household size (Tables 88–95)

Each census schedule required the interviewer to list together the members of each household, indicating which individual was head of the household. The term for "household" was *ménage* in French and *ᶜusra* in Arabic. A computer program was drawn up that constructed household units from this information, counted each one's members, and listed the following information for each household: location by census tract and residential area; number of persons in it; number of adults; number of children; composition according to proportions of adults and children; residential area type; household composition type (described below); attributes of the head of household (social group, sex, age group, occupational status, literacy, years of urban experience, marital status); ethnic category or categories of the members of the household (wholly Muslim, Jewish, French, other, and various mixtures – Muslim/Jewish, Muslim/French, Jewish/French, and other mixtures); language(s) spoken in the household (wholly Arabic, Berber, foreign, mixed families with persons speaking Arabic and Berber, and other mixtures); birthplace(s) of members of the household (wholly rural-born, Sefrou-born, other-town-born, France-born, born in other foreign areas, and the mixtures of rural/Sefrou, rural/other towns, Sefrou/other towns, Morocco/France, Morocco/other, and other mixtures); and the presence or absence of a servant of the household.

This tabulation of household size, composition, and other characteristics was made on the basis of a random selection of about 60% of the entire population of Sefrou.

Although I analyzed the relationships among all these characteristics of Sefrou's households, I report here only on several of the most important.

Table 88 shows that the average size of a household in Sefrou when broken down by social group varies from 2.66 persons per household for the French up to 5.21 for the Sefrou-born Arabic speakers. Fieldwork showed that many households of those long resident in Sefrou are living in rooms or houses adjacent to close relatives, and that, for many of these, the household is not a sharply bounded group and the census definition of household is too narrow. On the other hand, many households, especially among those groups who moved into Sefrou leaving most of their relatives behind, were isolated and self-contained. The census was not, however, designed to discover these patterns of interhousehold connections.

It is migration into town that lowers the average size of the household, rather than any difference in familial structure. This is shown by Table 89, in which are included data from the census of selected villages in the rural area surrounding Sefrou and from the large village of Bhalil nearby. It can be seen that the size of households in the villages is much the same as in Sefrou for the Sefrou-born Arabic speakers and the Sefrou-born Jews.

Table 90 displays a frequency distribution according to household size for each social group. The Sefrou-born Arabic speakers and the Sefrou-born Jews both have a much flatter distribution, with fewer one-person households and more households with more than eight members, than the other in-moving groups. The rural-born Muslims have high proportions of single-person households, and most of their households consist of only two to four persons.

Tables 91 and 92 show that the average number of persons per household varies quite neatly with the occupational status of the head of the household. The Jews, however, do not fit this pattern, for in 1960 low-status Jewish households had, on the average, more members than middle- or high-status Jewish families.

Table 93 takes a closer look at this relationship between household size and occupational status by comparing the frequency distributions of household sizes among the different social groups of each occupational status level. Higher proportions of very large households (eight or more members) are found among high-status Sefrou-born Arabic speakers, high-status Bhalil-born Arabic speakers, and medium-status Sefrou-born Jews. Higher proportions of single-person households are found among high-status Fez-born Arabic speakers (probably the teachers), low-status rural-born Berber speakers, low-status Bhalil-born Arabic speakers, and low-status other Muslims. The highest proportions of single-person households occur, as might be expected, among those classified as inactive in all social groups.

Table 94 compares average household sizes of persons from the major occupational sectors, according to social group. It shows that the rural-born Muslim groups have relatively smaller families irrespective of the kind of occupation the head pursues; for the Sefrou-born Arabic speakers, the earlier mentioned connection between occupational status and household size is again clearly illustrated.

Table 95 compares the average number of children per household according to social group. That the proportionately low number of children in the households of the rural-born Muslims is an effect of their movement into town is shown by a comparison with figures from the census of the rural areas around Sefrou.

Table 88. *Household size (averages): social groups compared (average number of persons per household)*

Social group of head of household	Average house-hold size	Number of house-holds
Major Muslim groups		
Sefrou-born Arabic speakers	5.21	848
Rural-born Arabic speakers	3.97	795
Rural-born Berber speakers	4.26	438
Minor Muslim groups		
Fez-born Arabic speakers	4.60	83
Bhalil-born Arabic speakers	3.96	128
Jews (Sefrou-born)	5.23	339
French (born in France)	2.66	24

Table 89. *Household size: urban-dwelling groups of rural origin compared with rural-dwelling groups (average number of persons per household)*

Social group of head of household	Average house-hold size	Number of house-holds
Living in Sefrou		
Rural-born Arabic speakers	3.97	795
Rural-born Berber speakers	4.26	438
Both	4.07	1,233
Bhalil-born	3.96	128
Living in villages		
Arabic speakers[a]	5.56	252
Berber speakers[a]	5.21	740
Both	5.30	992
Bhalil-born[b]	4.15	1,354

[a] Based on the census of eight selected villages in the region of Sefrou.
[b] Based on the census of the village of Bhalil.

Table 90. *Household size: social groups compared (percents within each social group)*

Social group of head of household	Percent of each household size				Number of households
	1	2–4	5–7	8+	
Major Muslim groups					
Sefrou-born Arabic speakers	5.7	39.7	35.5	19.1	848
Rural-born Arabic speakers	11.3	51.9	29.9	6.8	795
Rural-born Berber speakers	10.0	48.4	32.0	9.6	438
Minor Muslim groups					
Fez-born Arabic speakers	15.7	32.5	41.0	10.8	83
Bhalil-born Arabic speakers	14.1	50.8	26.6	8.6	128
Other Muslims	12.9	46.9	31.1	9.1	209
Jews (Sefrou-born)	8.8	39.2	27.1	24.8	339

Table 91. *Household size and occupational status: social groups compared (average number of persons per household in each cell; see Table 92 for numbers of households in each cell)*

Social group of head of household	Occupational status of household head[a]				Number of households
	Very high	High	Medium	Low	
Major Muslim groups					
Sefrou-born Arabic speakers	7.1	6.5	6.0	5.1	599
Rural-born Arabic speakers	6.5	5.0	4.3	4.1	389
Rural-born Berber speakers	5.3	4.9	4.7	4.2	245
Minor Muslim groups					
Fez-born Arabic speakers	8.0	4.8	4.7	4.0	62
Bhalil-born Arabic speakers	0.0	5.6	4.3	3.6	77
Jews (Sefrou-born)	6.0	5.5	5.8	6.4	244

[a] These levels of occupational status correspond to the categories used in the other tables in this study in the following way, referring to Table 34: very high, occupations 1–3; high, occupations 4–7; medium, occupations 8–10; low, occupations 11–15.

Table 92. *Household size (averages) and occupational status: social groups compared (number of households in each cell)*

Social group of head of household	Occupational status of household head[a]				Number of households
	Very high	High	Medium	Low	
Major Muslim groups					
Sefrou-born Arabic-speakers	8	121	194	276	599
Rural-born Arabic-speakers	2	118	78	191	389
Rural-born Berber-speakers	3	85	46	111	245
Minor Muslim groups					
Fez-born Arabic-speakers	1	34	16	11	62
Bhalil-born Arabic-speakers	0	12	9	56	77
Jews (Sefrou-born)	2	33	132	77	244

[a] These levels of occupational status correspond to the categories used in other tables in this study in the following way, referring to Table 34: very high, occupations 1–3; high, occupations 4–7; medium, occupations 8–10; low, occupations 11–15.

Table 93. *Household size and occupational status: social groups compared (percents within each occupational status level within each social group)*

Social group of head of household	Household size				Number of households
	1	2–4	5–7	8+	
High occupational status of household head					
Major Muslim groups					
Sefrou-born Arabic speakers	0.0	26.3	41.8	31.8	129
Rural-born Arabic speakers	4.1	43.3	34.1	17.5	120
Rural-born Berber speakers	4.5	40.9	40.9	13.6	88
Minor Muslim groups					
Fez-born Arabic speakers	25.7	17.1	40.0	17.4	35
Bhalil-born Arabic speakers	8.3	25.0	33.3	33.3	12
Other Muslims	10.6	42.4	27.3	19.7	66
Jews (Sefrou-born)	0.0	40.0	37.1	22.8	35
Medium occupational status of household head					
Major Muslim groups					
Sefrou-born Arabic speakers	1.5	33.5	38.7	26.3	194
Rural-born Arabic speakers	9.0	47.4	35.9	7.7	78
Rural-born Berber speakers	4.3	43.5	41.3	10.9	46
Minor Muslim groups					
Fez-born Arabic speakers	0.0	43.7	56.2	0.0	16
Bhalil-born Arabic speakers	11.1	44.4	22.2	22.2	9
Other Muslims	10.7	32.1	50.0	7.1	28
Jews (Sefrou-born)	1.5	40.2	29.5	28.8	132
Low occupational status of household head					
Major Muslim groups					
Sefrou-born Arabic speakers	2.9	43.8	26.6	16.7	276
Rural-born Arabic speakers	7.3	55.0	30.4	7.3	191
Rural-born Berber speakers	11.7	45.0	34.2	9.0	111
Minor Muslim groups					
Fez-born Arabic speakers	9.1	36.4	36.4	18.2	11
Bhalil-born Arabic speakers	12.5	57.1	26.8	3.6	56
Other Muslims	13.6	47.7	34.1	4.5	44
Jews (Sefrou-born)	1.3	24.7	36.4	37.7	77
No active working person in household					
Major Muslim groups					
Sefrou-born Arabic speakers	21.6	48.0	26.3	4.1	171
Rural-born Arabic speakers	18.6	54.1	24.7	2.6	344
Rural-born Berber speakers	15.3	58.9	22.1	3.7	163
Minor Muslim groups					
Fez-born Arabic speakers	17.6	52.9	23.5	5.9	17
Bhalil-born Arabic speakers	19.6	52.2	23.9	4.3	46
Other Muslims	17.7	56.4	22.6	3.2	62
Jews (Sefrou-born)	38.0	47.9	9.9	4.2	71

Table 94. *Household size for selected occupations: social groups compared (average number of persons per household within each cell)*

Social group of head of household	White collar em-ployee	Small farmer	Petty com-merce	Master craftsman (tradi-tional skills)	Worker (tradi-tional skills)	Worker (ser-vices)	Farm and other manual laborer
Household size							
Sefrou-born Arabic speakers	7.00	6.32	6.35	5.64	5.09	4.48	5.13
Rural-born Arabic speakers	4.07	5.45	4.34	4.23	4.05	3.83	3.83
Rural-born Berber speakers	5.25	4.80	5.06	3.85	4.03	4.30	4.26
Number of households							
Sefrou-born Arabic speakers	35	67	91	99	119	41	60
Rural-born Arabic speakers	38	31	44	34	57	37	67
Rural-born Berber speakers	12	30	29	14	27	13	53

Table 95. *Number of children per household: social groups compared (average numbers of children per household)*

Social group of head of household	Average Number of children	Number of house-holds
Sefrou population		
Major Muslim groups		
Sefrou-born Arabic speakers	2.43	848
Rural-born Arabic speakers	1.72	795
Rural-born Berber speakers	1.89	438
Jews (Sefrou-born)	2.44	339
Rural population (Muslim)		
Living in villages[a]		
Arabic speakers	2.61	252
Berber speakers	2.40	740
Both	2.45	992

[a] Based on the census of eight selected villages in the region of Sefrou.

Household composition (Tables 96–103)

In the same study of households described in the previous section it was possible to determine, within each household, which persons were married to one another, and therefore to enumerate how many married couples there were per household. It was then possible to count how many "other adults" (i.e., adults not listed as married to anyone else within the household) were also present. It was impossible, however, to determine what kin relationship, if any, these other adults had to the head of household or what relationship the two married couples had. Nonetheless, a rather abstract typology of household composition could be drawn up and social groups compared regarding the relative prevalence of these various types.

The households (representing a sample of 60 percent of Sefrou's population) were sorted into the types described in Table 96.

Given the imposed definition of "household" that is implicit in the census questions, the largest proportion of families in all groups are single conjugal families consisting of a married couple and several children. Tables 97 and 98 show that for all social groups, the proportion of households of the single conjugal family type ranges from 51.6 percent for Bhalil-born Arabic speakers to 35.4 percent for the Fez-born Arabic speakers. Compound conjugal families (i.e., those with two or more married couples residing together) are low in number and proportion. The social groups having the greatest proportions

of this latter sort of family, which may correspond to the anthropologist's "extended" family, are the Sefrou-born Arabic speakers (5.8 percent of all their households) and the rural-born Berber speakers (4.8 percent). Perhaps a better measure of "extendedness" is the category "conjugal family plus one or more other adults." Those groups with high proportions of this form of household are the Sefrou-born Arabic speakers (with 32.5 percent) and the Sefrou-born Jews (with 40.4 percent).

Single-person households are also differentially distributed, with the French having the highest proportion (29.4 percent) and the Fez-born Arabic speakers the next highest (15.9 percent). These are primarily men, as is shown in Tables 99 and 100, which give the same breakdowns but in greater detail. Groups with unusually high proportion of single-women households are the rural-born Berber speakers (7.1 percent), the Bhalil-born Arabic speakers (9.5 percent), and the Sefrou-born Jews (8.0 percent). Of course, as I have pointed out above, it is impossible to tell from the census the degree to which these single-member households represent social isolates, for they may be actually living in a room in a houseful of relatives.

Households that have more than one member, but include no married couple, are to be found in all groups, in fairly similar proportions, but those listed as having female heads greatly outnumber those with male heads of household.

Tables 101 and 102 provide some comparable statistics for the rural population in villages near Sefrou. They compare Berber-speaking with Arabic-speaking villages and show that there is no essential difference between them in household composition. Comparison of the village population with the urban groups of Table 97 reveals that more single conjugal families were reported by the census takers for the villagers than for the townspeople. This comparison should be made with the two urban-dwelling social groups who are not inmigrant to Sefrou, the Sefrou-born Arabic speakers and the Sefrou-born Jews. In both these urban cases the proportions of single conjugal families are much smaller than in the rural population. On the other hand, the proportions of households with no resident conjugal pair are markedly lower for the rural than for the urban groups.

Table 103 explores a different aspect of household composition in Sefrou. The question was asked of the data: How many households are made up of persons from different ethnic groups, from differing birthplaces, or speaking different primary languages? By far the largest proportion of households for almost all groups are homogeneous regarding these three characteristics.

However, there are interesting differences among the groups in proportions of mixed households.

The lines between the ethnic categories of Muslim, Jewish, and French are virtually never crossed. The exception is one family, one urban-born Berber speaker who has a French wife. There are much greater proportions of households in which some members are rural-born and some are urban-born (remembering that the people being counted are fifteen years and over). The two Sefrou-born groups – the Arabic-speaking Muslims and the Jews – have by far the lowest percentages of such mixed birthplace households.

For households with members speaking differing primary languages, a different pattern appears: The households headed by Berber speakers and containing an Arabic speaker are much more numerous than any other. This differential distribution of households with mixed birthplaces and mixed languages is probably best interpreted in terms of differential marriage patterns, which are discussed in the next section.

Table 96. *Types of households*

Simplified list	Detailed list	Criteria
Simple conjugal family	1. Couple, no children	One married couple, no children, no other adults
	2. Couple with children	One married couple, children, no other adults
Conjugal family plus other adults	3. Couple, no children, adults	One married couple, no children, other adults
	4. Couple, children, adults	One married couple, children, other adults

Table 96 (*cont.*)

Simplified list	Detailed list	Criteria
Compound conjugal family	5. Two couples, with or without children or other adults	Two married couples
	6. Three couples, with or without children or other adults	Three married couples
One-person household	7. Single man	One man
	8. Single woman	One woman
Nonconjugal family, female head	9. Women, no men, no children	More than one woman, no men, no children
	10. Women, men, no children	One or more women, no children, one or more men, no married couple, female head
	11. Women, no men, children	One or more women, children, no men
	12. Women, men, children	One or more women, children, one or more men, no married couple, female head
Nonconjugal family, male head	13. Men, no children, no women	More than one man, no children, no women
	14. Men, no children, women	One or more men, no children, one or more women, no married couple, male head
	15. Men, children, no women	One or more men, children, no women
	16. Men, women, children	One or more men, children, one or more women, no married couple, male head
Dormitory	17. Dormitory	No adults (persons over 15)

496 *Meaning and order in Moroccan society*

Table 97. *Household composition (simplified): social groups compared (percents within each social group; see Table 98 for numbers)*

Household composition	Social group of head of household							
	Sefrou-born Arabic speakers	Rural-born Arabic speakers	Rural-born Berber speakers	Fez-born Arabic speakers	Bhalil-born Arabic speakers	Other Muslims	Sefrou-born Jews	French
Single conjugal family	36.9	46.4	50.0	35.4	51.6	44.7	35.9	37.1
Conjugal family plus one or more other adults	32.5	24.3	21.3	28.0	18.3	24.5	40.4	25.7
Compound conjugal family (two or more married couples)	5.8	1.8	4.8	1.2	0.8	2.4	2.1	0.0
One-person household	5.5	10.9	9.9	15.9	13.5	13.0	8.9	28.6
Nonconjugal family, female head	11.8	12.2	11.2	8.5	11.1	9.2	11.0	8.6
Nonconjugal family, male head	7.5	4.1	2.5	11.0	4.8	6.2	1.8	0.0
Dormitory	0.0	0.4	0.2	0.0	0.0	0.0	0.0	0.0
Total	100.0	100.1	99.9	100.0	100.1	100.0	100.1	100.0

Table 98. *Household composition (simplified): social groups compared (numbers for Table 97)*

Household composition	Social group of head of household							
	Sefrou-born Arabic speakers	Rural-born Arabic speakers	Rural-born Berber speakers	Fez-born Arabic speakers	Bhalil-born Arabic speakers	Other Muslims	Sefrou-born Jews	French
Single conjugal family	311	365	218	29	65	93	121	13
Conjugal family plus one or more other adults	274	191	93	23	23	51	136	9
Compound conjugal family	49	14	21	1	1	5	7	0
One-person household	46	86	43	13	17	27	30	10
Nonconjugal family, female head	99	96	49	7	14	19	37	3
Nonconjugal family, male head	63	32	11	9	6	13	6	0
Dormitory	0	3	1	0	0	0	0	0
Total households	842	787	436	82	126	208	337	35

Table 99. *Household composition (detailed): social groups compared (percents within each social group; see Table 100 for numbers)*

Household composition	Social group of head of household							
	Sefrou-born Arabic speakers	Rural-born Arabic speakers	Rural-born Berber speakers	Fez-born Arabic speakers	Bhalil-born Arabic speakers	Other Muslims	Sefrou-born Jews	French
Simple conjugal family								
1. Couple, no children	7.0	12.2	15.8	4.9	13.5	13.0	9.8	14.3
2. Couple, with children	29.9	34.2	34.2	30.5	38.1	31.7	26.1	22.8
Conjugal family plus other adults								
3. Couple, no children, adults	4.9	5.0	3.2	1.2	3.2	4.8	7.7	8.6
4. Couple, children, adults	27.7	19.3	18.1	26.8	15.1	19.7	32.6	17.1
Compound conjugal family								
5. Two couples, with or without children, other adults	5.1	1.7	4.1	1.2	0.8	2.4	2.1	0.0
6. Three couples, with or without children, other adults	0.7	0.1	0.7	0.0	0.0	0.0	0.0	0.0
One-person household								
7. Single man	1.7	5.2	2.8	12.2	4.0	6.7	0.9	20.0
8. Single woman	3.8	5.7	7.1	3.7	9.5	6.2	8.0	8.6
Nonconjugal family, female head								
9. Women, no children, no men	0.6	0.9	1.4	2.4	0.8	1.4	3.9	2.8
10. Women, no children, men	2.9	2.7	1.1	0.0	1.6	2.4	1.8	2.8
11. Women, children, no men	5.3	6.5	6.9	4.9	4.0	3.8	3.6	2.8
12. Women, children, men	3.0	2.2	1.8	1.2	4.8	1.4	1.8	0.0
Nonconjugal family, male head								
13. Men, no children, no women	0.7	1.0	0.2	3.7	0.0	1.0	0.0	0.0
14. Men, no children, women	2.7	1.0	0.5	2.4	1.6	3.4	0.9	0.0
15. Men, children, no women	0.4	0.4	0.5	3.7	0.8	1.0	0.0	0.0
16. Men, children, women	3.7	1.7	1.4	1.2	2.4	1.0	0.9	0.0
Dormitory								
17. No adults	0.0	0.4	0.2	0.0	0.0	0.0	0.0	0.0
Total	100.1	100.2	100.0	100.0	100.2	99.9	100.1	99.8

Table 100. *Household composition (detailed): social groups compared (numbers for Table 99)*

Household composition	Sefrou-born Arabic speakers	Rural-born Arabic speakers	Rural-born Berber speakers	Fez-born Arabic speakers	Bhalil-born Arabic speakers	Other Muslims	Sefrou-born Jews	French
				Social group of head of household				
Simple conjugal family								
1. Couple, no children	59	96	69	4	17	27	33	5
2. Couple, with children	252	269	149	25	48	66	88	8
Conjugal family plus other adults								
3. Couple, no children, adults	41	39	14	1	4	10	26	3
4. Couple, children, adults	233	152	79	22	19	41	110	6
Compound conjugal family								
5. Two couples, with or without children, other adults	43	13	18	1	1	5	7	0
6. Three couples, with or without children, other adults	6	1	3	0	0	0	0	0
One-person household								
7. Single man	14	41	12	10	5	14	3	7
8. Single woman	32	45	31	3	12	13	27	3
Nonconjugal family, female head								
9. Women, no children, no men	5	7	6	2	1	3	13	1
10. Women, no children, men	24	21	5	0	2	5	6	1
11. Women, children, no men	45	51	30	4	5	8	12	1
12. Women, children, men	25	17	8	1	6	3	6	0
Nonconjugal family, male head								
13. Men, no children, no women	6	8	1	3	0	2	0	0
14. Men, no children, women	23	8	2	2	2	7	3	0
15. Men, children, no women	3	3	2	3	1	2	0	0
16. Men, children, women	31	13	6	1	3	2	3	0
Dormitory								
17. No adults	0	3	1	0	0	0	0	0
Total	842	787	436	82	126	208	337	35

Appendix: A statistical profile   499

Table 101. *Household composition (simplified): rural-dwelling population, based on census of eight selected villages in Sefrou region (percents within language category; see Table 102 for numbers)*

Household composition	Arabic	Berber	Total
Single conjugal family	42.0	41.4	41.5
Conjugal family plus one or more other adults	29.4	29.7	29.6
Compound conjugal family (two or more married couples)	15.9	10.6	11.9
One-person household	6.9	8.0	7.7
Nonconjugal family, female head	2.9	4.2	3.9
Nonconjugal family, male head	2.9	6.1	5.3
Dormitory	0.0	0.0	0.0
Total	100.0	100.0	99.9

(Language group of head of household)

Table 102. *Household composition (simplified): rural-dwelling population, based on census of eight selected villages in Sefrou region (numbers for Table 101)*

Household composition	Arabic	Berber	Total
Single conjugal family	103	305	408
Conjugal family plus one or more other adults	72	219	291
Compound conjugal family (two or more married couples)	39	78	117
One-person household	17	59	76
Nonconjugal family, female head	7	31	38
Nonconjugal family, male head	7	45	52
Dormitory	0	0	0
Total	245	737	982

(Language group of head of household)

Table 103. *Household composition: ethnic groups, birthplace, and language spoken (percents based on total number of households within each social group)*

Social group of head of household	Mixed ethnic composition (Muslim-Jewish-French)	Mixed birthplace composition (rural-urban)	Mixed language composition (Arabic-Berber)	Numbers
Major Muslim groups				
Sefrou-born Arabic speakers	0.0	9.2	2.7	848
Rural-born Arabic speakers	0.0	29.0	4.8	795
Rural-born Berber speakers	0.0	21.0	30.6	438
Minor Muslim groups				
Fez-born Arabic speakers	0.0	10.8	2.4	83
Bhalil-born Arabic speakers	0.0	11.7	2.3	128
Other Muslims	1.0	23.9	0.0	208
Other urban-born Arabic speakers	13.0	15.2	0.9	116
Sefrou-born Berber-speakers	0.0	28.3	65.2	46
Other urban-born Berber speakers	0.0	40.4	51.2	47
Jews (Sefrou-born)	0.0	0.9	10.1	335

(Household composition)

Marriage patterns (Tables 104–108)

In this portion of the study, a random sample of about 60 percent of the married couples of Sefrou (totaling 2,205 couples) was drawn out of the census, and the attributes of each husband and wife were tabulated against each other.

Tables 104 through 106 examine the direction of marriage choices of the various social groups. Table 104 gives percentages within each group of *husbands:* for example, what proportion of Sefrou-born Arabic-speaking men is married to women of the same social group, and for those who are not, from what social groups do the wives come? Table 105 shows the same base data with, however, the percentages computed in terms of the *wives:* for example, what proportion of Sefrou-born Arabic-speaking women is married to men of the same social group, and for those who are not, into what social groups have they married?

These tables show, first, that there is hardly any crossing of the ethnic group line by marriages among Muslims, Jews, and foreigners. The total of such mixed ethnic group marriages reaches only 0.4 percent of all marriages.

Second, overwhelming proportions of marriages are confined within each social group. The highest endogamy rate in Sefrou is that of the Sefrou-born Jews, 94.5 percent of whose men have Sefrou-born Jewish wives. They are unlikely even to marry Jews born elsewhere in Morocco. The next highest endogamy rate (83.4 percent) is that of the Sefrou-born Arabic speakers. The other social groups living in Sefrou but born elsewhere have lower endogamy rates, most ranging around 60 percent.

Some differences occur in the proportions and directions of mixed marriages, across birthplace lines and language lines. Tables 107 and 108, simplified selections of data from Tables 104 and 105, show some of these patterns. Sefrou-born Arabic-speaking men take more rural-born Arabic-speaking wives (6.6 percent) than rural-born Berber-speaking wives (1.2 percent). Rural-born Arabic-speaking men marry more Sefrou-born Arabic-speaking women (19.5 percent) than rural-born Berber-speaking women (5.1 percent). Rural-born Berber-speaking men marry more rural-born Arabic-speaking women (16.3 percent) than Sefrou-born Arabic-speaking women (10.0 percent).

Three of the smaller Muslim groups show distinctive differences in their marriage patterns. The Fez-born Arabic speakers are less endogamous than the larger groups, with only 47.2 percent of their wives also coming from Fez; they take more Sefrou-born Arabic speakers for wives (28.3 percent) than rural-born Arabic-speakers (11.3 percent) and hardly ever marry Berber speakers (1.9 percent). The Bhalil-born Arabic speakers have a higher rate of endogamy (60.0 percent) and a similar pattern of preference for Arabic speakers over Berber speakers. The Sefrou-born Berber speakers (of which we have only forty marriages in the study), on the other hand, have very low endogamy (10 percent), a strong pattern of choice of Sefrou-born Arabic speakers for wives (62.5 percent), and a preference for rural-born Berber speakers (15 percent) over rural-born Arabic speakers (2.5 percent).

The Sefrou-born Jews, as mentioned

above, have the highest endogamy rate (94.5 percent), and have taken a small number of the rural-born Jews as wives (1.1 percent). The rural-born Jews on the other hand have married a larger proportion of Sefrou-born Jewish women (36.4 percent) with a correspondingly lower endogamy rate (54.5 percent).

Table 104. *Marriage patterns: social groups compared: origins of wives (percents based on total numbers of husbands within each social group: see Table 106 for numbers)*

Social group of husband	Social group of wife																Total
	a	b	c	d	e	f	g	h	i	j	k	l	m	n	o	p	
Muslim groups																	
a	83.4	3.0	1.9	3.1	6.6	1.2	0.6	0.1	0.0	0.0	0.0	0.0	0.0	0.0	0.0	0.0	99.9
b	28.3	47.2	3.8	5.7	11.3	1.9	1.9	0.0	0.0	0.0	0.0	0.0	0.0	0.0	0.0	0.0	98.2
c	17.6	1.2	60.0	4.7	14.1	1.2	0.0	1.2	0.0	0.0	0.0	0.0	0.0	0.0	0.0	0.0	100.0
d	16.0	4.9	2.5	59.3	16.0	0.0	0.0	1.2	0.0	0.0	0.0	0.0	0.0	0.0	0.0	0.0	99.9
e	19.5	2.5	4.0	5.1	63.0	5.1	0.2	0.5	0.0	0.0	0.0	0.0	0.0	0.0	0.0	0.0	99.9
f	10.0	0.9	2.1	3.3	16.3	62.9	0.9	3.6	0.0	0.0	0.0	0.0	0.0	0.0	0.0	0.0	100.0
g	62.5	2.5	5.0	0.0	2.5	15.0	10.0	0.0	0.0	0.0	0.0	0.0	2.5	0.0	0.0	0.0	100.0
h	11.1	5.6	5.6	8.3	25.0	25.0	2.8	16.7	0.0	0.0	0.0	0.0	0.0	0.0	0.0	0.0	100.0
Jews																	
i	0.0	0.0	0.0	0.0	0.0	0.0	0.0	0.0	94.5	1.1	4.4	0.0	0.0	0.0	0.0	0.0	100.0
j	0.0	0.0	0.0	0.0	0.0	0.0	0.0	0.0	36.4	54.5	9.1	0.0	0.0	0.0	0.0	0.0	100.1
k	0.0	0.0	0.0	0.0	0.0	0.0	0.0	0.0	50.0	10.0	40.0	0.0	0.0	0.0	0.0	0.0	100.0
Foreigners																	
l	0.0	0.0	0.0	0.0	0.0	0.0	0.0	0.0	0.0	0.0	0.0	69.2	30.8	0.0	0.0	0.0	100.0
m	0.0	0.0	0.0	0.0	0.0	14.3	0.0	0.0	0.0	0.0	0.0	14.3	57.1	0.0	0.0	14.3	100.0
n	0.0	0.0	0.0	0.0	0.0	0.0	0.0	0.0	0.0	0.0	0.0	100.0	0.0	0.0	0.0	0.0	100.0
o	0.0	0.0	0.0	0.0	0.0	0.0	0.0	0.0	0.0	0.0	0.0	0.0	0.0	0.0	0.0	0.0	100.0
p	14.3	0.0	0.0	21.4	0.0	7.1	0.0	0.0	0.0	0.0	0.0	0.0	0.0	0.0	0.0	57.0	99.7

a, Sefrou-born Arabs; b, Fez-born Arabs; c, Bhalil-born Arabs; d, other urban Arabs; e, rural-born Arabs; f, rural-born Berbers; g, Sefrou-born Berbers; h, other urban Berbers; i, Sefrou-born Jews; j, rural-born Jews; k, other urban Jews; l, French born in France; m, North African French; n, other French; o, European-born foreigners; p, North African foreigners.

Table 105. *Marriage patterns: social groups compared: origins of husbands (percents based on total numbers of wives within each social group; see Table 106 for numbers)*

Social group of husband	Social group of wife															
	a	b	c	d	e	f	g	h	i	j	k	l	m	n	o	p
Muslim groups																
a	71.7	28.6	12.7	17.2	8.8	3.0	28.6	4.2	0.0	0.0	0.0	0.0	0.0	0.0	0.0	0.0
b	1.9	35.7	2.0	2.5	1.2	0.4	7.1	0.0	0.0	0.0	0.0	0.0	0.0	0.0	0.0	0.0
c	1.9	1.4	50.0	3.3	2.4	0.4	0.0	4.2	0.0	0.0	0.0	0.0	0.0	0.0	0.0	0.0
d	1.7	5.7	2.0	39.3	2.6	0.0	0.0	4.2	0.0	0.0	0.0	0.0	0.0	0.0	0.0	0.0
e	14.3	20.0	22.5	23.8	71.9	10.8	7.1	12.5	0.0	0.0	0.0	0.0	0.0	0.0	0.0	0.0
f	4.4	4.3	6.9	9.0	11.0	79.1	21.4	50.0	0.0	0.0	0.0	0.0	0.0	0.0	0.0	0.0
g	3.2	1.4	2.0	0.0	0.2	2.2	28.6	0.0	0.0	0.0	0.0	0.0	11.2	0.0	0.0	0.0
h	0.5	2.9	2.0	2.5	1.8	3.4	7.1	25.0	0.0	0.0	0.0	0.0	0.0	0.0	0.0	0.0
Jews																
i	0.0	0.0	0.0	0.0	0.0	0.0	0.0	0.0	95.2	18.7	66.7	0.0	0.0	0.0	0.0	0.0
j	0.0	0.0	0.0	0.0	0.0	0.0	0.0	0.0	3.0	75.0	11.1	0.0	0.0	0.0	0.0	0.0
k	0.0	0.0	0.0	0.0	0.0	0.0	0.0	0.0	1.8	6.2	22.2	0.0	0.0	0.0	0.0	0.0
Foreigners																
l	0.0	0.0	0.0	0.0	0.0	0.0	0.0	0.0	0.0	0.0	0.0	81.8	44.4	0.0	0.0	0.0
m	0.0	0.0	0.0	0.0	0.0	0.0	0.0	0.0	0.0	0.0	0.0	9.1	44.4	0.0	0.0	11.1
n	0.0	0.0	0.0	0.0	0.0	0.0	0.0	0.0	0.0	0.0	0.0	9.1	0.0	0.0	0.0	0.0
o	0.0	0.0	0.0	0.0	0.0	0.0	0.0	0.0	0.0	0.0	0.0	0.0	0.0	0.0	0.0	0.0
p	0.3	0.0	0.0	2.5	0.0	0.4	0.0	0.0	0.0	0.0	0.0	0.0	0.0	0.0	0.0	88.9
Total	99.9	100.0	100.1	100.1	99.9	99.7	99.9	100.1	100.0	99.9	100.0	100.0	100.0	0.0	0.0	100.0

a, Sefrou-born Arabs; b, Fez-born Arabs; c, Bhalil-born Arabs; d, other urban Arabs; e, rural-born Arabs; f, rural-born Berbers; g, Sefrou-born Berbers; h, other urban Berbers; i, Sefrou-born Jews; j, rural-born Jews; k, other urban Jews; l, French born in France; m, North African French; n, other French; o, European-born foreigners; p, North African foreigners.

Table 106. *Marriage patterns: social groups compared (numbers for Tables 104 and 105)*

Social group of husband	Social group of wife																Total
	a	b	c	d	e	f	g	h	i	j	k	l	m	n	o	p	
Muslim groups																	
a	556	20	13	21	44	8	4	1	0	0	0	0	0	0	0	0	667
b	15	25	2	3	6	1	1	0	0	0	0	0	0	0	0	0	53
c	15	1	51	4	12	1	0	1	0	0	0	0	0	0	0	0	85
d	13	4	2	48	13	0	0	1	0	0	0	0	0	0	0	0	81
e	111	14	23	29	358	29	1	3	0	0	0	0	0	0	0	0	568
f	34	3	7	11	55	212	3	12	0	0	0	0	0	0	0	0	337
g	25	1	2	0	1	6	4	0	0	0	0	0	1	0	0	0	40
h	4	2	2	3	9	9	1	6	0	0	0	0	0	0	0	0	36
Jews																	
i	0	0	0	0	0	0	0	0	256	3	12	0	0	0	0	0	271
j	0	0	0	0	0	0	0	0	8	12	2	0	0	0	0	0	22
k	0	0	0	0	0	0	0	0	5	1	4	0	0	0	0	0	10
Foreigners																	
l	0	0	0	0	0	0	0	0	0	0	0	9	4	0	0	0	13
m	0	0	0	0	0	1	0	0	0	0	0	1	4	0	0	1	7
n	0	0	0	0	0	0	0	0	0	0	0	1	0	0	0	0	1
o	0	0	0	0	0	0	0	0	0	0	0	0	0	0	0	0	0
p	2	0	0	3	0	0	0	0	0	0	0	0	0	0	0	8	14
Total	775	70	102	122	498	268	14	24	269	16	18	11	9	0	0	9	2,205

a, Sefrou-born Arabs; b, Fez-born Arabs; c, Bhalil-born Arabs; d, other urban Arabs; e, rural-born Arabs; f, rural-born Berbers; g, Sefrou-born Berbers; h, other urban Berbers; i, rural-born Jews; j, Sefrou-born Jews; k, other urban Jews; l, French born in France; m, North African French; n, other French; o, European-born foreigners; p, North African foreigners.

Table 107. *Marriage patterns: selected social groups compared: Muslims (percents based on total number of husbands in each social group; see Table 106 for numbers)*

Social group of husband	Social group of wife					
	Sefrou-born Arabic speaker	Rural-born Arabic speaker	Rural-born Berber speaker	Fez-born Arabic speaker	Bhalil-born Arabic speaker	Sefrou-born Berber speaker
Sefrou-born Arabic speaker	83.4	6.6	1.2			
Rural-born Arabic speaker	19.5	63.0	5.1			
Rural-born Berber speaker	10.0	16.3	62.9			
Fez-born Arabic speaker	28.3	11.3	1.9	47.2		
Bhalil-born Arabic speaker	17.6	14.1	1.2		60.0	
Sefrou-born Berber speaker	62.5	2.5	15.0			10.0

Table 108. *Marriage patterns: selected social groups compared: Jews (percents based on total number of husbands from each social group; see Table 106 for numbers)*

Social group of husband	Social group of wife	
	Sefrou-born Jews	Rural-born Jews
Sefrou-born Jews	94.5	1.1
Rural-born Jews	36.4	54.5

Index

The boldface number following each foreign term indicates the most complete definition of that term in the text.

ᶜadem, 37
Adlun family, 159, 310, 318; demography of, 320; economic organization of, 320, 338–41, 363–4; household composition in, 335–8; kinship terminology in, 360, 380–5; marriage choices and strategy in, 363, 389; marriage patterns of, 323–9, 374–5; names in, 341–56; as patronymic association, 341–56; residential pattern, 320, 329–30; visiting patterns in, 334–5; wedding payments of, 368; women in, 330–4
Adlun quarter, 318
ᶜadūl (sing. ᶜadel), 78–9, 81–2, 194, 365
agricultural productivity, 10–11
ᶜā'ila, 44, 347
ait, 347
Ait ben Assu, 35–40, 41–7
Ait Daud u Musa, 53–7
Ait Seghoushen, 53–7
Ait Yusi, 8, 14, 23–8, 36, 53–7, 58, 119, 135
Alawite Dynasty, 99, 135
Al-Fassi, Allal, 163
Al-Kettani, Abdel Hayy, 164
Al-Yusi, Qaid Umar, 14–15, 36, 69, 76, 118, 135
ᶜamal, 75
amīn (pl. umāna), 60, 77, 192–7, 206
ᶜamm, 347–8, 360
ᶜaql, 209
ᶜar, 42, 44, 46, 54, 76, 104, 55n25
Arabic, 199–212; transcription of, ix–x
Arabic-speakers, 23, 93–6, 143–5, 398–9
ᶜāreq, 347
ᶜarīfa, 79
ᶜasab, 359, 360, 361
asl, 92, 96, 346
'attat l-bit, 366
auctioneers, 186, 187

baraka, 29, 100, 137
bargaining, 221–9
bāṭel, 200, 201, 208, 211–12
bazaar, 123–4, 173–5, 182–3; change in, 139–40; clientele relations in, 217–21; geography of, 126, 127–9, 173–82, 265–307, 311–13; history of, 129; information in, 124–5, 198–9, 213–33, 308–10; occupational divisions in, 182–92; and socioethnic categories, 143–50; see also bargaining
Bekkai, Si M'barek, 16, 50, 69, 176
Ben Barka, Mehdi, 51
benī, 347
Berber Dahir, 15, 77, 162
Berber-speakers, 22–3, 93–6, 143–5
Bhalil, 8, 58, 95
birth ritual, 368
bit, 322, 323, 336
bled, 7, 8, 96–7
Bourdieu, P., 375
brideprice, 87, 322, 364, 365, 366, 368–9, 376
Brown, K., 1

caravans, 129–31, 132, 133, 135, 137–8, 170
Cassady, R., 226, 227
census: concept of social group in, 398–400; data collection and analysis, 397–400; ethnic identity in, 398; French classified in, 399; Jews classified in, 399; see also population
child custody and support, 42
child rearing, 315, 333
climate, see ecology
contracts: commercial, 133–6, 191; marriage, 366
Crapanzano, V., 1

dar, 322, 323
derb, 62, 63, 182, 318–9, 451

507

509